SIMPLIFIED DRAFTING AND BLUEPRINT READING

SIMPLIFIED DRAFTING AND BLUEPRINT READING

ABRAM H. BERMAN

Drafting Instructor
Sir Robert L. Borden Secondary School
Scarborough, Ontario

McGraw-Hill Ryerson Limited

Toronto Montreal New York St. Louis San Francisco
Auckland Bogotá Guatemala Hamburg Johannesburg
Lisbon London Madrid Mexico New Delhi Panama
Paris San Juan São Paulo Singapore Sydney Tokyo

SIMPLIFIED DRAFTING AND BLUEPRINT READING

Copyright © McGraw-Hill Ryerson Limited, 1983

All rights reserved. No part of this publication may be reproduced, stored in a retrieval system, or transmitted in any form or by any means electronic, mechanical, photocopying, recording or otherwise, without the prior written permission of McGraw-Hill Ryerson Limited.

Excepted from this copyright are the graphs found inside the back cover. Permission is hereby granted to instructors to reproduce these graphs for classroom use.

ISBN 0-07-092431-7

2 3 4 5 6 7 8 9 0 D 2 1 0 9 8 7 6 5 4

Printed and bound in Canada by John Deyell Company

Canadian Cataloguing in Publication Data

Berman, Abram H.
  Simplified Drafting and Blueprint Reading

Includes index.
ISBN 0-07-092431-7

1. Mechanical drawing.   2. Blue-prints.   I. Title.
T353.B47   604.2   C82-094432-7

TABLE OF CONTENTS

    Preface vii
1. Introduction, **1**
2. Use of Instruments, **5**
3. Lettering, **19**
4. Orthographic Drawing, Part 1   Rectangular Shapes, **24**
5. Reduced and Enlarged Scales, **58**
6. Circles, **65**
7. Orthographic Drawing, Part 2   Cylindrical Shapes, **78**
8. Dimensioning Rectangular Shapes, **88**
9. Dimensioning Cylindrical Shapes, **99**
10. Detail Working Drawings, **113**
11. Sectional Views, **136**
12. Screw Threads and Screw Thread Fasteners, **150**
13. Auxiliary Views, **166**
14. Assembly Working Drawings, **177**
15. Pictorial Drawings, **192**
16. Development of Objects, **219**
17. Architectural Drawing, **238**
18. Reading Construction Drawings, **273**
19. Reading Technical Drawings, **289**
    Index, **323**

PREFACE

This material is presented as a method of teaching the fundamentals of technical drawing. Its purpose is to guide the student, step by step, to successfully complete a number of projects and lead to an understanding of basic drafting. The projects are designed to be progressively more challenging bearing in mind that students will enjoy the challenge and remain receptive as long as they are convinced that the work is within their capabilities to complete.

Using progressive picture compositions, the lessons are graphically presented with a minimum of written instructions. This teaching method can be compared with the master apprentice arrangement before the age of technology: "*Look*, this is the way. Follow each step as I perform them and you, too, will be able to complete the project successfully."

ACKNOWLEDGEMENTS

I wish to thank a number of individuals for their valuable assistance in the preparation of this text.

Daniel F. Meadus for the many hours spent preparing a number of illustrations and projects.

Michèle Miodonski for the excellent illustrations of a non-technical nature used in the coloured margin and elsewhere in the book.

Ken Parton, Dwayne Edney and many other of my former students who have made this text possible, and the editorial staff of McGraw-Hill Ryerson, for their assistance and guidance.

The author and editors wish to thank Mr. Ronald B. Palace for his considerable contribution in preparing numerous finished drawings and for his review of the text and art manuscript of this book. (Mr. Palace is Assistant Technical Director at Albert Campbell C.I., Scarborough, Ontario).

TO MY WIFE DOLLY

for her understanding and sense of humour, expressed best, perhaps, by an old Scottish saying:

There is potential in each of us: some of us just need a little push.

CHAPTER 1
INTRODUCTION TO DRAFTING

WORDS TO LEARN

communicate (com-mú-ni-cate)
universal (u-ni-vér-sal)
describe (de-scríbe)
generation (gen-er-á-tion)

incline (iń-cline)
graphic (gráph-ic)
technician (tech-ní-cian)
vital (ví-tal)

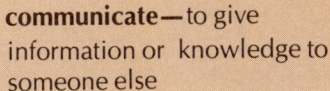

WHAT IS DRAFTING?

Many students entering the drafting classroom for the first time are faced with unfamiliar-looking desks and equipment. The question they ask themselves is: What is drafting?

Drafting is simply a method of **communicating** information. By using the drafting language we can tell other people what we want them to know. It may be said that drafting is the only truly **universal** language because it is the only language that is understood around the world.

What can drafting be like? It can be interesting, very enjoyable, and, most of all, it need not be difficult.

Drafting can be called "picture writing." From the beginning of time people used picture writing to **describe** what they saw and to record their thoughts and ideas. Some picture drawings date back thousands of years. They still exist today and are examples of how

communicate—to give information or knowledge to someone else

universal—worldwide
describe—to tell about in detail

generation—people of roughly the same age (compared to those of their parents' age)

incline—land or a ramp which slants upwards or downwards

graphic—using lines or pictures (or words) to describe something

technician—a person with great knowledge and skill in his or her trade

useful a tool they have been in our development.

Without picture writing to record inventions and ideas, very little of what people learned would have passed on from one **generation** to the next. Try to imagine life today without the wheel, the **incline** or the lever.

As you have seen, picture writing or drafting is the language used to communicate technical information. You may not realize it, but you have been using this **graphic** language of lines and symbols in everyday life. As you can see the message must be clear, accurate and quickly understood.

WHO USES DRAFTING?

We all use drafting: the skilled worker in the trades, the **technician**, and the homemaker. In addition to industrial uses, many things such as hobbies, do-it-yourself projects, even purchasing a new home or making an addition to an old one are made easier by understanding drafting.

If you look around the room you are in, you will see many objects. Likely, almost all of the objects were

2 INTRODUCTION TO DRAFTING

vital — of great importance

drawn first before they were built. The furniture, the lighting and plumbing, the fixtures, even the building itself were drawn first. Today, drafters are **vital** in nearly every area of our modern society. They produce the drawings from which our homes, factories, and offices are built. Expressways, bridges, and pipelines to carry gas or oil are constructed from their drawings. All of our appliances, from the washing machine to the latest in recording equipment, all began as ideas drawn by drafters.

CAN I BE A DRAFTER?

In answering this question, it should be clearly understood that the term drafter includes both men and women.

The student in drawing must have an open mind to learn the necessary steps and methods. This text is designed to teach drafting one basic step at a time. When you have mastered and practised the first step, you will find that you are ready and eager to take the next step. Drafting can be challenging; yet it need not be difficult. Most certainly it can be enjoyable and rewarding.

POINTS TO REMEMBER

- Drafting need not be difficult.
- Drafting makes use of graphic symbols and pictures to pass on information.
- Drafting is a universal language.
- Drafting develops skills and habits that will be useful in all walks of life.
- Drafting can help give you the confidence you need to accept a challenge and learn to master it.

QUESTIONS TO ANSWER

1. How did people communicate ideas and instructions before drafting was developed?
2. Why are technical drawings used?
3. List five occupations that would make use of technical drawings.
4. Think of the times you may have used a technical drawing and list as many as you can. (For example, a road map, a room layout of your school, etc.)
5. How can drafting help you?

REPLACE THE X'S WITH THE CORRECT TERM

1. You can XXXXXXXXXX *(communicate)* information by using the drafting language.

2. People used picture writing to XXXXXXX *(describe)* what they saw.

3. The language of lines and symbols is known as XXXXXXXX *(Drafting)*.

4. Drafting is a XXXXXXXXX *(universal)* language.

5. Drafters are XXXXX *(vital)* to the production of houses, factories, and office buildings.

6. People's ideas and thoughts have been passed on from one XXXXXXXXXX *(generation)* to another.

7. A XXXXXXXXXX *(technician)* is a skilled worker.

8. Inventions such as the wheel, the XXXXXXX *(graphics)* and the lever have made our lives easier.

CHAPTER 2
USE OF INSTRUMENTS

WORDS TO LEARN

misconception (mis-con-cép-tion)
insert (in-sért)
depress (de-préss)

misconception—an incorrect idea

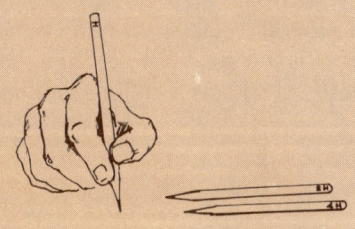

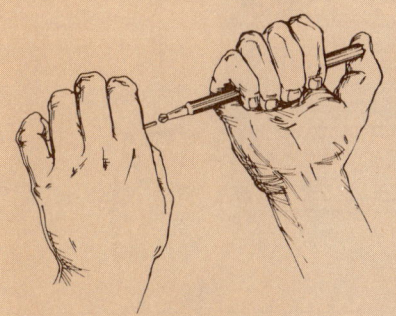

depress—to push down
insert—to put an object inside (or in between) other objects

To the beginner, the drafting room can appear frightening at first glance. The unfamiliar-looking desks and shiny instruments remind many people of a dentist's office. They expect that being there may not be a pleasant experience.

Set all your fears aside. We want to remove the self-doubts and **misconceptions** about drafting that may have kept you from exploring this subject before now. Let us begin by looking at a few of the instruments you will be using.

Wooden Pencils. Here is a familiar sight. Well, if you look closely, you will see numbers and letters stamped at one end of the pencil that you may not have noticed before. These numbers refer to the hardness or softness of the pencil's lead. Pencil leads are made from a mixture of carbon and clay. They can be made to any grade of hardness or softness, from very hard (9H) to very soft (7B). The pencils you will be using in drafting will be from the group: H, 2H, 3H and 4H. They will produce the lines you need, with the least amount of smudges and the cleanest results. Remember to sharpen the end of the pencil opposite the grade stamp.

Mechanical Pencils. A mechanical pencil is made up of an outer metal case with a set of jaws at the bottom and a push button at the top. When the button is **depressed**, the jaws open to allow a piece of lead to be **inserted**. The advantage of the mechanical pencil is

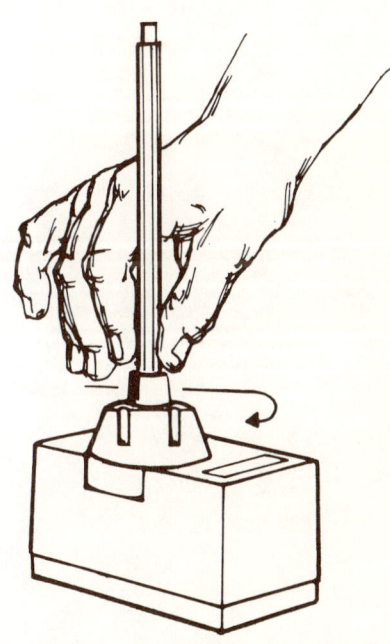

that the lead can be fully used up, no matter how short it becomes, and new leads can be inserted easily and quickly.

You don't necessarily become a better drafter by using a mechanical pencil, but using it will help you develop a professional image.

Mechanical drawing pencils can be sharpened using a mechanical lead pointer. Allow 10-15 mm of

5

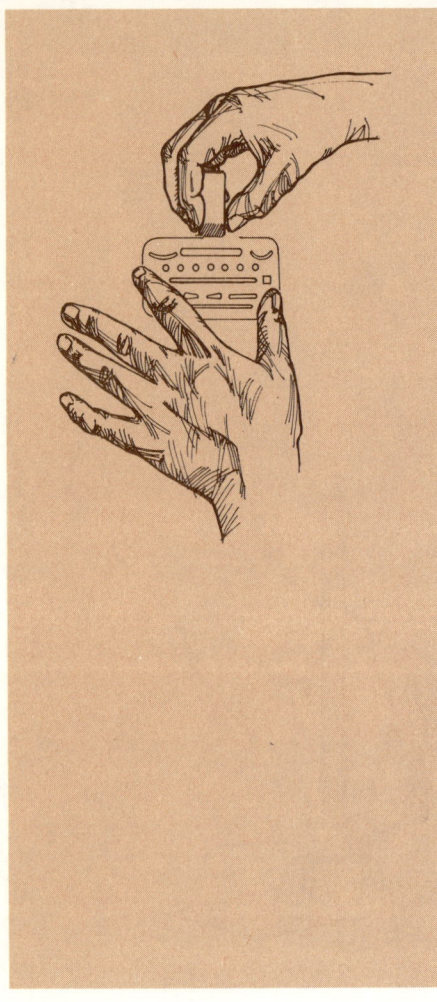

lead to extend out from the jaws of the mechanical pencil. If the lead is too short it will not sharpen. If the lead is too long, it will break off. Insert the mechanical pencil through the guide of the mechanical pointer. Be careful not to snap the lead. Hold the pencil between your fingers close to the guide of the pointer, as shown. Gently rotate the head of the pointer to sharpen the lead.

Erasers and Erasing Shields. Even professionals make mistakes, or for good reasons have to remove unwanted lines. A good soft eraser can be your best friend. An erasing shield will protect your good lines and allow you to erase unwanted lines. The result will be clean drawings of which you can be proud.

Courtesy: Keuffel and Esser Canada Incorporated

Fig. 2-1 *T-Square*

T-Squares. T-Squares are used to draw horizontal lines. The head of the T-Square is held firmly to the side of the drawing board and the horizontal line is drawn away from your body.

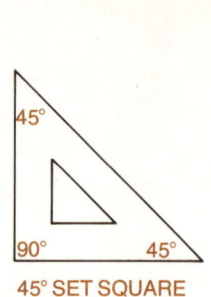 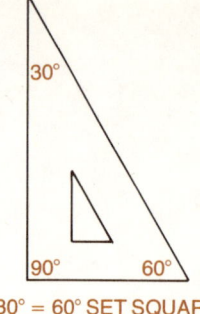

45° SET SQUARE   30° = 60° SET SQUARE

Fig. 2-2(a) *Set Squares*

Set Squares. Set squares are a pair of triangles made of a clear plastic. Look carefully at the set squares: they are not the same size or shape, but each has one angle of 90°.

One set square has two sides of equal length and two angles that are the same size. It is named the 45° set square. The other is the 30°—60° set square. Each side of the 30°—60° set square is different in length.

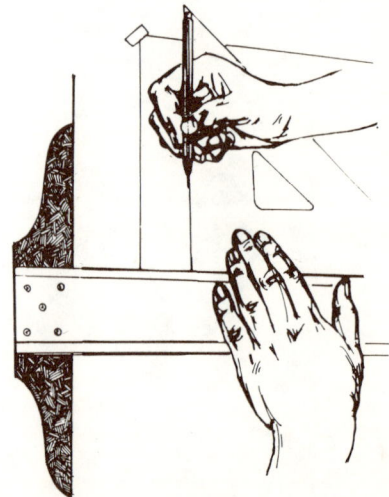

You can use either set square to draw vertical lines. Place the set square on the T-Square as shown, lean your pencil slightly away from you and draw the vertical lines.

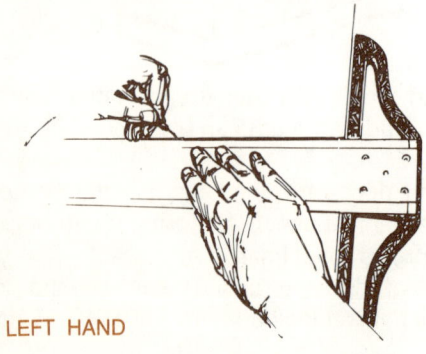 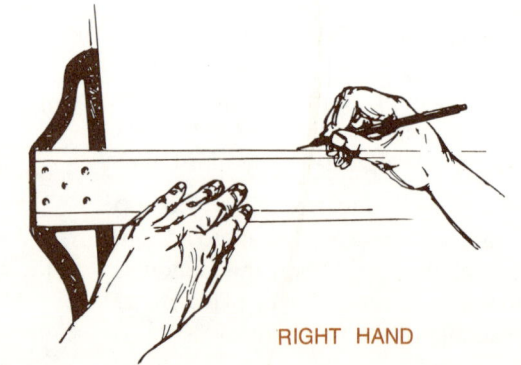

LEFT HAND   RIGHT HAND

6 USE OF INSTRUMENTS

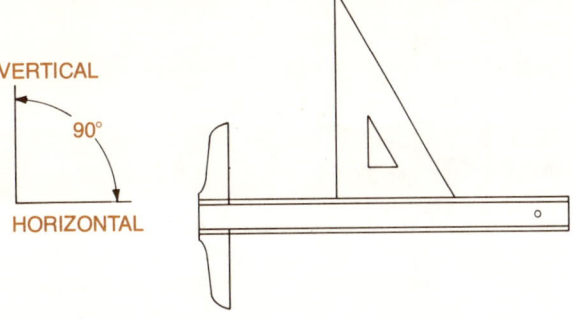

Fig. 2-2(b)

At this point you can draw horizontal lines and vertical lines. In Fig. 2-2(b) a horizontal line and a vertical line have been drawn to form an angle of 90°.

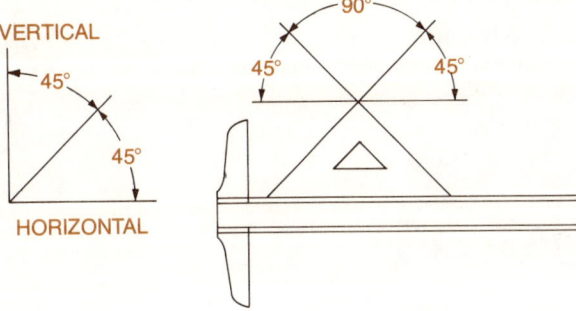

Fig. 2-2(c)

In Fig. 2-2(c) the 45° set square is placed so that we can draw a line that is 45° to the horizontal line and 45° to the vertical line.

With the 45° set square, you can draw 45° lines to form an angle of 90°.

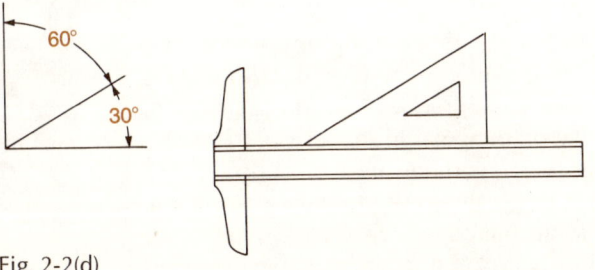

Fig. 2-2(d)

With the 30°—60° set square placed as shown, you can draw a line that is 30° to the horizontal line. Note that this line is 60° to the vertical line. Fig. 2-2(d).

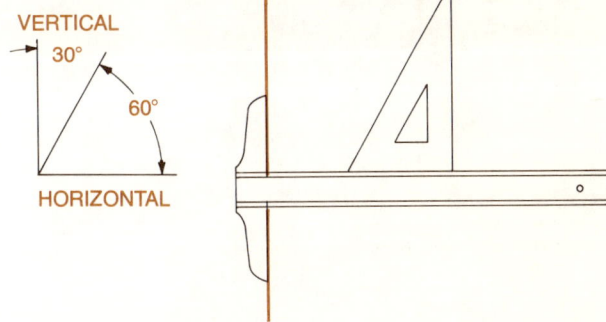

Fig. 2-2(e)

By placing the 30°—60° in this position, you can draw a line that is 60° to the horizontal line. Note that this line is 30° to the vertical line. Fig. 2-2(e).

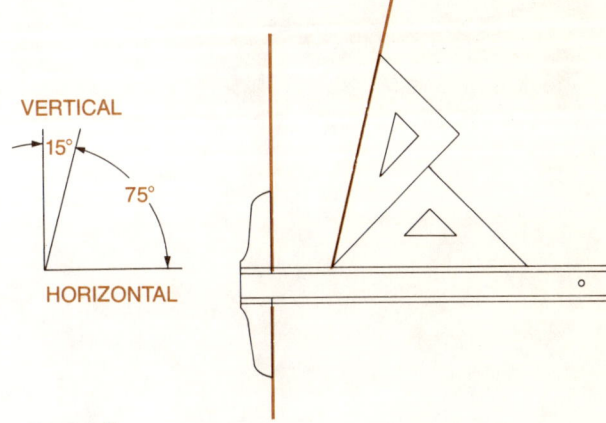

Fig. 2-2(f)

By placing the 30°—45° set squares together as shown, you can draw a line that is 75° to the horizontal line. Note that this same line is 15° to the vertical.

By placing the 30° and 45° set squares together as shown you can draw a line that is 15° to the horizontal line. Note that this same line is 75° to the vertical.

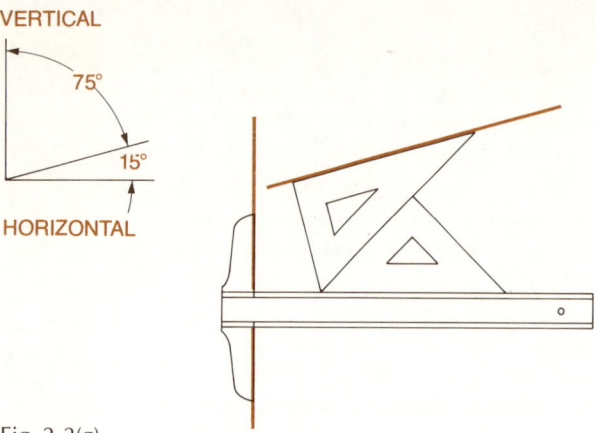

Fig. 2-2(g)

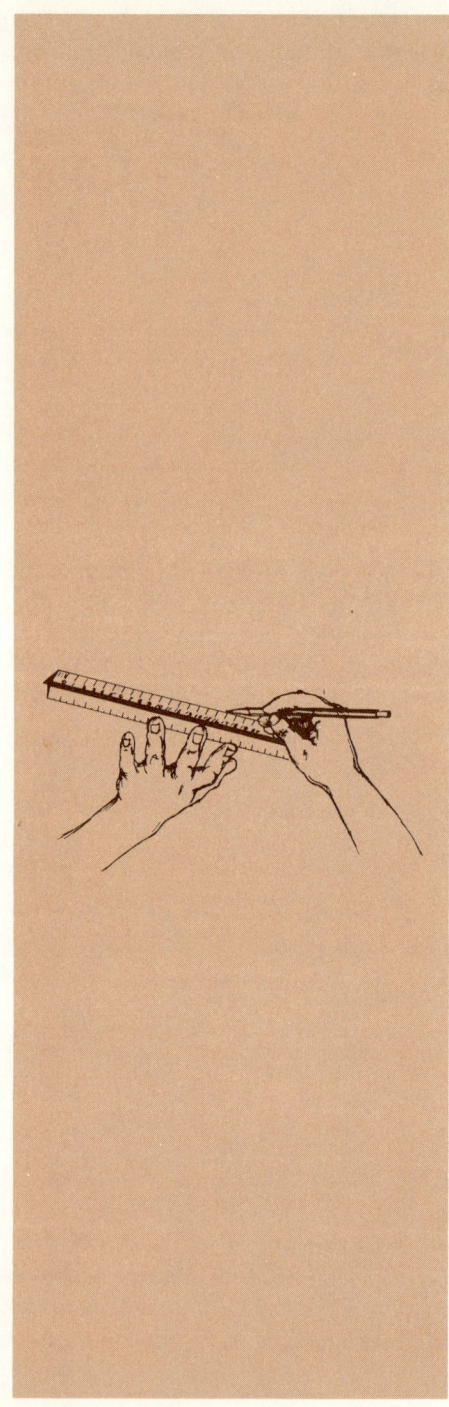

Don't throw up your hands in despair. You don't have to memorize the different positions of the set squares. After a little practice drawing your first projects, you will hardly have to think of which set square to use when drawing these commonly used angles.

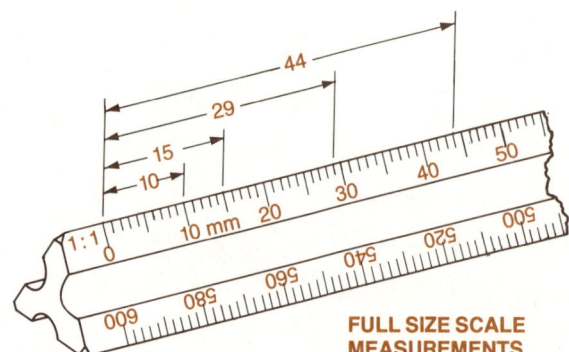

Fig. 2-3

The Scale. The scale is a measuring instrument. You may have called it a ruler in the past, but the scale is more than a ruler. It is a precise measuring instrument that is either flat or triangular in shape. The triangular scale is the one most commonly used in schools. There are times when this scale is used to draw objects at a reduced size to suit our paper size. On the other hand, quite often objects are too small to be drawn clearly in their full size. The scale can be used to create a larger view of the object. At this point we will only use the full size scale to draw objects to their actual size. The full size measuring edge is identified by the figures 1:1 in the left hand corner of the scale.

The full size scale is usually marked off to a length of 300 mm. Each division on the scale represents 1 mm. Remember that 10 mm is equal to 1 cm. All technical drawings that use metric units of measurement are usually drawn in millimetres unless noted otherwise. The scale is used to measure accurate distances. Never use the scale as an edge for drawing lines as the edge will not give a clear, crisp line.

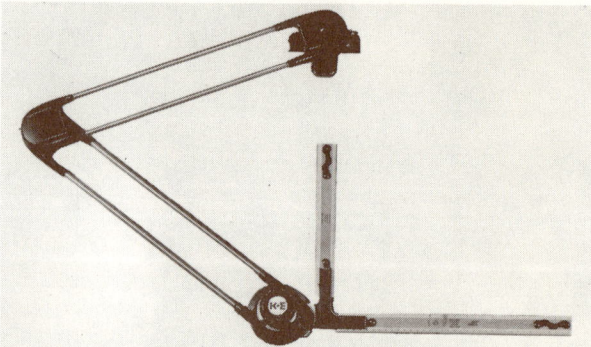

Courtesy: Keuffel and Esser Co.

Fig. 2-4(a) *Drafting Machine*

Courtesy: Keuffel and Esser Co.

Fig. 2-4(b) *Drafting Control Head*

The Drafting Machine. This handy machine has replaced the T-square and set squares on most drafting boards in industry and schools. The two scales are set at right angles, that is, 90° to each other.

Wherever the machine is moved on the drawing board, the scales will always be 90° to each other. The machine can be positioned to form any angle by moving the main control head with your finger tips. The machine is a scale, a T-square and set squares all in one. It can be locked at any angle you desire.

Today, computerized instruments (see Figures 2-5(a), (b)) are available. They can be used with most drafting machines. The artwork is still drawn by a drafter but these instruments can draw lines, and many kinds of symbols as well as lettering.

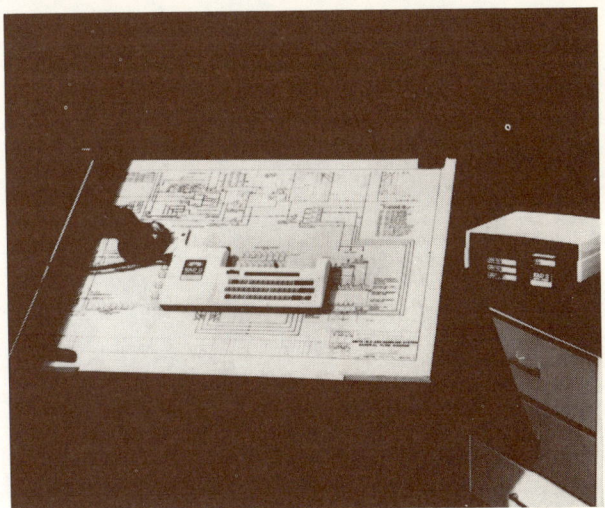

Courtesy: Koh-I-Noor Inc.

Fig. 2-5(b)

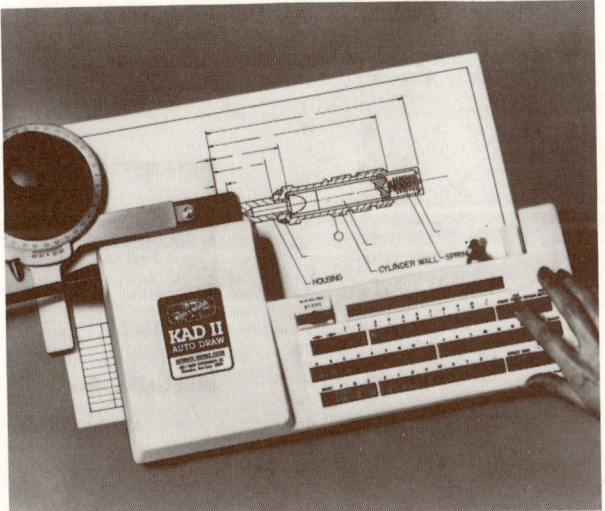

Courtesy: Koh-I-Noor Inc.

Fig. 2-5(a)

These are some of the instruments used to produce technical drawings. They are important, but only in the way you use them. We will give you a step by step outline for your first drawing project. Carefully follow the steps that are outlined in this example and then apply them in the projects at the end of the chapter.

DRAWING PROJECTS

The first series of projects are sometimes called templates or plane figures. Think of them as two dimensional figures. The length and height dimensions are shown but the width or thickness of the material is too minimal to be shown in the drawing. The thickness can be noted at the bottom of your paper in what is known as the title block.

We need only one view to completely describe two dimensional figures.

Ready to begin? Is the drawing surface clean? Are your hands clean? The instruments? Sharpen a medium hard pencil (3H or 4H) and place a soft eraser nearby.

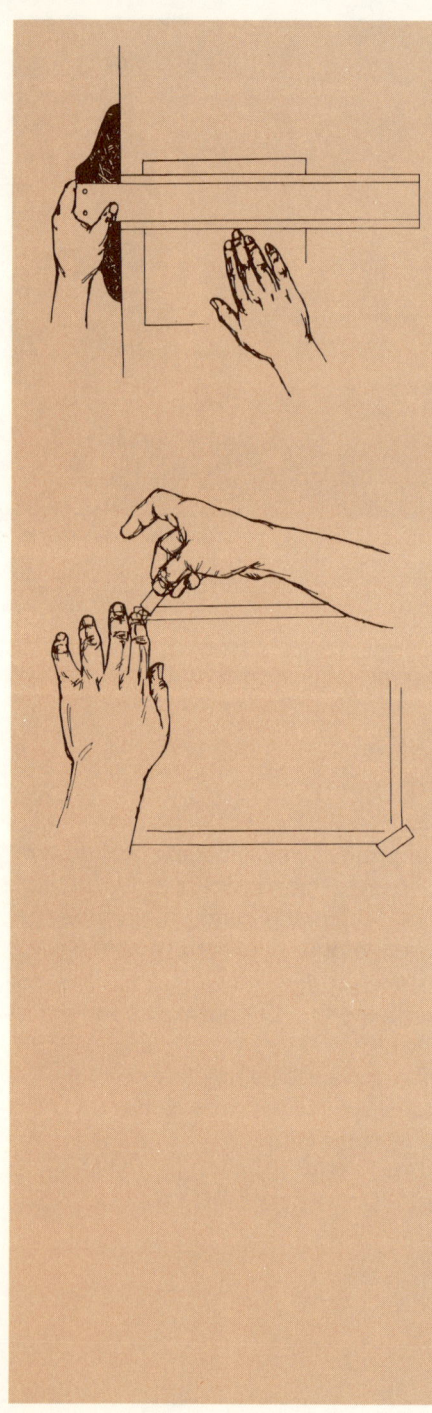

Steps in Placing the Drawing Paper on the Drawing Board

1. Place the drawing paper about 100 mm from the left side of the board.
2. Using the border of the paper as a guide, line the paper up with your drafting machine scale.
3. Hold the paper down while you place 4 small pieces of tape (about 30 mm long) across each corner. First tape top corners, then the bottom ones. The paper is now in position, squarely on the board, within easy reach.

It is possible to complete the projects in this chapter without following the steps as outlined, but control your eagerness. We want to avoid any mistakes and unhappy results. No one likes to start over again.

Helpful Hints

- Light, barely visible lines can be easily erased when necessary. As you construct your drawing, guide the pencil across the paper with a minimum of pressure. These lines are called **construction lines**.
- When measuring off distances try to measure along a line for accuracy.
- Mark off distances with a light stroke.
- Never press the lead point into the paper.
- When you use the eraser, some of the rubber particles will collect on the paper. You will find that the paper will stay cleaner if you allow a few of these particles to remain on the paper. Your instruments will ride on these particles and be less likely to smudge your linework.
- Keep a sheet of scrap paper handy for calculations, notes and testing your lead after sharpening.
- Check and recheck each dimension as you go along.

- The outline or visible shape of an object is darkened **only after the completed construction work has been checked for accuracy**. The finished line work is then drawn to stand out clearly. These lines are called **object lines**.

As we are about to start to draw the first project, there are several things we should look for. What is the project called? What are the overall dimensions?

What size of material would we need if we were asked to produce Template No. 1? We can see that the overall height is 114 mm. The overall length is 195 mm. Can you see how we calculated this last dimension? Given these two dimensions we can begin the drawing of the template by first spacing it on our paper. With these dimensions in mind we can start to space the drawing. Spacing a drawing is done for several good reasons:

1. To make sure that the view of the template can fit on the size of paper you have chosen.
2. To allow the drafter room to properly place the necessary dimensions and additional information.
3. The completed drawing will be easier to read and more pleasing to the eye.

Steps in Spacing a Single View Drawing

1. On the border, starting from the bottom right hand corner, measure off the length.
2. Measure the distance remaining on the line and find the mid-point of this distance. You simply divide the distance in half.
3. From this mid-point draw a light vertical line. (See Fig. 2-6)
4. On the border, starting from the top left hand corner, measure off the height.
5. Measure the distance remaining on the line and find the mid-point of this distance.
6. From this mid-point draw a light horizontal line. (See Fig. 2-7)

The two lines you have drawn form the lower left corner of your project. Erase all the measurement points from the border to avoid using them again.

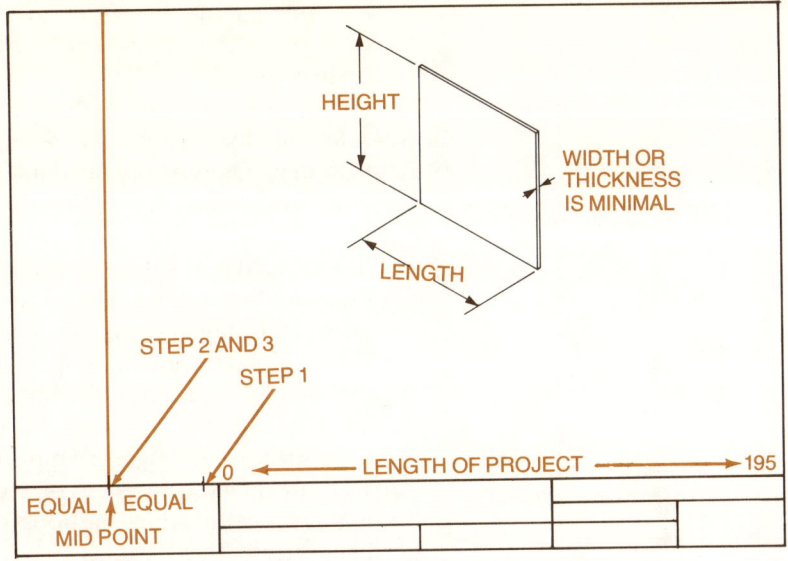

Fig. 2-6

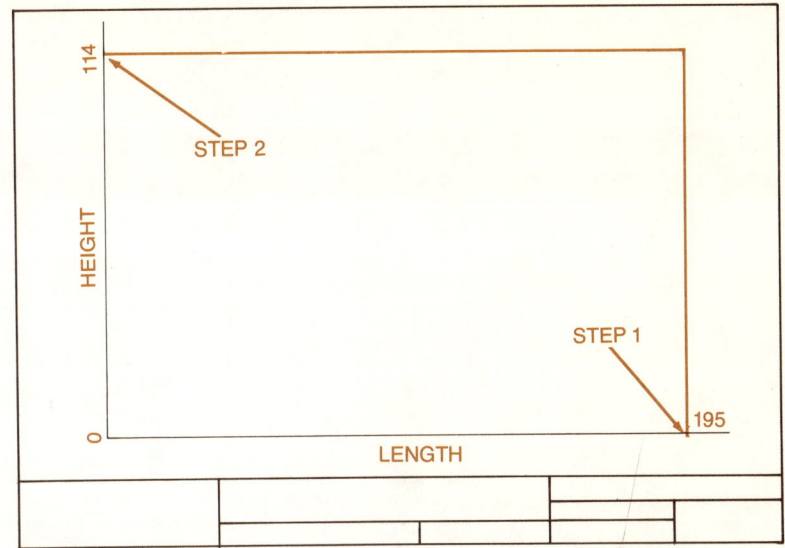

Fig. 2-8

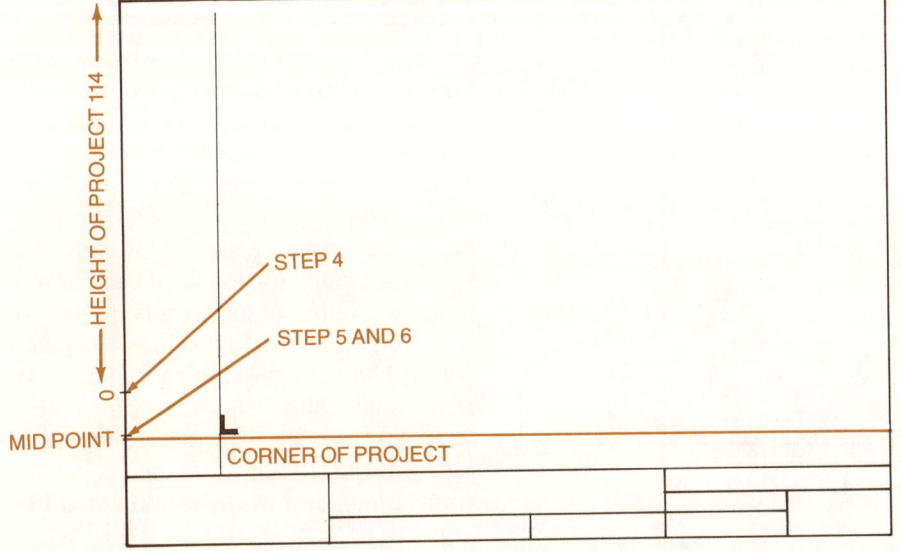

Fig. 2-7

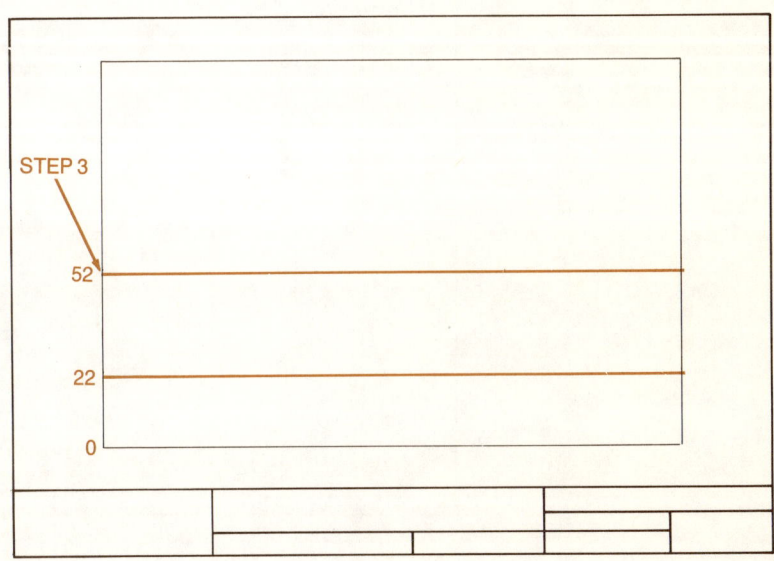

Fig. 2-9

DRAWING PROJECTS 11

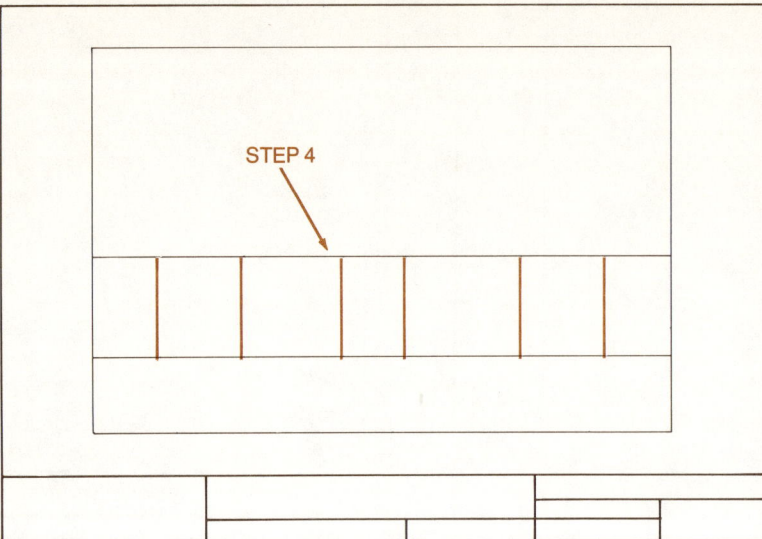

Fig. 2-10

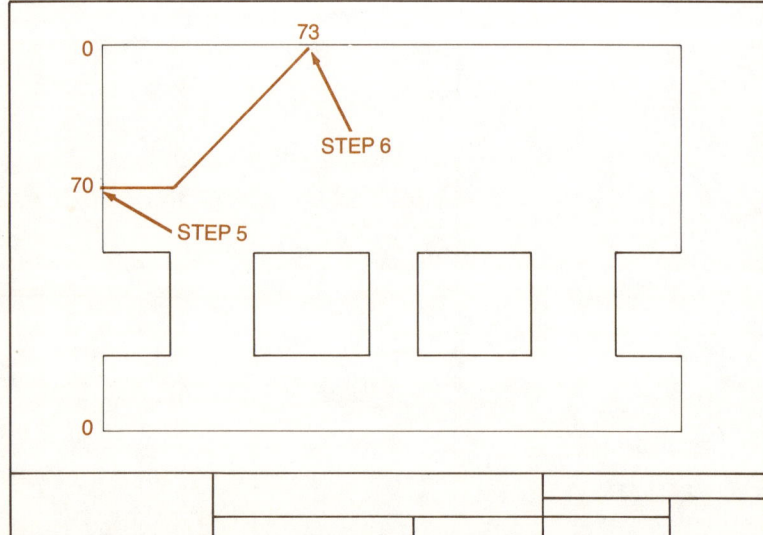

Fig. 2-11

Steps in Drawing Template No. 1

Now we can begin to draw the first project.

1. On the horizontal line from the corner, measure off the length of the template (195 mm). Draw a vertical line from this point. (Fig. 2-8)
2. On the vertical line from the corner, measure off the height of the template (114 mm). Draw a horizontal line from this point to complete the outline of the template. Check the measurements of the outline for accuracy. If these are not correct all the work that follows will be for nothing.
   - Read the drawing carefully. We note that the two slots and both rectangular holes are the same distance from the bottom of the template (22 mm). The slots and the holes are also the same height (30 mm). (Fig. 2-9)
3. Measure off these distances on the vertical line as shown and draw the horizontal lines lightly across the drawing.
   - Read the drawing again to find that the length of each slot is 25 mm. The space between the slot and the hole is 30 mm. Each rectangle is 35 mm long. (Fig. 2-10)
4. Measure these distances on the horizontal line as shown and lightly draw the vertical lines to complete the outlines of the slot and the holes. Remove the unnecessary lines between the slots and the holes.
   - Reading the drawing again you will see that the corner at the top left of the template has to be cut away. Note that there is a short horizontal line that is placed 70 mm from the bottom of the template. You are not given the length of this line. However, you will find that the sloping line is drawn at an angle of 45° from a point that is 73 mm from the left side of the template.
5. Measure the 70 mm distance off on the vertical line. Draw a light horizontal line from this point. (Fig. 2-11)
6. Measure the 73 mm distance off on the horizontal line. From this point draw a 45° line to the line just drawn to complete the outline of this corner.

7. Complete the remaining corner in the same manner. Check the accuracy of your measurements and remove all unnecessary lines and smudges.

• Darken the shape of the template using a sharp H or 2H pencil. Go over each line one or more times until the lines stand out clearly. Each line should be the same thickness. All corners must be closed. Use an erasing shield to remove any lines that extend past a corner.

• To complete the project the title block will have to be filled in. Steps for doing this operation are found in the next chapter.

POINTS TO REMEMBER

- Keep your hands, drawing board and instruments clean.
- Use your instruments properly. Avoid damaging them.
- Measure carefully and check your work often.
- Measure along existing lines if possible.
- Mark off dimensions lightly.
- Sharpen the pencil when necessary.
- Rotating the pencil slowly as you draw a line helps to keep it pointed.
- Spacing a drawing properly helps make it clear and easy to read.
- Use light construction lines to outline the whole project.
- Check and clean the drawing carefully before darkening the linework.

QUESTIONS TO ANSWER

1. What grades of pencil are most often used in drafting and why?
2. Which end of a wooden pencil would you sharpen? Why?
3. What are the advantages of using a mechanical pencil?
4. What purpose does an erasing shield serve?
5. Explain how a T-Square is used to draw horizontal lines.
6. Compare the 45° set square with the 30°—60° set square.
7. What common angles can be easily drawn using the T-Square and the set squares?
8. Explain the meaning of the statement: "The drafting machine is a scale, a T-Square and set squares all in one."
9. In what way is a scale more than just a ruler?
10. What is the smallest division on the full-size metric scale?
11. How long is the full-size scale in millimetres? In centimetres?
12. Think of and list four points that you should follow to take proper care of the instruments.
13. What steps should you take before you tape your drawing paper on the drafting board?
14. Describe the appearance of construction lines.
15. List four steps you should follow to keep your drawing clean right up to its completion.
16. Describe object lines. When are they drawn and how?
17. Why is it necessary to space a one view drawing?

REPLACE THE X'S WITH THE CORRECT TERM

1. Your XXXXXXXXXXXXX [*MISCONCEPTIONS*] about drafting are a result of not knowing enough about the subject.
2. When the button on the top of a mechanical pencil is XXXXXXXX [*depressed*] the jaws at the other end open to allow a piece of lead to be XXXXXXX [*inserted*].

PROJECTS

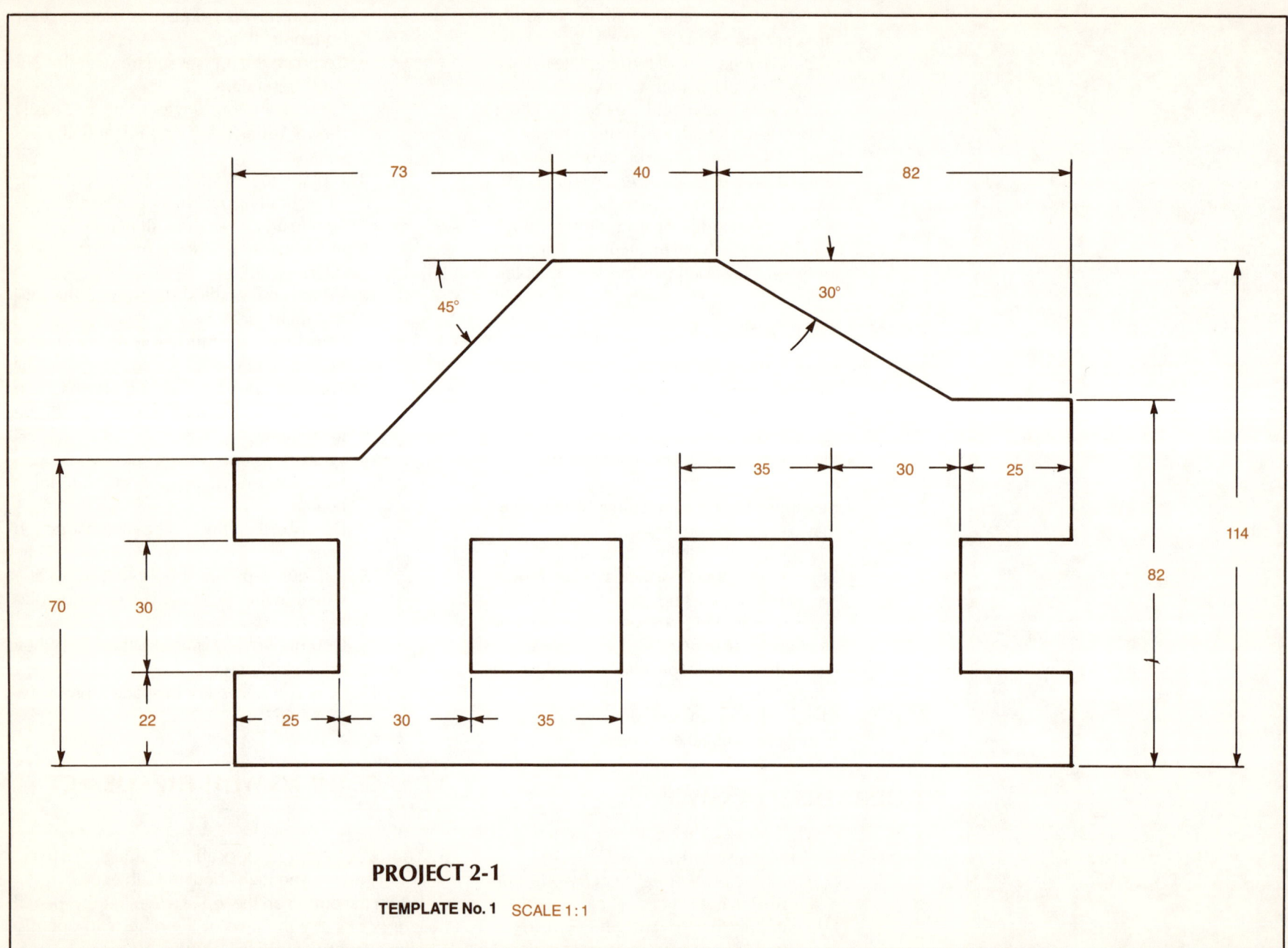

PROJECT 2-1

TEMPLATE No. 1 SCALE 1:1

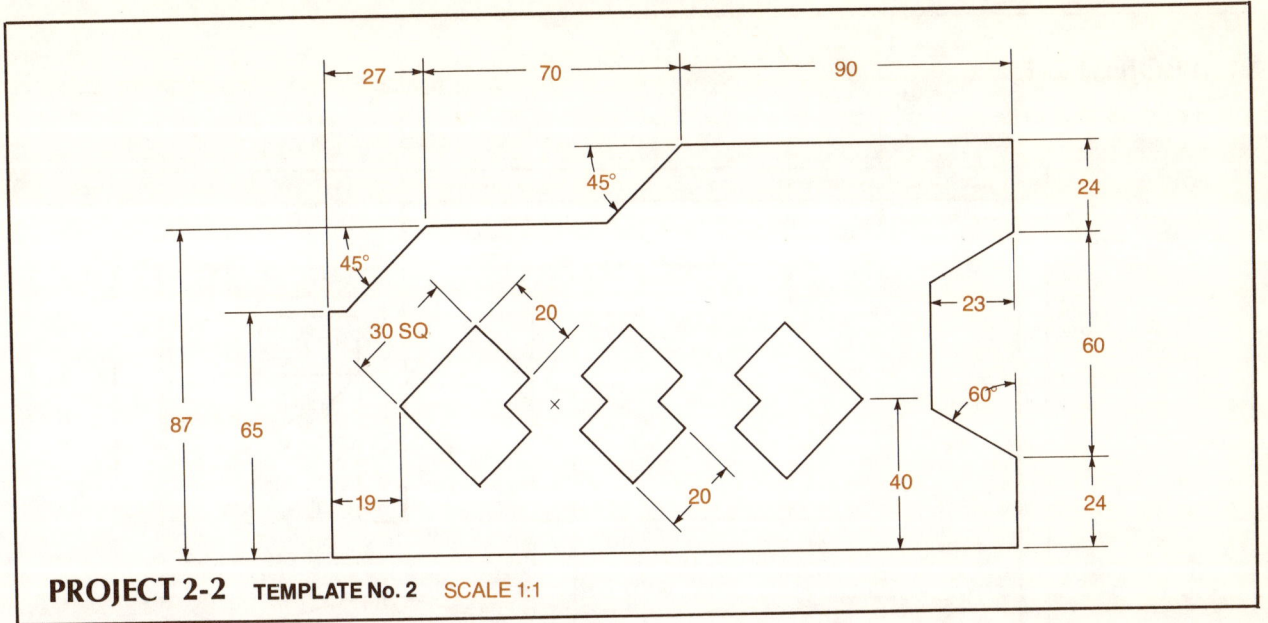

PROJECT 2-2 TEMPLATE No. 2 SCALE 1:1

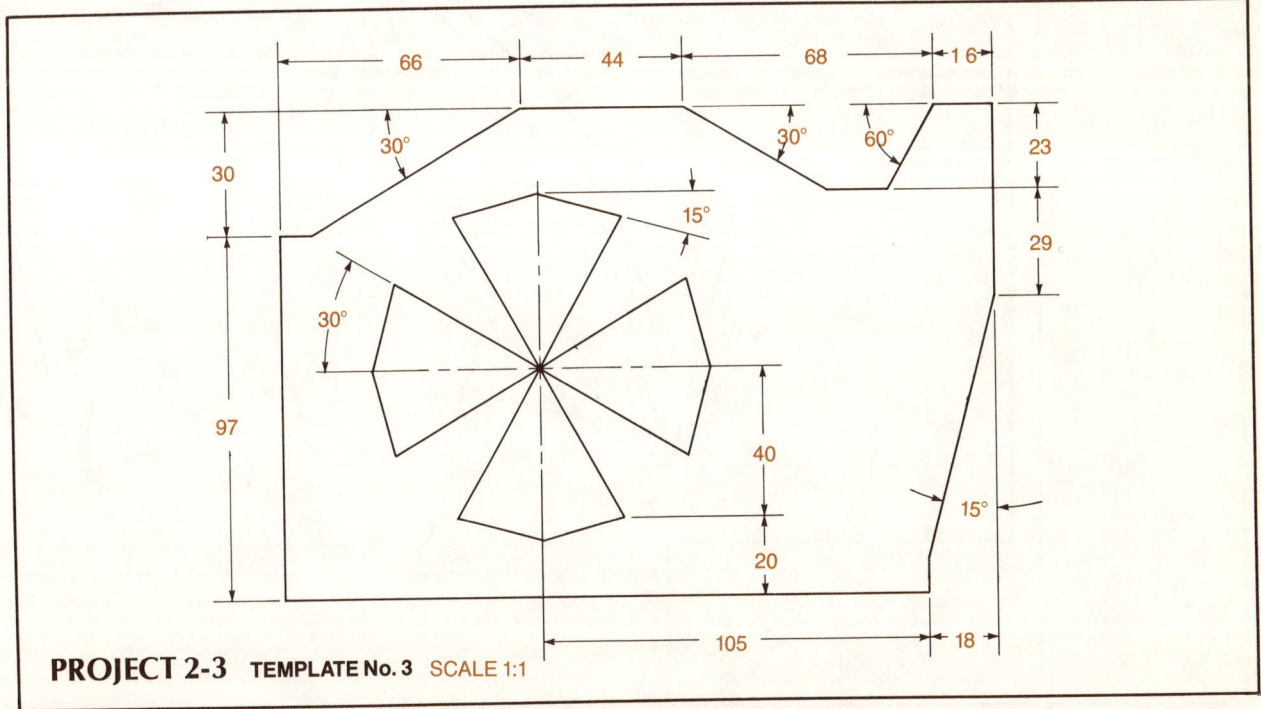

PROJECT 2-3 TEMPLATE No. 3 SCALE 1:1

PROJECTS 15

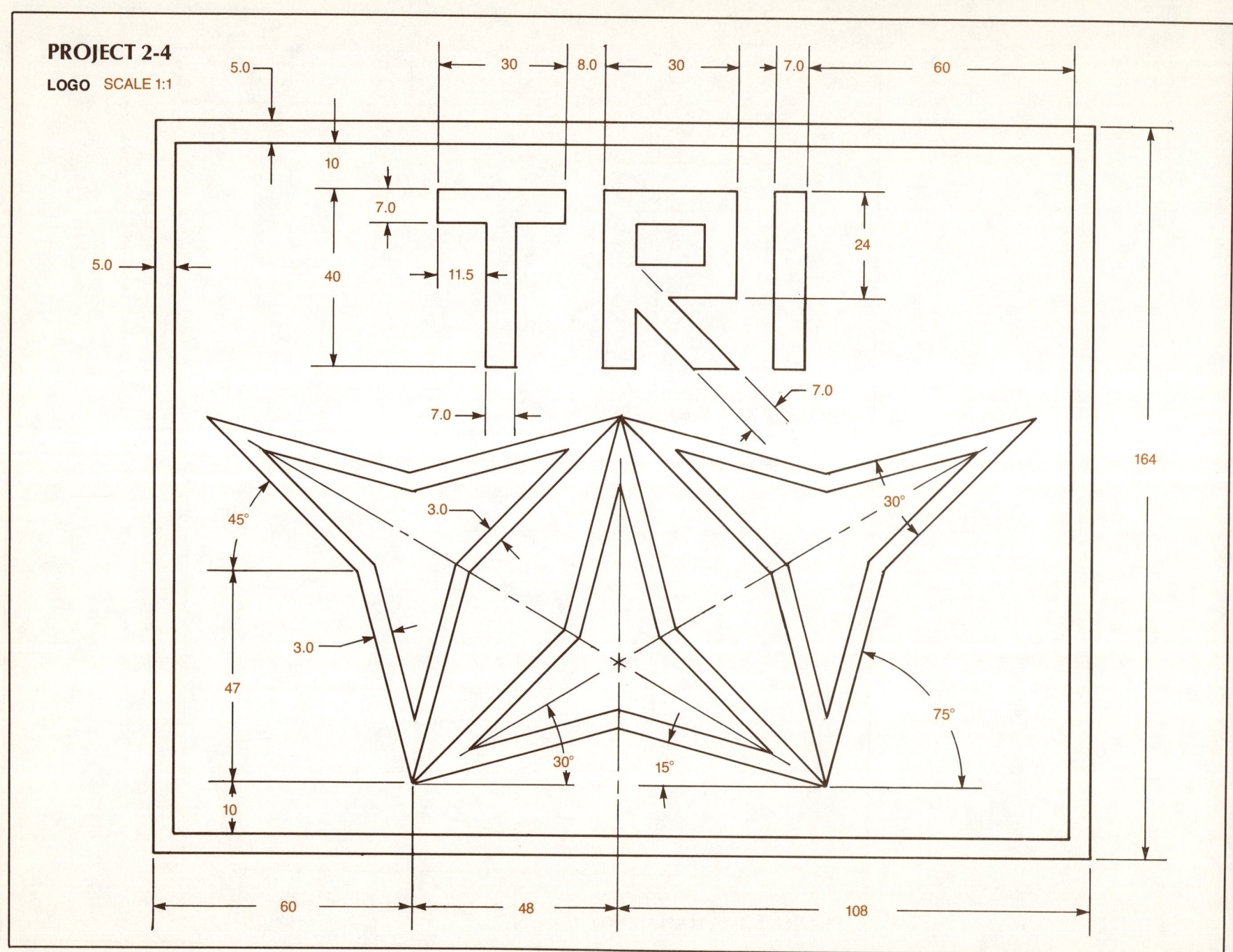

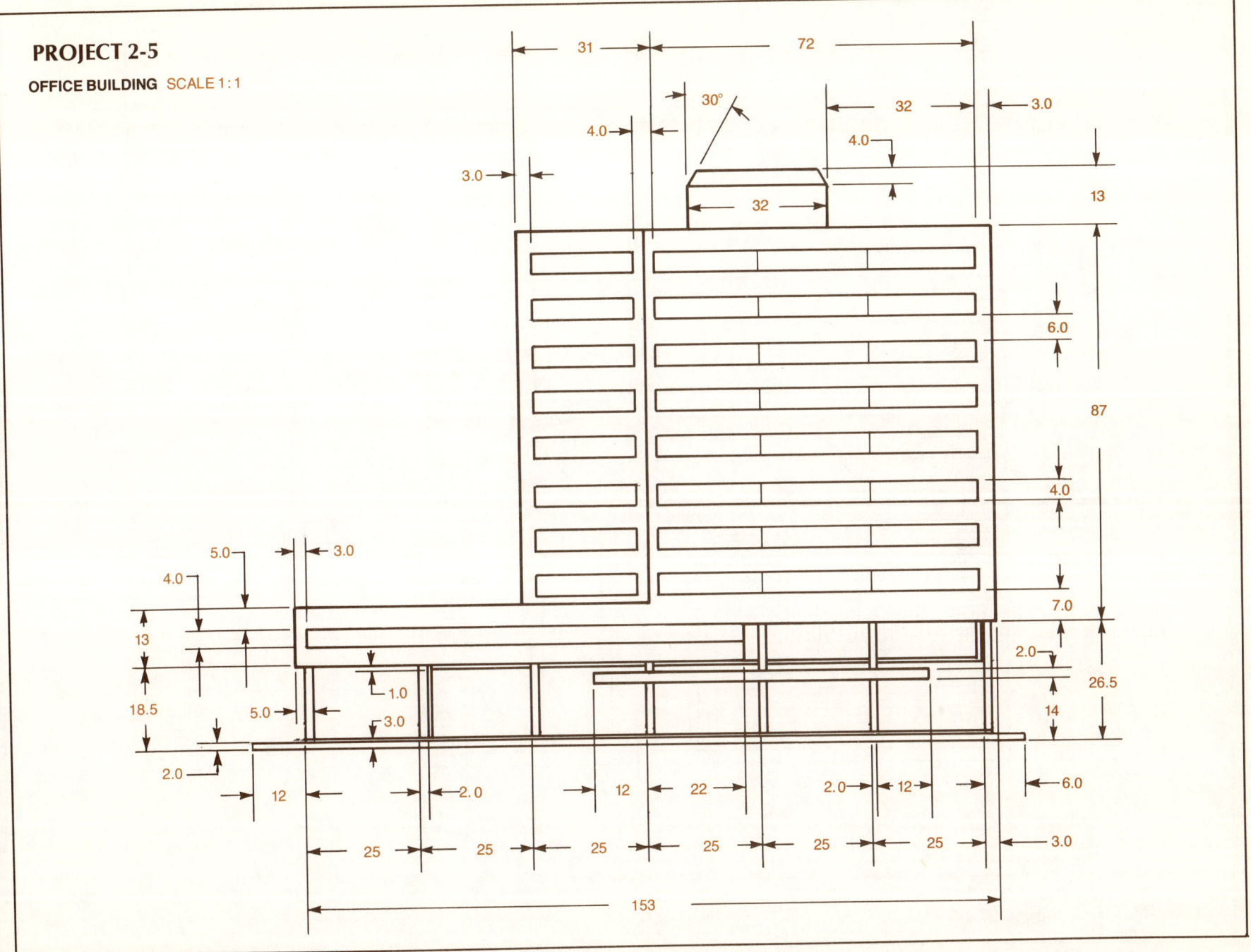

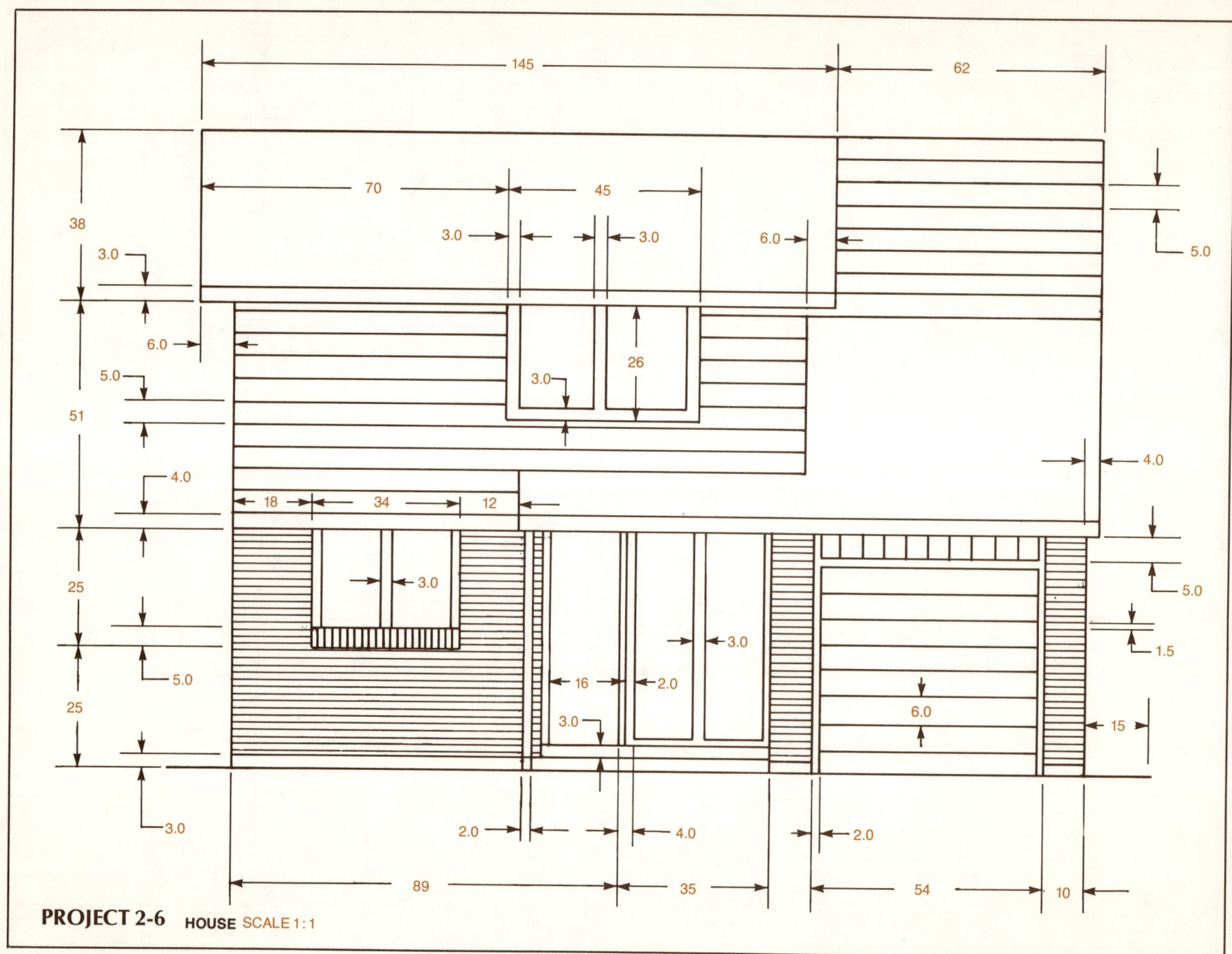

CHAPTER 3
LETTERING

WORDS TO LEARN

opportunity (op-por-tú-ni-ty)
flex
uniform (ú-ni-form)
inclined (in-clíned)

opportunity—a good chance

uniform—always the same

flex—to bend or exercise

A picture is worth a thousand words. This expression is very true of technical drawing. However, additional, clear, easy to read information is also lettered on technical drawings to complete the message supplied by the views.

The style of lettering used is called commercial Gothic. Only the capitals are used. This style is simple in shape and free of fancy details. Each letter is built from one or more single strokes.

ABCDEFGHI
JKLMNOPQR
STUVWXYZ&
1234567890

Fig. 3-1

If you have been unhappy with your lettering, you now have an **opportunity** to improve it. With a few helpful hints, and lots of practice, your lettering will soon be something you can be proud of. But most importantly, it will be easy to read.

Helpful Hints

- Lettering that is **uniform** in height is easier to read. Draw two light, barely visible guide lines before you start your lettering. Guide lines are usually 3.0 mm apart for most lettering. Guide lines for titles and headings can be drawn easily and of uniform height by using a guide lining aid.
- Rest your forearm on the drawing board and hold your pencil as shown. Beginners will find that their fingers become cramped at first. Take frequent breaks and **flex** your fingers. The finger muscles will soon strengthen with practice.

Fig. 3-2

19

Fig. 3-3

- Use only single strokes and press firmly. Do not repeat strokes.
- Most letters should be made as wide as they are high. However, the figure 1 and the letter I are made by a single stroke. The letters M and W are made slightly wider than they are high.
- Letters should be close together but not touching.

SPACE WORDS FOR EASY READING

ONE LETTER SPACE BETWEEN WORDS **CLOSE, BUT NOT TOUCHING**

Fig. 3-5

- Leave the space of one letter between words for easy reading.
- Leave the space of one letter between rows of lettering.

ROWS OF NOTES ARE SPACED APART BY THE SAME DISTANCE AS THE HEIGHT OF LETTERS USE A GUIDE LINER

EQUAL SPACES

Fig. 3-6

- Light, barely visible guide lines do not need erasing.

After some practice you should complete the projects from Chapter Two by preparing their title blocks.

inclined—put (or drawn) at an angle

LLL

AA

- Follow the construction of each letter as shown in the example. All vertical or **inclined** strokes are made from top to bottom. All horizontal strokes are made from left to right.

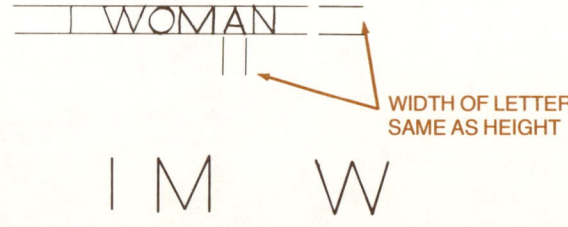

WIDTH OF LETTER SAME AS HEIGHT

I M W

Fig. 3-4

POINTS TO REMEMBER

- Light, barely visible *guide lines* will help you achieve uniform height in your lettering.
- Letter freehand using single strokes.
- Follow the examples of the capital letters slowly and carefully.
- Letters should be close together but not touching.
- Allow space between words.
- Allow a spacer row between rows in a note. If you don't, your note will be a jumble of letters.

QUESTIONS TO ANSWER

1. Why are guide lines used when lettering?
2. Why are capital letters used when lettering?
3. Why is lettering used on technical drawings rather than writing?
4. What is the suggested height of most lettering?
5. What are five important points to remember when lettering?

REPLACE THE X'S WITH THE CORRECT TERM

1. Guide lines will help you produce letters of **XXXXXXX** height.
2. By practising your lettering, you have an **XXXXXXXXXX** to improve your style.
3. When lettering, all strokes, whether vertical or **XXXXXXXX**, are made from top to bottom.
4. To prevent your fingers from becoming cramped, **XXXX** your fingers often.

LETTERING EXERCISES

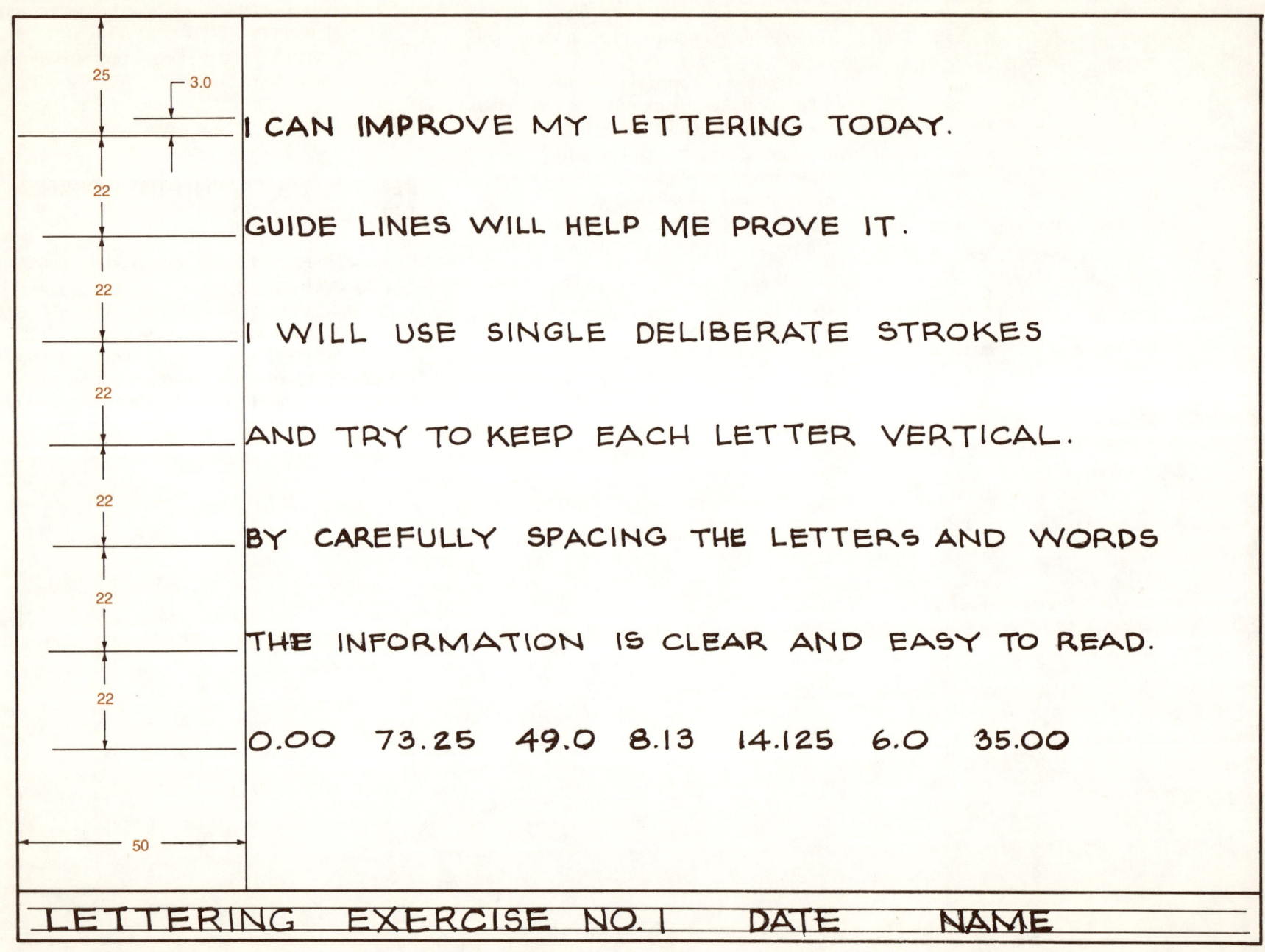

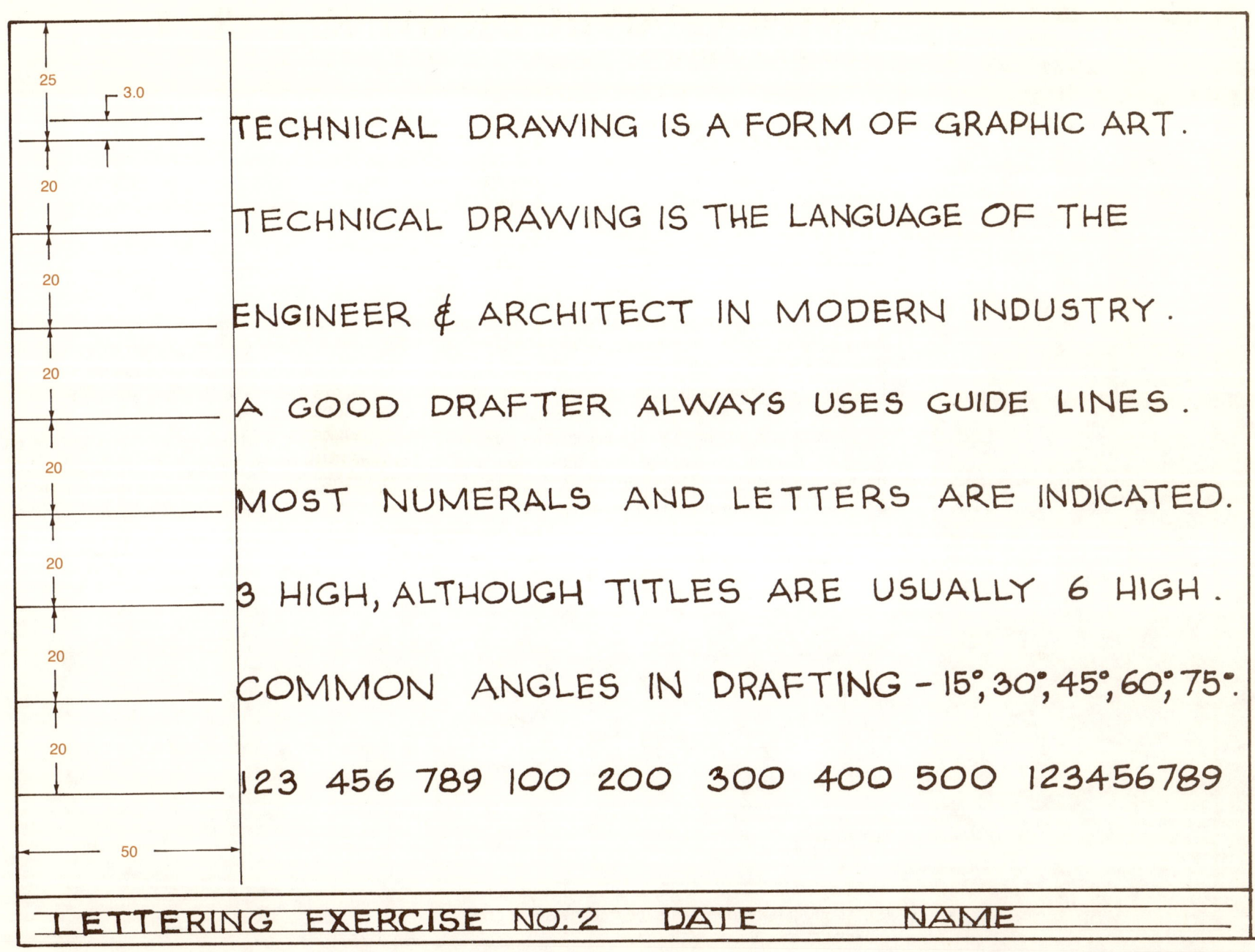

CHAPTER 4
ORTHOGRAPHIC DRAWING, PART 1
RECTANGULAR SHAPES

WORDS TO LEARN
impression (im-prés-sion)
foundation (foun-dá-tion)
distort (dis-tórt)
visualize (vís-u-al-ize)
project (pro-ject)

To help you understand the meaning of the term orthographic, let us first review what you have learned from the Projects in Chapter Two. These projects were basically two dimensional; that is, you were only concerned with the length and height dimensions. The width was too thin to be drawn. It is sometimes easier and just as clear to give the third dimension, the thickness of the material, in the **title block** or simply by a notation lettered neatly on the drawing.

Now that you have mastered the single view drawing, you are ready to draw objects that require three dimensions to describe them accurately.

What are these objects? They are all around us. If you were to group them by their general shape you would find, in simplest terms, that they are either **cylindrical** or **noncylindrical**. A cylindrical object has a shape that is round over most or all of its length (Fig. 4-2). A noncylindrical object has a basic shape

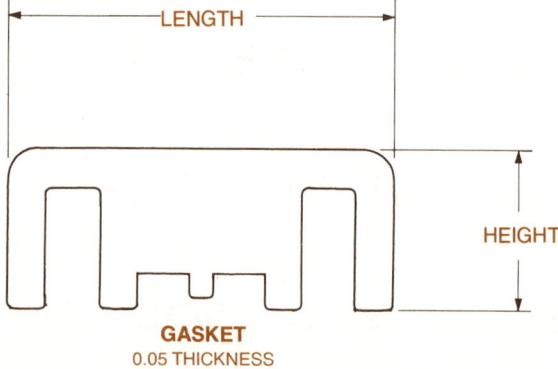

Fig. 4-1

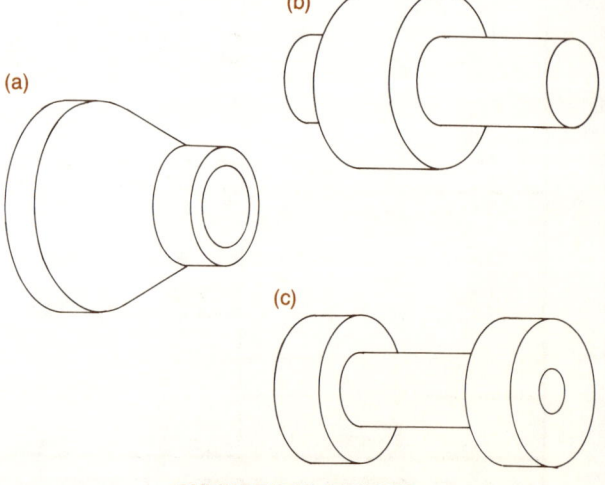

CYLINDRICAL OBJECTS

Fig. 4-2

A single view showing the length and width of an object and a note to indicate the thickness will completely describe the object's shape.

24

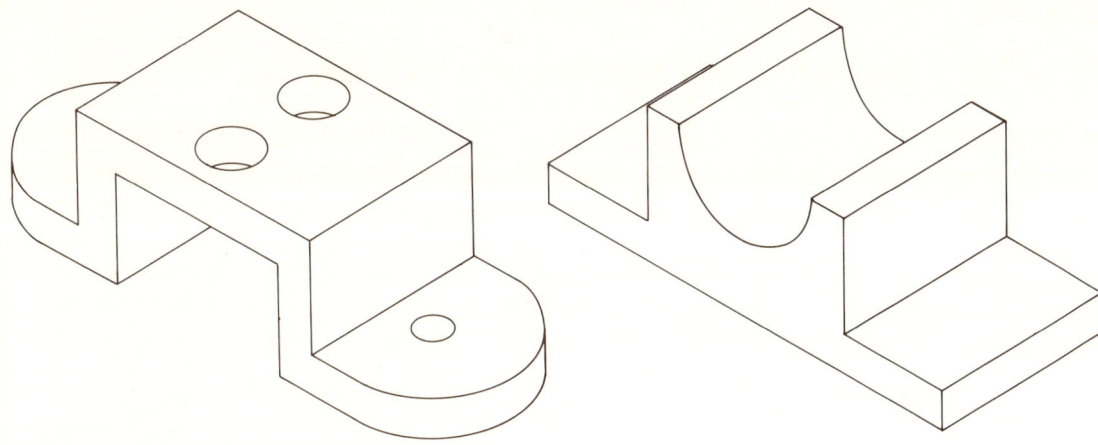

Fig. 4-3

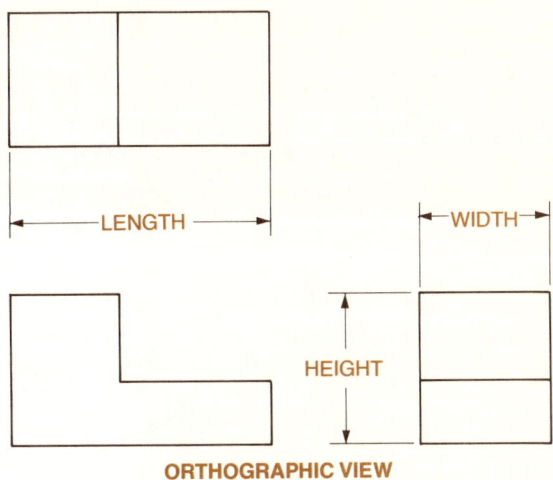

Fig. 4-4(b)

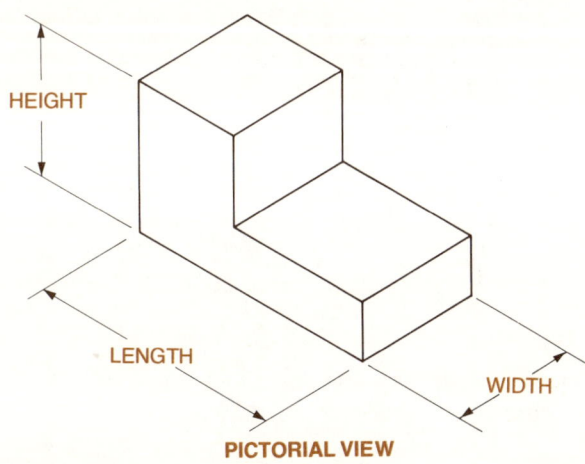

Fig. 4-4(a)

visualize—to picture in your mind

foundation—base upon which something stands

impression—a mental image of something or someone

that can be described as rectangular, although some may have round features (Fig. 4-3).

Can you think of some objects whose basic shape can be classified as either cylindrical or rectangular?

PICTORIAL VIEWS

The objects pictured in Figs. 4-2 and 4-3 provide a general **impression** of these shapes. These views are called pictorial views. They show the length, width and height of the object in one three dimensional view (Fig. 4-4(a)). Pictorial views cannot describe an object exactly or completely. The surfaces of objects are not shown in their true shape by a pictorial view. Also, quite often many of the features of an object are hidden from sight, and cannot be described.

ORTHOGRAPHIC VIEWS

Drafters have found that orthographic views can be used to describe any shape exactly and completely. As Fig. 4-4(b) shows, three separate views are used together and each view is two dimensional. When you have completed this chapter you will be able to look at the views of an orthographic drawing and create in your mind a visual image or picture of the object. This ability to **visualize** the shape and features of objects from reading orthographic drawings is the **foundation** of blueprint reading. Don't panic. We will begin with the most basic of objects. We will gradually progress step by step until you are familiar with the simple stages by which you can describe any object. Each project you will do is designed to use the skills learned earlier. New information will be introduced only when you are ready to proceed. Let us begin with a

ORTHOGRAPHIC VIEWS 25

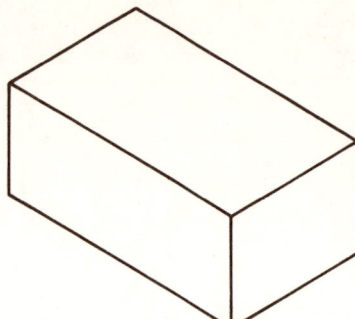

Fig. 4-5

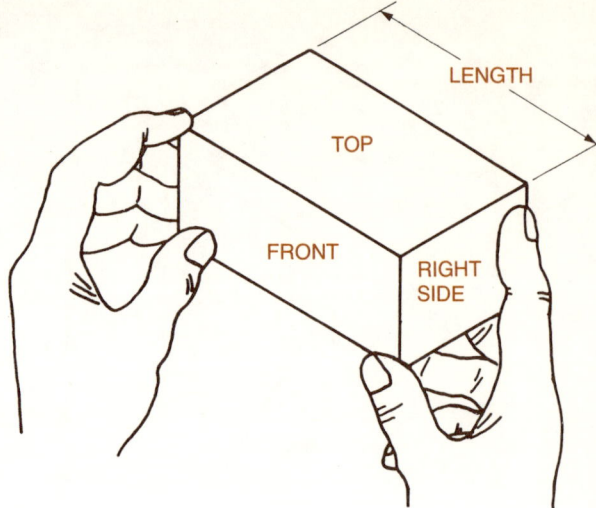

Fig. 4-7

Look at the object as it is held in Fig. 4-7. The distance between the fingers is the **length**. You can see that the length is the same for both the top and front sides (Fig. 4-8).

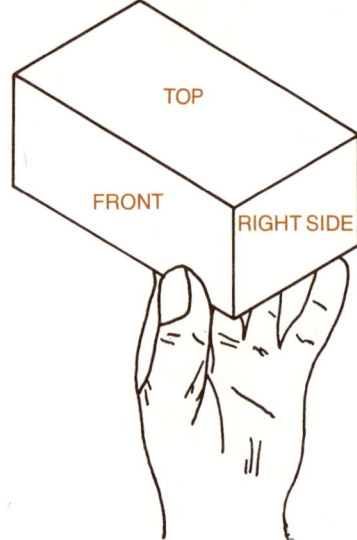

Fig. 4-6

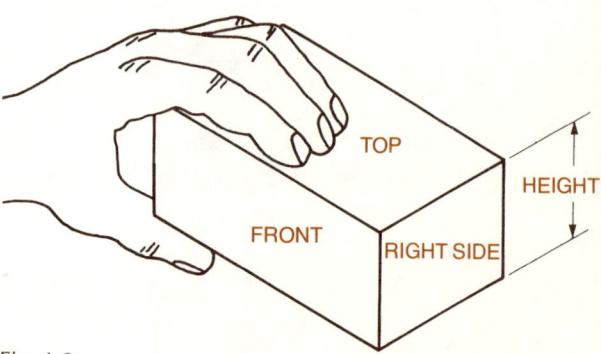

Fig. 4-8

simple block (Fig. 4-5). We will use the block to explain what we mean by orthographic drawings (Fig. 4-6).

If you held a rectangular solid block in your hand as shown in Fig. 4-6, you would realize that the object has six sides. These are the front and rear sides, the top and bottom sides and the right and left sides.

The three sides that are visible in Fig. 4-6 are called the front, the top and the right side. These are the sides we are most concerned with.

The distance between the fingers holding the object in Fig. 4-8 is the **height**. The height is the same for both the front and right sides.

In Fig. 4-9 the distance between the fingers holding the object is the **width**. Note that the width is the same for both the top and the right sides.

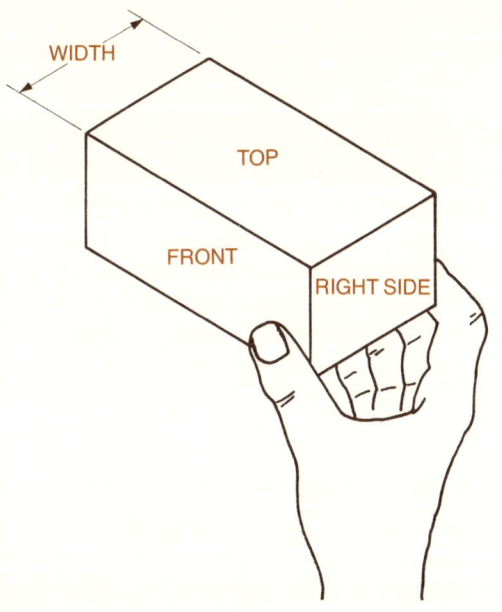

Fig. 4-9

Fig. 4-10

project—to transfer an image (or voice, object, etc.) from one position to another

distort—to give an appearance that is not true

Orthographic Projection. To help you understand the idea of orthographic projection the familiar rectangular block has been placed inside a hinged glass box. As you look at the block through the glass, the image of the block is **projected** onto the surface of the glass. To see the true shape of each side of the object, your line of sight must be at right angles to the side you are viewing. Only then is it possible to see its dimensions as they really are. This is very important to remember.

To explain this concept further, imagine yourself sitting in a movie theatre. If you sit in the side aisles, away from the centre of the screen, your view will be **distorted**. The closer you move towards the middle of the theatre, the truer the image will appear. It's the same in drafting. When you look at one surface and see only its outline and nothing more, then you are seeing its true shape. This view is called an **orthographic view**.

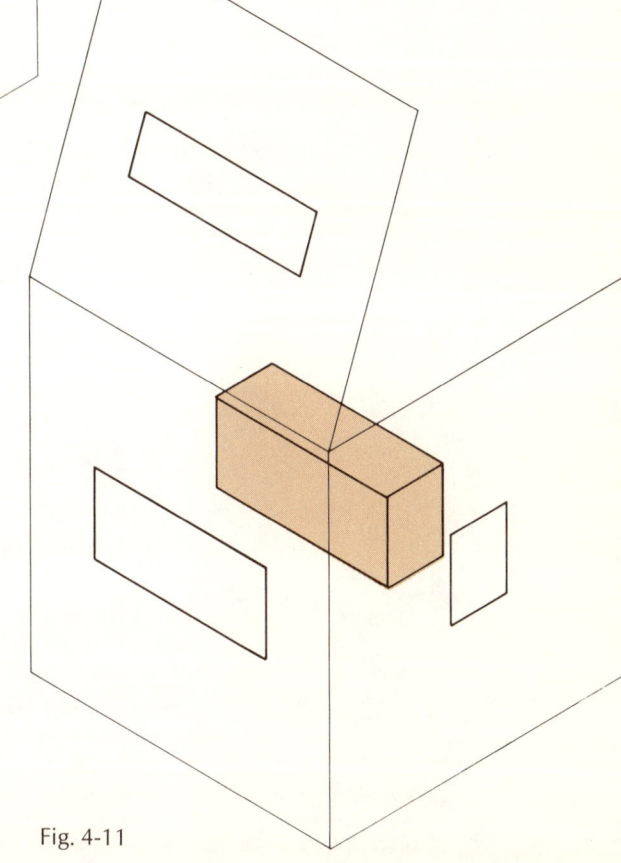

Fig. 4-11

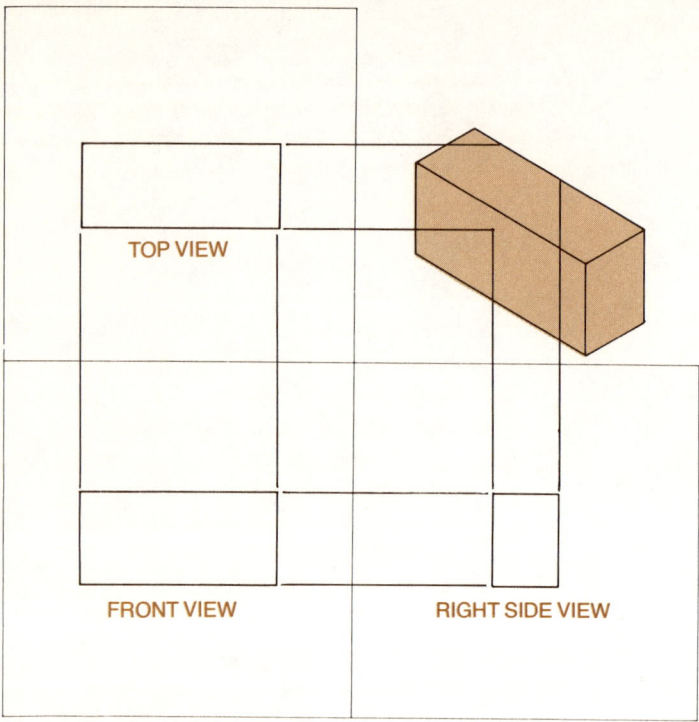

Fig. 4-12

Fig. 4-13

We can see as the glass box is opened out that the orthographic views are taking new positions. The top view has moved above the front view. The right side view is now to the right of the front view.

The line of sight has been left in Fig. 4-12 to help you to see how the dimensions can be projected from one view to the others. You can see from this that the length dimension is shared by both the front and top views. The height dimension is shared by the front and right side views. The width dimension is shared by the top and right side views. We can use these observations to draw the three orthographic views on a sheet of drawing paper.

Laying Out Three Orthographic Views

Later we will discuss the spacing of the views on the drawing paper. However, for the moment we will begin by drawing a vertical and a horizontal line as shown in Fig. 4-13. We have darkened in the corner where the two lines meet. Note that we have also darkened in a corner of the front side of the object in Fig. 4-14.

Before we begin, it is useful to remember that lines that are **parallel** to each other in the pictorial view are drawn **parallel** to each other in the orthographic view.

We can outline the three orthographic views simply by answering a few questions and applying the answers to the drawing.

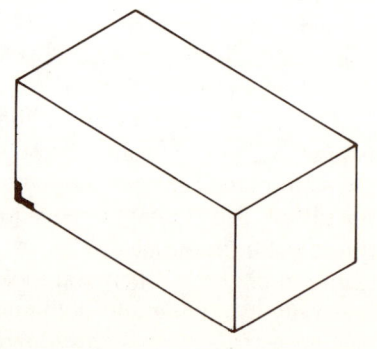

Fig. 4-14

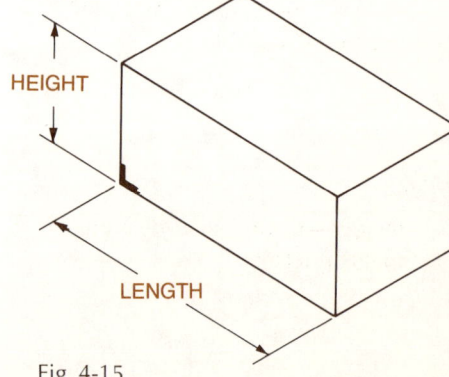

Fig. 4-15

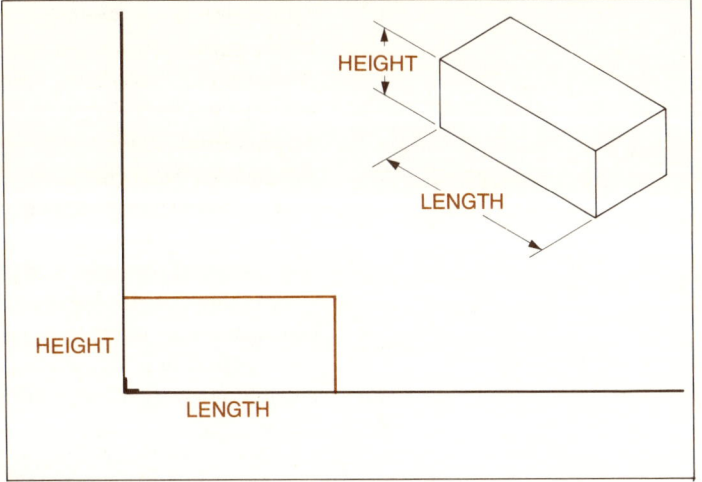

Fig. 4-16

Question: What two dimensions outline the front view?
Answer: The length and height dimensions.
Application: From the corner, mark off the height dimension on the vertical line. Mark off the length dimension on the horizontal line. From these two points draw lines parallel to the existing lines. You have now outlined the front view.

Views are usually spaced apart from one another to avoid crowding. You can begin the top view in the corner shown in Fig. 4-17.

Question: What dimension is common to the top view and the front view?
Answer: The length dimension.
Question: How can distances be transferred from one view to another view?
Answer: By using **projection lines**. These are light construction lines.
Application: Lightly project the length dimension up from the front view.

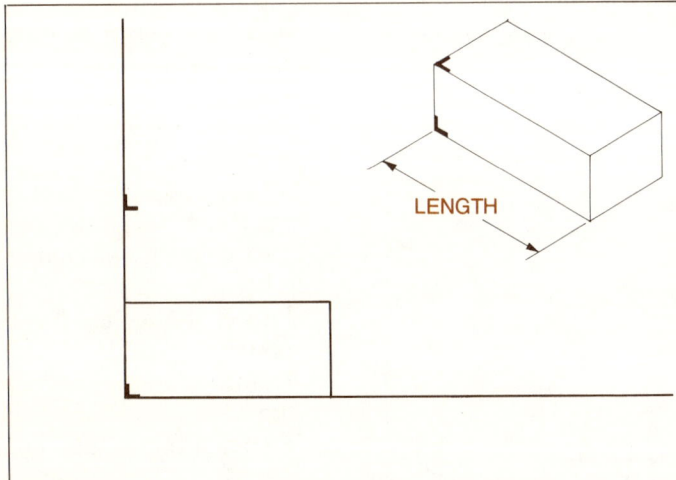

Fig. 4-17

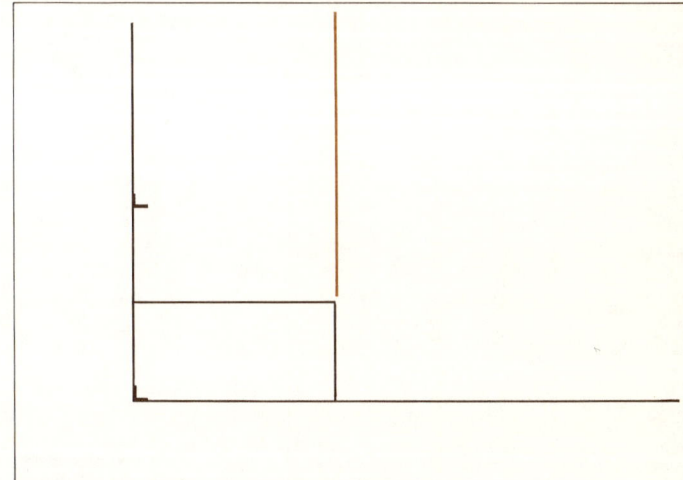

Fig. 4-18

ORTHOGRAPHIC VIEWS 29

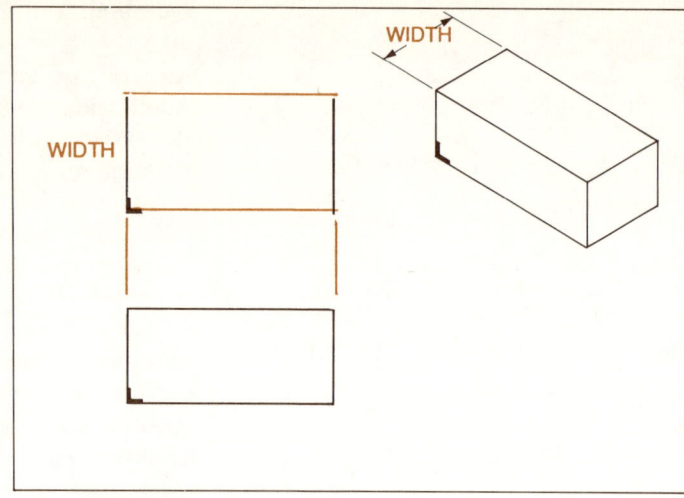

Fig. 4-19

Question: What other dimension is needed to outline the top view?
Answer: You need the width dimension.
Application: Mark off the width dimension from the corner in the top view. Draw horizontal lines from these points to complete the outline of the top view.
Question: What two dimensions are needed to draw the right side view?
Answer: The height and the width dimensions.

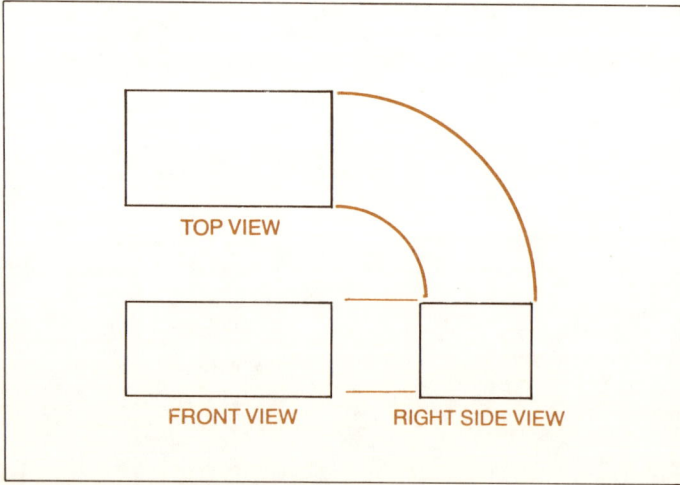

Fig. 4-20

Question: How can these dimensions be placed accurately and easily without measuring?
Answer: By projecting the height and the width dimensions from the other two views.
Application: Project the height dimension from the front view. With the aid of a compass, project the width dimension around from the top view as shown in Fig. 4-20. Draw the two vertical lines to complete the outline of the right side view.

The three orthographic views of the rectangular block are now complete and in the correct position.

Now that you know how easy it is to draw orthographic views of a rectangular object, we are sure that you would like to start working on your own. We have a series of projects for you to complete. To make your work easier the projects are designed to be completed on the prepared graph paper (Fig. 4-21).

All you need to do your drawings is a straight edge or a ruler and a soft pencil. There is no need to measure: the scales are on the border of the graph paper. Each square on the graph represents 5.0 mm. Each project in this series will have the same overall dimensions. These are shown in Fig. 4-22: length 120 mm, width 60 mm, and height 40 mm. Follow the steps in the example below and apply them to complete the projects.

1. From the darkened corner at the zero position in the front view, mark off the height and length. Mark 40 mm up for the height and 120 mm to the right for the length. Use the scale on the graph: there is no need to measure. Complete the front view (Fig. 4-23).
2. Project the length distance up to the top view position.
3. From the corner provided at the zero position in the top view, mark off the width dimension. Mark 60 mm from the zero. Finish the top view (Fig. 4-24).
4. To begin the right side view, project the height from the front view.
5. Project the width dimension from the top view. Follow the curve around and down to the right side view. Finish the right side view (Fig. 4-25).

30 ORTHOGRAPHIC DRAWING, PART 1

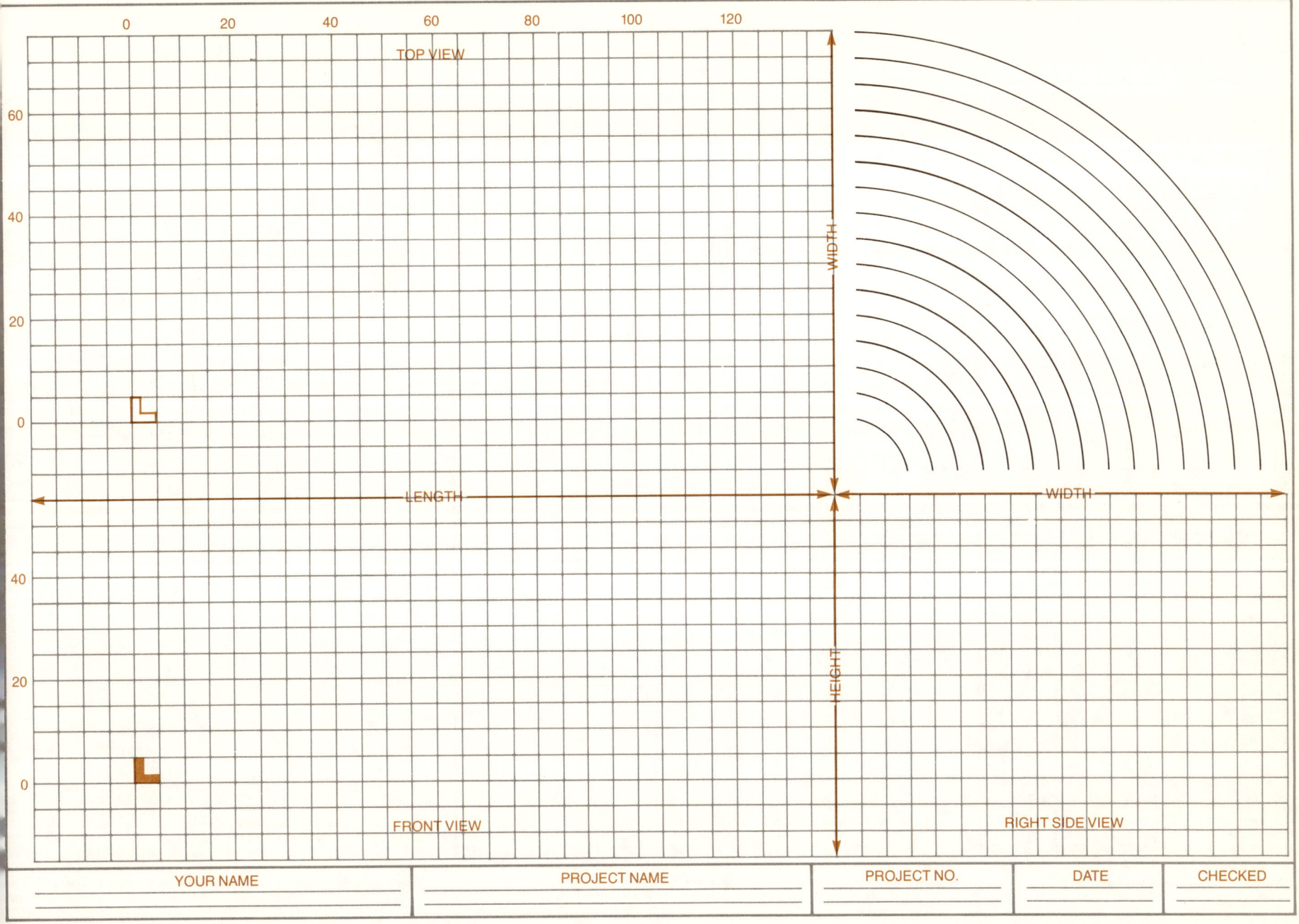

Fig. 4-21

ORTHOGRAPHIC VIEWS 31

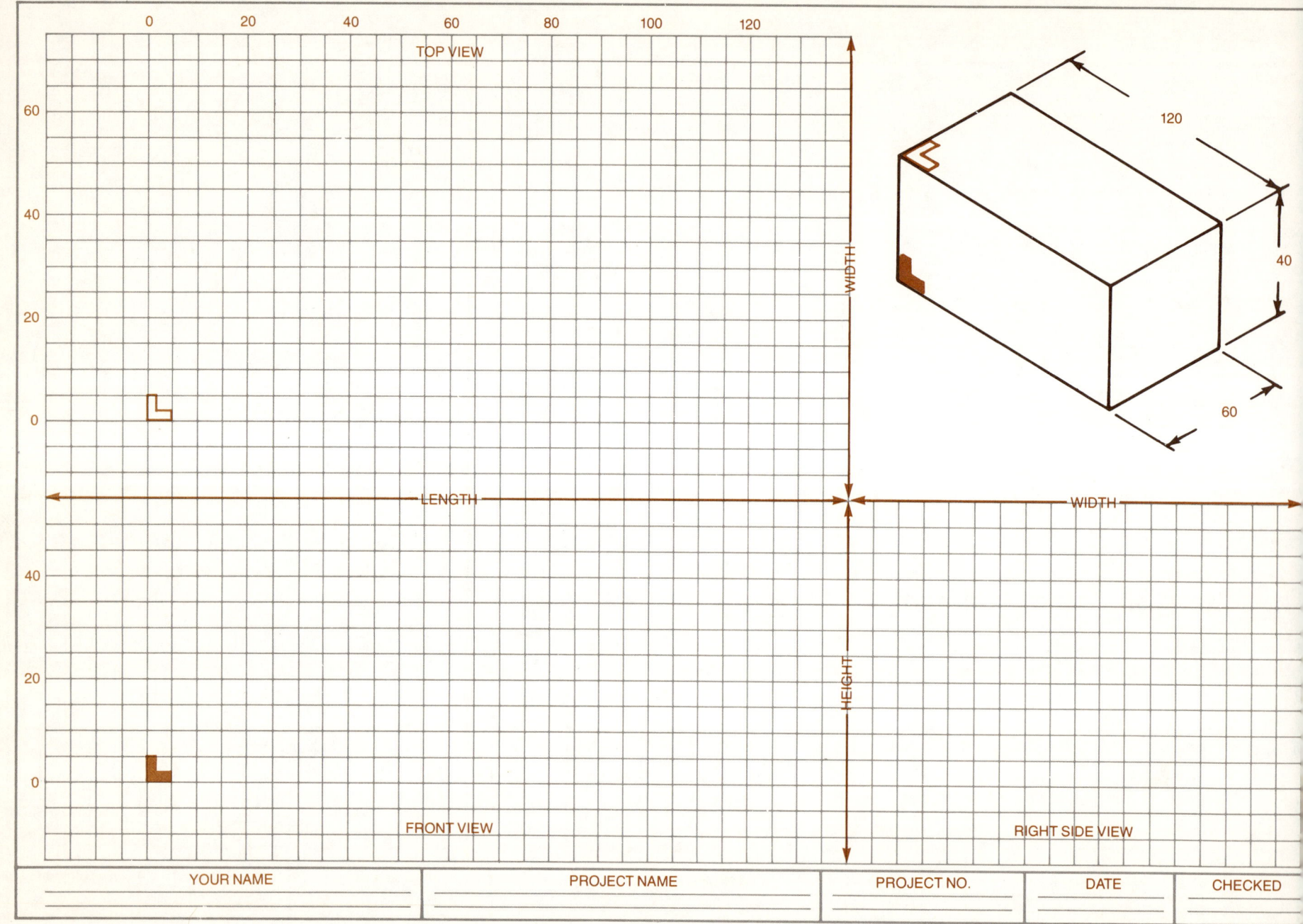

Fig. 4-22

32 ORTHOGRAPHIC DRAWING, PART 1

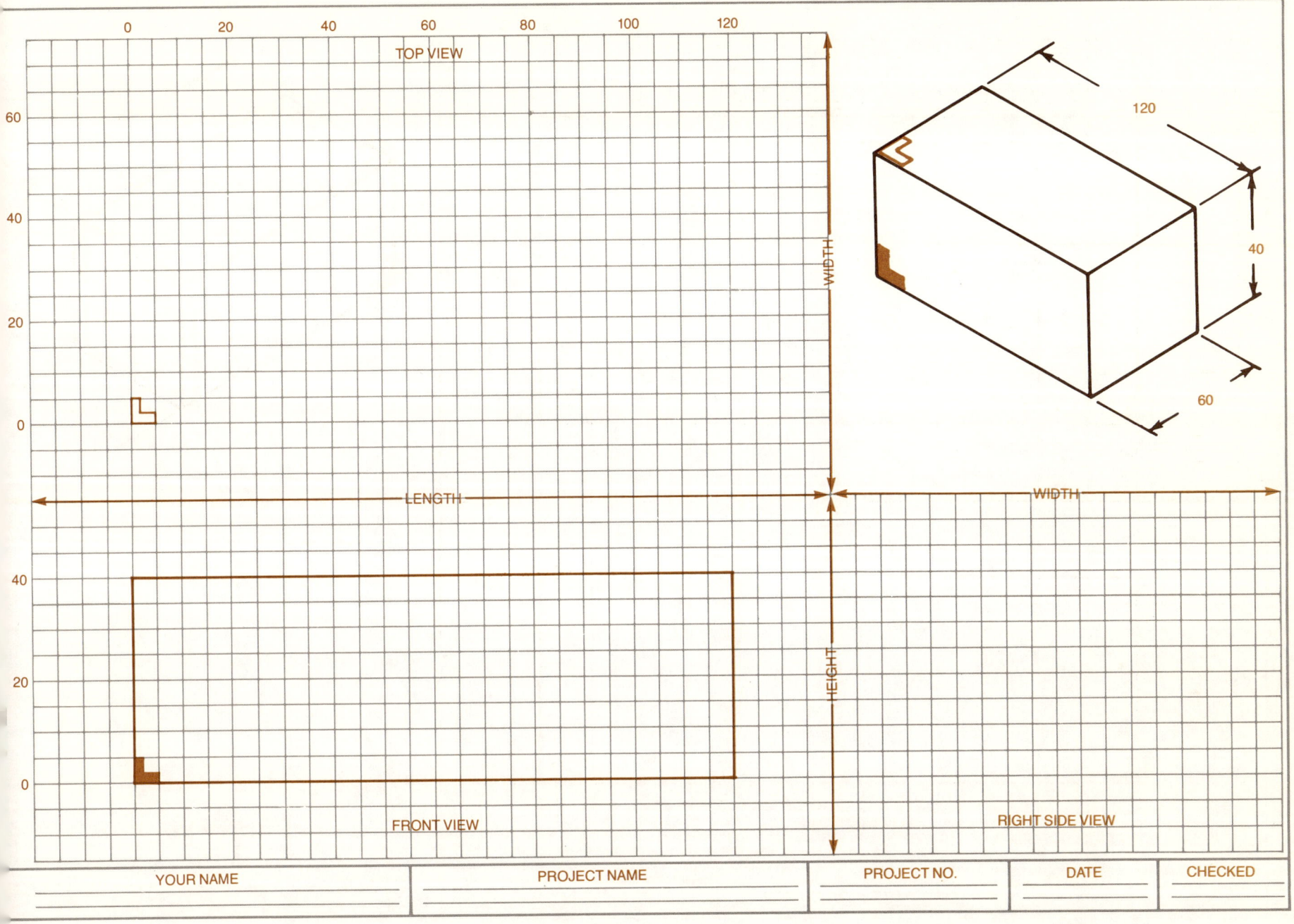

Fig. 4-23

ORTHOGRAPHIC VIEWS 33

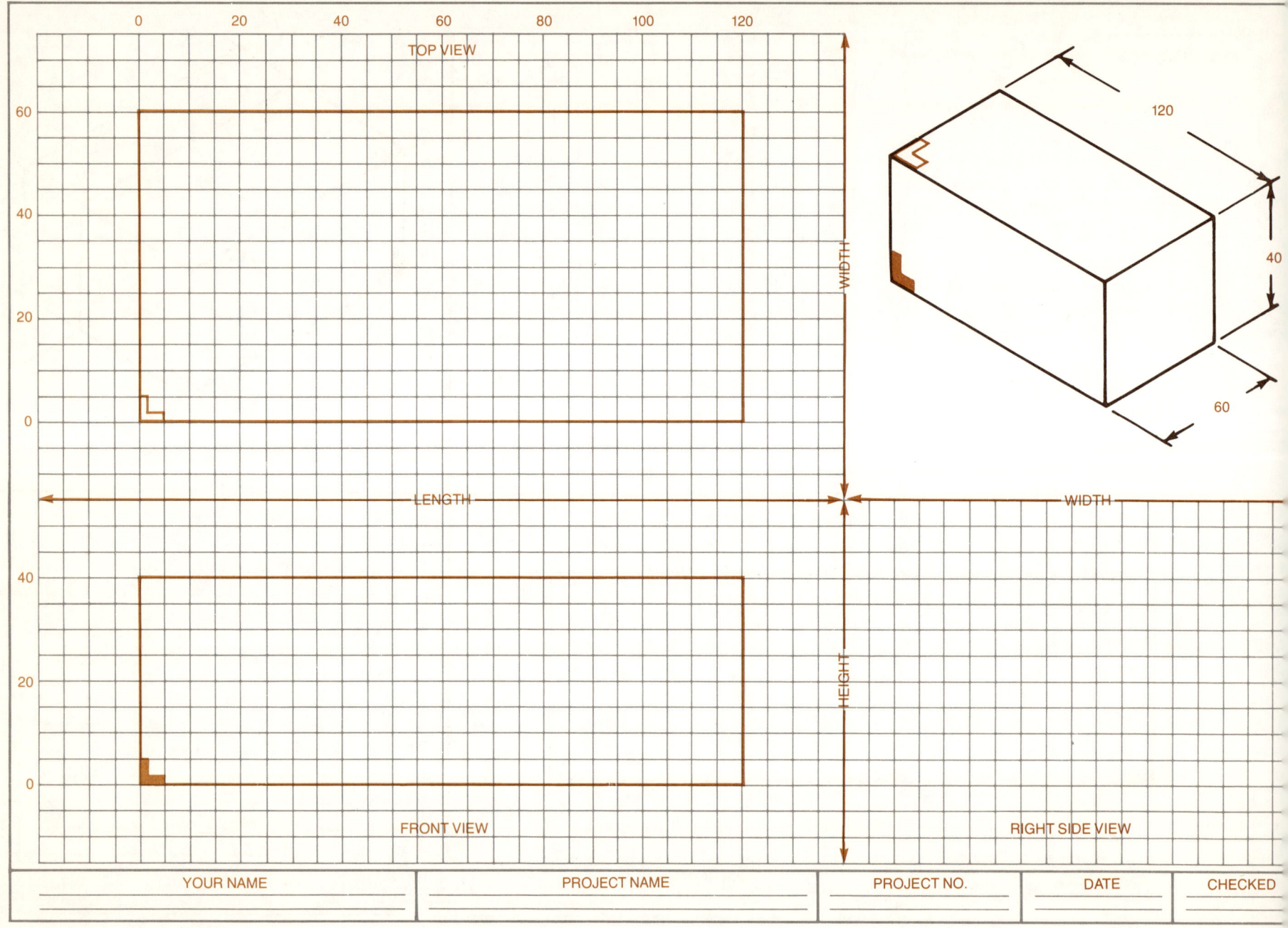

Fig. 4-24

34 ORTHOGRAPHIC DRAWING, PART 1

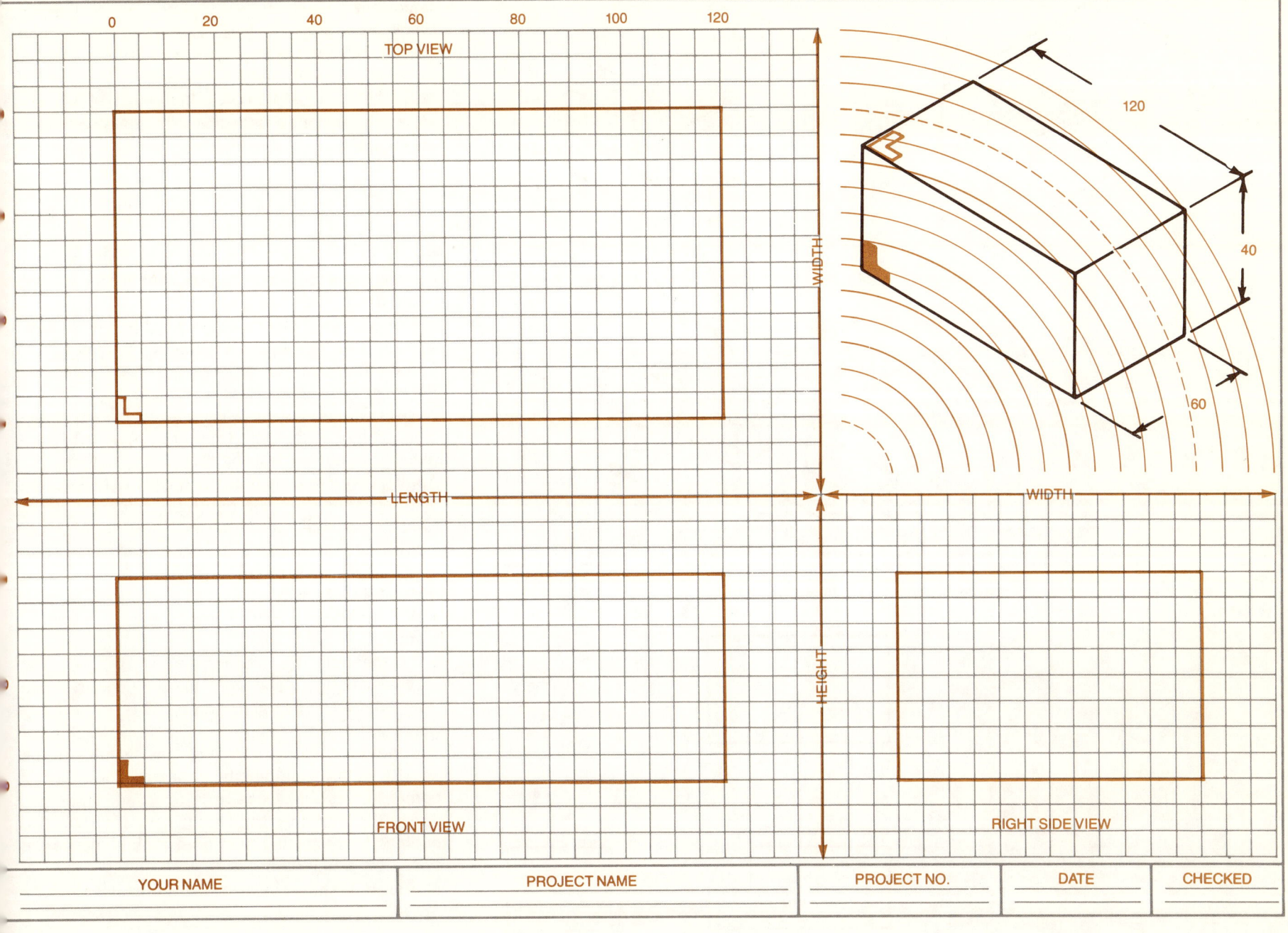

ORTHOGRAPHIC VIEWS 35

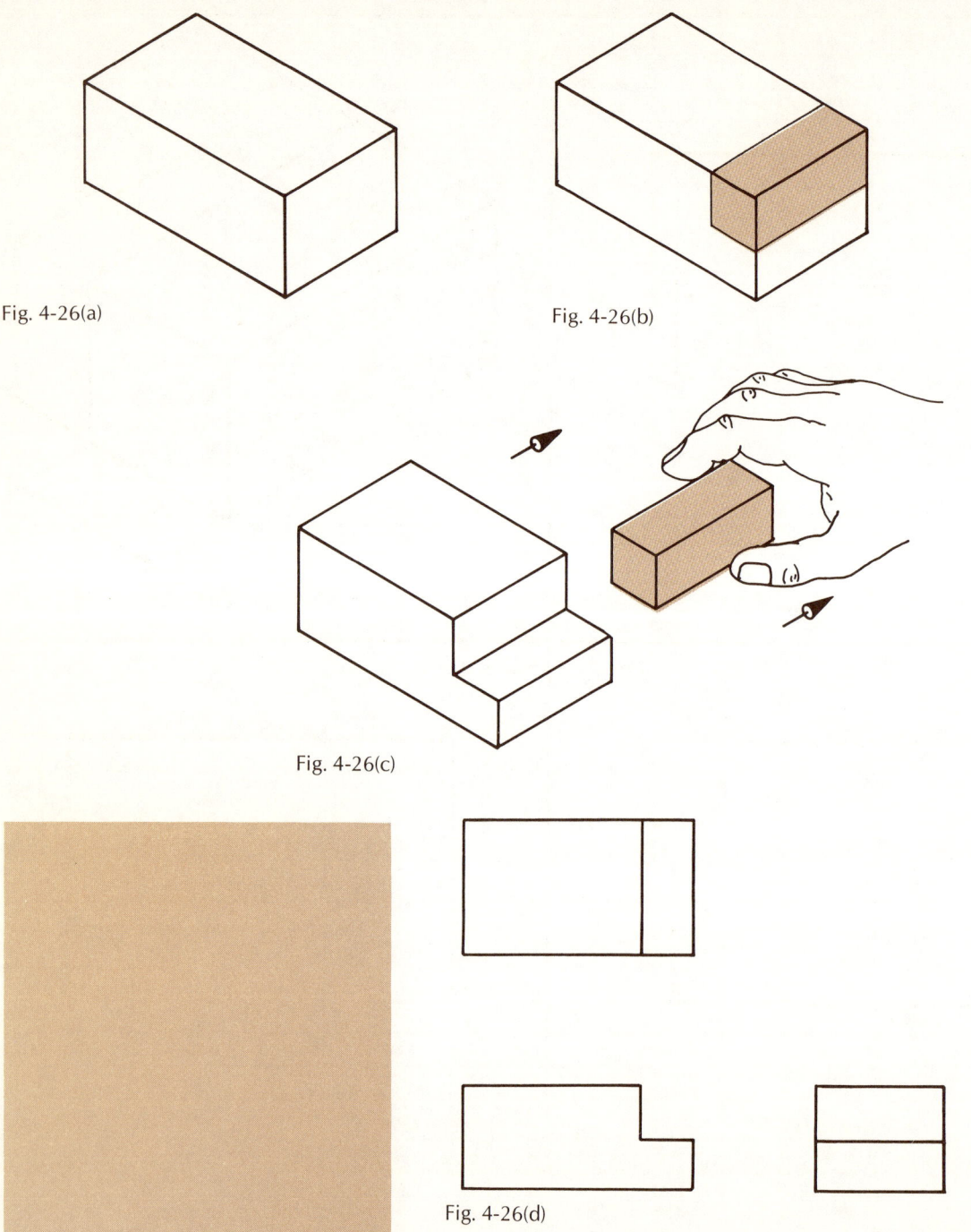

Fig. 4-26(a)

Fig. 4-26(b)

Fig. 4-26(c)

Fig. 4-26(d)

Important. This example was of a simple rectangular block. Later you will learn to draw more complex objects. However, always remember first to outline all three views of your project, as was done here. Do this before you start to complete the details of any one view. No matter how difficult a project may seem to be at first glance, you will find that laying out all of the three views will help you to complete the drawings successfully in less time.

In Fig. 4-26(a, b, c, d) the rectangular block has been altered. A corner of the object has been removed as shown in the pictorial drawings. The orthographic views give the same information. Your first project will be similar in shape to this example.

First, lay out all three views of the object. Treat them as if they were still a solid block.

Question: Which view of this object provides the most information about its shape?

Answer: The front view. The front view clearly shows that a corner of the object has been removed. Complete the front view first (Fig. 4-28).

Application: From each corner of the front view, project lines to the top and right side views (Fig. 4-29). Check to see if all three views are complete.

If you are still not sure of what you are doing, take another look at the project and give a little thought to these observations:

- When a line in a view changes direction, it forms a corner.
- A corner indicates an edge.
- When a corner is shown in one view, the edge will be indicated in the other views.

Important. Always outline first that view which gives you the most information about the features of the project. In this example, the front view shows that a corner of the object has been removed. Therefore, outline the front view first. The other views can then be outlined by projecting lines from each corner in the front view to the other views. Each corner in a view must be represented by a line in the other views.

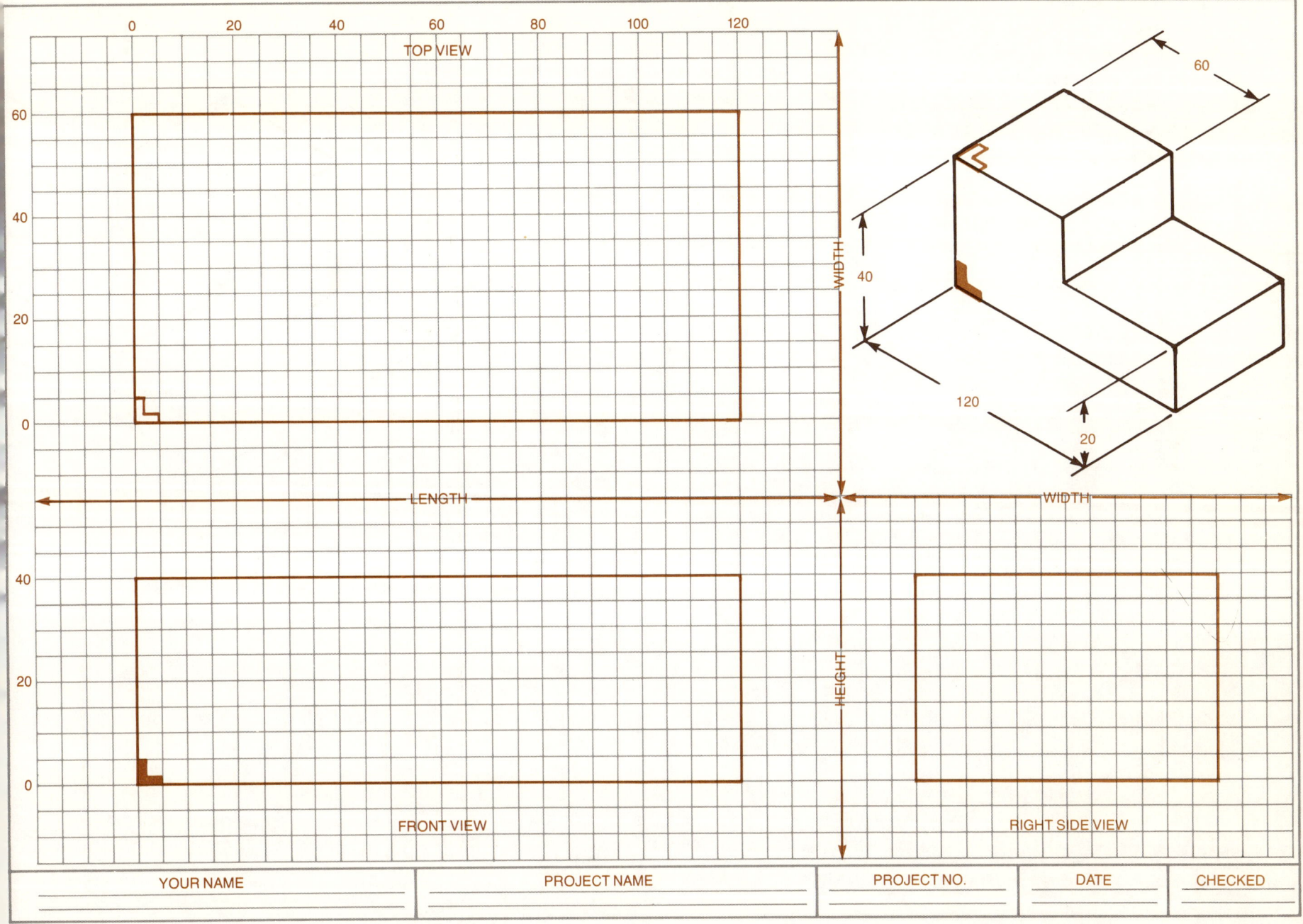

Fig. 4-27

ORTHOGRAPHIC VIEWS 37

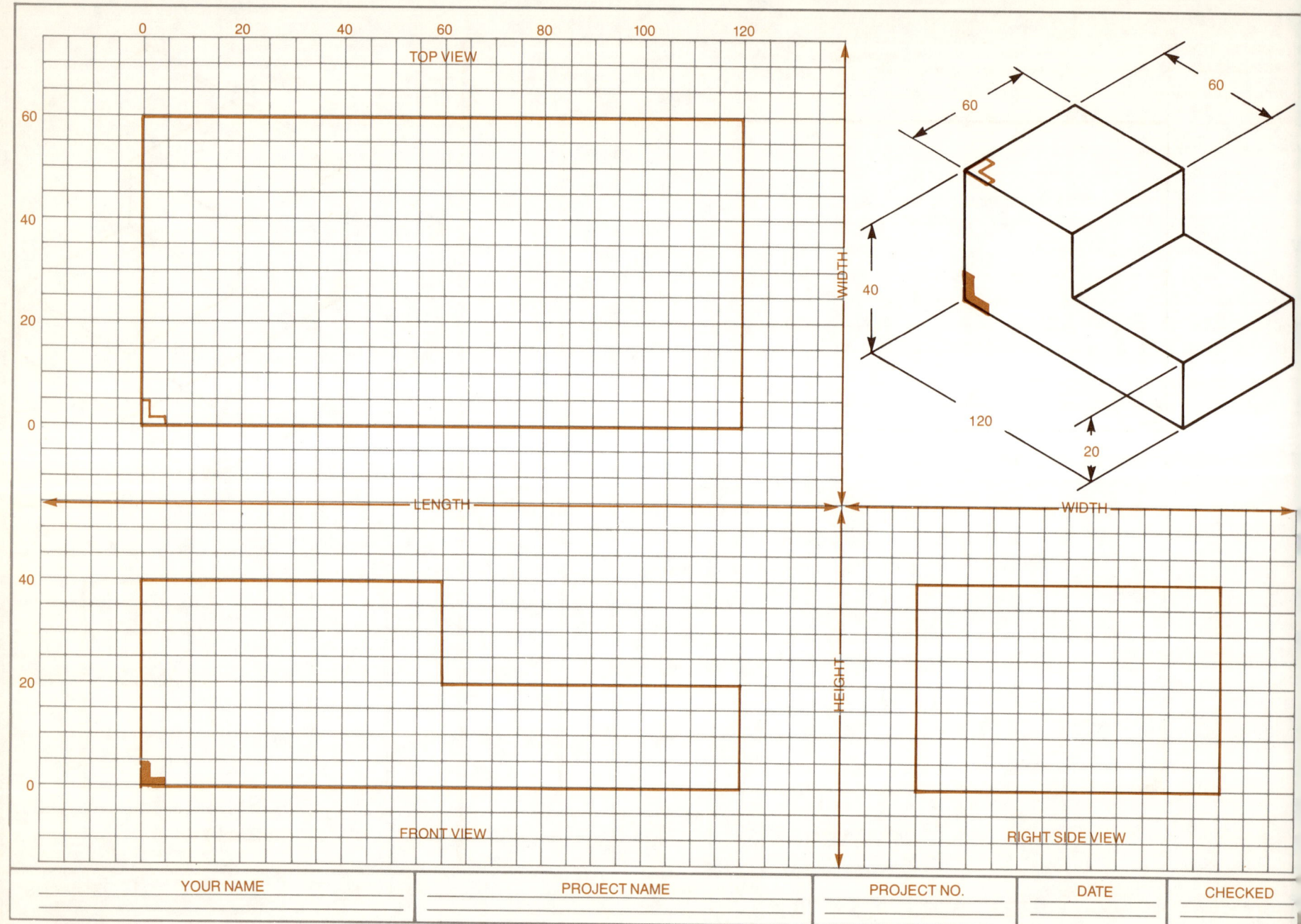

Fig. 4-28

38 ORTHOGRAPHIC DRAWING, PART 1

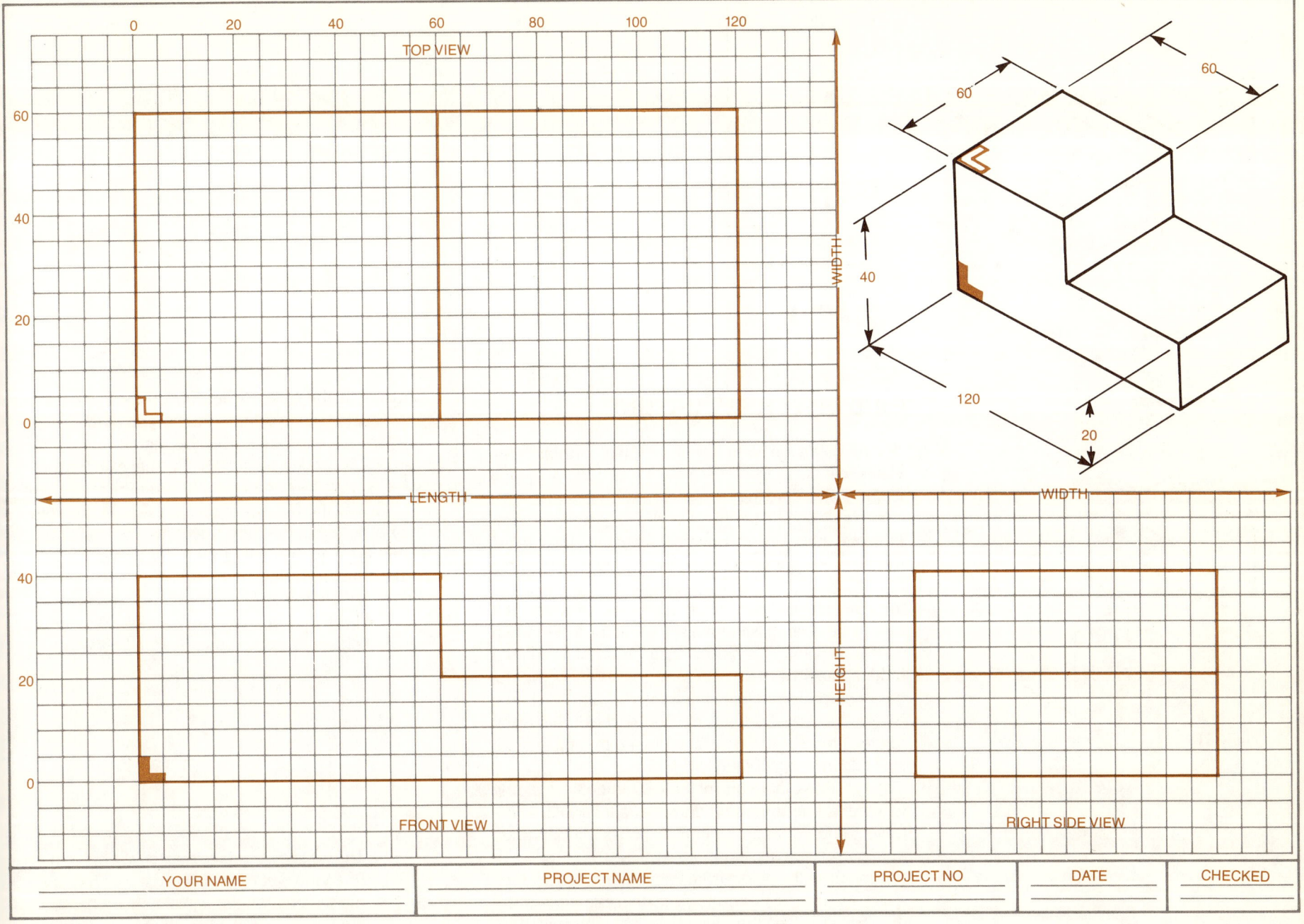

Fig. 4-29

ORTHOGRAPHIC VIEWS

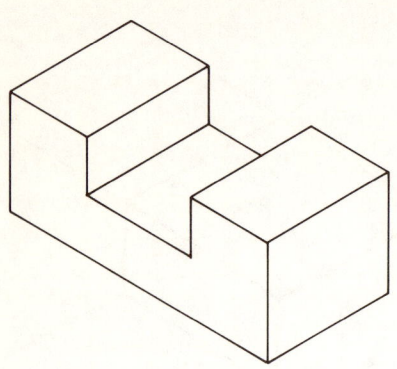

Fig. 4-30

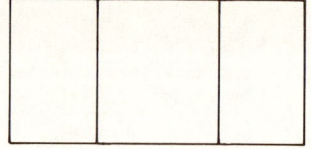

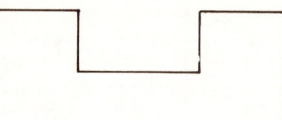
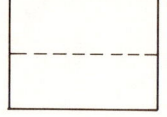

Fig. 4-31b

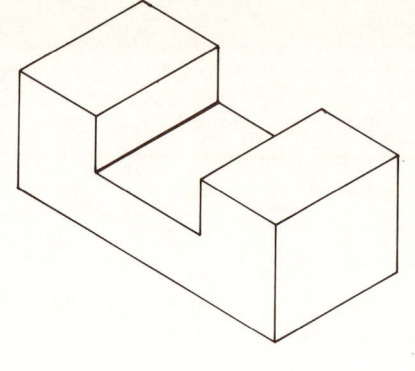

Fig. 4-32

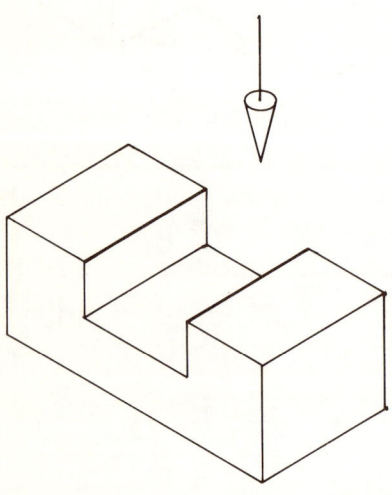

Fig. 4-31a

HIDDEN FEATURES AND LINES

Before going on with the spacing of orthographic views, we need to discuss how we can show hidden features on a drawing.

In Fig. 4-30, a dado block is shown. The front view indicates that a slot has been cut out of the block. In the top view the corners of the slot have been projected from the front view and are represented by two solid, thick lines. However, in the right side view the slot cannot be seen. It is hidden but it still must be shown on the drawing. This is done by using what is called a **hidden line**. In the right side view the corner of the slot has been projected from the front view and is shown by the thin line made up of short dashes. This is the hidden line. These dashes are 3 to 4 mm long and are spaced 1 mm apart. (See Fig. 4-31b).

If you think that you may have difficulty deciding whether a line should be drawn as a thick black line (object line), or as a thin line of dashes (hidden line), ask yourself this question:

Looking at the object from this position, would I see all the features (in this example the edges of the slot)? If the answer is yes, then the edges are represented by thick, solid object lines.

Looking at the object from the position shown in Fig. 4-32, all that is visible is the outline of the block.

Is there an edge in the block that is not visible because it is hidden from sight? In this example, the answer is yes. The corner at the bottom of the slot indicates that the bottom of the slot should be represented by a line in the right side view. As you cannot see this edge it must be shown by a hidden line.

When drawing hidden lines, there are a few general rules you should follow:

- Each end of a hidden line should touch an object line or another hidden line.

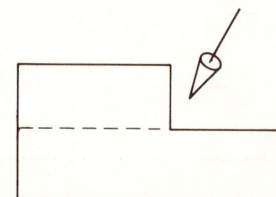

Fig. 4-33

- The edge of a surface may be visible in part of a view yet extend on past a corner as a hidden edge. If so, leave a space between the corner and the first dash of the hidden line.

40 ORTHOGRAPHIC DRAWING, PART 1

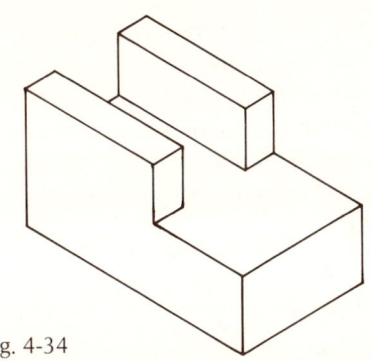

Fig. 4-34

- Corners of hidden lines are formed by dash lines that touch each other.

Fig. 4-35

- The dashes of hidden lines that are close together and parallel should be staggered. If they are not staggered they will appear to be a series of equal signs.

Fig. 4-36

Before continuing on to spacing Orthographic Views, turn to page 44 and complete the Graph Projects.

Spacing Orthographic Views

Using graph paper with the corners of the front and top views positioned has given you a great deal of orthographic drawing experience in a short period of time. To make orthographic projection possible the space between the front and the top views should be the same as the space between the front and the right side views. We suggest that you leave a space of 40 mm between views for most of the projects in this text.

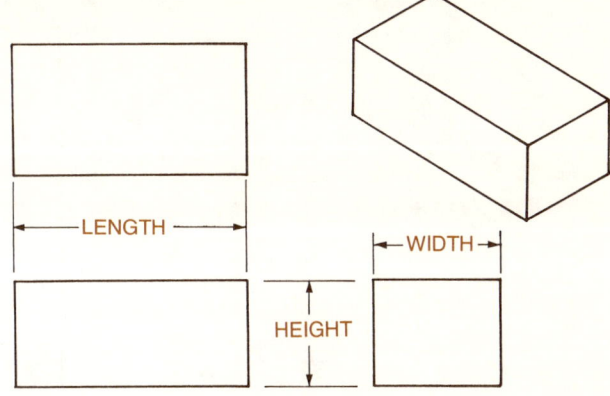

Fig. 4-37

Drafters usually try to centre the three views on the drawing paper for several reasons:
1. To make sure that the views can be drawn on the size of paper being used.
2. To allow the drafter room to properly place the necessary dimensions and notes.
3. The drawing will be more pleasing to the eye and easier to read.

Spacing three orthographic views is not difficult. What we need is a vertical and horizontal line on the drawing paper to form the corner of the front view.

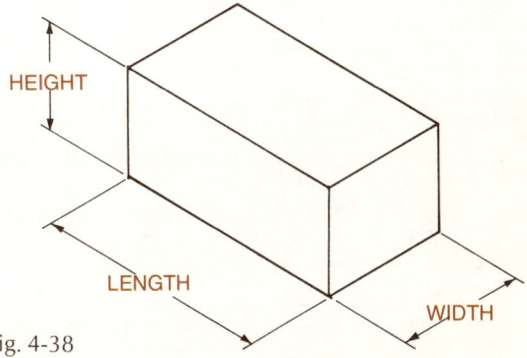

Fig. 4-38

Steps in Spacing Three Orthographic Views

Read the pictorial drawing of the project to find its overall dimensions. Remember that we will allow a 40 mm space between the views.

HIDDEN FEATURES AND LINES 41

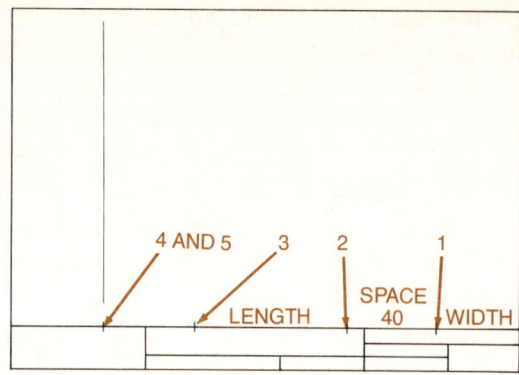

Fig. 4-39

1. On the border starting from the bottom right hand corner measure off the width.
2. From this point measure off the 40 mm space.
3. From this point measure off the length.
4. Measure the distance remaining on the line, and find the mid-point of the distance. That is, divide the distance in half.

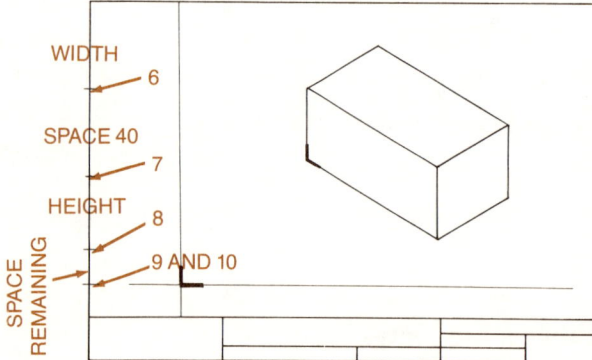

Fig. 4-40

5. From this mid-point draw a light vertical line.
6. On the border, starting from the top left hand corner, measure off the width.
7. From this point measure off the 40 mm space.
8. From this point measure off the height.
9. Measure the distance remaining on the line and find the mid-point of the distance. Again, you merely divide the distance in half.
10. From this mid-point draw a light horizontal line.
11. Remove all measurements and clean your drawing. You should now have only a light vertical line and a light horizontal line on your paper to begin laying out the three views.

Before you begin, remember to use light construction lines. They can be easily erased when necessary. Start at the corner formed by the vertical and horizontal lines you prepared earlier. Follow these steps.

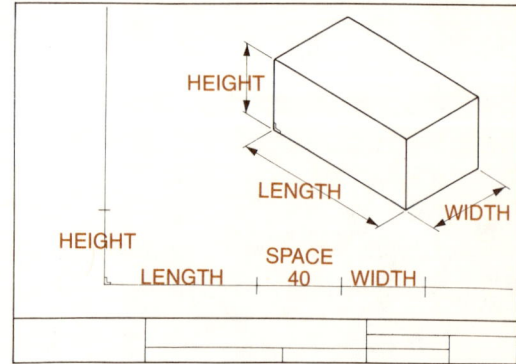

Fig. 4-41

1. Measure the height from the corner on the vertical line. Project the height across the page.
2. Measure the length from the corner on the horizontal line. From this point measure off the 40 mm space allowance and also the width dimension. Project vertical lines from each point on the horizontal line. You have now blocked in the front and the right side view. The top view can be completed simply by projecting the width dimension.

42 ORTHOGRAPHIC DRAWING, PART 1

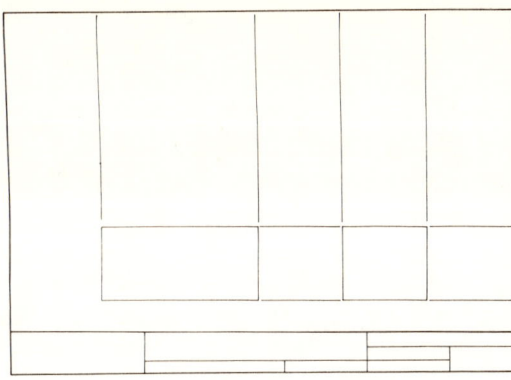

Fig. 4-42

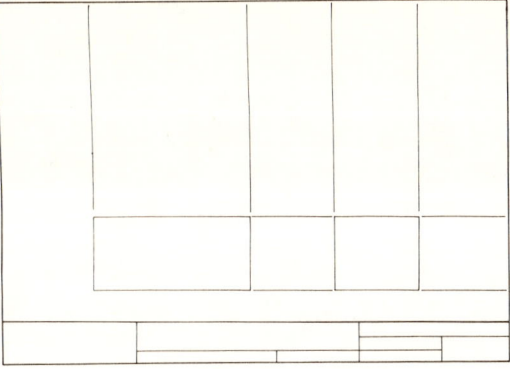

Fig. 4-44

3. From the corner in the front view, draw a light line at an angle of 45°.

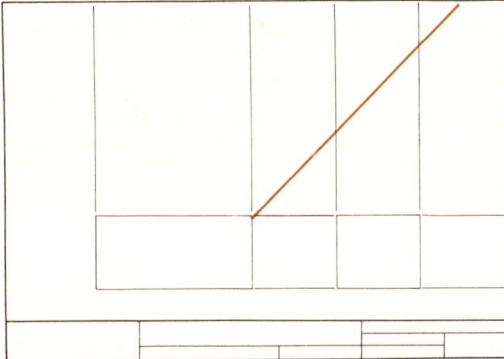

Fig. 4-43

4. Project the width dimension from the right side view to the 45° line. Project this distance horizontally to complete the top view outline. You will find that all width dimensions can be projected by this method using the 45° line.

Only when all three views are blocked in are you ready to complete the project. As you learned earlier on the graph paper, begin with the view that best describes the shape of the object.

GRAPH PROJECTS

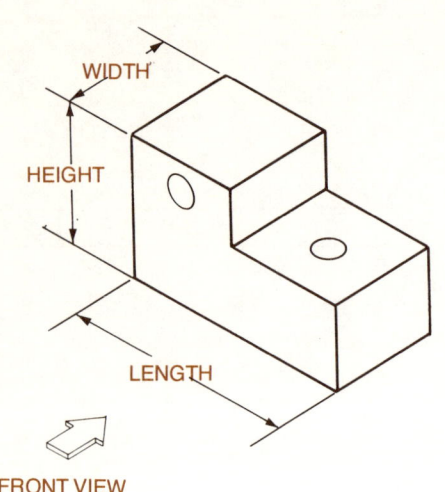

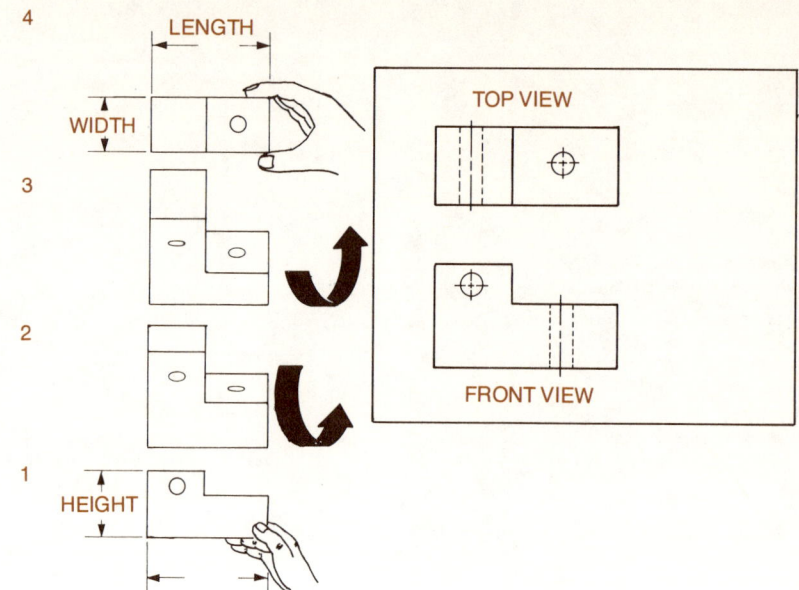

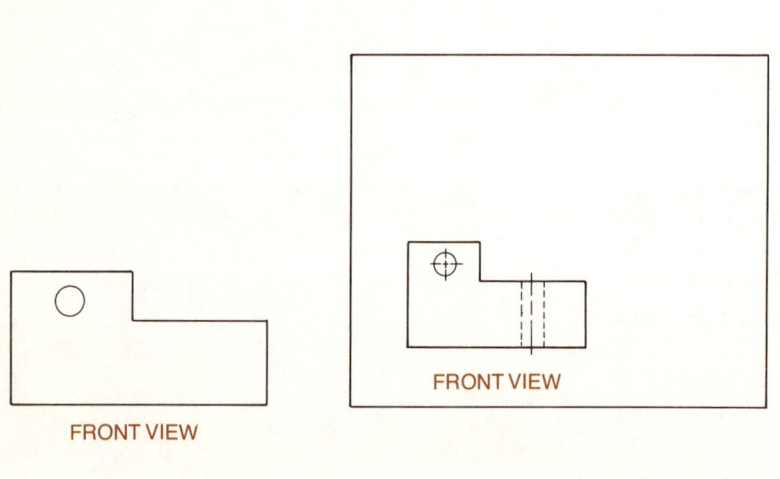

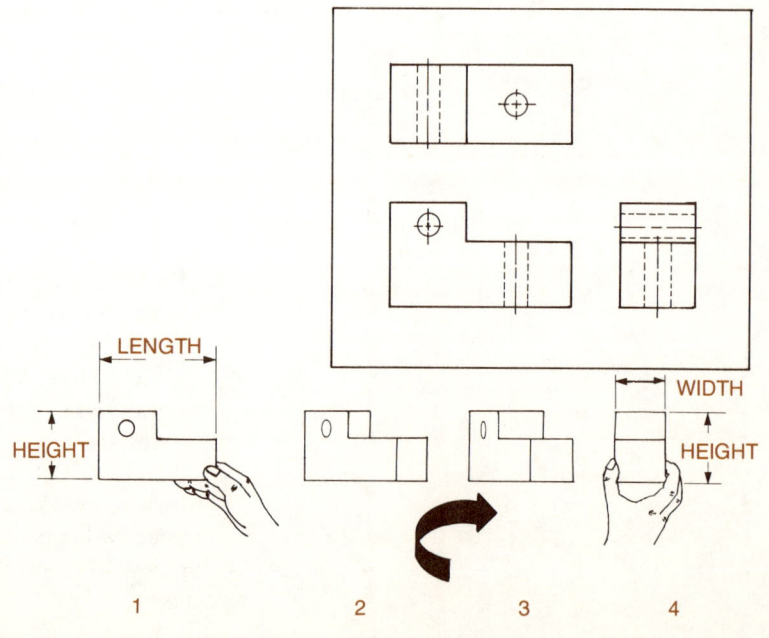

44 ORTHOGRAPHIC DRAWING, PART 1

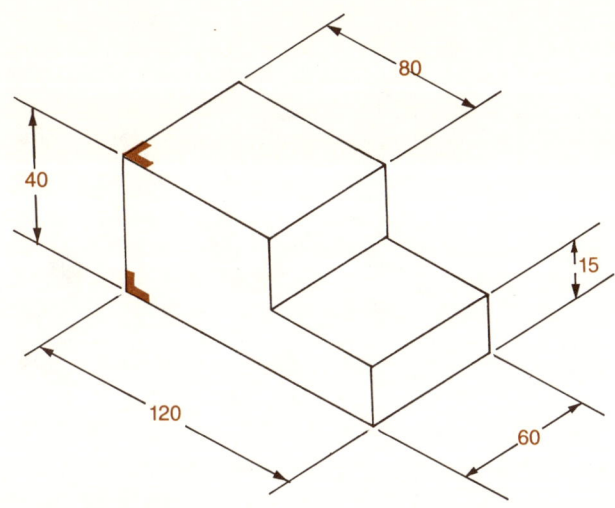

GRAPH PROJECT 1

END LAP MEMBER

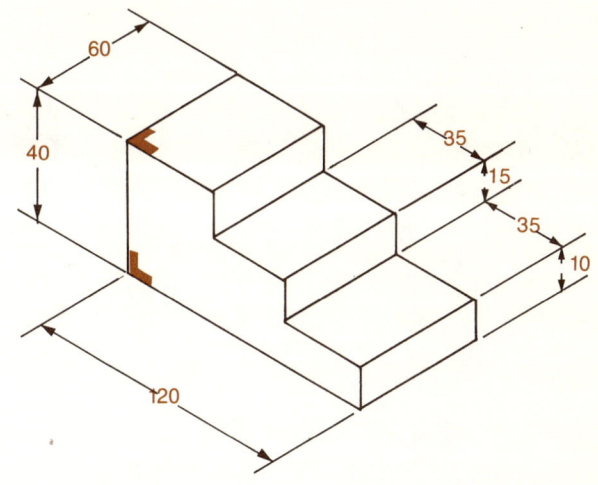

GRAPH PROJECT 3

TEE BLOCK

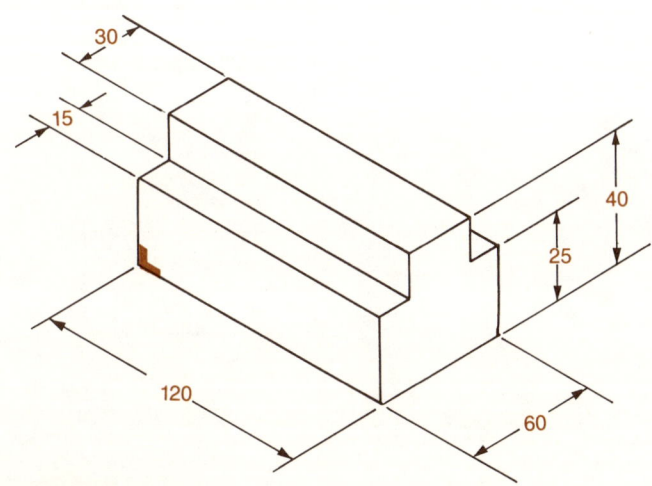

GRAPH PROJECT 2

STEP BLOCK

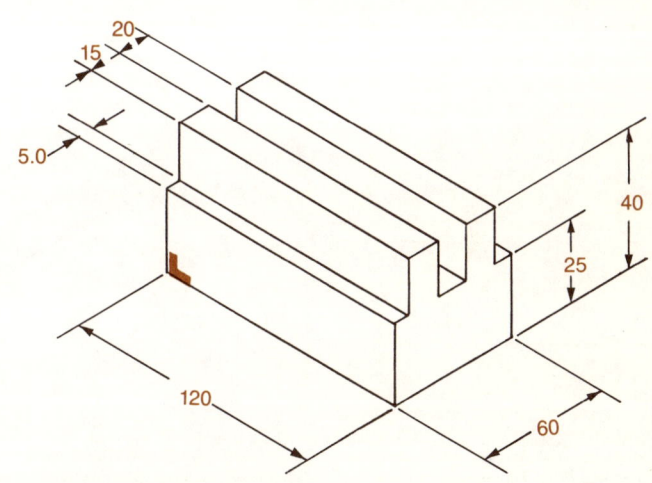

GRAPH PROJECT 4

SLOTTED BLOCK

GRAPH PROJECTS 45

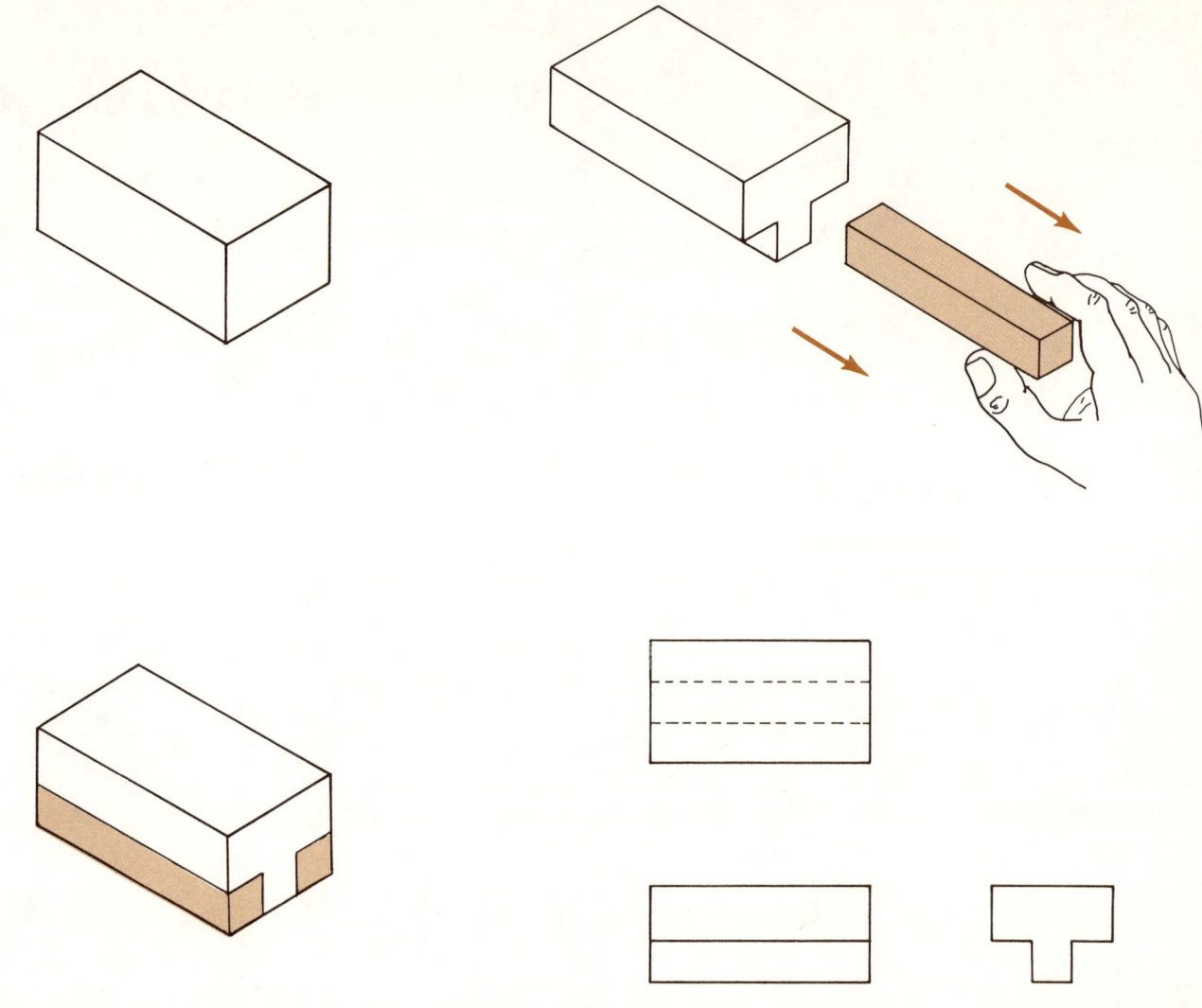

46 ORTHOGRAPHIC DRAWING, PART 1

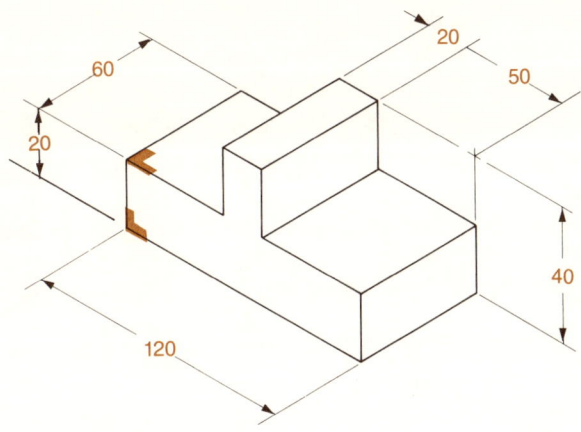

GRAPH PROJECT 5

TONGUED UNIT

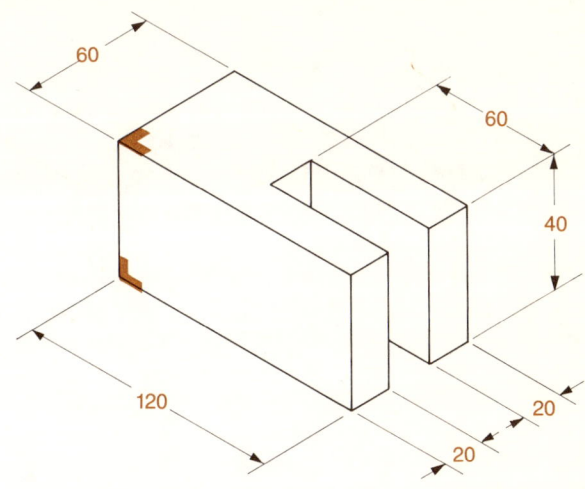

GRAPH PROJECT 7

OPEN MORTISE JOINT

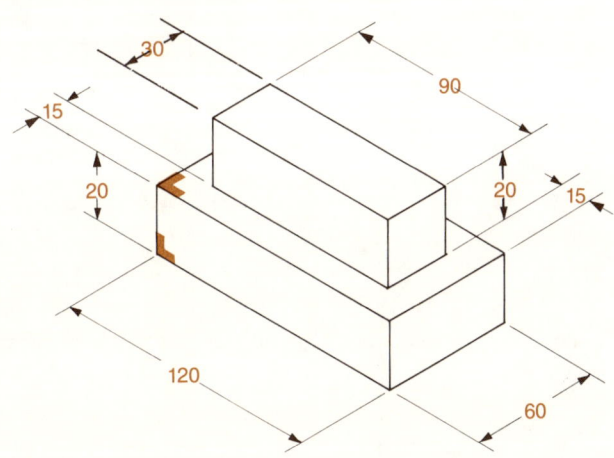

GRAPH PROJECT 6

TENON JOINT

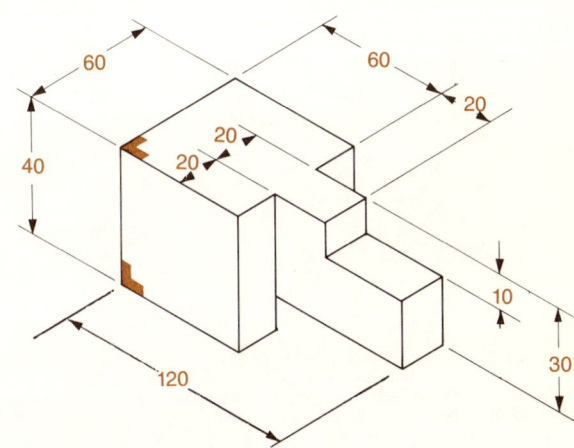

GRAPH PROJECT 8

CORNER JOINT

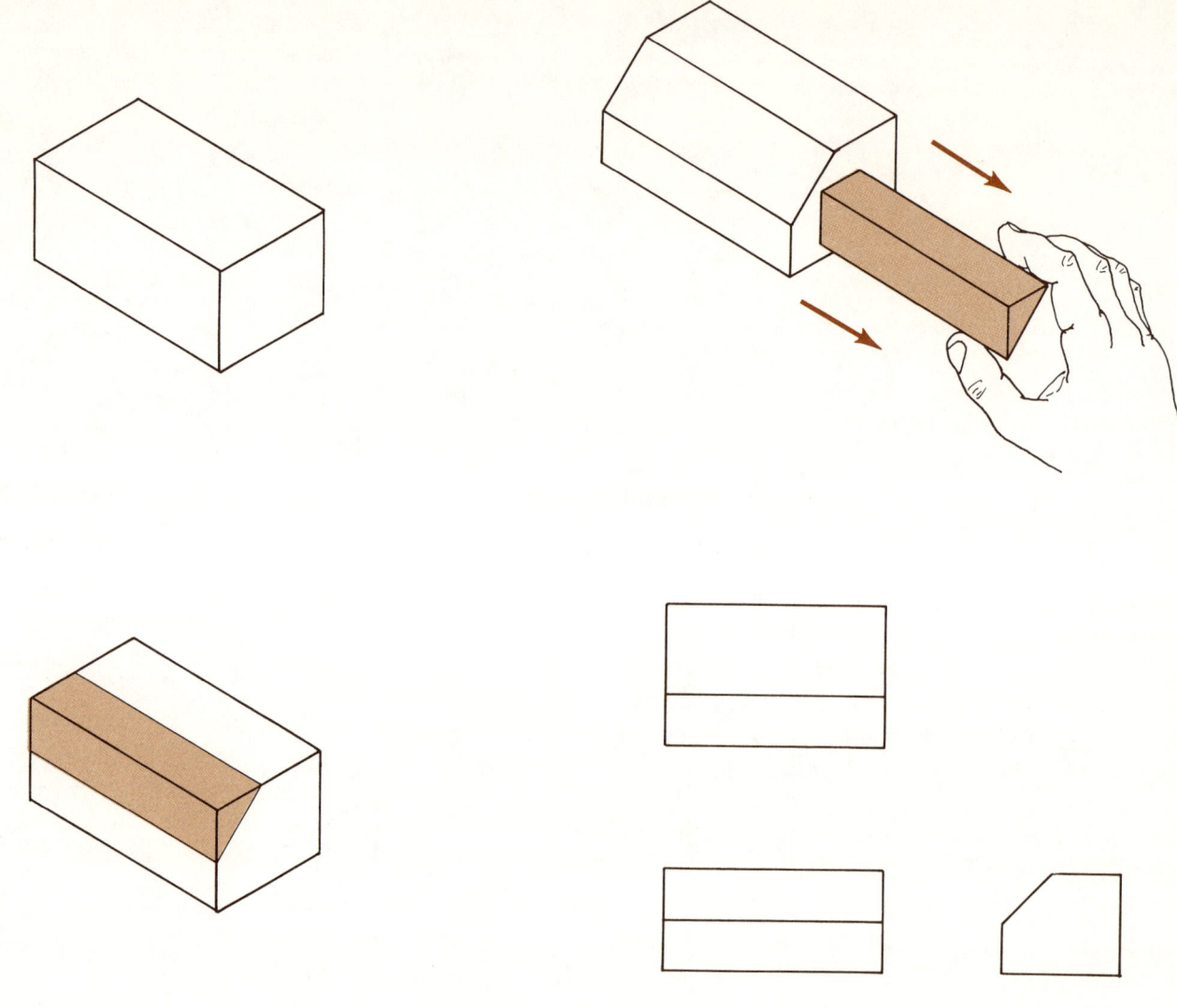

48 ORTHOGRAPHIC DRAWING, PART 1

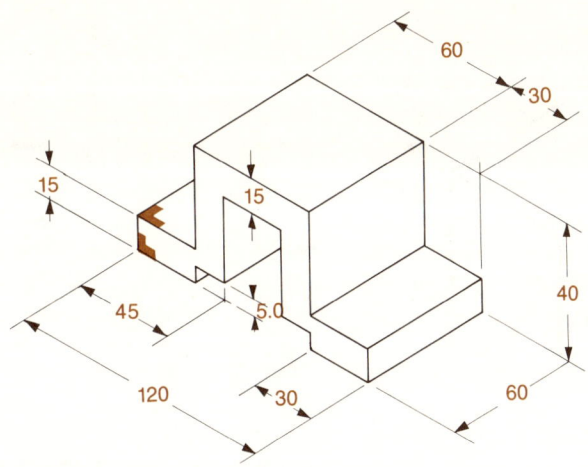

GRAPH PROJECT 9

GUIDE STAND

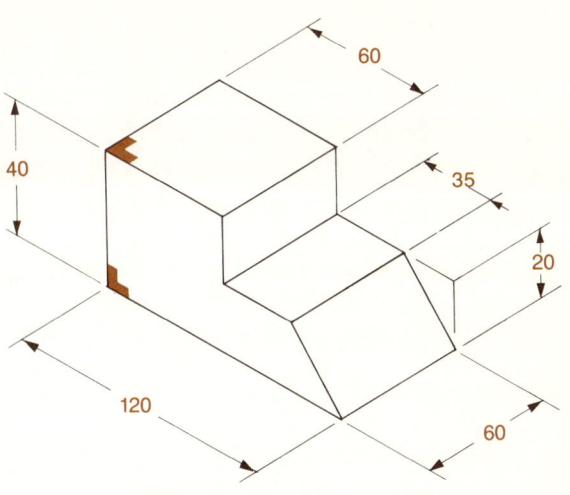

GRAPH PROJECT 11

LAP MITRE UNIT

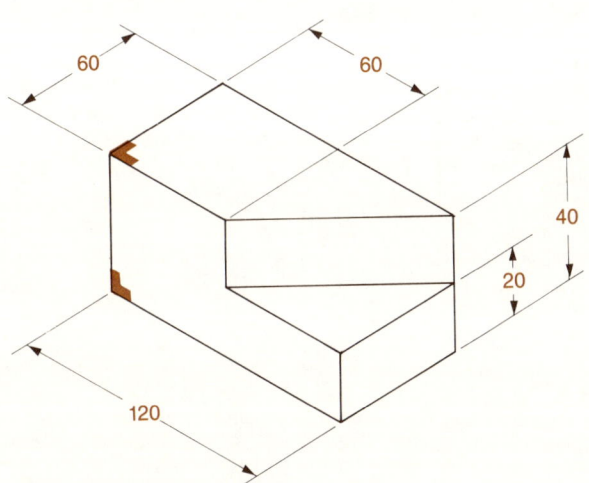

GRAPH PROJECT 10

ANGLE JOINT

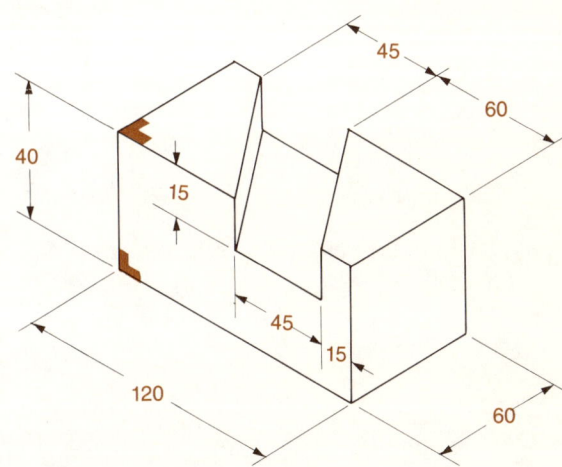

GRAPH PROJECT 12

GROOVED MEMBER

GRAPH PROJECTS 49

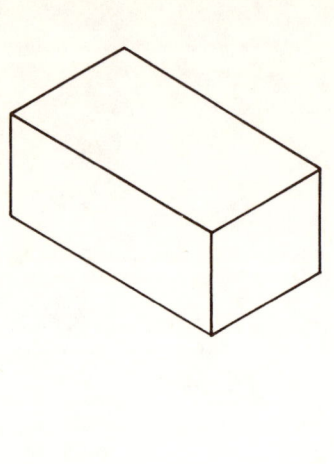
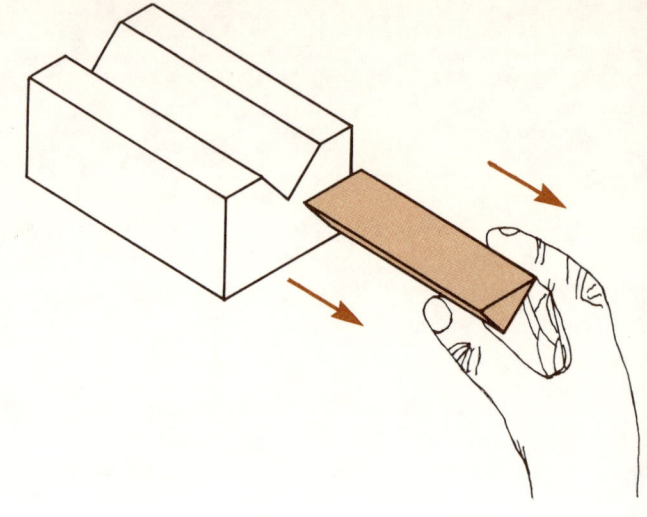
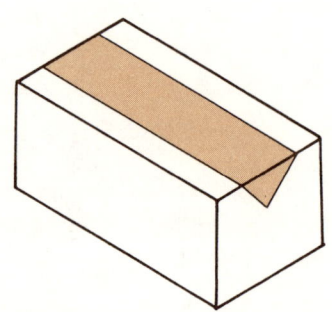
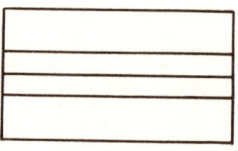
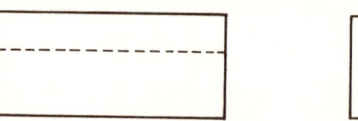

50 ORTHOGRAPHIC DRAWING, PART 1

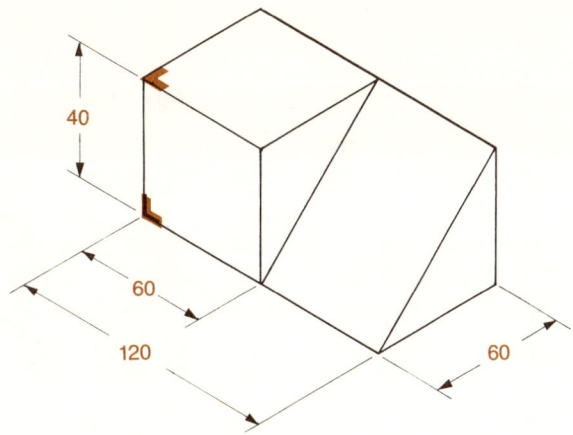

GRAPH PROJECT 13

BEVELLED BLOCK

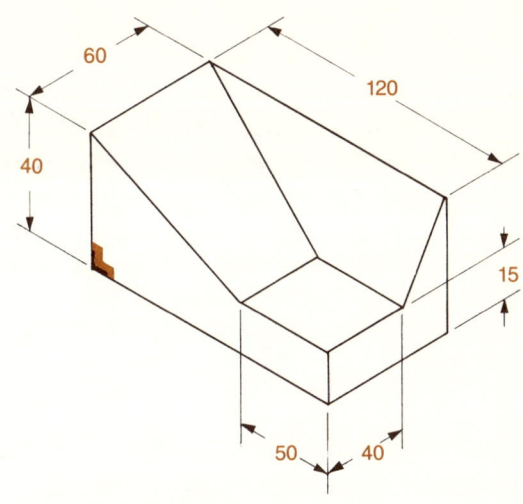

GRAPH PROJECT 15

ANGLE SLIDE

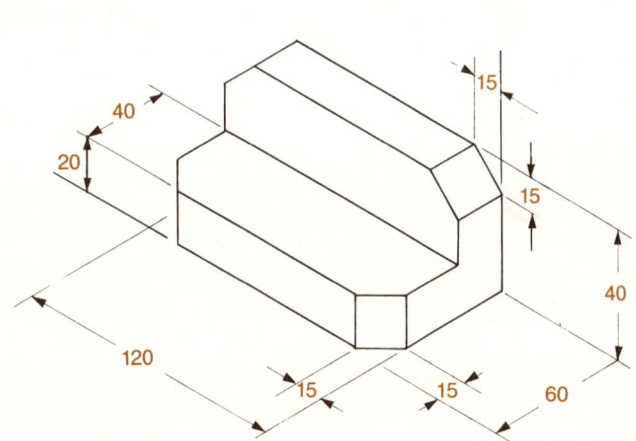

GRAPH PROJECT 14

ANGLE PIECE

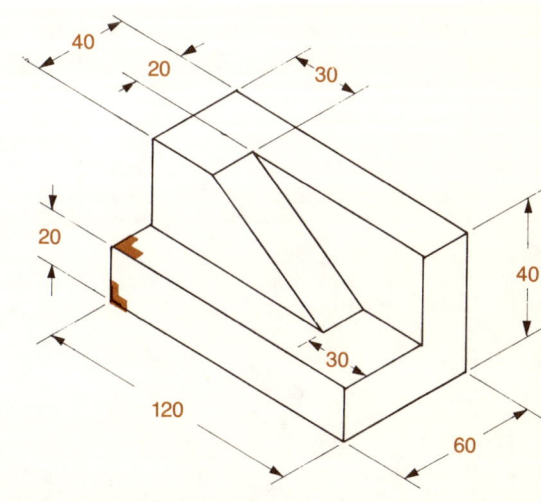

GRAPH PROJECT 16

END FIXTURE

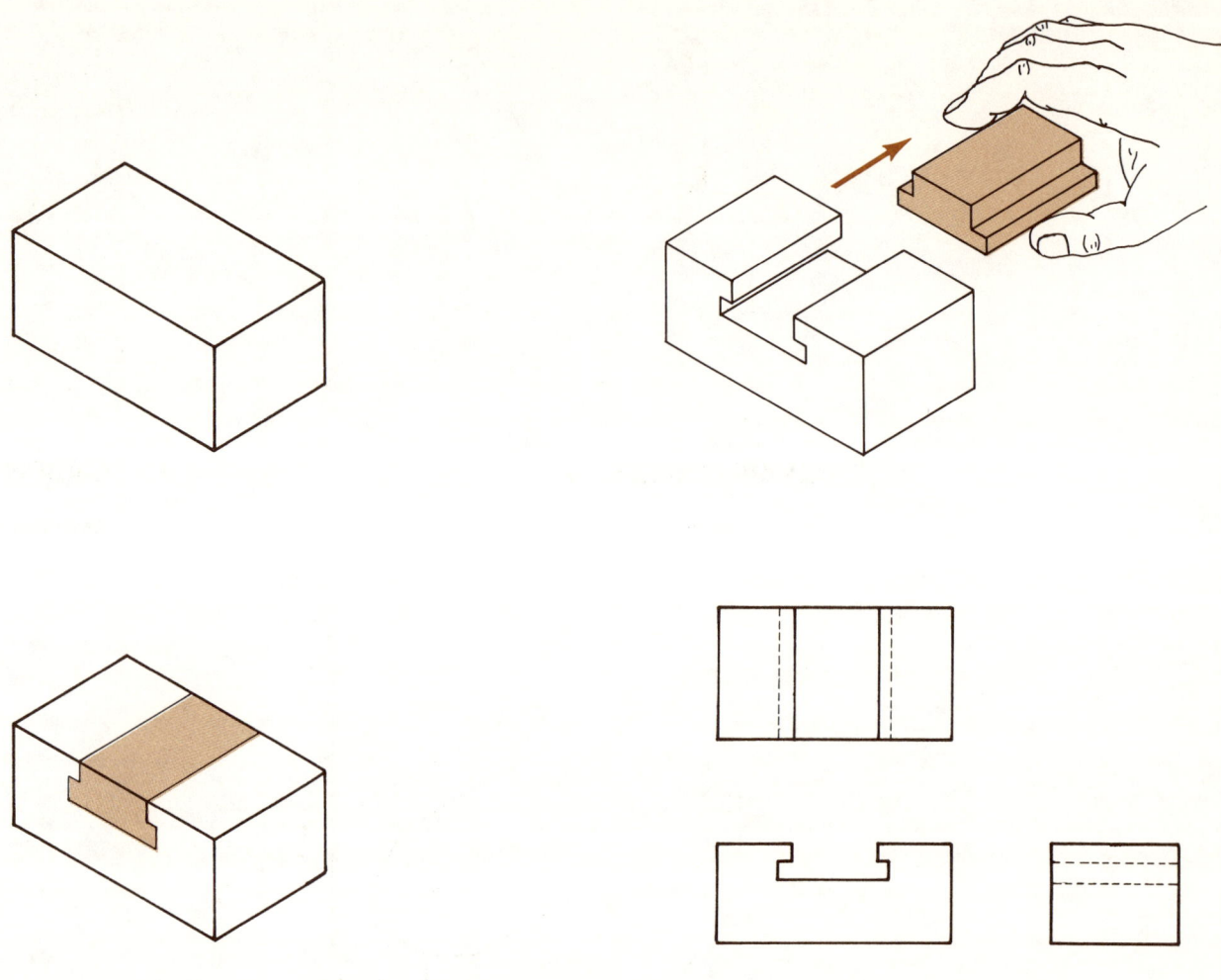

52 ORTHOGRAPHIC DRAWING, PART 1

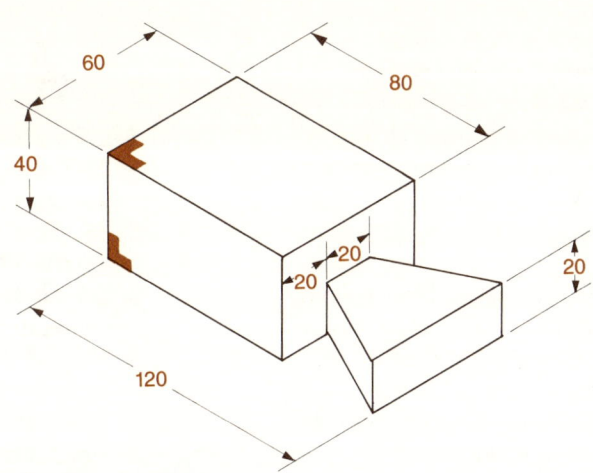

GRAPH PROJECT 17

DOVETAIL MEMBER

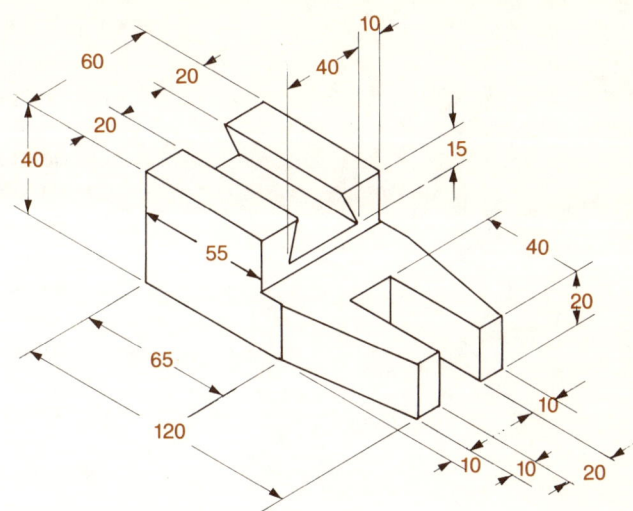

GRAPH PROJECT 19

DOVETAIL SUPPORT

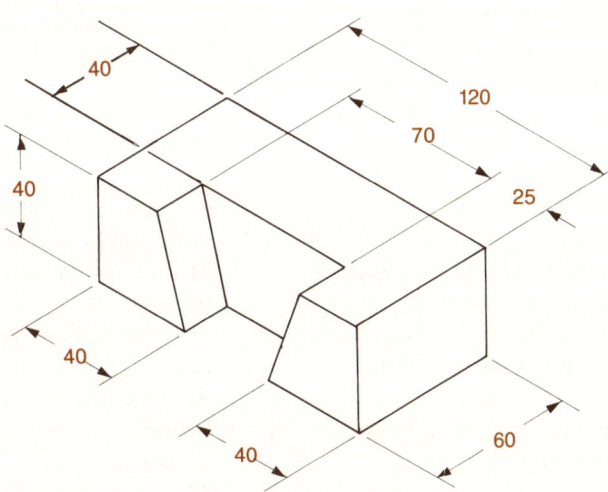

GRAPH PROJECT 18

ANGLE WEDGE

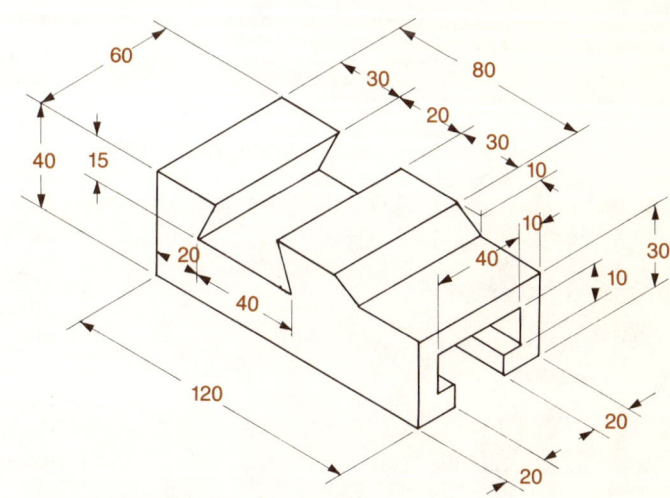

GRAPH PROJECT 20

TEE SLOT SLIDE

POINTS TO REMEMBER

- Many objects need more than one view to completely describe their features.
- Most non-cylindrical objects can be described as rectangular in shape.
- Pictorial views provide a general impression of the shape and features of an object.
- Orthographic views can be used to describe the shape and features of an object completely and exactly.
- Each orthographic view is two dimensional.
- To see the true shape of each surface of an object our line of sight must be at right angles to the surface we are viewing.
- Projection lines are used to project distances from one view to another.
- All the views of your drawing should be outlined before you attempt to complete any one view.
- The front view shows the length of the object and usually gives us the most information about the shape of an object.
- Hidden features of an object are represented by a series of dash lines.
- Orthographic views are spaced apart to make them easier to read and dimension.

QUESTIONS TO ANSWER

1. When is it possible to accurately describe an object using only one view?
2. List the names of the six orthographic views. Underline the three views that are usually drawn.
3. Copy these sentences and fill in the name of the missing overall dimension.
    (a) The front view and the top view share the **XXX** dimension.
    (b) The front view and the right side view share the **XXX** dimension.
    (c) The top view and the right side view share the **XXX** dimension.
4. Explain what is meant by each of the following terms:
    (a) projection
    (b) true shape
    (c) parallel
    (d) hidden lines
5. Why is it good practice to leave a space between orthographic views?
6. Once the three orthographic views are outlined, how would you decide which view to complete first?
7. Why is an edge in a view represented by a hidden line?
8. Why is it good practice to draw all construction lines as lightly as possible?
9. When would you darken all of the visible hidden lines?

REPLACE THE X'S WITH THE CORRECT TERM

1. If you sit in the side aisles of a movie theatre, your view will be **XXXXXXXXX**.
2. The image of a slide is projected onto a screen through a light source called a **XXXXXXXXX**.
3. The ability to **XXXXXXXXX** the shapes and features of objects from reading orthographic drawings is the **XXXXXXXXX** of blueprint reading.
4. Pictorial views give a general **XXXXXXXXX** of shapes.

PROJECTS

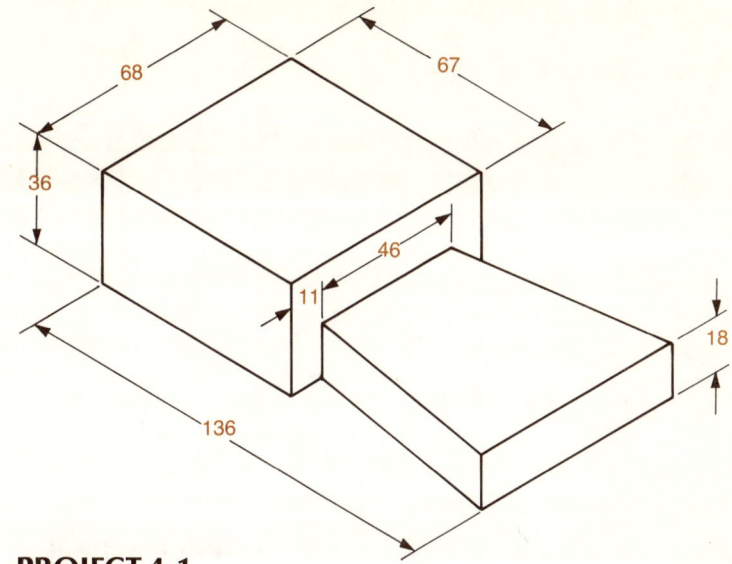

PROJECT 4-1

LAP DOVETAIL MEMBER **SCALE 1:1**

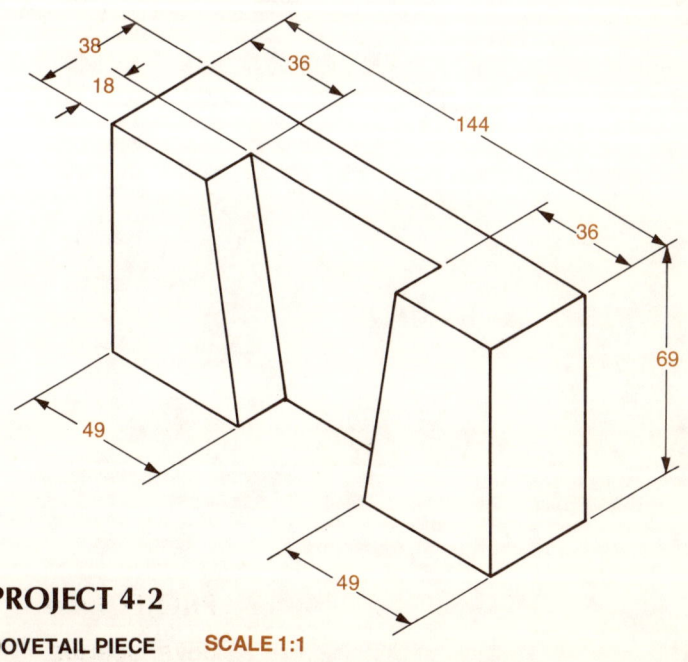

PROJECT 4-2

DOVETAIL PIECE **SCALE 1:1**

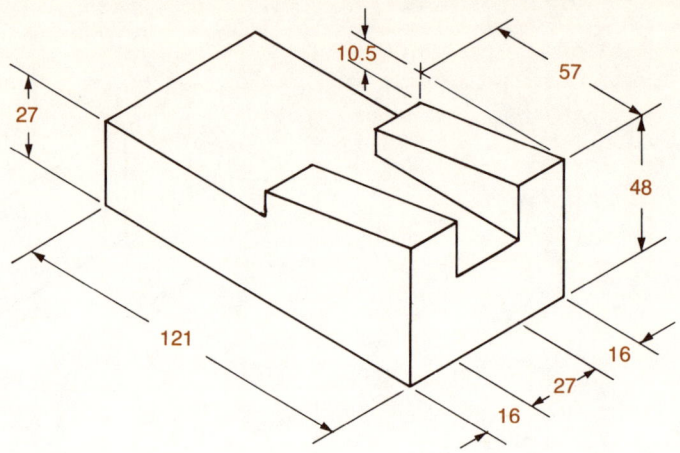

PROJECT 4-3

ANGLE BRACKET **SCALE 1:1**

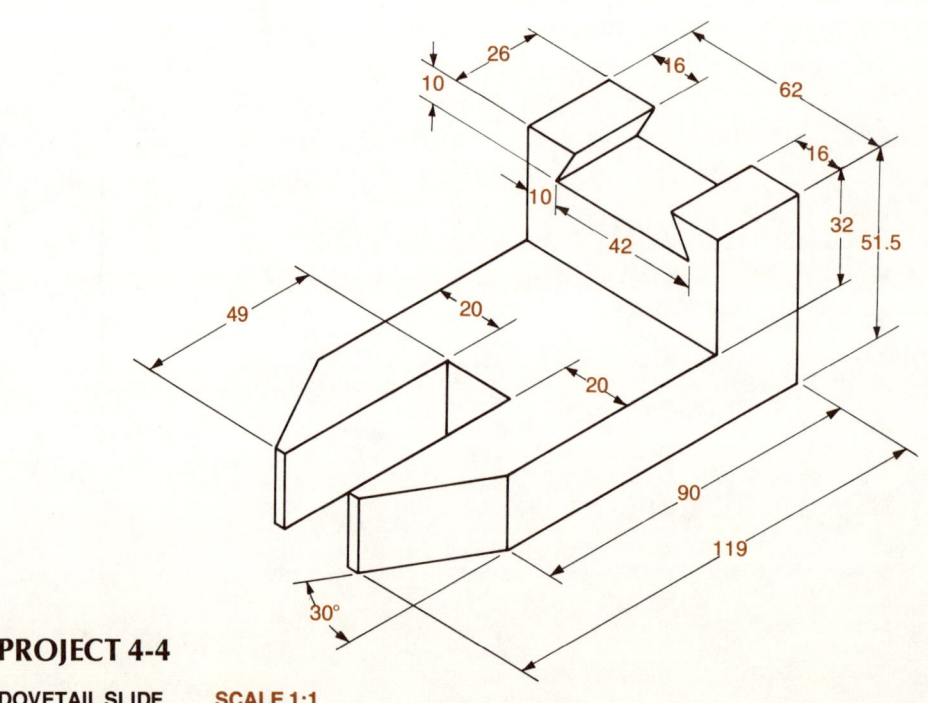

PROJECT 4-4

DOVETAIL SLIDE **SCALE 1:1**

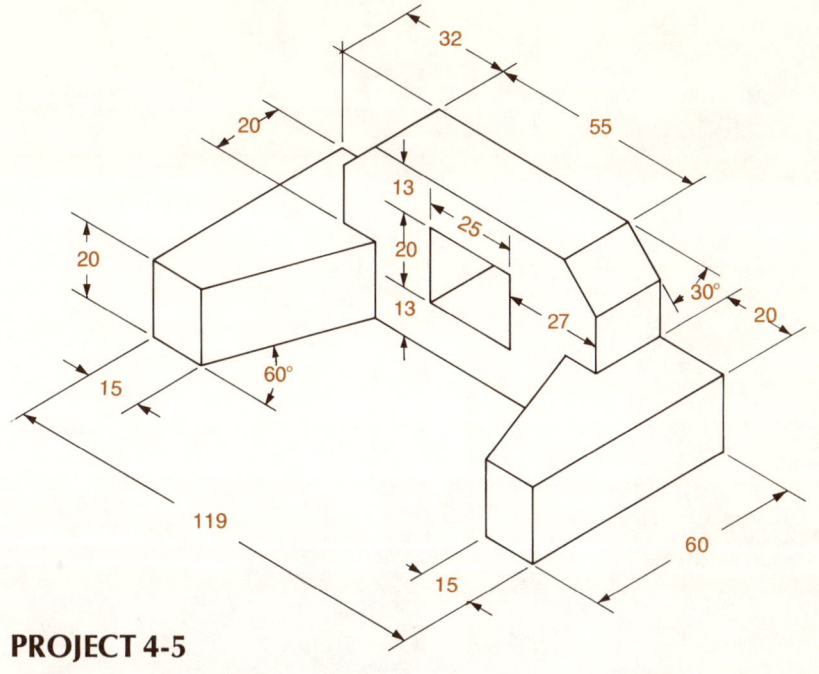

PROJECT 4-5

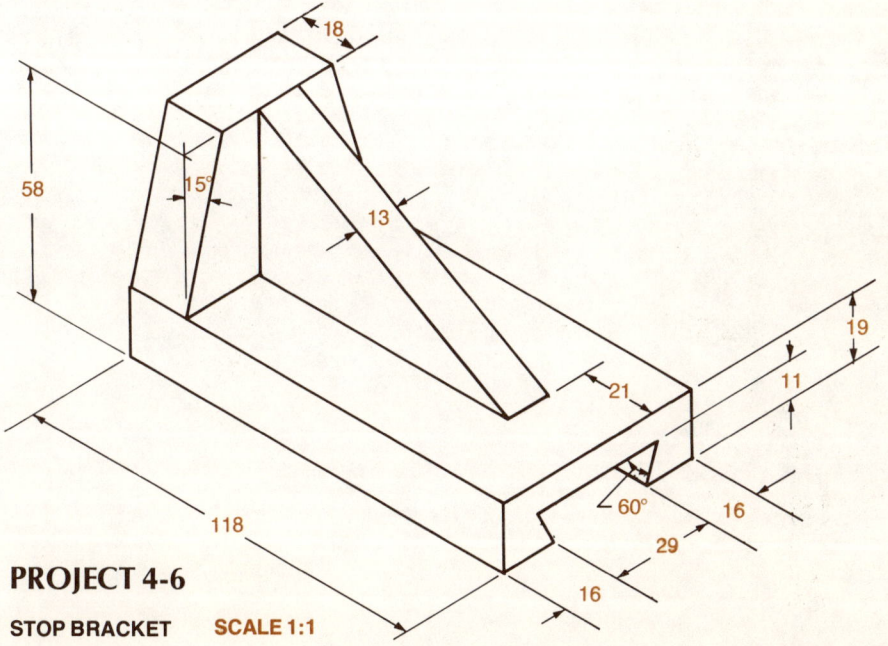

PROJECT 4-6

STOP BRACKET   **SCALE 1:1**

PROJECTS   57

CHAPTER 5
REDUCED AND ENLARGED SCALES

WORDS TO LEARN

proportion (pro-pór-tion)

proportion—the relative size of one thing as compared to another

We are all familiar with the word *scale*. Models of cars, planes, houses, etc., are made to scale. They are exact in every detail, but reduced in size in direct **proportion** to the actual object.

It is best, wherever possible, to draw objects to their actual dimensions. Objects that are drawn full size are noted on the drawing as scale 1:1. The scale 1:1 means that 1.0 mm on the drawing represents 1.0 mm of the actual object.

REDUCED SCALES

Many objects are too large to be drawn to their full size. The same information could be given by reducing the views to a more convenient size. Some of the scales used frequently are explained below.

Scale 1:2. One millimetre on the drawing represents 2.0 mm of the actual object. This means that the actual size of the object is twice the size represented on the drawing.

Scale 1:5. One millimetre on the drawing represents 5.0 mm of the actual object. This means that the actual size of the object is 5 times the size represented on the drawing.

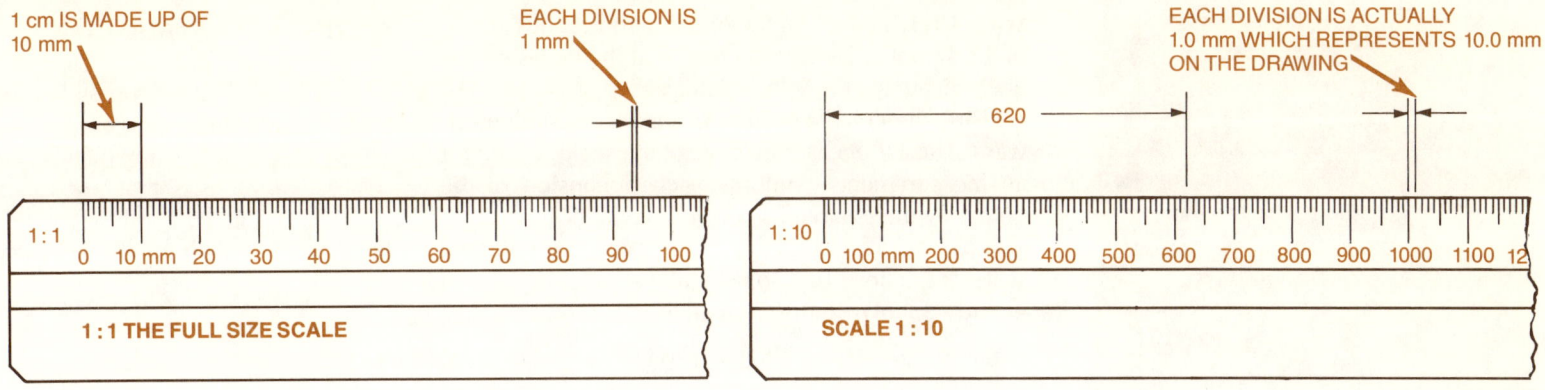

Fig. 5-1

Fig. 5-4 *1:10 Scale and Sample Readings*

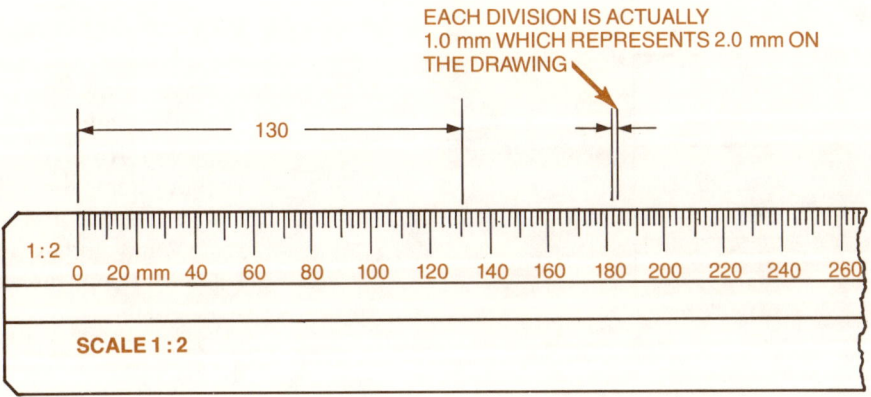

Fig. 5-2 *1:2 Scale and Sample Readings*

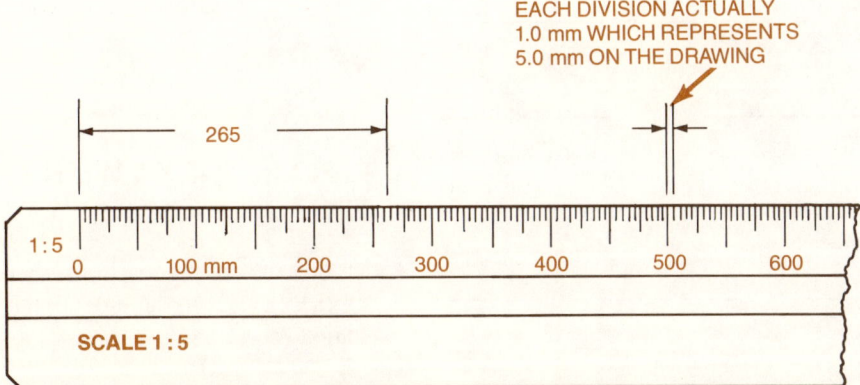

Fig. 5-3 *1:5 Scale and Sample Readings*

Scale 1:10. One millimetre on the drawing represents 10 mm of the actual object. This means that the actual size of the object is ten times the size represented on the drawing.

Other scales of 1:20, 1:50, 1:100 and 1:1000 can be useful as well. Just remember that, in each reduced scale, the second figure tells us by how much the actual object is larger than it is represented on the drawing.

ENLARGED SCALES

Quite often it is necessary to produce drawings to a scale that is larger than full size. Details of small objects are clearer and easier to dimension when they are drawn larger than their actual size. Objects can be drawn 2, 5, 10, 20 or more times their actual size. Some examples of enlarged scales are explained below.

Scale 2:1. 2.0 mm on the drawing represent 1.0 mm of the actual object. This means that the views on the drawing are shown twice their actual size.

Scale 5:1. 5.0 mm on the drawing represent 1.0 mm of the actual object. This means that the views on the drawing are shown five times their actual size.

ENLARGED SCALES   59

Scale 10:1. 10 mm on the drawing represent 1.0 mm of the actual object. This means that the views on the drawing are ten times their actual size.

Using the enlarged scales is really very straightforward. The 1:1 measuring edge of the scale is used for all measurements. Multiply each dimension of the object by the enlarged scale you have chosen — 2, 5, 10, 20, etc. For example, when using the enlarged scale 2:1, a line of an object that was actually 65 mm would be shown as 130 mm on the drawing.

$$2 \times 65 = 130$$

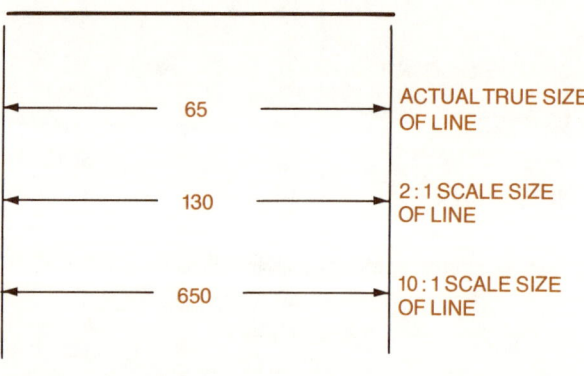

Fig. 5-5

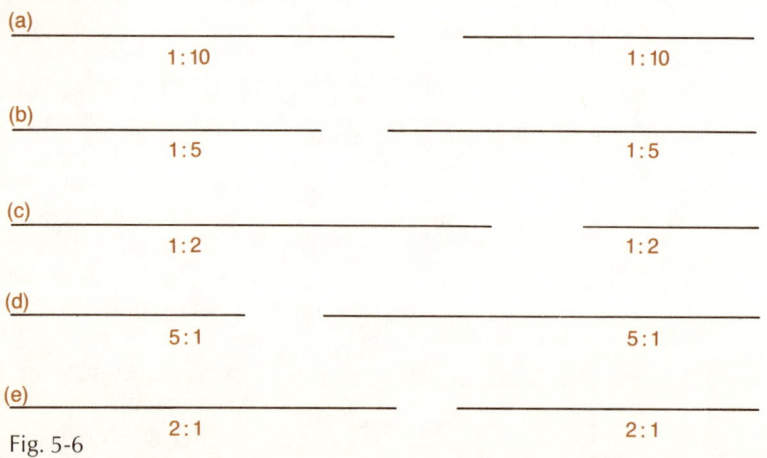

Fig. 5-6

POINTS TO REMEMBER

- Whenever possible use the 1:1 scale.
- Objects that are too large to be drawn full size are drawn to a reduced scale.
- Objects that are too small to be drawn clearly in full size are drawn to an enlarged scale using the 1:1 measuring edge.

QUESTIONS TO ANSWER

1. Why are objects sometimes drawn to a reduced or an enlarged scale?
2. List four items that could be drawn to a reduced scale and suggest the possible scale you would use for each.
3. List four items that could be drawn to an enlarged scale and suggest the possible scale you would use for each.
4. Explain in your own words the following scale notations:
   (a) 1:1   (c) 1:10   (e) 100:1
   (b) 10:1   (d) 1:5   (f) 1:50
5. Carefully scale each of the lines in Fig. 5-6, using the scale as noted. Record the actual size each line represents in millimetres.

REPLACE THE X'S WITH THE CORRECT TERM

Models of cars, planes, houses, etc., are made in direct XXXXXXXXXX to actual objects but on a reduced scale.

PROJECTS

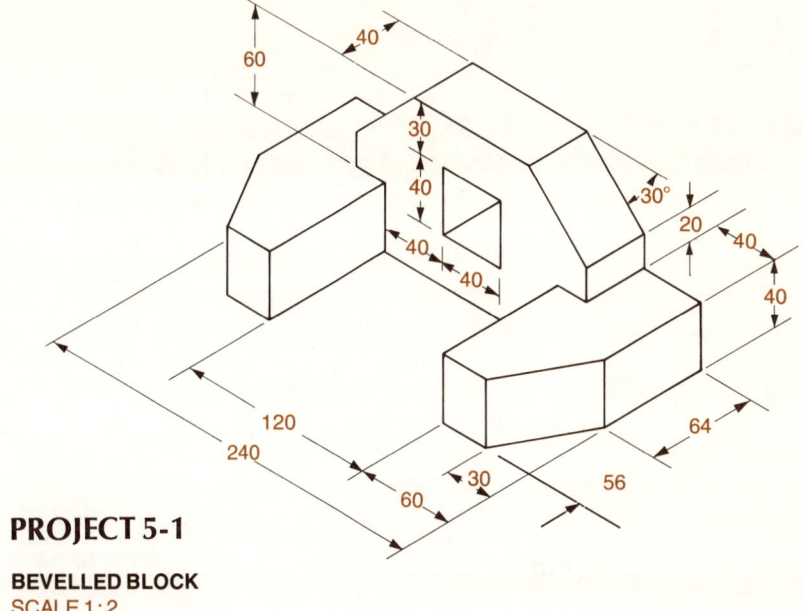

PROJECT 5-1

BEVELLED BLOCK
SCALE 1 : 2

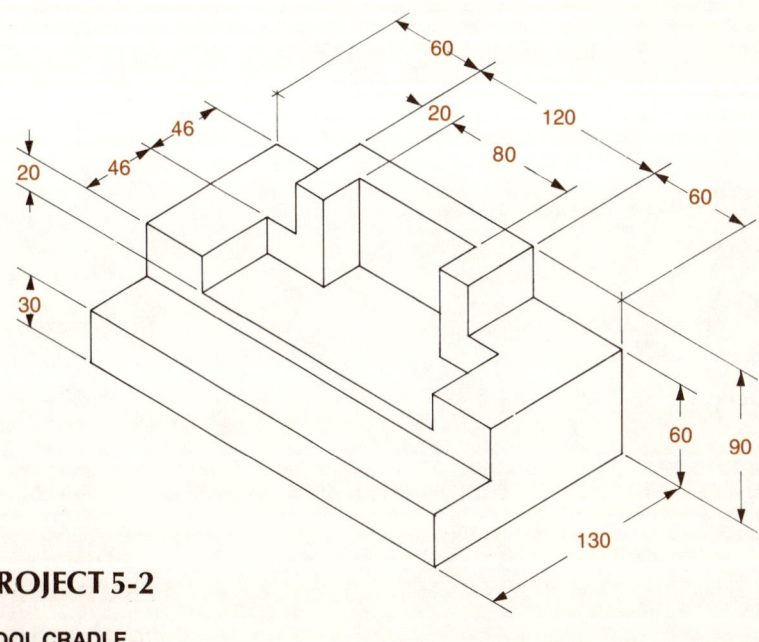

PROJECT 5-2

TOOL CRADLE
SCALE 1 : 2

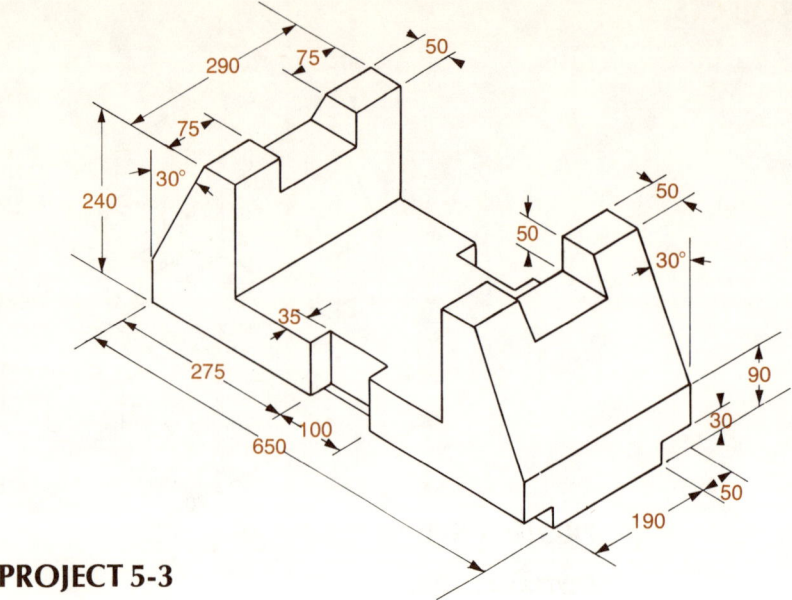

PROJECT 5-3

SLOTTED GUIDE
SCALE 1 : 5

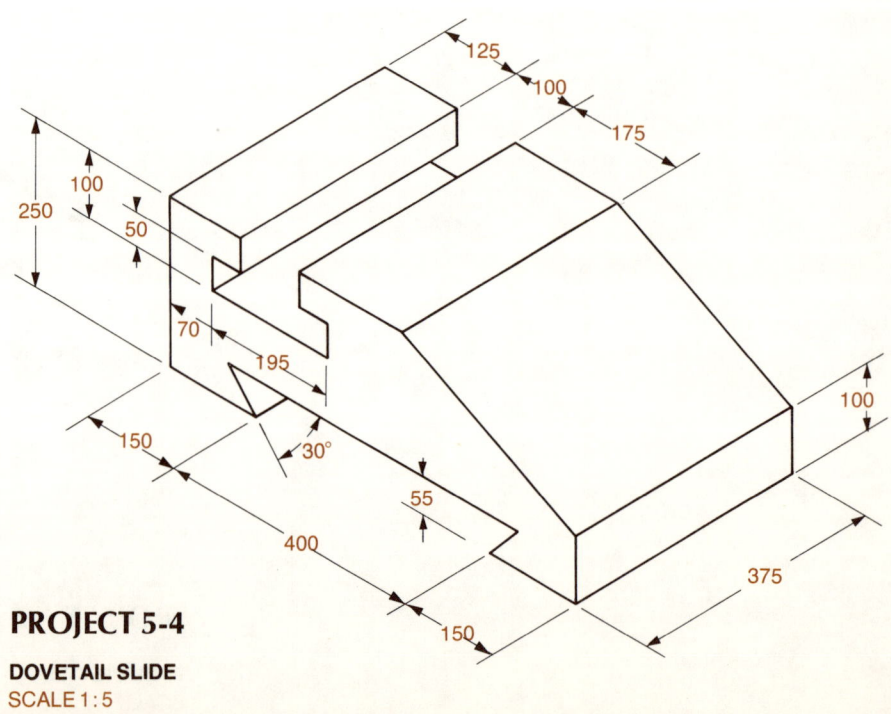

PROJECT 5-4

DOVETAIL SLIDE
SCALE 1 : 5

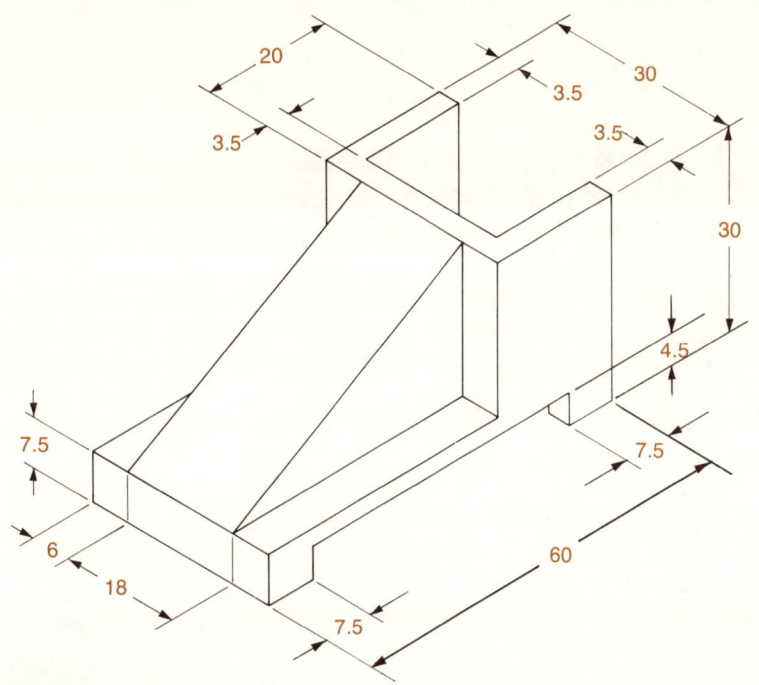

PROJECT 5-5

BEAM SUPPORT
SCALE 2:1

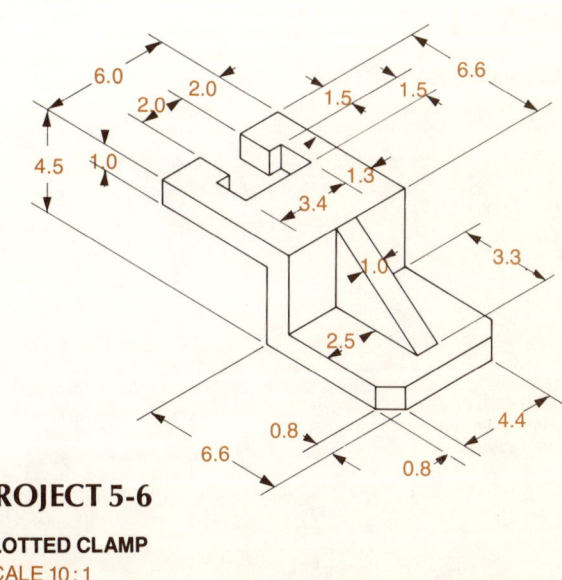

PROJECT 5-6

SLOTTED CLAMP
SCALE 10:1

PROJECTS 63

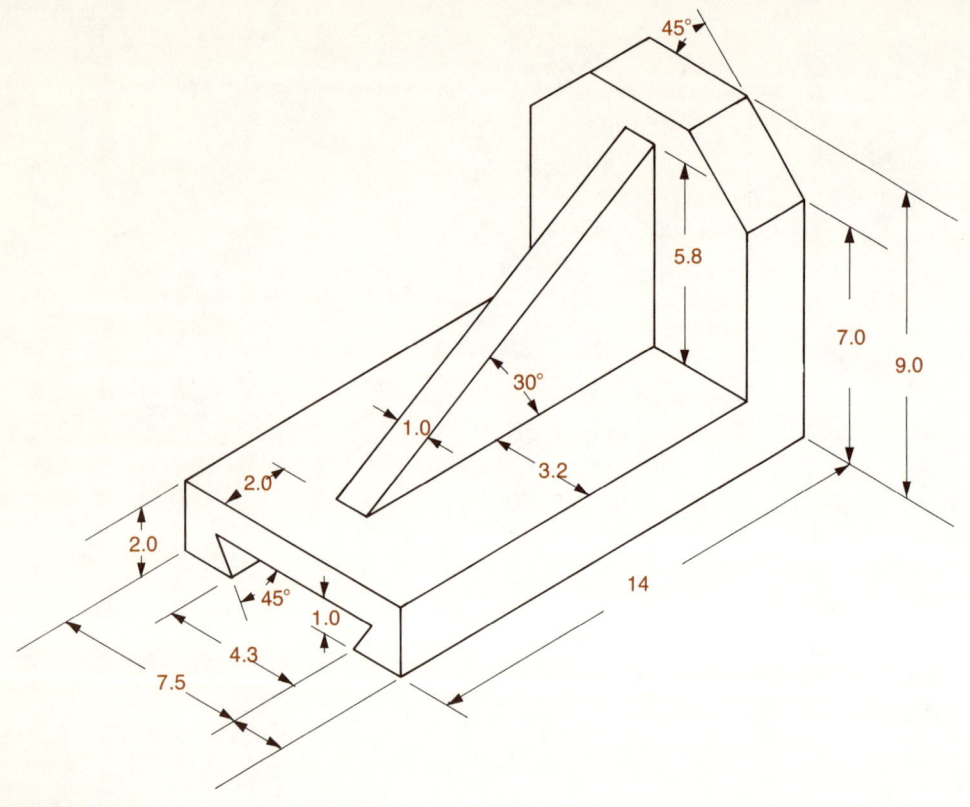

PROJECT 5-7

BRACE BRACKET
SCALE 10 : 1

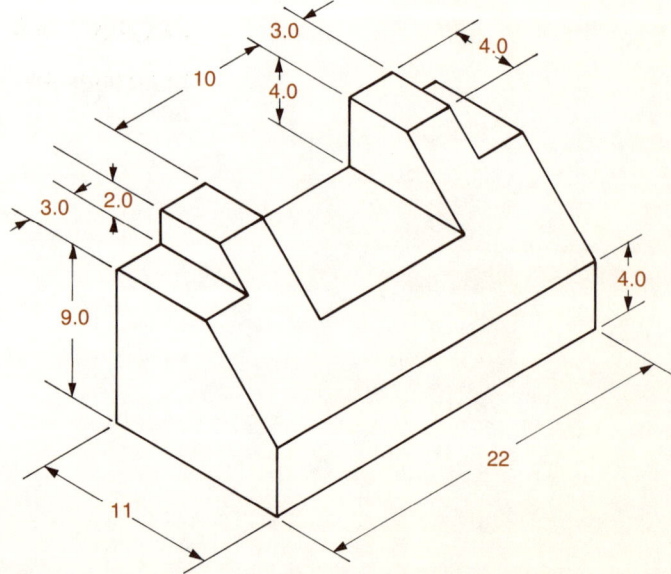

PROJECT 5-8

ANGLE BLOCK
SCALE 5 : 1

CHAPTER 6
CIRCLES

WORDS TO LEARN

circumference (cir-cúm-fe-rence) **chord** **rotate** (ró-tate)
radius (rá-di-us) **tangent** (tán-gent) **alternate** (ál-ter-nate)
diameter (di-ám-e-ter) **concentric** (con-cén-tric)
arc **intersect** (in-ter-séct)

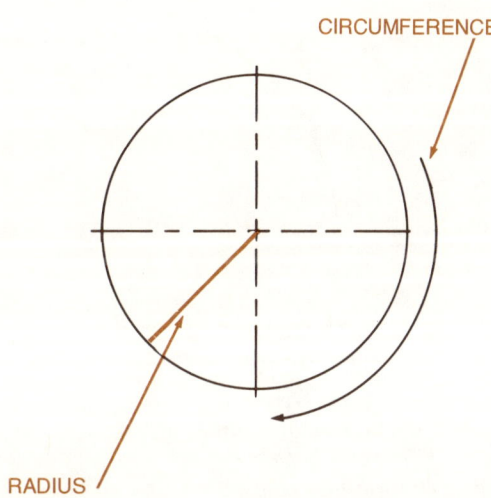

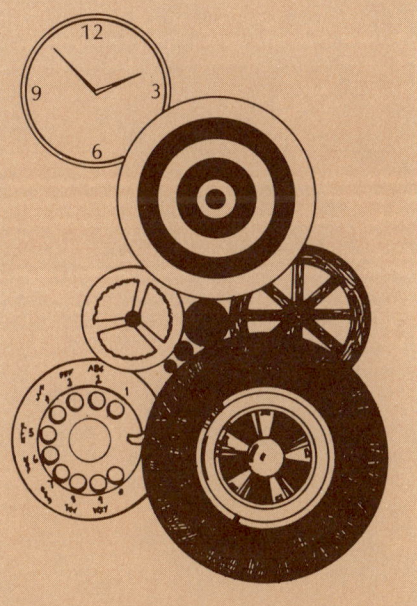

Fig. 6-1

Fig. 6-2

ABOUT THE CIRCLE

Up to this point we have been concerned with straight lines. Now we are going to tell you about some curved lines and a few additional straight lines that are related to the circle.

Circle: The circle is a closed curve. Each point on the curve is the same distance from a fixed point called the centre. The distance measured around the curve is called the **circumference**.

Radius: The **radius** is the distance along a straight line drawn from the centre of a circle to any point on the circumference. The symbol for radius is R.

Diameter: The **diameter** is the distance along a straight line joining any two points on the circumference, and passing through the centre of the circle.

65

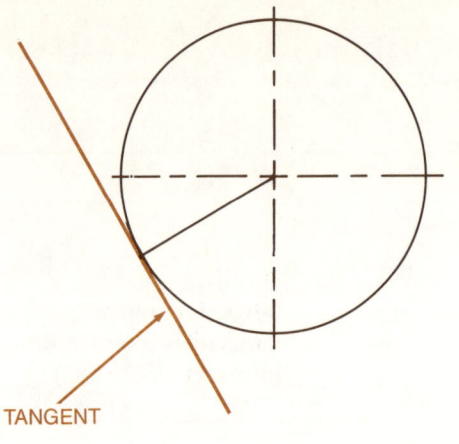

TANGENT

POINT OF TANGENCY

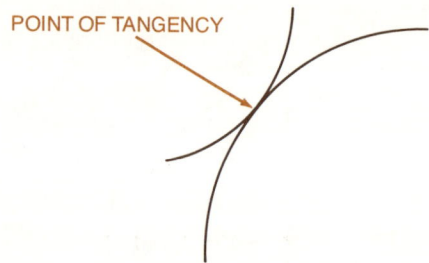

Fig. 6-3

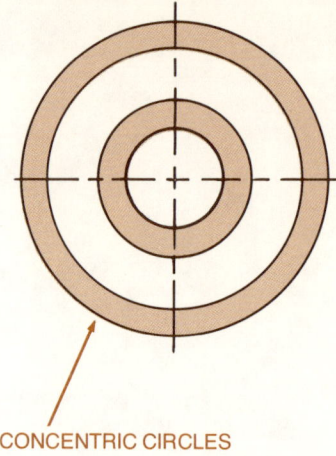

CONCENTRIC CIRCLES

Fig. 6-4

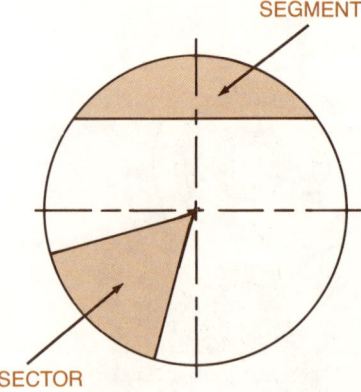

SEGMENT

SECTOR

Fig. 6-5

NOTE: the diameter of a circle is the radius × 2. Or, it can be stated the radius is the diameter ÷ 2. The symbol for diameter is Ø.

Arc: The **arc** is any part of the circumference of the circle.

Chord: The **chord** is a straight line joining any two points on the circle.

Tangent: A **tangent** to a circle is a straight line which touches the circle at one point only, but does not cut through it. Arcs of different circles can also be tangent to one another.

Concentric Circle: Concentric circles have a common centre. The radius of each circle is measured from the same centre.

Sector: A **sector** is the area contained by two radii and an arc.

Segment: A **segment** is the area contained by an arc and its chord.

THE COMPASS

Most circles and arcs are drawn using a bow compass. Look at its design: it is simple and functional. Surprisingly enough many people have problems using the bow compass. For this reason let us take a little time discussing how to prepare the compass for drawing, and how to use it so that you will be happy with the results.

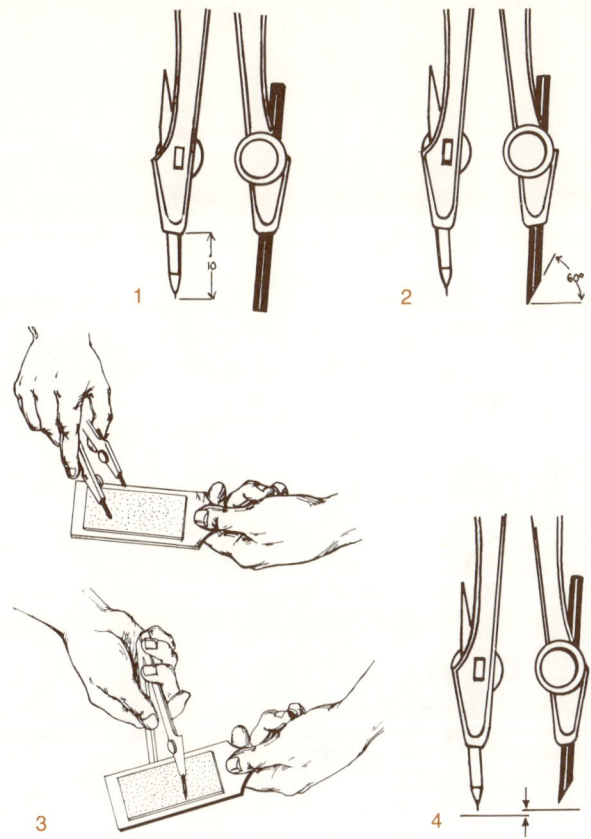

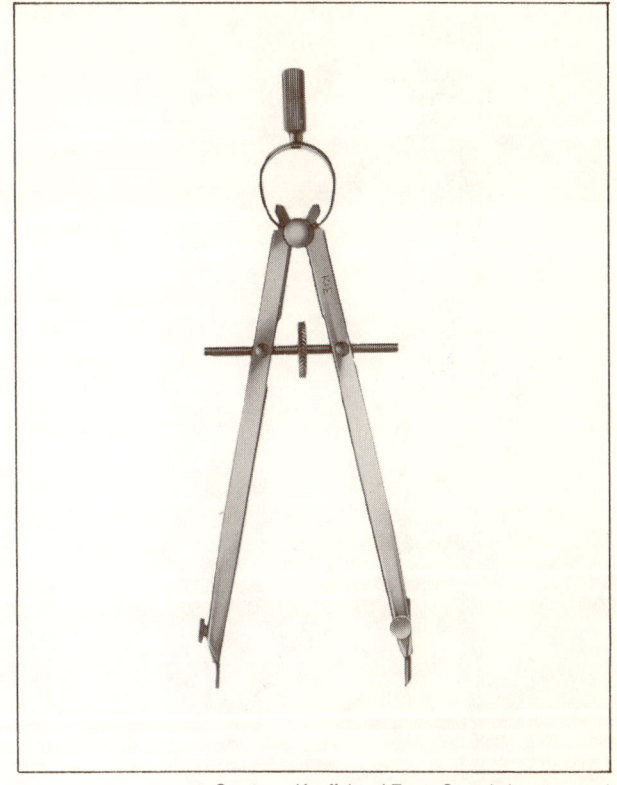

Courtesy: Keuffel and Esser Canada Incorporated

Fig. 6-6

Steps in Preparing the Compass for Use

1. The lead in the compass must be sharp. To sharpen the lead, first extend the lead a little beyond the needle point.
2. Hold the lead leg at an angle of 30° to a sanding block and gently stroke the lead back and forth, flattening the **outside** of the lead.
3. Hold the leg so that the sides of the lead can be stroked on the sandblock to form a V. First one side, then the other.
4. Adjust the lead so that it is slightly **shorter** than the needle point.

Steps in Using the Compass

We must know where to place the needle point, and also know the radius of the circle we want to draw. The size of a circle is described by its diameter. To find the radius of the circle, simply divide the diameter by two. For example, if the circle you wish to draw has a diameter of 80 mm, the radius is 80 ÷ 2 or 40 mm. The compass legs are always set to the radius of the circle being drawn.

1. Draw a vertical and a horizontal line at a right angle to each other to form a cross.
2. From the point where the two lines **intersect**, mark off the radius of the circle. Using

intersect—to cross each other (lines, paths, etc.)

THE COMPASS 67

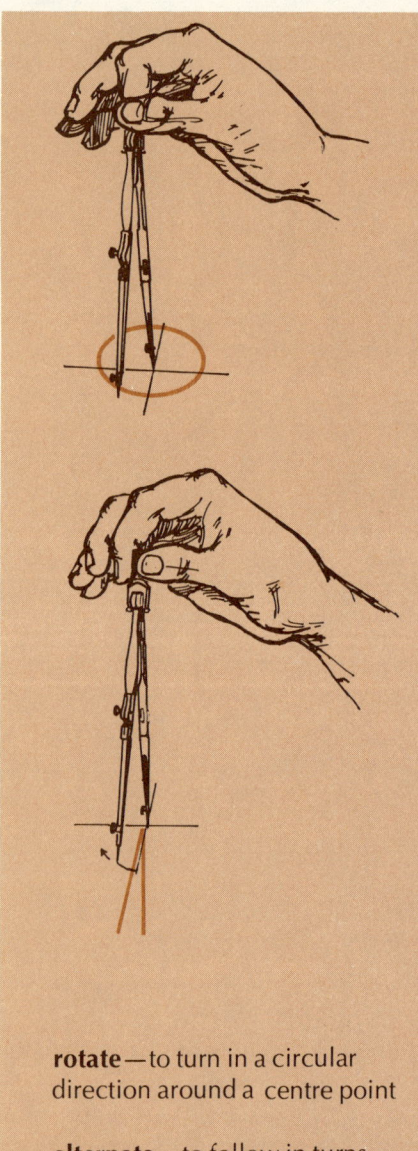

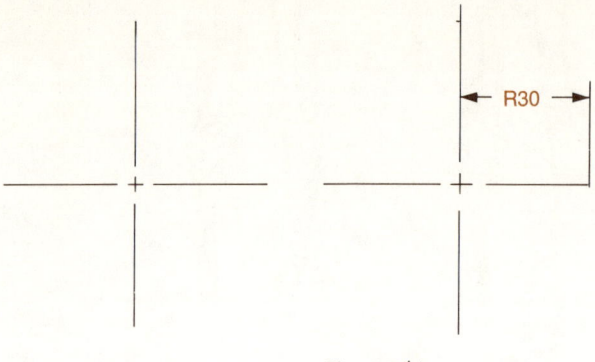

Fig. 6-7(a)   Fig. 6-7(b)

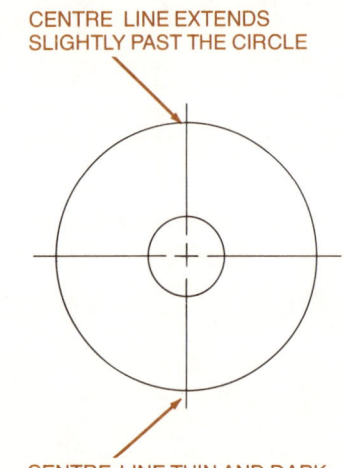

CENTRE LINE EXTENDS SLIGHTLY PAST THE CIRCLE

CENTRE LINE THIN AND DARK

Fig. 6-7(c)

rotate—to turn in a circular direction around a centre point

alternate—to follow in turns

our example from above, the diameter is 80 mm, which means that the radius is 40 mm. Set the 0 of the scale on the centre point and lightly mark off the radius along either of the intersecting lines.

3. Place the compass needle on the centre point and set the compass to the radius. Put a little pressure on the needle point but try not to go too deep into the drawing board. Tilt the compass slightly away from you in the direction you are rotating and draw the circle. Always **rotate** in one direction only. Never reverse the direction for the same circle or you may end up with a double line. If you feel it is necessary to darken the line repeat the rotation of the compass in the same direction as before.

Centre Lines

There are a number of points you should remember about centre lines.
- Centre lines are used to show the centres of cylinders and circular features.
- Centre lines are made up of **alternating** long and short dashes. The short dashes are about 2 mm to 4 mm long. The long dashes can vary from 10 mm to 100 mm according to the length of the feature through which they pass. Leave a space of 2 mm between the long and short dashes.
- Centre lines are thin dark lines that begin and end with a long dash. You can use a lead harder than 2H to produce a line that will be thinner than the outline of the object you draw.
- Centre lines project slightly past the view or feature. Again, the distance depends on the size of the view you have drawn. A distance of 2 mm to 5 mm is about right.

Bolt Circle

Bolt circle is another name for a circular centre line. A bolt circle is drawn for cylindrical holes or other cylindrical features that are located an equal distance from a common centre point. The bolt circle is drawn with alternate long and short dashes. The abbreviation for bolt circle is B.C.

Now let us apply the new terms you have just learned by adding this information to our familiar example.

68 CIRCLES

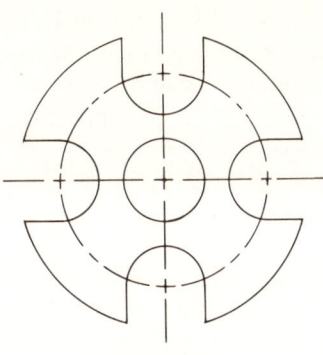

BOLT CIRCLE

Fig. 6-8

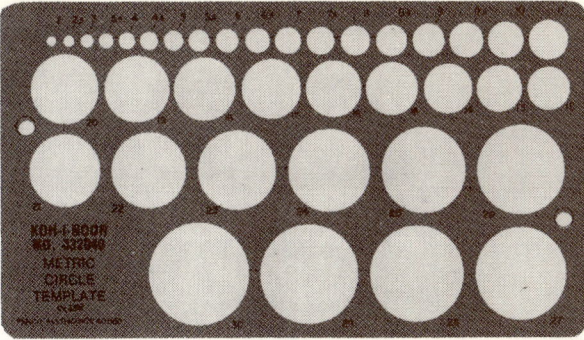

Courtesy: Keuffel and Esser Canada Incorporated

Fig. 6-10

The Circle Template

The circle template is used to draw relatively small circles without using a compass. It is a thin plastic sheet that has a series of holes cut out. Each hole is identified by its diameter. To use it, line up the cross lines on the circumference of the circle you have chosen, with the centre lines on your drawing. Hold the pencil against the side of the hole as you outline the circle.

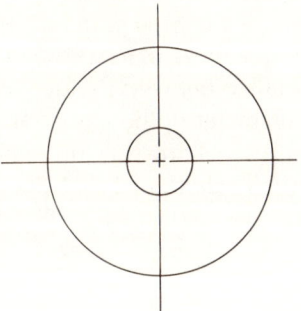

Fig. 6-9(a)

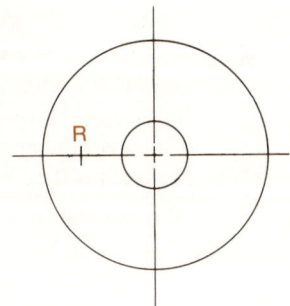

Fig. 6-9(b)

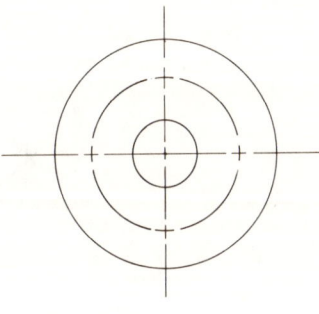

Fig. 6-9(c)

APPLICATION OF ARCS AND TANGENTS

Many objects have rounded corners. These corners are called **rounds** and **fillets**. An inside rounded corner is called a fillet. An outside rounded corner is called a round.

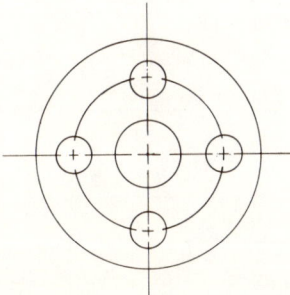

Fig. 6-9(d)

Draw a project using the following specifications: Ø 10, 4 holes **equally spaced**, 40 B.C.
1. It is really quite straightforward. The note tells us that four holes are to be drawn on a circular centre line that is 40 mm in diameter.
   Mark off the radius for the bolt circle Ø = 40. The radius is 40 ÷ 2 = 20.
2. Draw the bolt circle (light circular centre line).
3. Since the note specified four holes equally spaced from one another the holes must be 90° apart (360° ÷ 4 = 90°). Draw the holes where the bolt circle line intersects the horizontal and vertical centre lines.

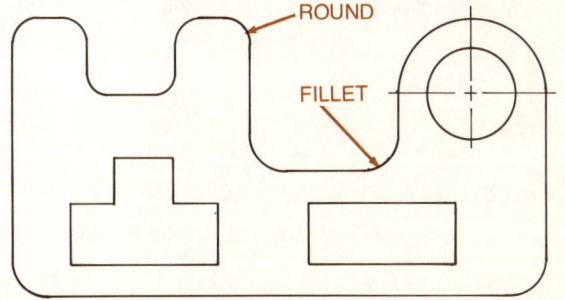

Fig. 6-11

APPLICATION OF ARCS AND TANGENTS 69

Rounded corners are less apt to chip, are safer to handle, often look better, and are stronger than square corners. On technical drawings rounds and fillets are represented by arcs drawn tangent to the sides forming the corner.

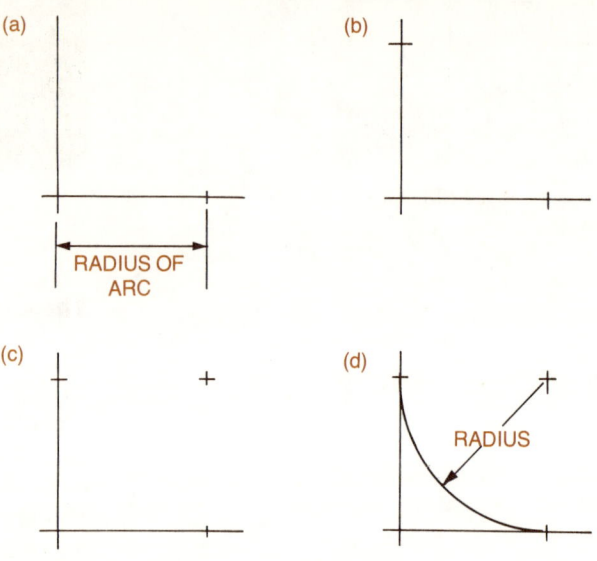

Fig. 6-12

Steps in Drawing an Arc Tangent To the Sides Of a Right Angle

A **right angle** is an angle of 90°.
1. Measure the radius of the arc along one side of the right angle.
2. Place the point of the compass at the corner of the right angle. Set the compass to the radius measured. Draw a light arc across each side of the angle.
3. Place the compass point where the arcs intersect the sides of the angle. From each point draw first one arc and then the other to intersect.
4. Place the compass point where the arcs intersect. Draw the desired arc tangent to the sides of the right angle.

Steps in Drawing an Arc Tangent To the Sides Of an Obtuse Angle

An **obtuse angle** is an angle of more than 90°.
1. Set the compass to the radius of the desired arc. Place the compass point anywhere along both sides of the obtuse angle. Draw two non-intersecting arcs.
2. Draw lines tangent to each of the two arcs, parallel to the sides of the obtuse angle.
3. Set the compass point at the point where the tangent lines intersect. Draw the desired arc tangent to the sides of the obtuse angle.

Tangents can also be drawn to the circumference of a circle to produce geometric shapes that are often useful in technical drawings. If we were to draw tangent lines to the circumference of a circle we would produce a square. The distance between the sides of the square is equal to the diameter of the circle. The distance between the sides is also known as the width across the flats. This is usually shortened to A/F (across flats).

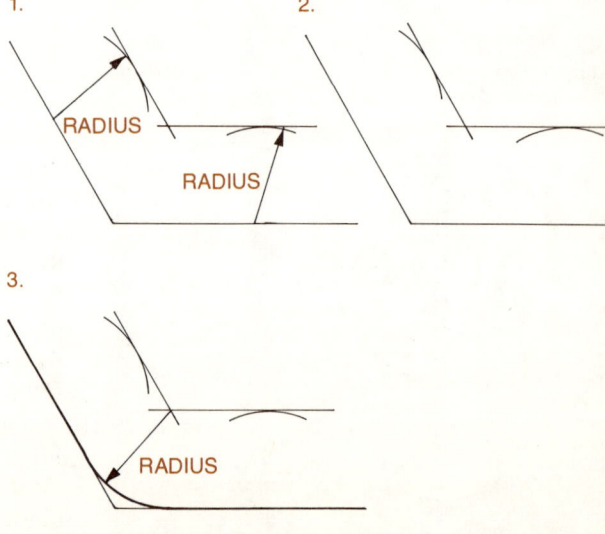

Fig. 6-13

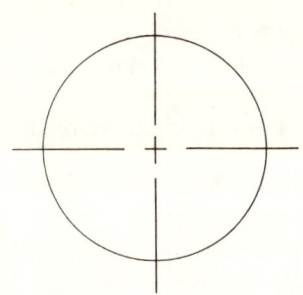
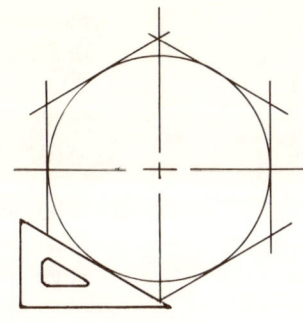
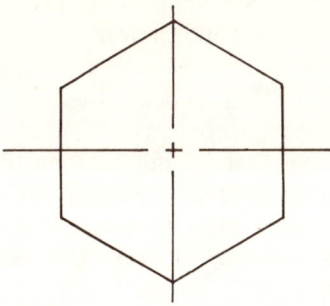

Fig. 6-14

Steps in Constructing a Regular Hexagon

A regular hexagon can easily be drawn when you know the width of it across the flats.

1. Locate the centre of the hexagon with vertical and horizontal centre lines.
Draw a light circle with a diameter equal to the A/F distance of the required hexagon.
2. Draw light vertical lines tangent to the circle.
3. Use the 30°–60° set square to lightly draw the remaining lines tangent to the circle.
4. Erase the unnecessary lines and complete the finished linework. Centre lines can remain if required.

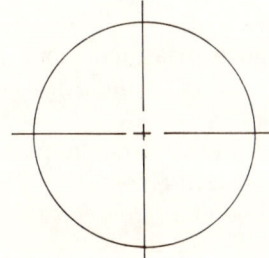

Fig. 6-15

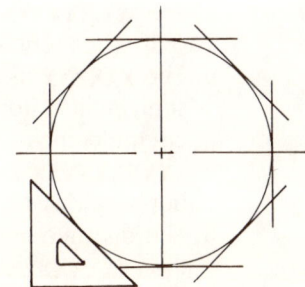
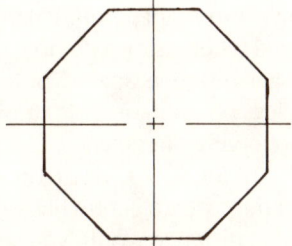

Steps in Constructing a Regular Octagon

A regular octagon can also easily be drawn when you know the width of it across the flats.

1. Locate the centre of the hexagon with vertical and horizontal centre lines. Draw a light circle with a diameter equal to the A/F distance of the required octagon.
2. Lightly draw vertical and horizontal lines tangent to the circle.
3. Use the 45° set square to lightly draw the remaining lines tangent to the circle.
4. Erase the unnecessary lines and complete the finished linework. Centre lines can remain if required.

POINTS TO REMEMBER

- The size of a circle is specified by its diameter.
- Given the diameter of a circle you can calculate the radius by dividing the diameter by two.
- Tangent lines touch the circumference of a circle at one point only but do not intersect.
- Keep the compass lead sharp.
- Adjust the compass lead so that it is slightly shorter than the needle point.
- Never adjust the compass against the edge of any scale. Always measure the radius off on a line and then set your compass to that distance.
- Use the compass with one hand, leaning the compass slightly in the direction you are rotating the lead.
- An arc is any part of the circumference of a circle.
- Centre lines begin and end with a long dash.
- Centre lines are thin and dark.
- Centre lines are used to show the centres of cylinders and circular features.
- Extend centre lines past the features of the object you have drawn.
- A bolt circle is a circular centre line drawn with alternate short and long dashes. It is often shortened to B.C.

- Use the circle template to save time when drawing arcs and circles.
- A fillet is an inside rounded corner. A round is an outside rounded corner.
- A right angle contains 90°. An obtuse angle is greater than 90° but less than 180°.
- An acute angle is one that is less than 90°.
- The size of regular hexagons and regular octagons is measured as the distance across the flats (A/F).

QUESTIONS TO ANSWER

1. Define each of the following terms in a short sentence:
   (a) arc
   (b) chord
   (c) tangent
   (d) diameter
   (e) circumference
   (f) bolt circle
   (g) width across the flats
   (h) regular hexagon
2. Explain why the diameter of a circle is twice the length of the radius of the circle.
3. How is the diameter of a circle different from the other chords in the same circle?
4. List five important points that must be kept in mind when using a compass.
5. At what distance apart would the compass legs be set in order to draw circles of the following diameters:
   (a) 36 (b) 58 (c) 79 (d) 210 (e) 94 (f) 20?
6. What purpose do centre lines serve?
7. To what distance would you set the compass to draw a bolt circle specified as:
   (a) 80 B.C. (b) 140 B.C. (c) 210 B.C.
8. A note specifies that the holes on a bolt circle are equal distance from each other. How many degrees separate the centres of each hole if there are:
   (a) 4 holes (b) 6 holes (c) 8 holes (d) 12 holes on a bolt circle?
9. What purpose does a circle template serve?
10. What are the names applied to outside and inside rounded corners?
11. Suggest three reasons why objects are often designed with rounded corners.
12. Name a common object whose shape is (a) hexagonal (b) octagonal.

REPLACE THE X'S WITH THE CORRECT TERM

1. An **XXX** is any part of the circumference of a circle.
2. Two lines that cross one another are said to **XXXXXXXXX**.
3. A **XXXXX** is a straight line joining any two points on the circle.
4. The **XXXXXXXX** is a straight line passing through the centre of a circle and joining any two points on the circumference.
5. Always **XXXXXX** the compass in one direction only when scribing a circle.
6. The **XXXXXX** is the distance measured along a straight line from the centre of a circle to the circumference.
7. **XXXXXXXXX** circles have the same centre point but have varying diameter measurements.
8. The distance measured around a circle is called the **XXXXXXXXXXXXX**.
9. A **XXXXXXX** to a circle is a straight line which touches the circle at one point only.
10. Centre lines are made up of **XXXXXXXXXX** long and short dashes.

PROJECTS

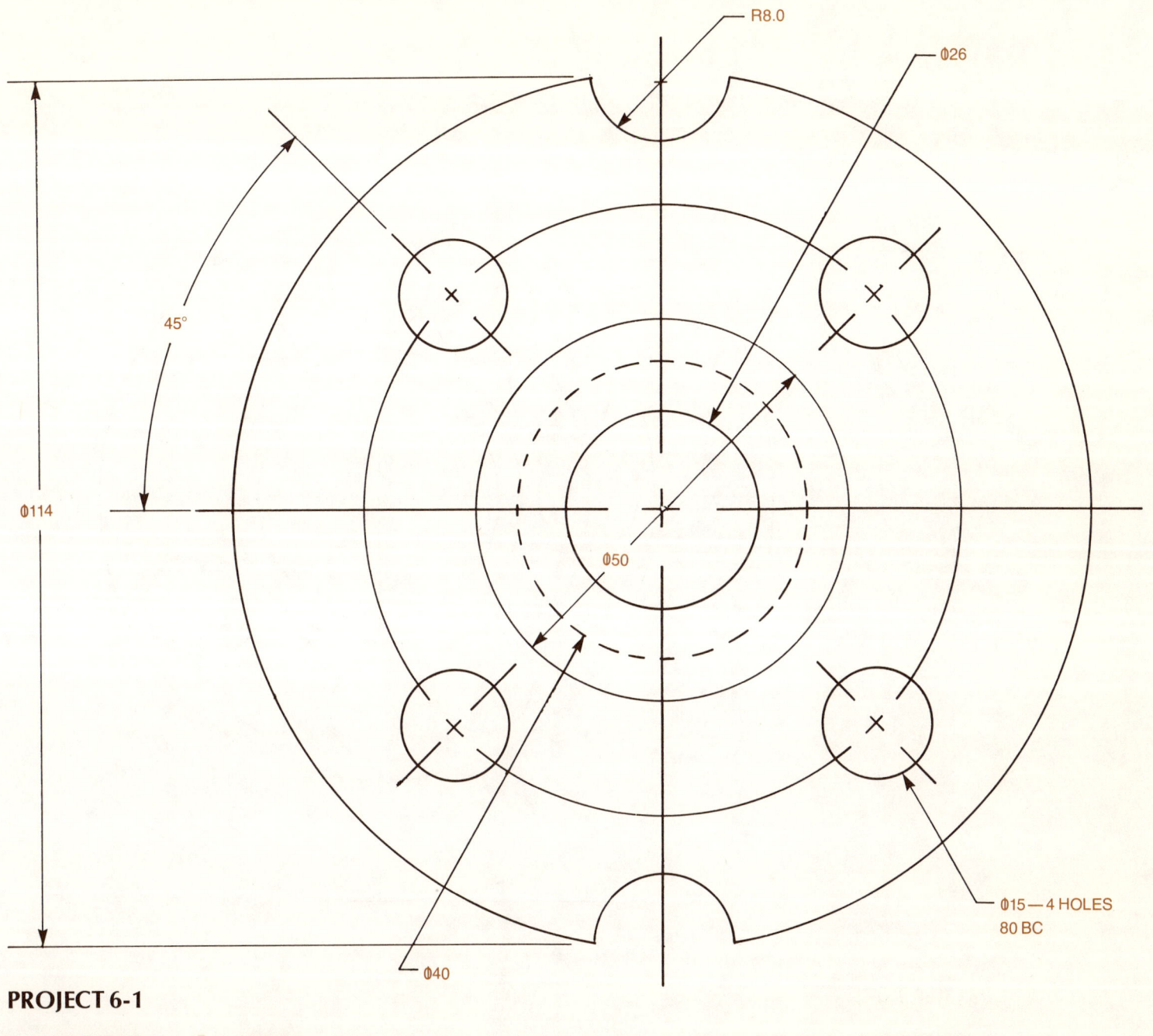

PROJECT 6-1

PLANE FIGURE No. 1   **SCALE 1:1**

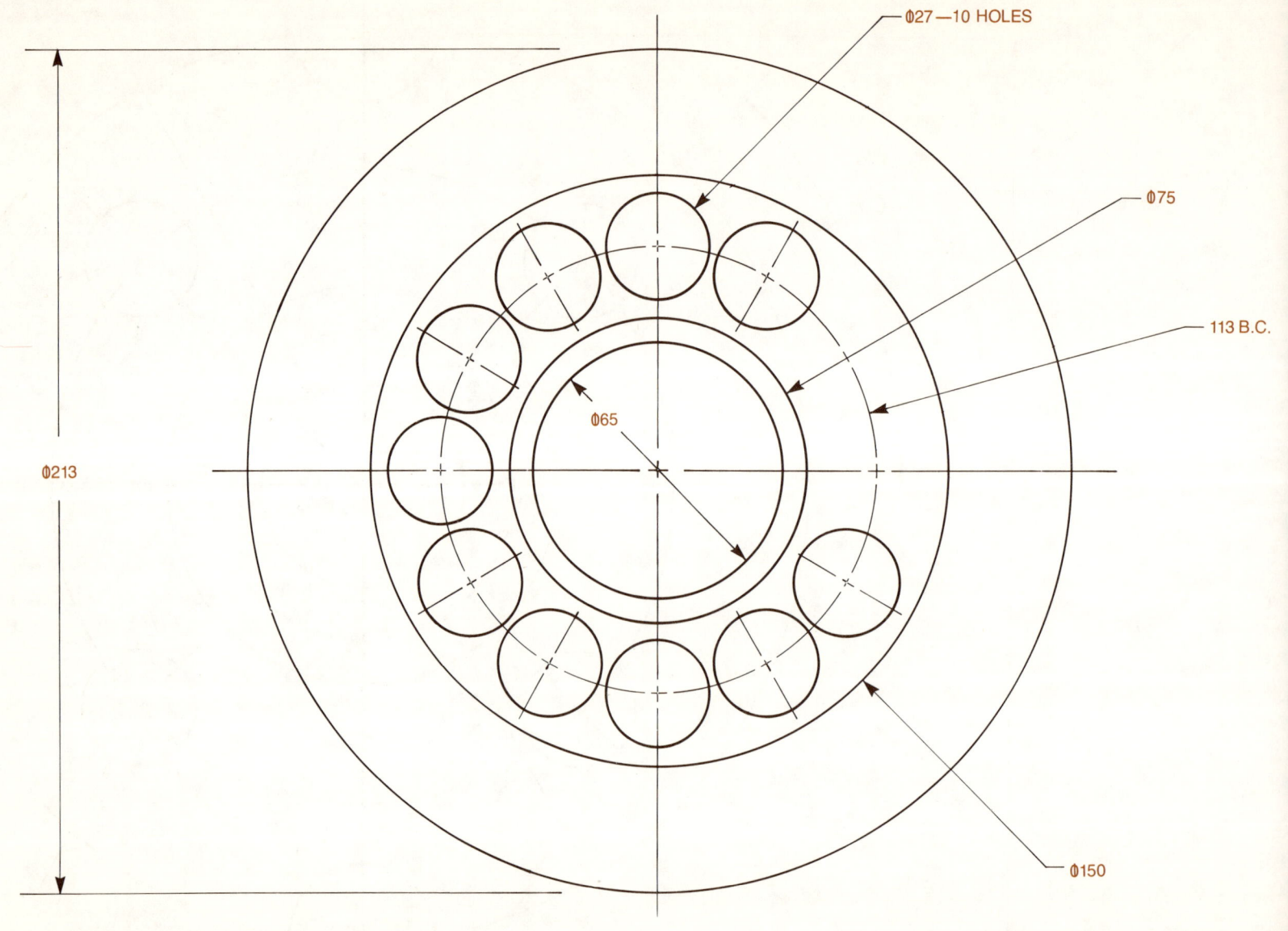

PROJECT 6-2

TELEPHONE DIAL   **SCALE 1:1**

74   CIRCLES

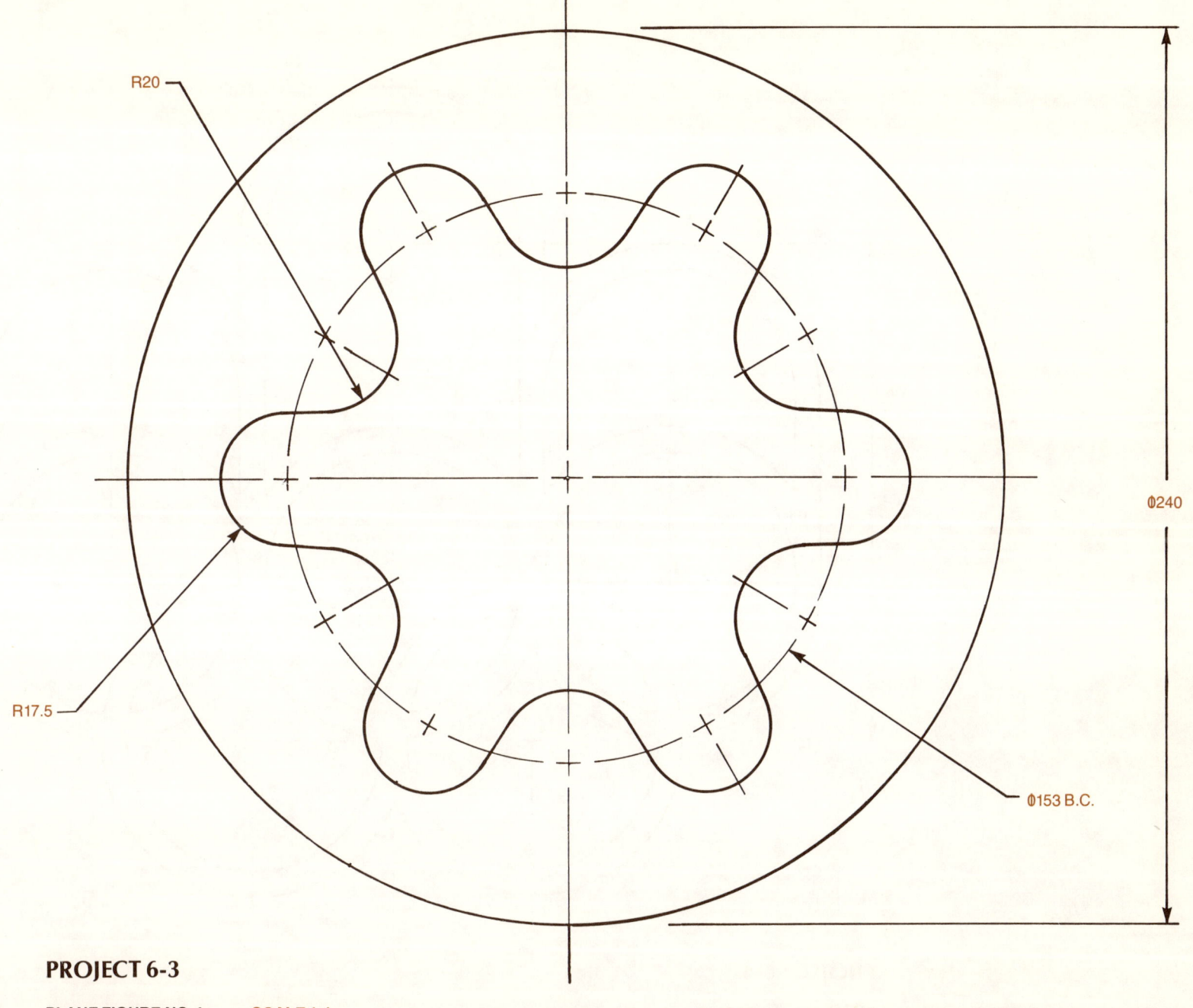

PROJECT 6-3

PLANE FIGURE NO. 1 **SCALE 1:1**

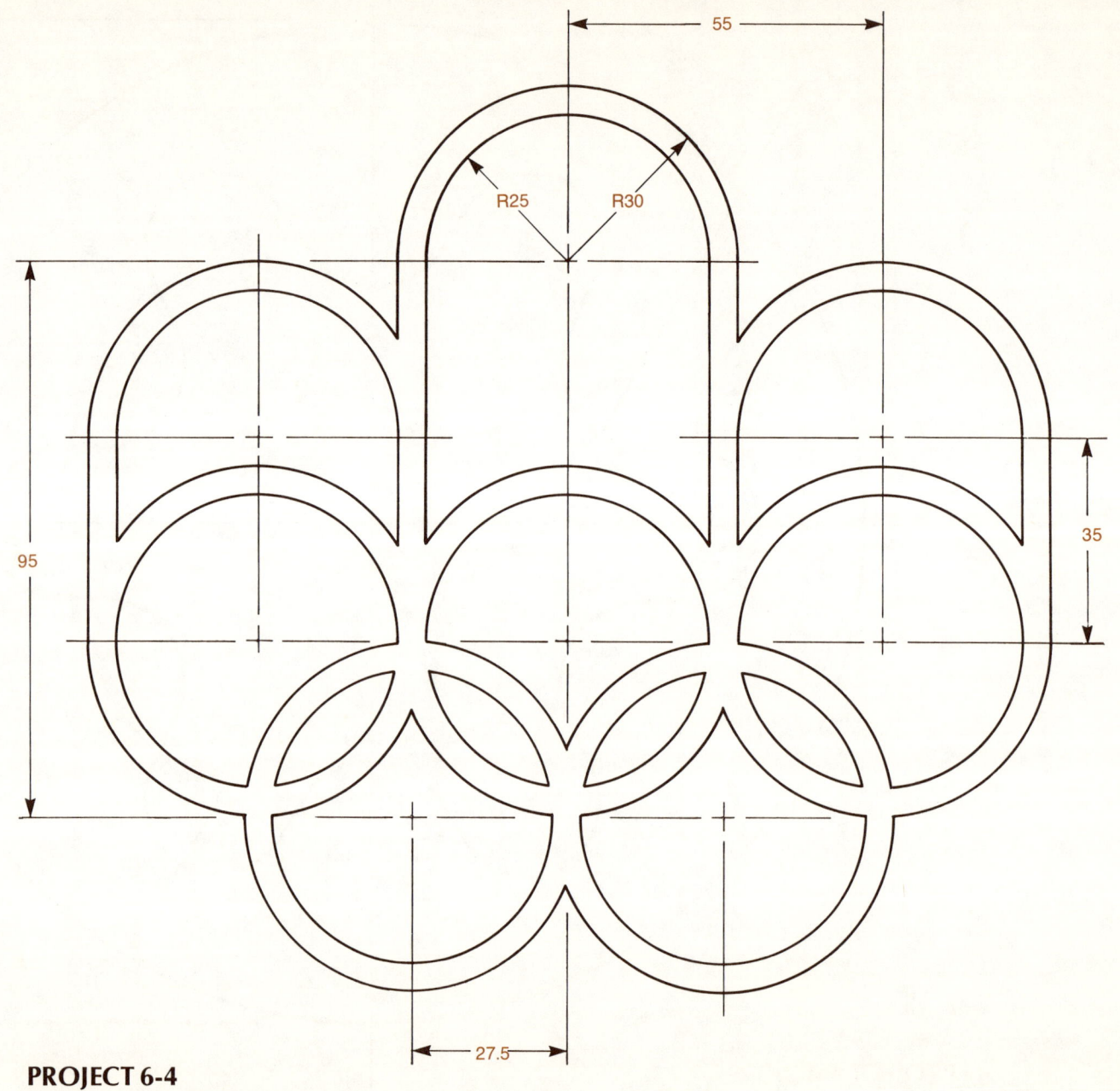

PROJECT 6-4

LOGO **SCALE 1:1**

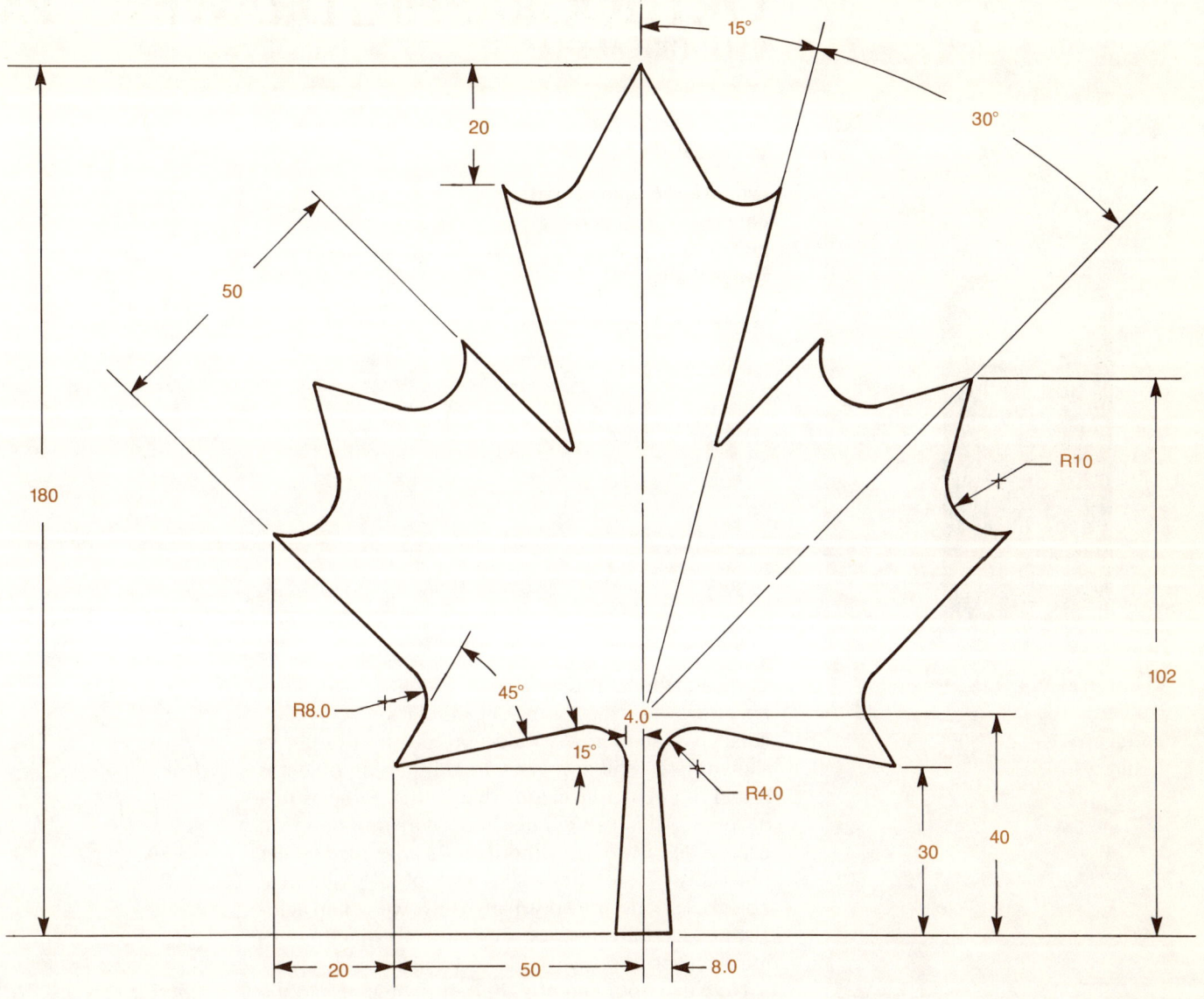

PROJECT 6-5

PLANE FIGURE NO. 2 **SCALE 1:1**

CHAPTER 7
ORTHOGRAPHIC DRAWING, PART II
CYLINDRICAL SHAPES

WORDS TO LEARN

cylindrical (cy-lín-dri-cal)
concentric (con-cén-tric)
hub (hub)
flange (flange)

cylindrical—having a rounded surface
concentric—having a common centre

OBJECT IS CYLINDRICAL IN SHAPE
Fig. 7-1

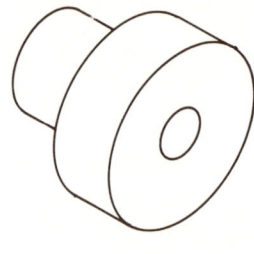

Fig. 7-2

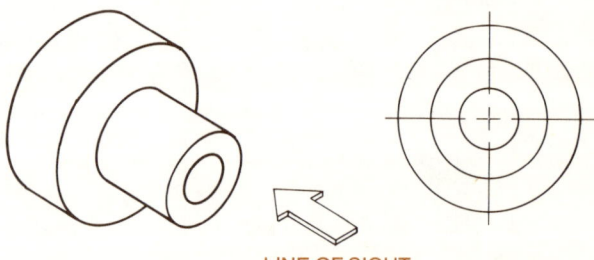

Fig. 7-3

Congratulations! You have come a long way to get this far. Now, let's look at some objects that are not rectangular in shape. How would you classify the object shown here? You may have noted that the object is round or circular in shape. That is true. Objects that have ends which are circular and have a round surface can be described as **cylindrical**. As with rectangular objects, we could draw six views of all cylindrical objects. Let's decide how many views we would actually need to fully describe a cylindrical object. Examine each end as shown in Fig. 7-2 and Fig. 7-3.

Note that your line of sight is at right angles to the end of the cylinder in Fig. 7-2 and Fig. 7-3. Both Fig. 7-2 and Fig. 7-3 show the true shape of this view of the cylinder as **concentric circles**. You will note that Fig. 7-3 shows all of the concentric circles as solid lines. There are no hidden features. Experience has taught you that this view is easier to read.

Now that you have selected one view, let us imagine that the cylinder is rotated 90° to give us the view showing the true shape of the front view.

78

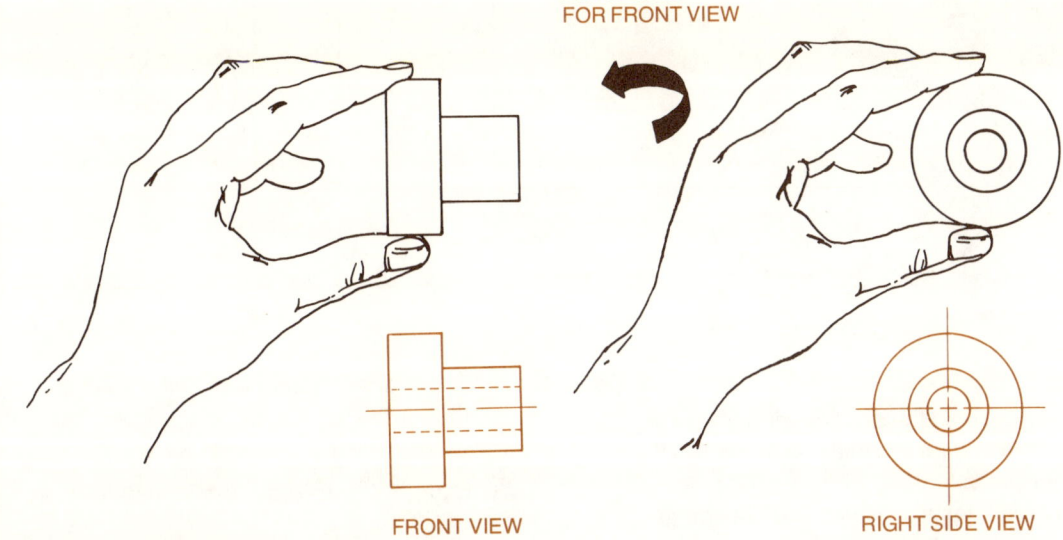

Fig. 7-4 *Revolved Cylinder*

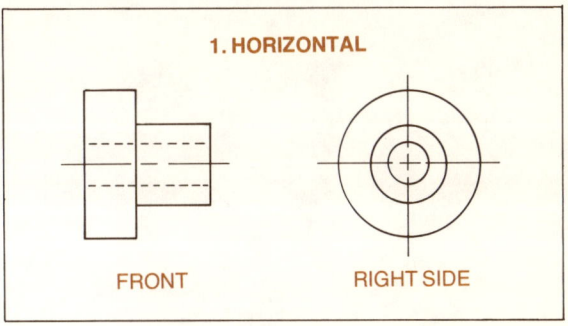

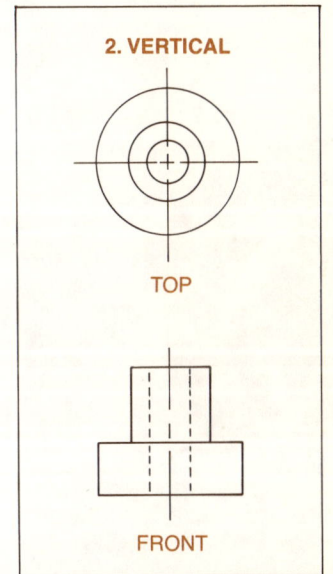

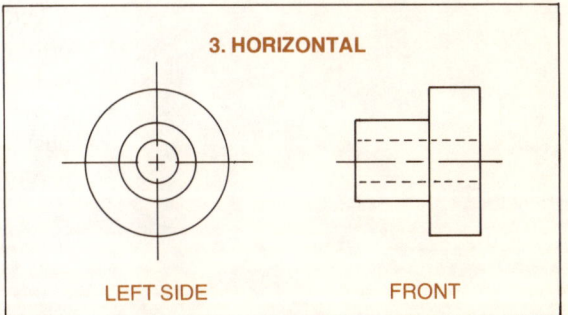

Fig. 7-5

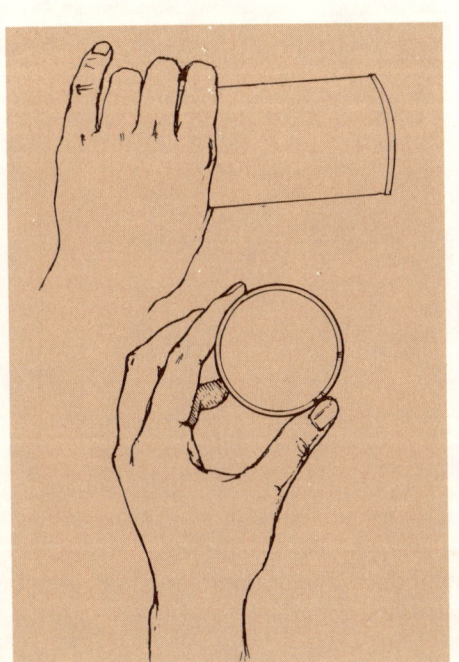

The view that shows the length of a cylinder is usually called the front view. You may have noticed that although the object is a cylinder, the front looks rectangular in shape. If you take a moment to go through the other possible ways to revolve the cylinder, you will see that each view will only duplicate the front view.

Simply stated, cylindrical objects need two views to describe them. One view looks circular and another view shows the length of the object and appears rectangular.

The positioning of the two views is a matter of choice. The two views can be drawn vertically or horizontally as shown in Fig. 7-5. Before you begin making your own decisions, let's do one drawing together step by step. Remember what you have learned in Chapter 6. The diameter of a circle is twice the radius.

CYLINDRICAL SHAPES 79

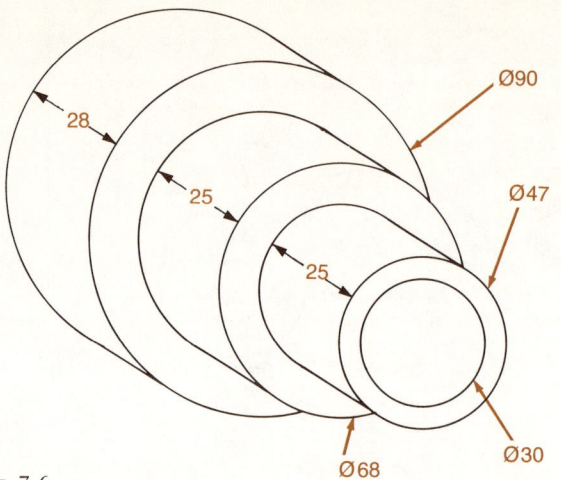

Fig. 7-6

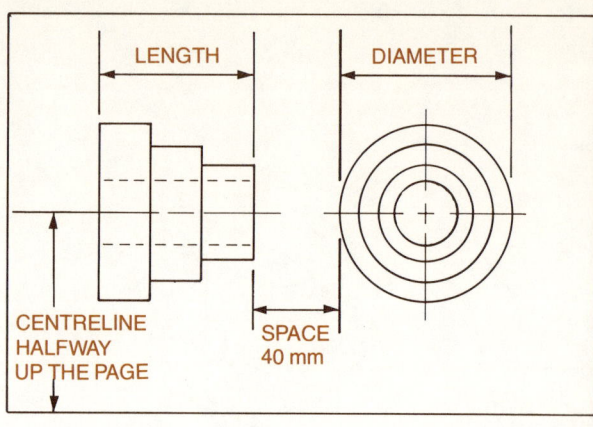

Fig. 7-7

Take a few minutes to read the pictorial drawing of a step bushing (Fig. 7-6) and jot down the answers to all these important questions:
1. What is the overall length of the step bushing?
2. What is the largest diameter?
3. What are the dimensions of the smaller diameters including the hole?

Note the radius for each diameter.

Your notes should look similar to this:

Overall length	= 78	
Largest Ø	= 90	R = 45
Next Largest Ø	= 68	R = 34
Smallest Step Ø	= 47	R = 23.5
Hole Ø	= 30	R = 15

With this information before you, drawing the orthographic views of the step bushing can be a simple task.

In Fig. 7-7, we have a completed drawing of the step bushing. As you look at the drawing, take note of several things:
1. The views are shown side by side, 40 mm apart.
2. The length is shown in the front view.
3. The diameter is shown in the side view.
4. The two views are drawn half-way up the page.
5. The space on either side of the two views is the same.

Now you are ready to draw the same views as in Fig. 7-7.

Steps in Spacing Two Orthographic Views

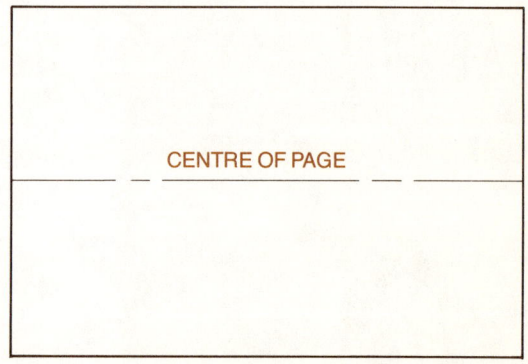

Fig. 7-8(a)

1. Measure the side of your paper. At the midpoint draw a light centre line horizontally across the paper.

80 ORTHOGRAPHIC DRAWING

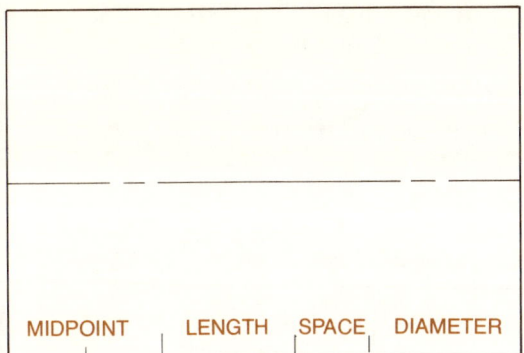

Fig. 7-8(b)

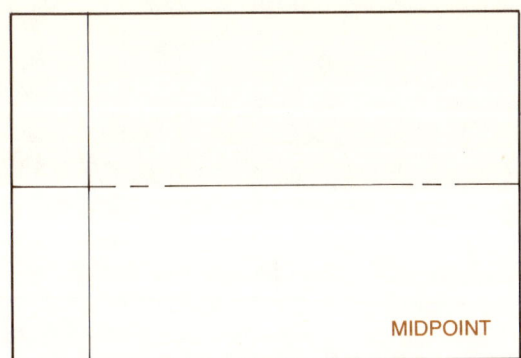

Fig. 7-8(c)

Steps in Laying Out Two Orthographic Views

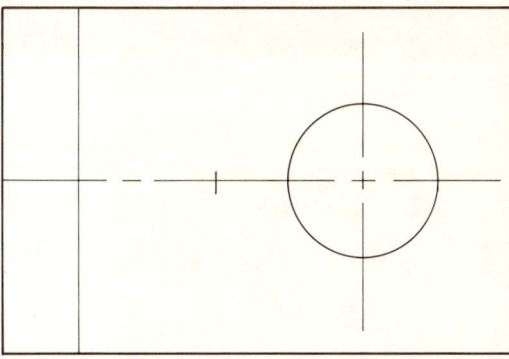

Fig. 7-9(a)

1. Set the point of the compass where the two centre lines intersect; adjust the compass to the radius and draw the circumference of the largest diameter.

2. On the border from the right, mark off the largest diameter (90 mm). Next add on the space desired between views (40 mm) and then add on the length (78 mm).

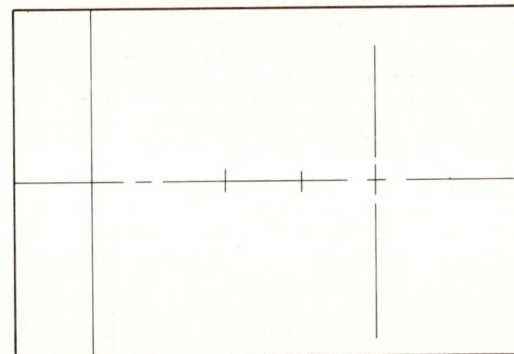

Fig. 7-8(d)

3. Measure the distance remaining on the line and find the mid-point of this distance and project this point to the horizontal centre line.
4. From this point on the centre line, measure off the length first, and then the space. From this point, add on the radius of the largest diameter (⌀90 ÷ 2) = 45. Draw a vertical centre line at this point.

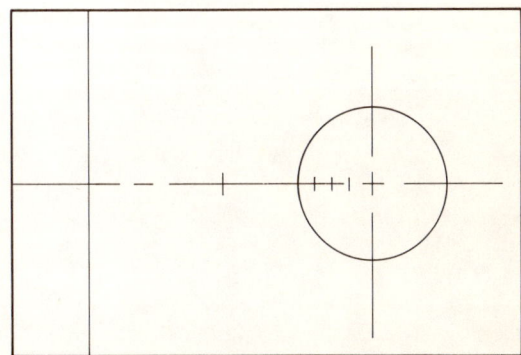

Fig. 7-9(b)

2. From the same centre line, mark off the radius of each of the other step diameters, including the hole diameter.

CYLINDRICAL SHAPES 81

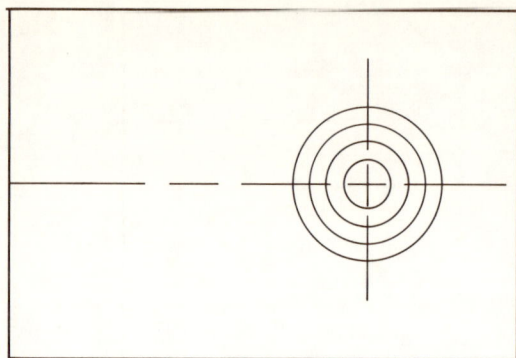

Fig. 7-9(c)

3. Draw each circumference in turn using the radius you have marked. Your side view is now complete. What you should have is four concentric circles whose diameters are: 90, 68, 47 and 30. Check these diameters with your scale. If you have made an error in measurement this is the time to catch it and correct the error.

Now for the front view. Look back at the finished drawing shown in Fig. 7-7. Note that the smallest hub is closest to the side view, stepping up to the next largest hub and then the largest hub. Just remember that the smallest hub is closest to the side view.

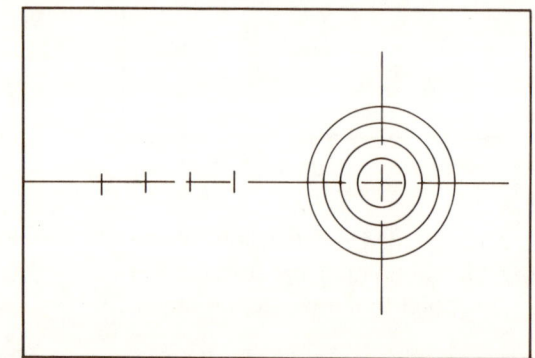

Fig. 7-9(d)

4. Mark off the space 40 mm along the horizontal centre line. From this point mark off in turn the length of each **hub** and the **flange**: first—25 mm, then 25 mm and finally 28 mm.

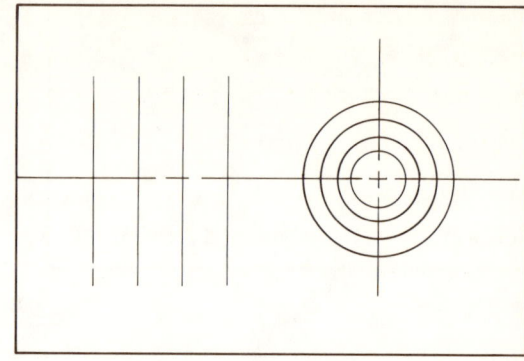

Fig. 7-9(e)

5. Draw light vertical lines through each of these points on the centre line.

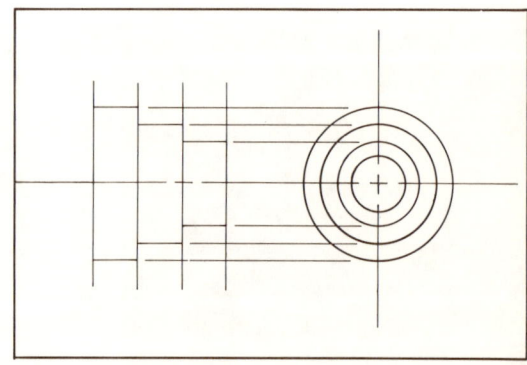

Fig. 7-9(f)

6. Starting with the largest step, project the diameter from the vertical centre line to the front view. Don't try to draw in all the projection lines. They may tend to confuse you. Just draw them in for the length of each step as needed.
7. The smallest circle on the side view, as you know, is the hole that passes through the step bushing. Since it is hidden from sight in the front view we can indicate the top and bottom of the hole by hidden lines.

flange—a rim or outer part of a wheel or pulley
hub—central part of a wheel or pulley

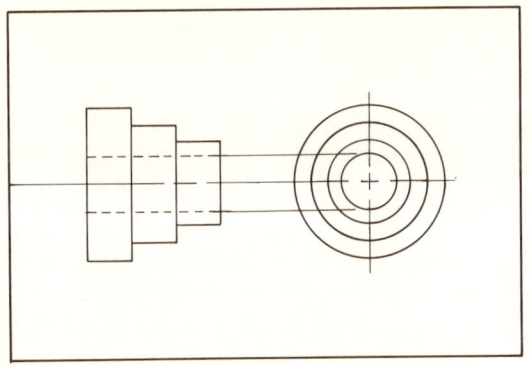

Fig. 7-9(g)

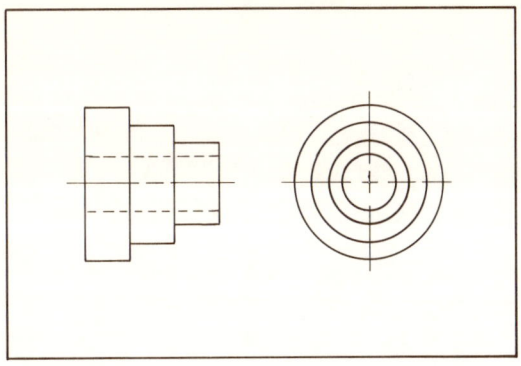

Fig. 7-9(h)

Note that the dashes touch at each end of the step bushing but do not touch any of the other visible lines.

8. To tell the reader that the object is cylindrical in shape we add centre lines as shown. We use vertical and horizontal centre lines in the side view and a horizontal centre line only in the front view.

Now, sit back and admire your work for a moment.

POINTS TO REMEMBER

- Most cylindrical objects need two views to best describe their shape.
- The front view usually shows the length of the cylindrical object.
- When deciding which views to draw, select those views which have fewer hidden lines. They are easier to read.
- The radius of a circle is equal to half its diameter.
- Vertical and horizontal centrelines are drawn on the view where the cylinder appears as a circle.
- A view of a hole that shows its length must have a centre line drawn through the hole.

QUESTIONS TO ANSWER

1. Explain what is meant by the term **cylindrical**.
2. How many views are usually required to fully describe a cylindrical object? Explain why.
3. Why is it necessary to space the views of any drawing carefully before completing any one view?
4. What is meant by the term **concentric circles**?
5. How would you describe the front view of a cylindrical object?
6. When drawing the views of a cylindrical object, which view would you outline first? Explain why.
7. Explain why centre lines
   (a) are necessary on views of cylindrical objects or features.
   (b) are drawn thin and dark.
   (c) consist of alternate long and short dashes.
   (d) extend a minimum of 3 mm beyond the view or feature they appear on.

REPLACE THE X'S WITH THE CORRECT TERM

1. The XXXXXX of an object is usually used to fasten one object to another.
2. Car wheels are fastened to the XXX of the axle.
3. Objects that have circular ends and round surfaces are known as XXXXXXXXXXX objects.

PROJECTS

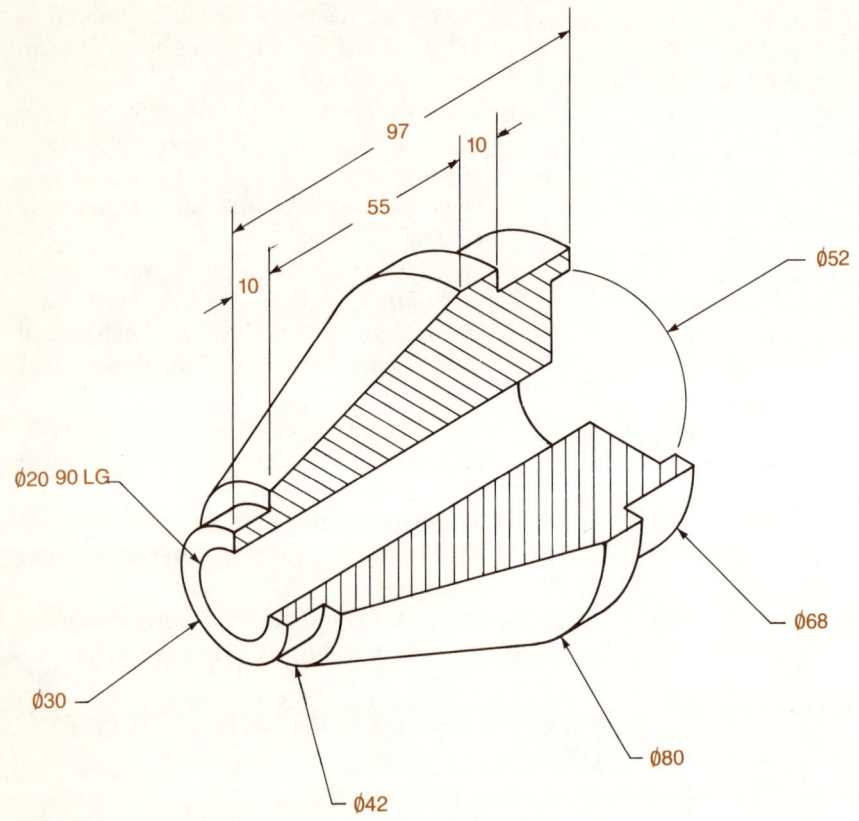

PROJECT 7-1

NOSE CONE **SCALE 1:1**

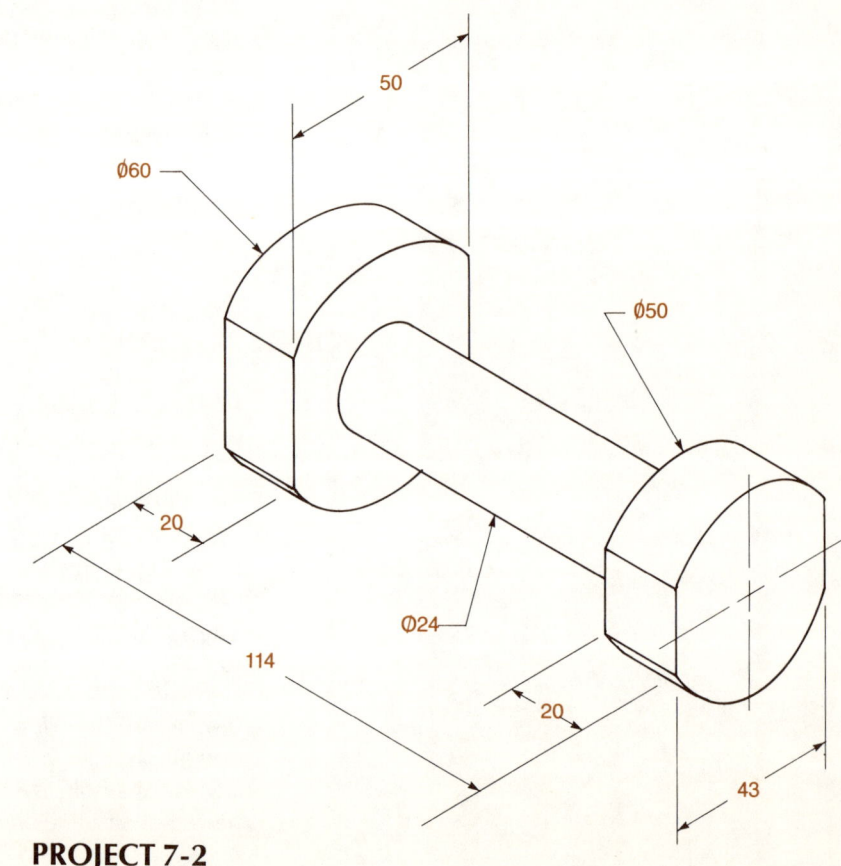

PROJECT 7-2

GAUGE **SCALE 1:1**

84 ORTHOGRAPHIC DRAWING

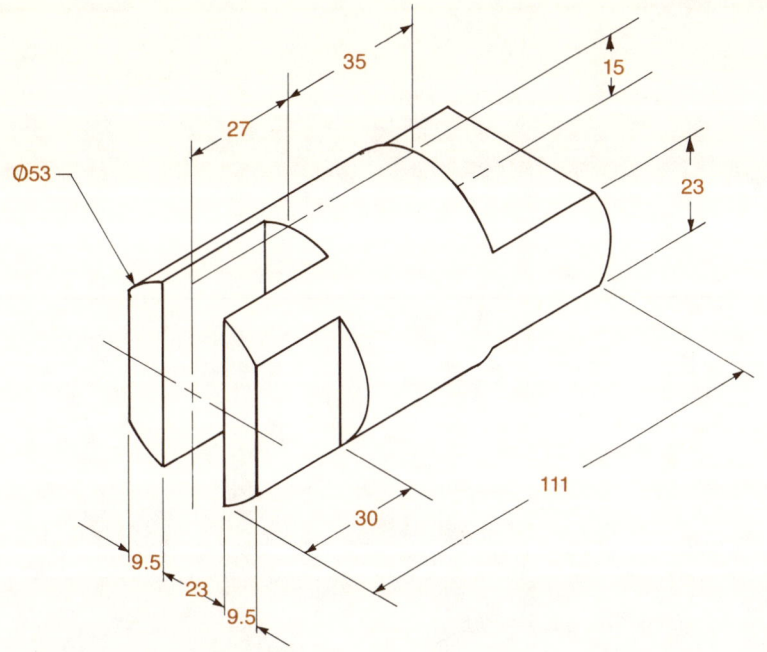

PROJECT 7-3

COUPLING **SCALE 1:1**

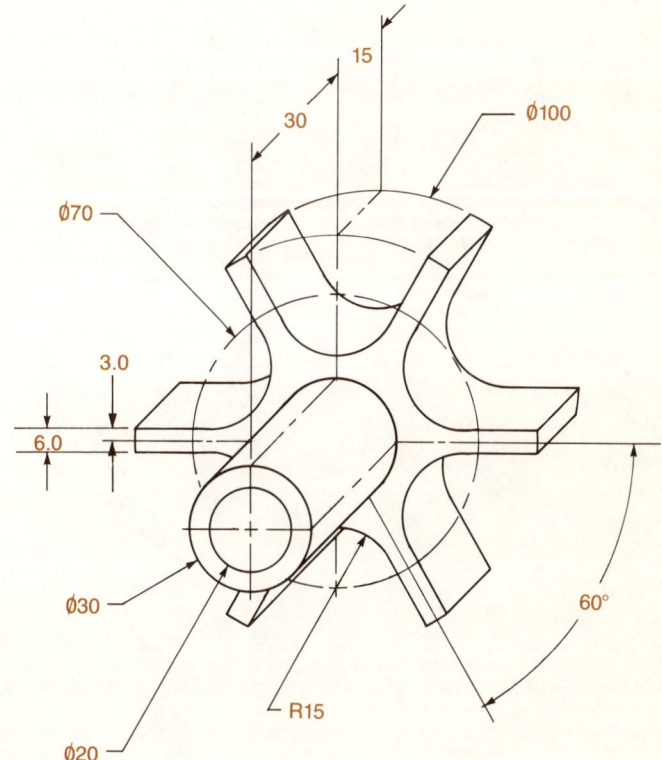

PROJECT 7-4

POLE PLATE **SCALE 1:1**

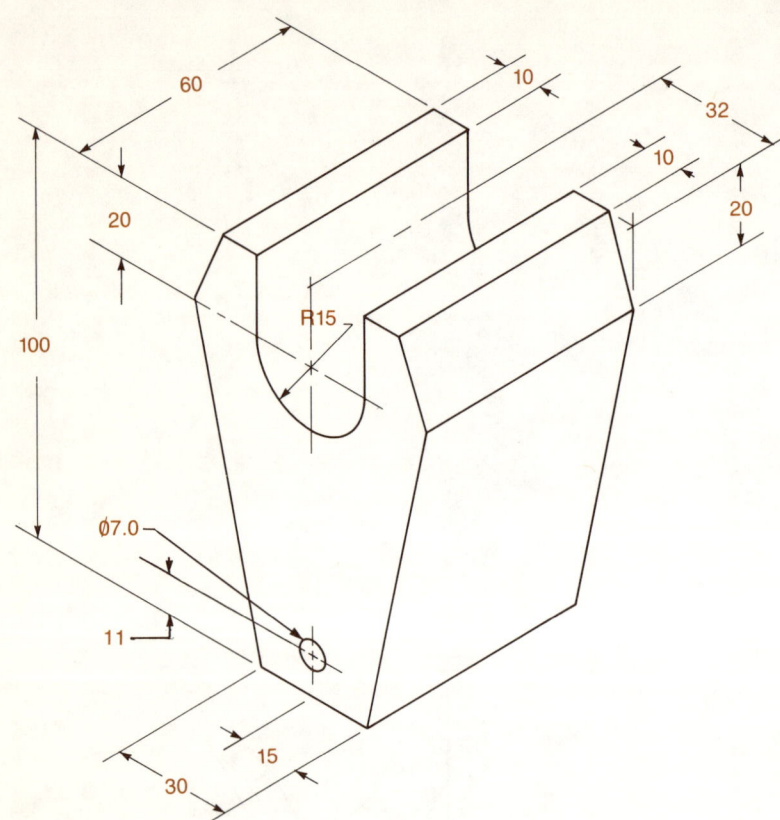

PROJECT 7-5

ANODE SCALE 1:1

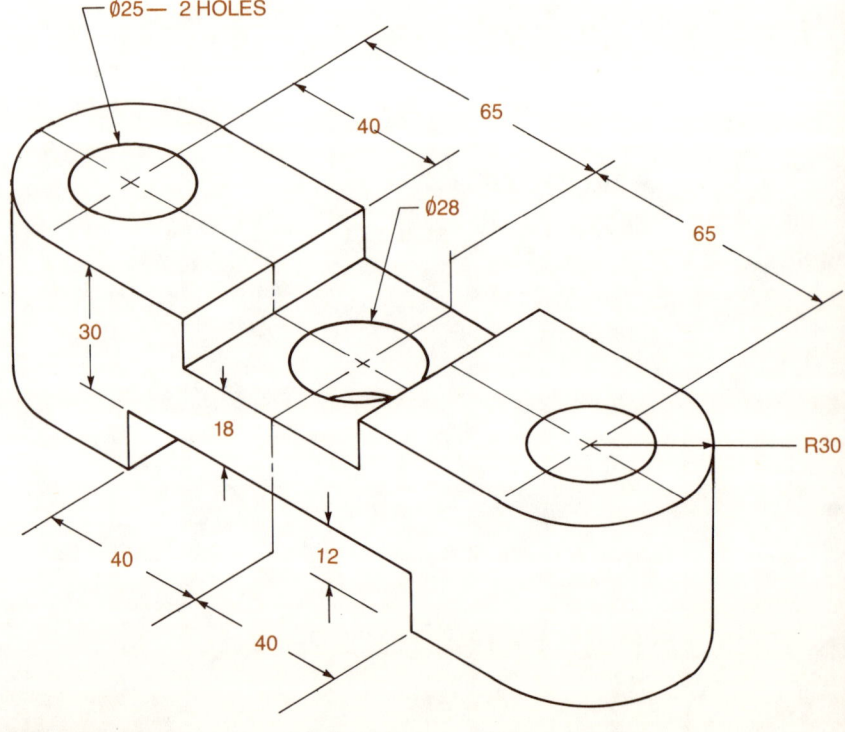

PROJECT 7-6

FIXED LINK SCALE 1:1

86 ORTHOGRAPHIC DRAWING

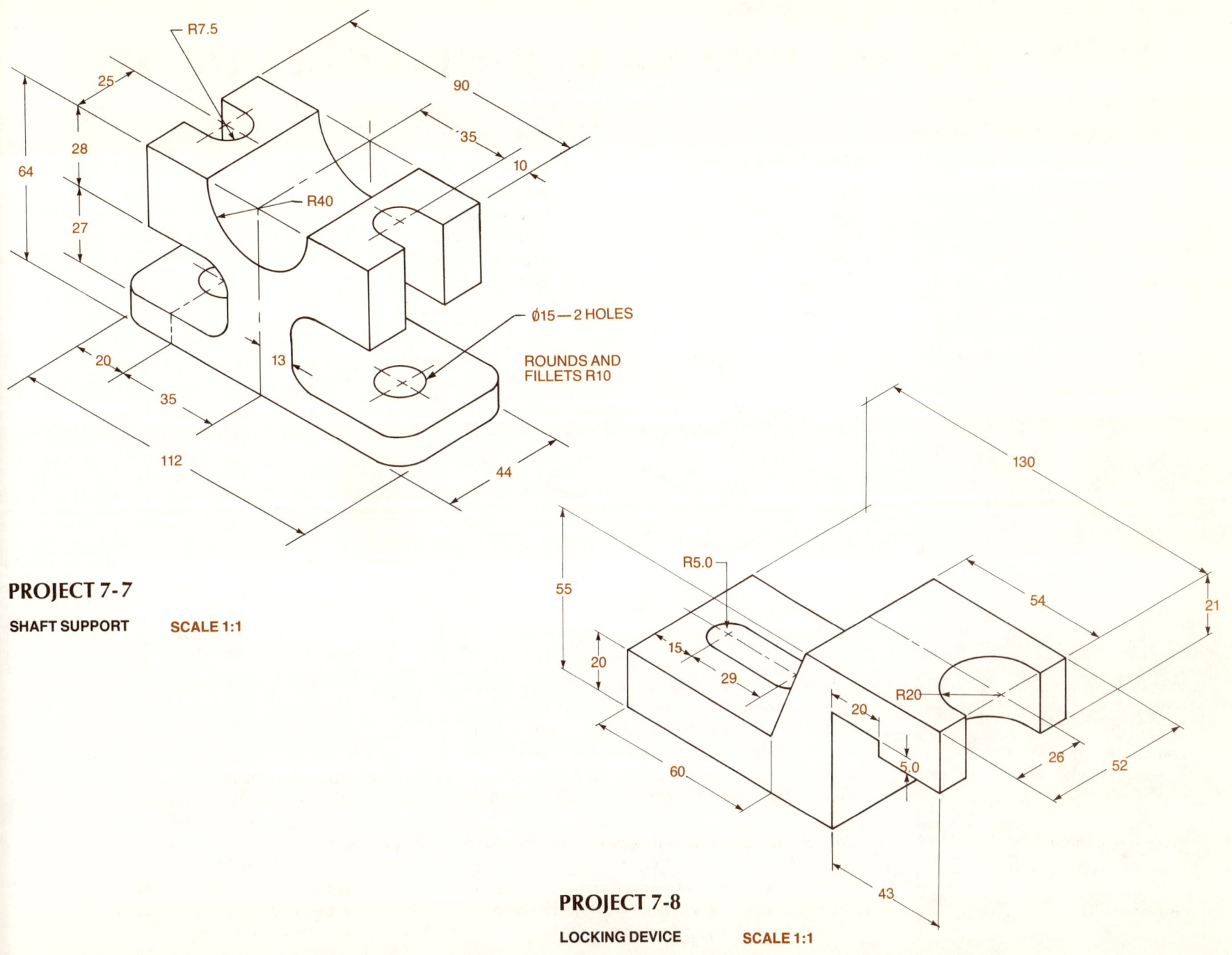

PROJECT 7-7

SHAFT SUPPORT   SCALE 1:1

PROJECT 7-8

LOCKING DEVICE   SCALE 1:1

CHAPTER 8
DIMENSIONING RECTANGULAR SHAPES

WORDS TO LEARN

avoid (a-voíd)
grasp
relate (re-láte)
clarity (clár-i-ty)
refer (re-fér)

comment (cóm-ment)
similar (sím-i-lar)
extend (ex-ténd)
stagger (stág-ger)
adjacent (ad-já-cent)

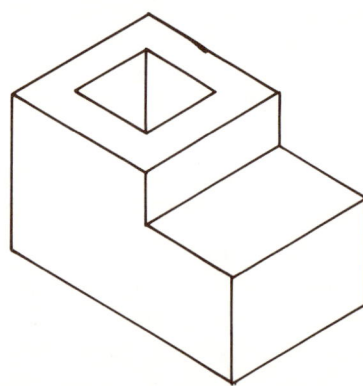

Fig. 8-1 *How would you dimension this object?*

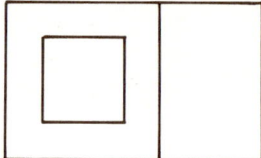

 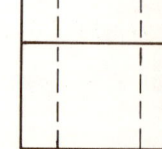

Fig. 8-2

avoid—to keep away from

comment—a statement made about something

grasp—to understand (hold)

similar—alike

We would all like to **avoid** dimensioning if we could. The usual **comment** made is that it is time-consuming and boring. That may be true, but you will have to admit that since the purpose of technical drawings is to communicate information, a drawing without dimensions is incomplete. It's like watching T.V. without sound.

Perhaps the easiest way to **grasp** the subject is to look at it from the point of view of the tradesperson reading your drawing. Put yourself in his or her place. What questions would you need answered if you were asked to make the object shown in Fig. 8-1?

Make a list and compare it with the one below. You may be surprised by the number of questions that need answers. Are your questions **similar** to these?

1. What are the overall dimensions—its length, width and height?
2. What is the height of this detail? The step?
3. How long is this detail?
4. What is the length of the hole and what is its distance from the edge?

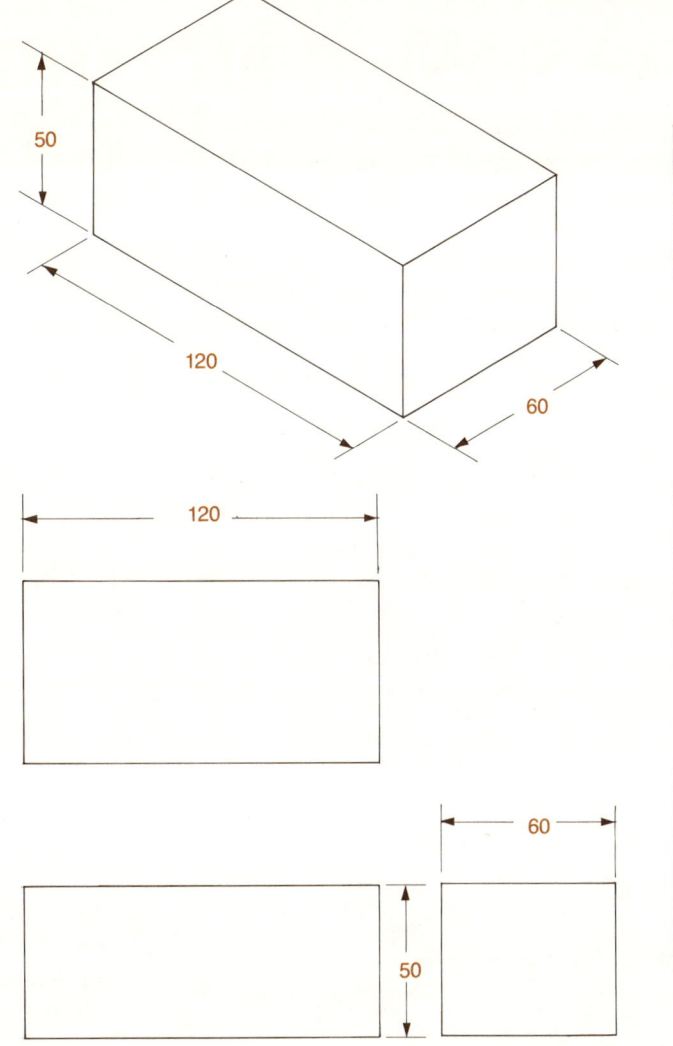

Fig. 8-3

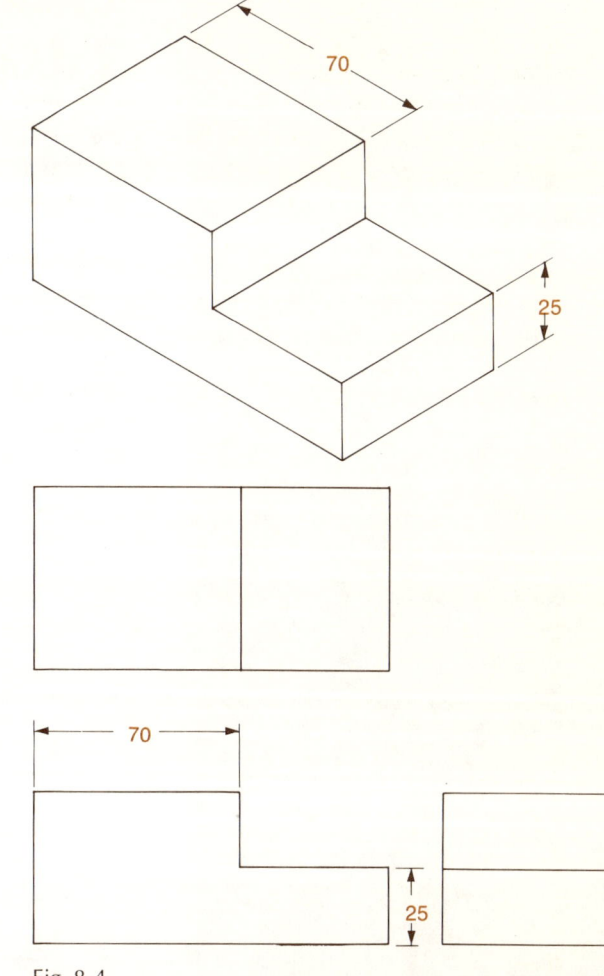

Fig. 8-4

5. What is the width of the hole and what is its distance from an edge?
6. How deep is the hole?

Now that you have asked the questions, let us try to supply all the answers. Remember, we want to avoid any misunderstanding that might lead to wasting time or material.

Orthographic views describe an object completely. We have drawn three views here to explain our project, and we should use all three views when dimensioning. We usually try to place all dimensions near the views—between the views and above the views if possible.

In Fig. 8-3, we look at the original rectangular block before the object is cut out of it. The overall dimensions are placed between and above the three views. These dimensions tell us what size to cut our material.

RECTANGULAR SHAPES

relate—to connect or compare in some way

Once the material is cut to the required size, you may next decide to cut the notch out of the block as shown in Fig. 8-4. You will need the two detail dimensions shown to know where to cut down and in. When the notch is removed, we check our object for accuracy by measuring the details. To make this easier, the drafter places the dimensions where the details are most clearly outlined. In our project, these details are best shown in the front view.

By reading the drawing (Fig. 8-2) you discover that the hole is square and goes right through the object from top to bottom. The shape of the hole is visibly outlined by solid lines in the top view and the hidden outline tells us the depth of the hole. The dimensions for the length and width of the hole are placed next to the visible outline of the hole in the top view (Fig. 8-5). Now that we know the size of the hole, we must know exactly where to place it.

By **relating** the hole to the closest sides we can easily check its size and position once it has been cut out. The hidden outline tells us that the hole is a through hole; therefore, there is no need to dimension its depth.

Does this still sound difficult? Look again, one step at a time, and with practice you will be dimensioning with ease.

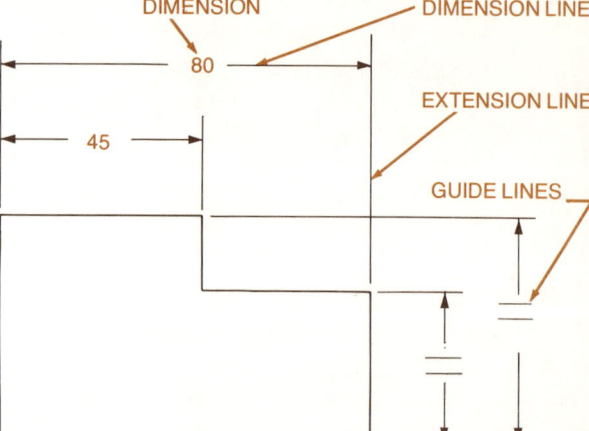

Fig. 8-6

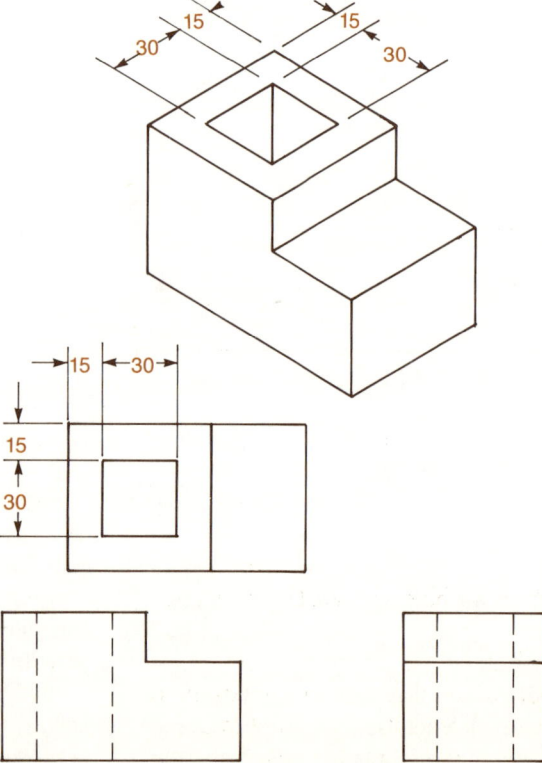

Fig. 8-5

Method of Dimensioning

We often extend our hands when talking to help describe the size of objects in our conversation. In drafting we use lines for the same purpose.

Extension lines. Two thin, black lines are drawn out from a view to limit the size we are describing. Leave a space between the outline and the start of the extension line. Even if the extension line crosses over an outline to extend out from a detail, leave a space. In order to add clarity, we allow the extension lines to project past the dimension line by about 2 mm.

Dimension lines. The dimension line is a thin, black line drawn with arrowheads at both ends touching the extension lines. A break is left in the dimension line to allow space for the dimension figure. In order to help

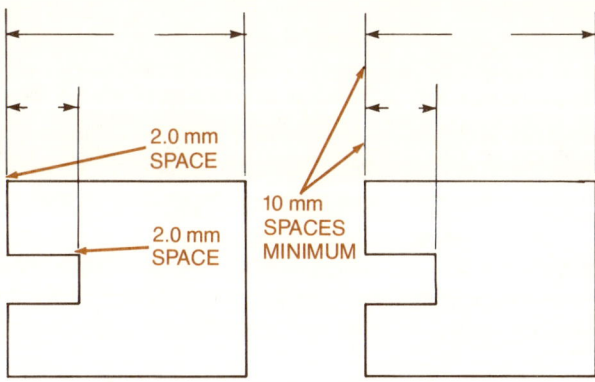

Fig. 8-7

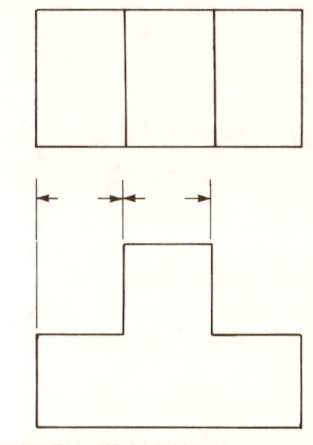

Fig. 8-8

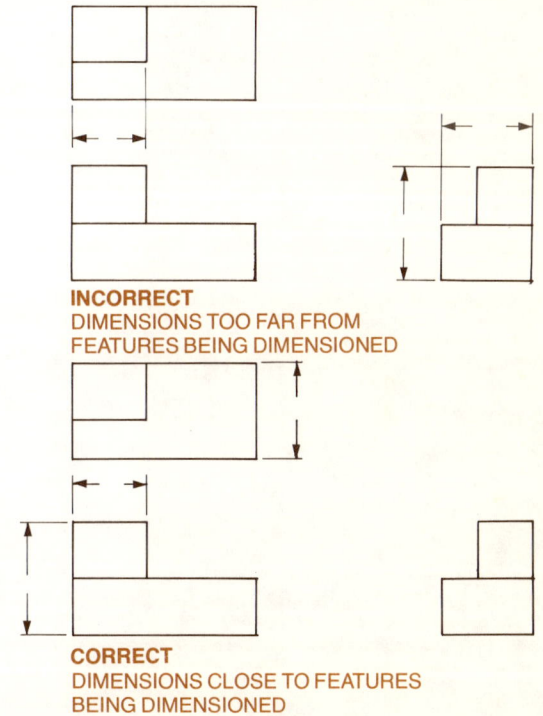

HERE THE FRONT VIEW SHOWS THE SHAPE MORE CLEARLY

Fig. 8-9

avoid crowding the views, we can draw the dimension lines at least 10 mm from the view. If we need another dimension line next to the first, again leave a 10 mm space.

Remember that we draw outlines as thick lines to stand out and clearly describe the shape. We want to keep our views easy to read. For this reason, both extension and dimension lines are drawn thin and sharp.

Arrowheads. Arrowheads are solid, pointed and must touch the extension lines.

Dimension figures. These are lettered in the space between the dimension lines. They should be lettered between light guide lines which are drawn parallel to the top of the page.

Helpful Hints

Now you can see that dimensioning is not difficult after all. Here are a number of points to remember:
- You will find that one view outlines a detail better than another. Place the dimension next to the view where the shape is shown most clearly.
- Avoid extension lines that take you too far from the feature being dimensioned. It is better to be close.

INCORRECT
DIMENSIONS TOO FAR FROM FEATURES BEING DIMENSIONED

CORRECT
DIMENSIONS CLOSE TO FEATURES BEING DIMENSIONED

Fig. 8-10

RECTANGULAR SHAPES 91

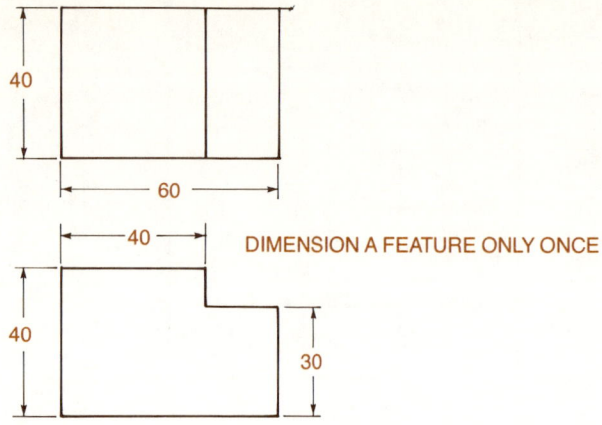

DIMENSION A FEATURE ONLY ONCE

Fig. 8-11

- Dimension a feature only once. Don't repeat yourself.

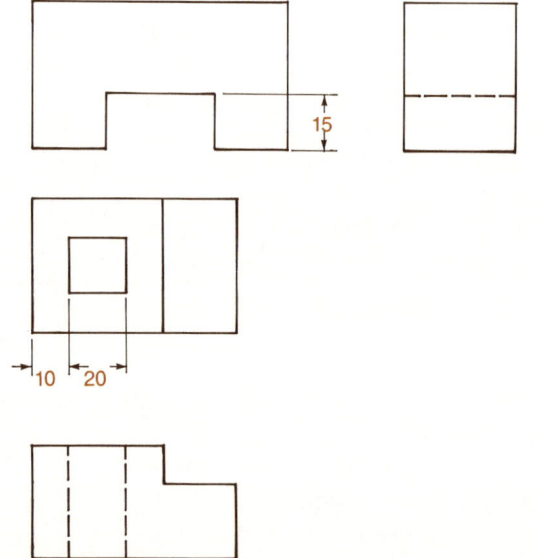

Fig. 8-12

- Dimension to visible outlines rather than hidden lines if possible. They are easier to read.

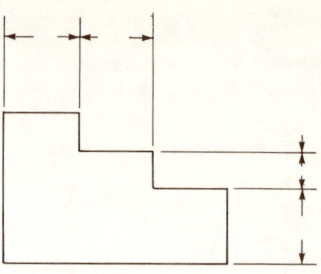

Fig. 8-13

- Detail dimensions in a row are easier to read than staggered dimensions.

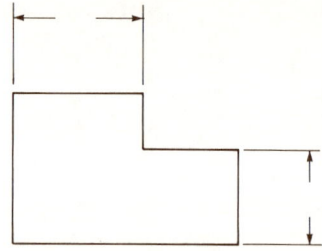

Fig. 8-14

- Dimension what you can measure rather than the space.

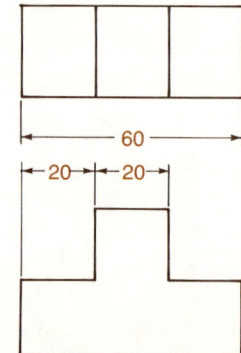

Fig. 8-15

- Omit one detail dimension in a chain. It is not good practice to complete the chain. The dimension at either end is unnecessary.

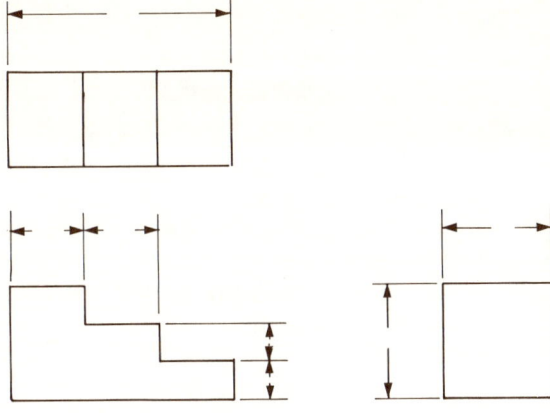

Fig. 8-16

- Dimension all necessary features. You will find quite often that some dimensions are unnecessary.

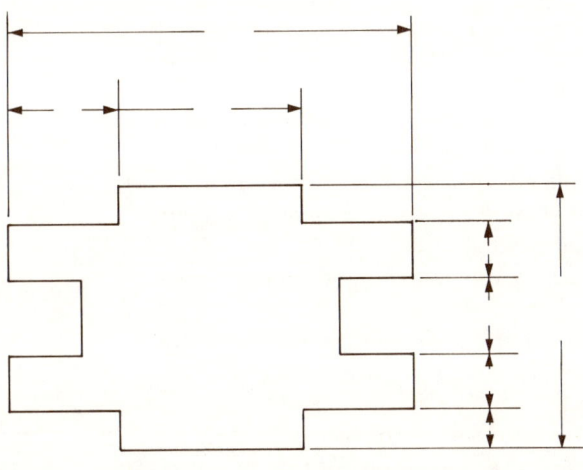

Fig. 8-17

- Some objects have features that are obviously the same at either end. There is no need to dimension both; one will do.

Dimension Figures

We have placed a great deal of importance on extension and dimension lines. It is true that they are important, but the actual dimension figures are even more important. Quite often the positioning of the lines depends on the size of the dimension. The space is usually large enough so that the dimension lines, the dimension figure and the arrowheads can be placed between the extension lines. The dimension figures are placed centrally between the extension lines.

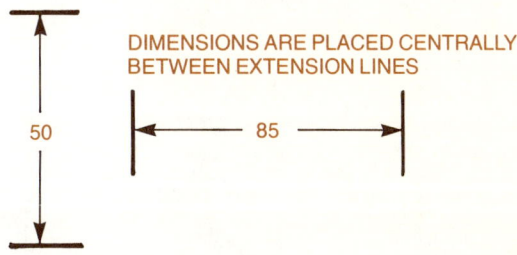

Fig. 8-18

Metric dimension figures always have at least two digits. If a dimension is less than one, we place a zero before the decimal point (e.g., 0.5).

0.4   0.6   0.25   0.98

Fig. 8-19

Whole numbers from one to nine are shown with a zero after the decimal point (e.g., 2.0).

2.0   3.0   5.0   9.0

Fig. 8-20

Whole numbers greater than nine are shown as plain whole numbers, single decimal numbers or double decimal numbers (e.g., 13, 15.0, 20.00).

21   21.2   13.25

Fig. 8-21

RECTANGULAR SHAPES 93

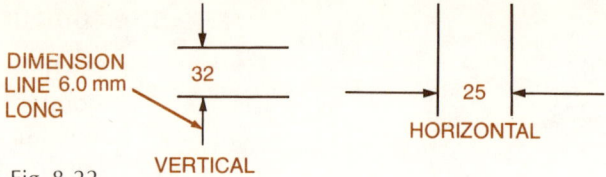

Fig. 8-22

Quite often we find some features that need special treatment. When the feature being dimensioned is too small to place the dimension within the dimension line, we can draw the dimension line arrowheads outside the extension lines and allow room inside for the dimension.

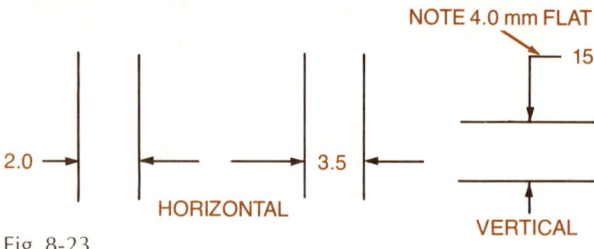

Fig. 8-23

If the space is too small for the dimensions to be placed between the extension lines, the dimension and the dimension line arrowheads can be placed outside the extension lines.

The dimensioning of angles may also need to be done differently, depending on the size and position of the angle. The dimension line is drawn as an arc using a compass. The arc is drawn to any convenient radius to suit the size of the angle.

You can refer to the following examples when necessary.

Note. Keep in mind that all dimensions on a technical drawing are understood to be in millimetres unless otherwise noted.

Note. The dimensions specified on technical drawings are the actual full size dimensions of the object, no matter what scale was used to prepare the drawing.

Note. Technical drawings properly dimensioned require no additional calculations by the reader.

You have probably read more than enough to absorb by simple reading. Follow the steps in dimen-

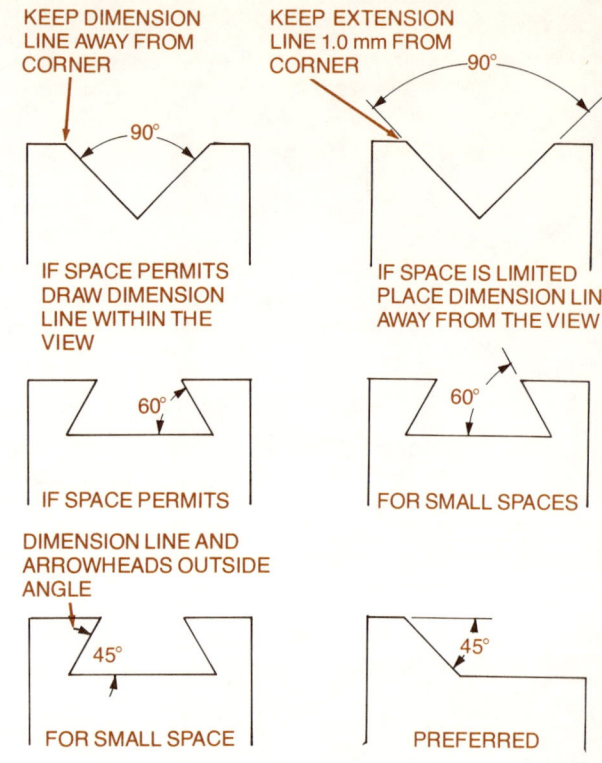

Fig. 8-24

sioning below whenever you dimension a drawing. You will soon find that it won't be necessary to memorize a lot of rules.

Steps in Dimensioning

1. Lightly draw in all extension and dimension lines wherever you think they are needed.
2. Erase those extension and dimension lines that are unnecessary.
3. Lightly draw all of the guide lines for the dimension figures.
4. Carefully letter in all dimension figures.
5. Darken in all of the extension and dimension lines.

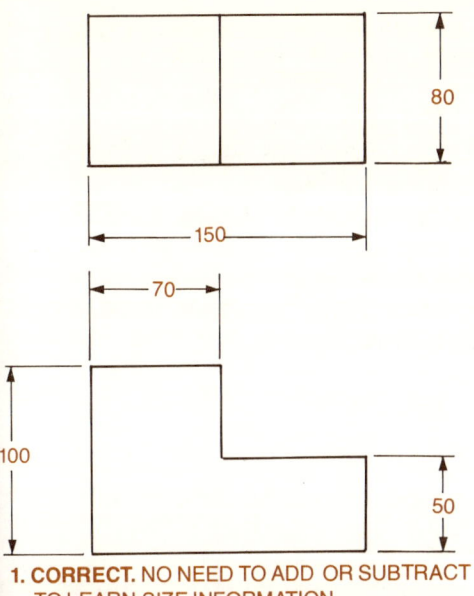

1. CORRECT. NO NEED TO ADD OR SUBTRACT TO LEARN SIZE INFORMATION

Fig. 8-25(a)

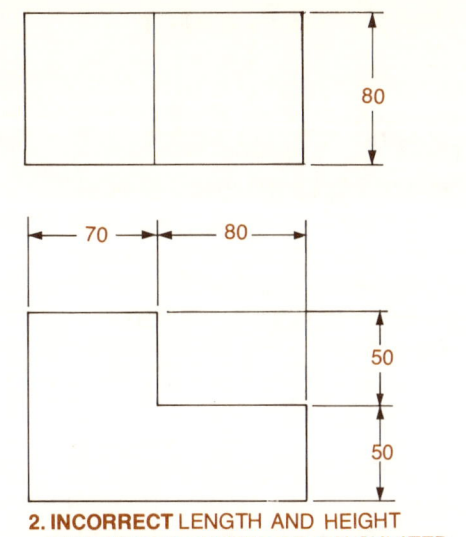

2. INCORRECT LENGTH AND HEIGHT DIMENSIONS HAVE TO BE CALCULATED

Fig. 8-25(b)

6. Draw in all of the arrowheads as carefully as you can.

That's it. You can now begin dimensioning with ease. Good luck.

POINTS TO REMEMBER

- In metric drawings all dimensions are in millimetres, unless otherwise noted.
- The scale of a drawing may be greater or less than full size, but the actual full size dimension must be used.
- It should be unnecessary for someone reading your drawing to make any additional calculations.
- When dimensioned, your drawing should be clear, complete and easily understood.
- Extension and dimension lines are drawn thin and black to contrast with the thick visible outline.
- Always use guidelines for the dimension figures.
- All dimensions should be lettered parallel to the top of the page.
- Neat, sharp, pointed arrowheads add to the clarity of a drawing.

QUESTIONS TO ANSWER

1. Why is it necessary to dimension technical drawings?
2. What are the names for all the overall dimensions?
3. Give two practical reasons for placing dimensions away from the views and between the views if possible.
4. Why is it necessary to draw extension and dimension lines thin and black?
5. Explain the different purposes that the extension and dimension lines serve.
6. Describe the appearance and the position of (a) arrowheads, (b) dimension figures, when dimensioning a technical drawing.
7. Why is it good practice to leave a space between the outline of a view and the extension line?
8. Why are dimension lines placed a minimum of 10 mm from a view and from an adjacent dimension line?
9. List six important rules to keep in mind when dimensioning a drawing. Explain the importance of each rule.
10. Is it necessary to place the millimetre symbols after each dimension on a drawing? Explain the reason for your answer.
11. If a drawing is drawn to a scale of 2:1, should the dimension figures be twice the actual size of the object? Explain your answer.
12. Why is it often necessary to place dimension lines, arrowheads and dimensions outside of extension lines instead of between the extension lines?

REPLACE THE X'S WITH THE CORRECT TERM

1. A diving board XXXXXXX out from the side of a pool.
2. Sometimes it is hard to XXXXX the meaning of a word.
3. Nails and screws are XXXXXXX in that they hold pieces of material together.
4. A horse and a mule look XXXXXXX in many ways, but are not identical.
5. Good speakers will improve the XXXXXXX of sound from a stereo.
6. If you are unsure of the meaning of a word, you can XXXXX to a dictionary.
7. XXXXXXXXX office hours would reduce traffic problems at the rush hour.
8. We can XXXXX danger by obeying warning signs.
9. A garage can be built as part of a house or XXXXXXX to the house.
10. After a sports game, broadcasters offer their XXXXXXX on the game.

96 DIMENSIONING

PROJECTS

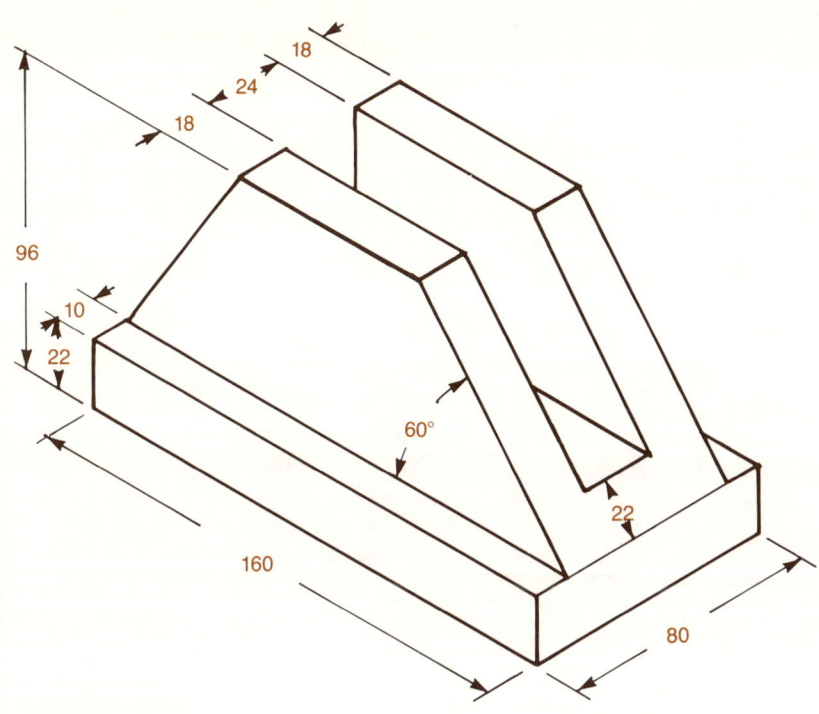

PROJECT 8-1

GUIDE BLOCK SCALE 1:2

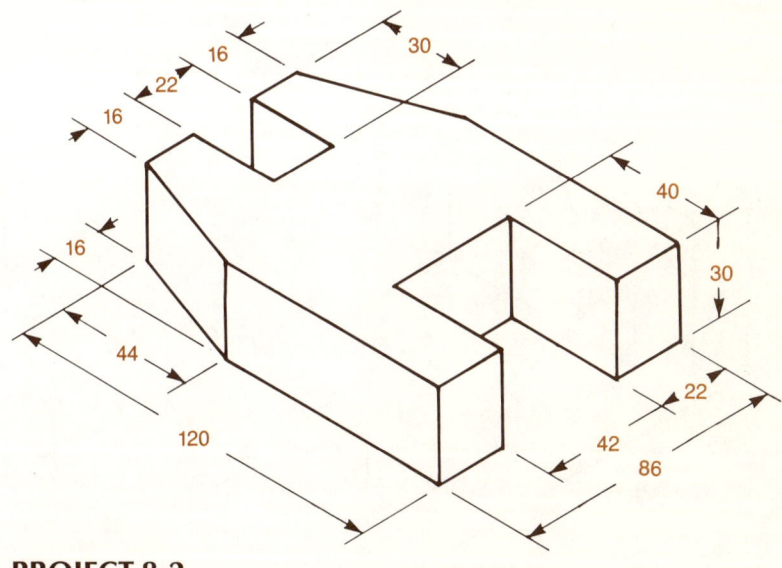

PROJECT 8-2

ARBOUR PRESS BASE SCALE 1:2

PROJECTS 97

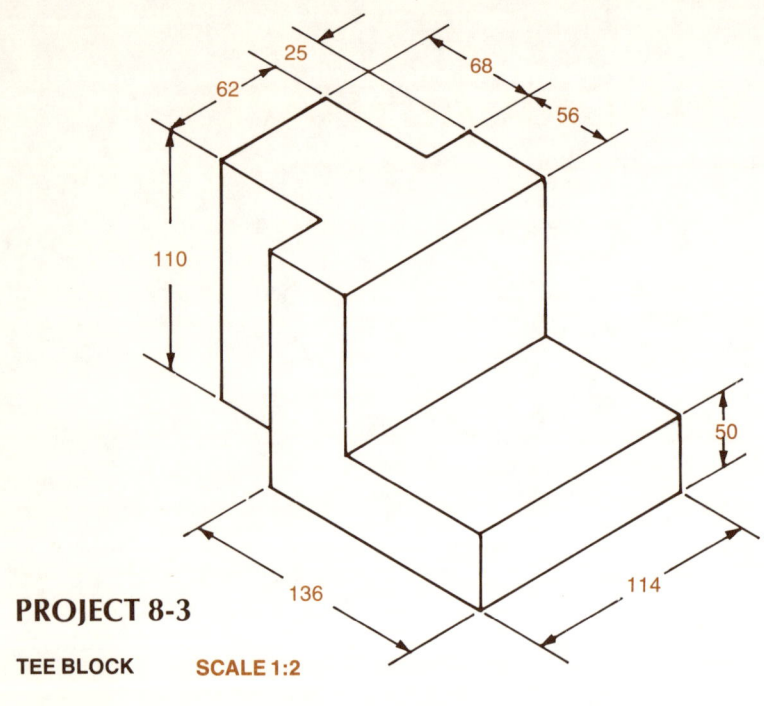

PROJECT 8-3

TEE BLOCK SCALE 1:2

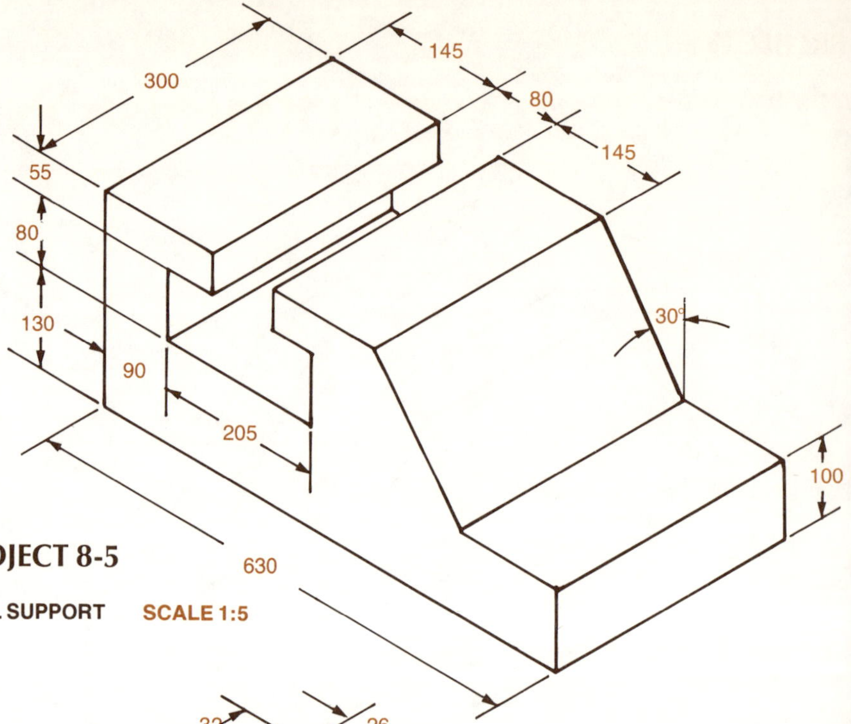

PROJECT 8-5

TOOL SUPPORT SCALE 1:5

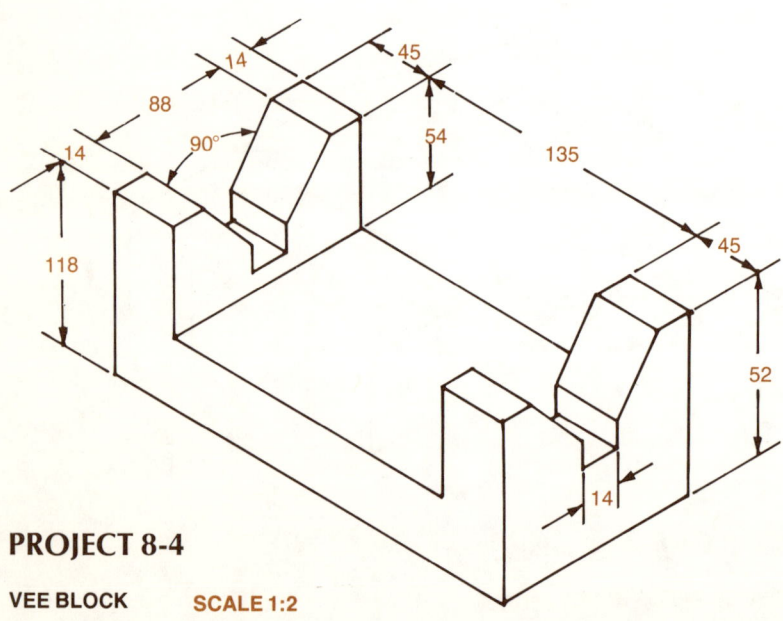

PROJECT 8-4

VEE BLOCK SCALE 1:2

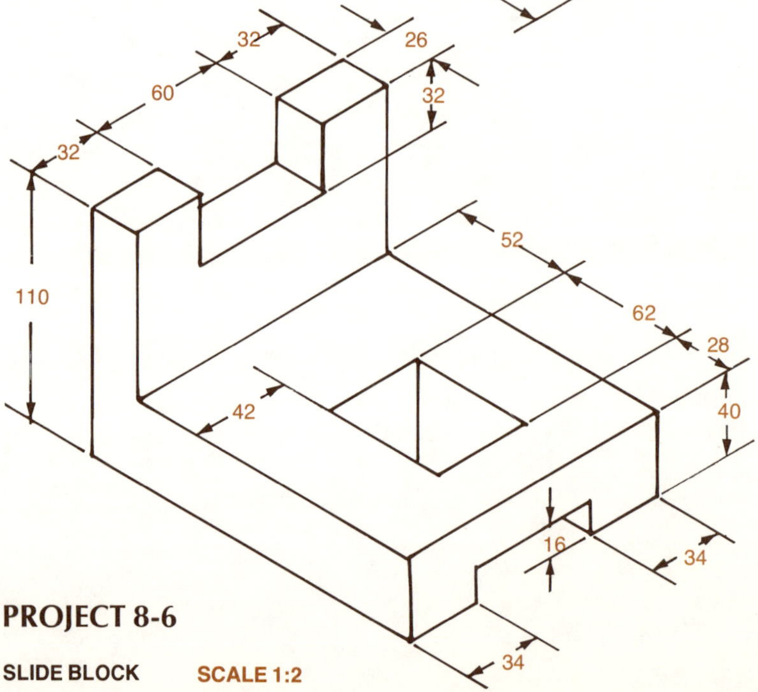

PROJECT 8-6

SLIDE BLOCK SCALE 1:2

CHAPTER 9
DIMENSIONING CYLINDRICAL SHAPES

WORDS TO LEARN
cylindrical (cy-lín-dri-cal)
illustrate (íl-lus-trate)
contour (cón-tour)

cylindrical—circular—or roller-shaped body, either hollow or solid

As you learned earlier, dimensioning is extremely important. Now for some bad news and some good news. The bad news first. You will have to learn some additional methods of dimensioning in order to dimension **cylindrical** objects and shapes. The good news is that what you have **already** learned about dimensioning can be applied to dimension cylindrical objects and shapes.

You will remember that all objects have three overall dimensions: length, width and height. Because of the shape of most cylindrical objects the height and width dimensions are the same as the diameter. Cylindrical objects can be described using two dimensions: the length and the diameter.

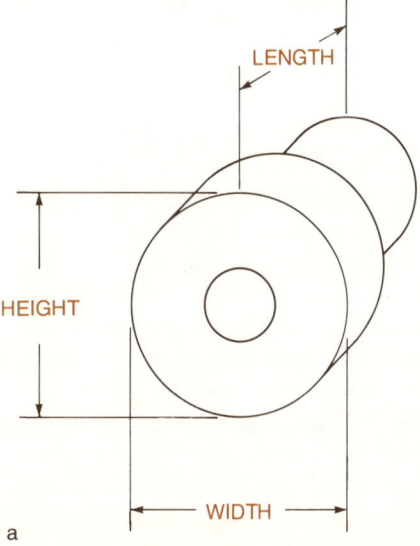 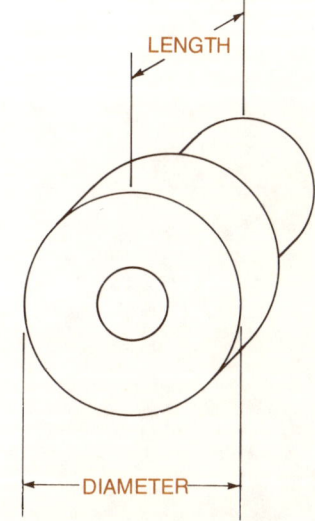

Fig. 9-1

99

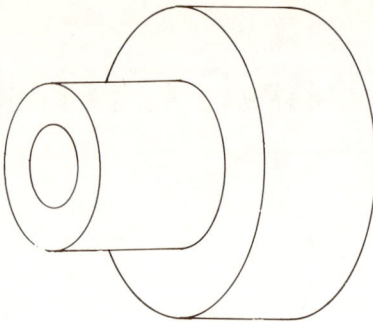

Fig. 9-2

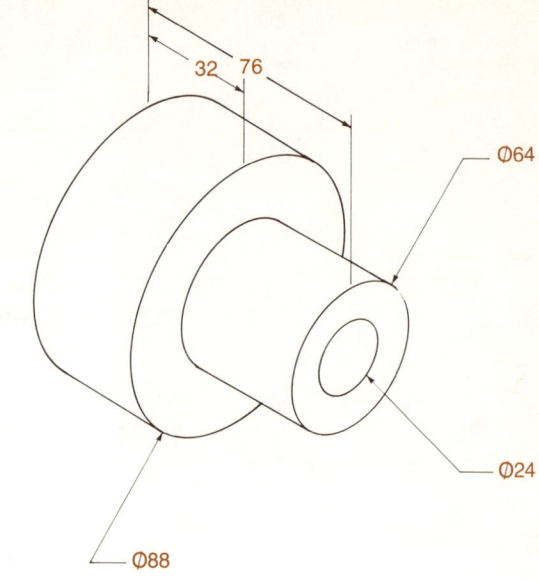

Fig. 9-3

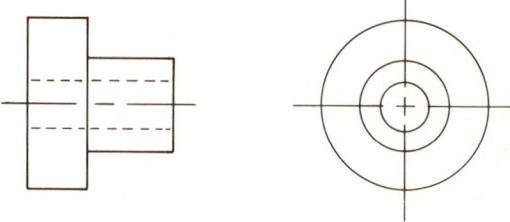

Fig. 9-4

How would you dimension the object in figure 9-2? Again, the easiest way to understand the subject is to look at it from the point of view of the tradesperson reading your drawing. What dimensions would you need to know if you were asked to produce this object? A list of questions could be prepared to help you to answer:

1. What is the diameter of the flange?
2. What is the overall length of the object?
3. What is the diameter of the hole?
4. What is the length of the flange? The answers to these questions can be easily found from the pictorial view (Fig. 9-3). The problem is: Where do we place these dimensions on the orthographic views (Fig. 9-4)?

Here are some points to remember:
- We want to avoid any misunderstanding that might waste time or material.
- Since in our example (Fig. 9-4) we have drawn two views to describe the object, we should use both views when dimensioning.
- We usually try to place all dimensions away from the views—between the views, and above the views if possible.
- All objects have three overall dimensions: the length, width and height. The length of the bushing is required. The height and width of the bushing are referred to as the diameter.

Method of Dimensioning

Cylindrical holes. Cylindrical holes are dimensioned as circles on the view where they appear.

Leader line. A leader line is drawn pointing to the centre of the hole and touching the circumference of the hole. The leader line is a thin line with an arrowhead at the end which points to the hole. The leader line extends out from the view any convenient dis-

illustrate—to show or describe
contour—the outline of a body or figure

tance and a 3.0 mm "flat" is drawn leading to the dimension figure.

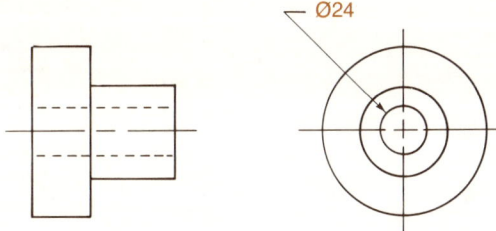

Fig. 9-5

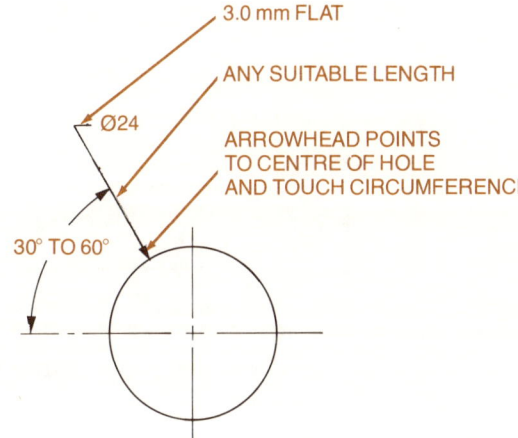

Fig. 9-6

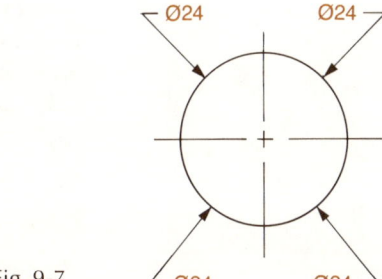

Fig. 9-7

The leader could have been placed in any of four areas, depending on the space available. If necessary, the flat on a leader may be reversed.

The exterior cylindrical **contours** of the part; that is, the diameters of the hub and the flange, are dimen-sioned off the front view using extension and dimension lines as shown in Fig. 9-8.

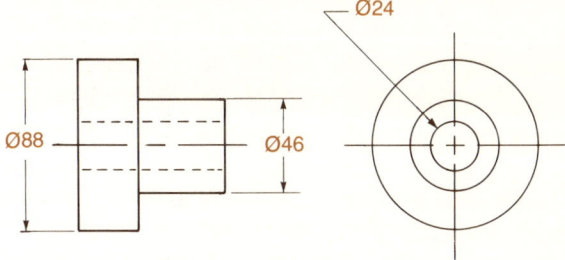

Fig. 9-8

- The length of the flange and the above overall length are placed above the front view as shown in Fig. 9-9. That was pretty easy to understand.

Let's look at another object and see how it can be dimensioned as well.

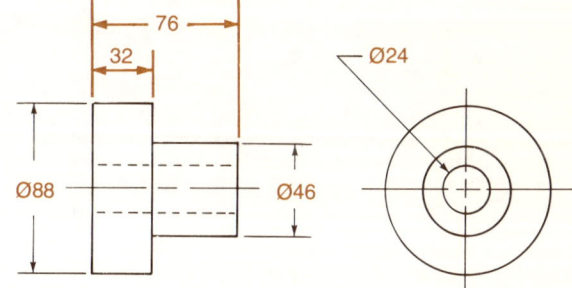

Fig. 9-9

Four holes have been produced on the flange. The holes are the same size, Ø12, and are situated on a circular centre line called the **bolt circle** (B.C.).

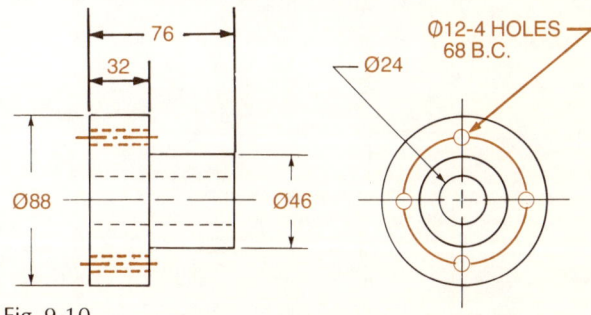

Fig. 9-10

METHODS OF DIMENSIONING 101

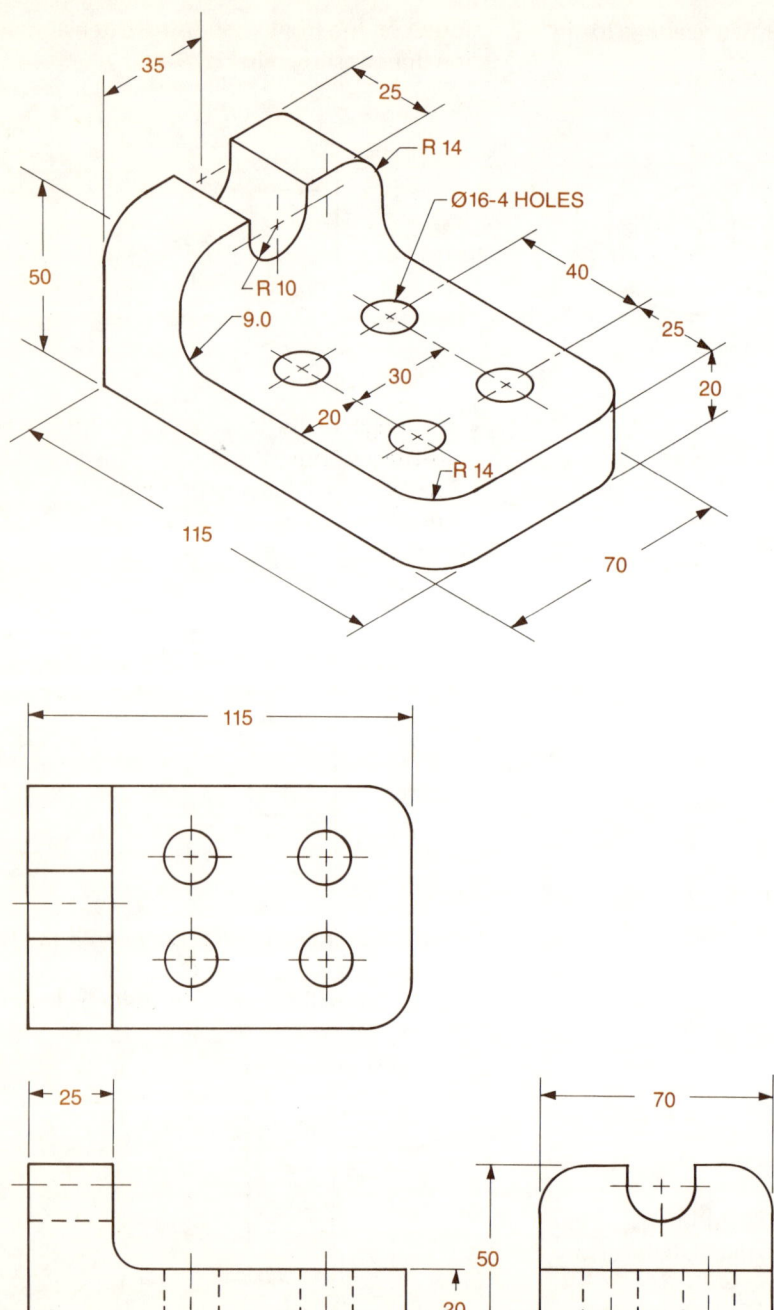

Fig. 9-11

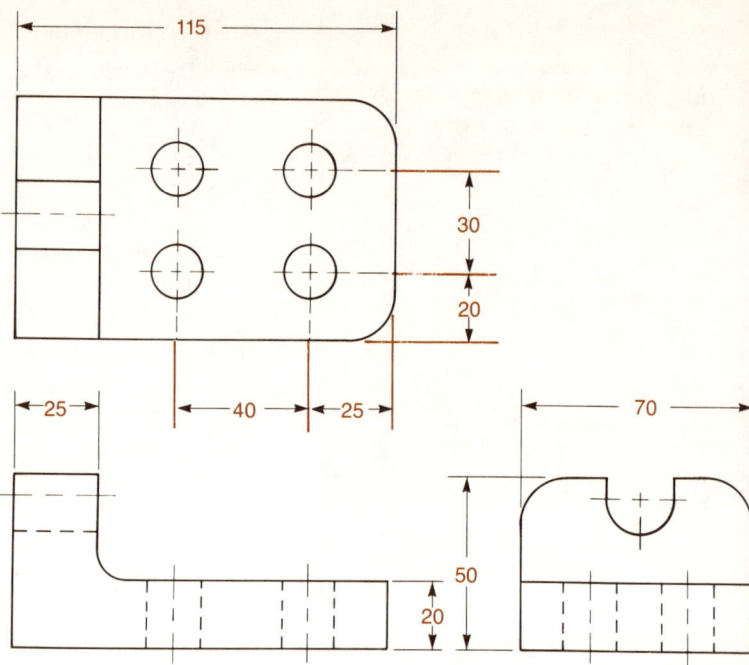

Fig. 9-12

How to Dimension Holes on a Bolt Circle

As you can see in Fig. 9-10, a leader line is drawn pointing to the centre of one of the holes, the arrowhead touching the circumference.

As the holes on the bolt circle are all the same size it is only necessary to dimension one of them. The leader note states the diameter of the holes, the number of holes involved, and the diameter of the bolt circle on which they are situated.

How to Dimension Holes and Arcs

There are many instances where holes and arcs appear on drawings. To **illustrate** how to dimension holes and arcs in other situations we can dimension the part as shown in Fig. 9-11.

Once again, look at the project from the tradesperson's point of view and you will discover what dimensions are necessary to produce the part. From past experience you can readily place the detail and overall dimensions. What diameter are the holes? Where are they located?

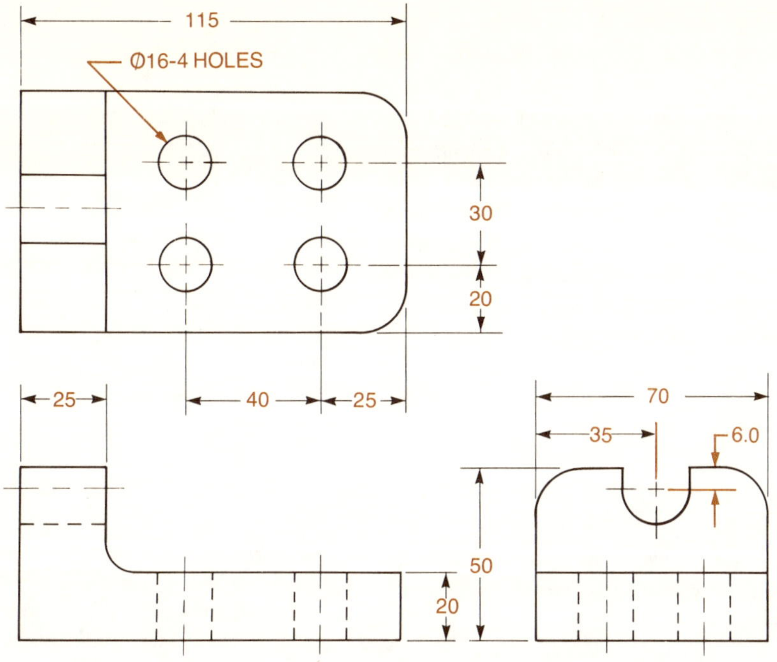

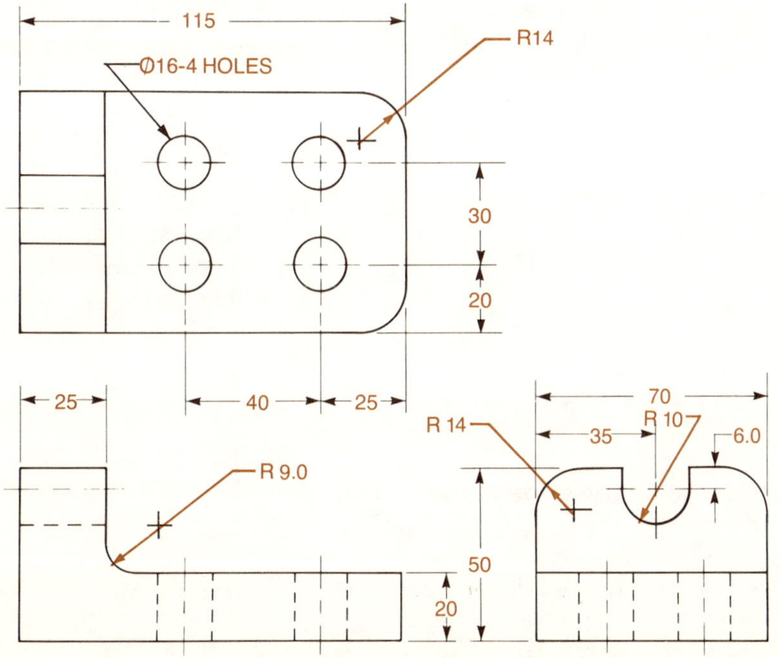

Cylindrical holes on a straight centre line are located by noting the distance between the centres of the holes. The centre lines serve as extension lines. Extend the centre lines off the views and place the dimension between the extension lines as you would normally. Dimension the distance from one of the holes to the side of the view. Holes are usually tied in this manner to one important side of the object.

The location of the centre lines for the slot can be related to the sides of the guide support.

Remember. Holes are dimensioned as a circle on the view where they appear. A leader line can be drawn to any one of the holes noting the diameter and number of holes involved.

Arcs are dimensioned by noting their radius. A cross 3.0 mm long is drawn at the centre point of the arc. A straight line joins the centre point to the arc. An arrowhead is placed at the end of this line touching the arc. The radius of the arc is placed on this line if space permits.

Often, the radius line is too small and confined to allow for the dimension to be placed on the line. The radius line can be lengthened past the arc to become a leader line. The dimension figures are then noted beside the flat of the leader as in Fig. 9-14.

Fig. 9-13

Fig. 9-14

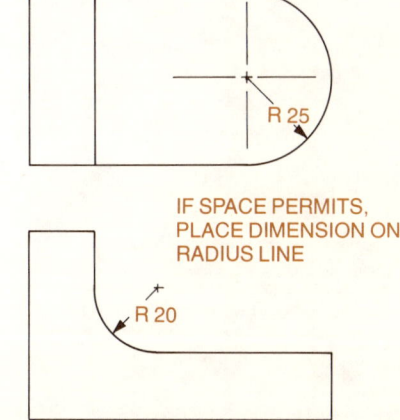

Fig. 9-15

METHODS OF DIMENSIONING 103

You will have noticed that the corners of many objects have been rounded off by arcs. The arcs forming outside corners are called **rounds**. The arcs of inside corners are called **fillets**. The radii of these arcs are usually dimensional as shown by the examples in Fig. 9-15. It is possible at times to dimension rounds and fillets by a note, placed wherever space permits on the drawing. The use of a note can save dimensioning time. If the radii of all the rounds and arcs are the same, for example, R 6.0, the note could read:

ROUNDS AND FILLETS R 6.0.

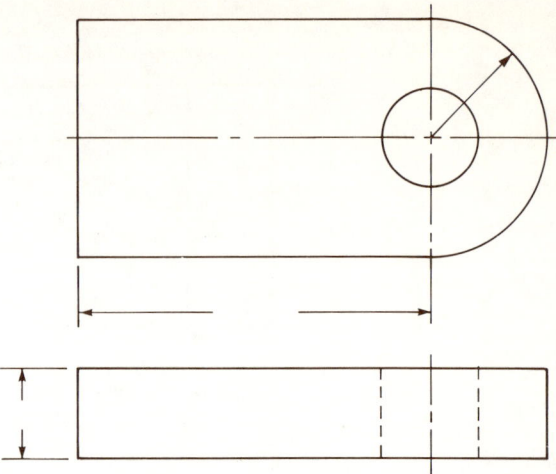

Fig. 9-17

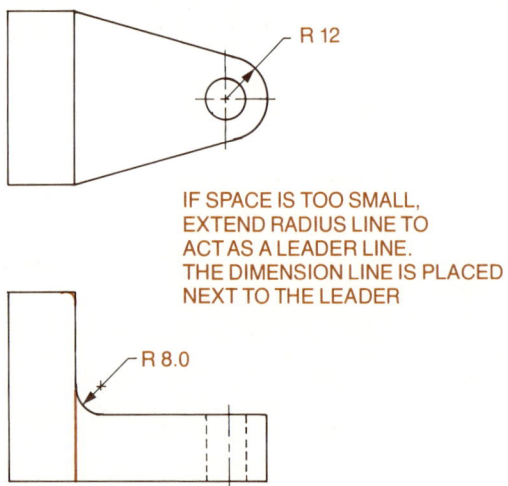

IF SPACE IS TOO SMALL, EXTEND RADIUS LINE TO ACT AS A LEADER LINE. THE DIMENSION LINE IS PLACED NEXT TO THE LEADER

Fig. 9-16

How to Dimension Semi-Cylindrical Objects

Objects that are partly cylindrical in shape do not need all three overall dimensions. One or two overall dimensions can be left off the drawing.

In Fig. 9-17 the overall height dimension is required. The overall length dimension is not needed. The radius of the arc added to the other dimensions in the top view can tell us the overall length. The radius of the semi-circle in the top view x 2 will supply the overall width dimension.

Here are a few more examples of semi-cylindrical shapes. In each example, look to the radius of a semi-cylindrical contour to indicate whether one or more overall dimensions is unnecessary.

Before you rush off to dimension eagerly every drawing in sight we suggest you review the steps in dimensioning outlined in Chapter 8.

We have listed them again below, along with a few necessary additions. Follow each step carefully. Errors are difficult to correct once they have been made.

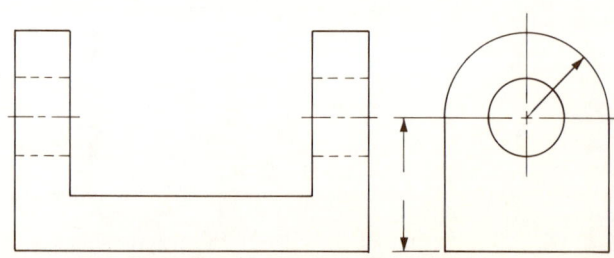

IN THIS EXAMPLE THE OVERALL HEIGHT AND WIDTH DIMENSIONS ARE UNNECESSARY

Fig. 9-18

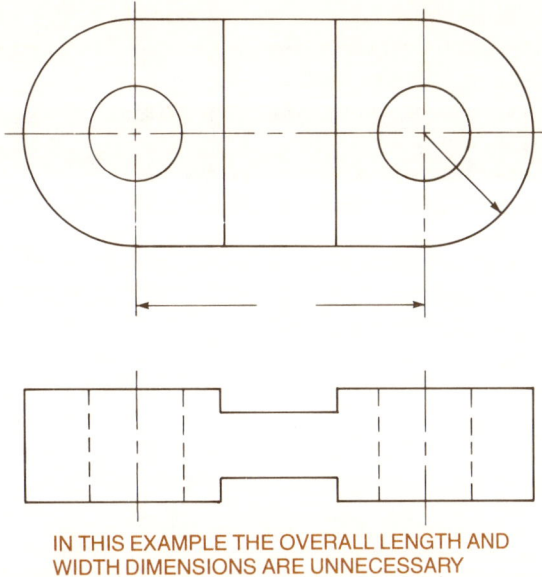

IN THIS EXAMPLE THE OVERALL LENGTH AND WIDTH DIMENSIONS ARE UNNECESSARY

Fig. 9-19

Steps in Dimensioning Cylindrical Objects

1. Lightly draw in all extension, dimension and leader lines wherever you think they are needed. Because centre lines often serve as extension lines it is best to draw centre lines lightly as well. Remember to place all dimension lines at least 10 mm from a view. Leave 10 mm between one dimension line and the next parallel dimension line.
2. Erase those extension, dimension and leader lines that are unnecessary.
3. Lightly draw all of the guide lines for the dimension figures.
4. Carefully letter in all dimension figures.
5. Darken in all of the extension, dimension, leader and centre lines.
    Remember each of these lines should be thin and black.
    Centre lines become extension lines without a break in the line.
6. Draw in all of the arrowheads as carefully as you can. Arrowheads should be sharp and narrow and must touch the line they are dimensioning. The point of the arrowhead ends at a centre line extension line or arc where necessary.

POINTS TO REMEMBER

- Holes that are cylindrical are dimensioned as circles on the view where they appear.
- Diameters of the exterior cylindrical **contours** are dimensioned on the front view.
- Cylindrical holes and arcs are dimensioned by leader lines.
- Rounds and fillets which have the same radius can be dimensioned by a note, to save time.
- Centre lines can be used as extension lines to locate holes and other cylindrical features.
- Extension lines, dimension lines and centre lines are drawn thin and dark to contrast with the thick visible outline.
- Extension lines begin about 2 mm away from a view and end about 2 mm past a dimension line.
- All dimensions should be lettered parallel to the top of the page.
- When dimensioned, your drawing should be clear, complete and easily understood.

QUESTIONS TO ANSWER

1. How many overall dimensions are necessary to describe a cylindrical object? Name them.
2. Where should dimensions be placed when drawing a view?
3. A leader line is drawn pointing to a hole. Where does it point? What does it touch? How is it drawn?

4. How would you locate cylindrical holes that are on a straight centre line?
5. How is an arc dimensioned?
6. In what ways can rounds and/or arcs of the same radius be dimensioned on a drawing?
7. How many overall dimensions are needed to describe a semi-cylindrical object? Why?

REPLACE THE X'S WITH THE CORRECT TERM

1. Pictures in a comic strip **XXXXXXXXXX** the story.
2. A paint can and a piston are both **XXXXXXXXXXX** in shape.
3. The **XXXXXXX** of hills can be represented on a special map that shows different heights of land.

PROJECTS

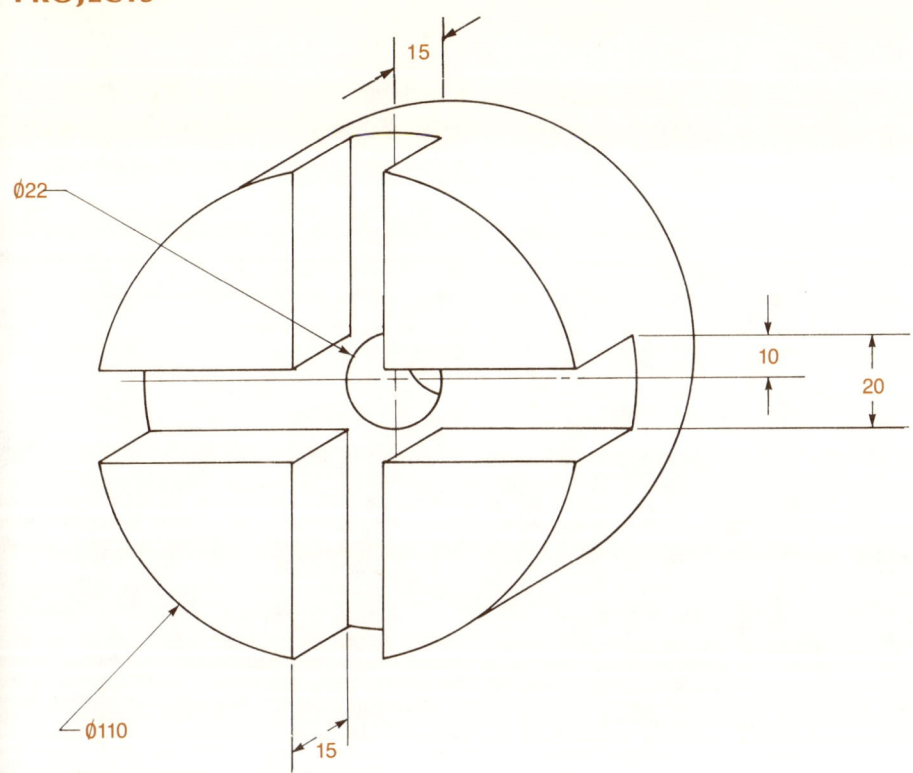

PROJECT 9-1

CROSS SLIDE   **SCALE 1:1**

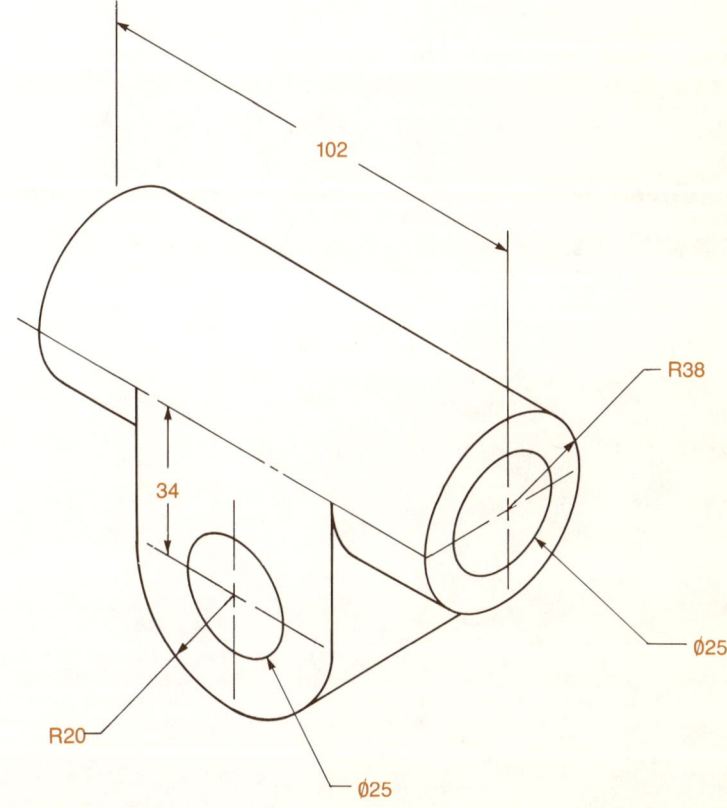

PROJECT 9-2

SHAFT POSITIONER   **SCALE 1:1**

PROJECTS   107

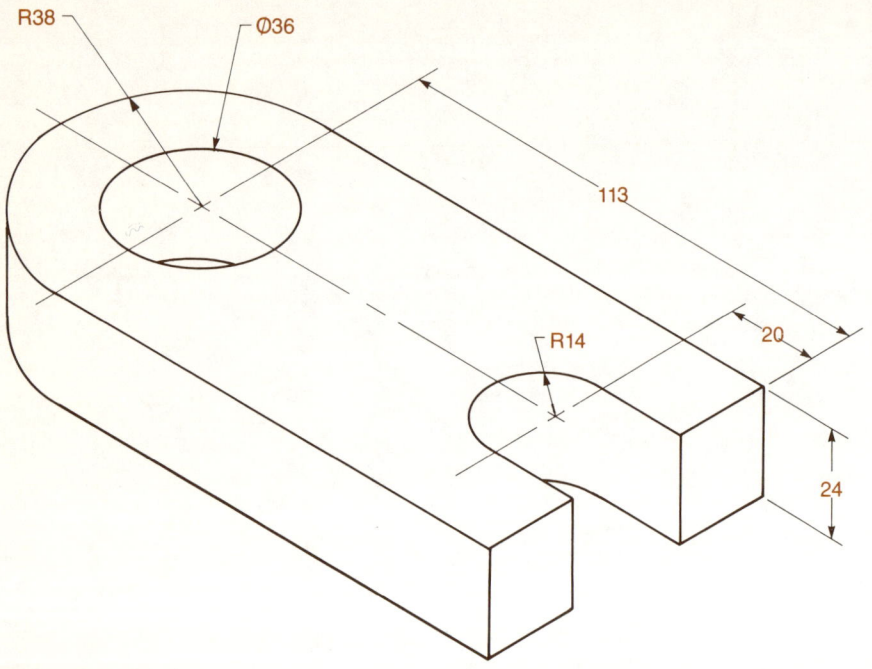

PROJECT 9-3

CLAMP **SCALE 1:1**

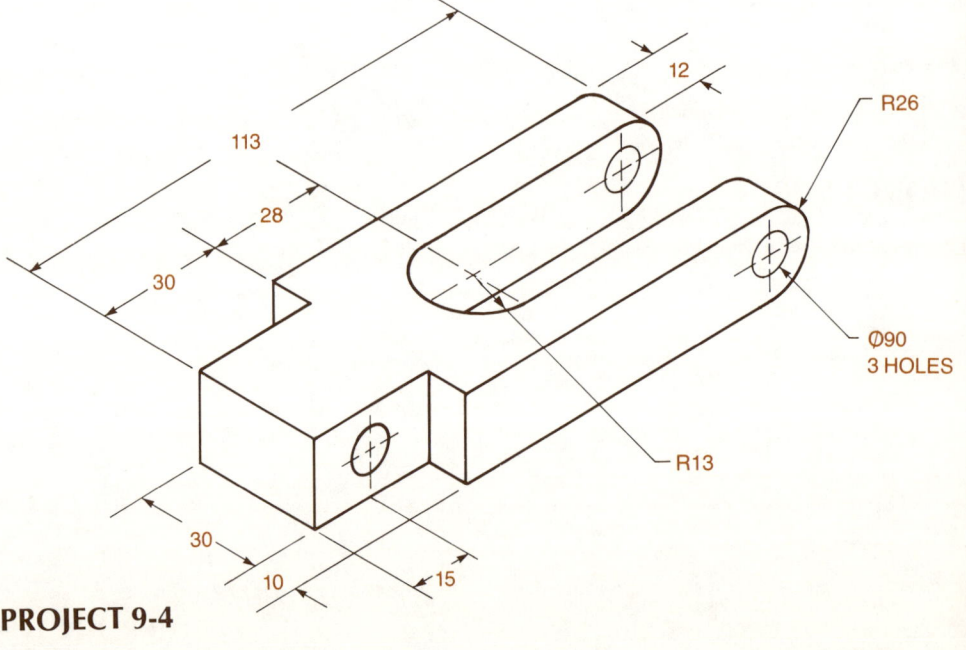

PROJECT 9-4

FORK LINK **SCALE 1:1**

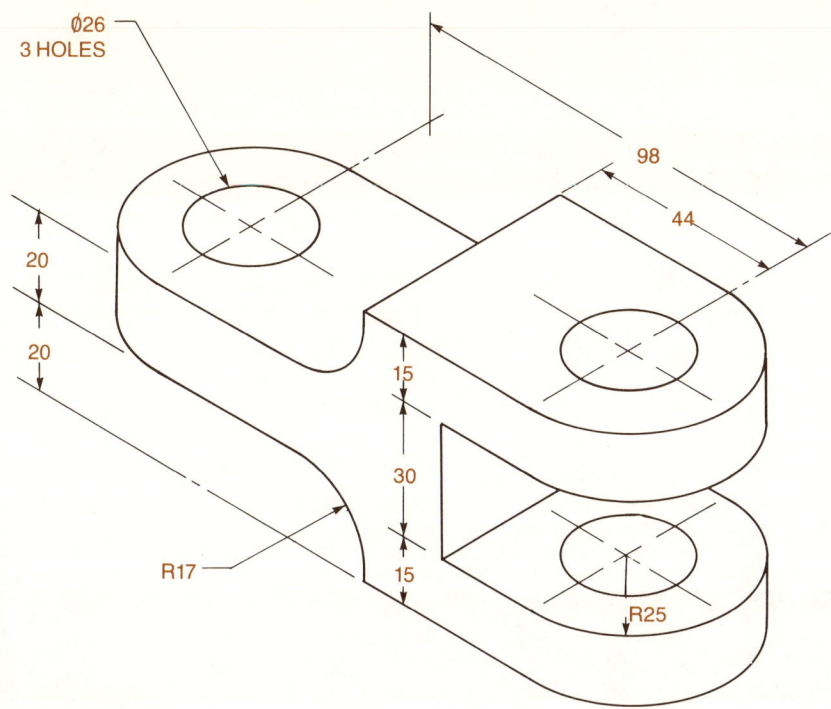

PROJECT 9-5

CIRCULAR LINK **SCALE 1:1**

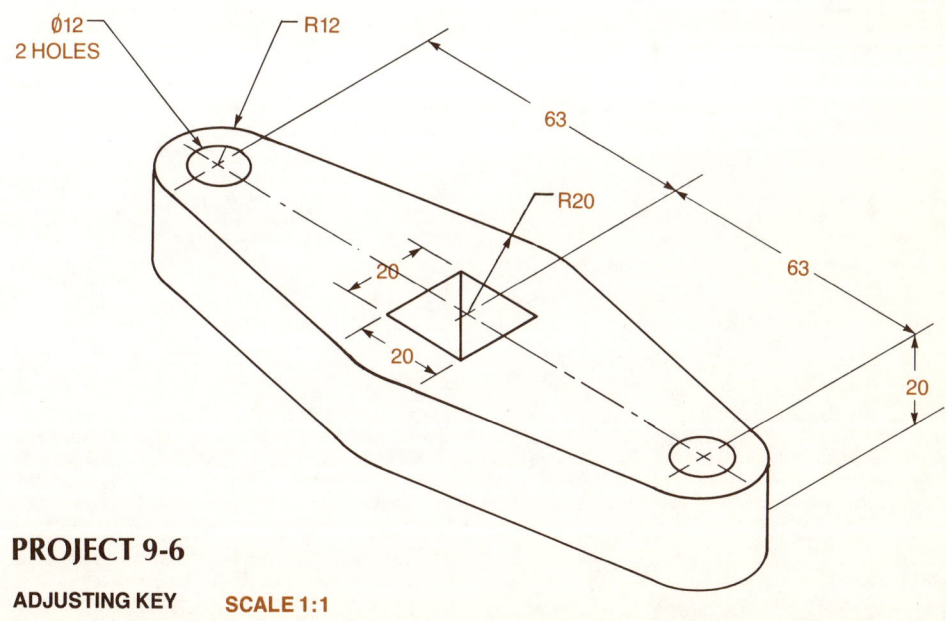

PROJECT 9-6

ADJUSTING KEY **SCALE 1:1**

PROJECTS 109

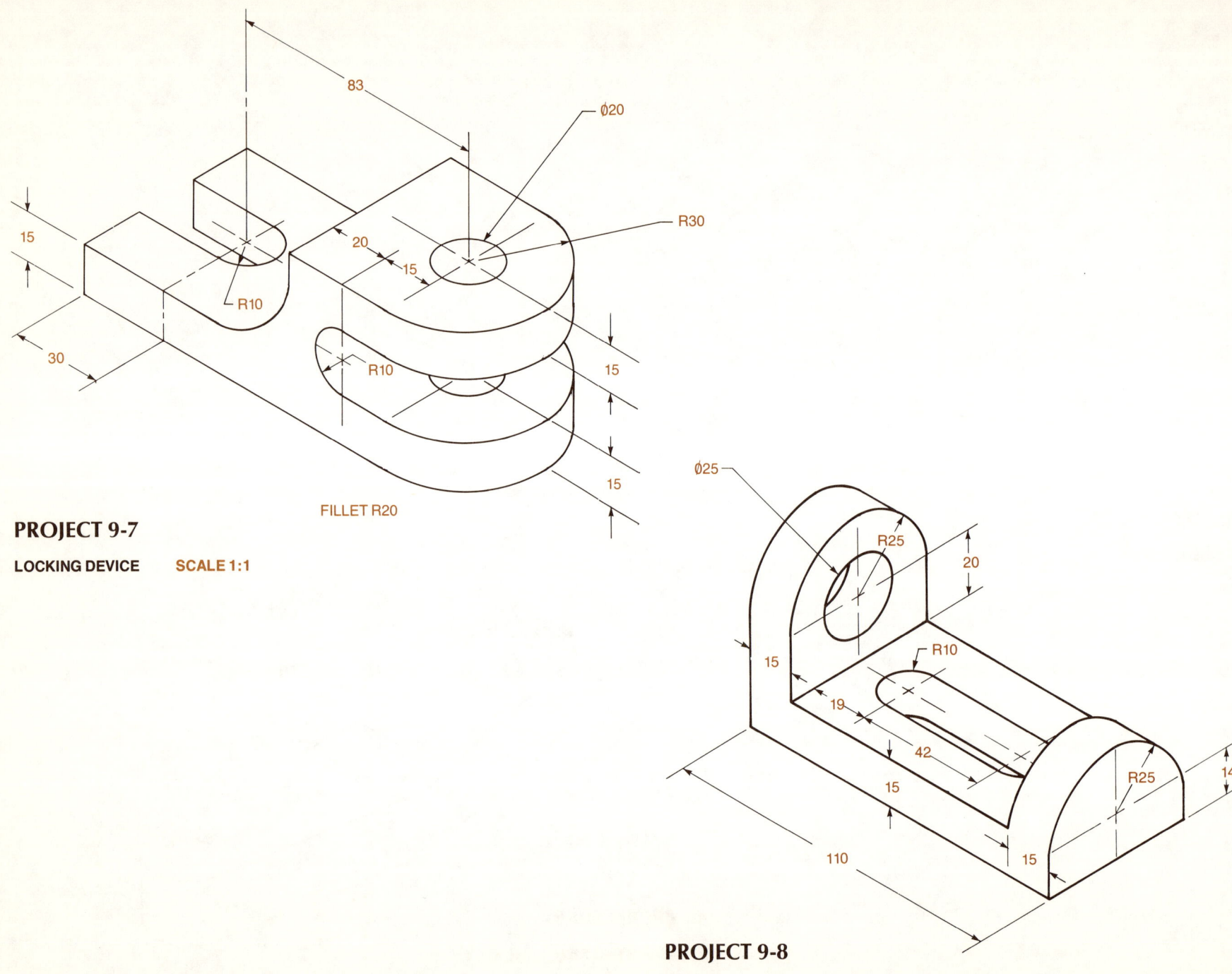

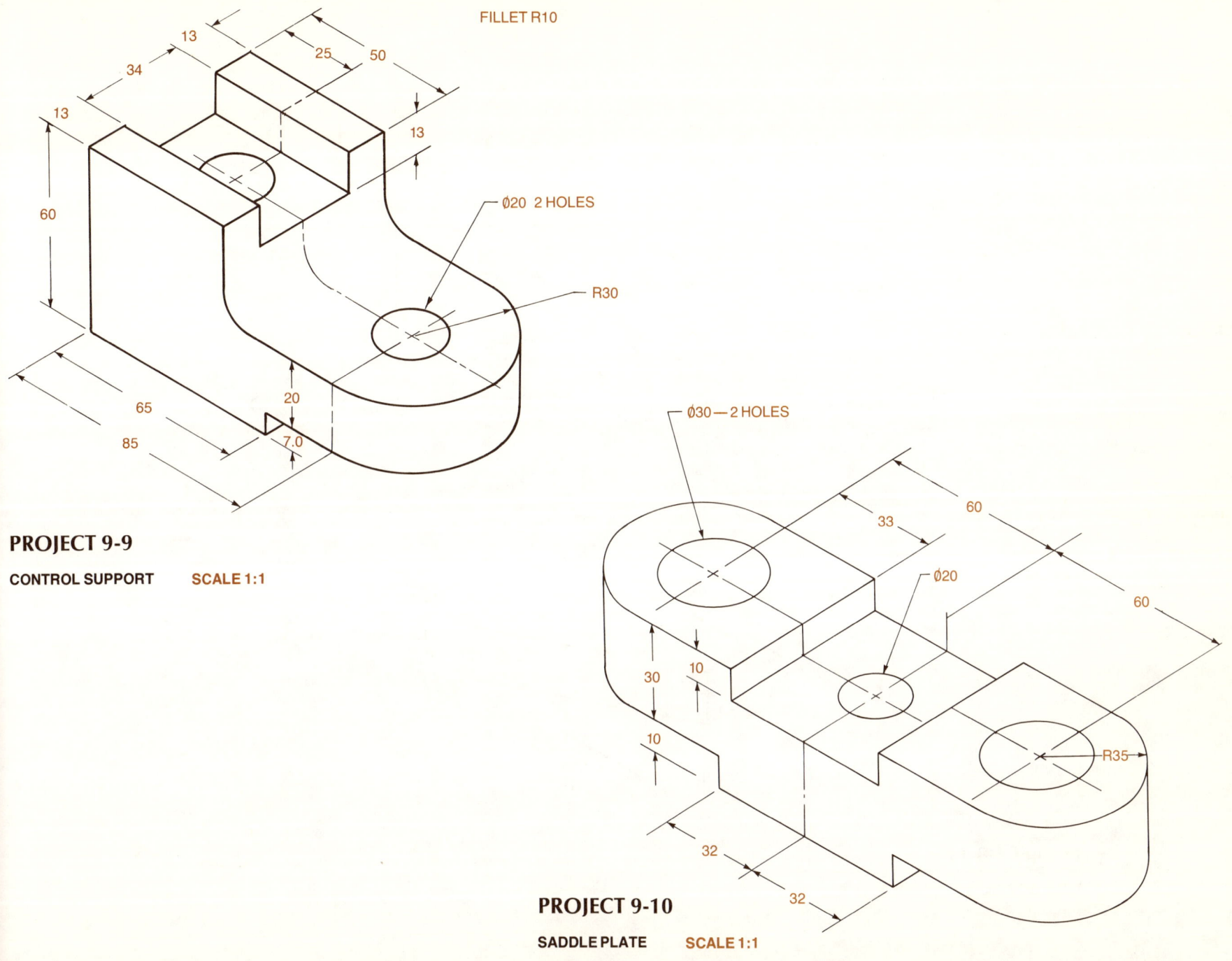

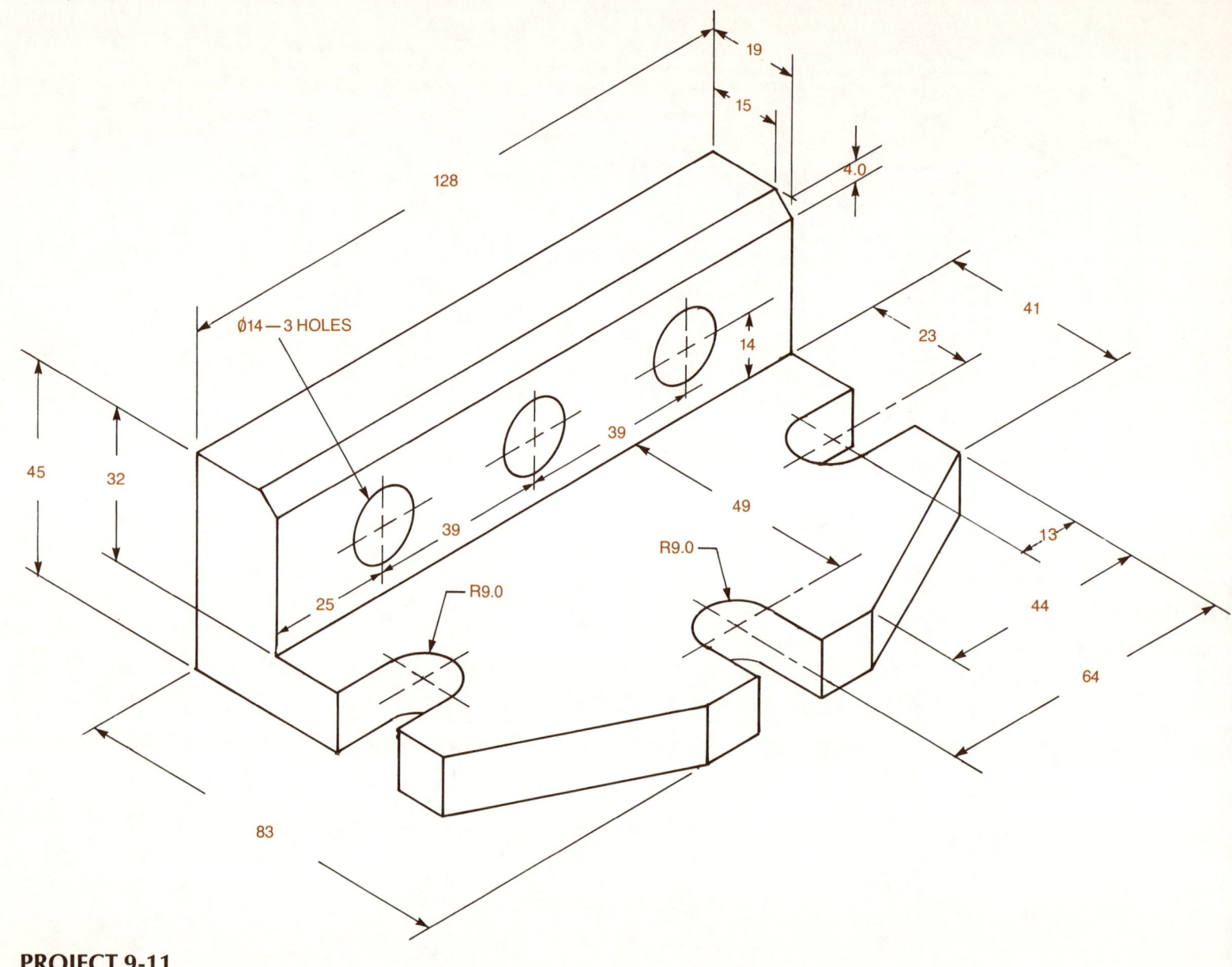

PROJECT 9-11

LOCK BRACE **SCALE 1:1**

CHAPTER 10
DETAIL WORKING DRAWINGS

WORDS TO LEARN

manufacture (man-u-fác-ture)
perform (per-fórm)
characteristic (char-ac-ter-ís-tic)
extreme (ex-tréme)
malleable (mál-le-a-ble)

pliable (plí-a-ble)
inclined (in-clíned)
indicate (ín-di-cate)
molten (mól-ten)

manufacture—to make
(literally, to make by hand)

Working drawings are used in both mechanical drafting and architectural drafting. In architectural, these are often called construction drawings, and we will study these in Chapter 17.

In mechanical drafting, two types of working drawings are used: **detail** working drawings and **assembly** working drawings. Look at the airplane in the photograph. In general terms, before it even can leave the assembly plant, it has to go through two different stages of construction.

First, every part, whether little or big, has to be made to accurate measurements. For this, **details** of the parts are needed. Second, all the parts have to be **assembled** or put together in the proper way. In Chapter 14 we will look at assembly working drawings. Right now we will think about the drawings needed for that first stage of **manufacturing**.

As you can see from this detail working drawing, its purpose is to provide workers with information necessary to make the finished part. Keep these points in mind:

- The views of the drawing accurately show its shape.
- All the necessary dimensions are given.
- The scale is noted.
- The material is identified from which the finished part will be made and the part is named.
- All other information which is needed is given, usually as notes on the drawing.

Behind the detail working drawings is the story of the materials and the methods used to produce the parts themselves.

It would be true to say that skilled tradespeople use detail working drawings and the necessary tools to produce parts from basic raw materials. True, yes, but

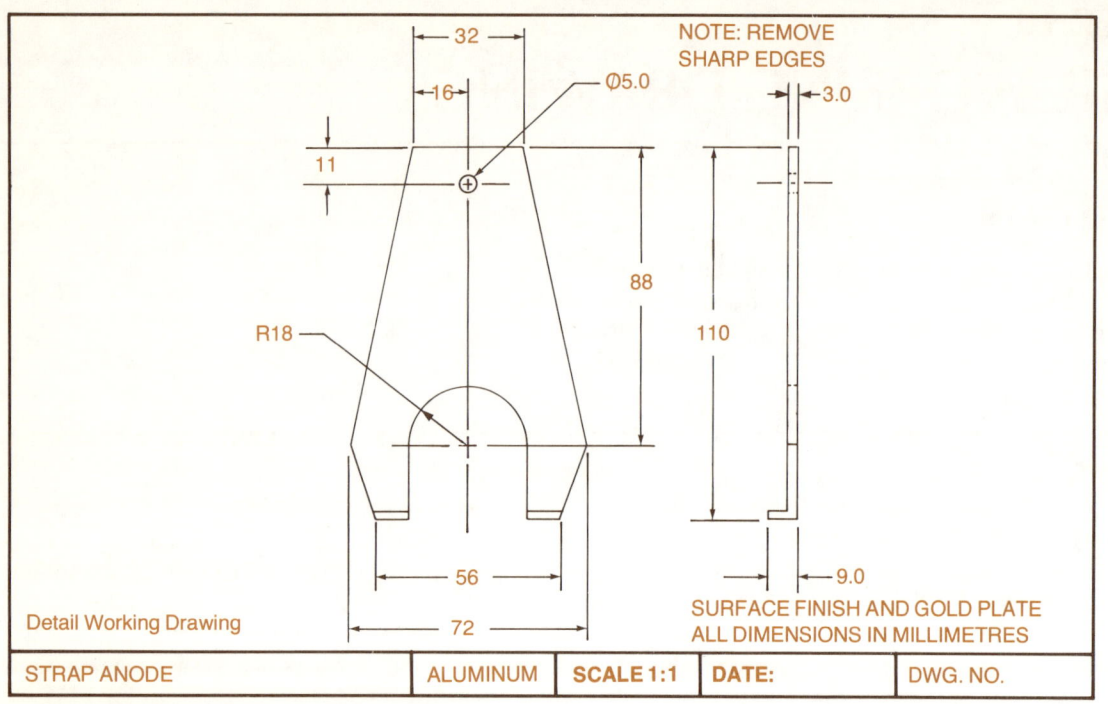

Fig. 10-1 Assembly drawing

that still doesn't answer the question: how does any individual part "happen"? The answer is, it doesn't just happen. It is born out of necessity. We need it for a specific purpose.

From the beginning of time, people have used the raw materials they have found about them to produce tools, weapons and utensils. The last illustration shows a man using a lever to increase his lifting power. In each example, the person came up with an idea for a tool that would suit his or her purpose.

An individual part, then, is born as an idea in someone's mind. The method of production and the material from which the part is made is then considered by the designer before the part is produced.

Perhaps we could relate to the decision process a little by using a specific example, like an airplane or an automobile. To conserve energy and use less fuel, engineers are redesigning thousands of parts of cars, trucks, trains, ships, and airplanes to improve their performance and reduce their mass. They must also consider a great many other **characteristics** of the materials used before deciding on the changes.

- Mass—will the part be lighter, yet will it **perform** as well as, or better than, before?
- Availability—is the material readily available in quantity?
- Machinability—can the part be machined by available production methods?
- Stability—will the part remain in the same form after production or will it be affected—by **extreme** heat, for example?

New materials are being developed almost daily to meet the demands of industry. There are too many to describe in this chapter, but it would be useful to list some of the most common metals in use.

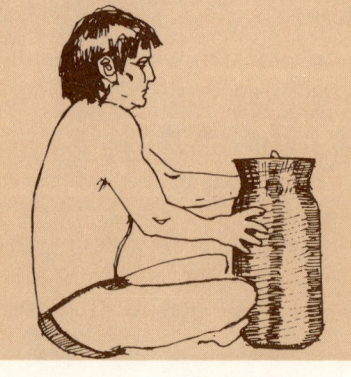

perform—to carry out (a task)
characteristic—a feature of a person or object by which that person or object could be identified

extreme—the farthest in any direction

DETAIL WORKING DRAWINGS

malleable—capable of being shaped or formed

pliable—easily bent or shaped

MATERIALS

Metals are usually divided into two groups, ferrous or non-ferrous.

Ferrous Metals

Metals that contain iron are called ferrous. Ferrous metals have magnetic properties.
Pig Iron. Pig iron is produced from iron ore. It is the basic ingredient of steel.
Cast Iron. Cast iron is produced by mixing pig iron with scrap iron. It is brittle but it is used for a wide variety of shapes and forms that do not have to withstand sudden loads.
Malleable Iron. Malleable iron is basically the same as cast iron. It has less carbon content, which makes it less brittle and easier to bend and form.
Steel. Steel is essentially made of iron. Carbon is an important element in steel because the amount of carbon in the steel determines its hardness. Steel that contains less than 0.50% carbon is called **mild steel**. This steel can be easily forged and machined. Steel with a higher carbon content is hard steel, commonly called **tool steel**. Tool steel is steel that can be further hardened to be used in the manufacture of tools.

Non-Ferrous Metals

Non-ferrous metals contain little or no iron. Non-ferrous metals do not have magnetic properties and also resist corrosion.
Aluminum. Aluminum is produced from bauxite. It has one-third the mass of steel. It can be alloyed with other metals to increase its hardness and flexibility.
Note. An alloy is an element that is combined with or added to another element to provide it with additional desirable qualities.
Bronze. Bronze is an alloy of copper and tin. It can be cast and easily machined.
Brass. Brass is an alloy of copper and zinc. Brass machines easily and it can also be cast.

METHODS OF PRODUCTION

You have learned that a machine part or item can be produced from a variety of materials. When a material has been selected for a particular part the designer must decide on the method of producing that part. There are various methods to consider. We will look at some of the most common methods. These are:
- Forging
- Casting
- Welding
- Machining
- Stamping

The method chosen to produce any part depends on:
(1) the basic shape of the part;
(2) how many parts are required;
(3) the function of the part.

Whatever method is used, the part must be produced quickly and at the least cost.
Forging. Forging is the operation of hammering the metal into the required shape. The metal can be heated until it is as soft as Plasticine to make it more *pliable*.

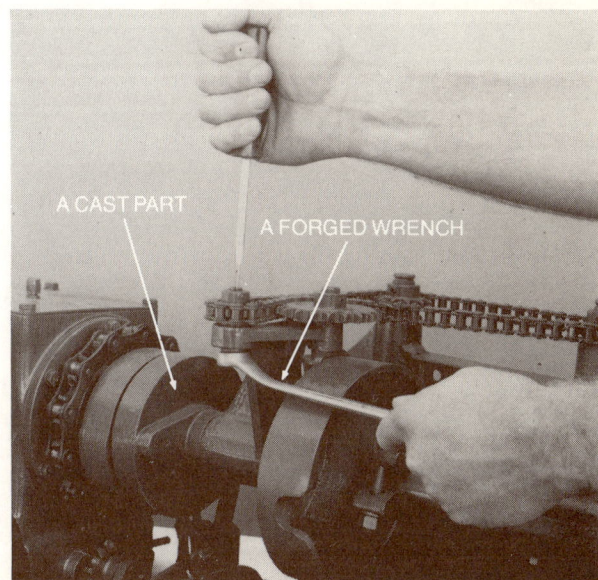

Fig. 10-2

Some metals can be forged in their cold state but need much more force and energy to change their shape. The benefits of forgings, which have the utility of strength and need little further reworking, outweigh the benefits of castings, which tend to be cheaper.
Casting. Casting is the process of making a part by melting a metal until it is **molten** and pouring it into a mould of the required shape. Casting is a cheap and quick method of making many different shapes that would be difficult to produce otherwise.

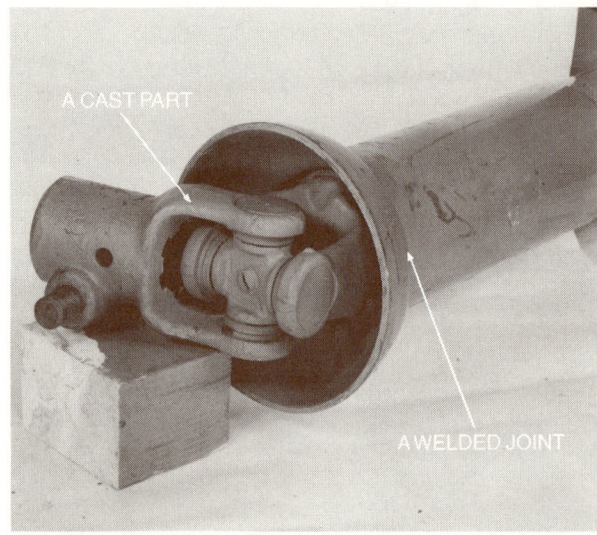

Fig. 10-3

Welding. Welding is the process of joining metals together to form various shapes by adding another metal and applying heat. It can also be done by applying heat to fuse the metals. This method produces parts lighter and stronger than if they were cast or forged.
Machining. Machining is the shaping of metal by removing metal from standard stock. Four basic types of machine tools are used to do this: the lathe, milling machine, shaper and drill. Machining can be used to mass produce individual parts to a required shape and to exact dimensions.

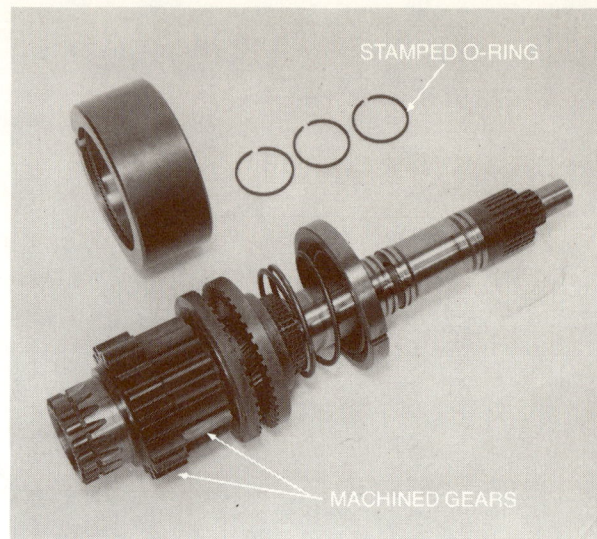

Fig. 10-4

Stamping. Stamping produces parts in mass quantities from flat sheet metal. Presses of many kinds are used to cut, punch and bend the metal into the required shape.

MACHINING METHODS

These methods can produce parts that are complete and ready for use. However, some parts, because of their design and function, need additional machining before the part is complete. We can look at some of these machining methods, why they may be used and how this information would appear on your drawings.
Drilling. Drilling is one of the most common machining operations. It is used to make a circular hole. Usually, the part is held stationary and is cut by the revolving drill. Holes may be cut through the part so that fasteners such as bolts, screws, etc., can pass through the part (see Fig. 10-5(a)). If the hole is cut into the part but not through it, it is called a **blind hole** (see Fig. 10-5(b)). The blind hole may be a seat for a dowel or it could have an internal thread cut in it to suit a cap screw or stud, etc.

116   DETAIL WORKING DRAWINGS

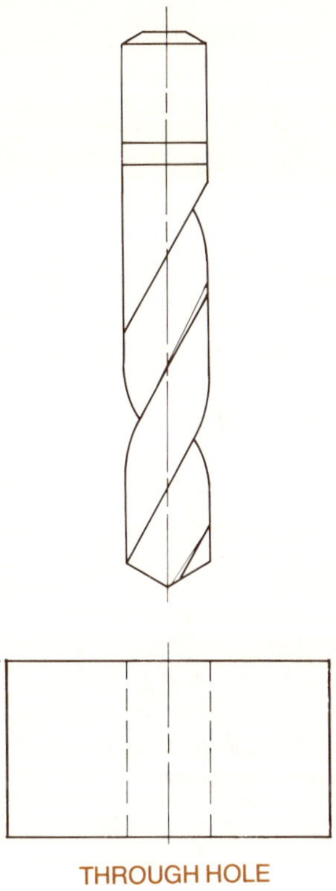

On the drawing, the drill diameter would be noted as a circle on the view where the hole appears. The leader points to the centre of the hole, the arrowhead touches the circumference, and the information follows the flat of the leader. The diameter symbol, Ø, comes first, followed by the diameter of the drill. If the hole is a blind hole, the depth is also noted.

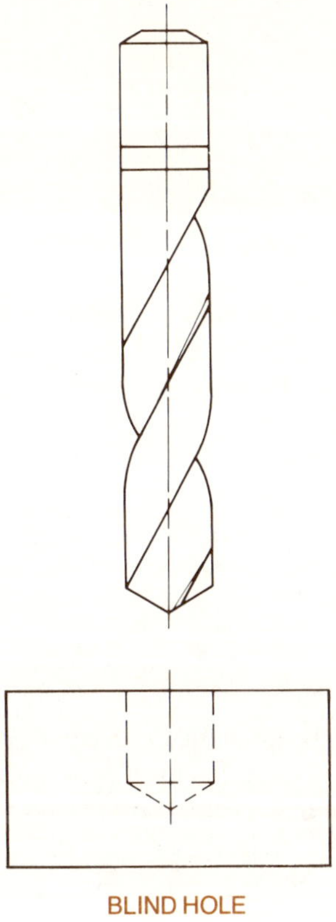

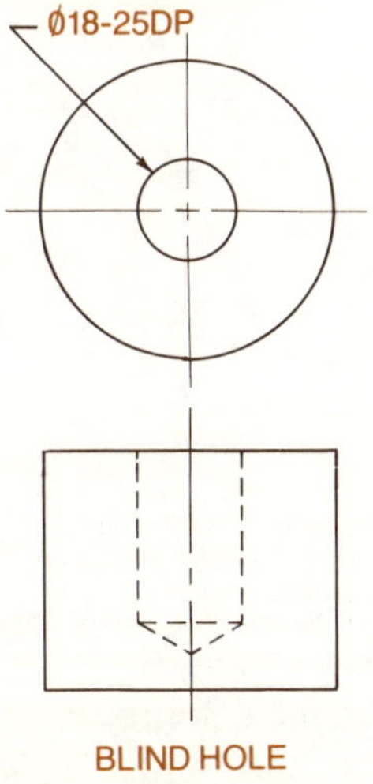

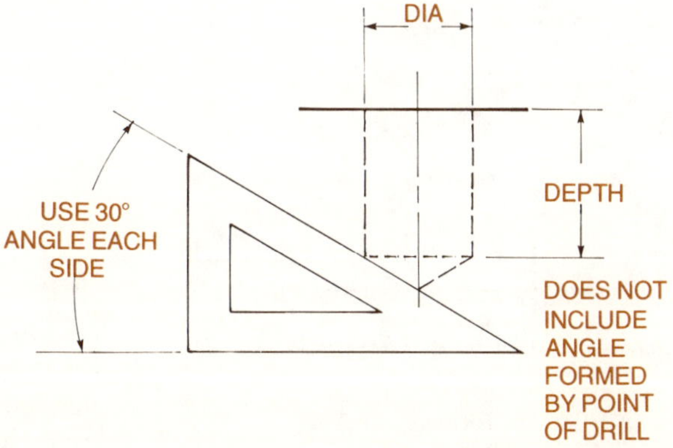

THROUGH HOLE

Fig. 10-5(a)

BLIND HOLE

Fig. 10-5(b)

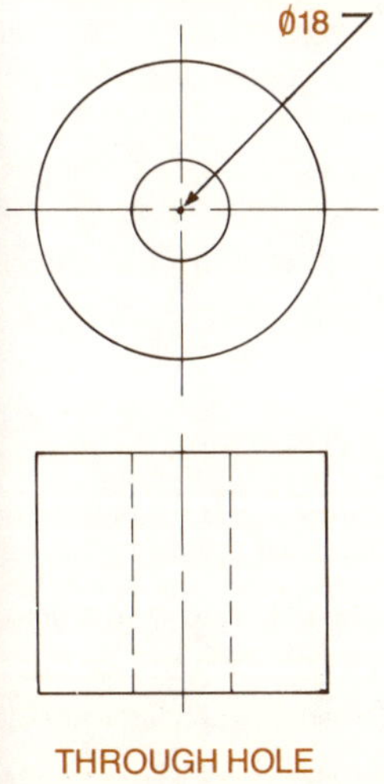

Ø18

Ø18-25DP

THROUGH HOLE

Fig. 10-6(a)

BLIND HOLE

Fig. 10-6(b)

USE 30° ANGLE EACH SIDE

DIA

DEPTH

DOES NOT INCLUDE ANGLE FORMED BY POINT OF DRILL

Fig. 10-6(c)

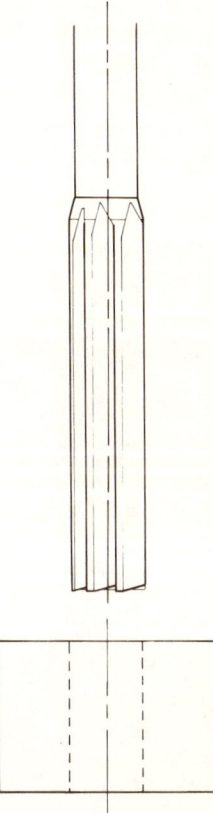

Fig. 10-7

Reaming. Reaming is a method of enlarging a cylindrical hole to a more accurate size. A tool called a reamer is used. The reamer cuts a very small amount of material away as it passes through the hole. This creates a fine surface finish.

Note in Fig. 10-8 that the leader shows two dimensions following the diameter symbol, Ø. These are the limit sizes of the reamed hole. In this example the note

MACHINING METHODS 117

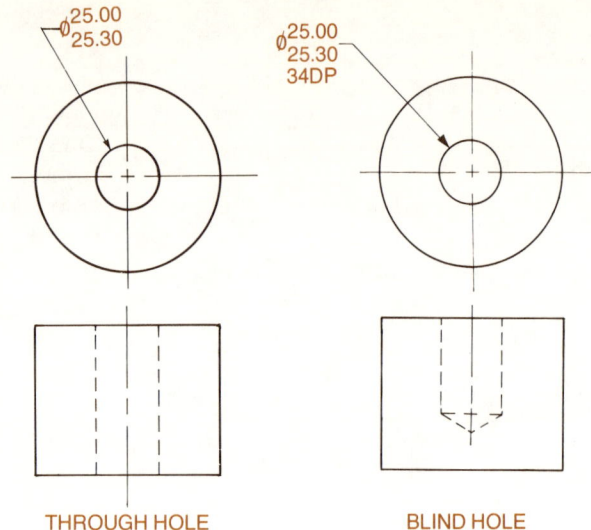

THROUGH HOLE   BLIND HOLE

Fig. 10-8(a)   Fig. 10-8(b)

tells the machinist that the hole may be reamed up to a maximum size of Ø 25.30. It may be reamed to the minimum size of Ø 25.00. This allows the machinist a certain amount of possible error (0.30), but the part will still be acceptable. If the hole is a blind hole, note the depth.

Boring. Boring is similar to reaming. Cylindrical holes larger than Ø 50 that must be accurate and have a fine finish are bored. The accuracy of the hole depends on the adjustment of the tool in the boring bar.

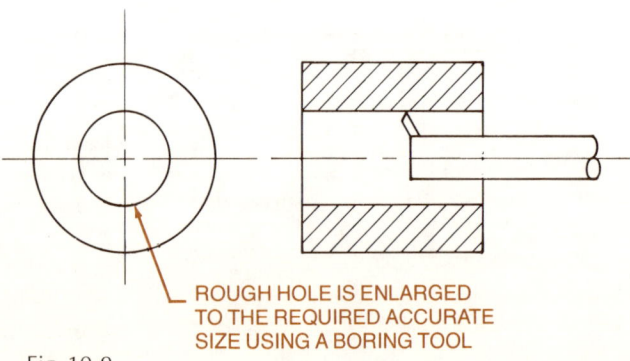

ROUGH HOLE IS ENLARGED TO THE REQUIRED ACCURATE SIZE USING A BORING TOOL

Fig. 10-9

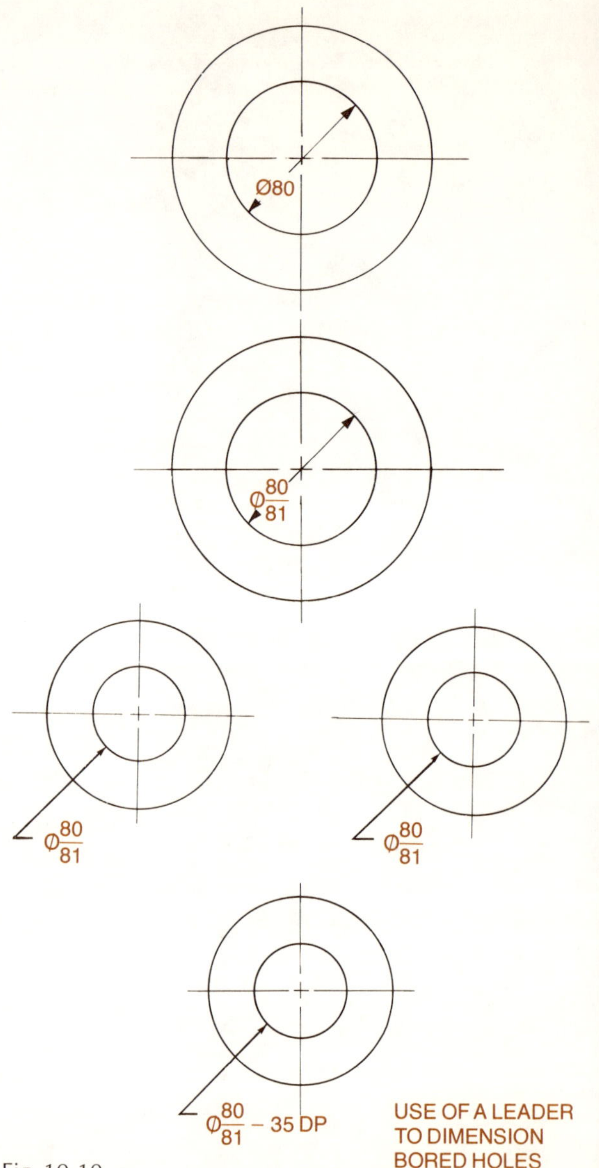

USE OF A LEADER TO DIMENSION BORED HOLES

Fig. 10-10

Note in Fig. 10-10 that the leader shows the diameter of the bored hole. If a greater degree of accuracy is needed, the maximum and minimum sizes are noted. Again, if the hole is a blind hole the depth of the hole is added.

118   DETAIL WORKING DRAWINGS

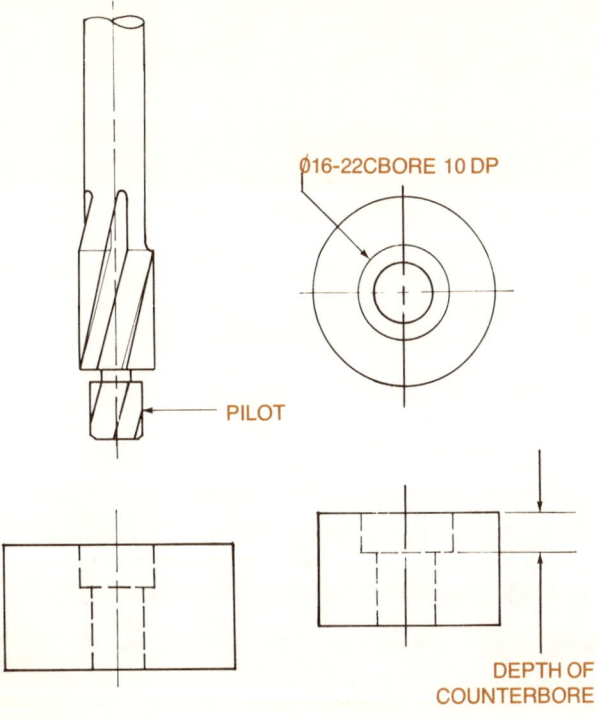

Fig. 10-11   Fig. 10-12

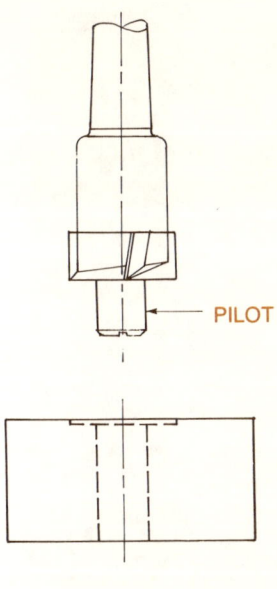

Fig. 10-13

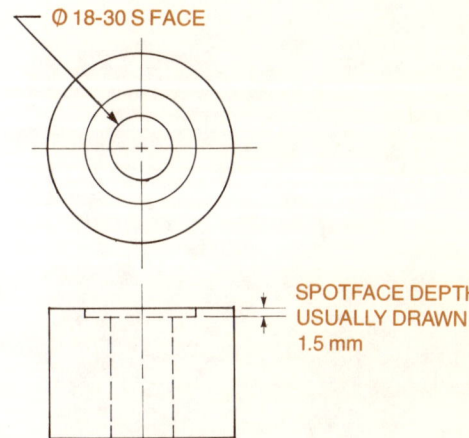

Fig. 10-14

Counterboring. Counterboring enlarges the diameter of an existing cylindrical hole to a desired depth at one or both ends. This allows parts, or the heads of bolts, etc., to sit below the surface. This improves the appearance and safety of the design. As well, it allows parts to be assembled without interference.

Note in Fig. 10-12 at the existing hole and the counterbored hole are drawn as circles first, and then projected to the other views. The counterbored depth is shown. The leader line indicates the diameter of the hole, the diameter of the counterbore, and the depth of the counterbore.

Spotfacing. Spotfacing is an operation similar to counterboring except that the depth of the enlarged hole is kept very shallow. This operation cleans up the area around the hole to provide a smooth surface for mating parts to be seated.

Note in Fig. 10-14 that the hole and the spotface are drawn first as circles and then projected to the other views. The spotface is usually drawn 1.5 mm deep. The leader line notes the diameter of the hole and the diameter of the spotface. It is unnecessary to note the depth of the spotface unless it is of special importance to the part.

MACHINING METHODS 119

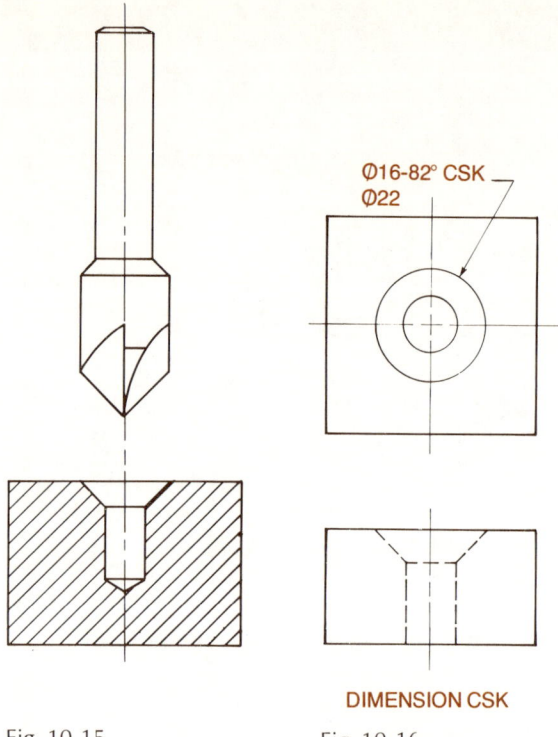

Fig. 10-15 Fig. 10-16

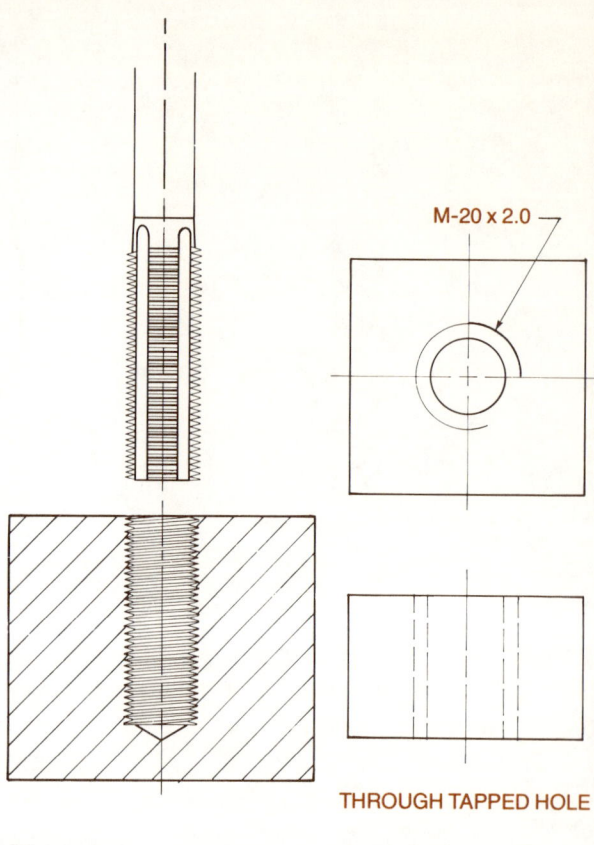

Fig. 10-17 Fig. 10-18

Countersinking. Countersinking enlarges an existing hole with a cone shaped tool called a rose cutter. The cone shaped opening of a countersunk hole allows a tapered part such as the head of a screw to sit below the surface of the part. Like counterboring, this improves the appearance and safety of the design. As well, it allows parts to be assembled without interference.

Note in Fig. 10-16 that the hole and the countersink are first drawn as circles and then projected to the other views. The included angle of the countersink is drawn at 90°. The leader line indicates the diameter of the hole, the diameter of the countersink and the actual included angle of the countersink. When it is necessary the depth of the countersink is noted.

Tapping. Tapping is the method of cutting a thread into a hole so that a bolt or screw can be screwed into it.

Note in Fig. 10-18 that the hole is shown as a circle. To indicate that the hole is tapped, a slightly larger circle is drawn. Note that the circle is left incomplete. This is the symbol for the **internal thread**. The circles are projected to the other views and appear as two hidden lines. The leader line notes the metric diameter, the distance between the threads, and the depth of the tapped hole if necessary.

Chamfering. Chamfering is a method of creating a bevelled edge. Chamfering makes the part safer to handle, less likely to chip, and allows parts to be assembled easily.

The chamfer can be **inclined** at any angle. The most common angles are 60°, 45° and 30°.

incline—drawn on an angle

120 DETAIL WORKING DRAWINGS

indicate—to point out or show

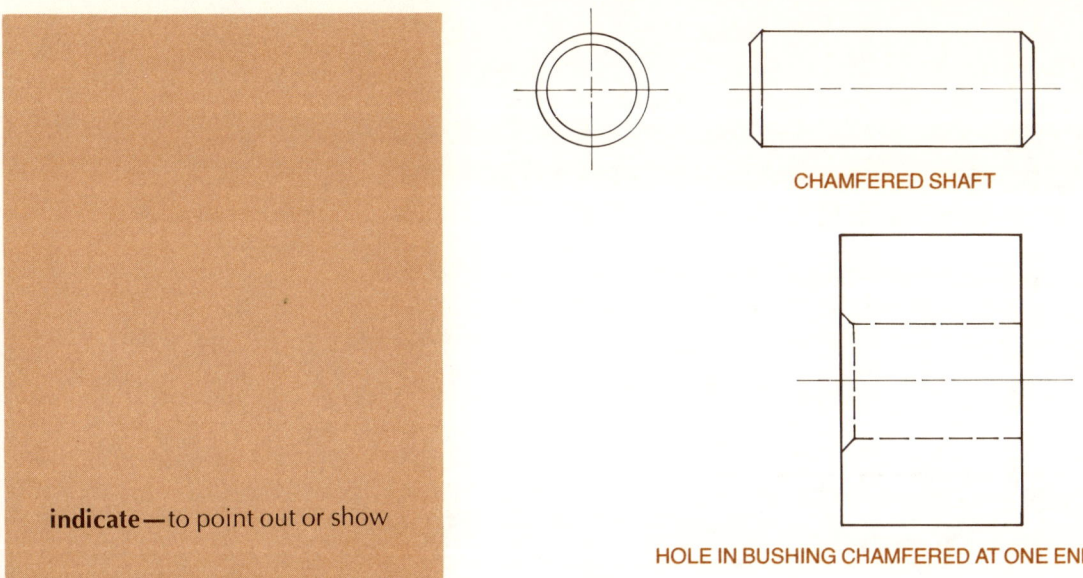

CHAMFERED SHAFT

HOLE IN BUSHING CHAMFERED AT ONE END

Fig. 10-19

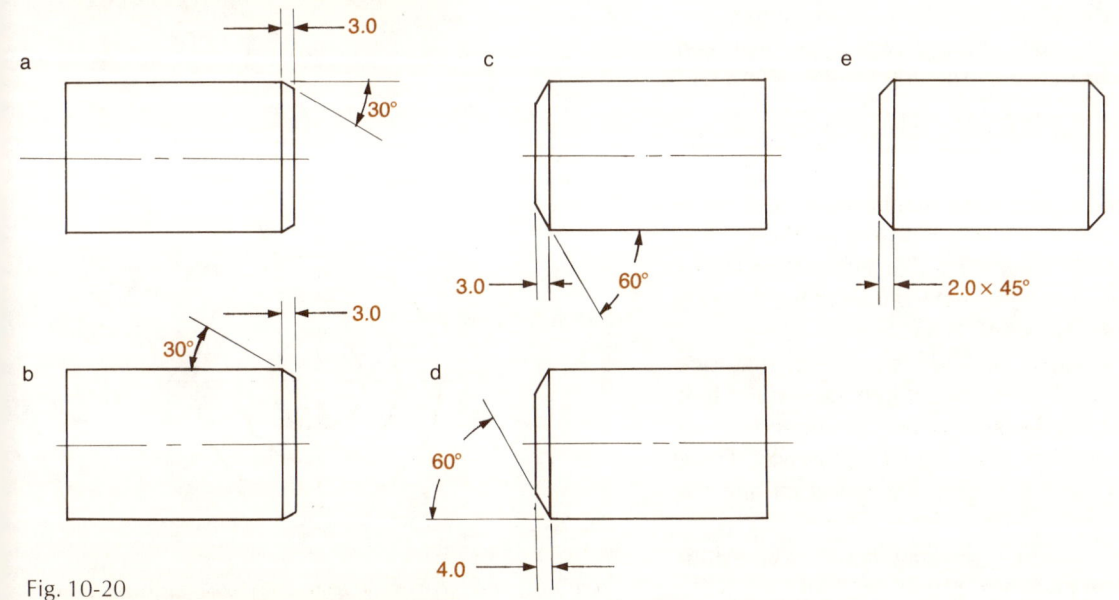

Fig. 10-20

Note in Fig. 10-20 that there are several methods of dimensioning chamfers. Whatever the size of the chamfer, any of these methods can be used.

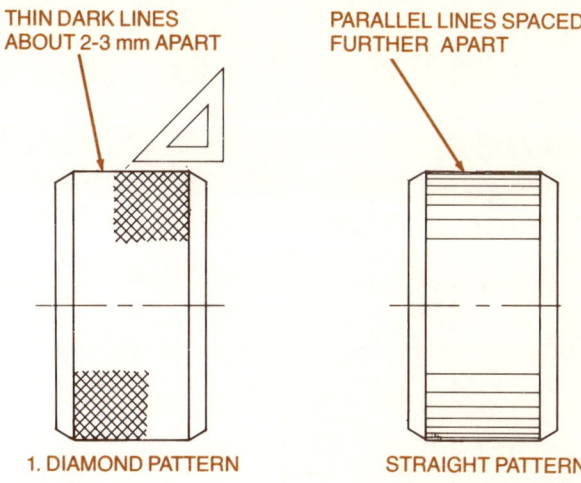

1. DIAMOND PATTERN   STRAIGHT PATTERN

Fig. 10-21

Knurling. Knurling is a machine operation of cutting into a part to produce a ridged surface. The knurled part is easier to grip and is more attractive in appearance. The ridges can be either straight or diamond patterned.

Note in Fig. 10-18 that it is not necessary to show the entire knurled area. A small number of diagonal lines in opposite corners of the knurled surface will **indicate** a diamond knurl. A few straight lines at each end of the knurled area is sufficient to indicate the straight knurl. A leader line notes the type and size of the knurl.

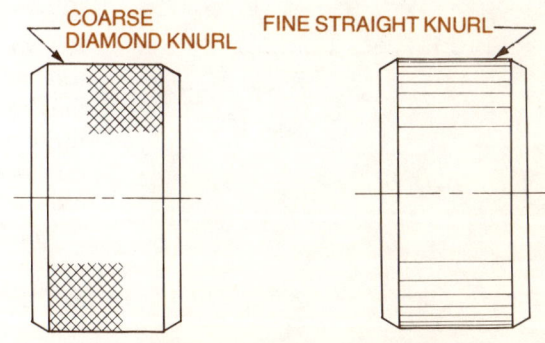

TO DIMENSION KNURLED FEATURES

Fig. 10-22

MACHINING METHODS 121

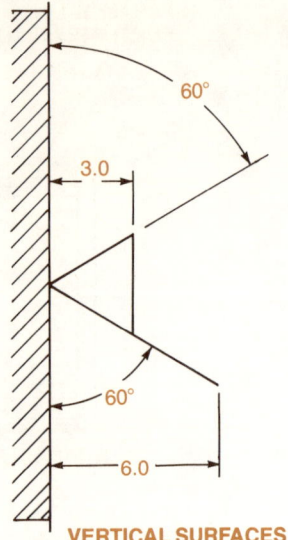

VERTICAL SURFACES

Fig. 10-23(a)

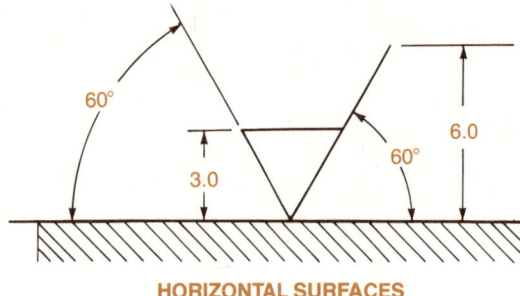

HORIZONTAL SURFACES

Fig. 10-23(b)

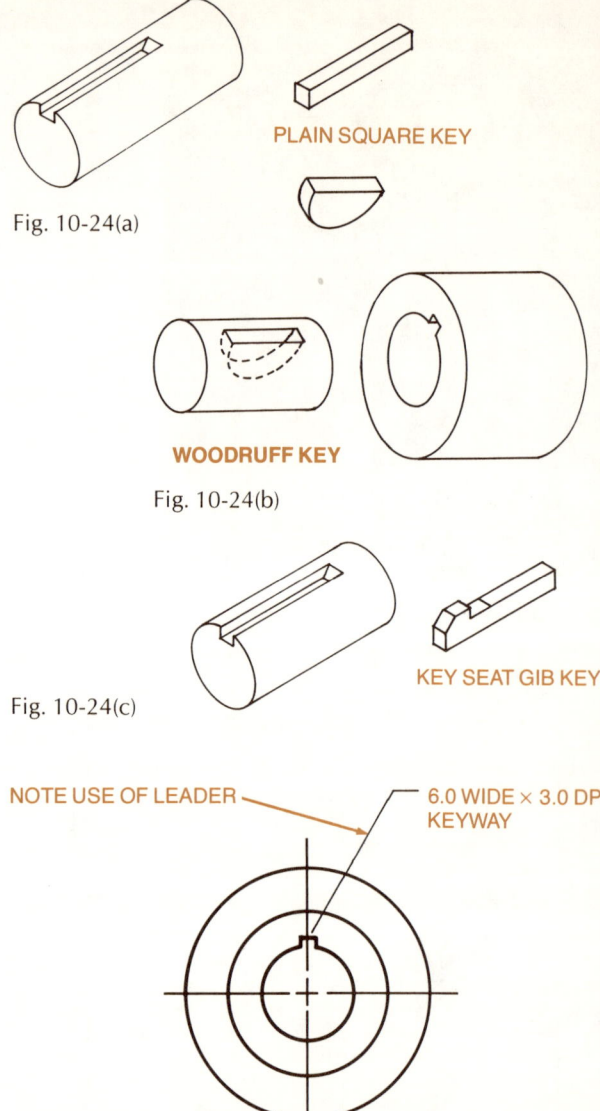

Fig. 10-24(a) **PLAIN SQUARE KEY**

Fig. 10-24(b) **WOODRUFF KEY**

Fig. 10-24(c) **KEY SEAT GIB KEY**

Fig. 10-25 — NOTE USE OF LEADER — 6.0 WIDE × 3.0 DP KEYWAY

Finishing. Finishing is the process of machining the rough surface of a part. Parts that are cast or forged often need to be finished. The entire surface of a part can be machined if necessary.

Note in Fig. 10-23 that surfaces that are to be machined are identified by a finished symbol ∀. This is placed on the surface to be machined wherever the surface is shown as an object or hidden line. If it is necessary to finish every surface of the part, the letters F.A.O. are placed just above the border of the drawing (F.A.O stands for Finish All Over).

Keyway and **Keyseat.** Keys are metal parts that lock rotating parts together. A slot cut into the shaft to seat the key is called the **keyseat**. A slot cut into the side of the mating cylindrical part is called the **keyway**. Three common keys are: the square, the woodruff and the gib.

Note in Fig. 10-25 that a leader line shows the width and the depth of the keyway or keyseat for the square and gib key. The woodruff key is noted by a stock number.

Boss and **Pad.** A **boss** is a raised circular projection above the surface of a casting or forging. The boss can be machined to provide a smooth seat for the head of a bolt.

A **pad** is a raised projection above the surface of a casting or forging. The pad can be machined to provide a smooth surface for two or more bolt heads.

122 DETAIL WORKING DRAWINGS

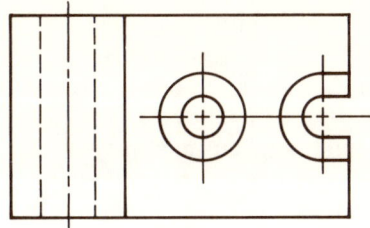
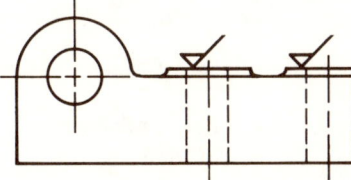

Fig. 10-26

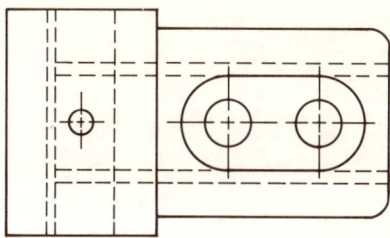
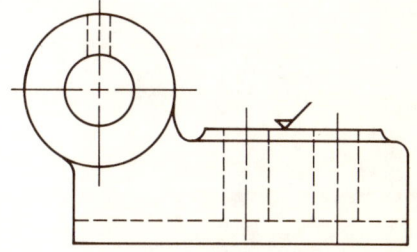

Fig. 10-27

The advantages of the boss and pad are clear: both reduce the amount of machining required. Only the area around the holes need be machined.

Note on the above drawings that the finish symbol is placed on the surface of the boss or pad. The symbols must appear in all views where the surface is shown as an edge.

POINTS TO REMEMBER

- Both detail working drawings and assembly working drawings are used in mechanical drafting.
- Detail working drawings provide the information needed to make a part.
- Before making a part, the designer must consider the material to be used and the method of production.
- Metals are usually grouped as ferrous or non-ferrous.
- Ferrous metals contain iron ore and have magnetic properties.
- Parts are produced by casting, forging, machining, welding and stamping.
- Parts are machined by drilling, reaming, boring, counterboring, countersinking, tapping, chamfering and knurling.
- Holes in parts are either through holes or blind holes.
- When lettering the diameter of a hole, the diameter symbol Ø comes before the diameter figure.

QUESTIONS TO ANSWER

1. Name the two types of working drawings used in mechanical drafting.
2. What is the purpose of each of these working drawings?
3. Give four examples of raw materials that early primitive people used for their tools, weapons and utensils.
4. What are the important reasons for people to continue to develop new objects?
5. Describe the term **ferrous**.

6. Define the following terms:
   (a) steel   (b) tool steel
   (c) aluminum   (d) bronze
   (e) brass   (f) alloy
7. List three conditions that determine the method by which a part is to be produced.
8. How do the processes of casting and forging differ?
9. Why are many parts formed by the welding process rather than by the casting or forging methods?
10. Name four items that are produced by the stamping process.
11. What is meant by the term **blind hole**?
12. What common purpose do reaming and boring serve? How do the two methods differ?
13. Compare the appearance and purpose of spotfacing to counterboring.
14. What is the purpose of countersinking a hole?
15. Explain the following terms:
    (a) tapping   (b) chamfering
    (c) knurling   (d) finishing
    (e) boss   (f) pad

REPLACE THE X'S WITH THE CORRECT TERM

1. If you were to boil water and then freeze it you would be going from one **XXXXXXX** to the other.
2. A car engine that has been tuned **XXXXXXXX** well.
3. Hammering a **XXXXXXXXX** metal will tend to change its shape rather than break it.
4. A car speedometer **XXXXXXXXX** the speed at which the car is moving.
5. **XXXXXXXX** ramps make it easier for people in wheel chairs to use public buildings.
6. When rock in a volcano gets hot enough, it becomes **XXXXXX** , or liquid.
7. Toffee is a **XXXXXXX** candy.
8. A **XXXXXXXXXXXXXX** of a happy person is a smiling face.
9. Ford of Canada **XXXXXXXXXXX** cars.

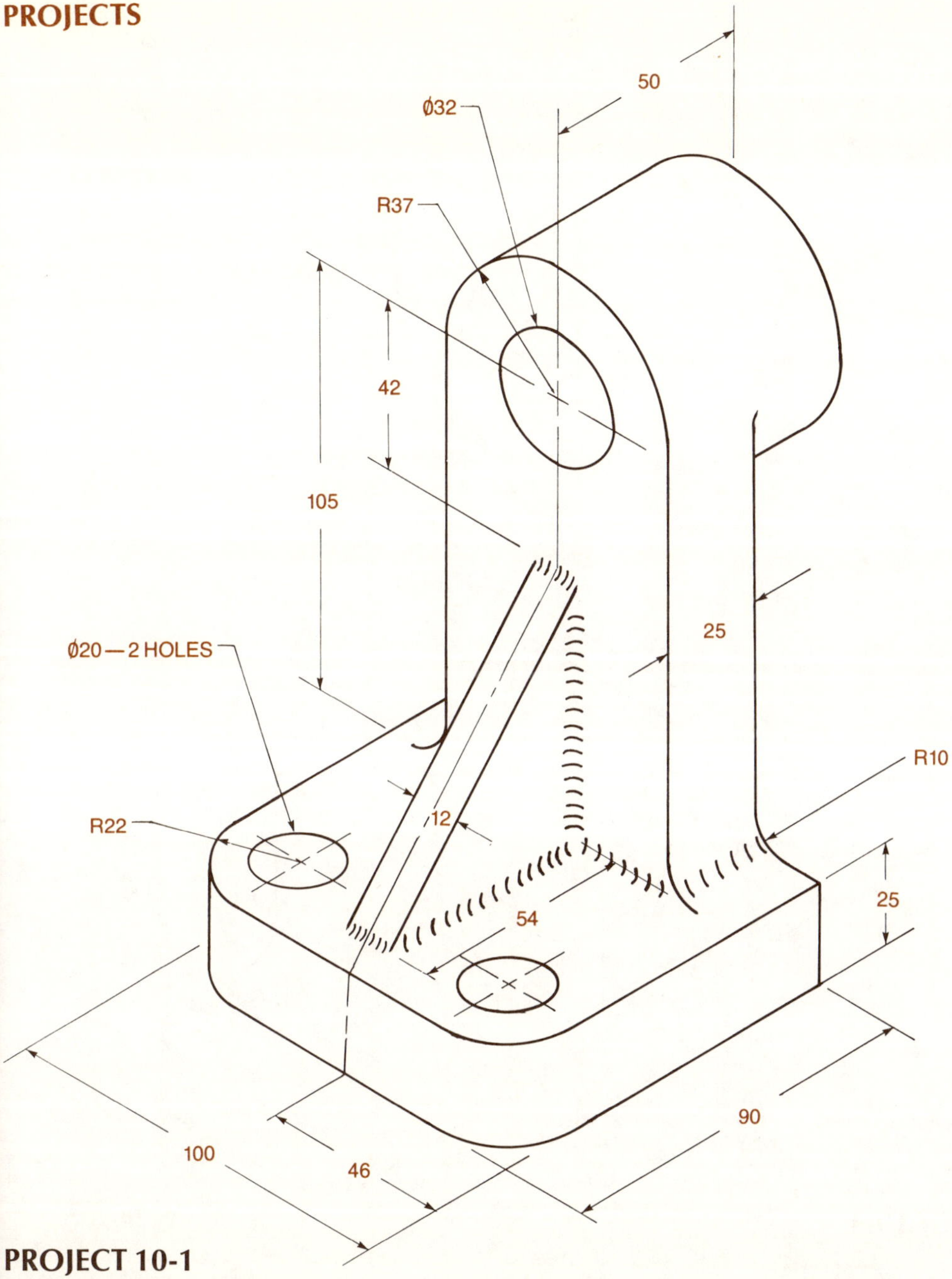

PROJECTS

PROJECT 10-1

CONTROL ARM **SCALE 1:1** MTL. CAST STEEL FILLETS NOT DIMENSIONED

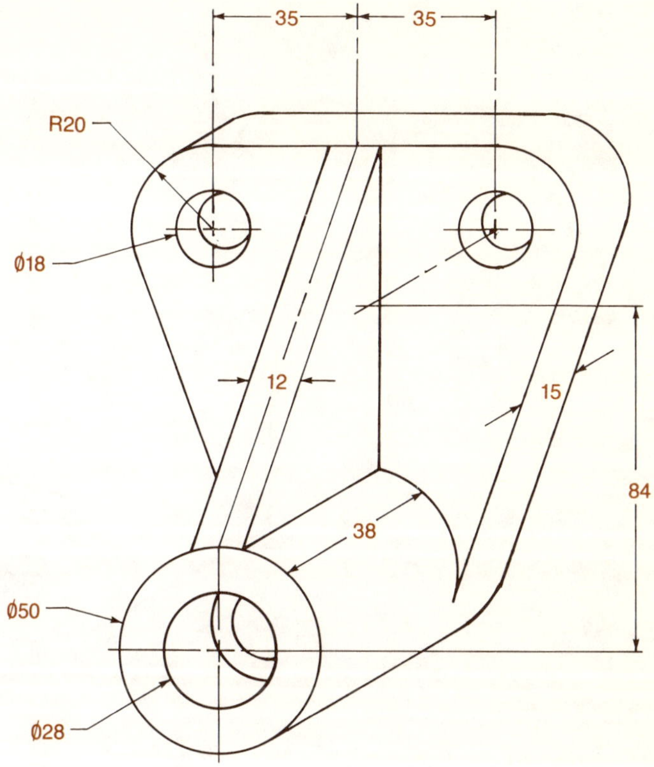

PROJECT 10-2

BRACKET **SCALE 1:1** MTL. CAST ALUMINUM F.A.O.

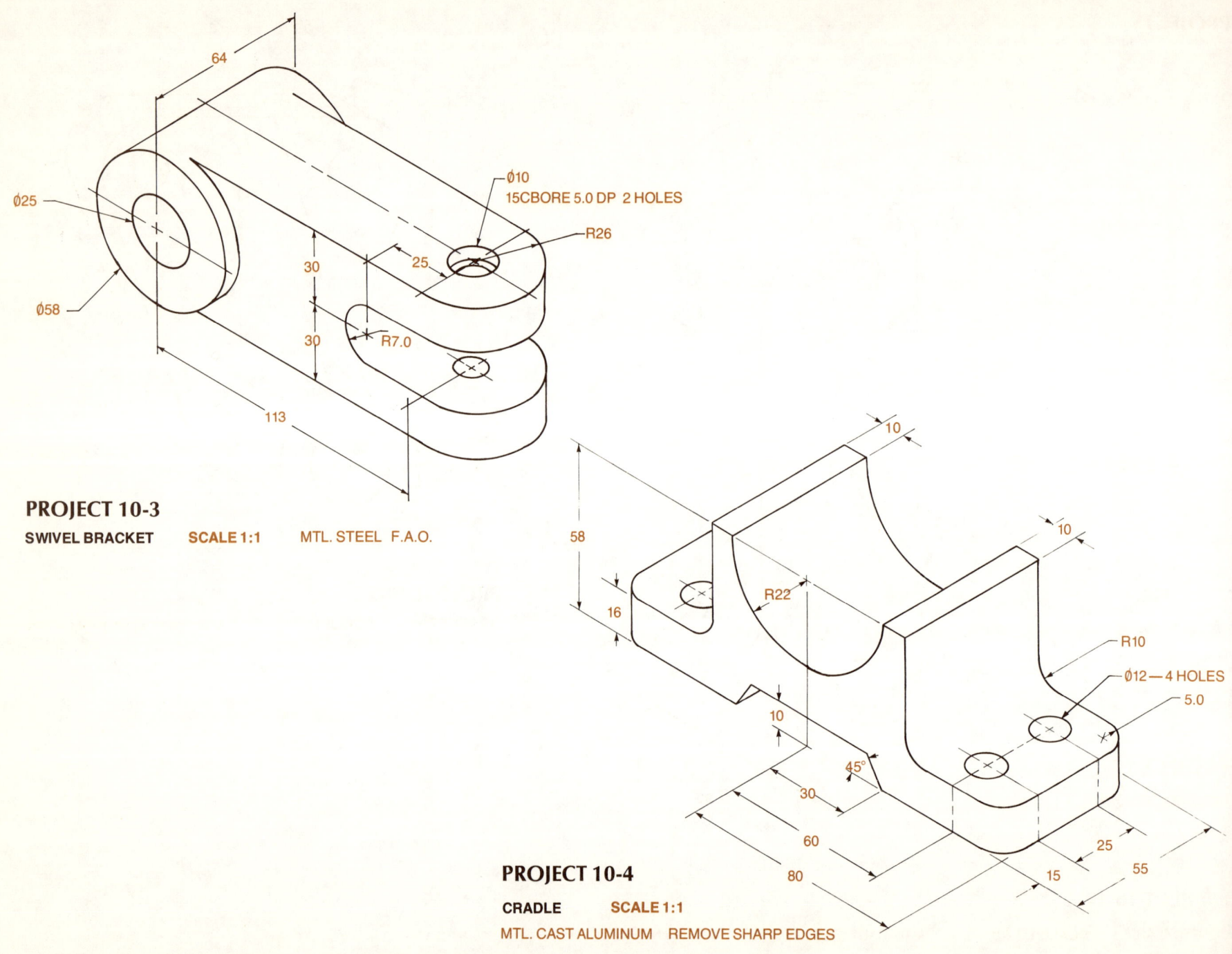

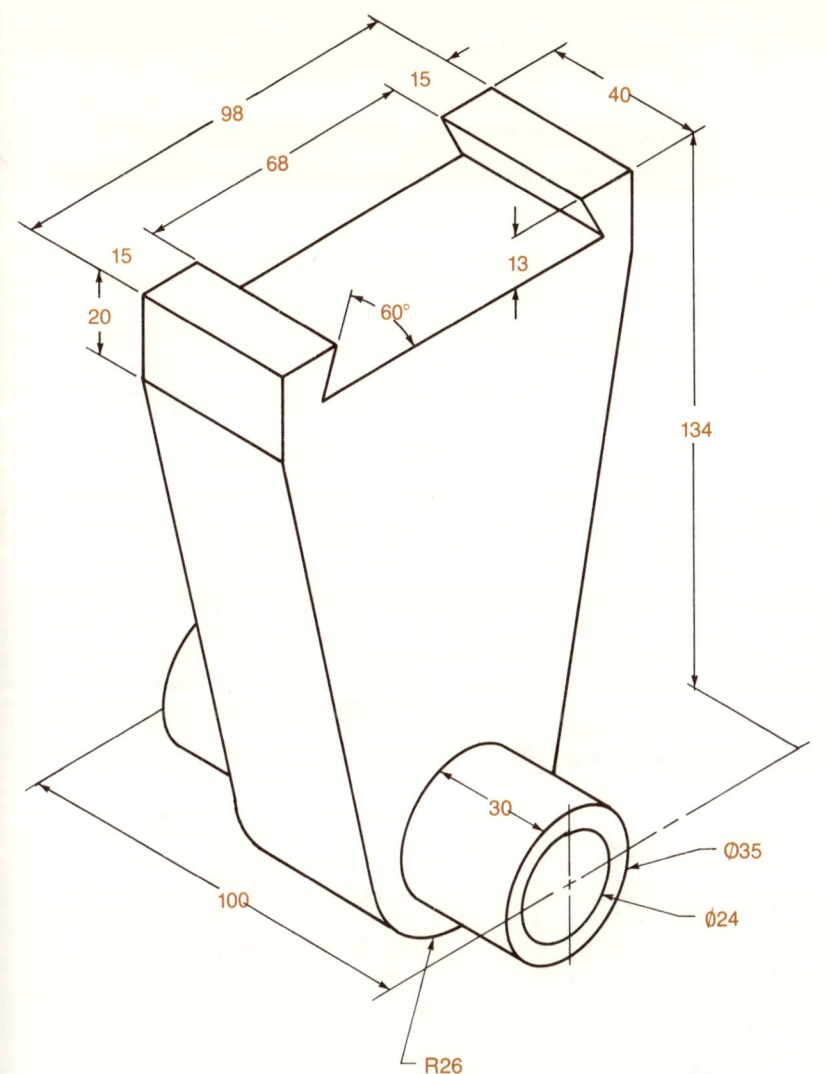

PROJECT 10-5

DOVETAIL SUPPORT **SCALE 1:1**

MTL. CAST IRON
SHOW FINISH SYMBOLS
WHERE NECESSARY

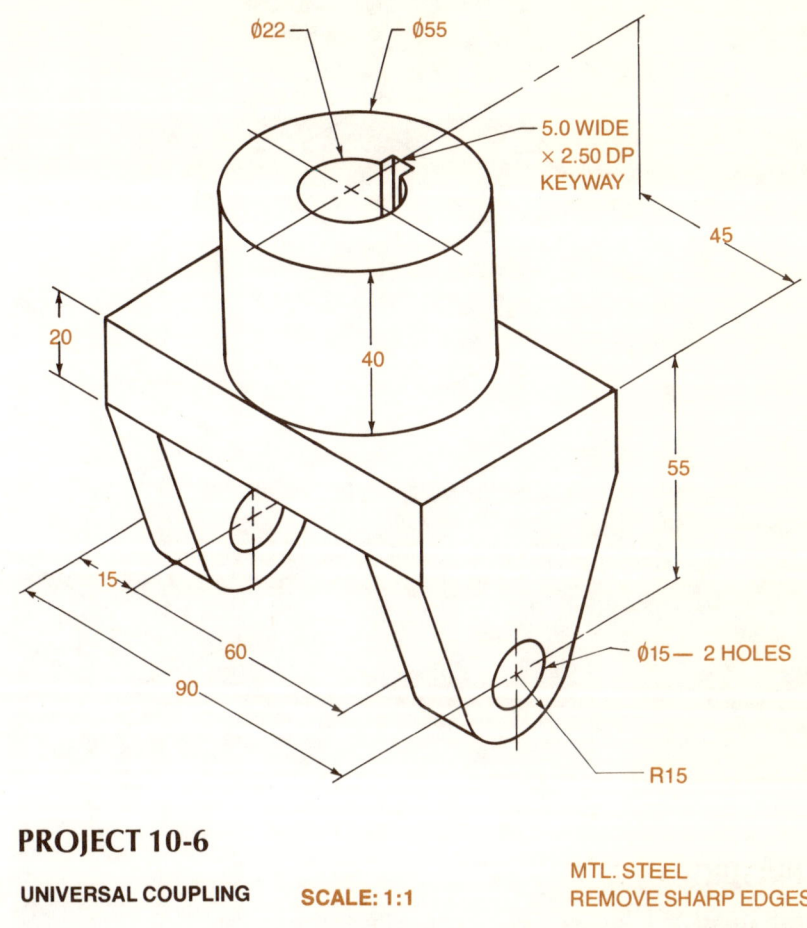

PROJECT 10-6

UNIVERSAL COUPLING **SCALE: 1:1**

MTL. STEEL
REMOVE SHARP EDGES

PROJECTS 127

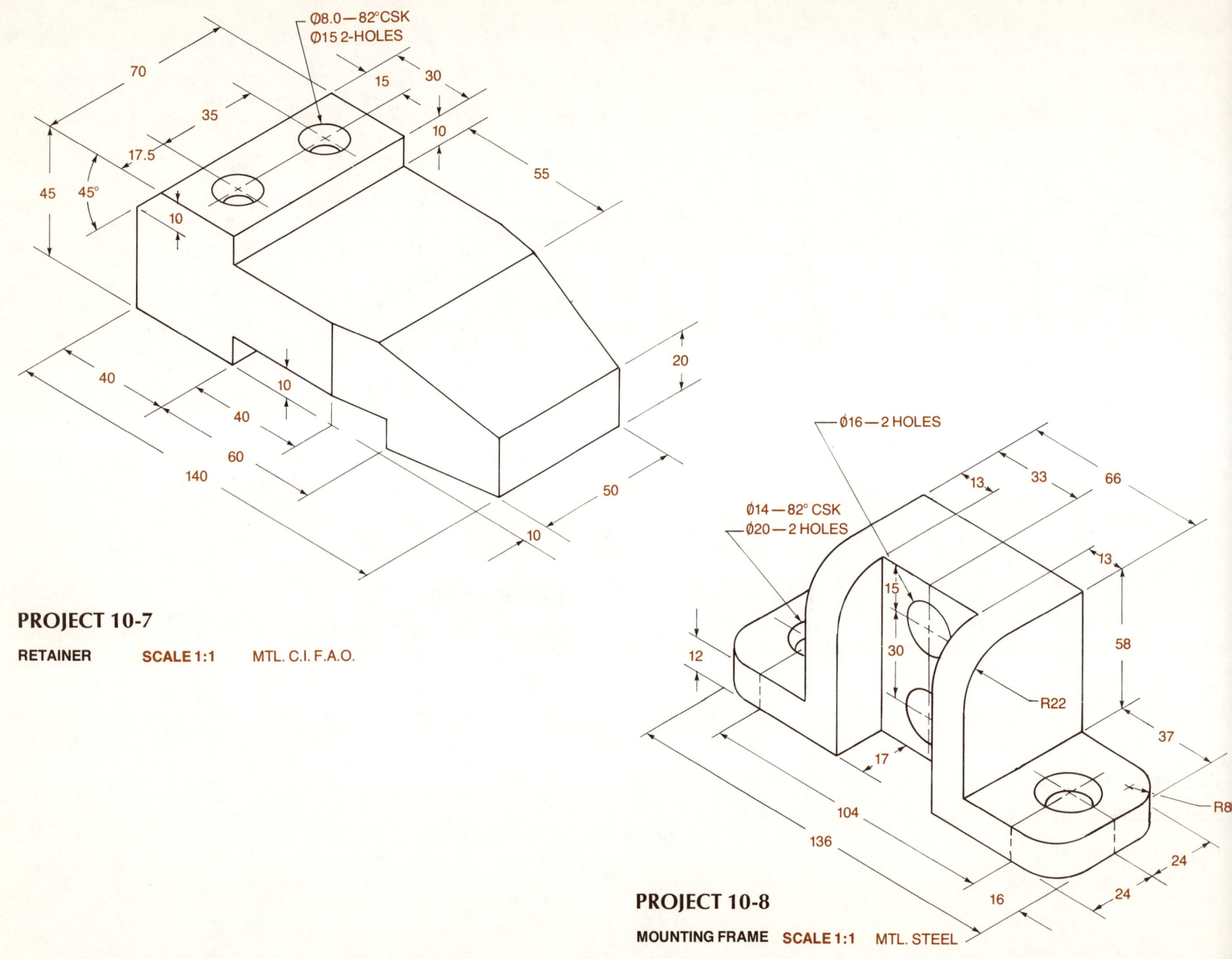

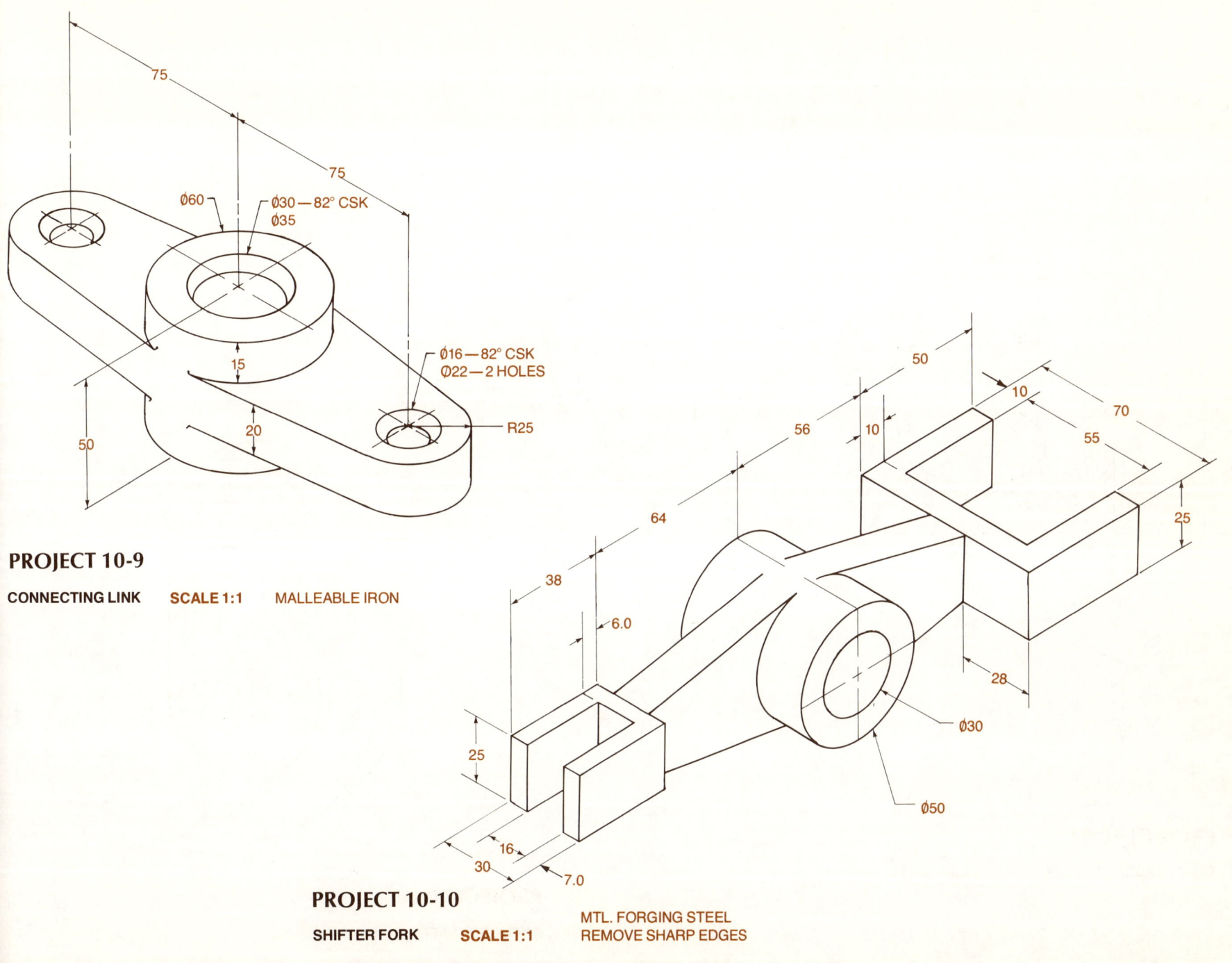

PROJECT 10-9

CONNECTING LINK   **SCALE 1:1**   MALLEABLE IRON

PROJECT 10-10

SHIFTER FORK   **SCALE 1:1**   MTL. FORGING STEEL
REMOVE SHARP EDGES

PROJECTS 129

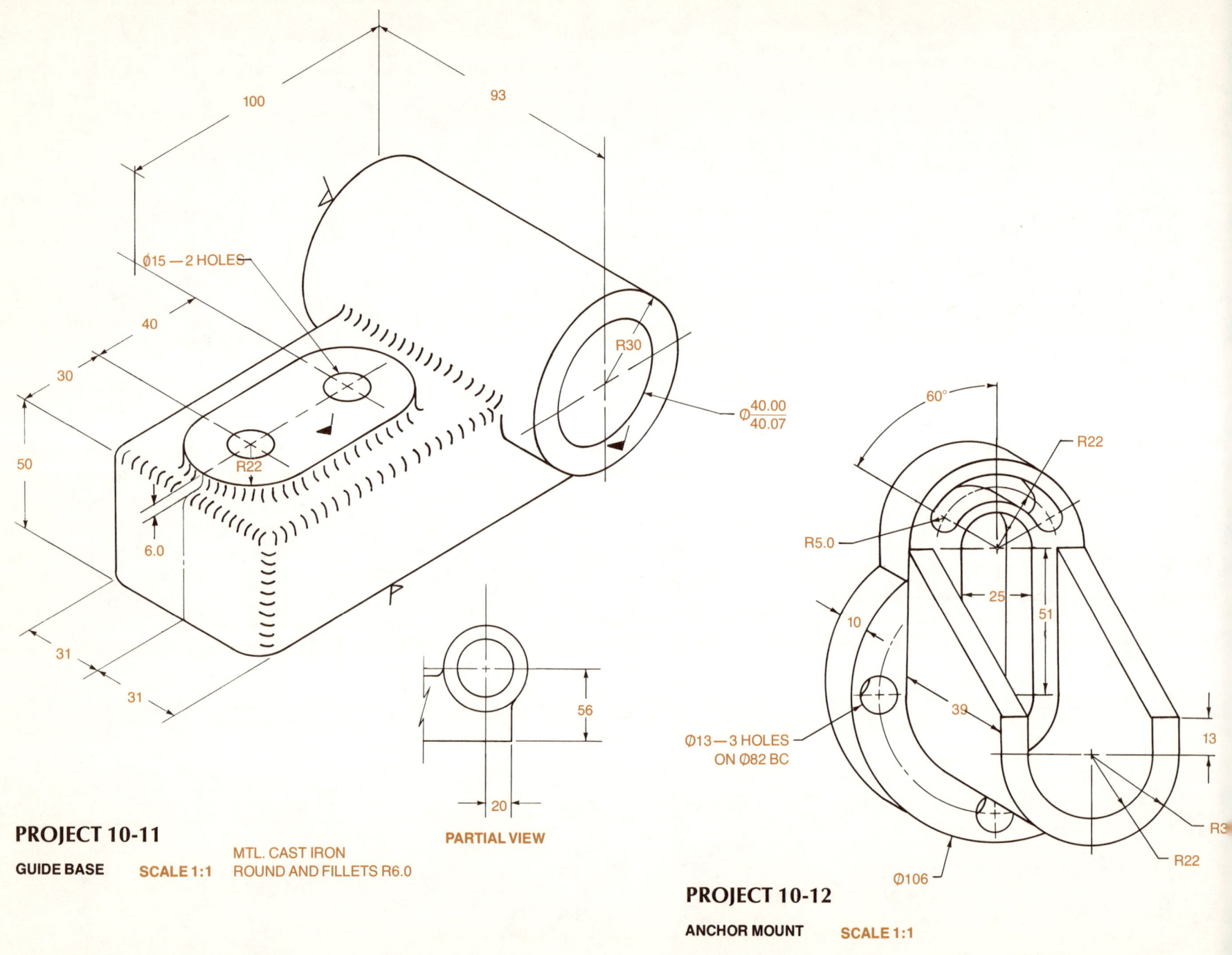

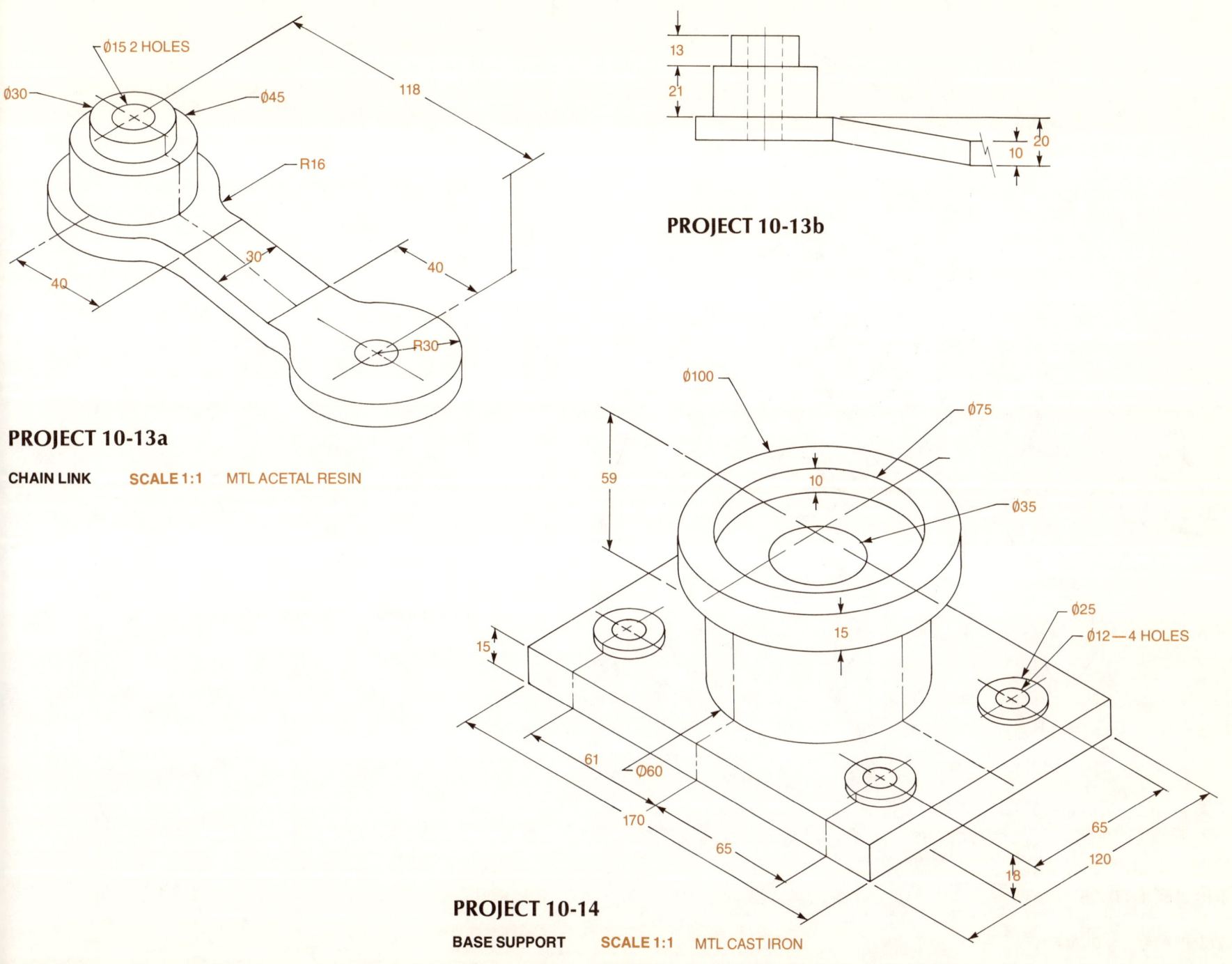

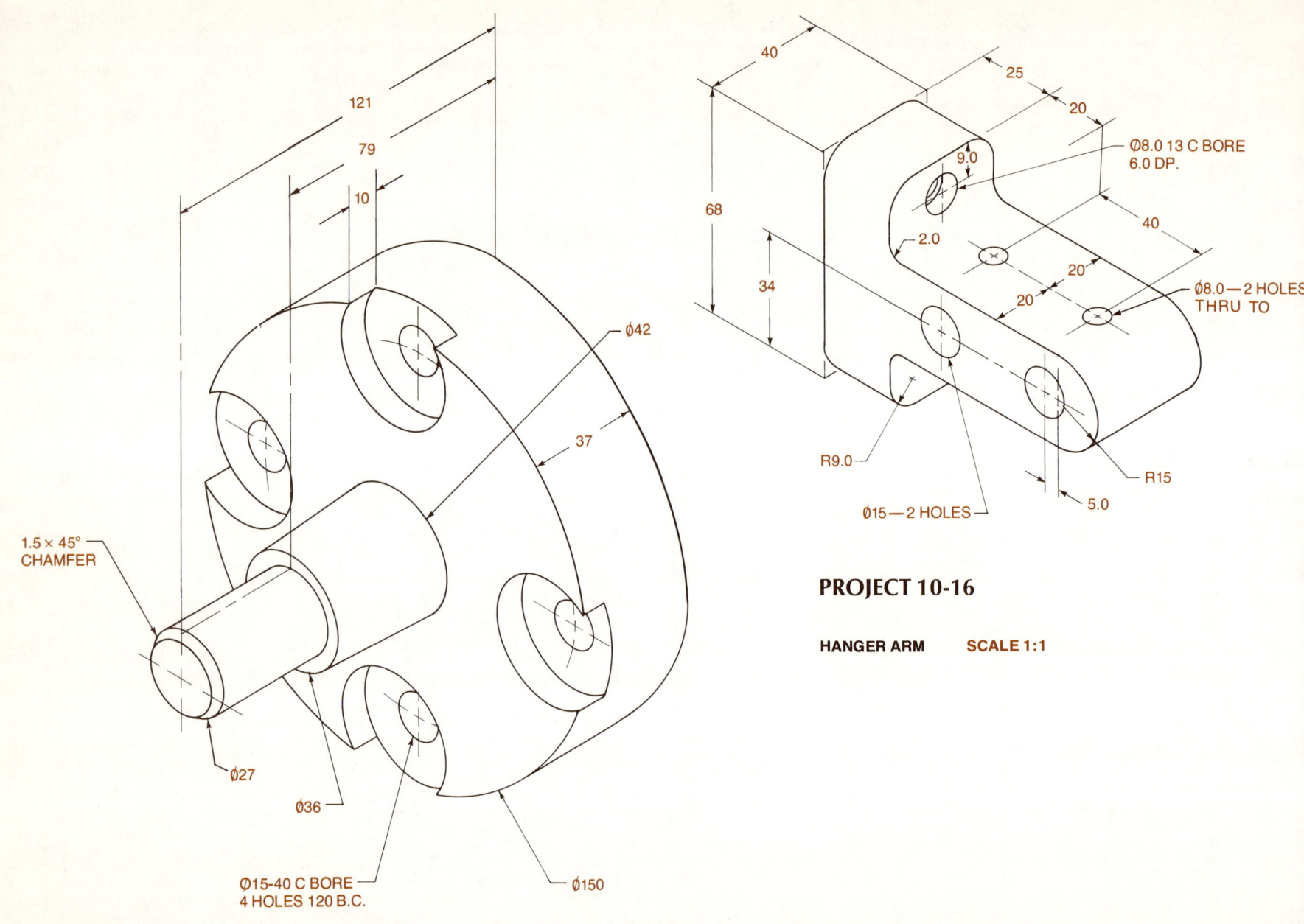

PROJECT 10-15

END PLATE   SCALE 1:1

PROJECT 10-16

HANGER ARM   SCALE 1:1

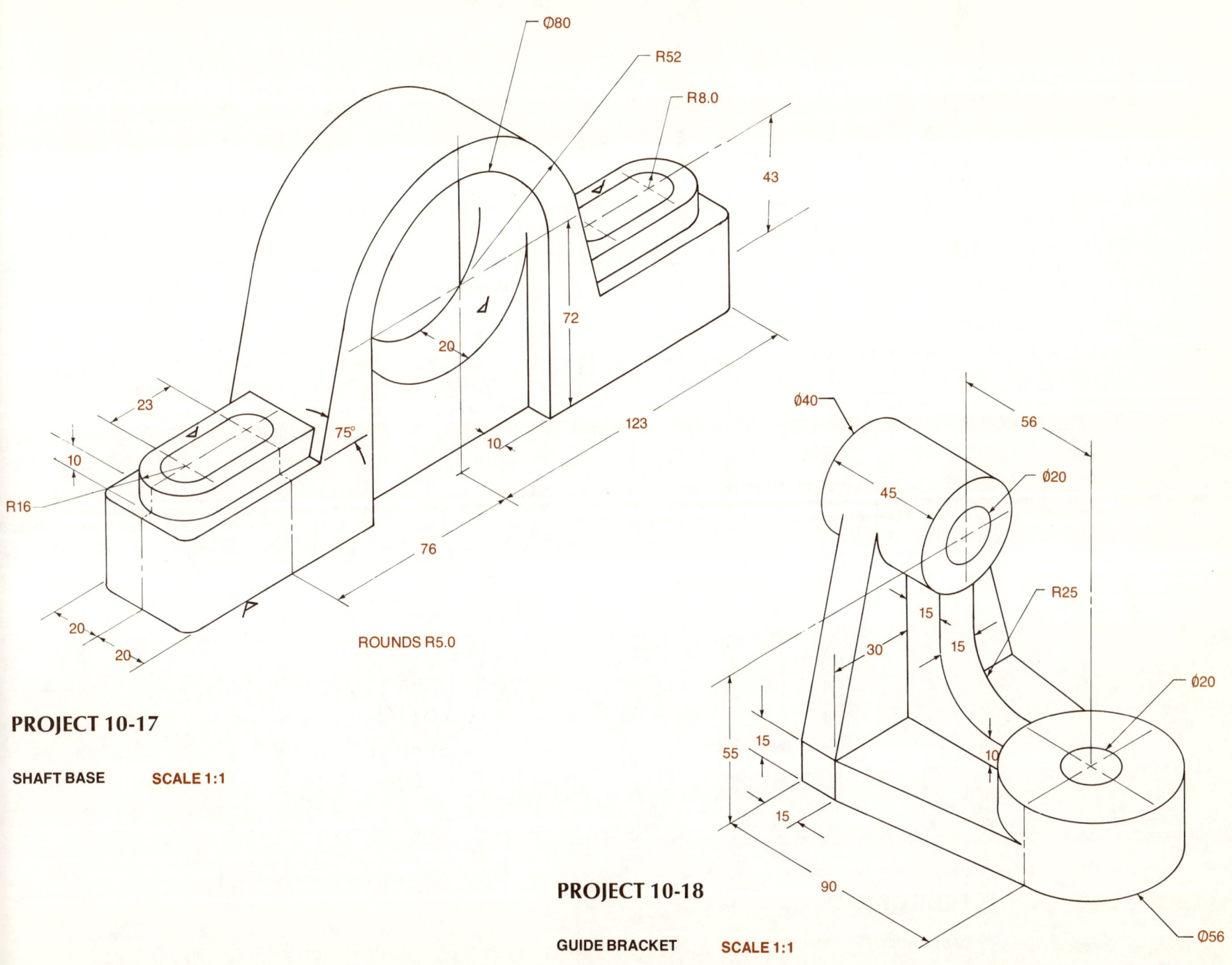

PROJECT 10-17

SHAFT BASE **SCALE 1:1**

PROJECT 10-18

GUIDE BRACKET **SCALE 1:1**

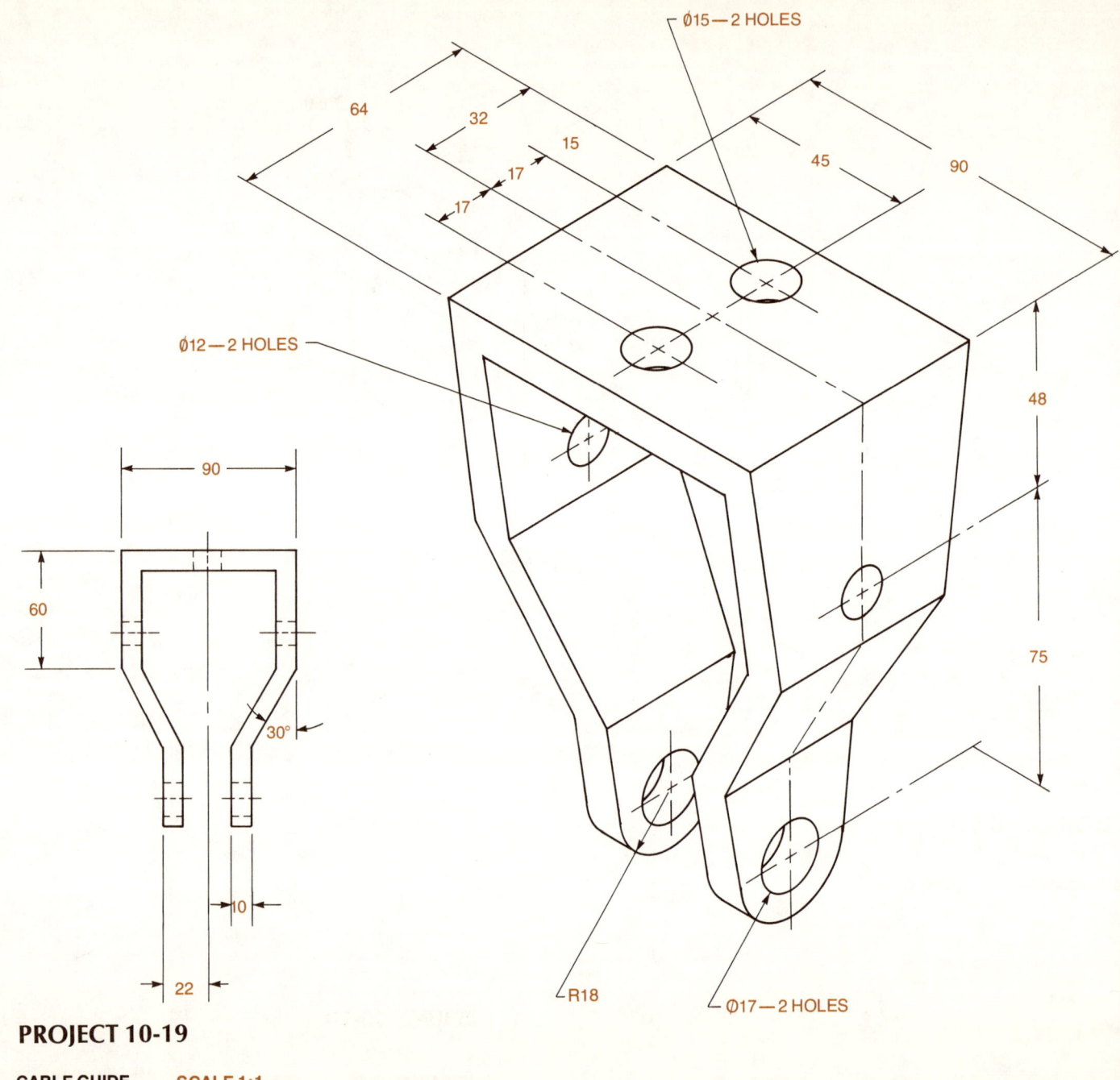

PROJECT 10-19

CABLE GUIDE SCALE 1:1

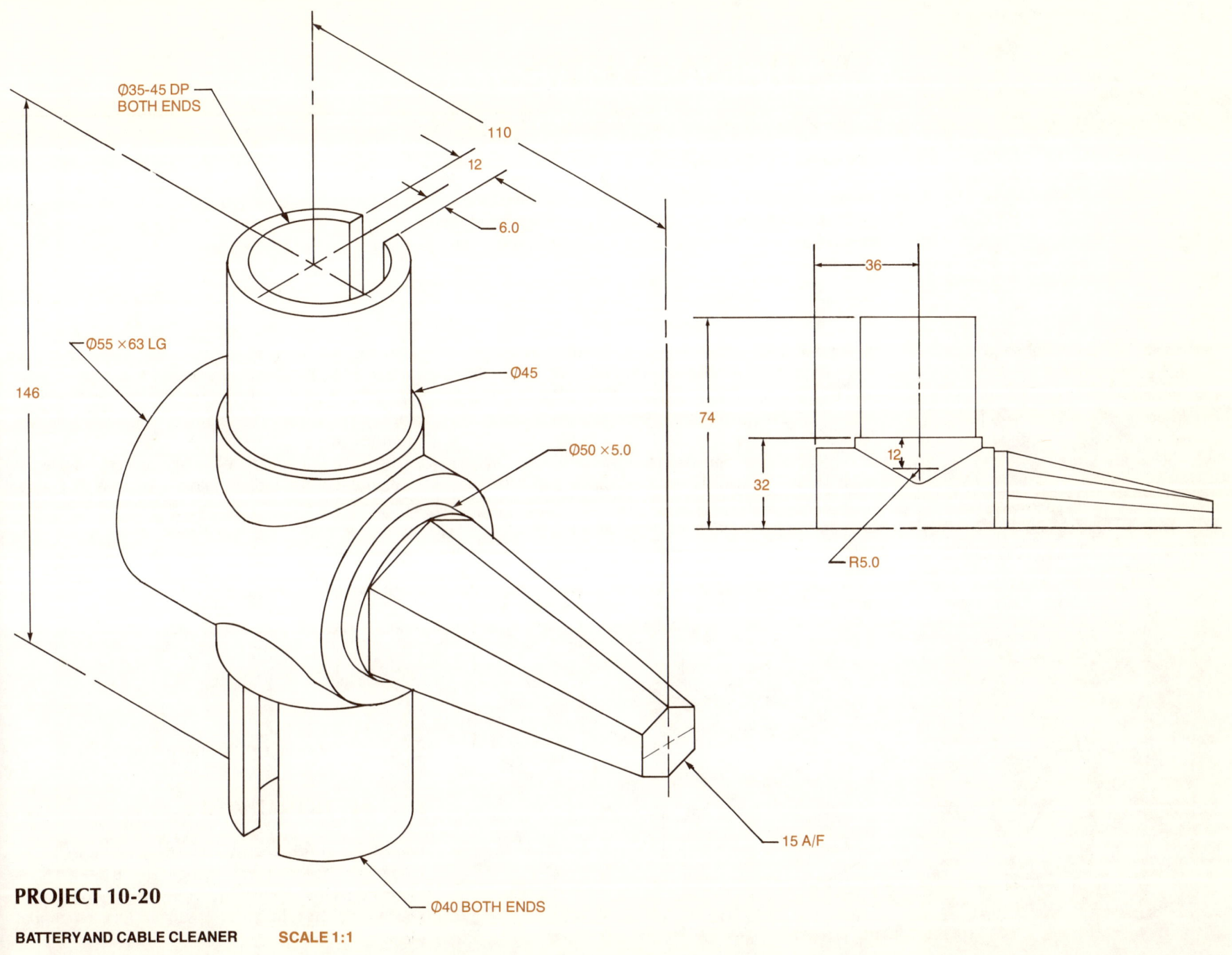

CHAPTER 11
SECTIONAL VIEWS

WORDS TO LEARN

reveal (re-véal)
indicate (ín-di-cate)
revolve (re-vólve)
interior (in-té-ri-or)

clarity (clár-i-ty)
diagonal (di-ág-o-nal)
offset (óff-set)

reveal—to expose or show something that has been hidden
interior—the part of an object within its sides or boundaries

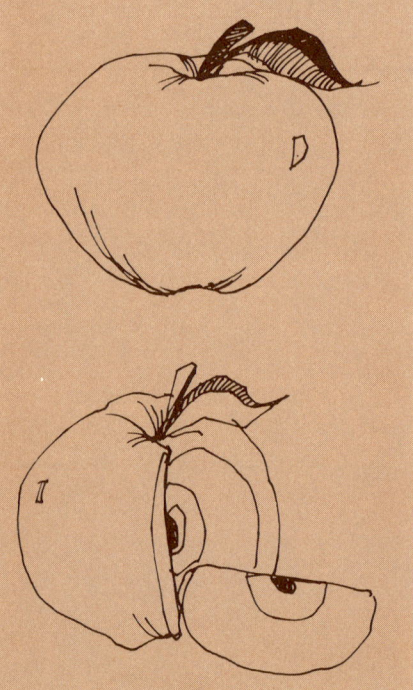

You are probably quite pleased with your drawings to this point. Your relatives and friends are no doubt impressed and you are enjoying this well-earned praise. So, let's pause a moment and review a few facts.

When drawing some objects it is necessary to use a great many hidden lines to explain their inside features. Drawings that have too many hidden lines are confusing and difficult to understand.

To avoid this problem, sectional views are often used to make these drawings easier to read. Sectional views are created by using our imagination. Part of an object is imagined to be cut away to **reveal** its hidden **interior**.

There are different types of sectional views used to explain better the hidden features of objects. Follow along as we try to describe why and how each type is used.

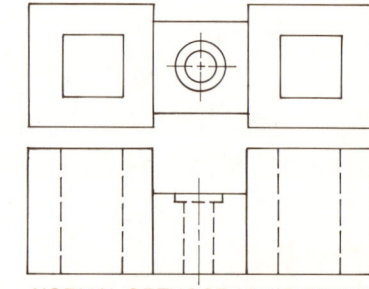

Fig. 11-2 NORMAL ORTHOGRAPHIC VIEWS

FULL SECTIONAL VIEWS

Look at Fig. 11-2. The two orthographic views accurately describe the object, but note all the hidden lines in the front view. Now allow your imagination to take you through the following steps to produce a sectional view.

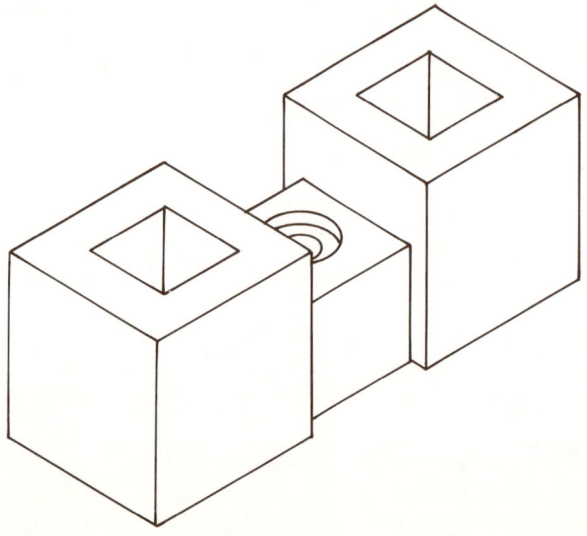

Fig. 11-1

136

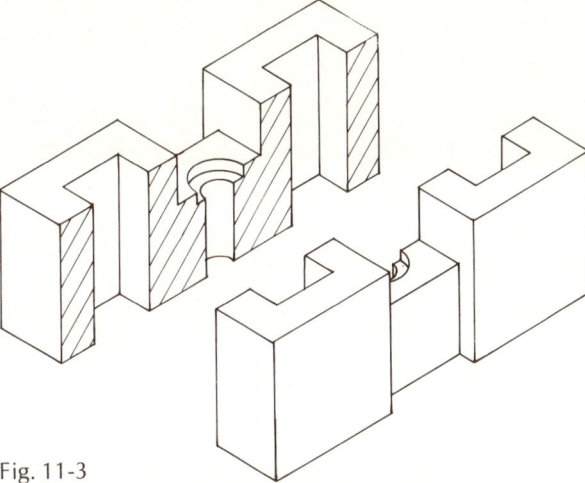

Fig. 11-3

Imagine that the object has been cut along in a straight line, from one end to the other, for its entire length.

Imagine that the half of the object nearest you has been removed and you are now able to look at the remaining half, as in a normal orthographic view.

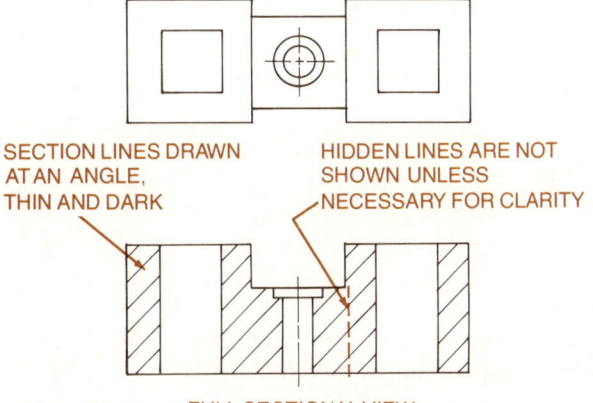

SECTION LINES DRAWN AT AN ANGLE, THIN AND DARK

HIDDEN LINES ARE NOT SHOWN UNLESS NECESSARY FOR CLARITY

FULL SECTIONAL VIEW

Fig. 11-4

Edges and features that were hidden before are now visible and are shown as solid lines.

The **diagonal** lines are drawn to **indicate** the solid areas of the part. These diagonal lines are called section lines. Edges that are still hidden from sight are not shown unless they are absolutely needed for **clarity**.

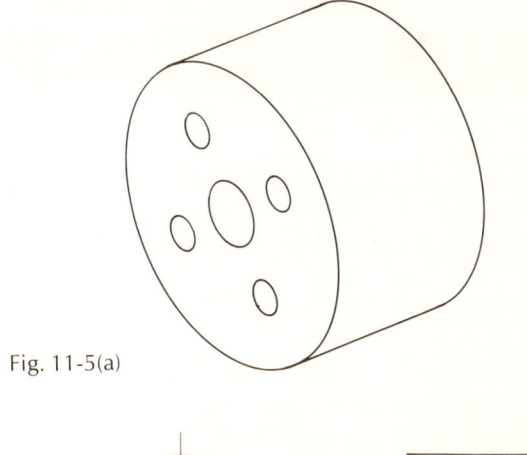

Fig. 11-5(a)

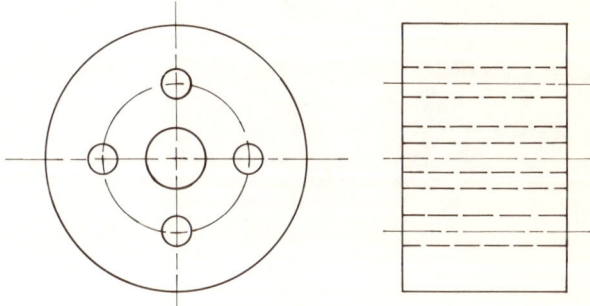

Fig. 11-5(b)

Full Sectional View of a Cylindrical Object

Here is a cylindrical object. Use your imagination again in the same way as before.

Imagine that you have cut the object in a straight line along the centre line. This is done across its full diameter. Imagine that the half of the object nearest you has been removed and you are now able to look at the remaining half as in a normal orthographic view. Edges and features that were hidden before are now visible and are now shown as solid lines. Thin diagonal lines are used to indicate the solid areas of the part. Edges that are still hidden from sight are not shown in the sectional view unless needed for clarity.

---

diagonal—a slanted straight line

indicate—to show (usually with detail)

clarity—clearness

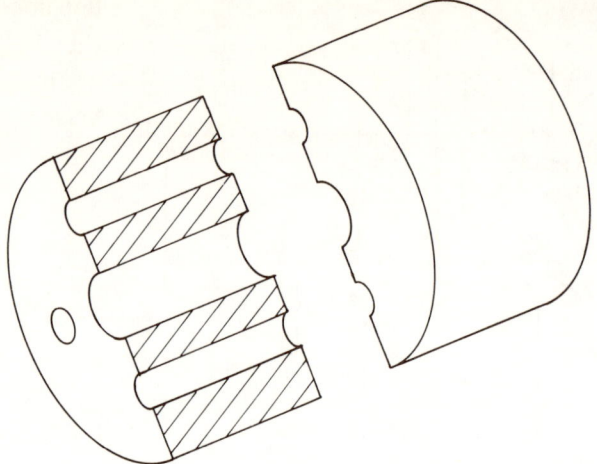

Fig. 11-6

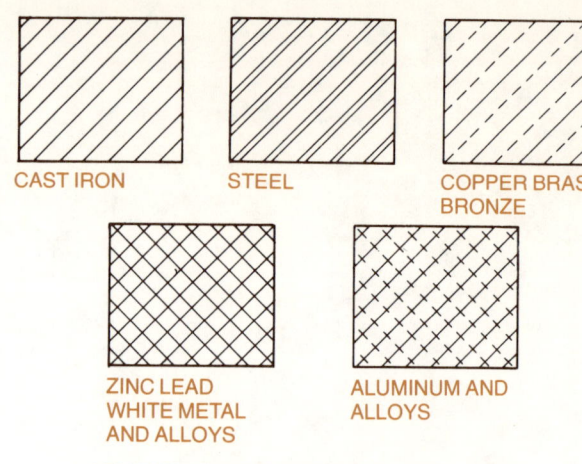

CAST IRON   STEEL   COPPER BRASS BRONZE

ZINC LEAD WHITE METAL AND ALLOYS   ALUMINUM AND ALLOYS

MOST FREQUENTLY USED SECTION LINES

Fig. 11-8

imagined to have cut. You will get the idea very quickly.

Webs and Spokes in Section

A web or spoke is a thin flat part of an object that is used to support and strengthen the object. To avoid any misunderstanding about the thickness of webs or spokes we do not section line them. You will easily see why in Fig. 11-9(a, b, c, d, e).

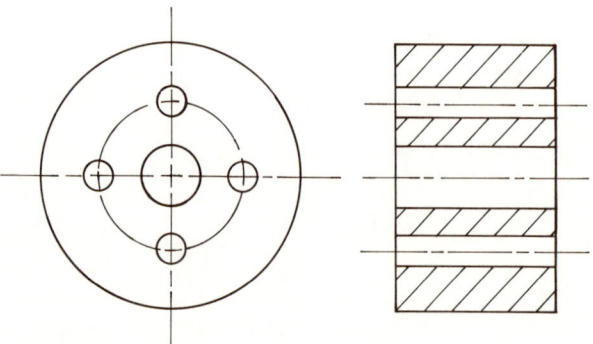

Fig. 11-7

Section lines. As you have seen, section lines are used to indicate the solid areas of a part. Section lines are thin and dark, and are usually drawn at an angle of 45°. We can identify every type of material from which a part is made by using standard section line symbols.

Now all that may sound confusing, but just remember that when half of an object is imagined to be cut away, we can see what was once hidden from sight. All visible edges are shown as solid outlines. Section lines indicate the solid areas of the part that you

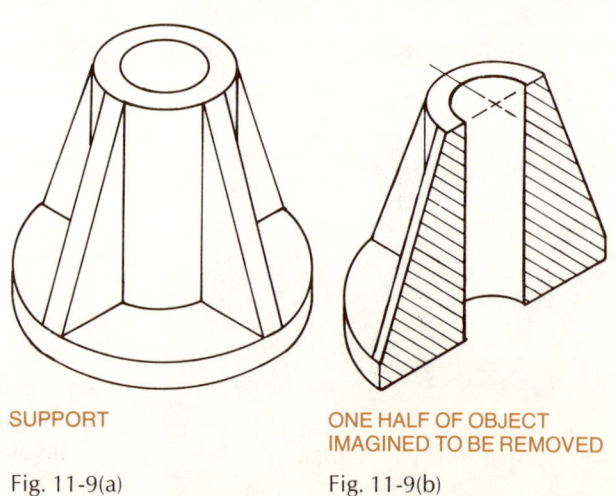

SUPPORT   ONE HALF OF OBJECT IMAGINED TO BE REMOVED

Fig. 11-9(a)   Fig. 11-9(b)

138   SECTIONAL VIEWS

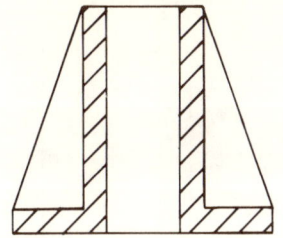

CORRECT SECTIONAL VIEW NOTE THE WEB IS NOT SECTION LINED

Fig. 11-9(c)

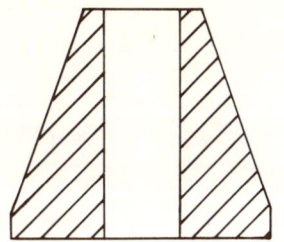

ACTUAL SECTIONAL VIEW OFFERS MISLEADING INFORMATION OF THE SHADE OF THE SUPPORT

Fig. 11-9(d)

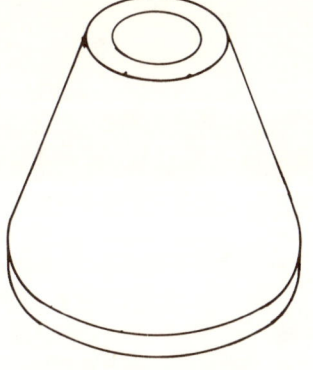

SECTION-LINING THE WEB GIVES FALSE IMPRESSION THAT THE SUPPORT IS BELL-SHAPED

Fig. 11-9(e)

Offset Sectional View

Up to this point, we have introduced you to objects that have features that are located in a straight line. For this reason we have imagined these objects cut along a straight line to prepare a sectional view. When hidden interior features are not in a straight line, we refer to them as **offset** (see Fig. 11-11). To prepare a full sectional view for this situation, we simply offset the path of the cutting line to pass through as many of the hidden features as possible. We call the sectional view obtained by this method an offset sectional view.

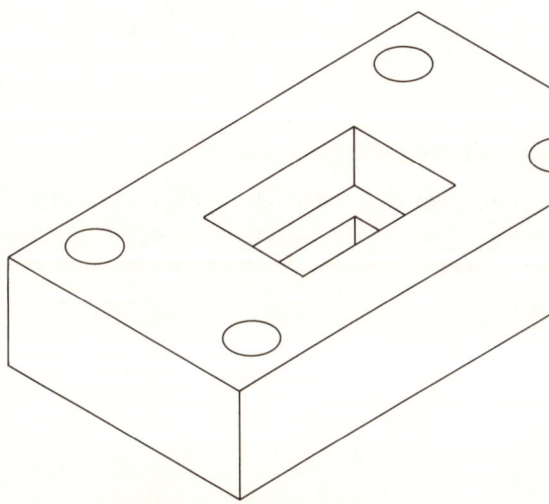

INTERIOR FEATURES ARE NOT IN A STRAIGHT LINE

Fig. 11-10(a)

offset—not located on a common line

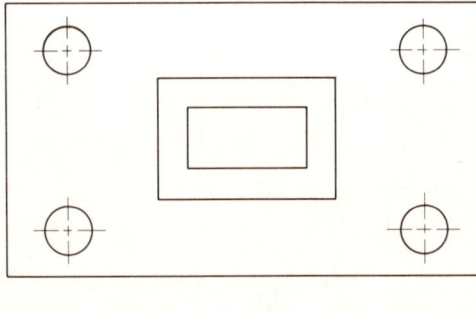

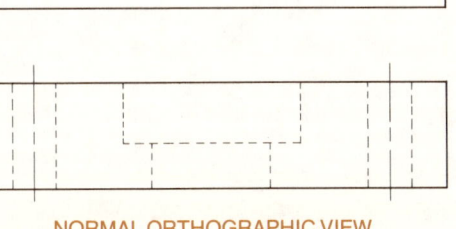

NORMAL ORTHOGRAPHIC VIEW

Fig. 11-10(b)

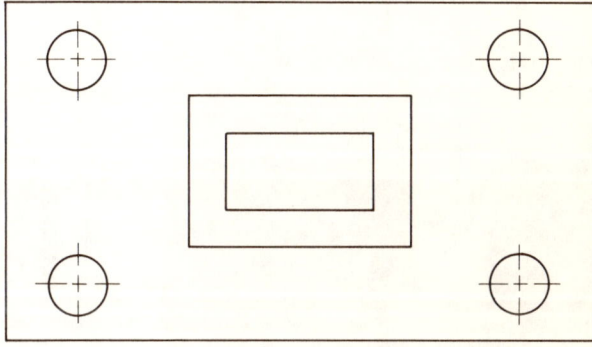

THIS FULL SECTIONAL VIEW OFFERS ONLY A PARTIAL DESCRIPTION OF THE INTERIOR FEATURES OF THE OBJECT.

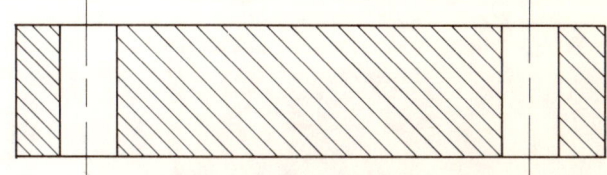

THIS FULL SECTIONAL VIEW OFFERS ONLY A PARTIAL DESCRIPTION OF THE INTERIOR FEATURES

Fig. 11-11

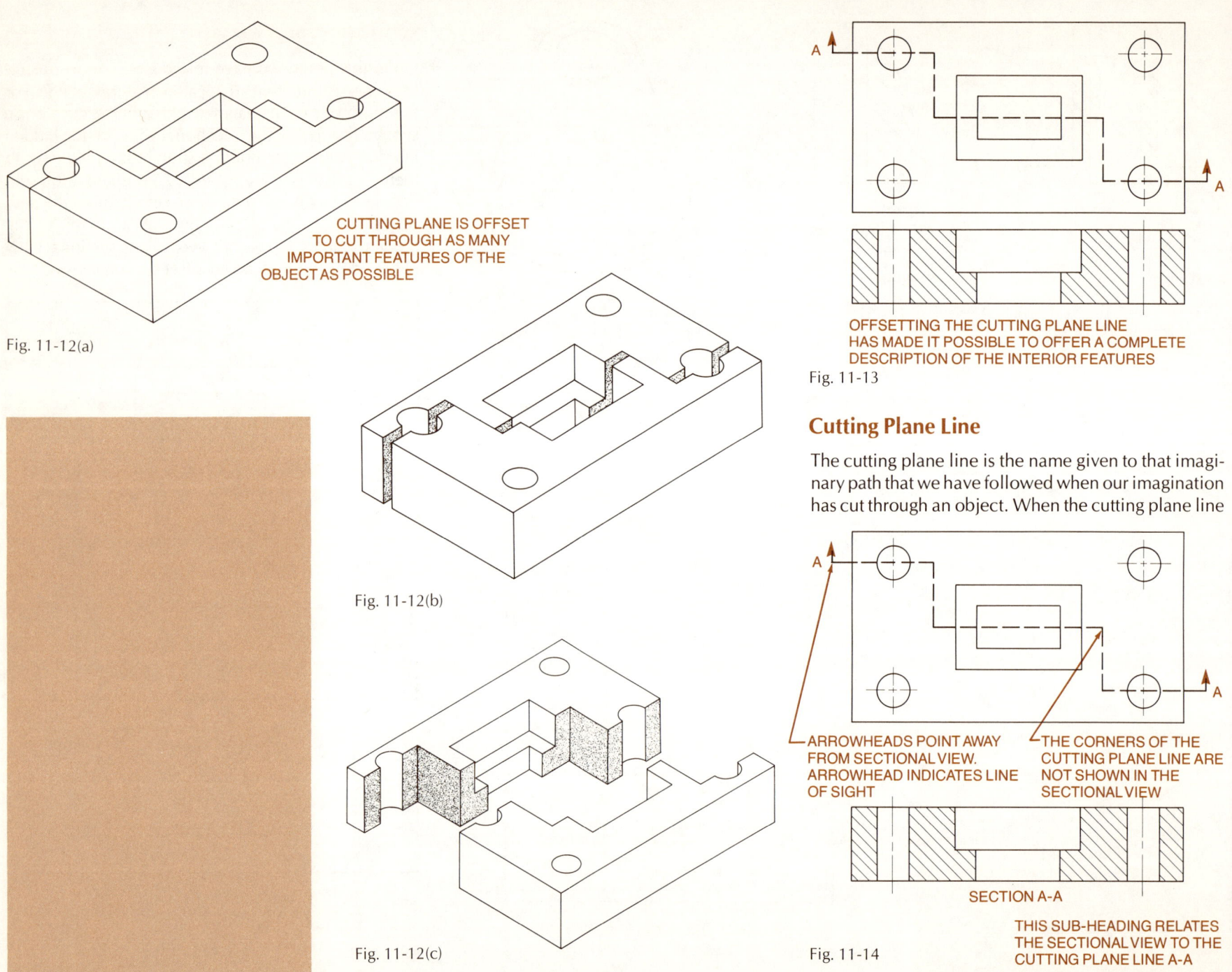

Fig. 11-12(a)

CUTTING PLANE IS OFFSET TO CUT THROUGH AS MANY IMPORTANT FEATURES OF THE OBJECT AS POSSIBLE

Fig. 11-12(b)

Fig. 11-12(c)

OFFSETTING THE CUTTING PLANE LINE HAS MADE IT POSSIBLE TO OFFER A COMPLETE DESCRIPTION OF THE INTERIOR FEATURES

Fig. 11-13

Cutting Plane Line

The cutting plane line is the name given to that imaginary path that we have followed when our imagination has cut through an object. When the cutting plane line

ARROWHEADS POINT AWAY FROM SECTIONAL VIEW. ARROWHEAD INDICATES LINE OF SIGHT

THE CORNERS OF THE CUTTING PLANE LINE ARE NOT SHOWN IN THE SECTIONAL VIEW

SECTION A-A

THIS SUB-HEADING RELATES THE SECTIONAL VIEW TO THE CUTTING PLANE LINE A-A

Fig. 11-14

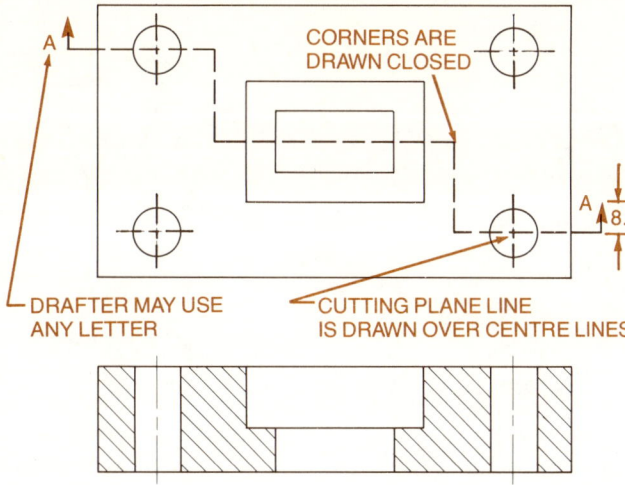

Fig. 11-15

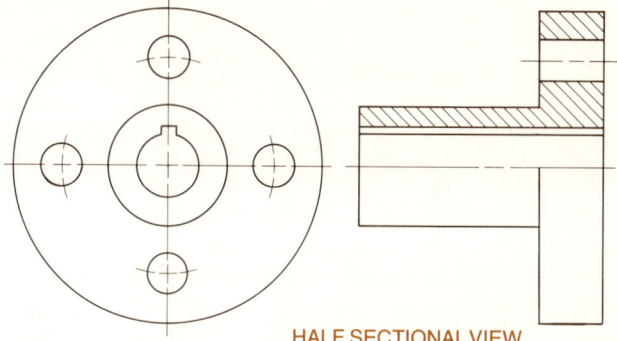

HALF SECTIONAL VIEW

Fig. 11-16(a)

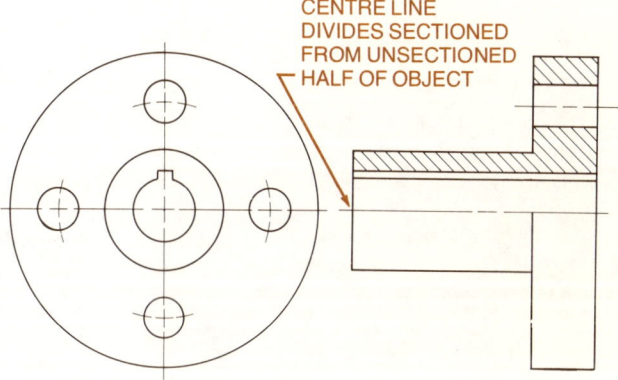

SIDE VIEW IS UNCHANGED

A CUTTING PLANE LINE IS UNNECESSARY

Fig. 11-16(b)

is offset, a broken line is used. The cutting plane line is an extra thick line with arrowheads at each end of the line indicating the direction of sight for the sectional view.

When producing a full sectional view, the cutting plane line is drawn only when necessary. Usually the line we imagined to have cut along is obvious to the reader and need not be drawn.

For offset sectional views, however, a cutting plane line is always used to clarify the path of the imaginary cut.

HALF SECTIONAL VIEW

Half sectional views are used to explain the interior features of objects that are symmetrical in shape. A centre line divides the sectional view into two halves. One-half of the view up to the centre line shows the interior of the object. The other half of the sectional view shows the exterior of the object.

Note in Fig. 11-17 that one-quarter of the object is imagined to be removed. The half sectional view is useful because it describes both the interior and exterior of an object in one view. Half sectional views are used mostly for drawings that describe parts assembled together into a unit.

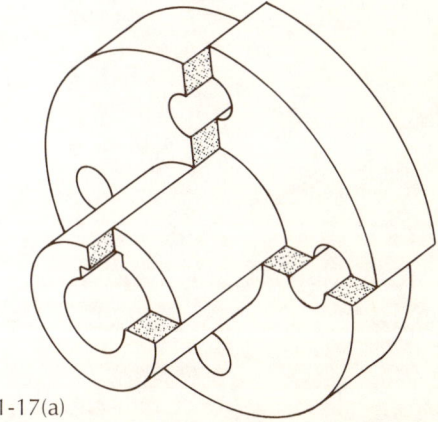

Fig. 11-17(a)

HALF SECTIONAL VIEWS 141

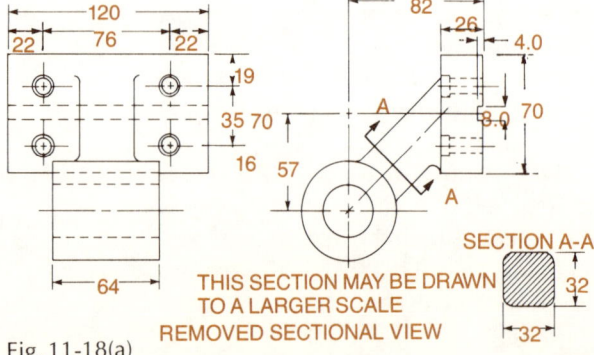

Fig. 11-17(b)

Revolved and Removed Sections

A **revolved sectional view** is used to describe the shape of an object at any location. Imagine that you have cut a slice out of the object. Imagine further that the slice is **revolved** 90° to allow us to view the slice as if it were a side view. This revolved view is drawn directly on the orthographic view where you have imagined the cut to be made.

A **removed sectional view** is similar to a revolved sectional view. A slice of an object has been imagined to be cut at any desired location. The slice is revolved 90° to allow us to view the slice as if it were a side view.

revolve—to turn on a set path around a central point

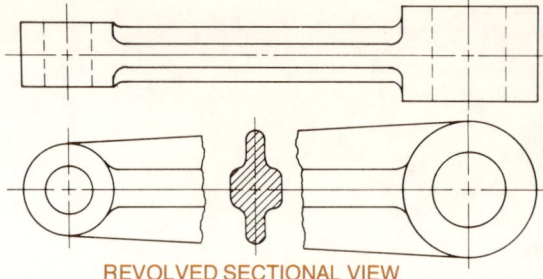

Fig. 11-18(b)

The sectional view is removed from the other view to an open area on the drawing. The revolved sectional view can be drawn to an enlarged scale for clarity. The advantages of a removed sectional view are:
- A clearer enlarged description of the shape of an object is produced.
- The enlarged scale and additional space make dimensioning easier.

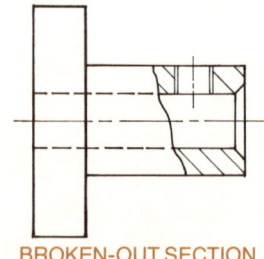

Fig. 11-19

Broken-Out Sectional Views

Where a sectional view of a portion of an object is needed, a broken-out section may be used. We merely imagine that a part of the exterior is broken away. The interior of that portion of the object is exposed as if the exterior was gone. A freehand irregular line is drawn to show the edge of the break.

You will soon learn to appreciate the value of sectional views. Unfortunately, reading about the different types of sectional views can never have the excitement and satisfaction of drawing itself, but it does give you more tools to work with. Now it is time to use these new tools to produce even better, clearer drawings than before.

POINTS TO REMEMBER

- Sectional views make technical drawings clearer and easier to understand.
- We imagine that parts of objects have been cut away to reveal their inner features.
- Edges and features that were hidden before are now visible and are shown as visible lines.
- Section lines indicate the solid areas of a part.
- Webs and spokes are not usually sectioned.
- Cutting plane lines are drawn thick and black, with arrowheads pointing in the direction the cut section is viewed.
- Cutting plane lines are usually not necessary in full and half sectional views.
- Half sectional views are used to help explain symmetrical objects. They are most often applied to drawings of assembled parts.

QUESTIONS TO ANSWER

1. Why are sectional views used on technical drawings?
2. Why are hidden lines usually not used in sectional views?
3. How are solid areas represented in sectional views?
4. Why are webs and spokes not section-lined?
5. In a drawing, how would you draw (1) a straight cutting plane line, (2) an offset cutting plane line?
6. In what particular way are half section views useful?
7. What two advantages does a removed sectional view have?
8. How do you draw the edge of the break in a broken-out sectional view?

REPLACE THE X'S WITH THE CORRECT TERM

1. The hands on a clock XXXXXXXX the time.
2. A straight line joining the opposite corners of a rectangle is a XXXXXXXX line.
3. Peeling an orange XXXXXXX the hidden fruit.
4. Seats in a theatre are XXXXXX to make it easier to see the screen.
5. Television dials can be adjusted to improve the XXXXXXX of the sound or picture.
6. The earth XXXXXXXX around the sun.
7. The XXXXXXXX of new cars is as roomy as the earlier large cars.

REVIEW QUESTIONS 143

PROJECTS

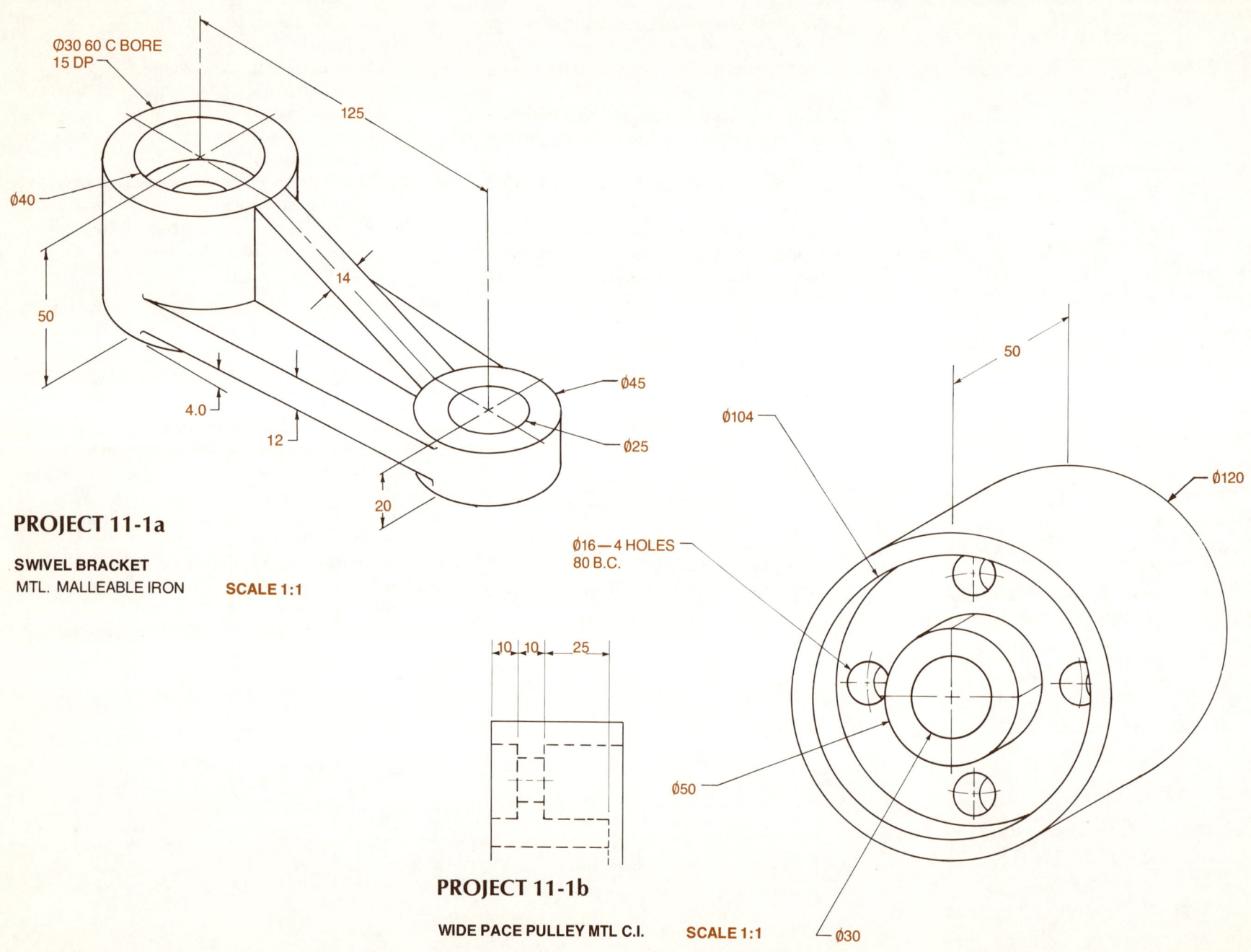

PROJECT 11-1a

SWIVEL BRACKET

MTL. MALLEABLE IRON   **SCALE 1:1**

PROJECT 11-1b

WIDE PACE PULLEY MTL C.I.   **SCALE 1:1**

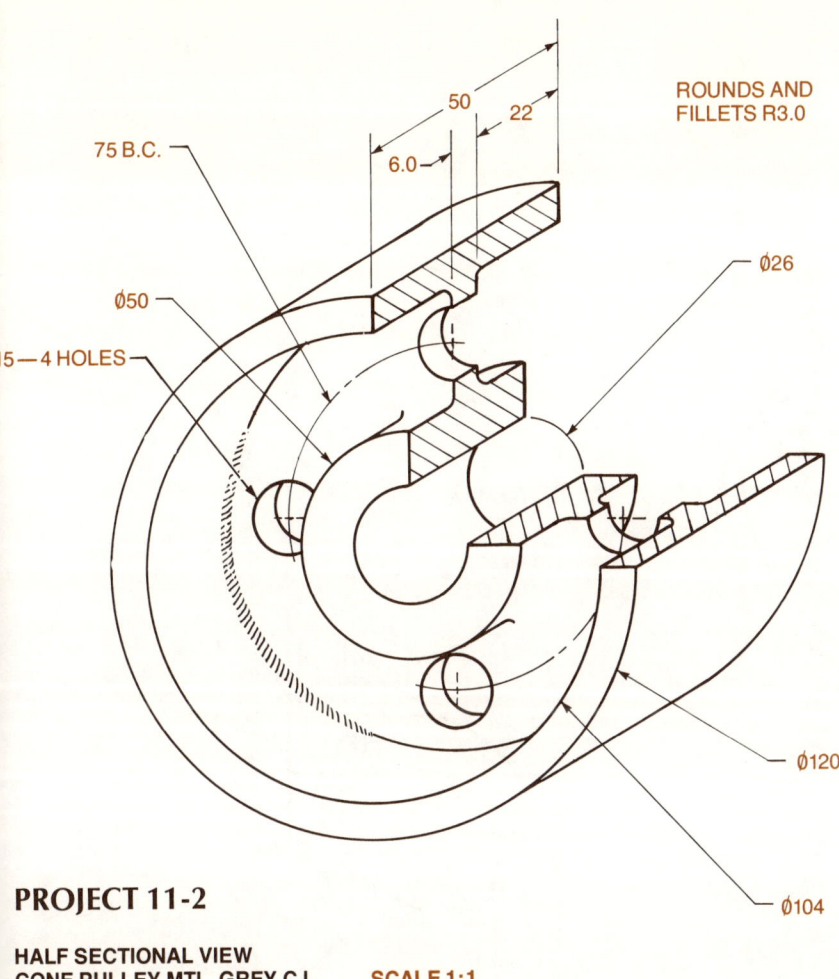

PROJECT 11-2

**HALF SECTIONAL VIEW
CONE PULLEY MTL. GREY C.I.** **SCALE 1:1**

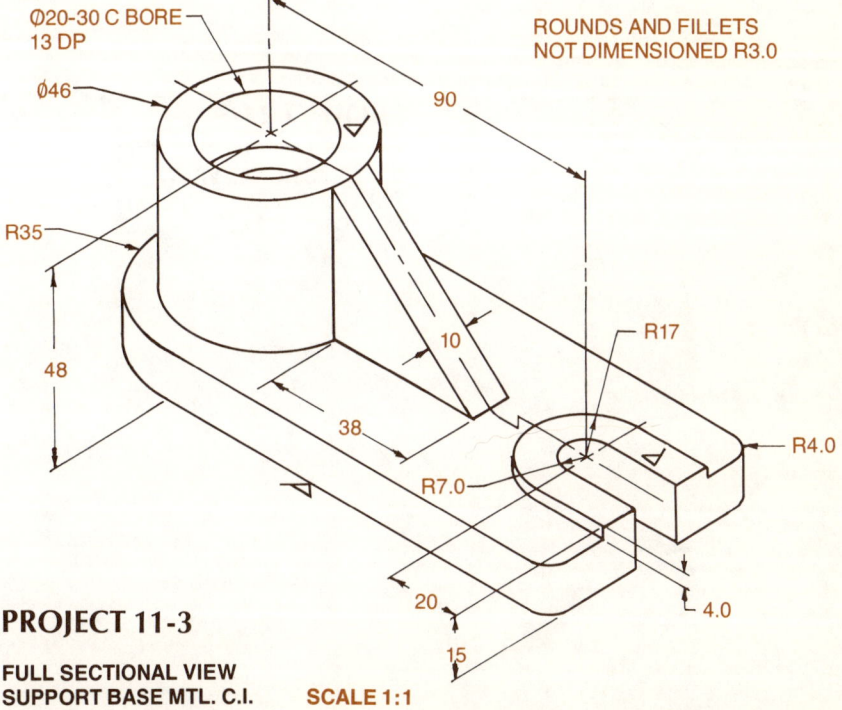

PROJECT 11-3

**FULL SECTIONAL VIEW
SUPPORT BASE MTL. C.I.** **SCALE 1:1**

PROJECTS 145

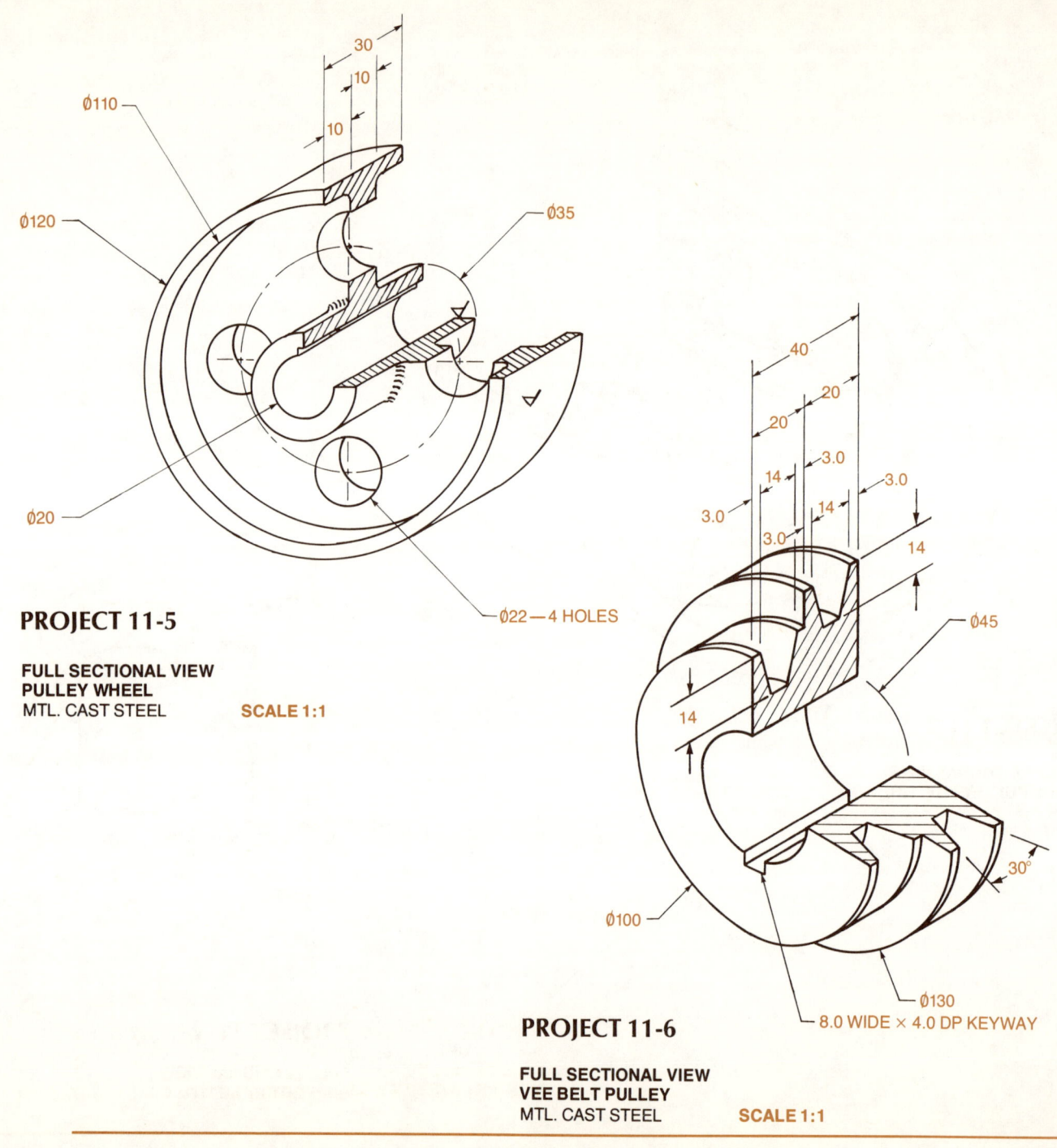

PROJECT 11-5

**FULL SECTIONAL VIEW
PULLEY WHEEL**
MTL. CAST STEEL SCALE 1:1

PROJECT 11-6

**FULL SECTIONAL VIEW
VEE BELT PULLEY**
MTL. CAST STEEL SCALE 1:1

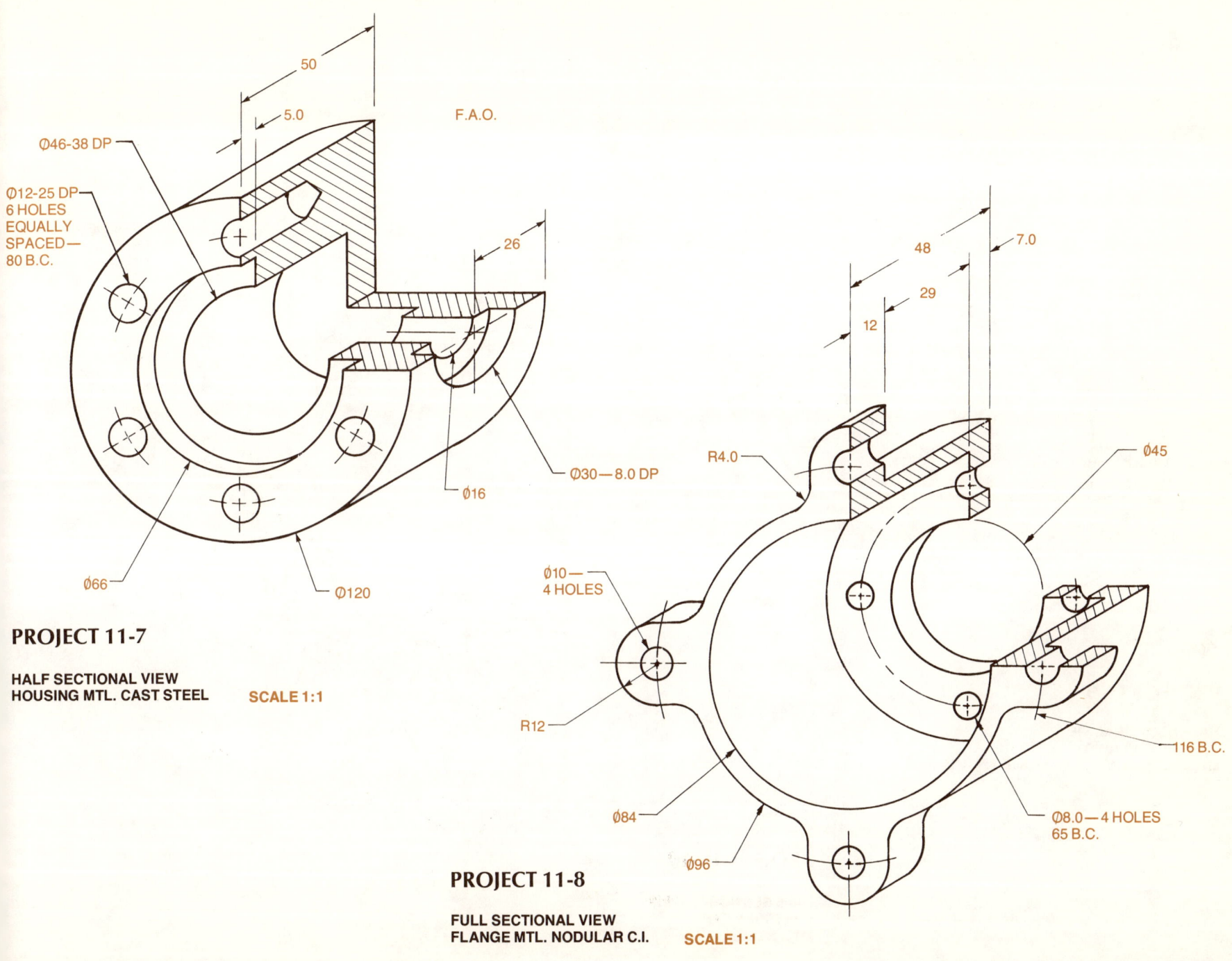

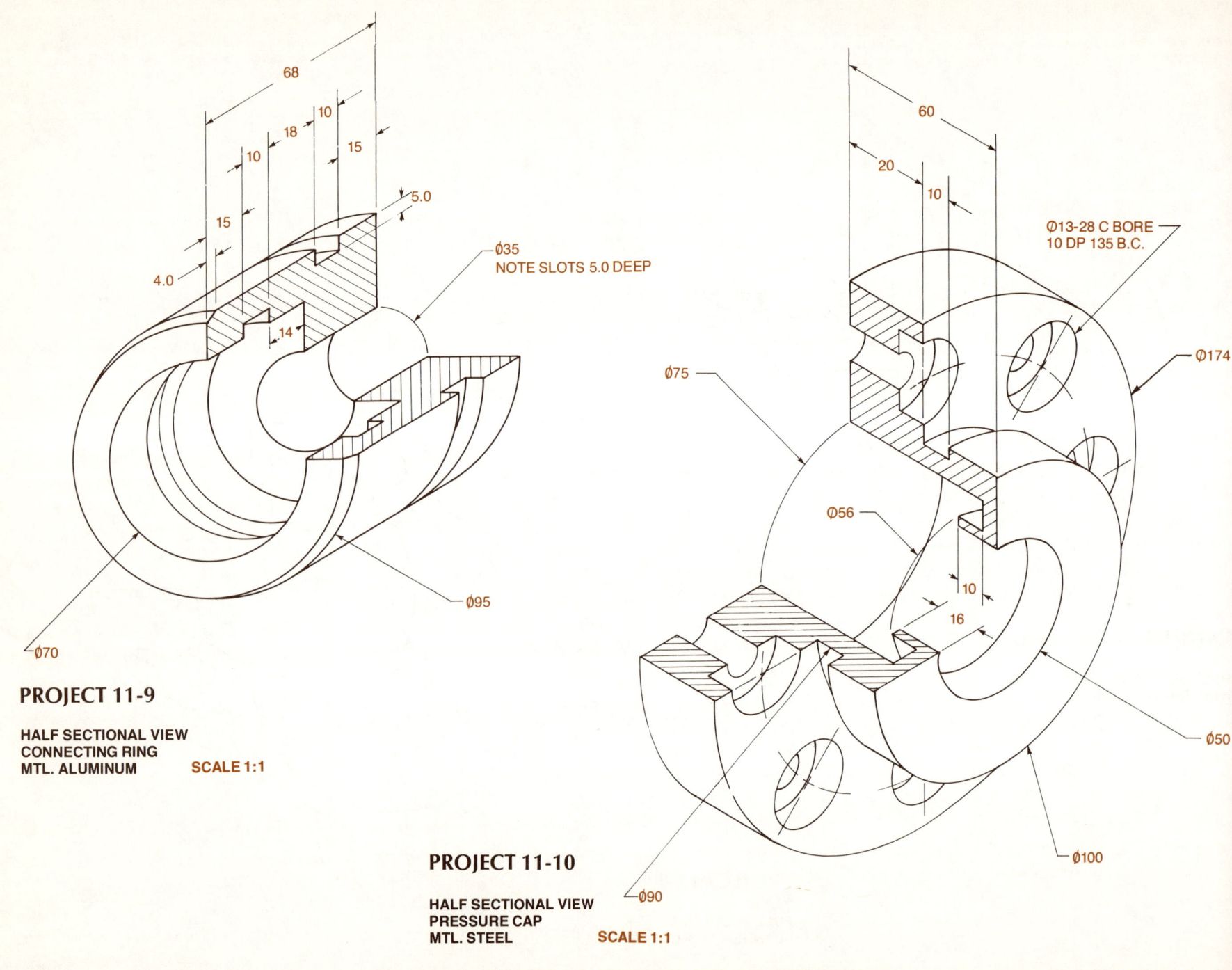

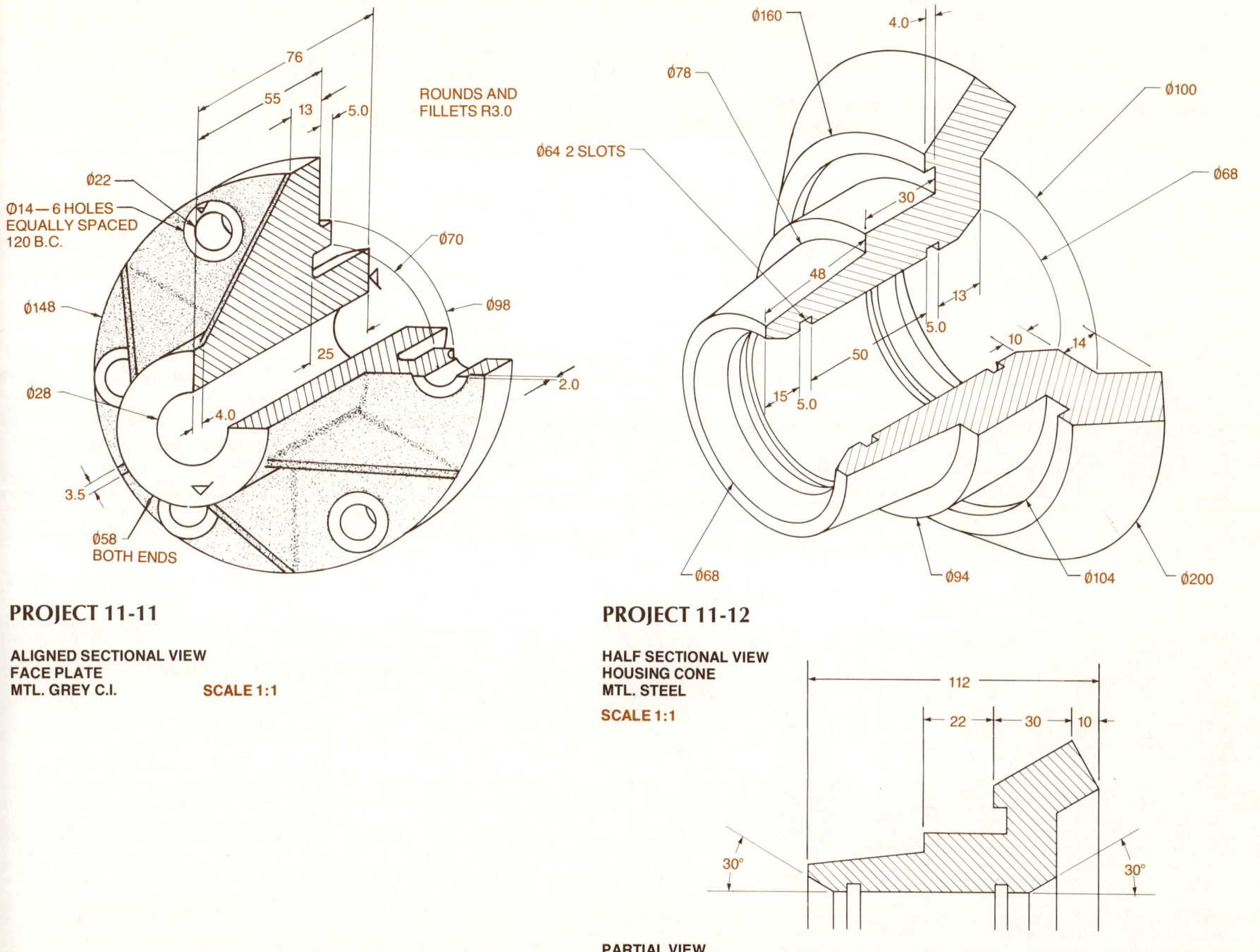

CHAPTER 12
SCREW THREADS AND SCREW THREAD FASTENERS

WORDS TO LEARN
transmit (trans-mít)
standard (stán-dard)
schematic (sche-mát-ic)
clearance (cléar-ance)

transmit—to pass along

standard—of an accepted normal quality, size, etc.

Screw threads are so much a part of our daily lives that we take them for granted. We use screw threads 1) to **transmit** power, 2) to adjust parts in relation to one another, and 3) to fasten parts together. With a little thought, you could easily give examples for each of the three uses of a screw thread.

Since there are actually over 500 000 different types of screw thread fasteners in **standard** use, we should be familiar with some of the most commonly used types.

The shape of the fastener or thread may vary but they all share common features and terms.

Pick up any item that has a screw thread. Examine it while we go over the terms used to describe its features. The thread appears as a ridge winding in a spiral called a **helix**.

Crest. The top of the ridge is called the crest of the thread.

Root. The bottom of the ridge is called the root of the thread.

Thread depth. The distance from the crest to the root is the thread depth.

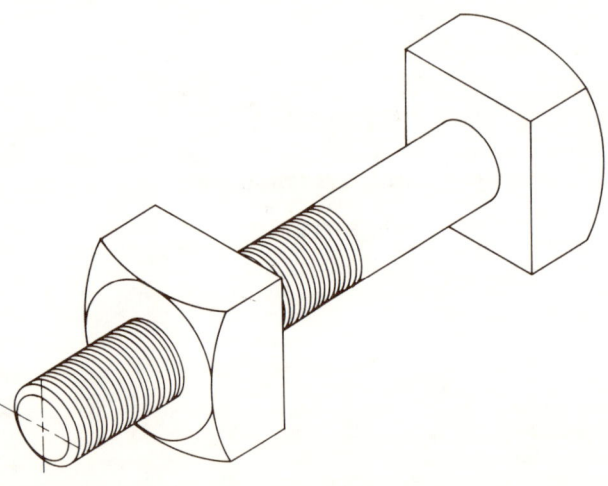

Fig. 12-1

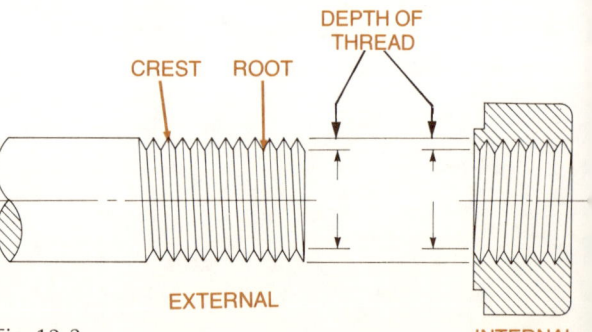

Fig. 12-2

150

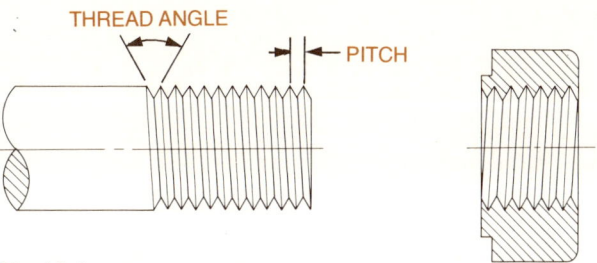

Fig. 12-3

Thread pitch. The distance between a point on a thread and a point in the same position on the thread next to it is called the pitch.

Thread angle. The angle formed by the crests of two adjacent threads and the root in between is called the thread angle.

Minor diameter and **Major diameter.** The root diameter, which is smaller than the crest diameter, is called the minor diameter. This allows us to call the crest diameter the major diameter.

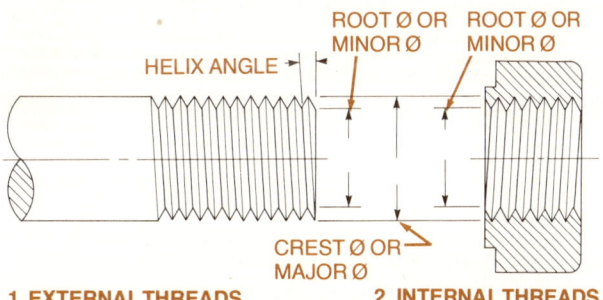

Fig. 12-4

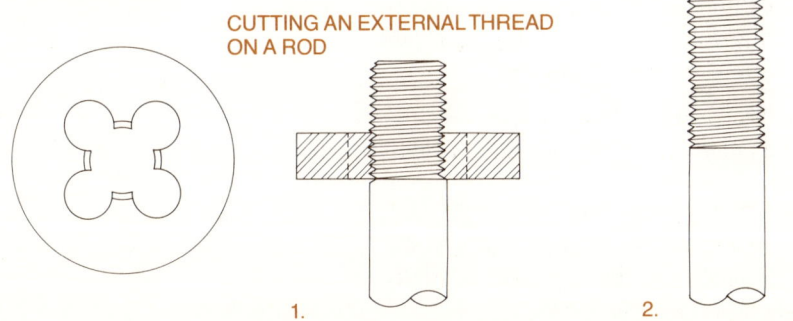

Fig. 12-5(a)

CUTTING AN INTERNAL THREAD
Fig. 12-5(b)

External and **Internal Threads.** As you might guess, the external thread is one that has been cut on the outside of a cylinder such as a bolt or rod. The internal thread is a thread that has been cut on the inside of a cylindrical hole, such as a nut.

Right and **Left Hand Threads.** Again, this explains itself. A right hand thread on a bolt will allow the bolt to screw into a matching screw thread of a nut when turned to the right. A left hand thread on a bolt will allow the bolt to screw into a matching screw thread of a nut when turned to the left.

Coarse and **Fine Threads.** Metric threads are available in two series; course pitch and fine pitch. Two bolts may appear the same because they have the same major diameter and the same length of thread but will still be different. The fine pitch series has more threads on the bolt than the bolt of a coarse series. To save you time and effort, we have provided sizes for the standard parts required in the projects of this book.

Metric Screw Thread Dimensions

If a drafter were to label a screw thread as M 20 × 2.0, what would that mean? The capital letter M shows that the thread is metric. The first number, in this example

MAJOR DIAMETER	FINE PITCH	COARSE PITCH
8.0	1.25	1.0
10	1.25, 1.0, 0.75	1.25
11	1.0, 0.75	1.5
12	1.5, 1.25, 1.0	1.75
14	1.5, 1.25, 1.0	2.0
15	1.0	1.5
16	1.5, 1.0	2.0
17	1.0	1.5
18	2.0, 1.5, 1.0	2.5
20	2.0, 1.5, 1.0	2.5
30	3.0, 2.0, 1.5	3.5
40	4.0, 3.0, 2.0	4.5
48	3.0	5.0

SOME EXAMPLES OF METRIC SCREW THREAD MAJOR DIAMETERS AND THEIR PITCH SIZES.
NOTE: ONLY THE FINE PITCH MAY HAVE MORE THAN ONE PITCH SIZE

Fig. 12-6 *Table of thread proportions*

20, is the size of the major diameter in millimetres. The second number, in this example 2.0, gives the required pitch size. If the thread had to be a left hand thread, the letters LH would have been added.

Steps in Drawing a Screw Thread—Pictorial Method

There are several methods of representing a screw thread. The pictorial method looks most like an actual thread but takes longer to draw. The **schematic** method and the simplified method take much less time and give the reader the same information. You can use the table of thread proportions to find the pitch and depth sizes for a variety of major diameters.

1. Draw two parallel lines to represent the major diameter of the thread. Add the centre line.
2. On the bottom line, from the right end, mark off the pitch distance. Repeat the pitch distance on the line for as many threads as you wish to draw.

schematic—in the form of a diagram (not meant to represent the object exactly, but to give the important features)

PICTORIAL METHOD OF DRAWING SCREW THREADS

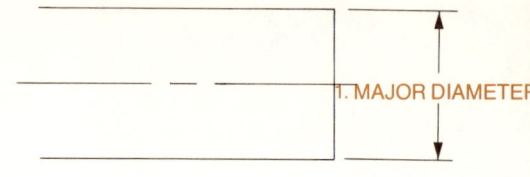

Fig. 12-7(a)

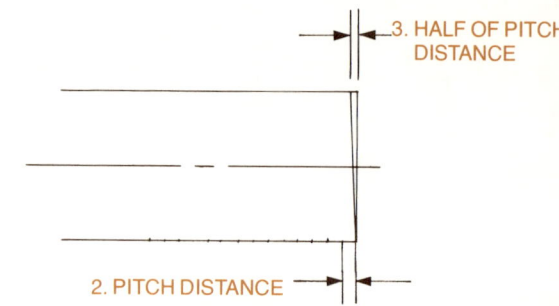

Fig. 12-7(b)

3. On the top line from the right end, mark off a distance equal to one-half of the pitch length.
4. Join this point to the right end of the bottom line. This is the crest line of the thread.

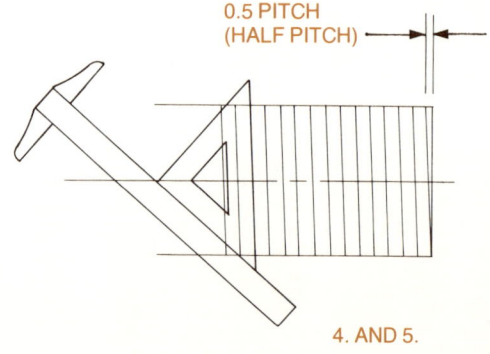

Fig. 12-7(c)

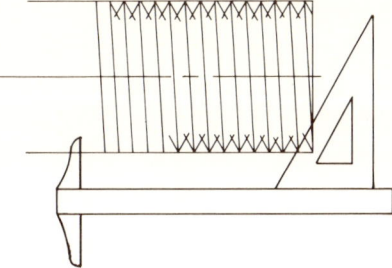

Fig. 12-8

5. From each point on the bottom line, draw the remaining crest lines parallel to the first crest line.

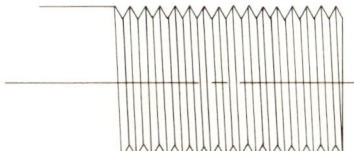

Fig. 12-9

6. For each thread, draw the thread angle which is contained between the crest lines. The thread angle is 60°.
7. Draw a line joining the top root to the bottom root between each crest.

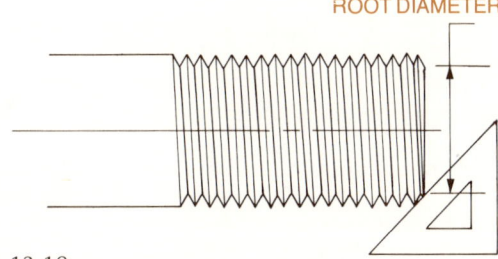

Fig. 12-10

8. From the minor diameter, you can construct the 45° chamfer. When you complete the finished linework, draw the root lines thicker than the crest lines.

Steps in Drawing a Screw Thread— Schematic Method

This method takes less time to draw yet still gives the same information.

1. Draw two parallel lines to represent the major diameter of the thread. Add the centre line.

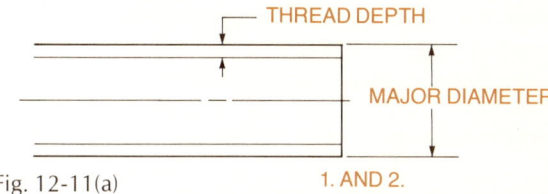

Fig. 12-11(a)   1. AND 2.

2. Use the table of thread proportions to find the depth of thread needed and add two very light parallel lines to the drawing to represent the thread depth.
3. Draw a 45° chamfer at the end of the screw.

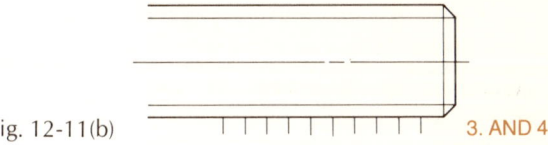

Fig. 12-11(b)   3. AND 4.

4. From the thread proportions table, choose the correct pitch distance. Mark off the pitch distances starting from the chamfer.
5. Draw light vertical lines from each pitch point to represent the crest lines.

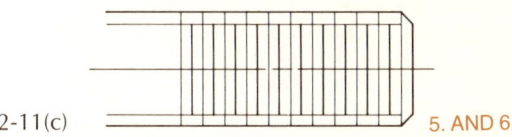

Fig. 12-11(c)   5. AND 6.

6. Use the scale to find the mid-point between the crest lines. Draw light vertical lines from these points to represent the root lines. When finished, the crest lines should appear as thin dark lines. The root lines should appear as object lines, thick and dark. Erase the light thread depth lines.

Steps in Drawing a Screw Thread— Simplified Method

This method, as you might expect, is the most popular method of representing screw threads. It takes the least amount of time to draw yet gives all the necessary information.

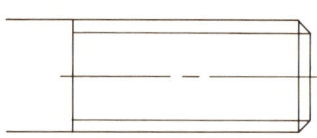

Fig. 12-12

Fig. 12-14 Bolt and nut

1. Draw two parallel lines to represent the major diameter of the thread. Add the centre line.
2. Use the table of thread proportions to find the depth of thread needed and add two light parallel lines to the drawing to represent the thread depth.
3. Draw a 45° chamfer at the end of the screw thread.
4. Draw a vertical line to represent the end of the thread.

clearance—the amount of space between one object and another

FASTENERS

Now that you can draw screw threads, let us examine how they can be applied.

Bolts and Nuts. Parts can be fastened together by a bolt and a nut. The bolt passes through a **clearance** hole in each part and the nut is turned onto the bolt to hold the parts together. Bolts and nuts are available in hexagonal and square styles. They allow parts to be fastened together without using threaded holes. (Fig. 12-14).

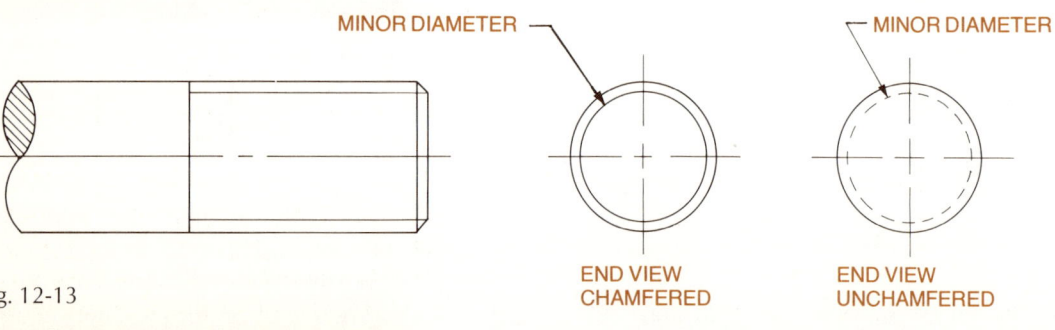

Fig. 12-13

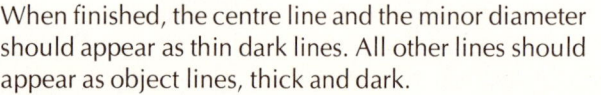

When finished, the centre line and the minor diameter should appear as thin dark lines. All other lines should appear as object lines, thick and dark.

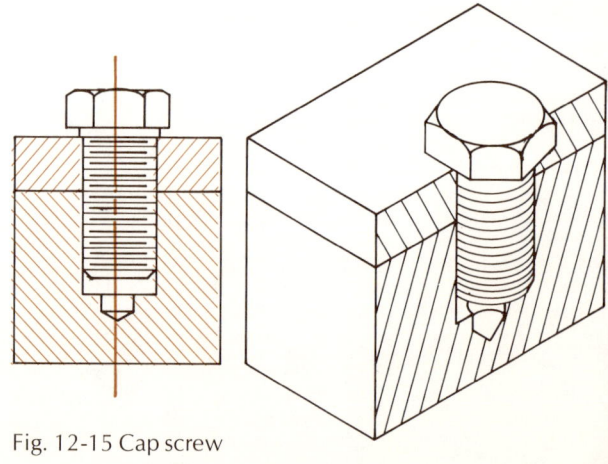

Fig. 12-15 Cap screw

154   SCREW THREADS AND SCREW THREAD FASTENERS

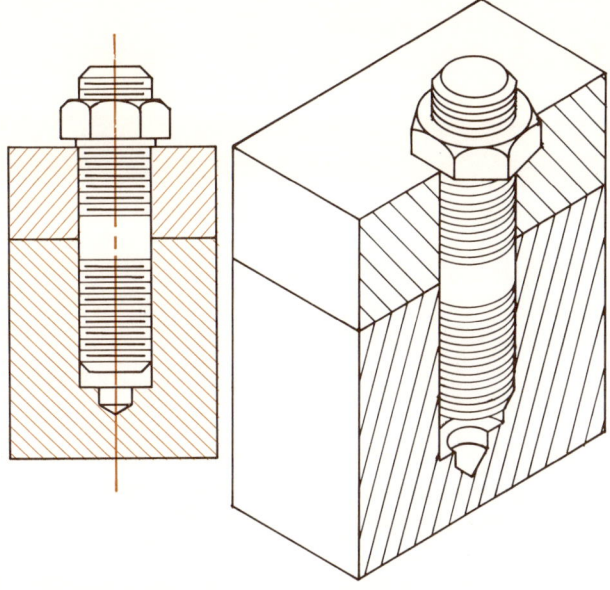
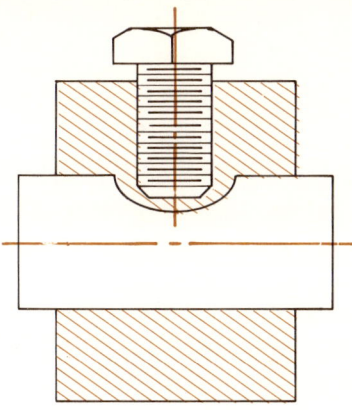

Fig. 12-17 Set screw

Fig. 12-16 Stud and nut

Cap screws. In Fig. 12-15 two parts are fastened together using a cap screw. The cap screw passes through the clearance hole of the one part and turns into the threaded hole of the second part to hold the two parts together. The cap screw is available in a variety of styles so that they may be turned by using a screwdriver or wrench. Only one hole need be threaded. This eliminates the need for a nut.

Studs. A stud is a rod that has rolled threads at both ends. The stud passes through the clearance hole of one part and turns into the threaded hole of the second part. The parts are held together by turning a nut onto the other end of the stud. The top part can be released by removing the nut, and that stud serves as a guide when parts are to be assembled. (Fig. 12-16).

Set screws. Set screws lock parts together. In Fig. 12-17 the set screw turns through the tapped hole of the top part into the slot of the second part. Set screws are available in a variety of point styles. Only the square head set screw has a head; the other types do not.

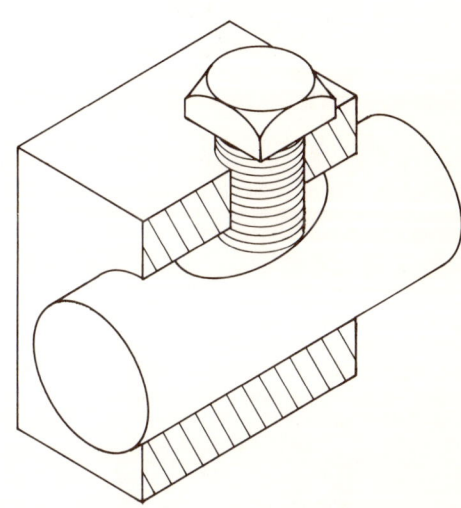

Fig. 12-18

Machine Screws. These very common fasteners are really small bolts. The body of the machine screw is threaded over its entire length. Machine screws are used for light fastening duties with or without a nut.

There are other types of fasteners available, but these are some of the most common. Now to help you in drawing fasteners, we have included detailed steps for two of them.

FASTENERS 155

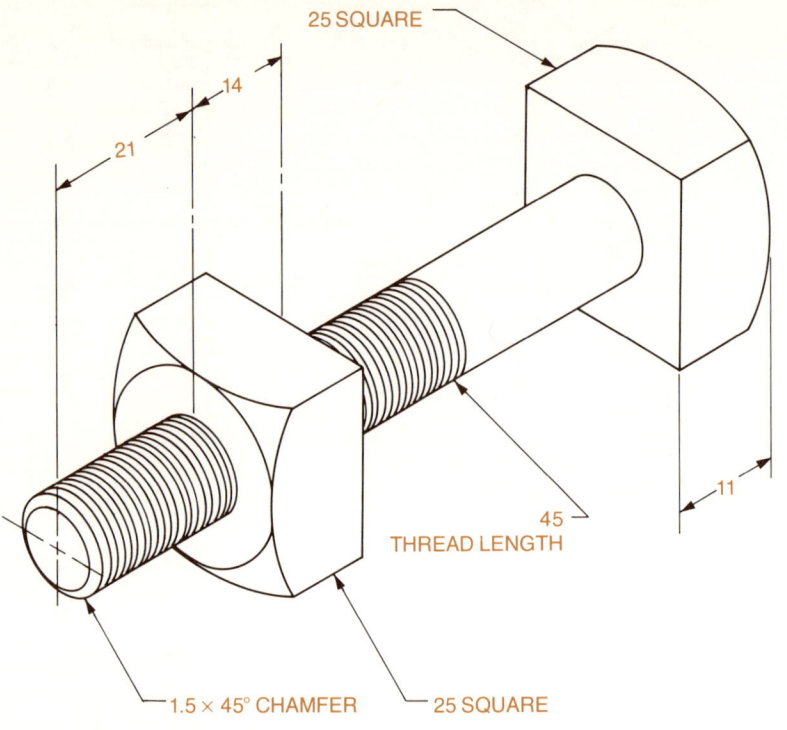

Fig. 12-19

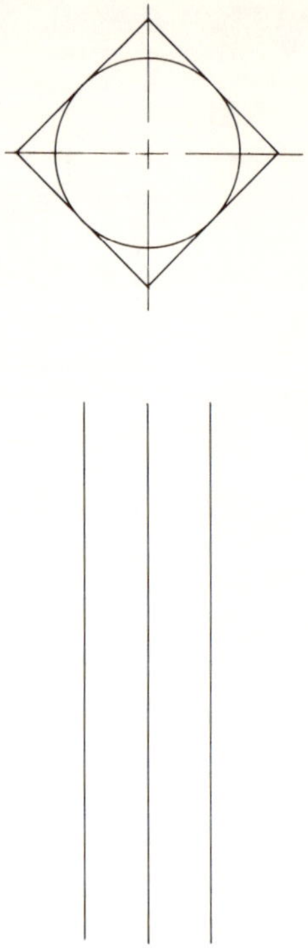

Fig. 12-22 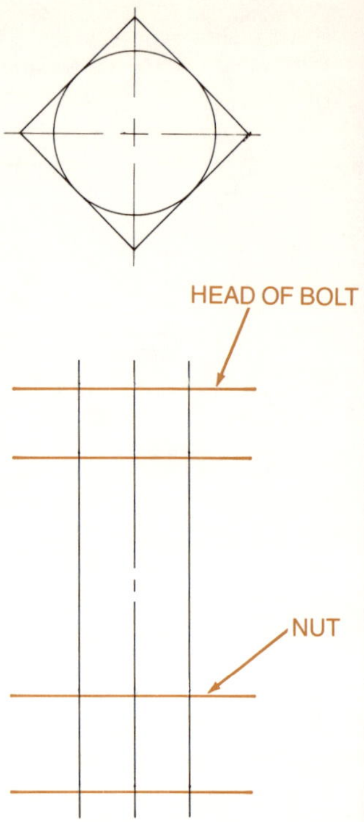   Fig. 12-21

Steps in Drawing a Square Head Bolt & Nut

Using the dimensions in Fig. 12-19,
1. Draw the top view of the square head of the bolt across the corners as shown in Fig. 12-20.

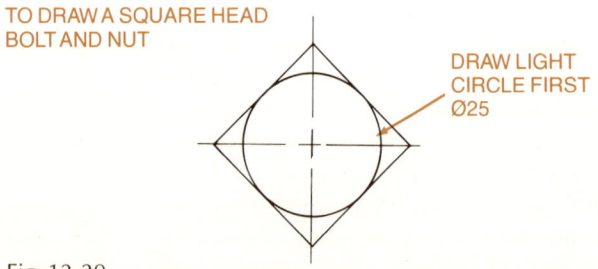

Fig. 12-20

2. Draw a vertical centre line and the major diameter lines of the bolt in the front view position.
3. Draw two horizontal lines for the head of the bolt. Draw two horizontal lines for the nut wherever you want to position the nut on the bolt. (Look at Fig. 12-19 again.)
4. Project the corners of the bolt head in the top view to the head and nut in the front view.
5. Use the 30°–60° set square as shown to find the centre for the arcs.
6. Place the compass point in each centre and set the compass so that the arcs are tangent to the horizontal lines as shown for the bolt and nut.

156 SCREW THREADS AND SCREW THREAD FASTENERS

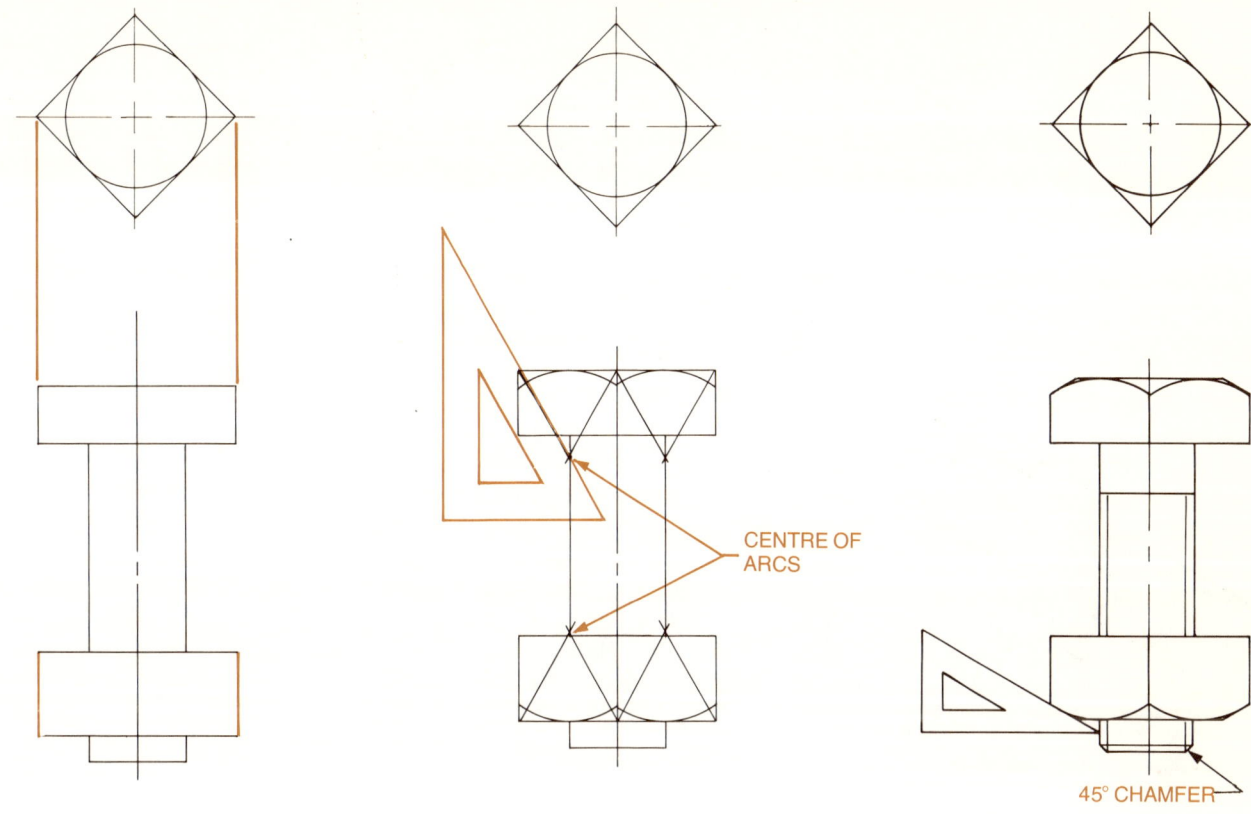

Fig. 12-23

Fig. 12-24

Fig. 12-25

7. Use the 30°—60° set square to bevel the corners tangent to the arcs.

8. Draw the screw thread on the bolt. Use the simplified method. Chamfer the end of the bolt.

FASTENERS 157

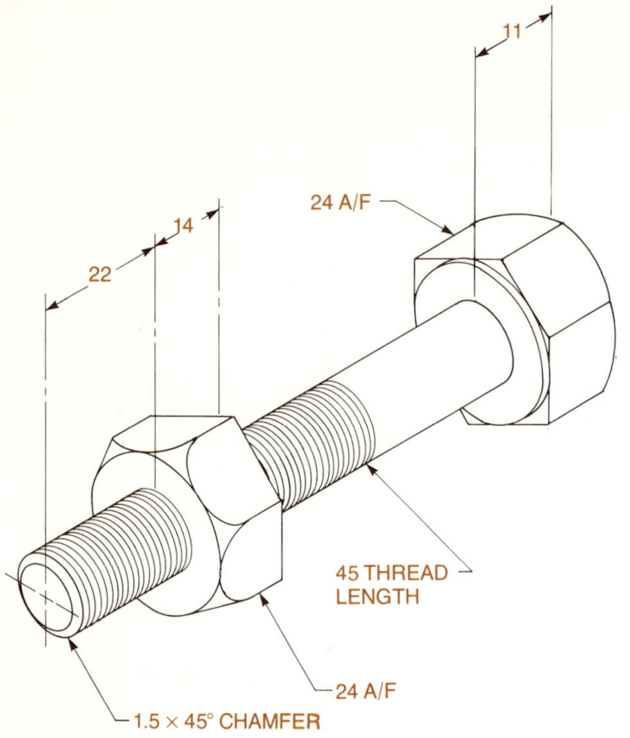

Fig. 12-26

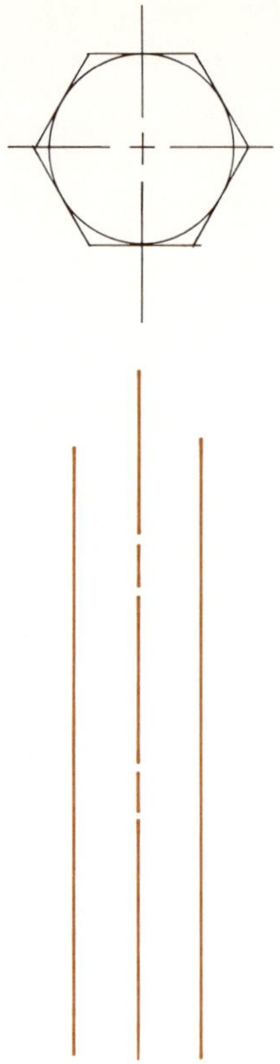

Fig. 12-28 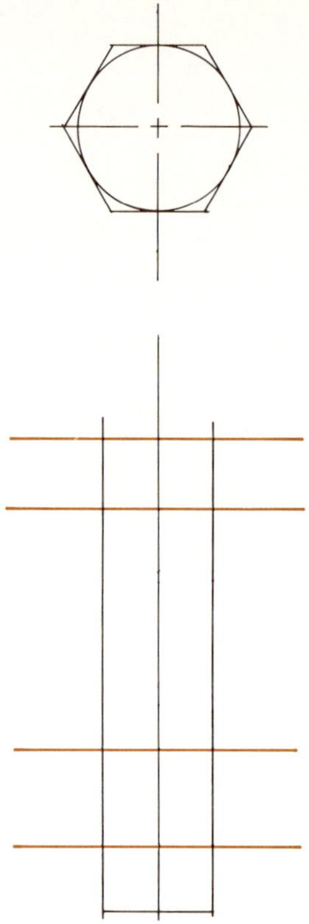   Fig. 12-29 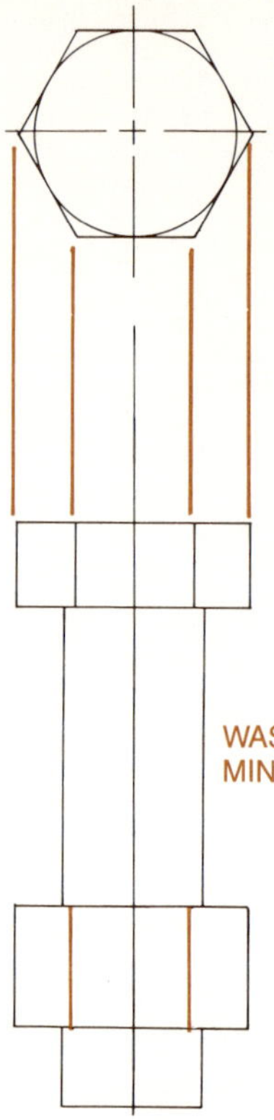   Fig. 12-30 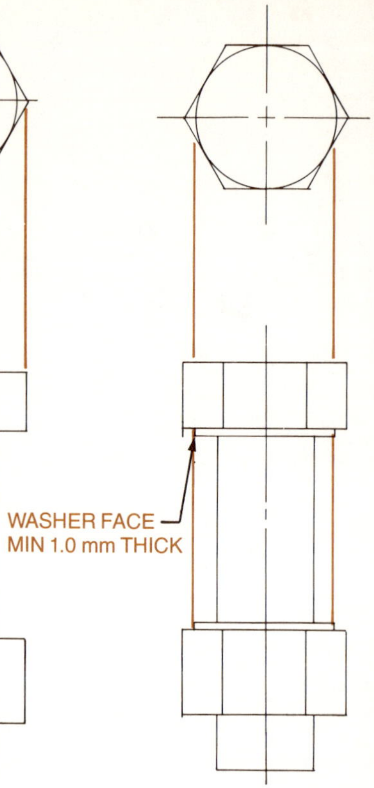   Fig. 12-31

WASHER FACE MIN 1.0 mm THICK

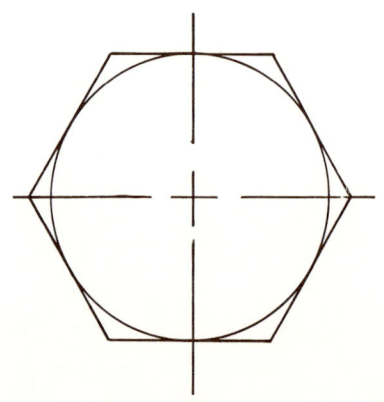

Fig. 12-27

Steps in Drawing a Hexagon Bolt & Nut

Note: The hexagon nut and bolt head have an added feature; a washer face. The washer face provides a smooth surface so that the head of the bolt and the nut will sit flush against the parts they are fastening.

Using the dimensions in Fig. 12-26,
1. Draw the top view of the hexagonal head of the bolt across the corners as shown in Fig. 12-27.

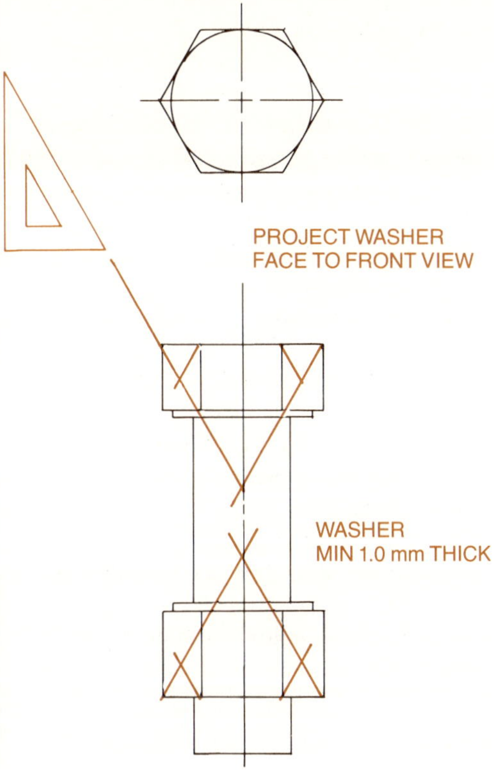

PROJECT WASHER
FACE TO FRONT VIEW

WASHER
MIN 1.0 mm THICK

Fig. 12-32

Fig. 12-33

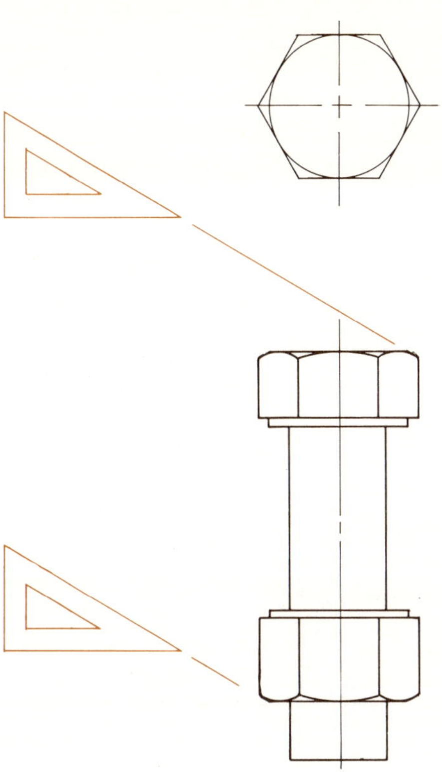

Fig. 12-34

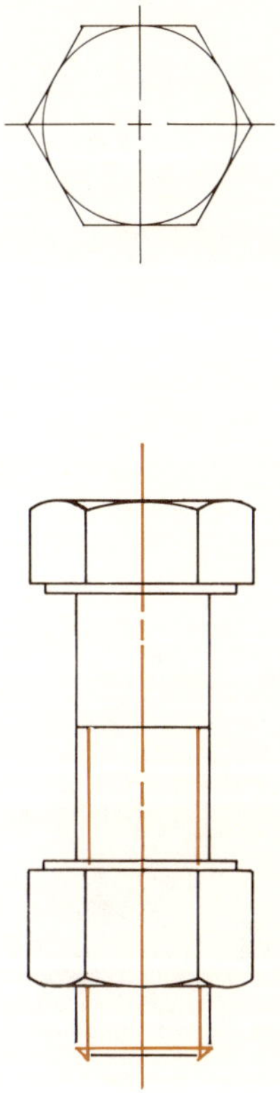

Fig. 12-35

2. Draw a vertical centre line and the major diameter lines in the front view position.
3. Draw the two horizontal lines of the head of the bolt. Draw two horizontal lines for the nut wherever you want to position the nut on the bolt. (Look at Fig. 12-26 again.)
4. Project the corners of the bolt head in the top view to the bolt head and nut in the front view.
5. Project the diameter of the washer face in the top view to the bolt head and nut in the front view. The washer face is shown as 1.0 mm thick.

6. Use the 30°—60° set square as shown to find the centre for the arcs.
7. Place the compass point in each centre and set the compass so that the arcs are tangent to the lines as shown for the bolt and nut.
8. Use the 30°—60° set square to bevel the corners tangent to the arcs.
9. Draw the screw thread on the bolt. Use the simplified method. Chamfer the end of the bolt.

FASTENERS 159

POINTS TO REMEMBER

- Parts can be put together or taken apart easily when fastened with screw thread fasteners.
- Screw threads make it possible to transmit power from the source to where it is needed. (A good example is the screw in a vise. The force created by turning the handle is passed on by the screw to the jaw of the vise.)
- Pictorial thread representation takes more time to draw than the schematic or simplified method.
- The pitch of a screw thread is the distance from any point on a thread to a point in the same position on the next thread.
- Dimensions for screw threads are listed in tables of thread proportions.
- A tapped hole is a threaded hole.
- Clearance holes allow parts to pass into or through them.
- Bolts do not require tapped holes.
- Cap screws do not require nuts.
- Studs can align parts together as well as be used as fasteners together with nuts.
- Set screws lock parts together when they are positioned in a slot in one of the parts.

QUESTIONS TO ANSWER

1. List the three main uses of screw threads. Give an example for each.
2. In a simple sentence explain what is meant by the following terms:
   (a) crest   (d) thread pitch
   (b) root   (e) major diameter
   (c) depth of thread (f) minor diameter
3. Sketch neatly an example of each of the three methods of representing a screw thread on a rod. Label each example with the following information:
   (a) major diameter
   (b) minor diameter
   (c) depth of thread
4. Bolts and nuts as well as cap screws are used to fasten parts together. How do they differ from each other? Give two applications that you know of for each of the two types of fasteners.
5. Define the following terms:
   (a) stud (b) set screw (c) machine screw (d) clearance hole.
6. Completely explain the thread designation M 16 × 2.0.

REPLACE THE X'S WITH THE CORRECT TERM

1. XXXXXXXX parts are parts that are made in quantity and are alike in every way.
2. XXXXXXXX holes are made slightly larger than the parts that are to pass into or through them.
3. XXXXXXXX drawings use outlines to give a general impression of items.
4. The drive shaft in a car XXXXXXXX turning power from the engine to the wheels.

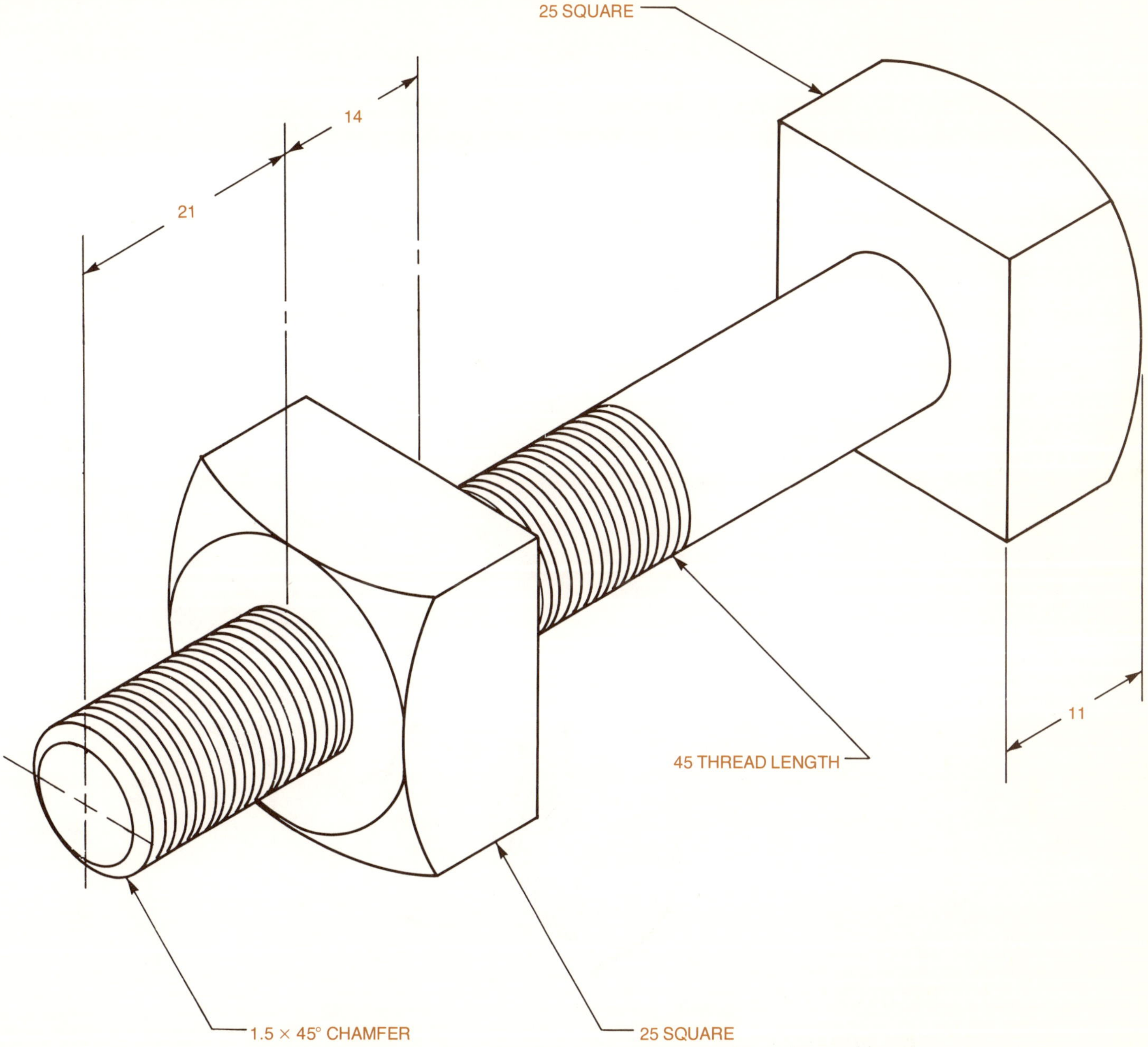

PROJECTS

PROJECT 12-1

REGULAR SQUARE HEAD BOLT AND NUT
M-16 × 2.0-70 LG   **SCALE 1:1**

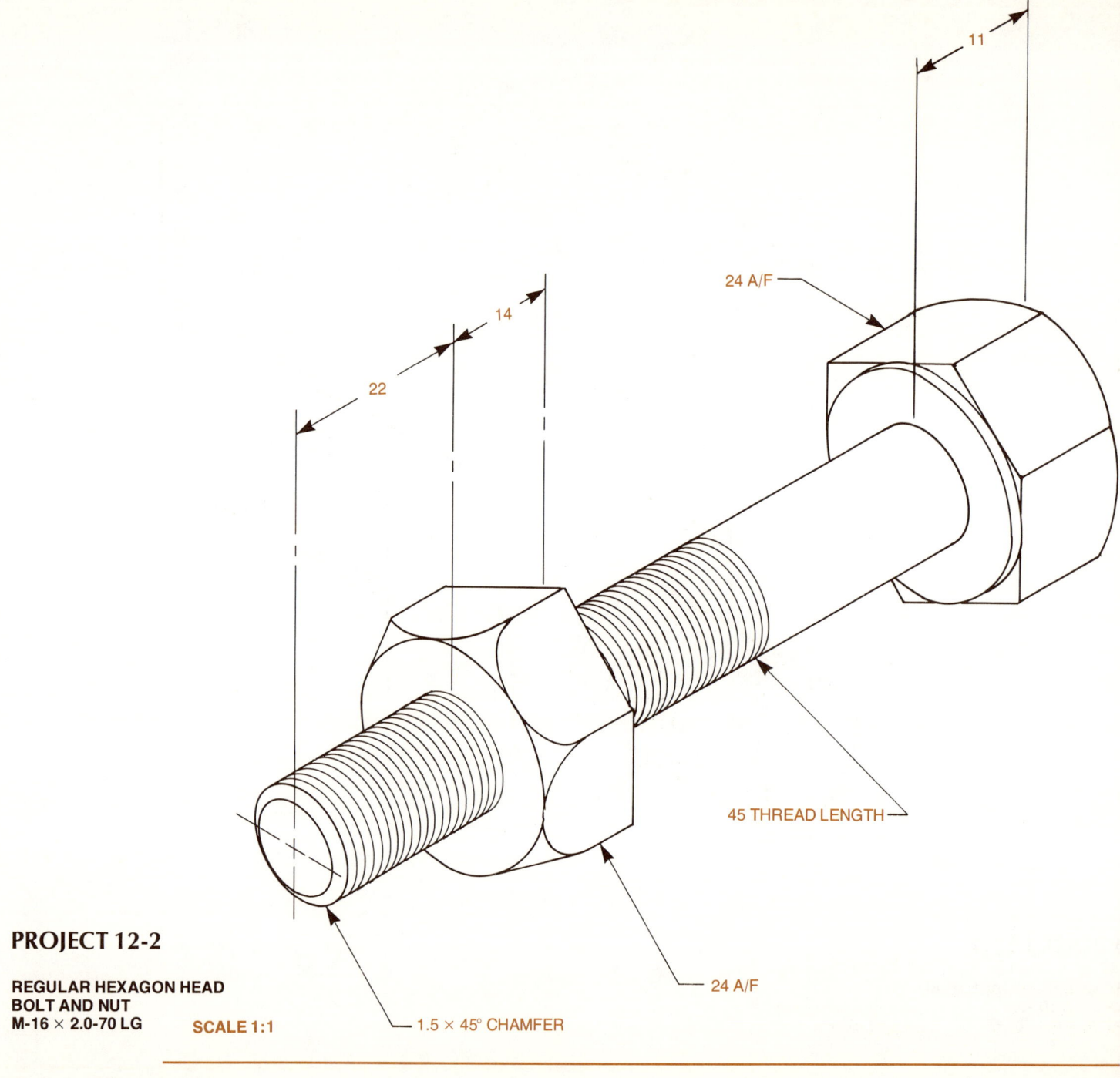

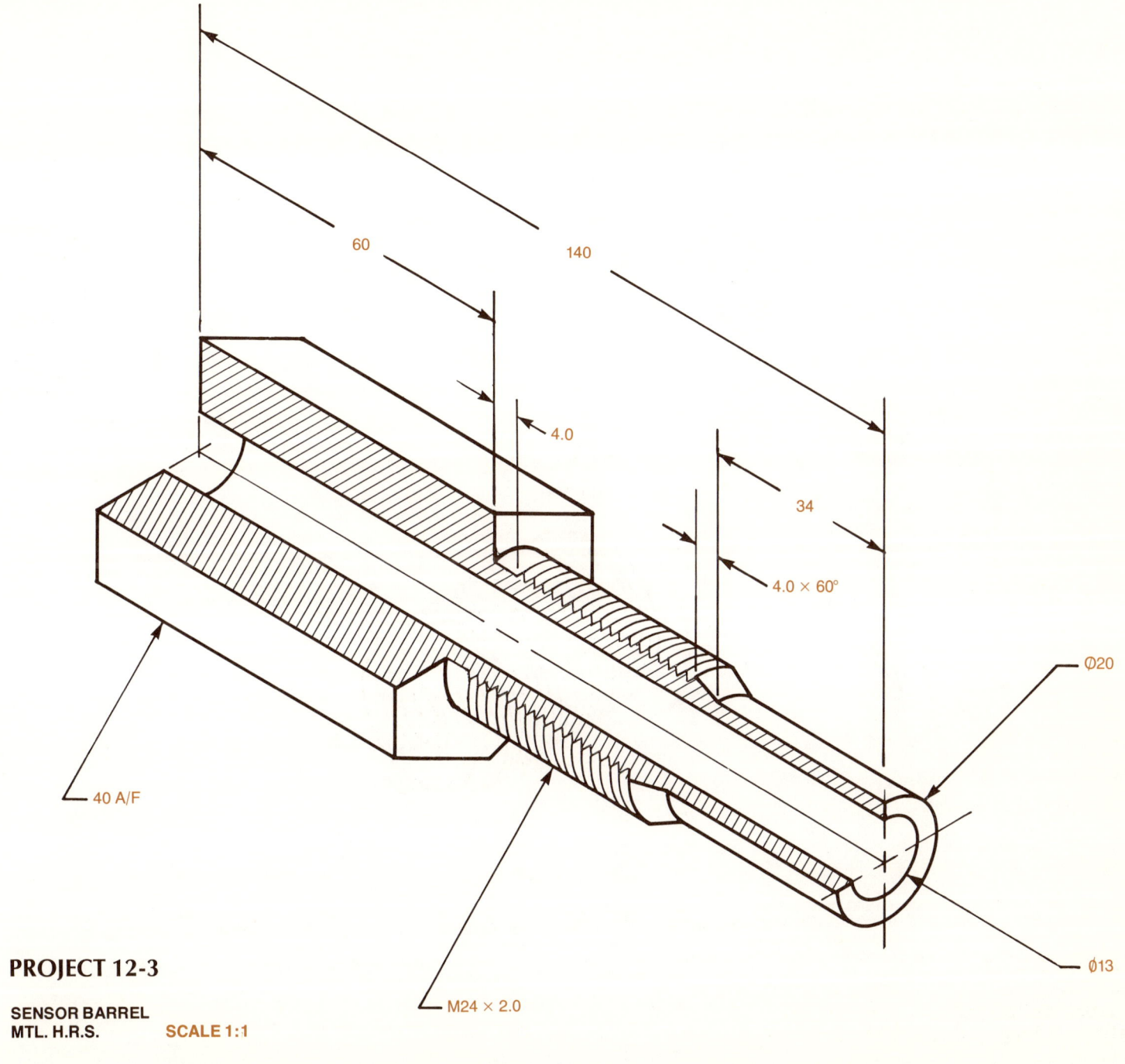

PROJECT 12-3

SENSOR BARREL
MTL. H.R.S. **SCALE 1:1**

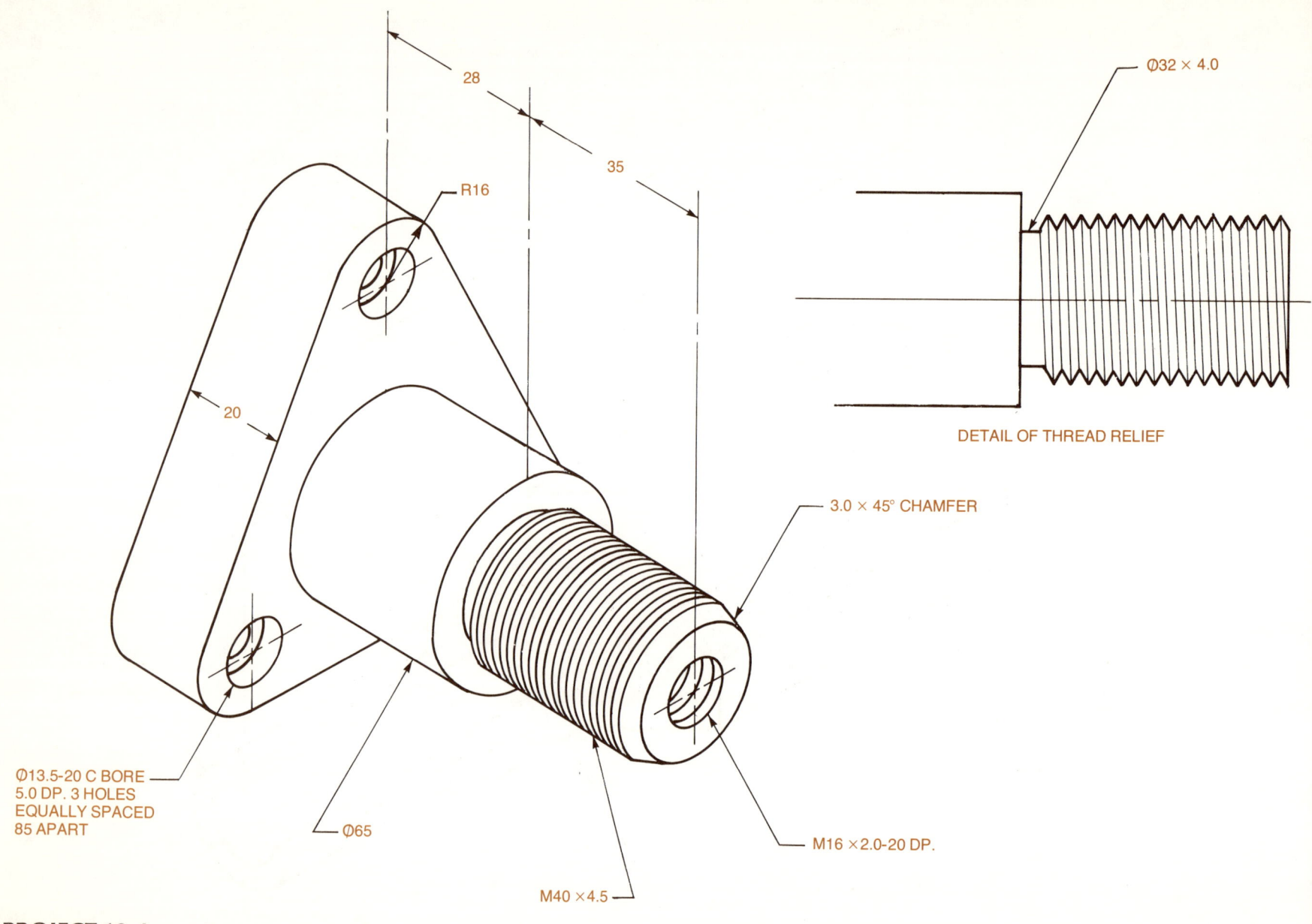

DETAIL OF THREAD RELIEF

PROJECT 12-4

CONNECTING BRACKET
MTL. S.A.E. 1006   **SCALE 1:1**

164   SCREW THREADS AND SCREW THREAD FASTENERS

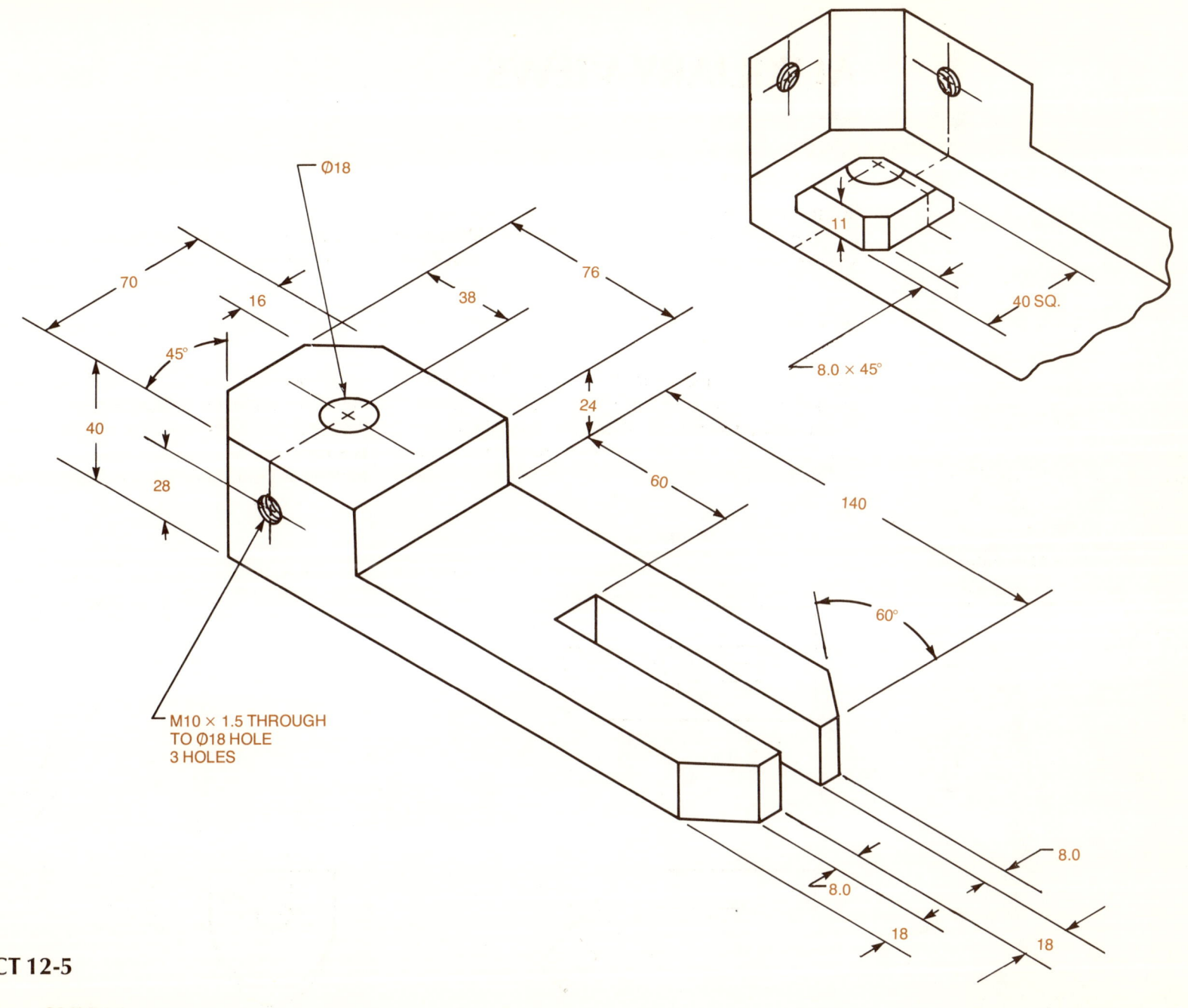

PROJECT 12-5

TRIP KEY **SCALE 1:1**

CHAPTER 13
AUXILIARY VIEWS

WORDS TO LEARN

incline (ín-cline)
auxiliary (aux-íl-ia-ry)
analyze (án-a-lyze)
distorted (dis-tór-ted)
elliptical (el-líp-ti-cal)
convenient (con-vén-ient)

One day you'll find yourself looking at the orthographic views you have just drawn and thinking that something isn't quite right. It's not very hard to spot the problem. Chances are that the object has one or more **inclined** surfaces.

Inclined surfaces are not accurately described by any of the normal orthographic views. In these views the surface appears **distorted**. An extra view called an **auxiliary** view is needed. It is merely another way of looking at the inclined surface. From this position our

inclined—put or drawn on an angle

distorted—not in its true shape

auxiliary—additional, one that gives help

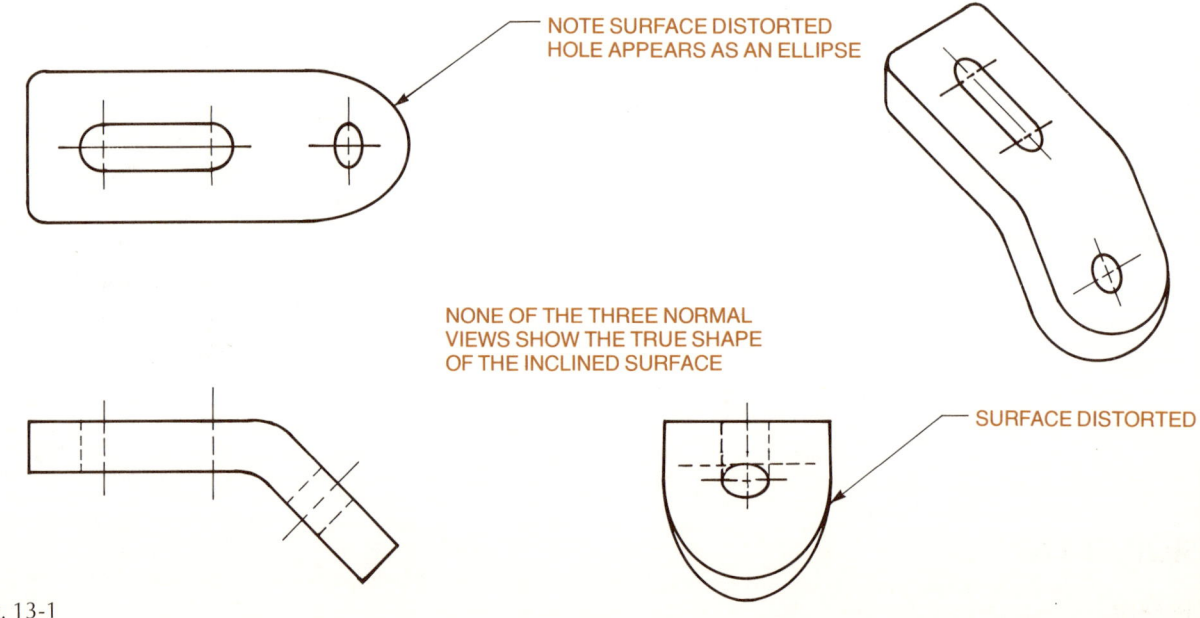

Fig. 13-1

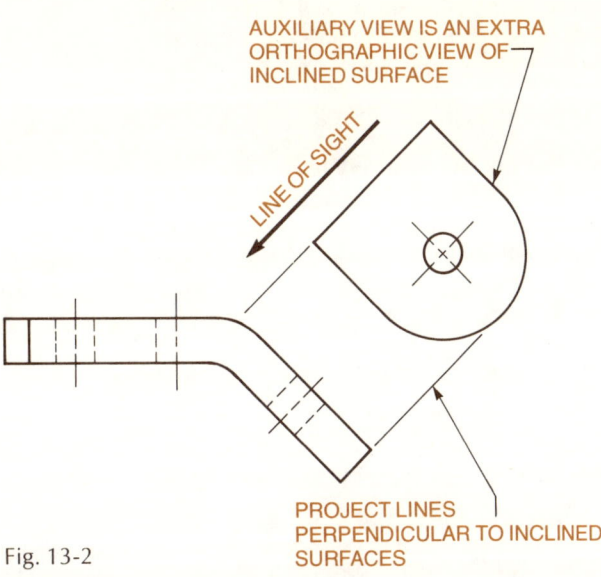

Fig. 13-2

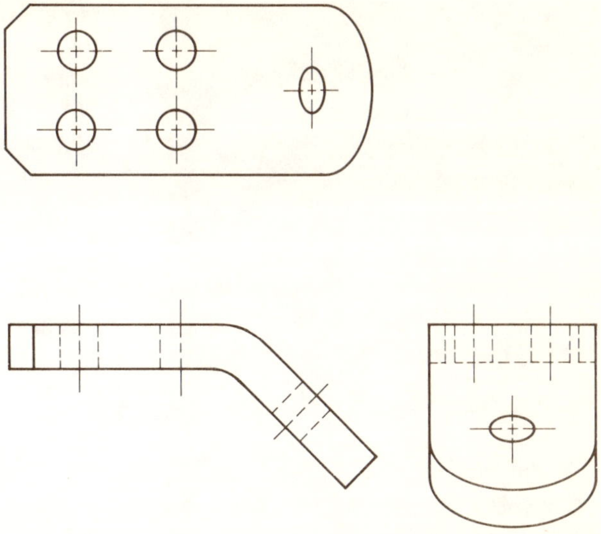

AUXILIARY VIEW IS AN EXTRA ORTHOGRAPHIC VIEW OF INCLINED SURFACE

LINE OF SIGHT

PROJECT LINES PERPENDICULAR TO INCLINED SURFACES

Fig. 13-3

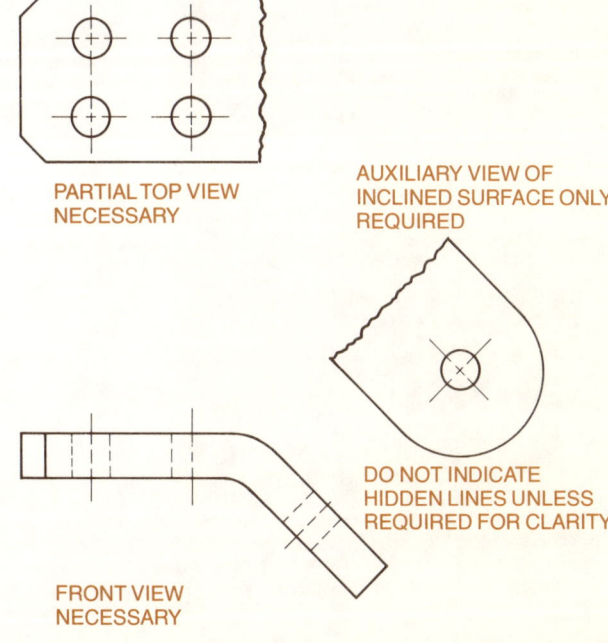

PARTIAL TOP VIEW NECESSARY

AUXILIARY VIEW OF INCLINED SURFACE ONLY REQUIRED

DO NOT INDICATE HIDDEN LINES UNLESS REQUIRED FOR CLARITY

FRONT VIEW NECESSARY

Fig. 13-4

elliptical—having the shape of an ellipse (egg-shaped or oval)

analyze—to separate into parts so as to understand the whole

line of sight is perpendicular (at right angles or 90°) to the inclined surface. Only then can we see the true shape of the inclined surface accurately. Let's look at an object that would call for an auxiliary view.

The top view is partly useful. The exact size of the four holes and their true position is accurately described. But as you can see, in this view the inclined surface appears distorted. The surface appears shortened and the holes look **elliptical** or oval. The right side view adds very little of value. The hole again appears as an ellipse and there are far too many hidden lines that only make the view harder to read. This view can be eliminated.

Let's **analyze** the situation further. First, we need the front view. It is true and accurate. Note that the inclined surface appears as an edge. Secondly, since only part of the top view is correct, we can keep that part and imagine the distorted part to be broken away and unnecessary. Now we are ready to deal with that part of the object that requires extra help, the inclined surface. You're right, an auxiliary view will show the inclined surface accurately and completely.

AUXILIARY VIEWS

Note. To save valuable time and for the sake of clarity the auxiliary view need only show that part of the object which is inclined. Therefore, a break line can be drawn to limit the partial view. The rest of the view is unnecessary.

Steps in Drawing an Auxiliary View

Now it's time to follow the steps in drawing an auxiliary view. They are really very simple, logical and easy to learn.

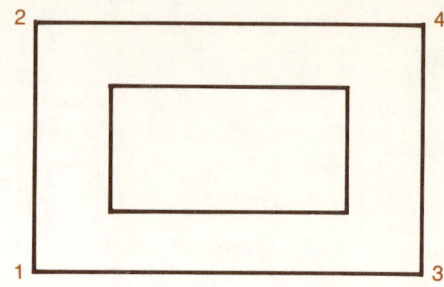

Fig. 13-7(a)

2. Draw the top view.

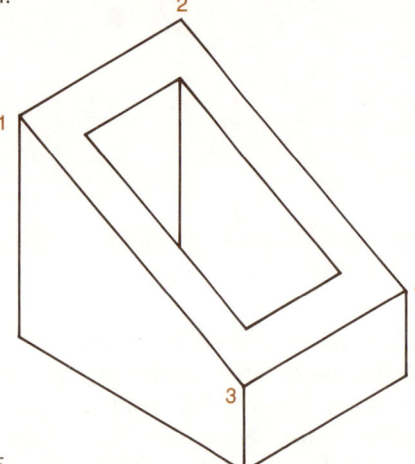

Fig. 13-5

1. Draw the view that shows the inclined surface as an edge. In this example it is the front view. (see Fig. 13-6).

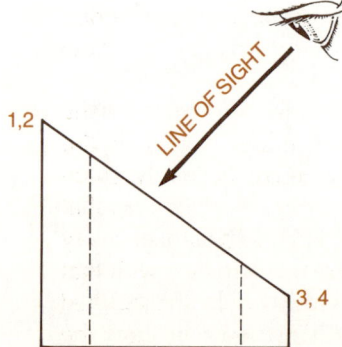

Fig. 13-6

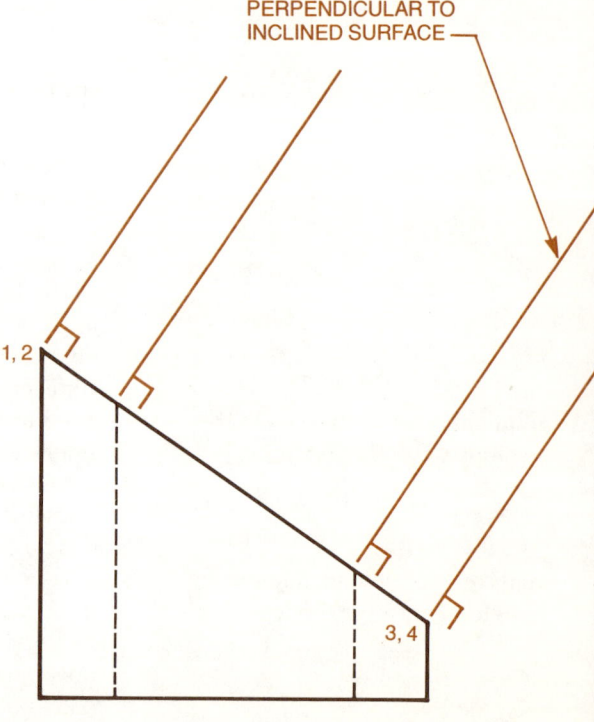

Fig. 13-7(b)

3. Project construction lines perpendicular to the inclined surface.

168 AUXILIARY VIEWS

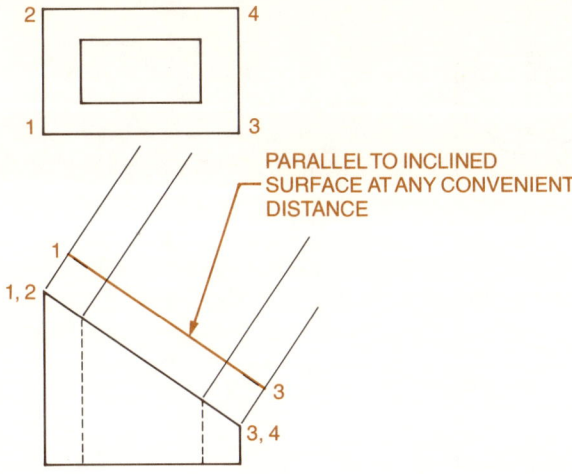

Fig. 13-8

convenient—useful or suited to one's needs

4. Draw a line parallel to the inclined surface at any **convenient** distance. This line will form one side of the auxiliary view.

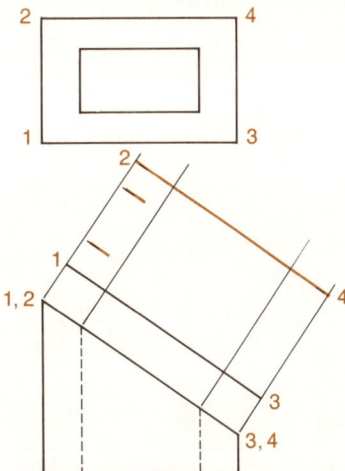

Fig. 13-9

5. Transfer the width dimensions from the top view to the auxiliary view. You can use your compass or dividers for this purpose.

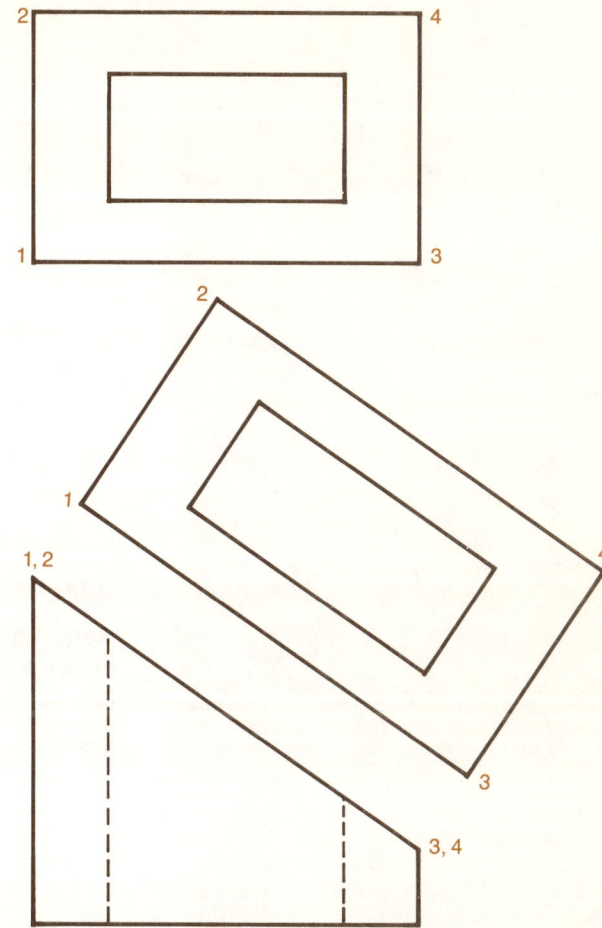

Fig. 13-10

6. Block in the auxiliary view by drawing lines through these points parallel to the inclined surface. Now that you've mastered this example you're probably anxious to try one on your own. Wait just a bit. You will need to know a little about curves in auxiliary views. It's just as simple to learn.

AUXILIARY VIEWS 169

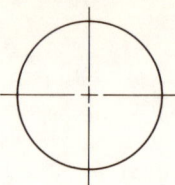

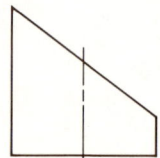

Fig. 13-11

Steps in Drawing a Circle or an Arc in an Auxiliary View

Note. The inclined surface appears as a circle in the top view but, in reality, its true shape is an ellipse. In this example it is the ellipse that has to be drawn.

STEP 1

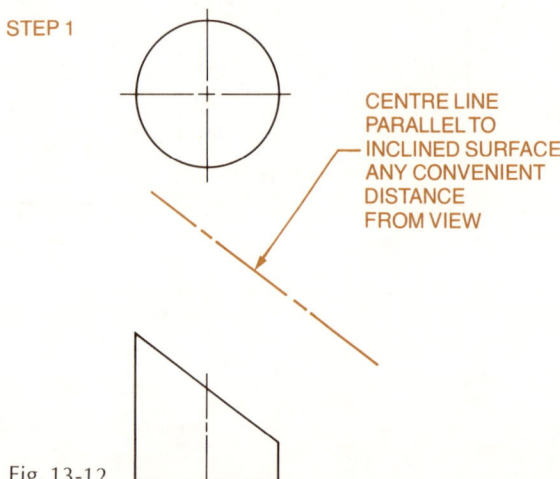

CENTRE LINE PARALLEL TO INCLINED SURFACE ANY CONVENIENT DISTANCE FROM VIEW

Fig. 13-12

1. Draw a line at a convenient distance away from, and parallel to, the inclined surface shown in the front view. This line will serve as the centre line for the auxiliary view.

STEP 2

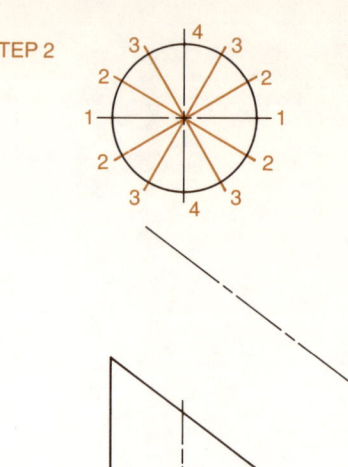

Fig. 13-13

2. Divide the circumference into 12 equal 30° sectors. In our example each point on the circumference is numbered to help you to follow the remaining steps.

STEP 3

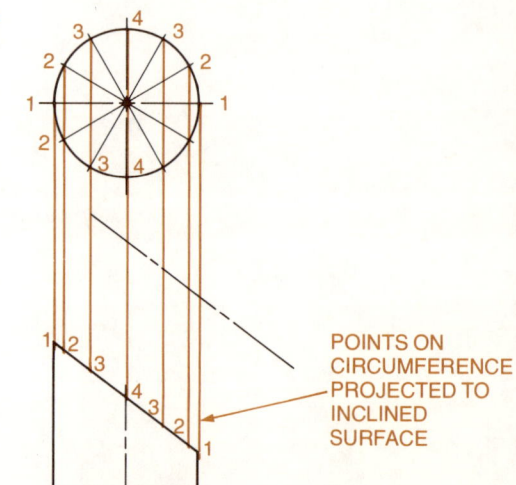

POINTS ON CIRCUMFERENCE PROJECTED TO INCLINED SURFACE

Fig. 13-14

3. Project lines from these points on the circumference down to the inclined surface of the front view.

170 AUXILIARY VIEWS

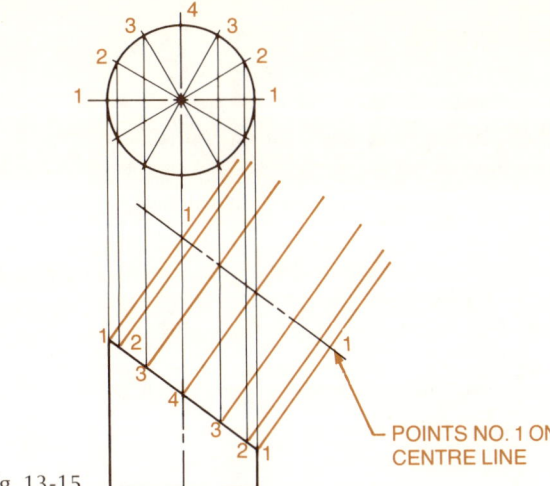

the other points on the circumference. As before transfer the distance down the projection line and along to the centre line of the auxiliary. Mark each distance off on both sides of the centre line.

Fig. 13-15

4. Extend the projection lines perpendicular to the inclined edge through the centre line of the auxiliary view.
5. Note that points numbered on the top view are on the horizontal centre line. Follow down the projection lines to the inclined edge and up to their new positions on the auxiliary view centre line.

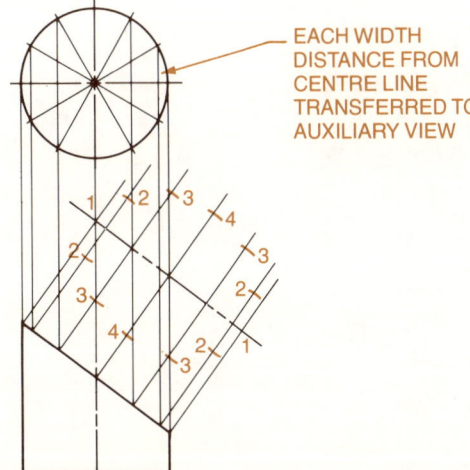

Fig. 13-16

6. Using a compass measure the width distance from the centre line in the top view to

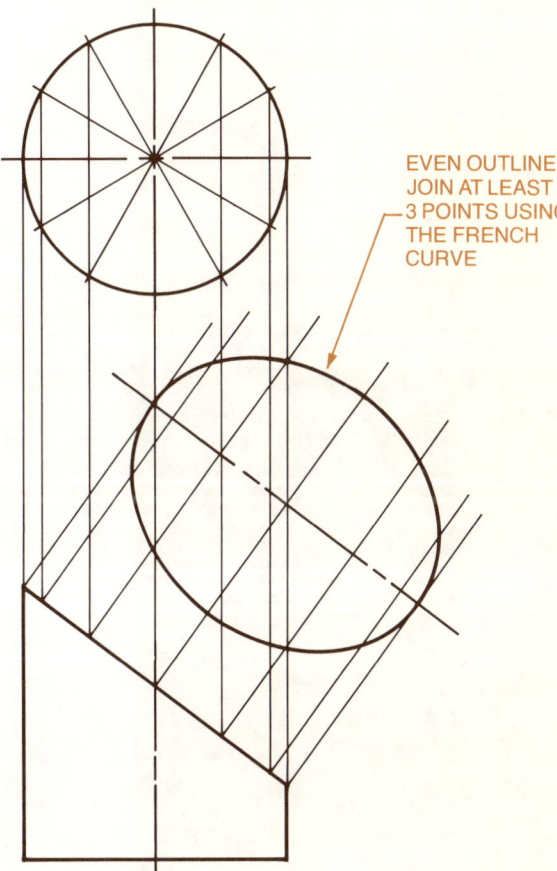

Fig. 13-17

7. When all the points have been transferred to the auxiliary view, join them using a French curve to form a smooth continuous curve.

Now you know it all. Concentrate on what you are doing. Follow the steps.

AUXILIARY VIEWS 171

POINTS TO REMEMBER

- Inclined surfaces are not accurately described by any of the normal orthographic views.
- Auxiliary views are extra views that accurately describe the features of sloping surfaces.
- Partial orthographic views should be used together with the necessary auxiliary views to save time.
- Auxiliary views need only show the part of the object that is inclined.

QUESTIONS TO ANSWER

1. What is meant by the term **auxiliary?**
2. What special purpose does an auxiliary view serve?
3. Give two reasons why an auxiliary view usually describes only the inclined surface of an object rather than the entire object.
4. Neatly sketch the orthographic views to describe the following objects. Add the necessary auxiliary views.

REPLACE THE X'S WITH THE CORRECT TERM

1. The shape of an egg is described as **XXXXXXXXXX**.
2. Looking into a curved mirror will give you a **XXXXXXXXX** image of yourself.
3. It is **XXXXXXXXXX** to live close to a bus stop.
4. A problem can be **XXXXXXXX** by examining each of its parts carefully.
5. Trucks usually gear down when going down a steep **XXXXXXX**.
6. Many people belong to the **XXXXXXXXX** police force in their city.

1.
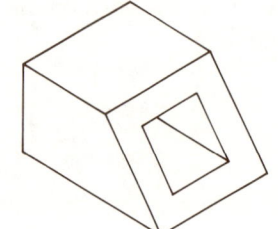

2.
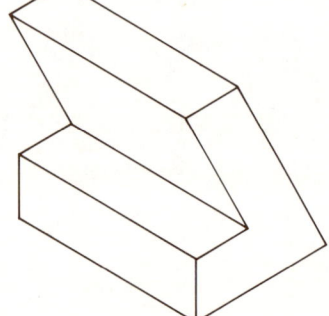

3.
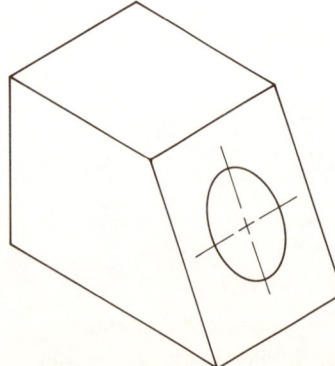

4.
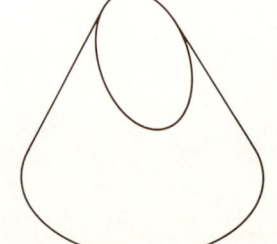

PROJECTS

INSTRUCTIONS
For each project, draw the necessary views. Include a partial auxiliary view. Dimension the drawing.

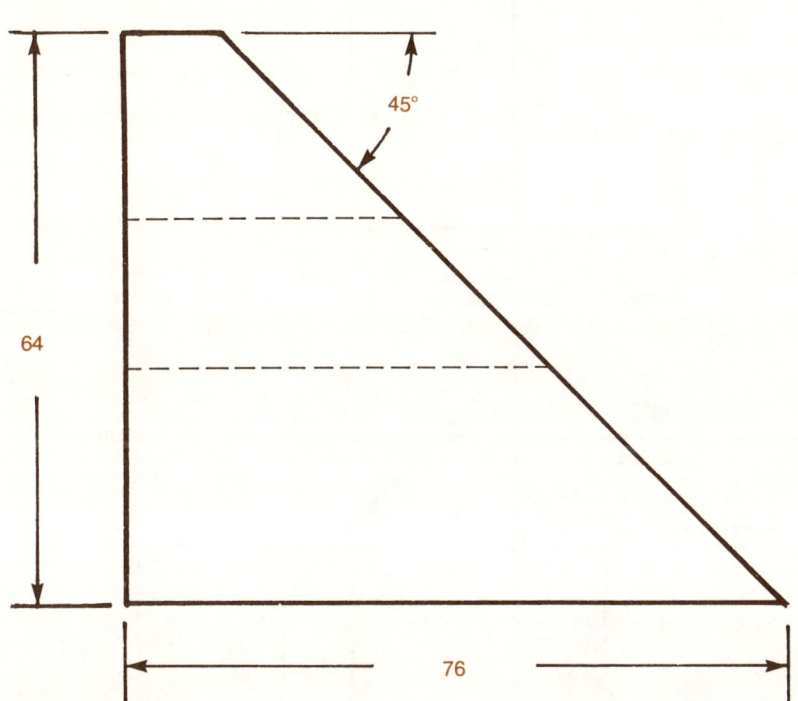
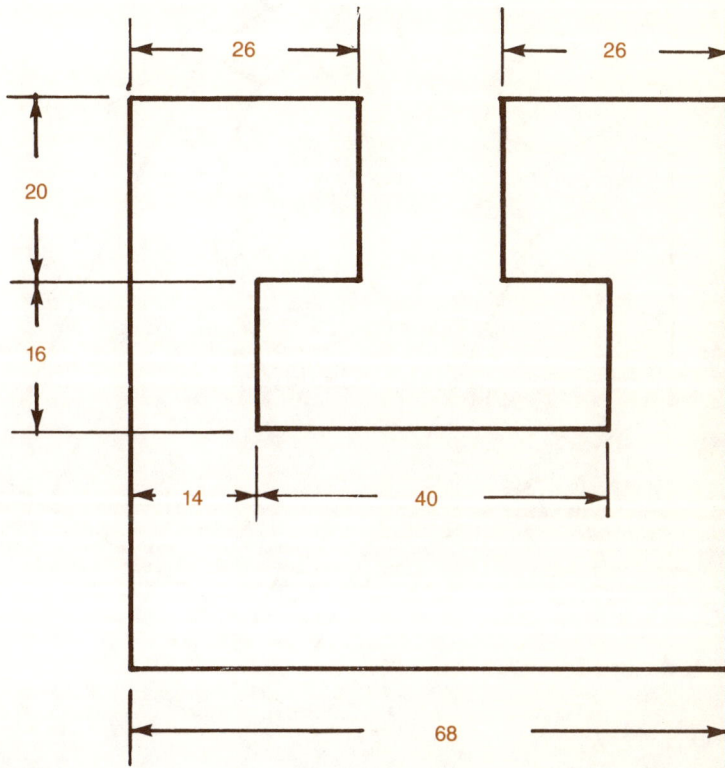

PROJECT 13-1
ANGLED TEE BLOCK   **SCALE 1:1**

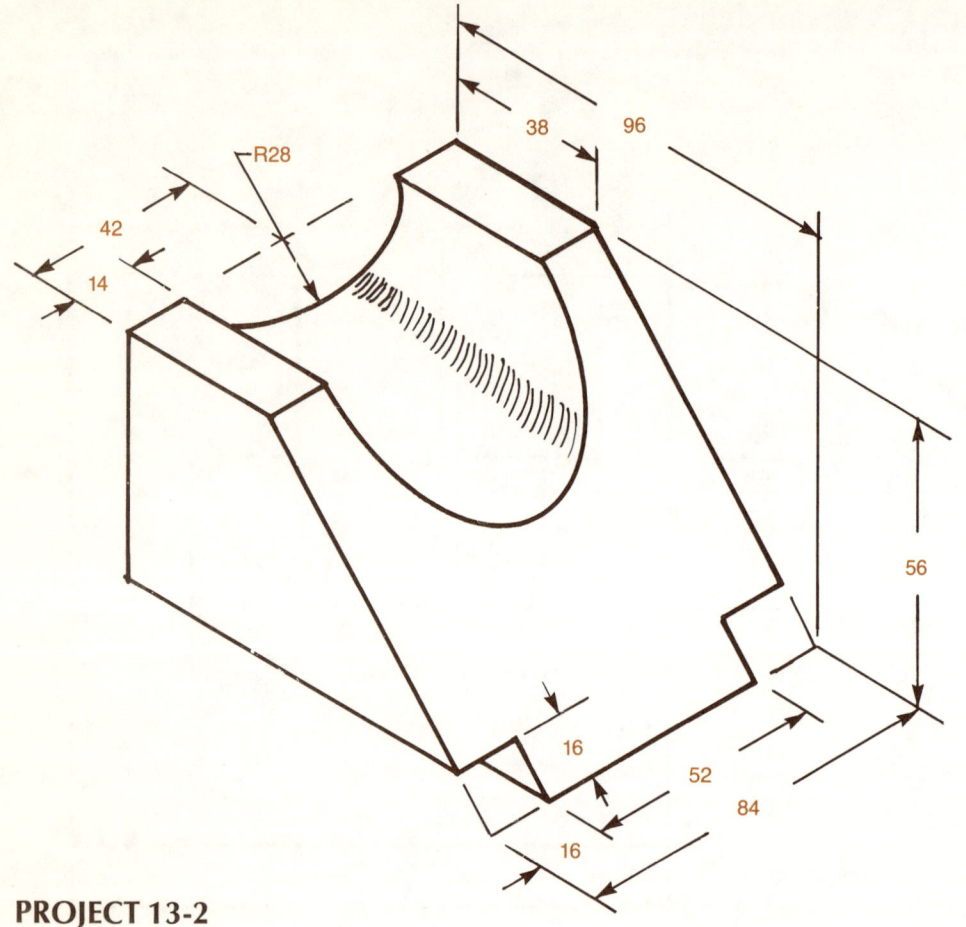

PROJECT 13-2

INCLINED REST **SCALE 1:1**

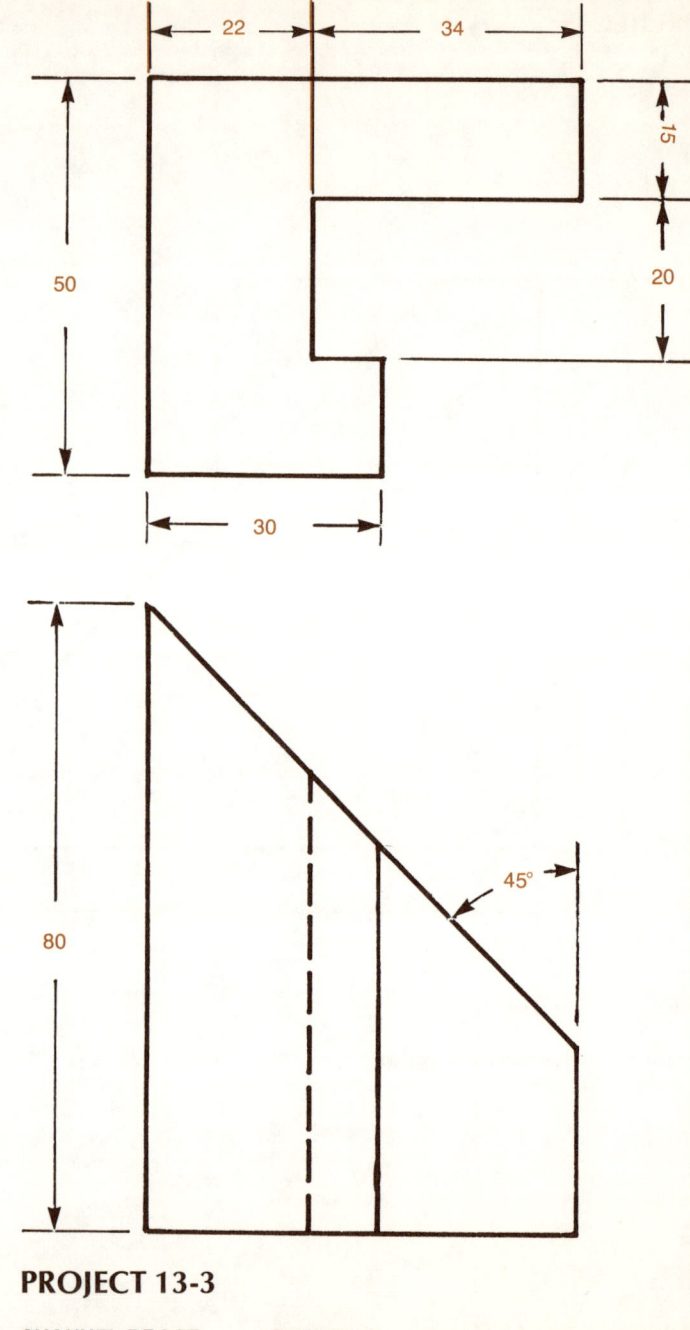

PROJECT 13-3

CHANNEL BRACE **SCALE 1:1**

174 AUXILIARY VIEWS

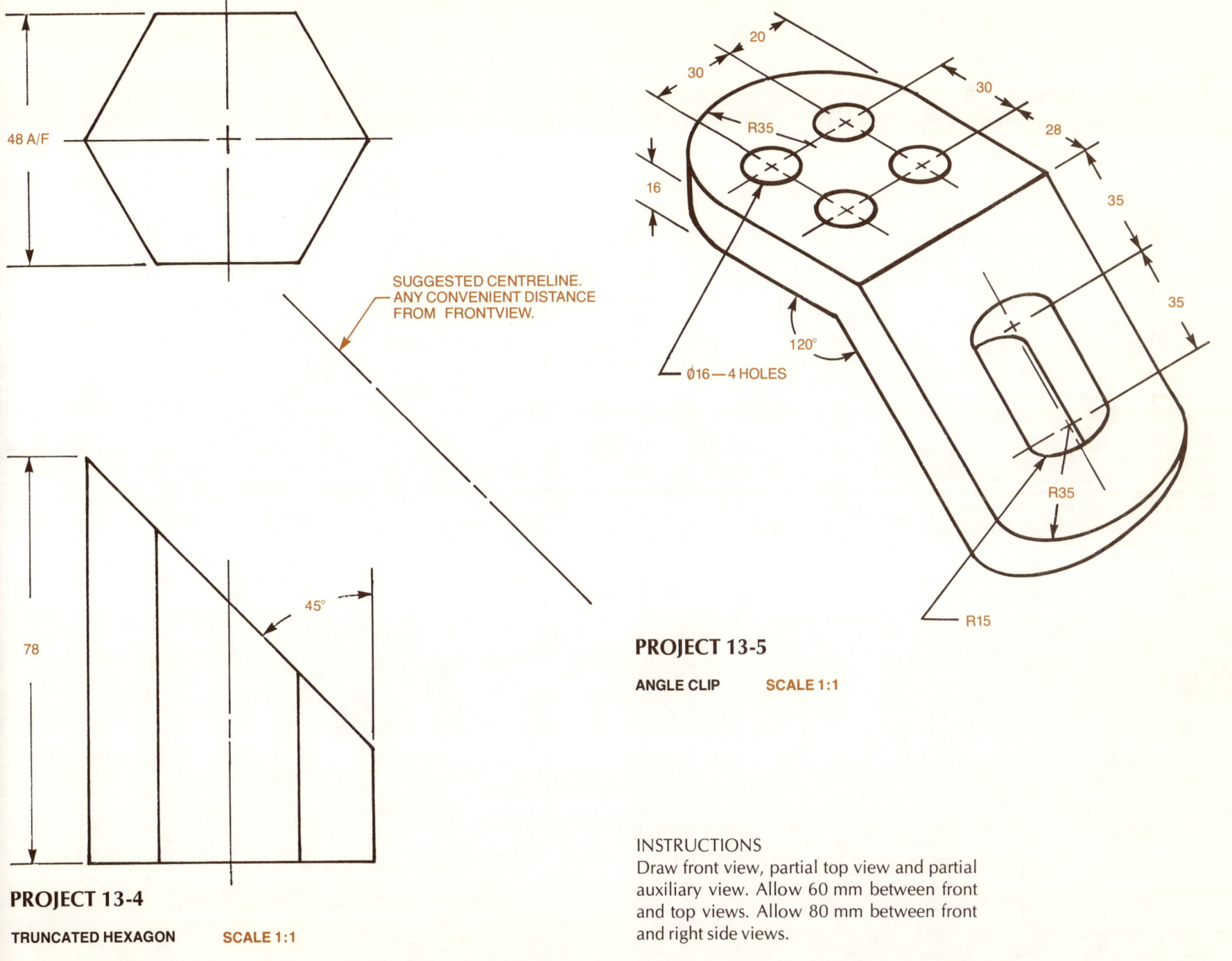

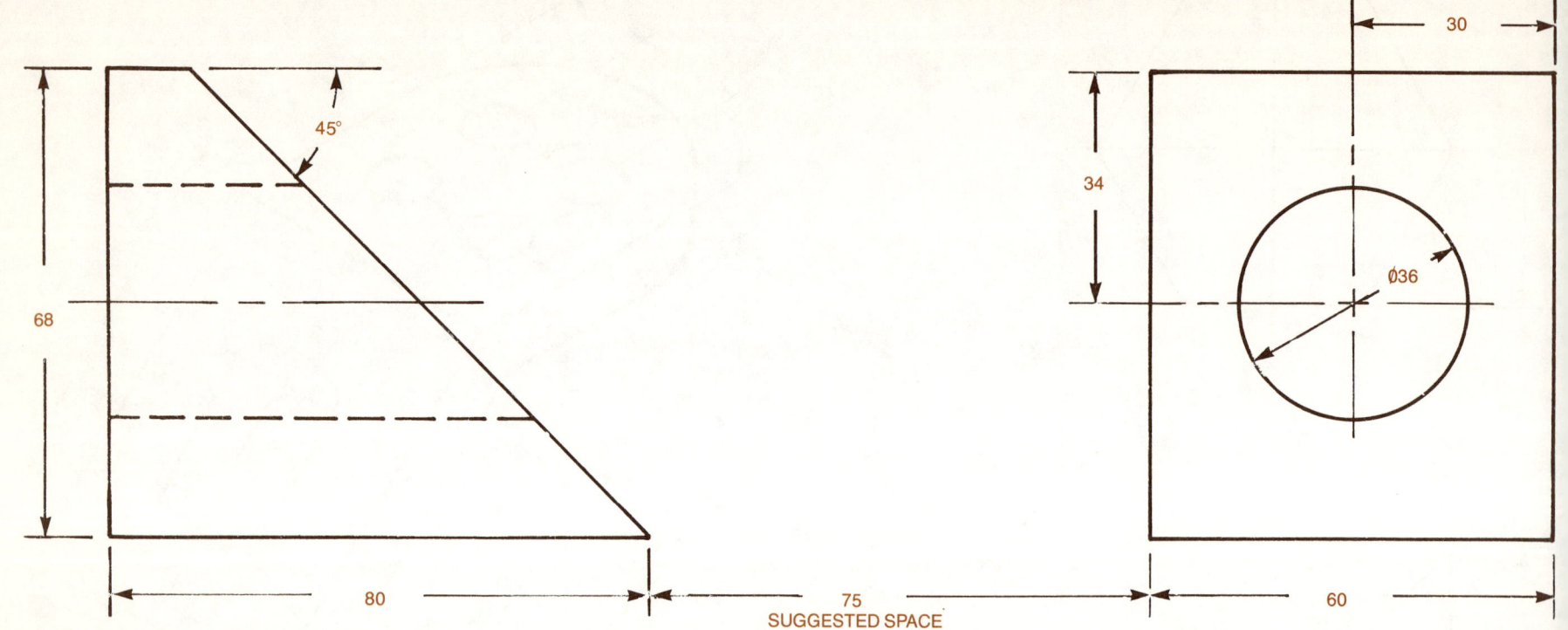

PROJECT 13-6

ANGLED SPACER **SCALE 1:1**

CHAPTER 14
ASSEMBLY WORKING DRAWINGS

WORDS TO LEARN

itemize (í-tem-ize)
fundamental (fun-da-mén-tal)
abbreviation (ab-bre-vi-á-tion)

---

itemize—to break down a grouping into the individual items that make it up

abbreviation—a short form

This chapter describes how individual parts are joined together to make a complete unit. It is brief, straightforward, and you will find it enjoyable.

Many of us, as youngsters, loved to take interesting things apart to see what "made them tick". Putting them back together again, however, was often a problem. Perhaps if we had had an assembly drawing to work from, the task of putting parts together in working order would have been easier. How does an assembly drawing help to make a completed unit?

- It provides a parts list that **itemizes** and describes each part that is needed to assemble the unit.
- It provides one or more views that describe the shape of the assembled unit.
- It shows clearly how each part in the unit is positioned in relation to the other parts in the assembled unit.
- It identifies by number each individual part of the assembled unit.
- It states any additional information that helps to explain the assembled unit and, when necessary, states how the assembled unit works.

THE PARTS LIST

Before any unit can be assembled, each of its individual parts must be brought together. We need a shopping list of sorts to itemize each part that makes up the assembled unit.

A simple format is prepared by the drafter before the drawing is begun. It is placed on the right side of the drawing, either above the title block or at the top of the drawing. Each part of the assembled unit is listed by a number and its name. The material that each part is made of is noted. The quantity required of each part is listed as well. Often a part for a unit will have to be purchased. This item is usually listed as **standard** in the materials column. Its complete description must be noted in the name column so that the purchaser can order the part. Items that are standard include screws, ball bearing, keys, etc. Whenever possible, acceptable **abbreviations** are used in the parts list columns.

Figure 14-2 is an example of a parts list. There are other more detailed lists for complicated mechanisms but, for our purposes, we offer this simple format and its dimensions, which you can follow for the projects in this chapter.

177

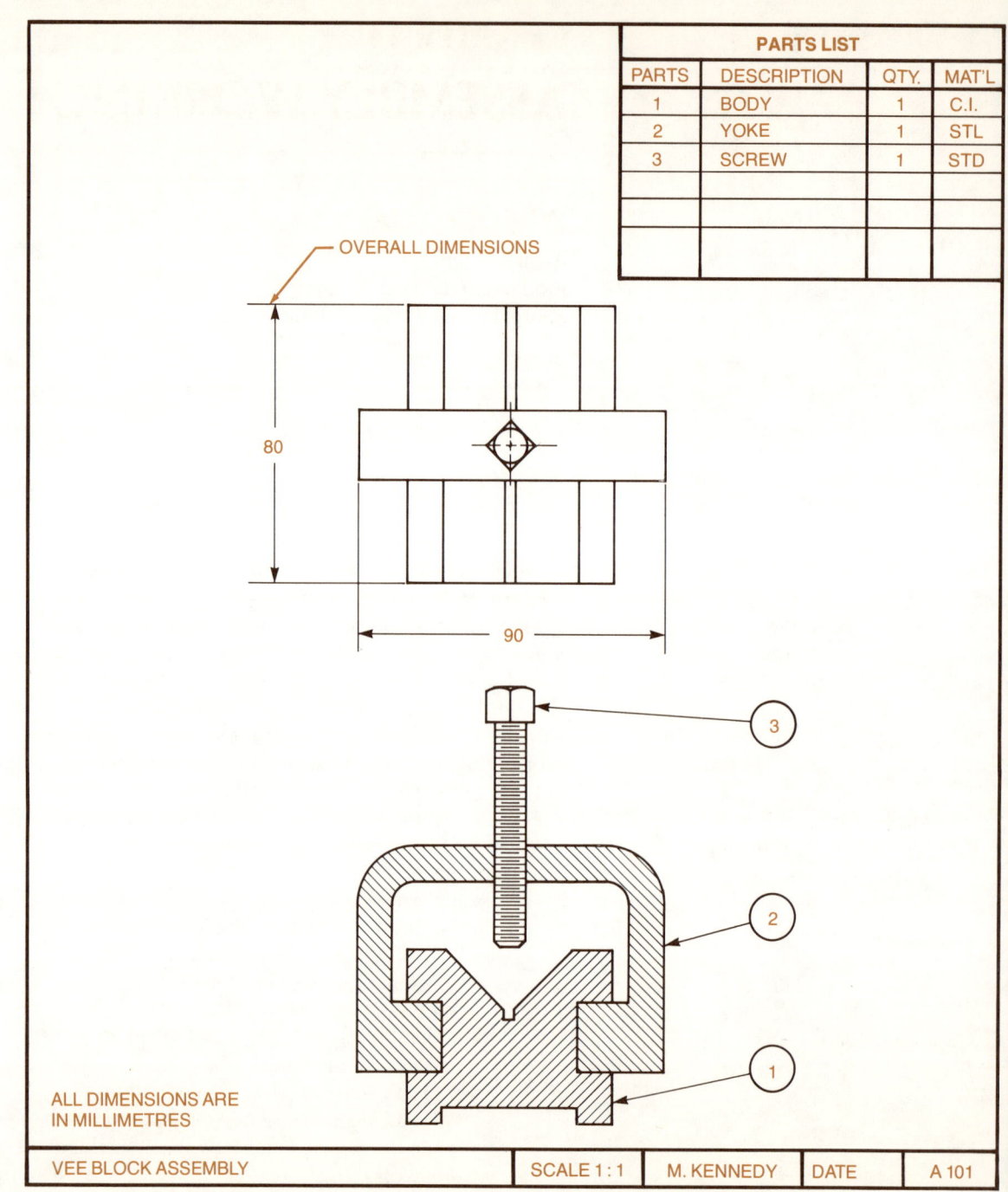

Fig. 14-1

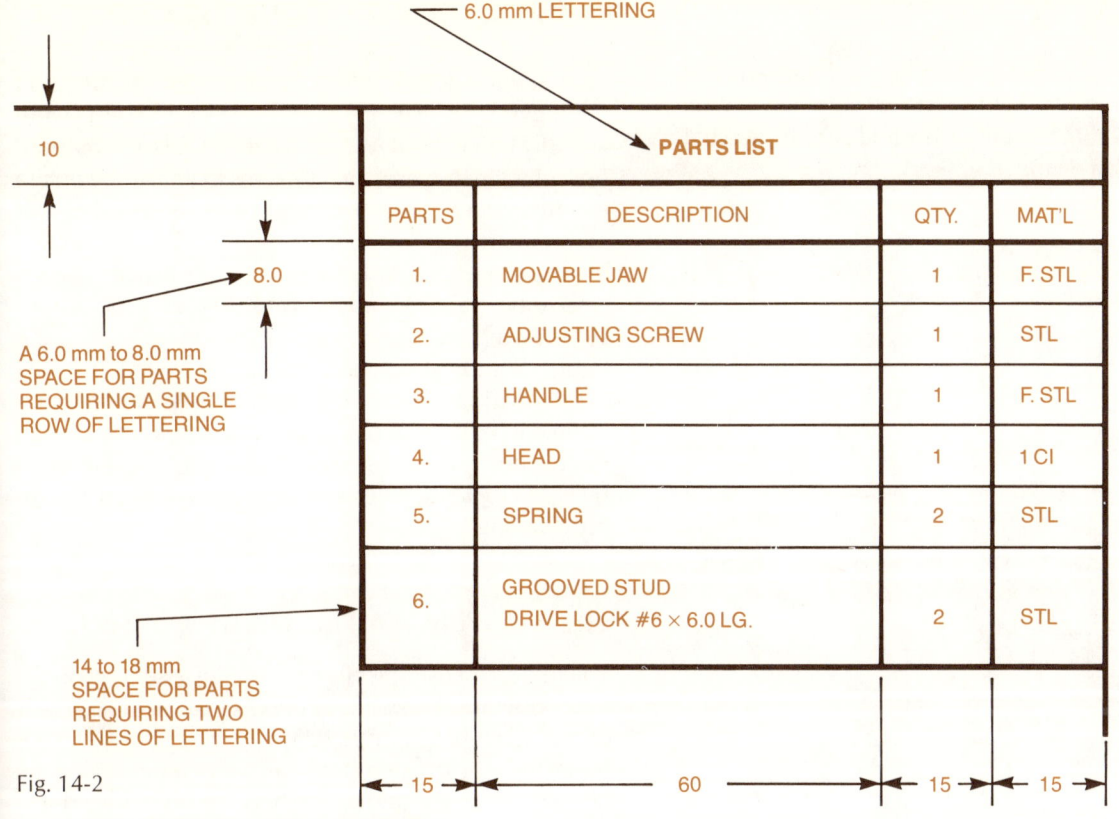

Fig. 14-2

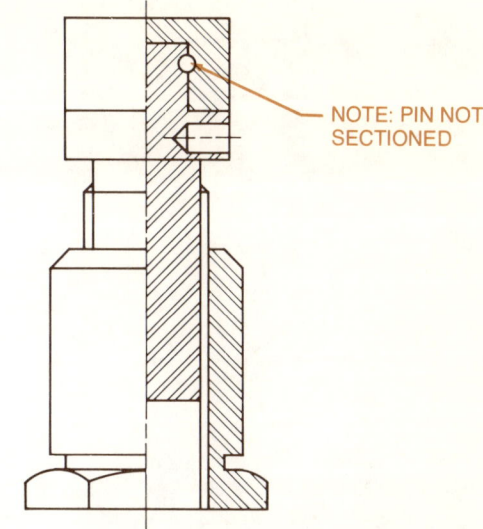

Fig. 14-3

Parts identification. Each part in the assembled unit is given an identifying number. The numbers are placed within a circle called a **balloon** close to the part in the assembly. A **leader line** is drawn from the circle to the part. It is recommended to use a Ø12 balloon.

The balloons and leader lines can be laid out so that identifying each part is a breeze. But don't let yourself be carried away by drawing arrowheads into the assembly from every direction. The drawing might end up looking like the target in a turkey shoot. Follow these hints to get the best results.

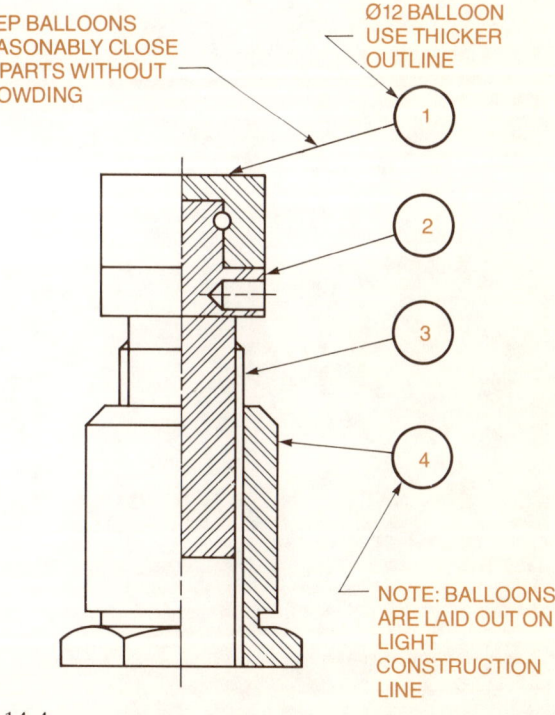

Fig. 14-4

THE PARTS LIST 179

Helpful Hints

1. Keep the balloons in line with one another. Draw a light construction line about 25 mm from the view and centre each balloon on the line.

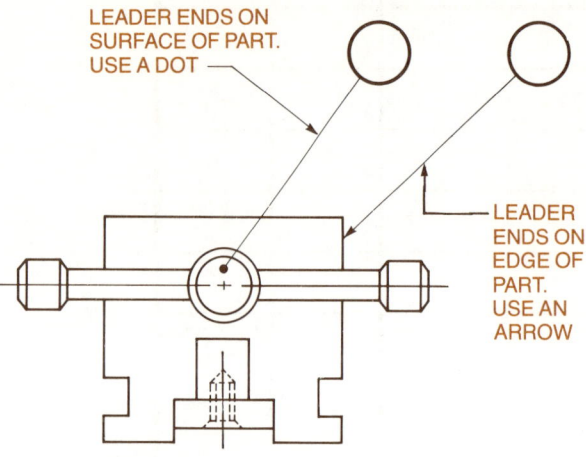

Fig. 14-5

2. Try to keep each balloon in numbered order if possible.
3. Try to avoid long leader lines by placing each balloon close to the part being identified.
4. When drawing leader lines, use slightly different angles for each leader line.
5. Avoid using horizontal or vertical leader lines.
6. Use straight leader lines whenever possible. A slight bend can be used in a leader line if it is necessary for the sake of clarity.
7. An arrowhead is used at the end of a leader line when the leader line touches the edge of a part.
8. A dot is used at the end of a leader line when the leader line crosses over the edge of a part onto a surface.

fundamental—a basic idea or concept

THE ASSEMBLY WORKING DRAWING

From a set of detailed working drawings for a unit you will be able to visualize each part as if the parts were actually before you. As a rule one part is larger or more important in the sense that it seems logical to begin the assembly with this part. Using one or more views, put all the parts together to form the unit. For the sake of clarity, unnecessary, hidden lines are usually left off assembly views. Dimensions are not placed on assembly drawings except to indicate, when necessary, the limits of movement or distance. For example, the assembly drawing of a vise would indicate the maximum and minimum openings of the jaws. The overall dimensions of an assembled unit and the distance between locating holes are often placed on an assembly drawing.

The Assembly Working Drawing in Section

The reason for using sectional views in assembly drawing is obvious. We want to make clear how each part of the assembled unit is related to the others. A sectional view of an assembled unit is a beautiful thing. Its hidden secrets are laid bare. There are no hidden lines. Each part is section-lined to indicate the material of which it is made. Note that the angle of the section lines on mating parts in the assembly vary in spacing and direction to avoid confusion.

Solid parts in the assembled units such as shafts, keys, and threaded fasteners usually are left unsectioned.

Steps in Drawing an Assembly Working Drawing

What you have just learned is most important. The information is basic to most situations you will have to cope with. Now that you have mastered these **fundamentals** it's time to practise them to get to the successful stage that we promised you earlier.

Fig. 14-6

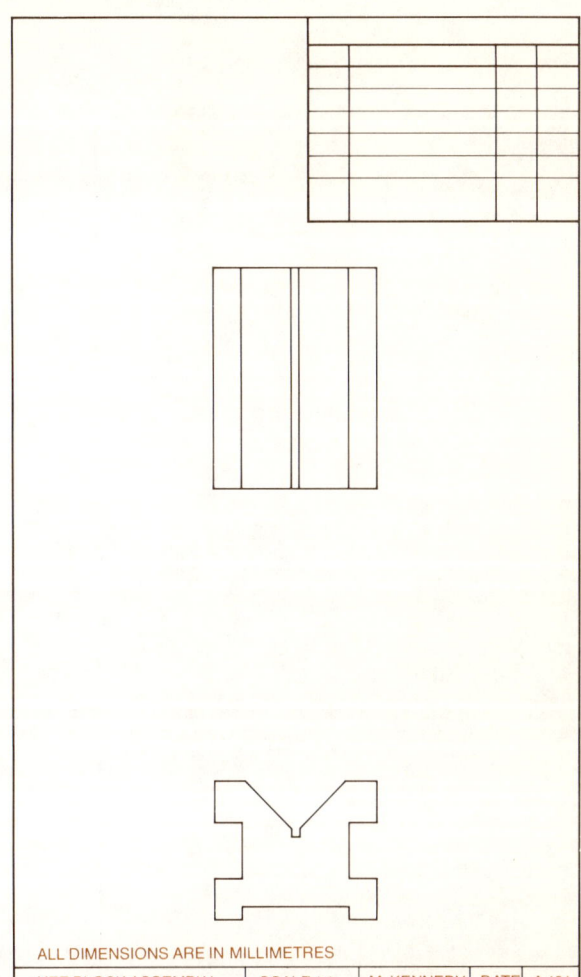

Fig. 14-7

Assembly working drawings are usually prepared from the detail working drawings for each of the parts making up the assembled unit. For our purpose we can look at the pictorial views of the parts that make up the Vee Block. Follow the steps in producing an assembly drawing of the Vee Block.

1. Lay out a parts list in the top right hand corner. This gives you an idea of how much space you have remaining on the sheet. For this example only one view is necessary.

2. The main part in this assembly would appear to be part (1), the body. Draw the front view of the body.

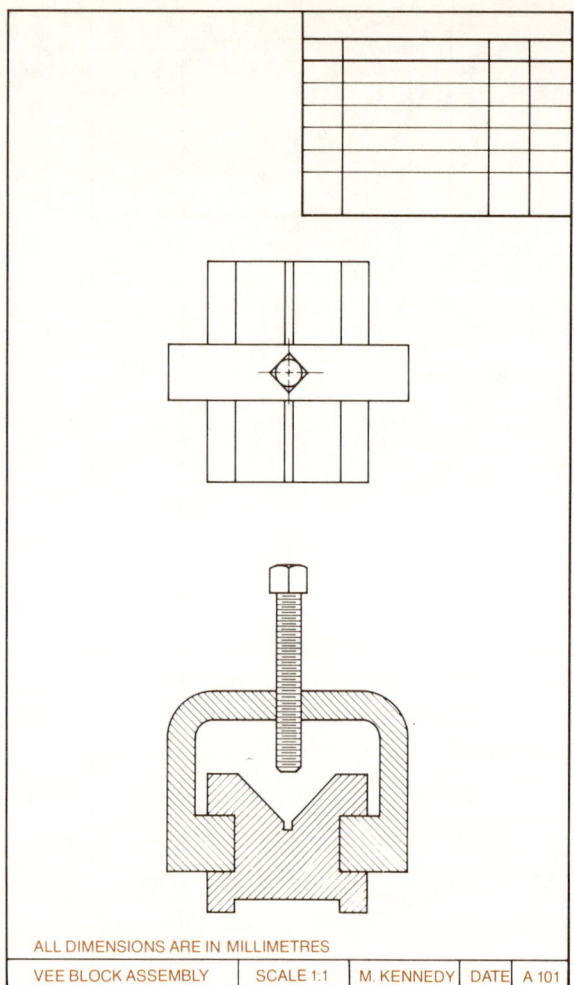

Fig. 14-8

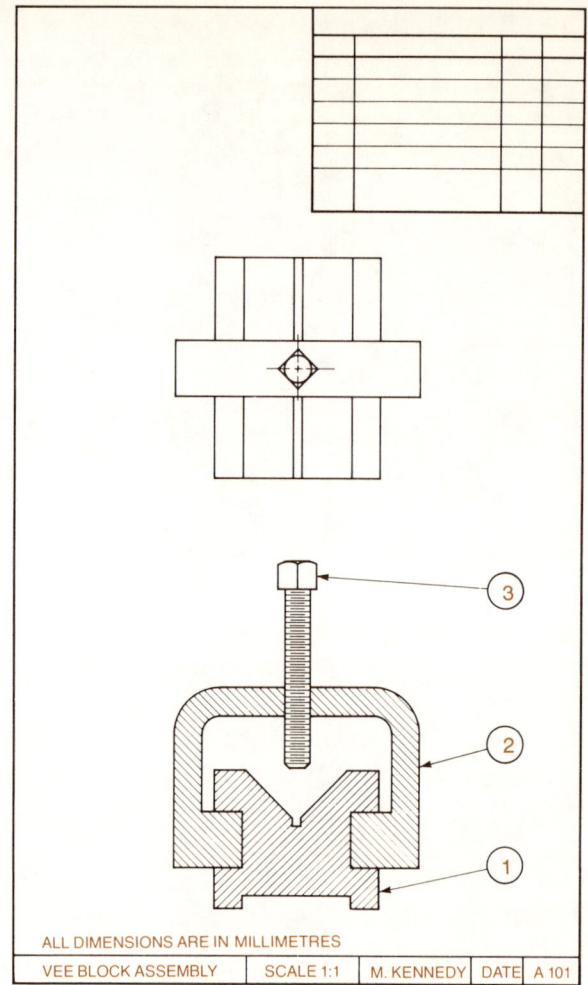

Fig. 14-9

3. Fit the yoke, part (2), onto the body. Part (3), the screw, is then drawn into position.

4. Add the parts balloons and leader lines. Plan the positioning carefully.

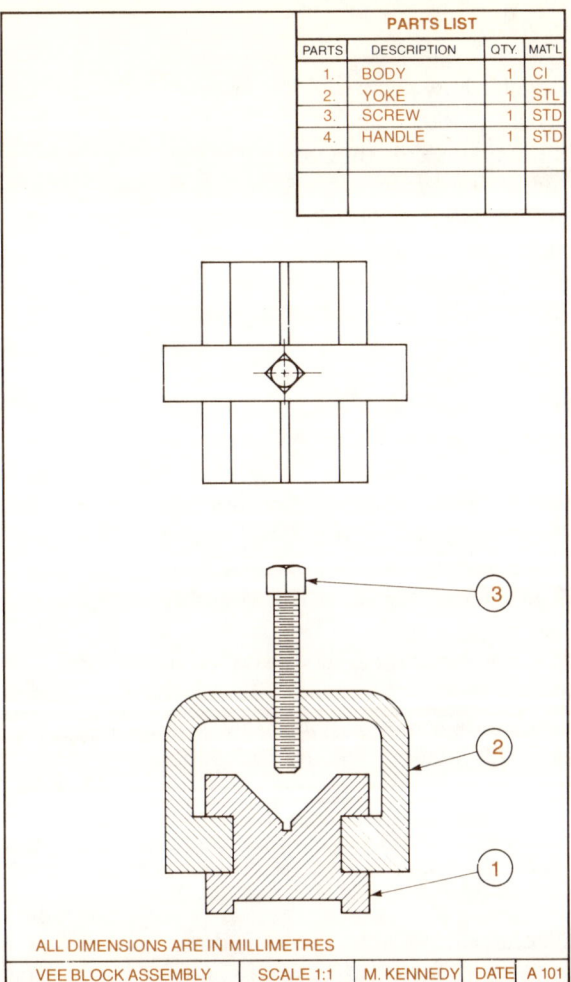

Fig. 14-10

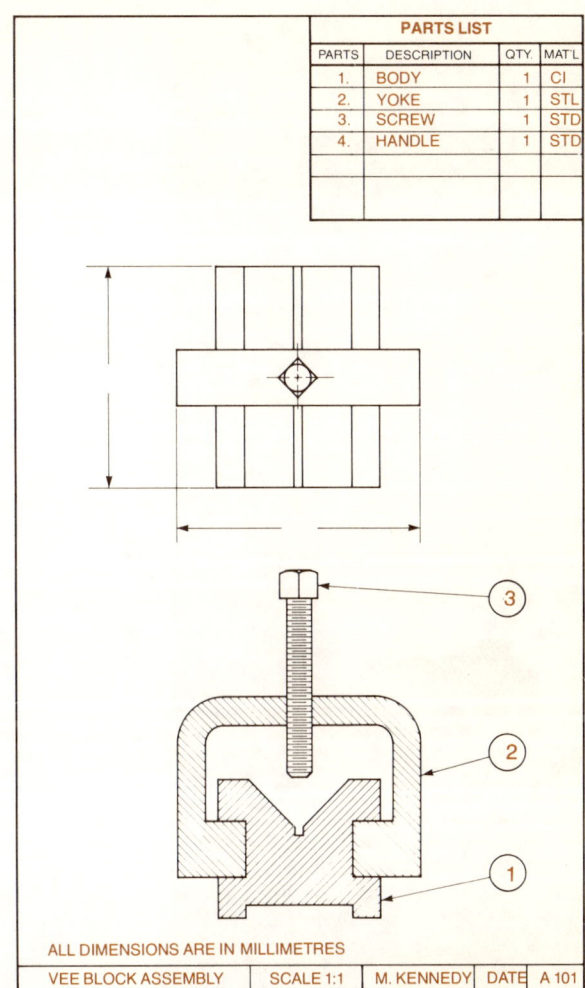

Fig. 14-11

5. Letter in the information required in the parts list. Note that this part's list format allows space for parts to be added to the list when required. In our example the handle did not have to be drawn in detail. We did note it as a part in the parts list.

6. Add any additional information that will help explain the function and features of the assembled unit. This additional information can be placed in a note on the drawing. Dimensions that relate to the function of the assembly are added to the drawing.
7. Check the completed assembly drawing.

THE ASSEMBLY WORKING DRAWINGS 183

POINTS TO REMEMBER

- An assembly drawing shows the arrangement of parts to form a unit.
- Assembly working drawings, as a rule, need not be dimensioned.
- Hidden lines are not drawn in assembly drawing unless they are absolutely necessary.
- Block in the parts list before drawing the views.
- Position the identification balloons in straight lines around the views.
- The leader lines should be drawn at an angle.
- Alternate the angle of the section lines of adjacent parts in a sectional assembly view.
- Keys, shafts, fasteners and other solid parts are not usually section-lined in assembly drawings.
- Parts that are standard can be described in the parts list.
- Notes and dimensions can be added as reference information to the assembly drawing.

QUESTIONS TO ANSWER

1. What is the purpose of an assembly drawing?
2. What dimensions can be placed on an assembly drawing?
3. Why is a parts list necessary?
4. How are the materials of different parts identified on a sectional assembly drawing?
5. Why are hidden lines usually not drawn on assembly drawings?
6. When would a dot be used at the end of a leader line?
7. What reference information can be added to an assembly drawing?
8. How are the identification numbers of parts shown on the assembly drawing?
9. Suggest a reason why standard parts are not drawn in detail.
10. Why must a parts list give the complete specification for the standard parts required in an assembled unit?

REPLACE THE X'S WITH THE CORRECT TERM

1. "Don't" is the **XXXXXXXXXXX** of the words "do not".
2. Catalogues **XXXXXXX** all the products a store sells.
3. It is important to learn the **XXXXXXXXXXX** of a subject before getting into its complex details.

PROJECTS

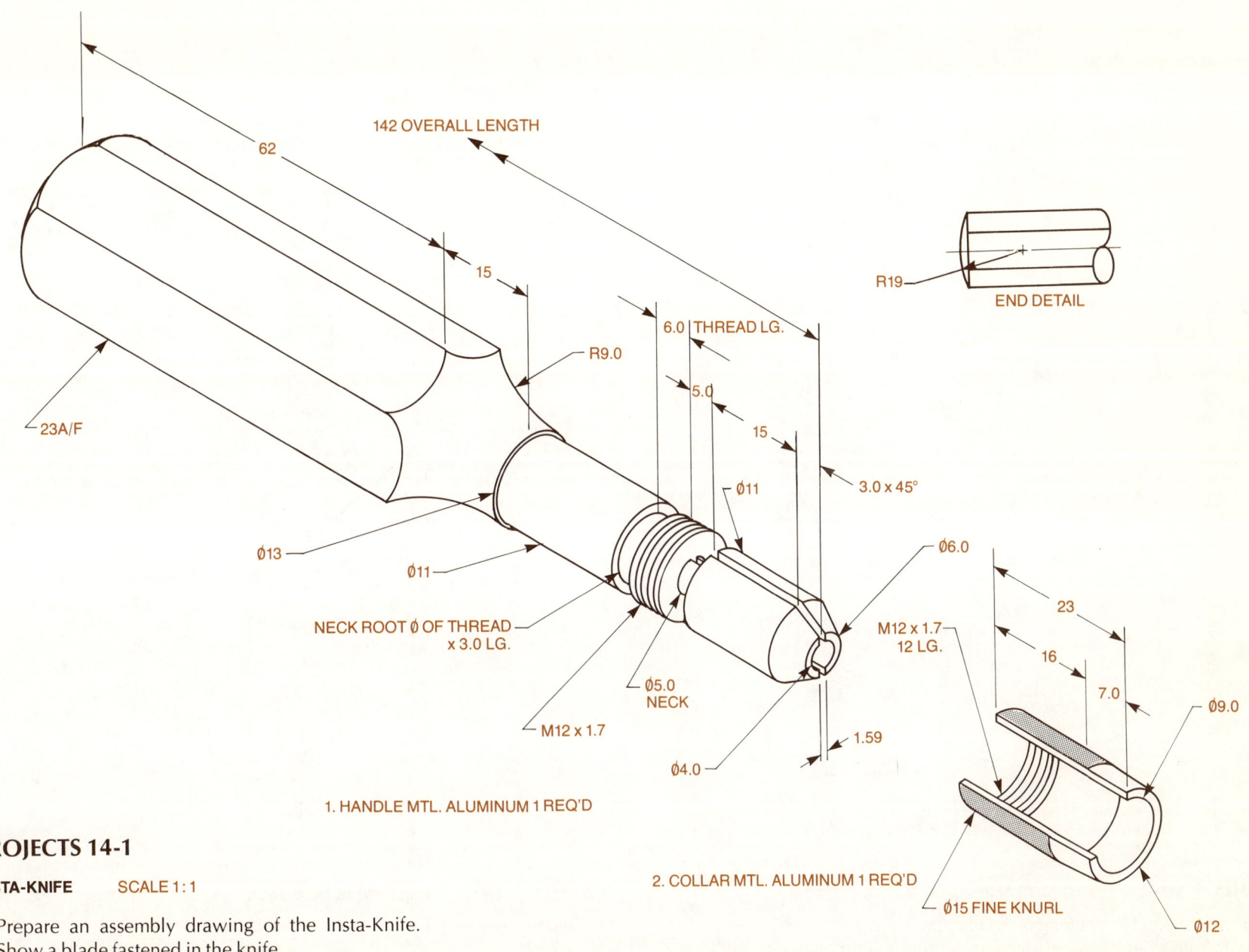

PROJECTS 14-1

INSTA-KNIFE   SCALE 1:1

1. Prepare an assembly drawing of the Insta-Knife. Show a blade fastened in the knife.

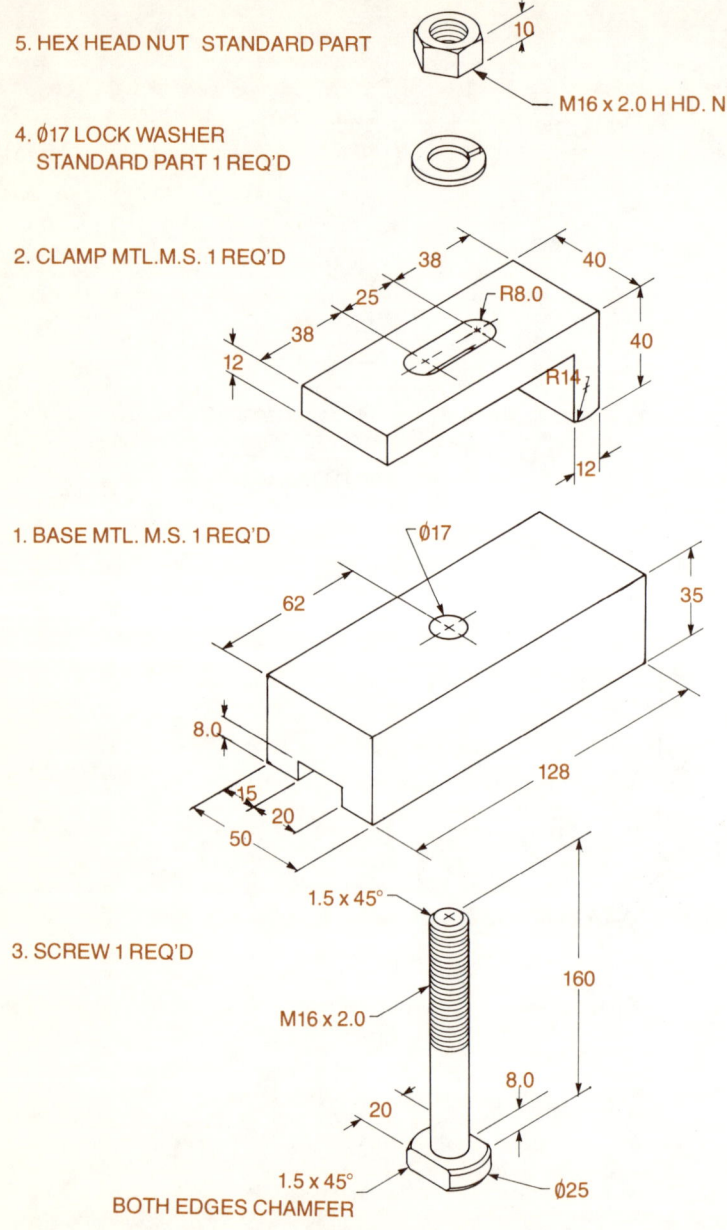

PROJECT 14-2 SPECIAL CLAMP SCALE 1:1

1. Draw an assembly drawing of the clamp.
2. On the finished drawing, show maximum clamp opening.

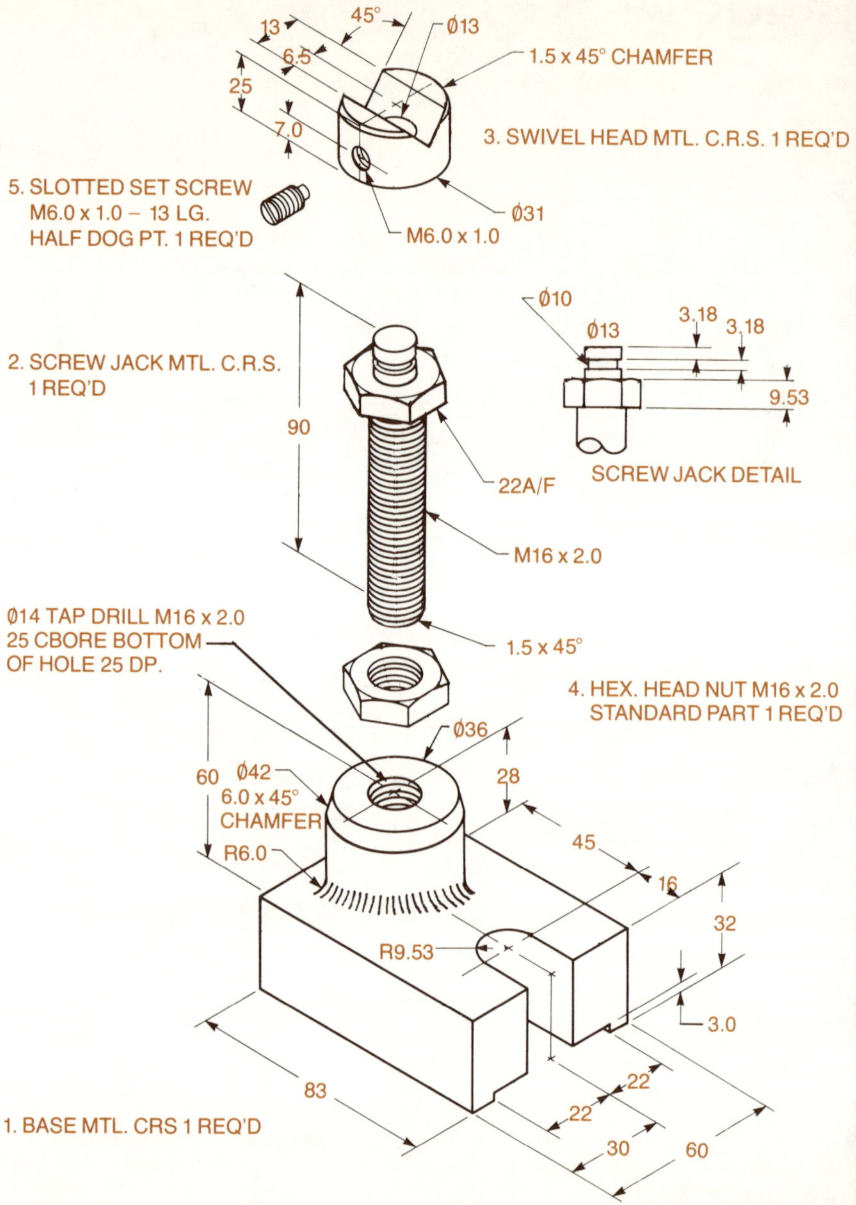

PROJECT 14-3 MACHINE-SCREW JACK SCALE 1:1

1. Prepare an assembly drawing of the machine-screw jack.

186 ASSEMBLY WORKING DRAWINGS

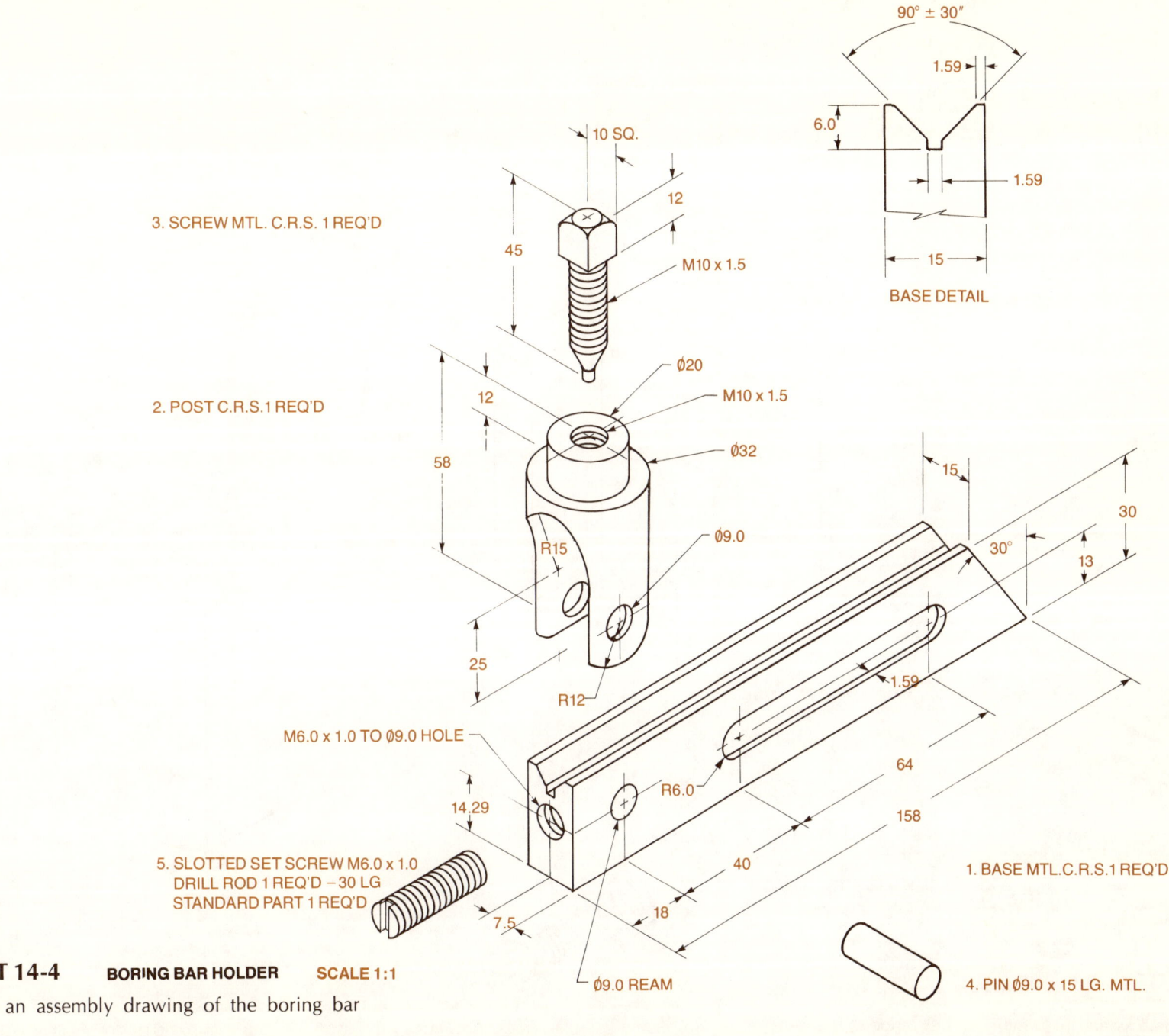

PROJECT 14-4 BORING BAR HOLDER SCALE 1:1

1. Prepare an assembly drawing of the boring bar holder.

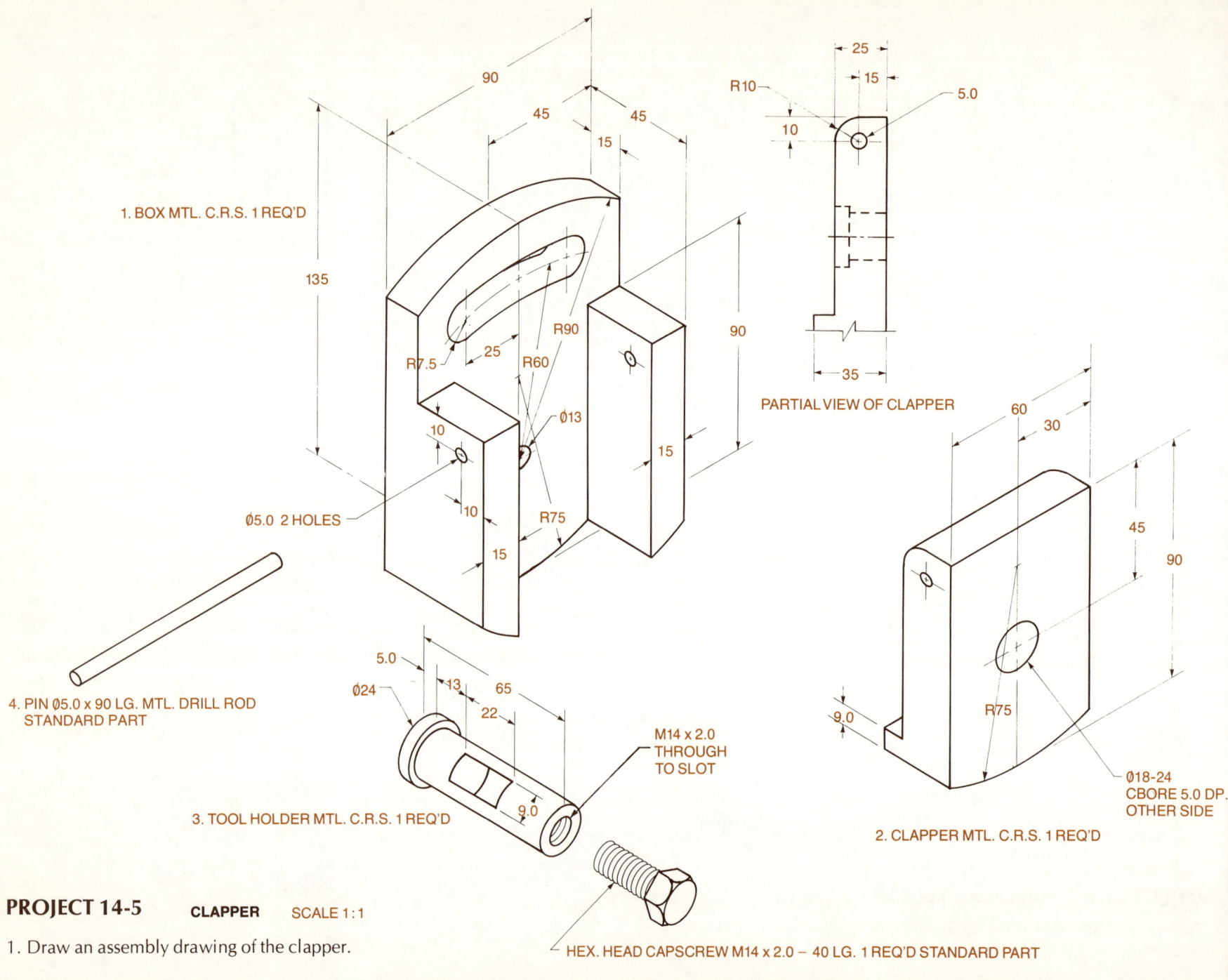

PROJECT 14-5 **CLAPPER** SCALE 1:1

1. Draw an assembly drawing of the clapper.

188 ASSEMBLY WORKING DRAWINGS

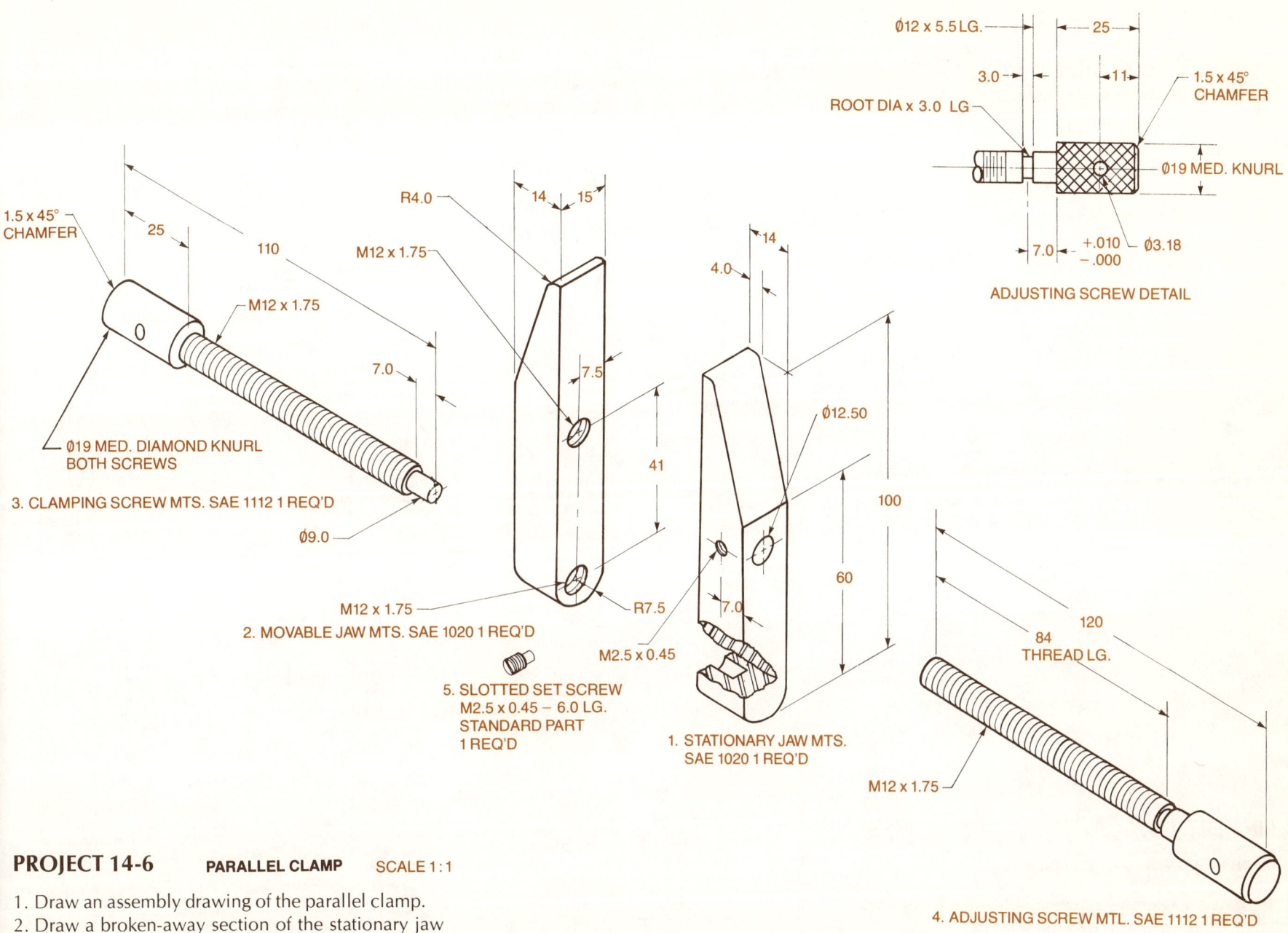

PROJECT 14-6 PARALLEL CLAMP SCALE 1:1

1. Draw an assembly drawing of the parallel clamp.
2. Draw a broken-away section of the stationary jaw showing the clamping screw in position.

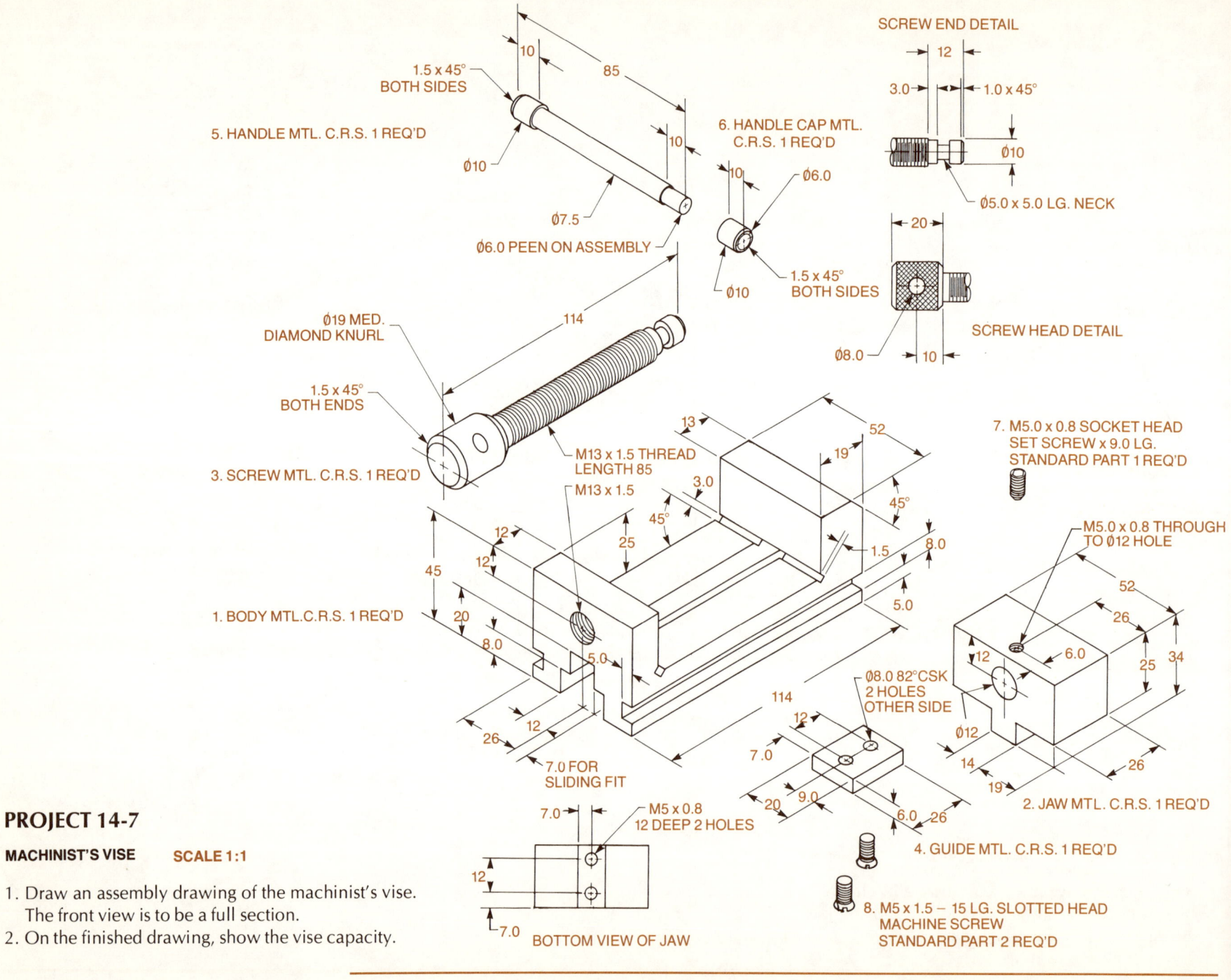

PROJECT 14-7

MACHINIST'S VISE   SCALE 1:1

1. Draw an assembly drawing of the machinist's vise. The front view is to be a full section.
2. On the finished drawing, show the vise capacity.

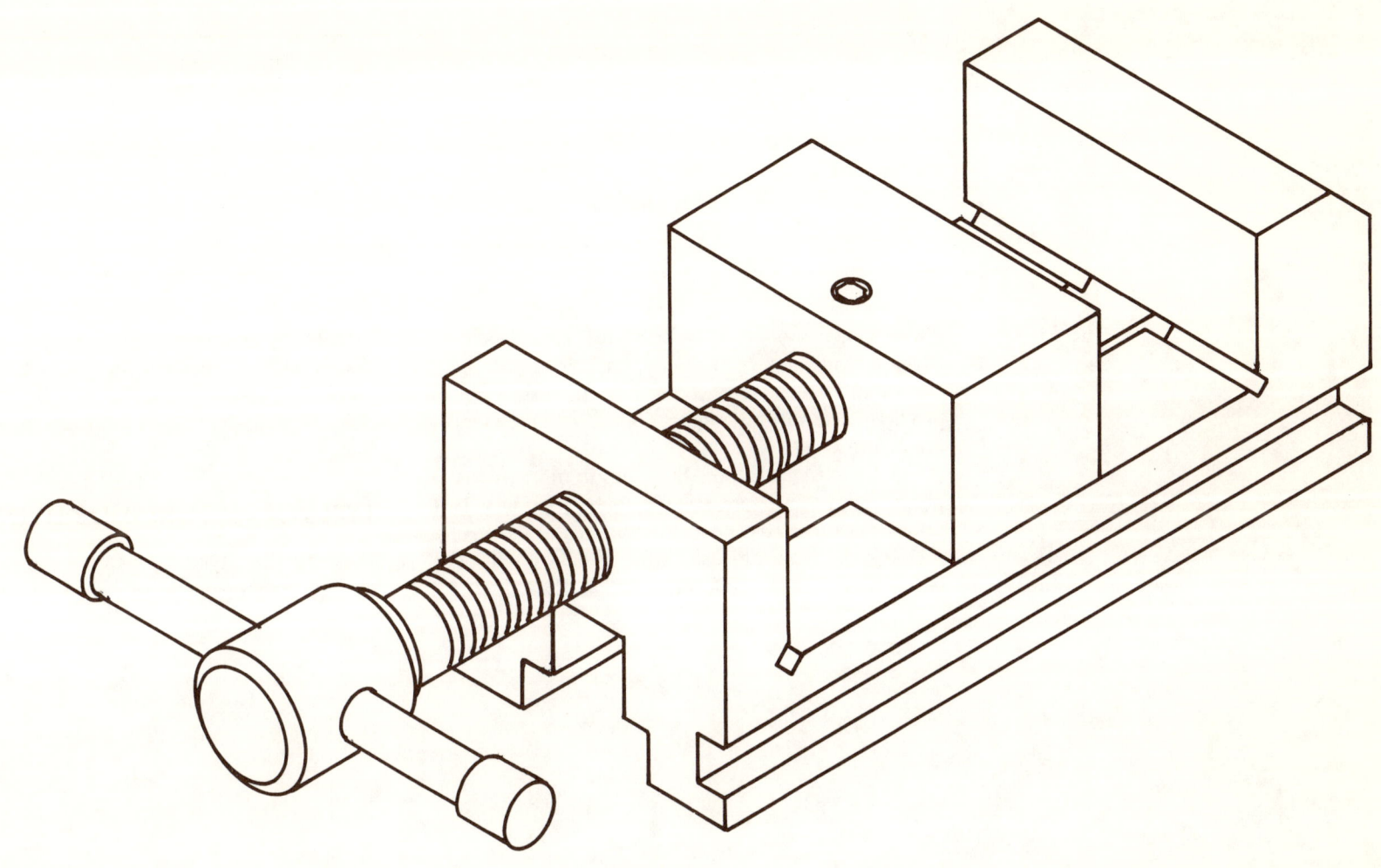

PICTORIAL OF ASSEMBLED VISE

CHAPTER 15
PICTORIAL DRAWINGS

WORDS TO LEARN

axis (plural **axes**) (áx-is) (ax-és)
recede (re-céde)

"You, too, can become an artist in 5 easy lessons." Perhaps you have read this claim before and said, "Not me." You may be right. But you can learn to produce pictorial drawings that are as realistic as most artists' drawings.

You have seen pictorial drawings in many types of publications. They are used in parts manuals, text books, how-to-assemble instructions, catalogues, etc. Pictorial drawings are used wherever they will help people to understand information. (Fig. 15-1)

Pictorial drawings help people without orthographic skills to visualize any object. With your orthographic experience to help, you will be amazed at how quickly you can progress in producing pictorial drawings.

TYPES OF PICTORIAL DRAWINGS

There are three types of pictorial drawings: isometric, oblique and perspective. (Fig. 15-2a, b, c,)

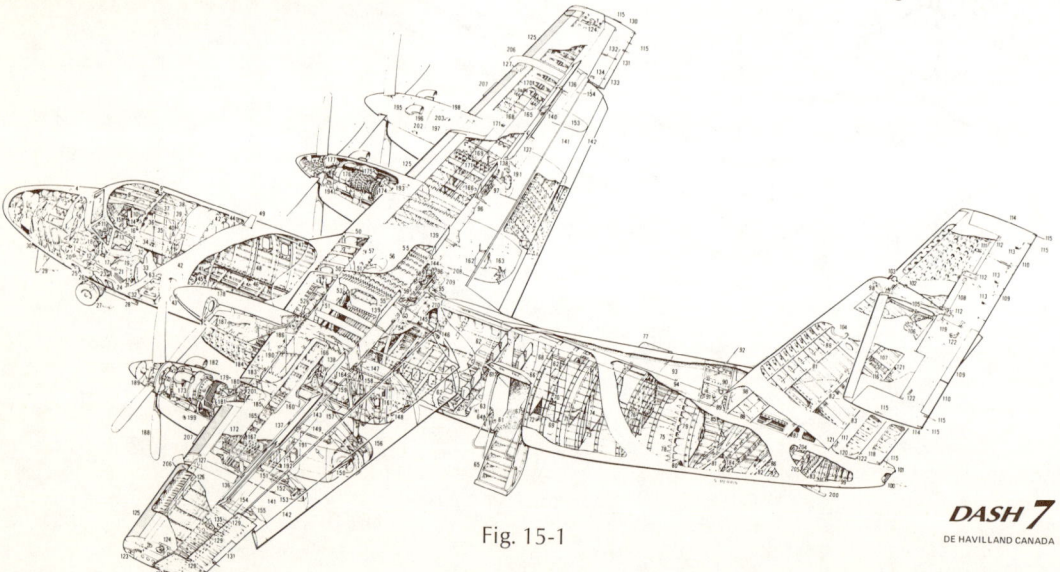

Fig. 15-1

DASH 7
DE HAVILLAND CANADA

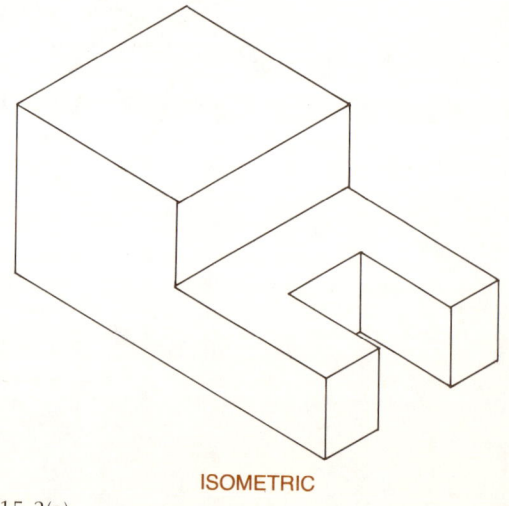

ISOMETRIC

Fig. 15-2(a)

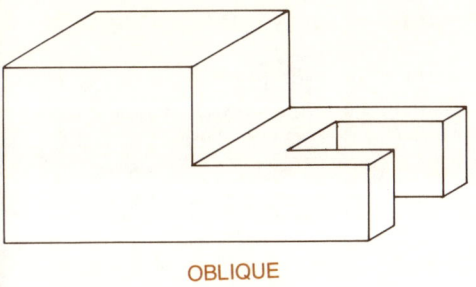

OBLIQUE

Fig. 15-2(b)

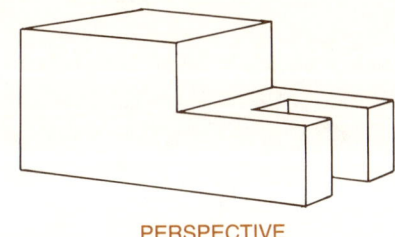

PERSPECTIVE

Fig. 15-2(c)

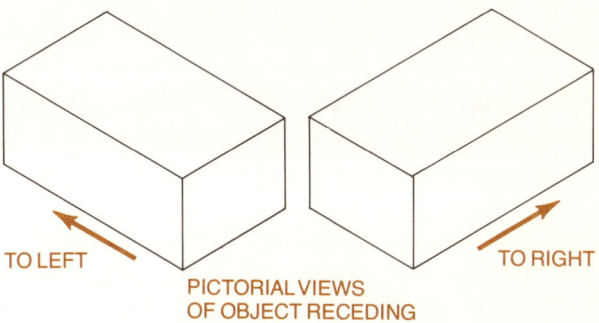

TO LEFT   TO RIGHT

PICTORIAL VIEWS
OF OBJECT RECEDING

Fig. 15-3(a)

ISOMETRIC DRAWINGS

Isometric means **equal measure**. If you will read the text carefully and follow the steps faithfully we can promise you success. Become impatient, take short cuts, and you may get lost. Stay with us.

Objects may be visualized in several positions as in Fig. 15-3(a).

The block can be visualized **receding** to the left or receding to the right. There is no real difference in this example. It is merely a matter of choice. If we had a preference, perhaps isometric views receding to the left would be better understood by beginners. This isometric drawing shows the top, front and right side surfaces. These are the surfaces you have become used to drawing orthographically.

We can best learn how to make isometric drawings by using orthographic views as our guide. Before we begin our first drawing, keep in mind these truths:
- points that are joined together in orthographic views are also joined together in the isometric drawing.
- lines and surfaces that are parallel to one another in the orthographic views are parallel to one another in the isometric drawing. (Fig. 15-3(b))

To prepare an isometric drawing of a rectangular object, first examine Fig. 15-4. It is a rectangular solid. The overall length, width and height are shown.

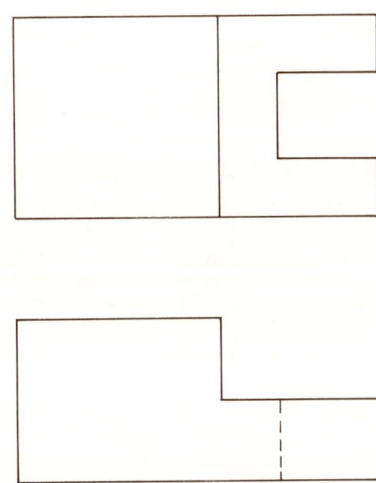

ORTHOGRAPHIC

Fig. 15-2(d)

recede—to slope (or move) backward

Perspective pictorials are both artistic and realistic; they show objects almost exactly as they would appear to the eye.

However they take some time to produce and are a little more difficult than the other two methods. For these reasons this chapter will describe only isometric and oblique pictorial drawings.

Each method has its advantages and disadvantages. We will begin with the simplest and, for some, the most satisfying method, isometric.

TYPES OF PICTORIAL DRAWINGS   193

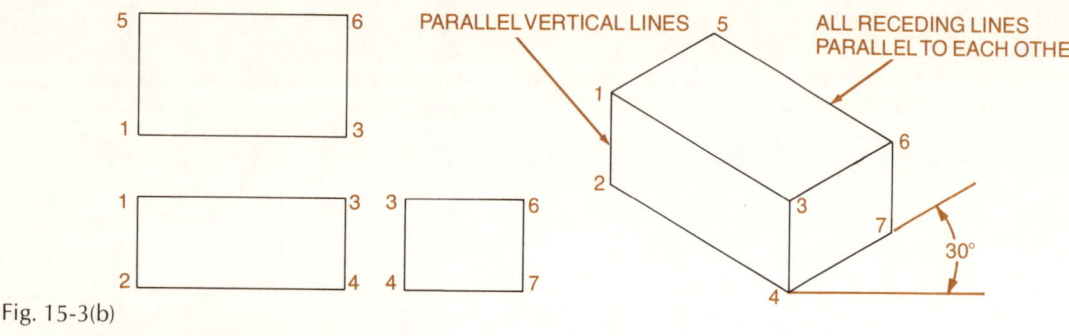

Fig. 15-3(b)

Steps in Producing an Isometric Drawing

1. We need a starting point. For our example it can be placed 20 mm up from the bottom border and 100 mm from the right side border. (Fig. 15-5)

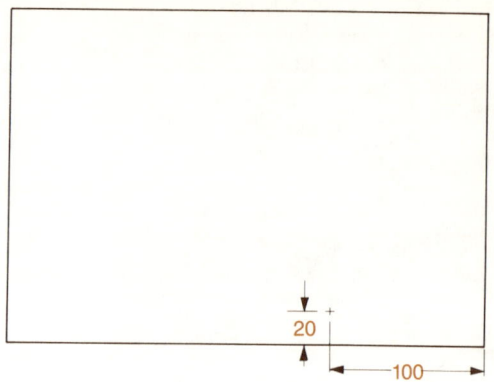

Fig. 15-5

axis — a line which serves in placing an object in position around that line

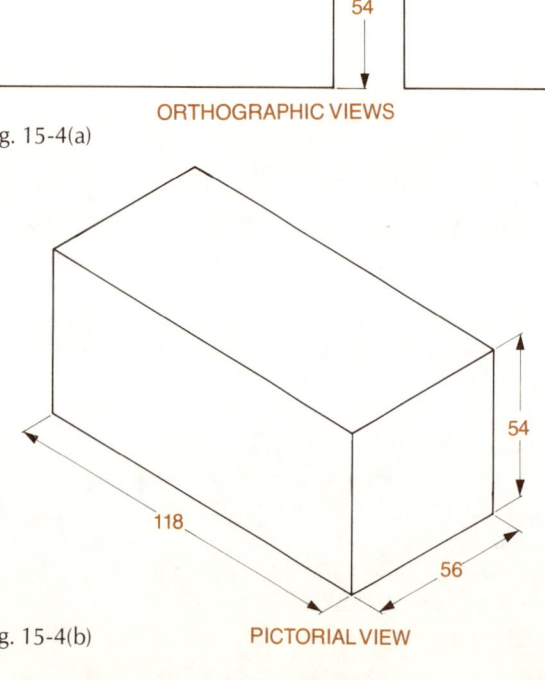

Fig. 15-4(a)

ORTHOGRAPHIC VIEWS

Fig. 15-4(b)

PICTORIAL VIEW

2. Draw isometric **axes**. This is easier than it sounds. Lightly draw three lines from the starting point; a vertical line and two lines at 30° to the horizontal. (Fig. 15-6)

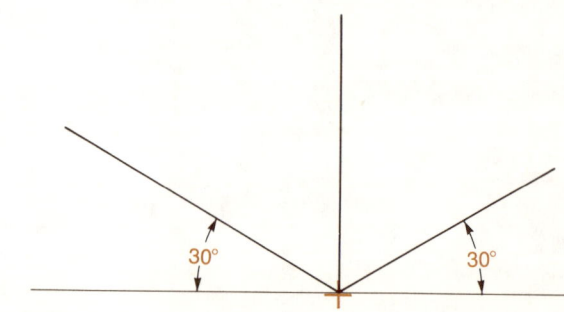

Fig. 15-6

3. From the starting point of the axes measure up the vertical line to mark off the height. On the line receding to the left mark off the length. On the line receding to the right mark off the width. (Fig. 15-7)

194   PICTORIAL DRAWINGS

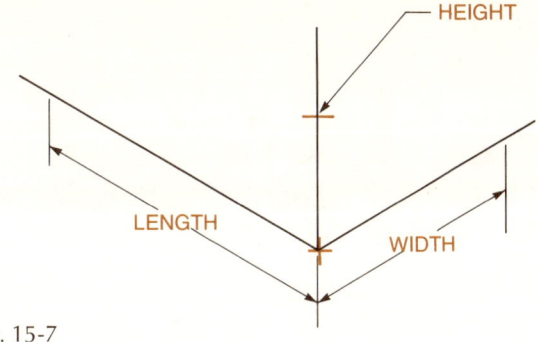

Fig. 15-7

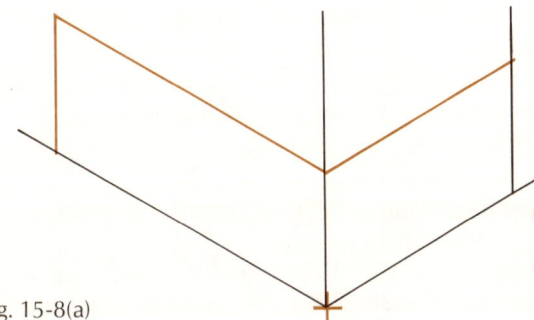

Fig. 15-8(a)

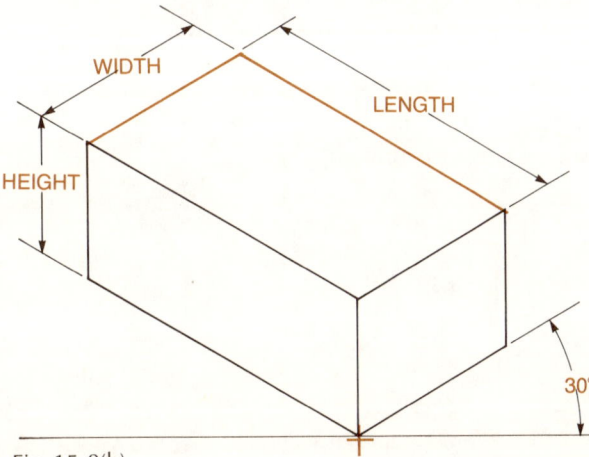

Fig. 15-8(b)

4. From the points you have just marked, draw lines parallel to each of the three lines of the isometric axes. (Fig. 15-8) (a & b)

5. Complete the isometric box by drawing the remaining two lines again parallel to the isometric axes. Always begin an isometric pictorial by drawing an isometric box using the overall dimensions of the object.

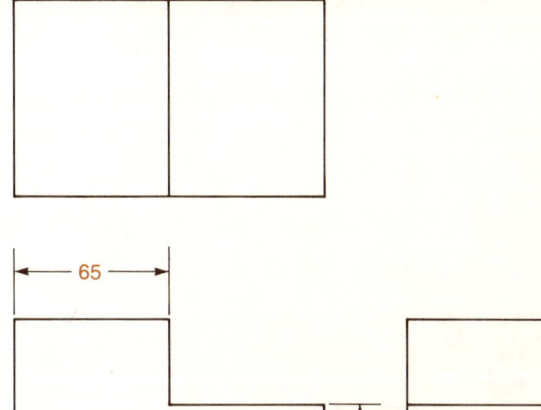

Fig. 15-9

6. Note the changes in the orthographic views (Fig. 15-9). The front view tells us that a corner has been cut out of the object. The height of the detail is 35 mm. The detail length of the step is 65 mm. Transfer these distances to the isometric box. (Fig. 15-10)

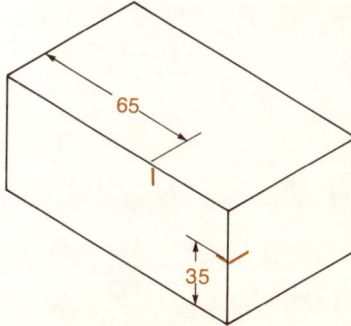

Fig. 15-10

TYPES OF PICTORIAL DRAWINGS   195

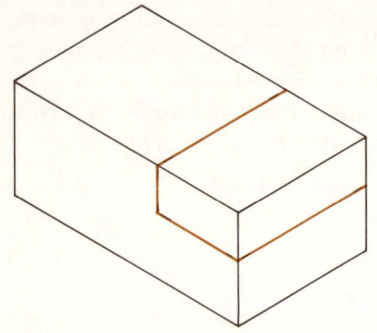

Fig. 15-11

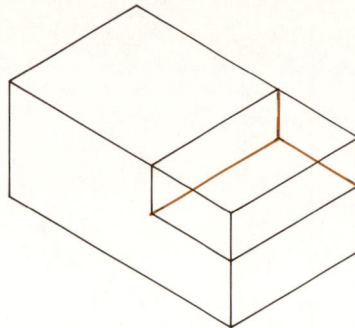

Fig. 15-12

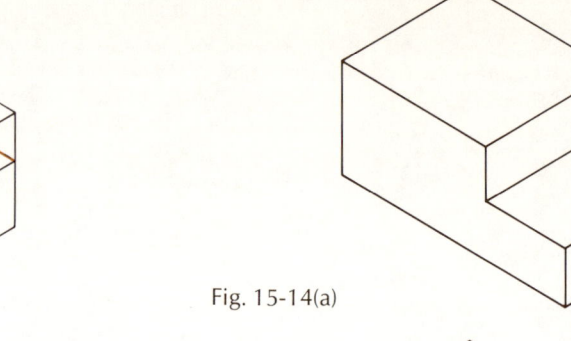

Fig. 15-14(a)

Note. Measurements are always made on the isometric axes or on lines that are parallel to the isometric axes.

7. From these two points draw lines parallel to the isometric axes. (Fig. 15-11)
8. Look at the orthographic drawings in Figure 15-9. Lines that are parallel to each other in the orthographic views are drawn parallel to each other in the isometric drawing. (Fig. 15-12). Note that all the lines on this isometric view are either vertical lines or have been drawn at an angle at 30° to the horizontal. It will take you only a moment or two to let the simplicity of these steps sink in. Ready to move on?

We can remove slots from the object and demonstrate that the changes to the orthographic views can easily be shown in the isometric drawing.

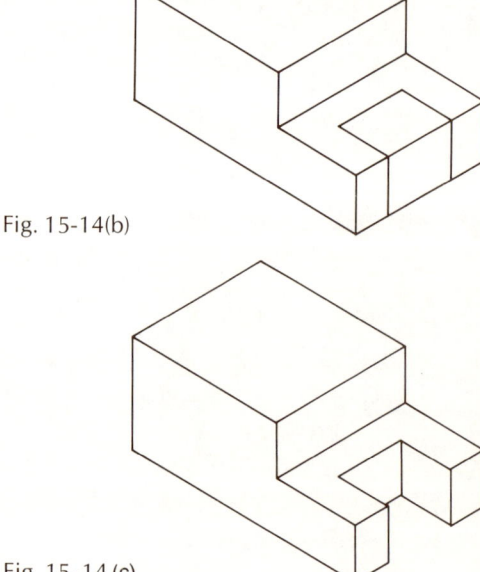

Fig. 15-14(b)

Fig. 15-14 (c)

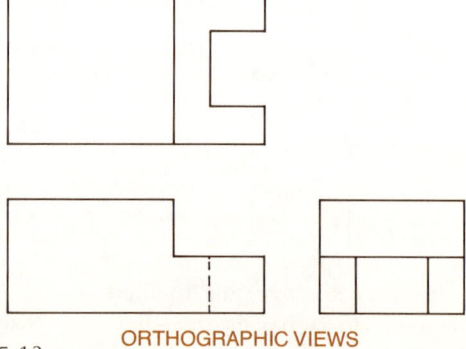

ORTHOGRAPHIC VIEWS

Fig. 15-13

Here is a quick review. Just follow the steps carefully.

1. Lightly draw the isometric axes.
2. Lightly draw the isometric box.
3. Transfer all detail dimensions onto the isometric axes or lines parallel to the axes.
4. Erase all unnecessary construction lines.
5. Darken the outline of the object.

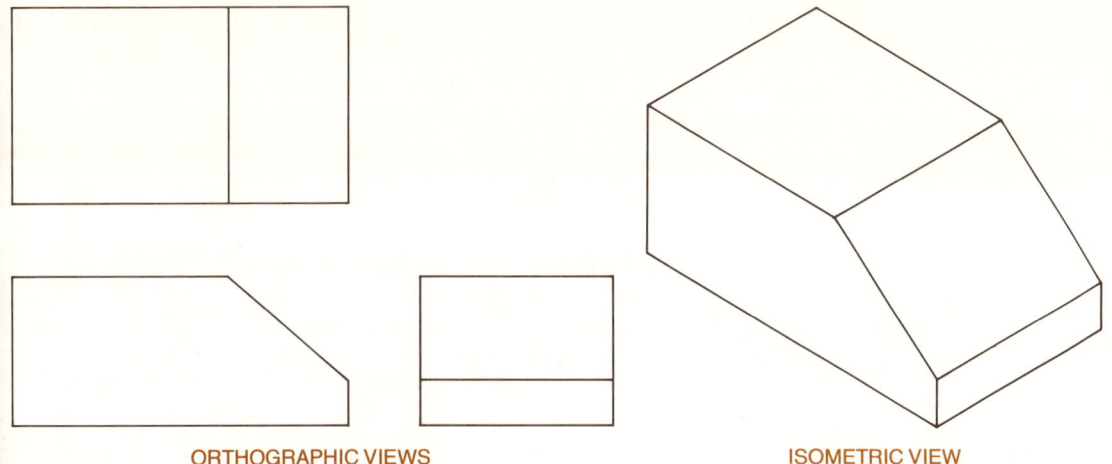

ORTHOGRAPHIC VIEWS   ISOMETRIC VIEW   Fig. 15-16(b)

Fig. 15-15

Drawing Inclined Surfaces in Isometric Views

Many objects have inclined or sloping surfaces. In the orthographic views these sloping surfaces appear as lines that are not parallel to any isometric axis. (Fig. 15-15) Inclined lines can be drawn on isometric views using the angle dimensions given in orthographic views.

Figure 15-16 shows how sloping lines are located and drawn.

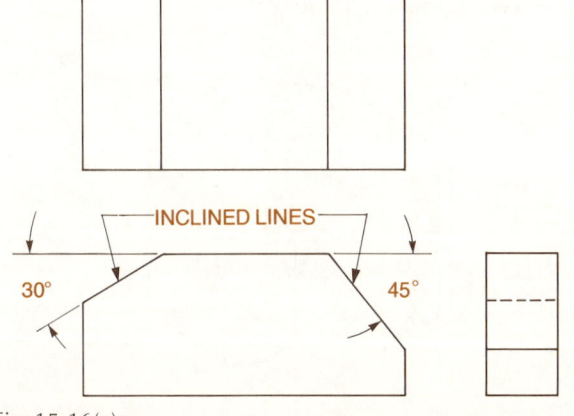

Fig. 15-16(a)

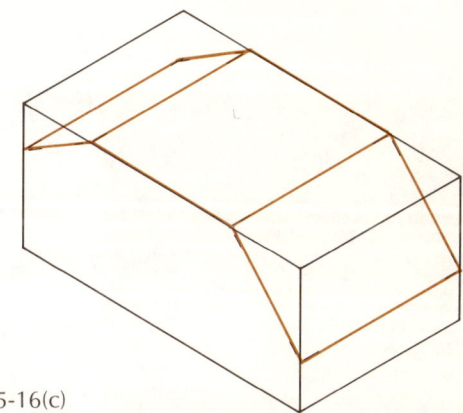

Fig. 15-16(c)

Steps in Drawing an Inclined Surface

1. Centre the isometric axes as before.
2. Construct the isometric box as before.
3. Locate the top and bottom ends of the sloping lines by measuring along the isometric lines.
4. Join these points with straight lines. The points that are joined in the front view are joined in the isometric view.
5. Complete the isometric view.

Remember. Lines that are parallel in the orthographic views are parallel in the isometric view.

TYPES OF PICTORIAL DRAWINGS   197

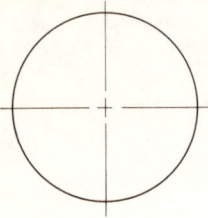

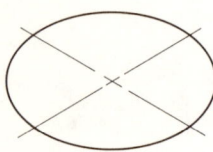

Fig. 15-17

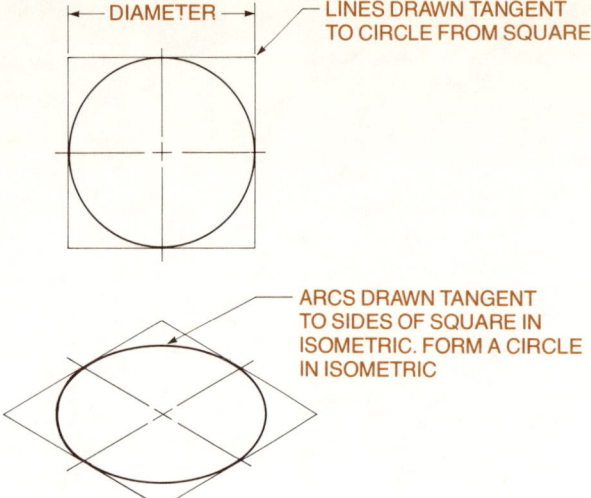

Fig. 15-18

Circles in Isometric Views

In isometric drawings a circle appears in the shape of an ellipse. (Fig. 15-17)

If we were to draw tangent lines to a circle, as in Fig. 15-18, we would have produced a square. You can see that the diameter of the circle is equal in length to each side of the square. Strangely enough we have just found the clue to drawing a circle in isometric. That is, to draw a circle in isometric we must first construct a square in isometric. Each side of the square would be equal in length to the diameter of the circle you want to draw. The most common positions for circles in isometric are shown by the cube as illustrated in Fig. 15-19.

Don't give up at this point. You can follow a few simple steps to construct a perfect isometric circle.

Steps in Drawing Isometric Circles in the Top Position

1. Draw two isometric centre lines. (Fig. 15-20)

Fig. 15-20

2. Mark the radius of the circle off on the centre lines. (Fig. 15-21)

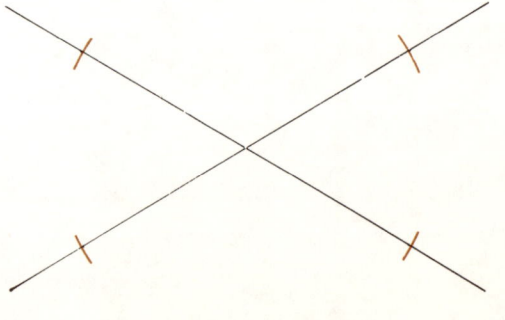

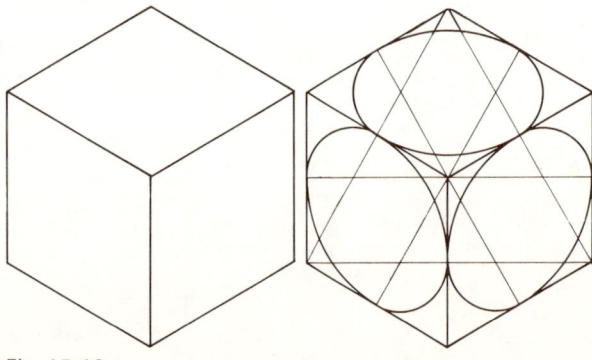

Fig. 15-19

Fig. 15-21

198 PICTORIAL DRAWINGS

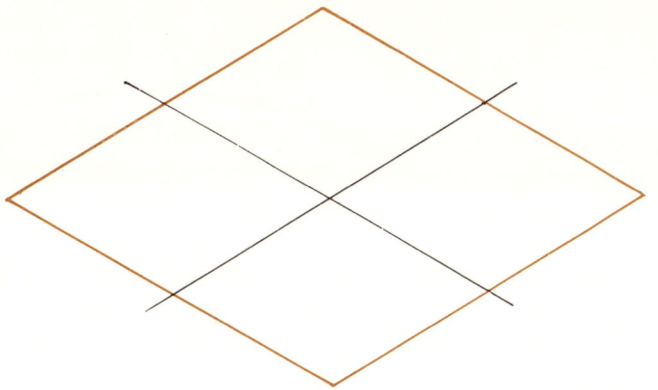

Fig. 15-22

3. Construct an isometric square by drawing isometric lines through these points (Fig. 15-22). Take a minute to study the square you have just drawn. Each side must be exactly the same size. Check them. Notice that the isometric square has two pairs of angles: two large angles called **obtuse angles** and two smaller angles called **acute angles**. An obtuse angle is larger than 90°; an acute angle is smaller than 90°.
4. From the corner of each of the obtuse angles construct lines to the centres of the opposite sides. (Fig. 15-23). You now have the four centre points necessary to construct the isometric circle. All that is left to do is to draw the four arcs to form the isometric circle.
5. Place the compass point in the corner of one obtuse angle. Set the compass to the length of the line and draw the arc tangent to the sides of the angle as shown in Fig. 15-24.

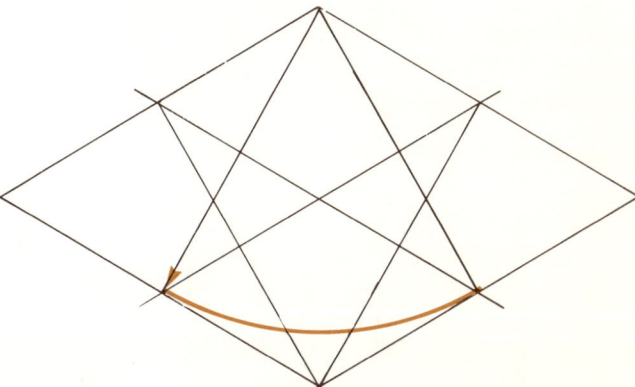

Fig. 15-24

6. Place the compass in the corner of the other obtuse angle. Using the same radius as before, draw the arc as shown in Fig. 15-25. The two remaining centre points are located by the intersecting construction lines.

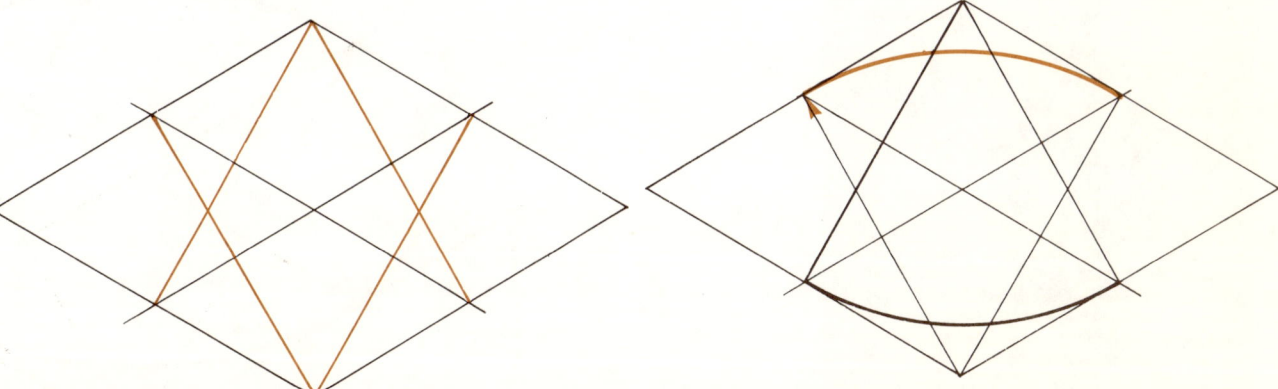

Fig. 15-23

Fig. 15-25

TYPES OF PICTORIAL DRAWINGS

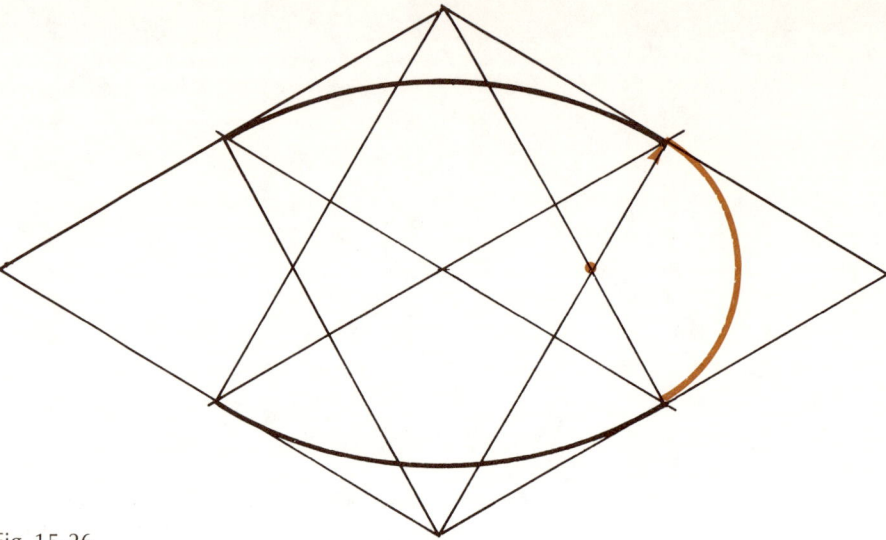

Fig. 15-26

7. Place the compass point at the intersection of the construction lines. Set the compass to the length of the line and draw the arc tangent to the sides of the acute angle as shown in Fig. 15-26.

8. Place the compass point at the intersection of the other two construction lines. Using the same radius as in step 7, draw the last arc tangent to the sides of the angle shown in Fig. 15-27.

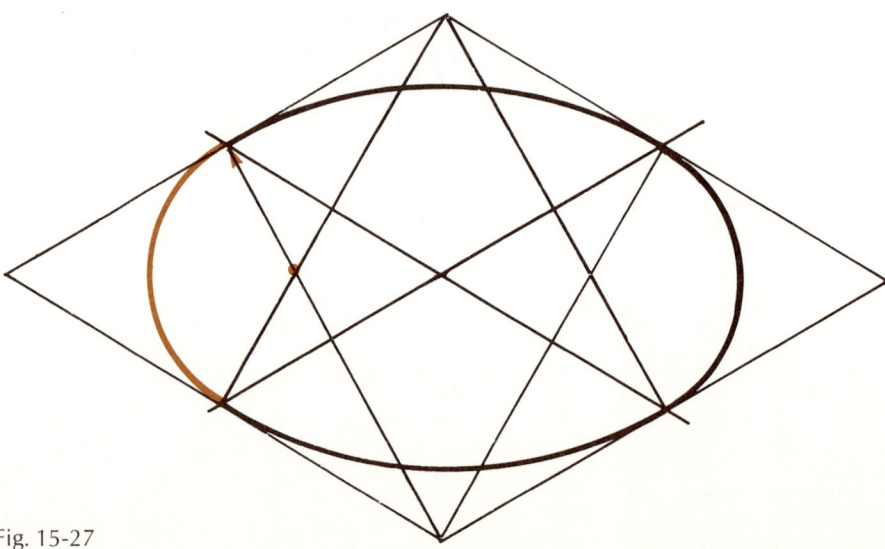

Fig. 15-27

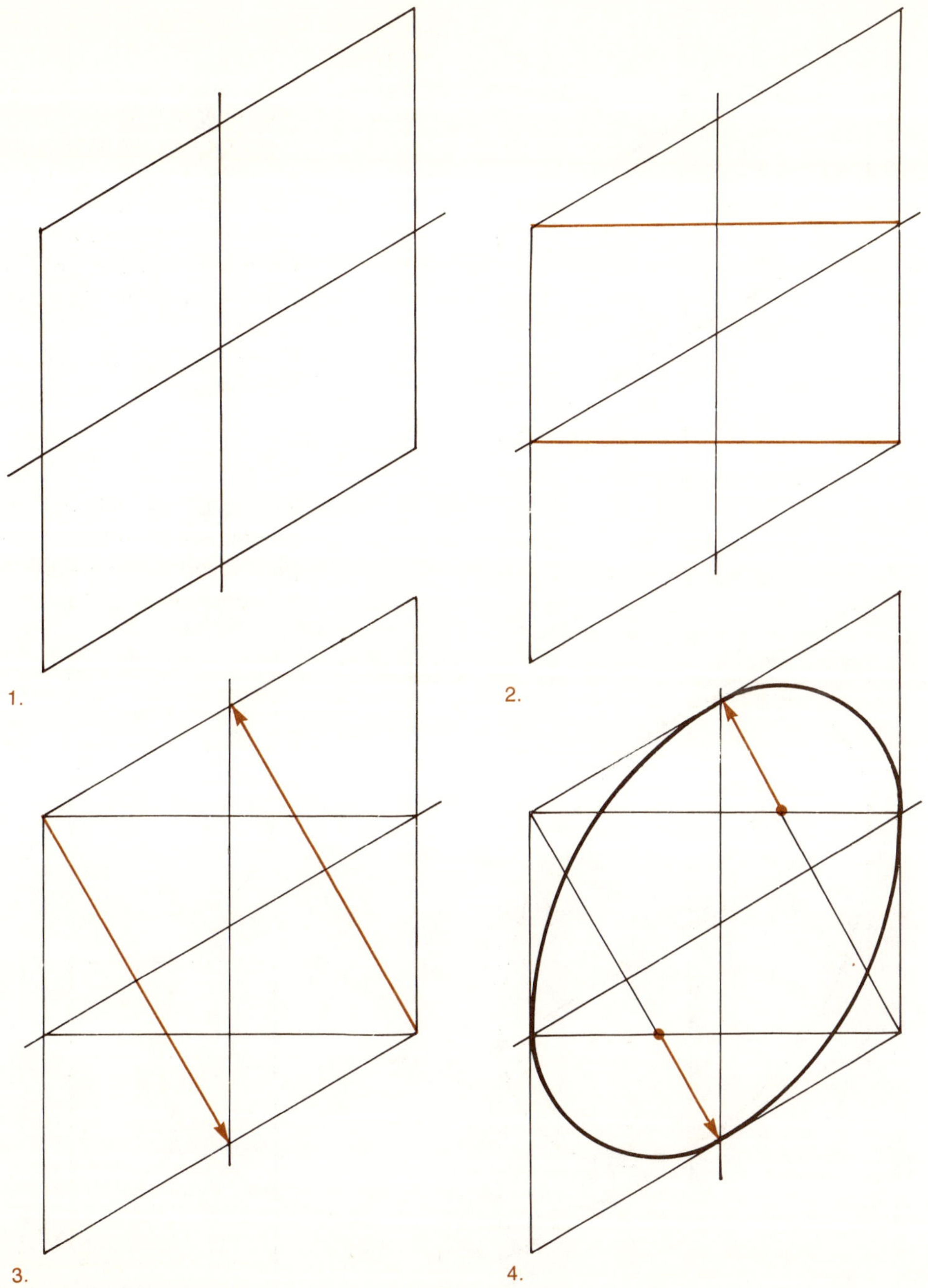

Steps in Drawing Isometric Circles in the Right Position

1. Draw the two isometric centre lines.
2. Construct an isometric square on the centre lines. **Remember.** The length of the isometric square is equal to the diameter of the circle.
3. From the corners of the two obtuse angles draw construction lines to the opposite sides. This locates the centre points for the circle.
4. Draw the four arcs as shown using the same steps as for the top position.

Fig. 15-28(a)

TYPES OF PICTORIAL DRAWINGS

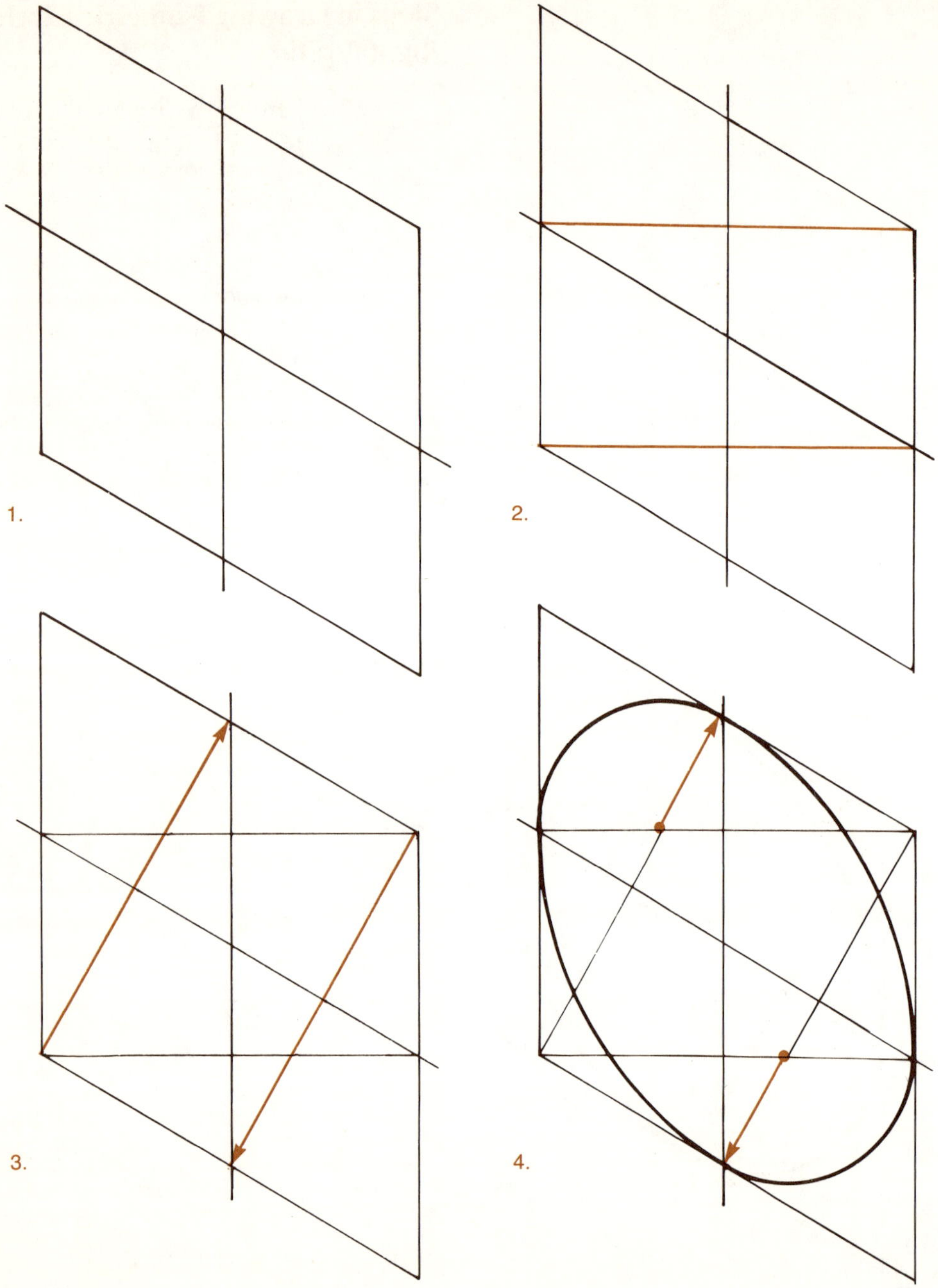

Steps in Drawing Isometric Circles in Left Position

1. Draw the isometric centre lines.
2. Construct an isometric square on the centre lines. The sides of the square are equal to the diameter of the circle.
3. From the corner of the two obtuse angles draw construction lines to the opposite sides. This locates the centre points for the circle.
4. Draw the four arcs as shown using the same steps as for the top position.

Steps in Drawing an Isometric Cylinder

1. Visualize the cylinder from the orthographic views in Fig. 15-29. In this example, the top position would appear to be the best position. (Fig. 15-30)

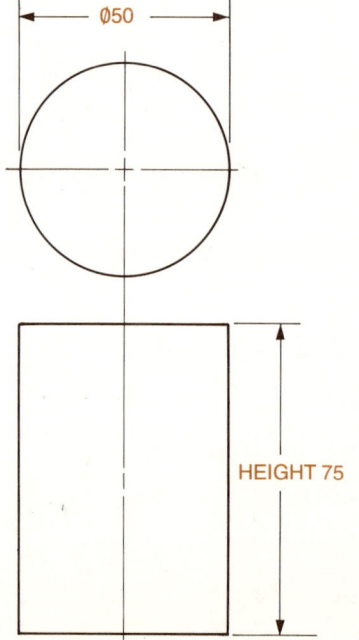

Fig. 15-28(b)

Fig. 15-29

202   PICTORIAL DRAWINGS

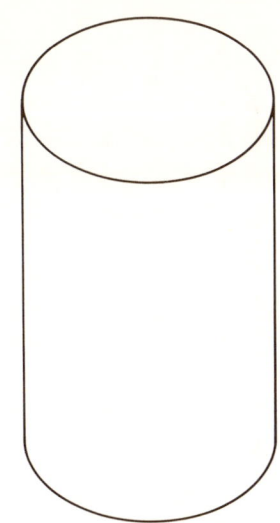

Fig. 15-30

2. Construct the isometric square for the top face of the cylinder. The sides of the square are 50 mm long, equal to the diameter of the cylinder.
3. Locate the centre points for the circle as usual.
4. Draw the arcs tangent to the sides of the square to form the circle.

(Fig. 15-31a) To draw the bottom edge of the cylinder we need to locate three new centre points.

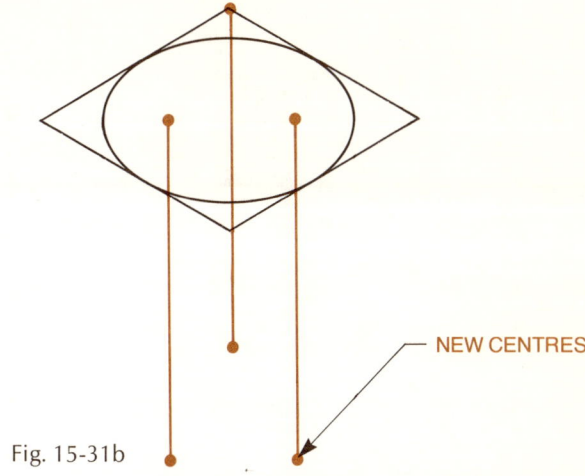

Fig. 15-31b — NEW CENTRES

5. Project light lines from three of the centre points used to construct the top circle. Because the cylinder is in the top position, these lines project straight down parallel to the vertical axis. From the centre points, measure down and mark off the height distance, in this example 75 mm. These are the new centre points for the arcs that form the bottom of the cylinder.
6. Set the compass to the radius of the large arc. Move down the projection line to the new centre. Draw the arc.

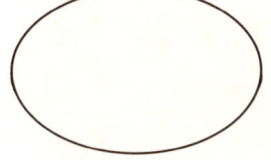

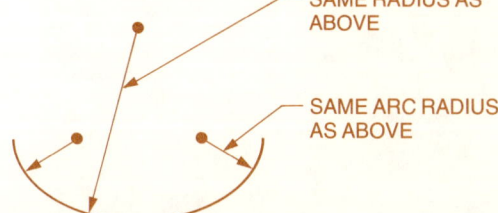

Fig. 15-31c

SAME RADIUS AS ABOVE

SAME ARC RADIUS AS ABOVE

TYPES OF PICTORIAL DRAWINGS 203

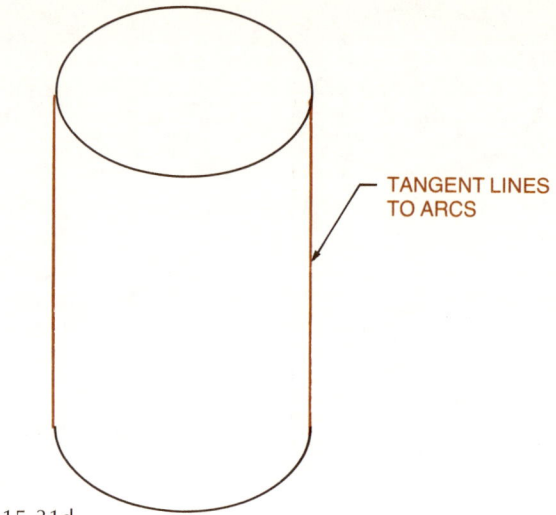

Fig. 15-31d

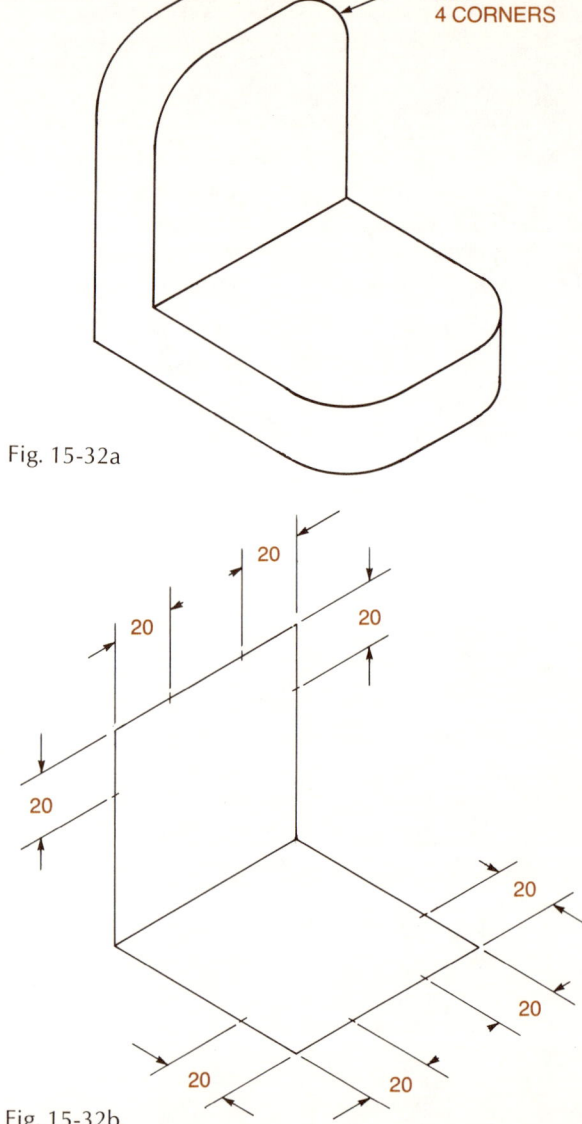

Fig. 15-32a

Fig. 15-32b

7. Set the compass to the radius of the smaller arc. Move down the projection line to the new centre. Draw the arc tangent to the other arc.
8. Use the same radius as in step 6. Move down the projection line to the new centre. Draw the arc tangent to the other arc.
9. Draw tangent lines from the arcs in the top position to the arcs below. Note that only three arcs were necessary to form the bottom edge.

Steps in Drawing Arcs in Isometric

Any arc can be drawn given the radius and the centre point. In our example the radius for each corner is 20 mm. The centres for the arcs can be located very easily.

1. From each corner, mark off the radius distance along the isometric lines, 20 mm.
2. Contruct lines perpendicular to the lines from the points you have marked off.
3. Place the compass where the lines intersect in each corner. Set the compass to draw the arc tangent to the sides of the corner.

Isometric Template. We are sure you have enjoyed the results of your efforts. To save time, however, in the future you can use an isometric template. Once you understand the basics of isometric circles you will find the isometric template a valuable aid.

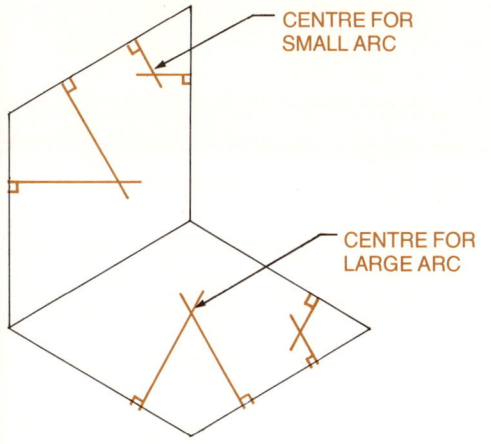

Fig. 15-32c

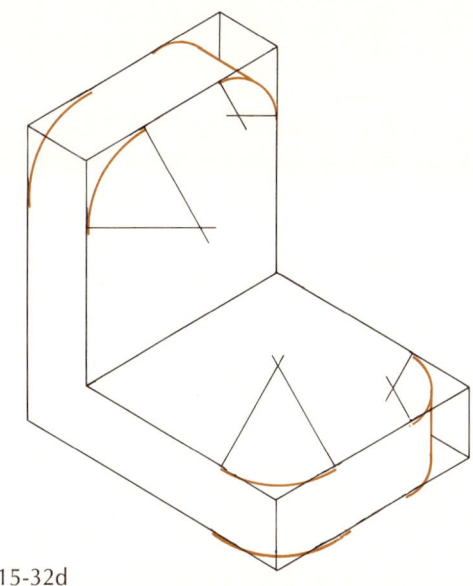

Fig. 15-32d

at a 30° or 45° angle. Oblique pictorials are used to advantage in objects having circular contours and features.

Note. To reduce distortions often created by the receding lines, the length of each receding line is reduced by half.

This type of oblique pictorial is called **cabinet projection**. It is important to decide which view of an object gives the most information before drawing the pictorial. As in isometric drawing, the receding edges can slope towards either the right or left as a matter of choice.

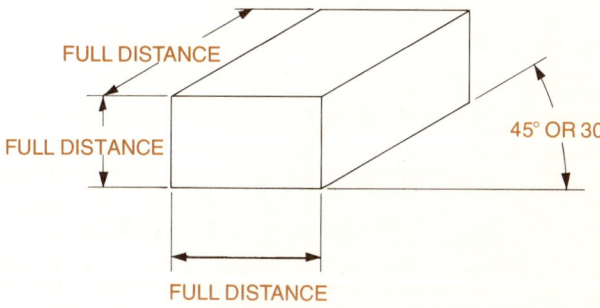

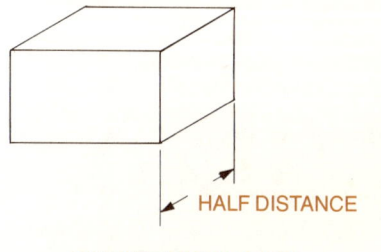

Fig. 15-34

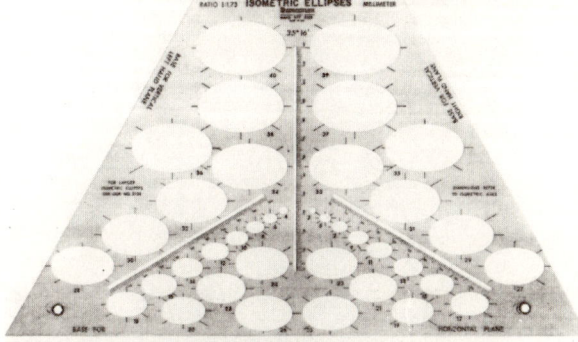

Fig. 15-33

OBLIQUE DRAWINGS

The oblique pictorial is a simple method of describing objects that are neither too complicated nor too large. One surface of the objects is drawn orthographically and all the receding edges are drawn parallel, usually

Steps in Drawing a Cabinet Projection of a Rectangular Object

1. Lightly draw the cabinet box. Use the full height and full length measurements.
2. Lightly draw the receding lines at an angle of 45° to the base line. Mark off half the

OBLIQUE DRAWINGS   205

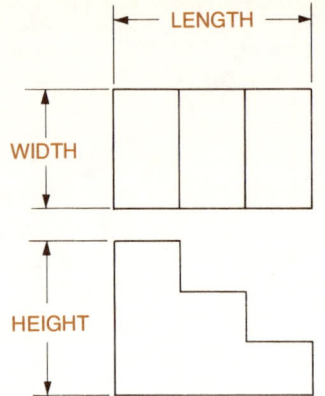

Fig. 15-35

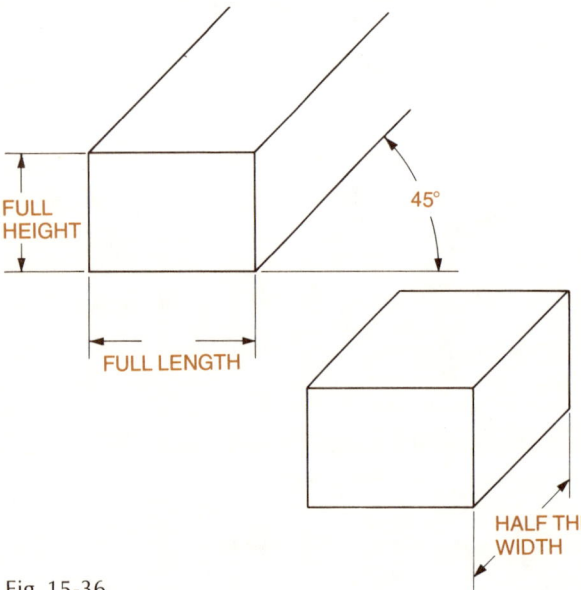

Fig. 15-36

width distance along the receding line and complete the cabinet box.
3. Construct the front view on the front face of the cabinet box.
   Lightly complete the outline of the pictorial using parallel lines.
   Remove unnecessary construction lines and complete the finished linework.

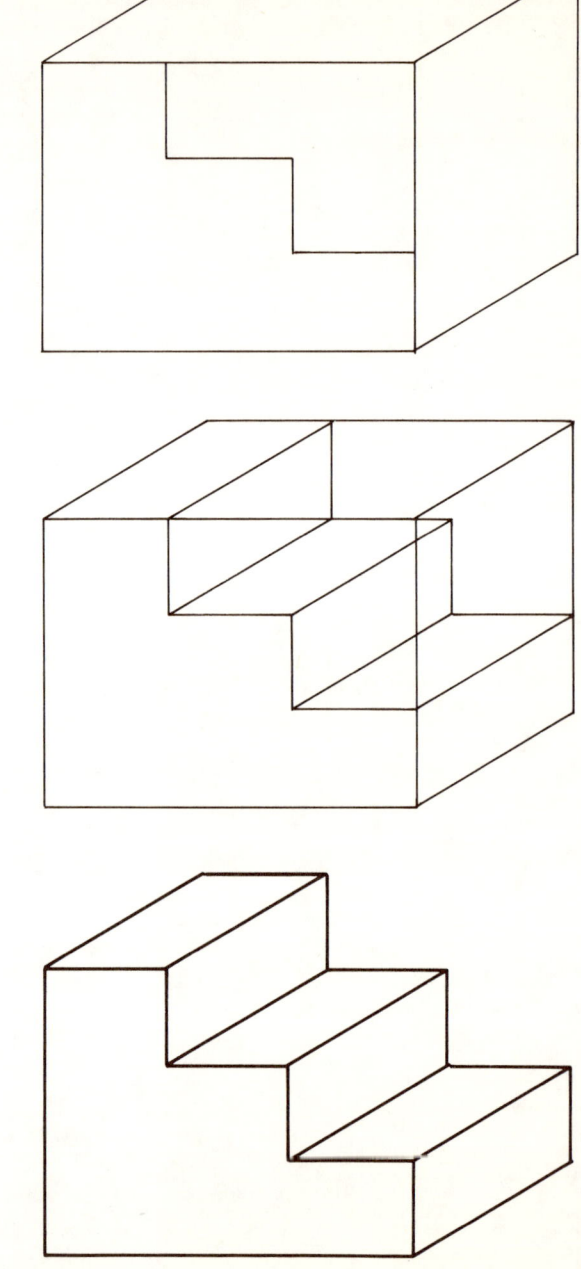

Fig. 15-37

Steps in Drawing a Cabinet Projection of a Cylindrical Object

For best results the circular contours of the object should be drawn orthographically on the front face of the pictorial as full or partial circles. Receding edges can slope either to the right or the left as a matter of choice.

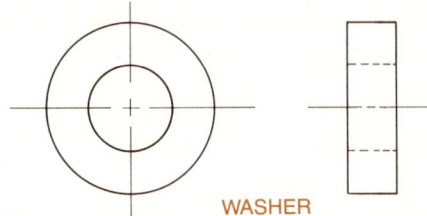

WASHER

Fig. 15-38

1. Construct light horizontal and vertical centre lines and draw the front face of the object, in this case a washer.

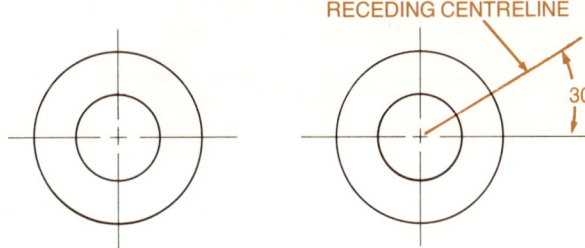

Fig. 15-39

2. From the centre point of the washer draw a receding centre line. Any angle could be used, but for this example the angle is 30°.

Fig. 15-40

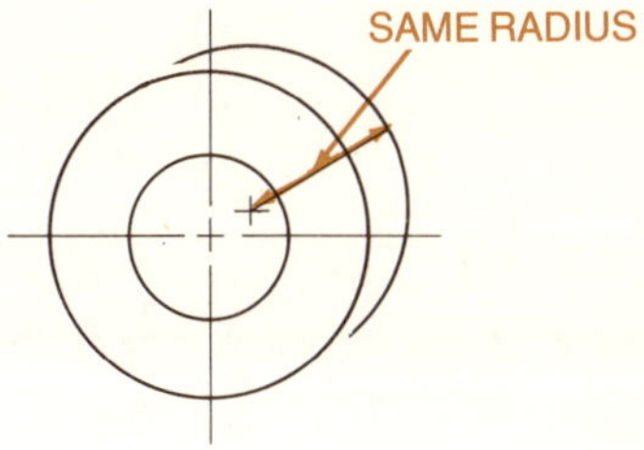

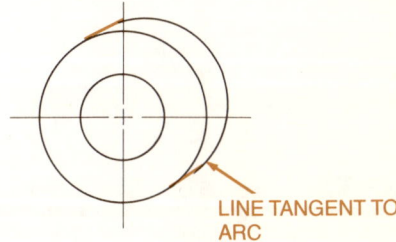

Fig. 15-41

3. Measure half the length of the washer along the receding line for the centre point.
4. Draw the rear contour of the washer using the new centre and the same radius used on the front face.

Fig. 15-42

5. Draw tangent lines from the front face to the arcs completing the washer outline.

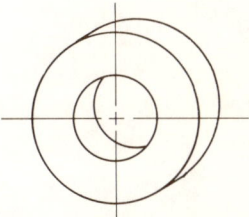

Fig. 15-43

6. Follow the method learned from the above steps to draw the rear contour of the hole in the washer.
7. Remove unnecessary construction lines and complete the finished linework.

OBLIQUE DRAWINGS

POINTS TO REMEMBER

- Pictorial drawings are used to help people visualize what objects look like.
- The three types of pictorial drawings are isometric, oblique and perspective.
- Isometric pictorial is the most popular, although perspective is the most realistic.
- Measurements in isometric must be made on an isometric axis or on a line parallel to an axis.
- Lines that are parallel in the orthographic views of an object are drawn parallel in the isometric view of that object.
- Circles in isometric drawings are drawn as ellipses.
- Oblique pictorials are usually used to describe objects that have circular contours or features.
- Oblique pictorials often produce the most distortion because the receding lines appear too long.
- Receding distances in oblique pictorials are usually shortened to half of the actual distance.

QUESTIONS TO ANSWER

1. Explain what is meant by the statement: "Pictorial drawings help people without orthographic skills to visualize any object."
2. List the three methods of producing pictorial drawings. Which is the most popular?
3. When is oblique projection used for pictorial drawings rather than isometric projection?
4. What is the main disadvantage of oblique pictorials? How does cabinet projection relieve the problem?
5. Which type of pictorial do drafters usually prefer?
6. Describe how sloping surfaces are drawn in isometric drawings.
7. Why is it advisable to begin isometric pictorials with a lightly drawn isometric box?
8. How many centres are required to draw a circle in isometric projection? Describe the appearance of the circle.

HOW TO USE THESE WORDS

1. Both vertical and horizontal **XXXX** lines are used when plotting a graph.
2. When the tide goes out the water **XXXXXXX** from the ocean beach.

PROJECTS

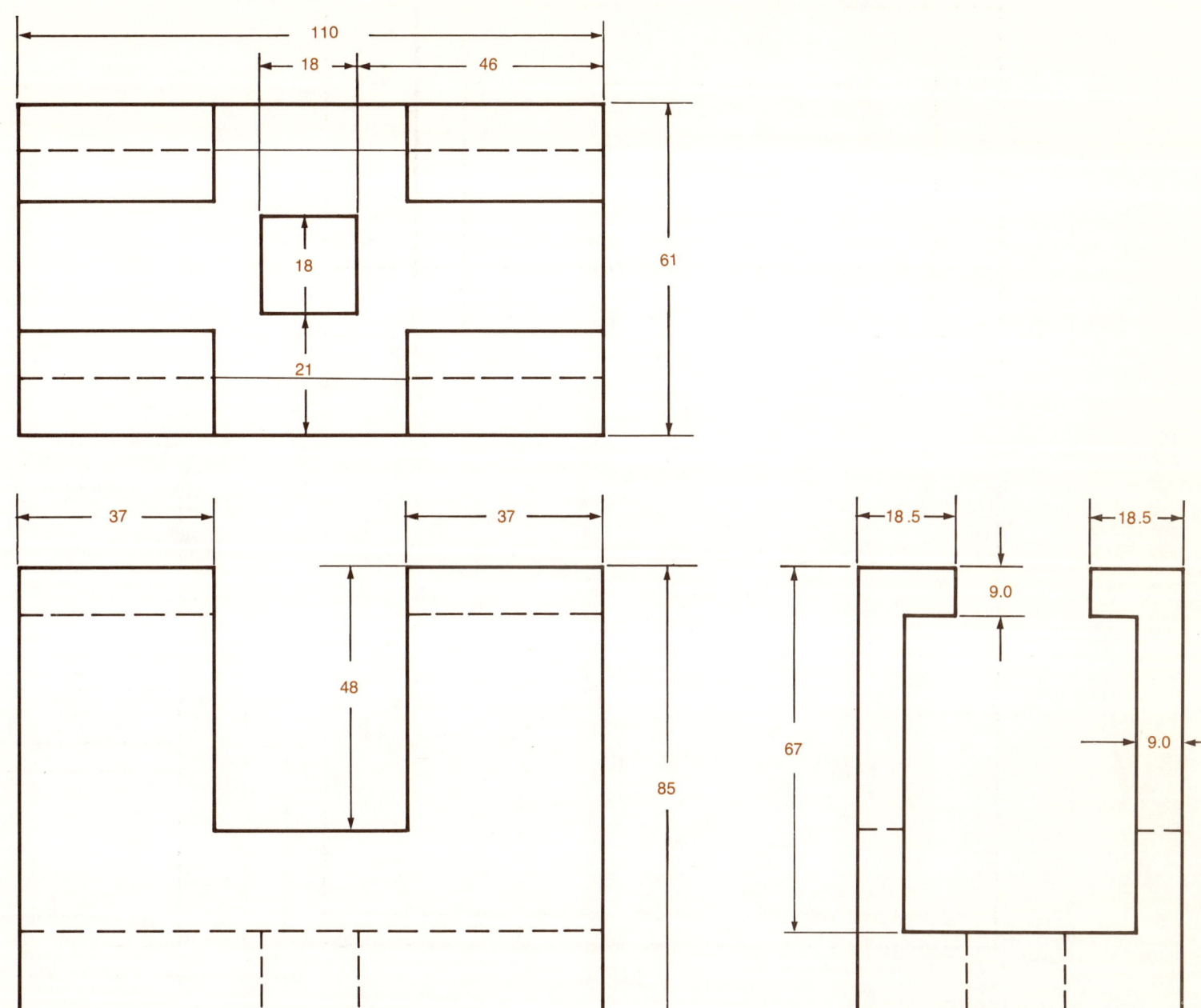

PROJECT 15-1

ISOMETRIC TRACK HANGER

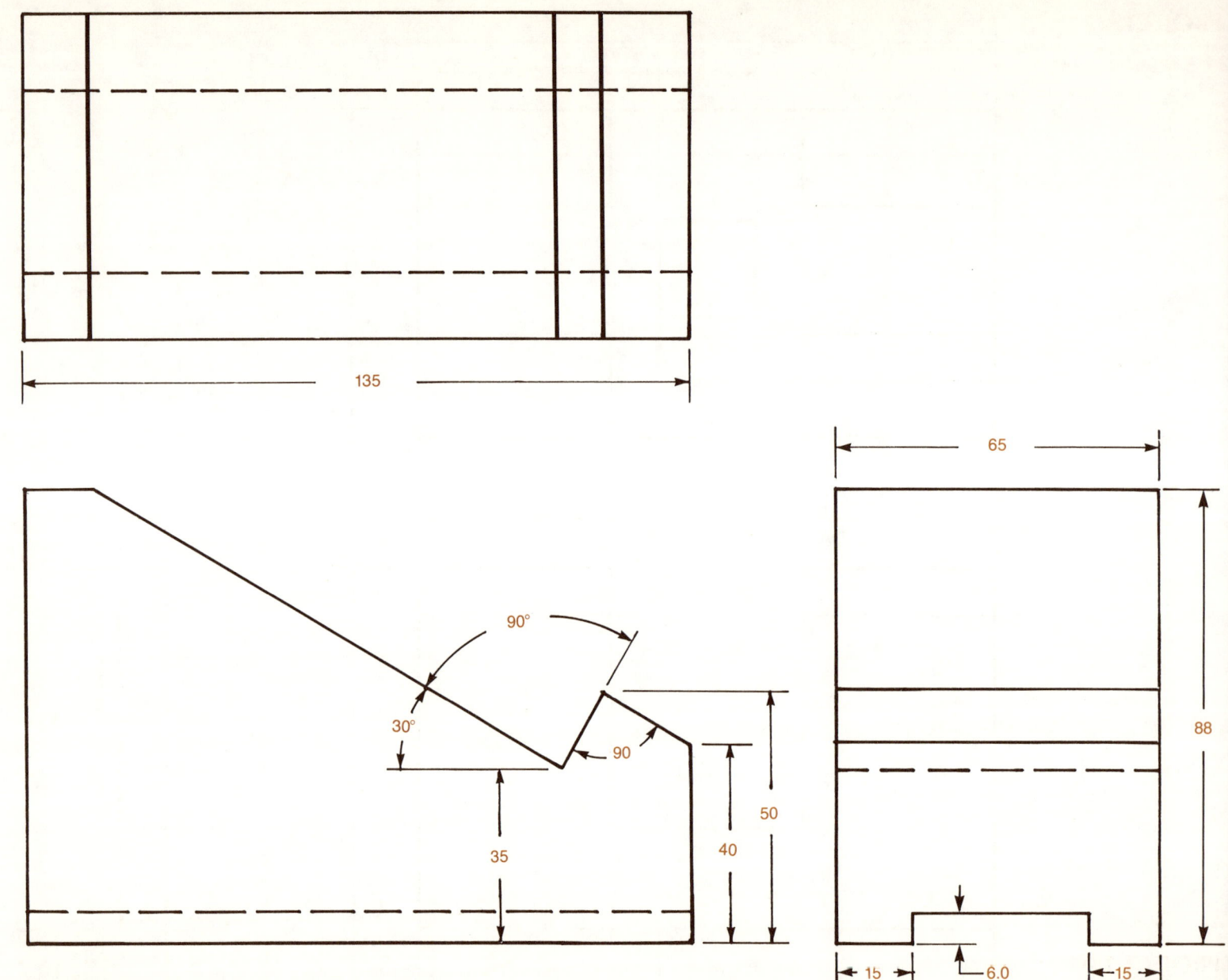

PROJECT 15-2

ISOMETRIC WORK REST

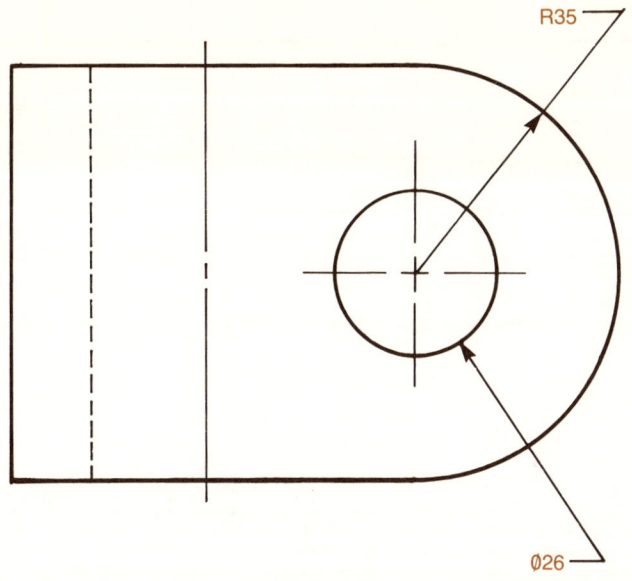

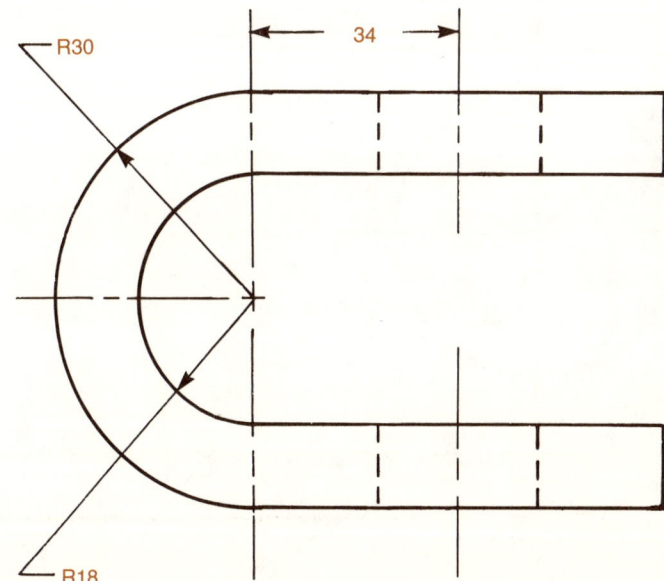

PROJECT 15-3

ISOMETRIC ROD SUPPORT

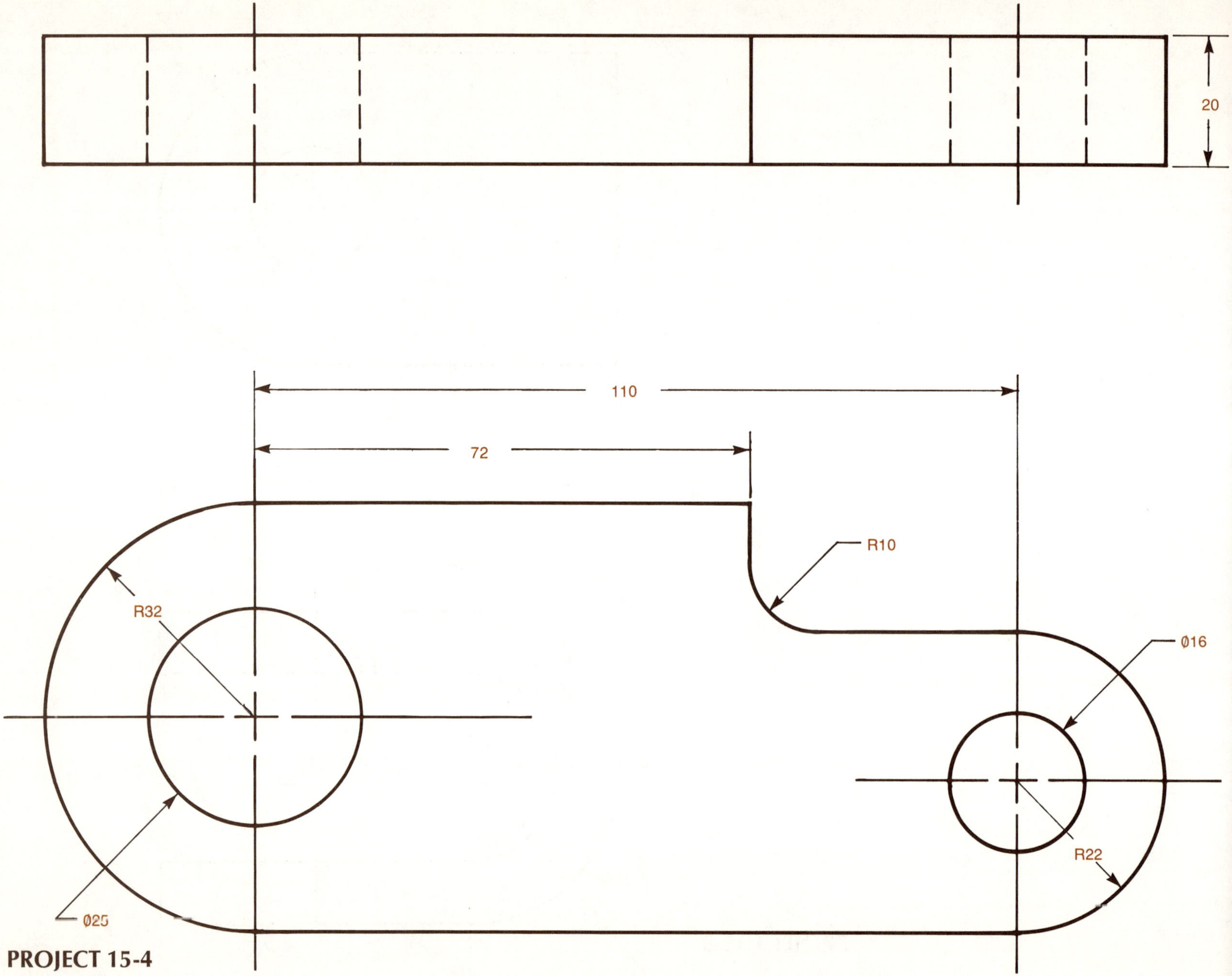

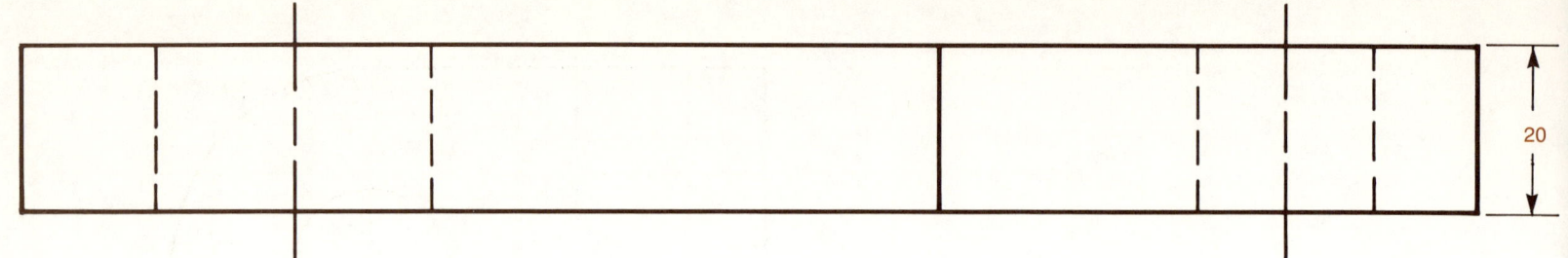

PROJECT 15-4

ISOMETRIC YOKE

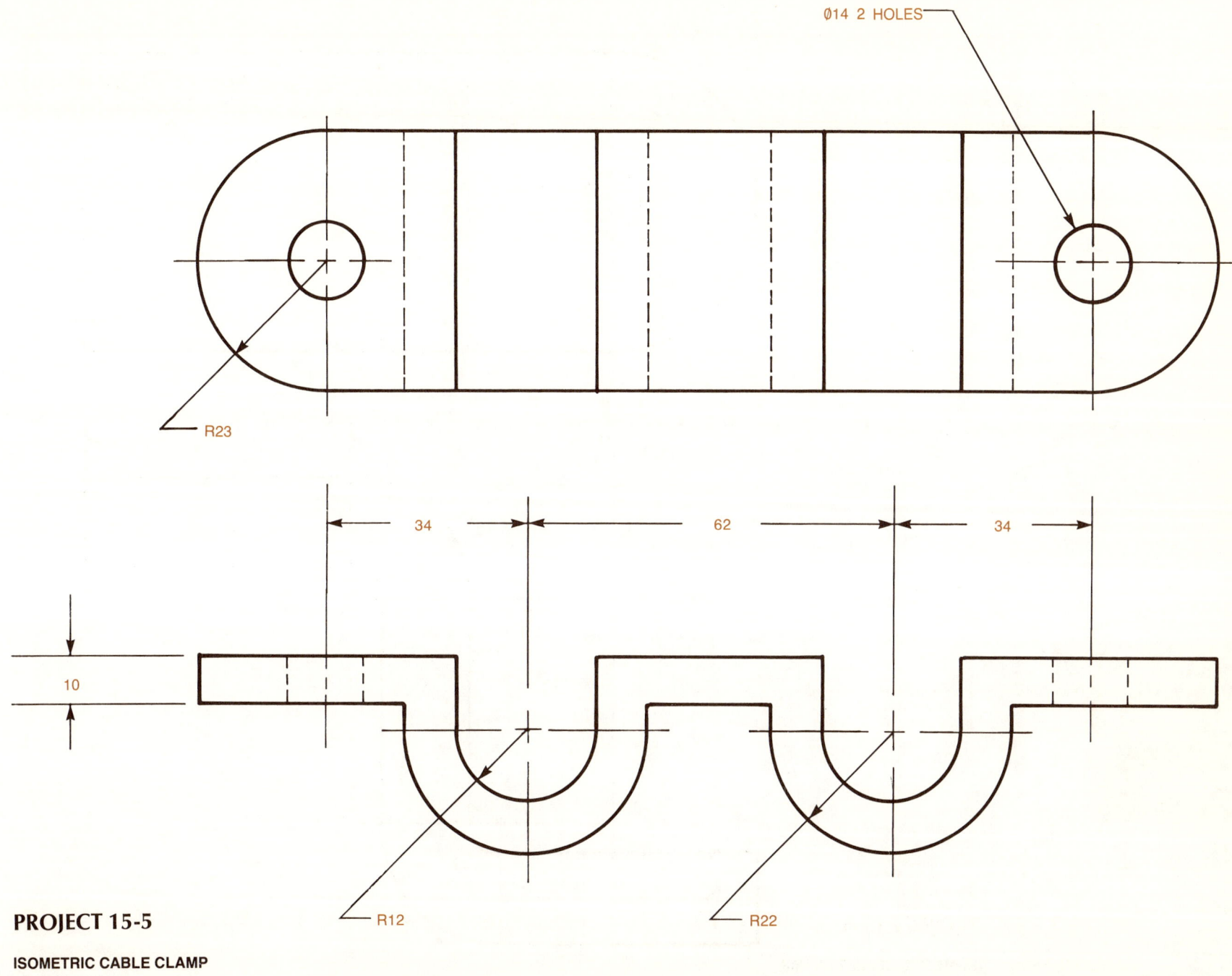

PROJECT 15-5

ISOMETRIC CABLE CLAMP

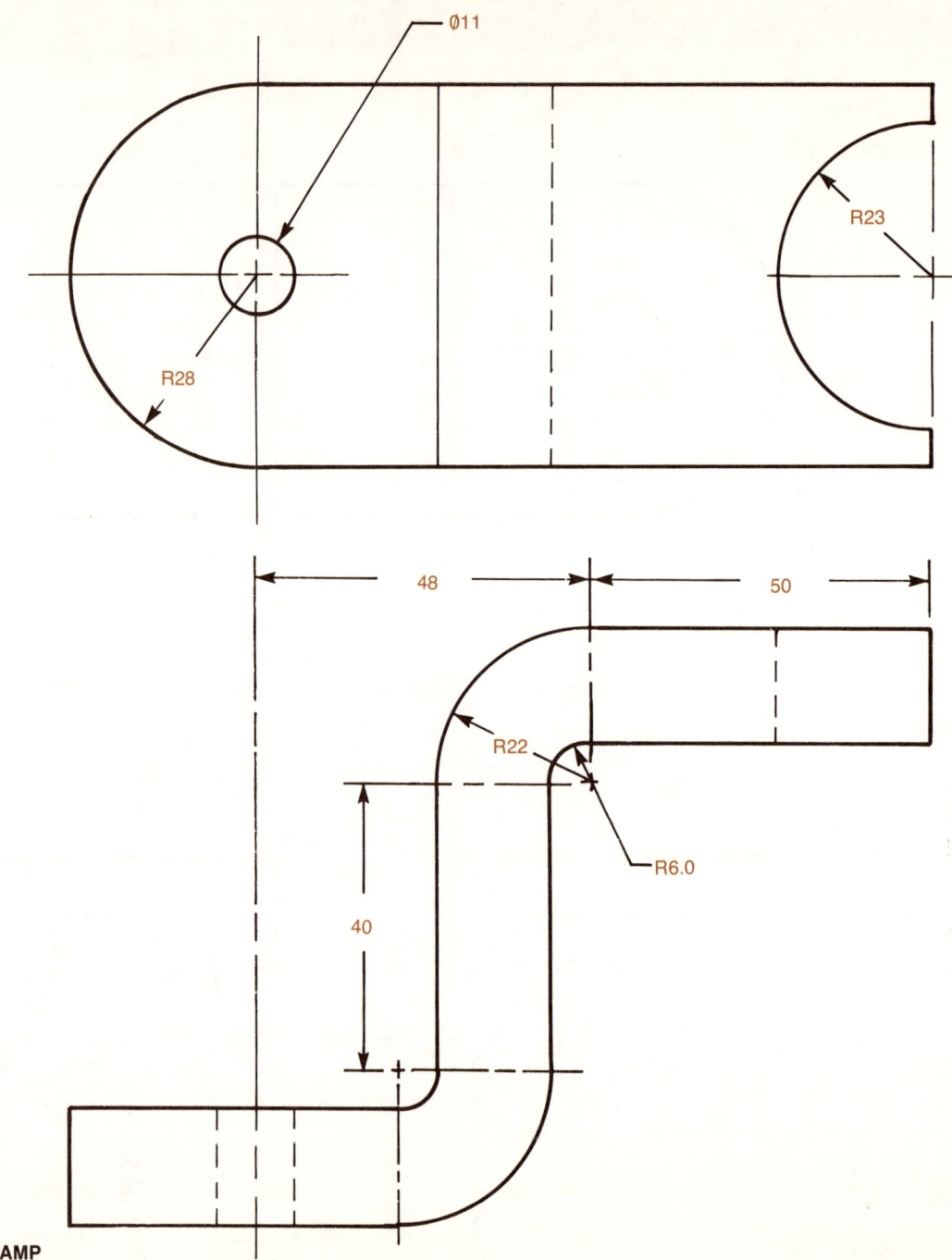

PROJECT 15-6

ISOMETRIC OFFSET CLAMP

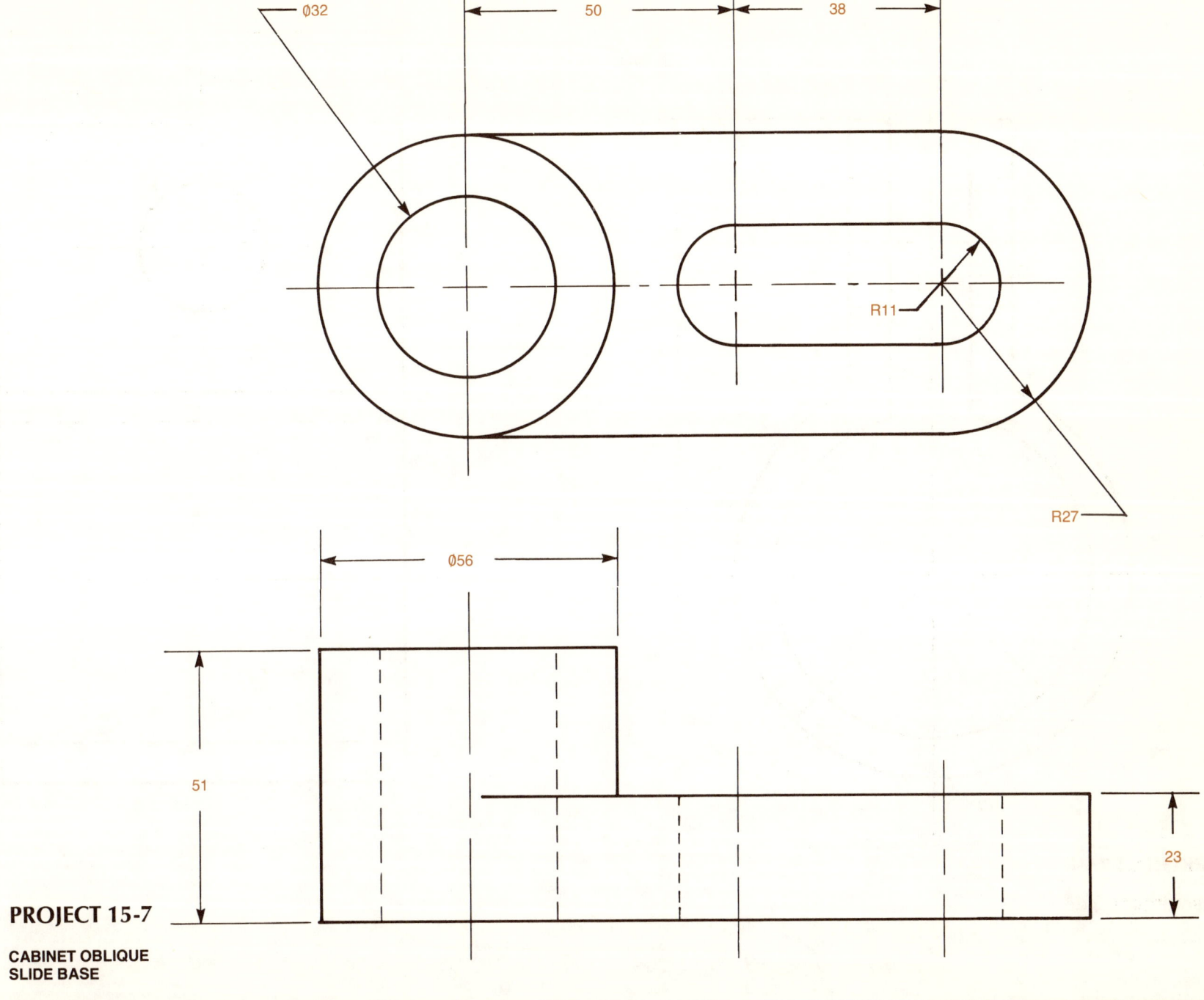

PROJECT 15-7

CABINET OBLIQUE SLIDE BASE

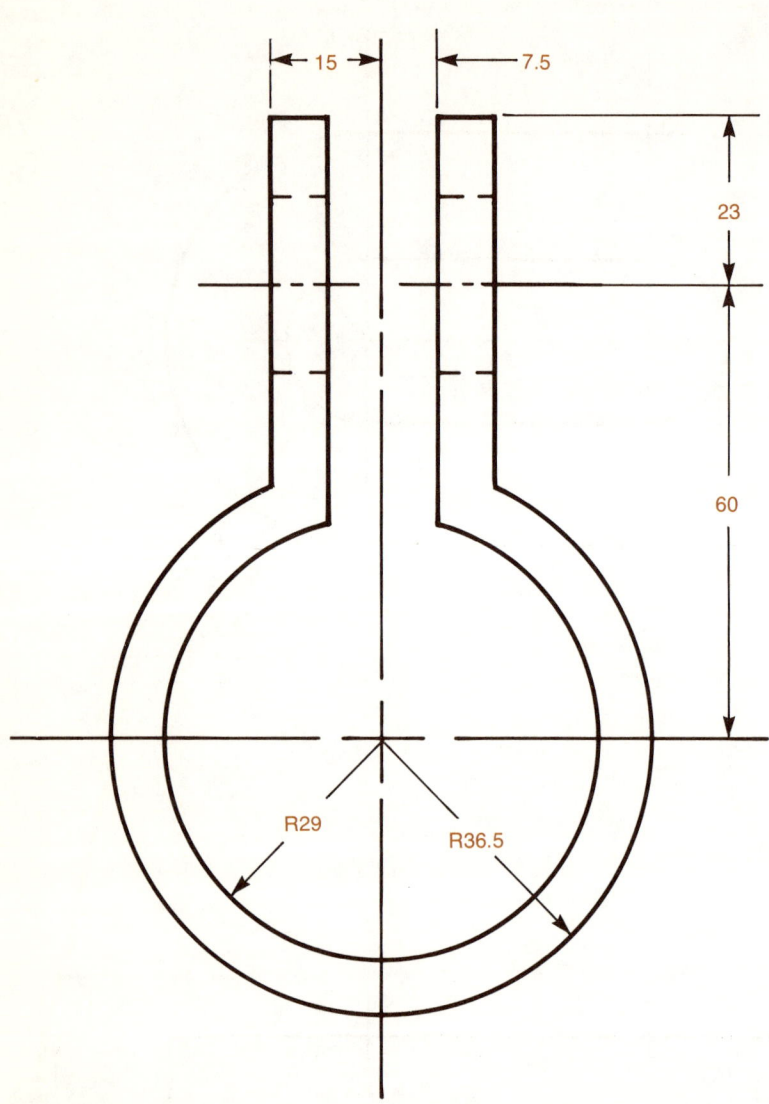
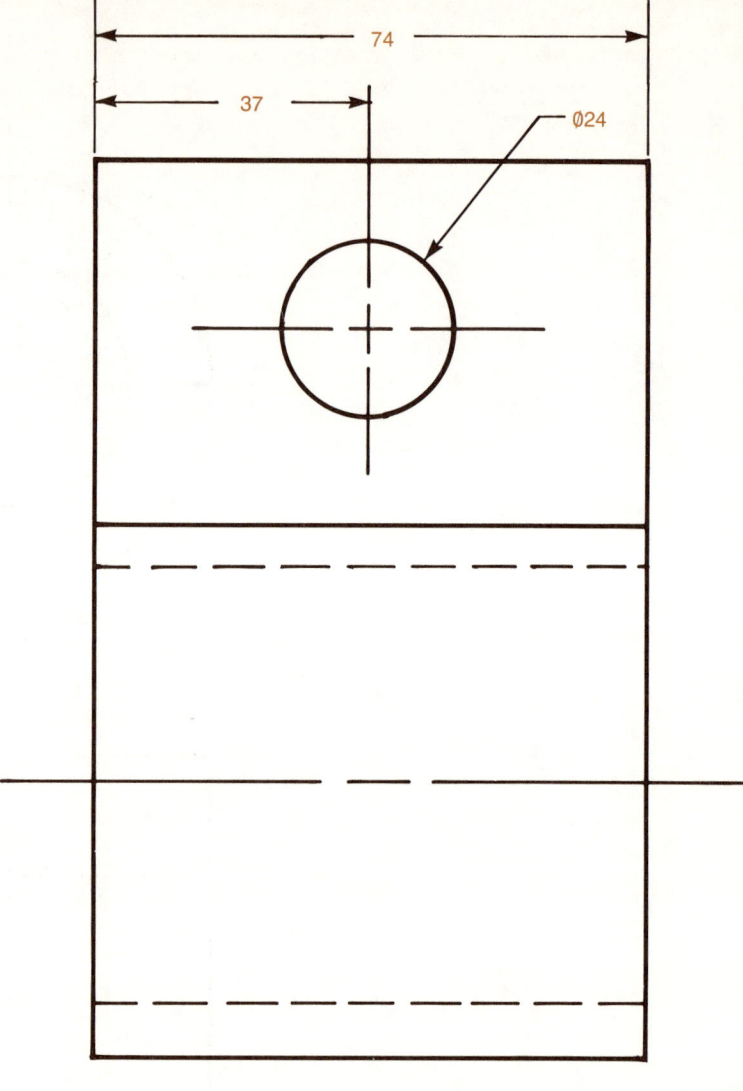

PROJECT 15-8

ISOMETRIC CLAMP

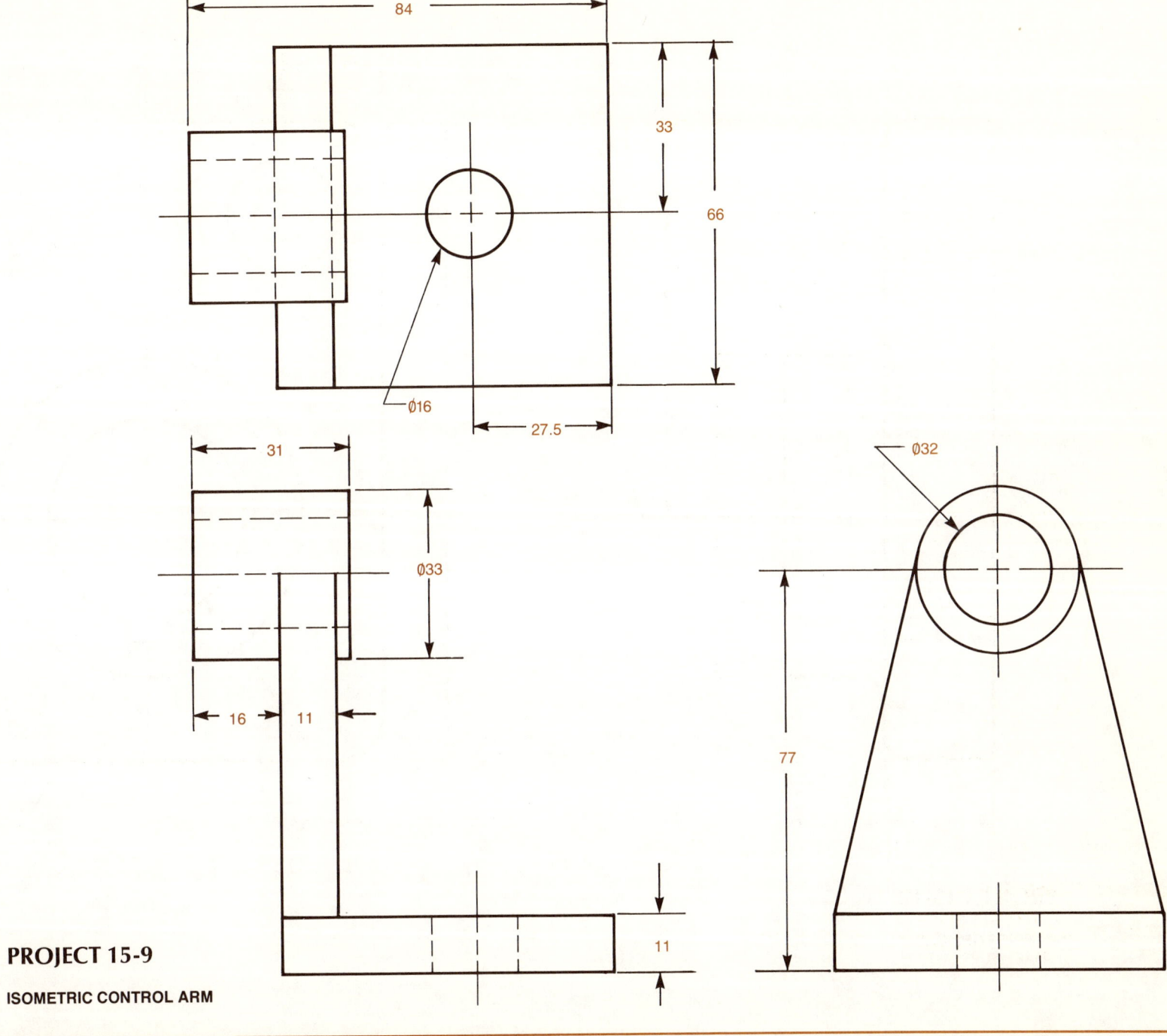

PROJECT 15-9

ISOMETRIC CONTROL ARM

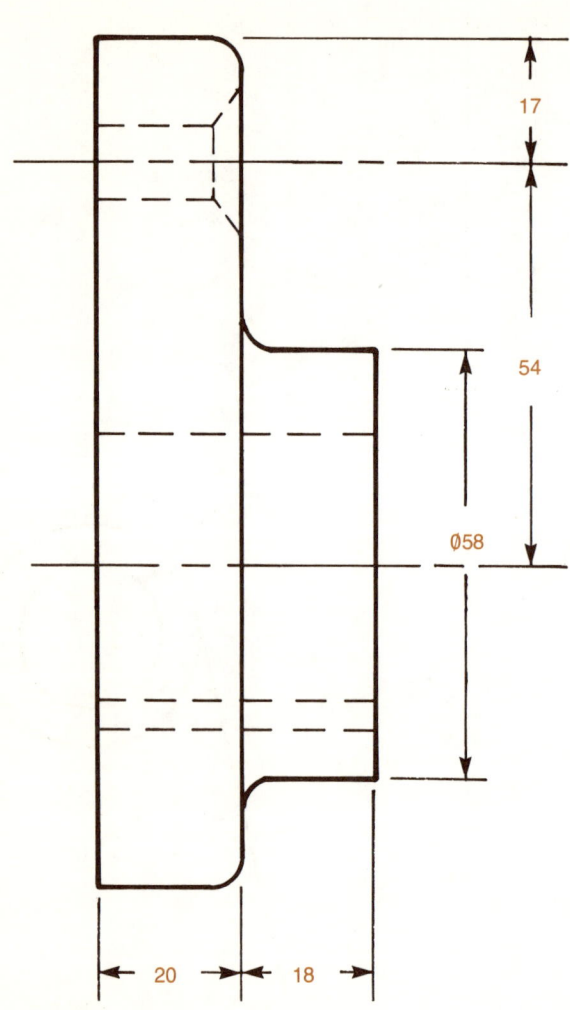
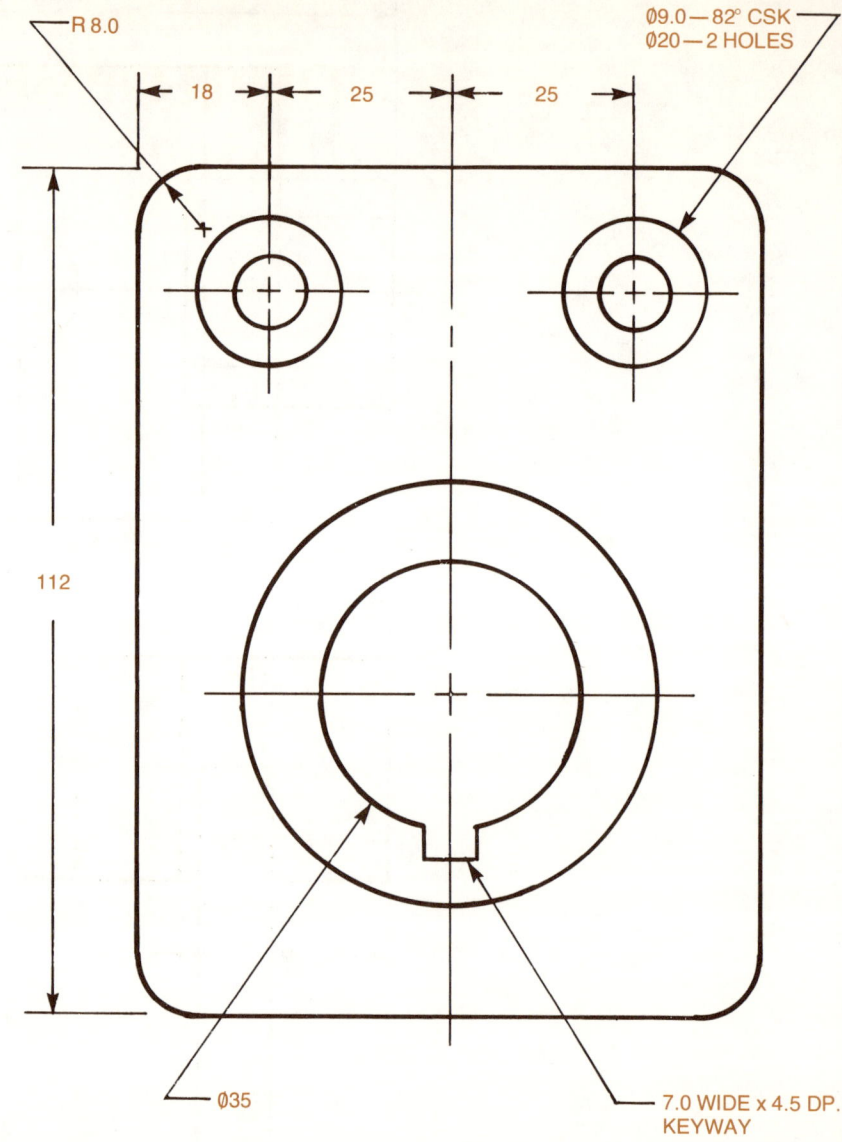

PROJECT 15-10

**CABINET OBLIQUE
SHAFT SUPPORT**

218 PICTORIAL VIEWS

CHAPTER 16
DEVELOPMENT OF OBJECTS

WORDS TO LEARN
enclose (en-clóse)
truncated (trun-cá-ted)
allowance (al-lów-ance)

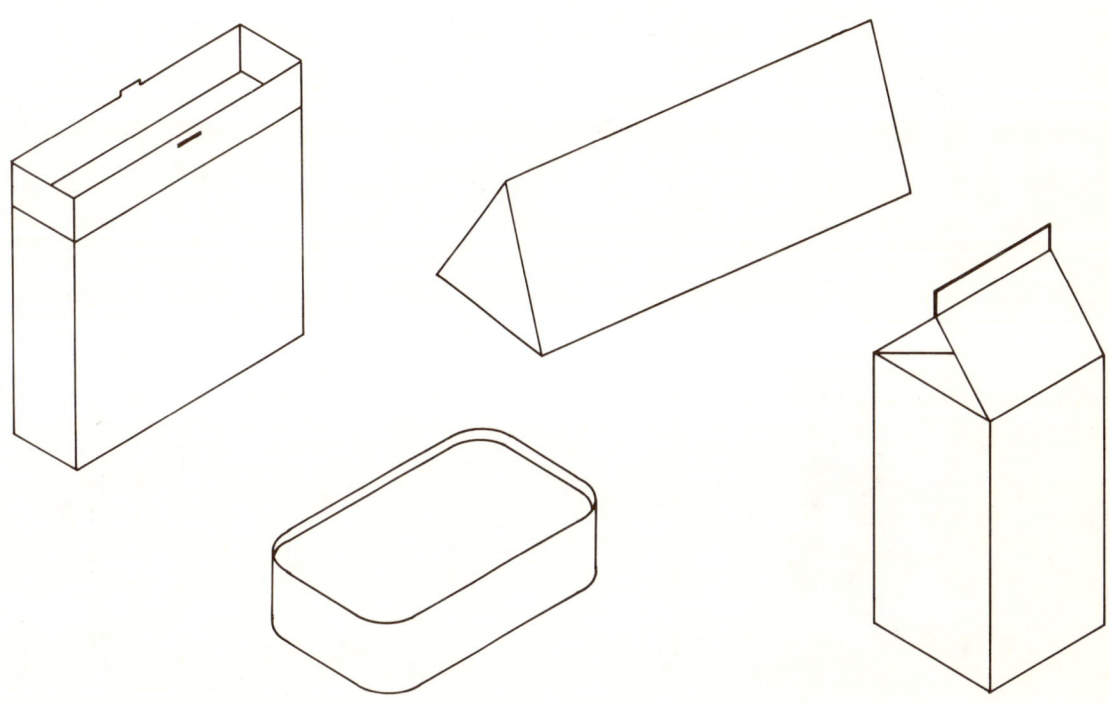

Fig. 16-1

Don't let the title of this chapter puzzle you. We will be dealing with items that you see and use every day.
You have probably developed some of these objects on your own in the past. The development of an object is the opening out or unfolding of its surface or surfaces to its original flat state.

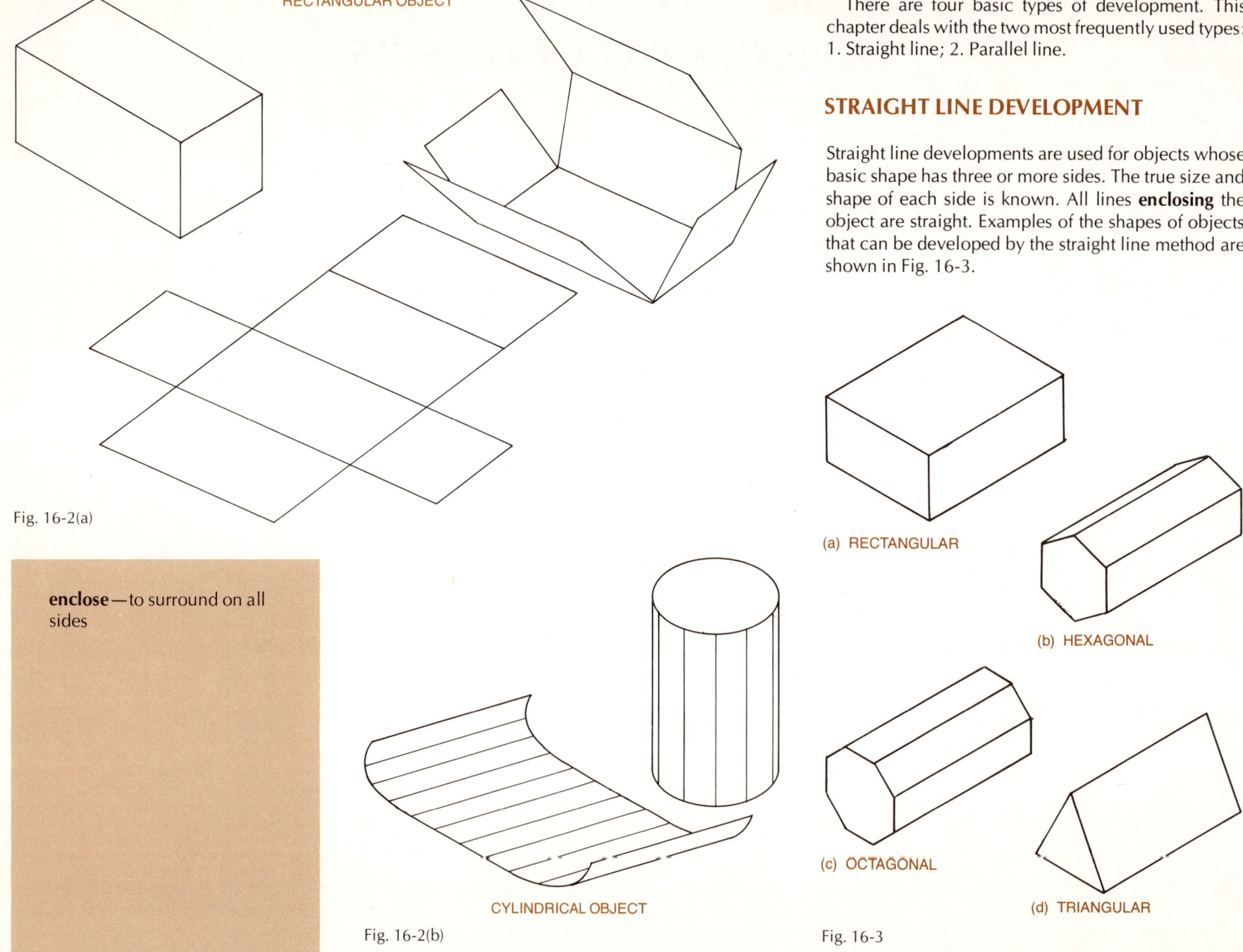

RECTANGULAR OBJECT

Fig. 16-2(a)

enclose—to surround on all sides

CYLINDRICAL OBJECT

Fig. 16-2(b)

There are four basic types of development. This chapter deals with the two most frequently used types: 1. Straight line; 2. Parallel line.

STRAIGHT LINE DEVELOPMENT

Straight line developments are used for objects whose basic shape has three or more sides. The true size and shape of each side is known. All lines **enclosing** the object are straight. Examples of the shapes of objects that can be developed by the straight line method are shown in Fig. 16-3.

(a) RECTANGULAR

(b) HEXAGONAL

(c) OCTAGONAL

(d) TRIANGULAR

Fig. 16-3

220 DEVELOPMENT OF OBJECTS

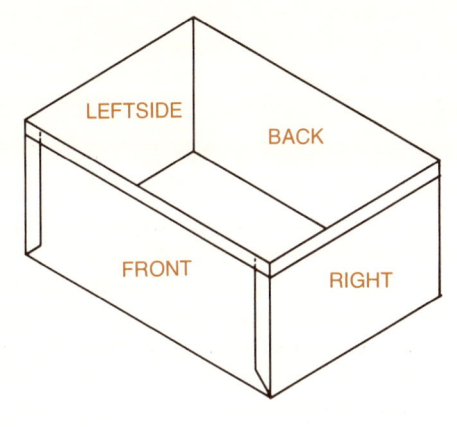

Fig. 16-4(a)

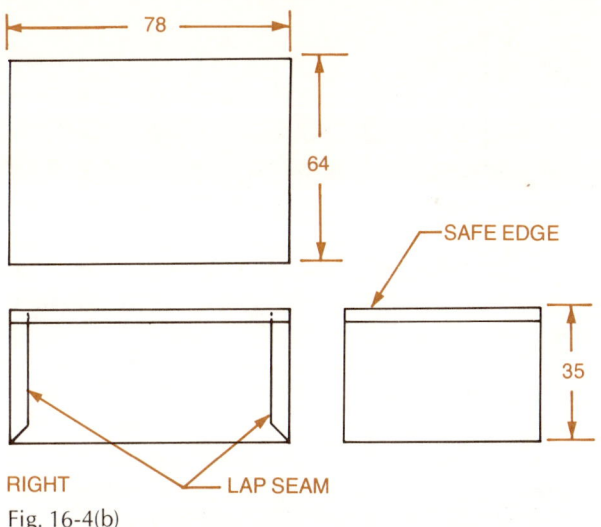

Fig. 16-4(b)

An example of a rectangular object is the simple tray shown in Fig. 16-4(a and b). Follow the development of the tray as it unfolds in Fig. 16-5 (a and b). The completed development drawing with folding instructions, seam and edge allowance is shown in Fig. 16-5(c). Now you will think it doesn't look so simple anymore. It may look complicated at first, but as you have learned before, if you take a problem and progress one step at a time you will find once again how great it is to discover how clever you really are. Ready?

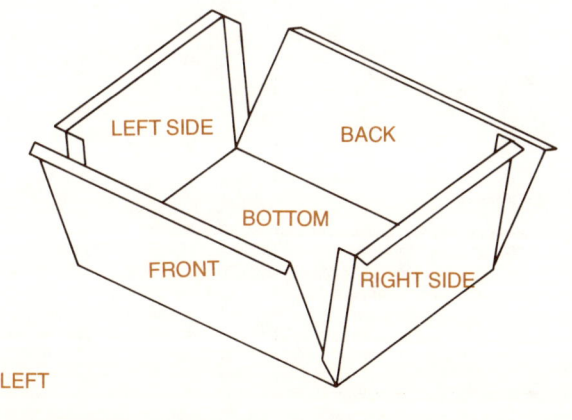

Fig. 16-5(a)

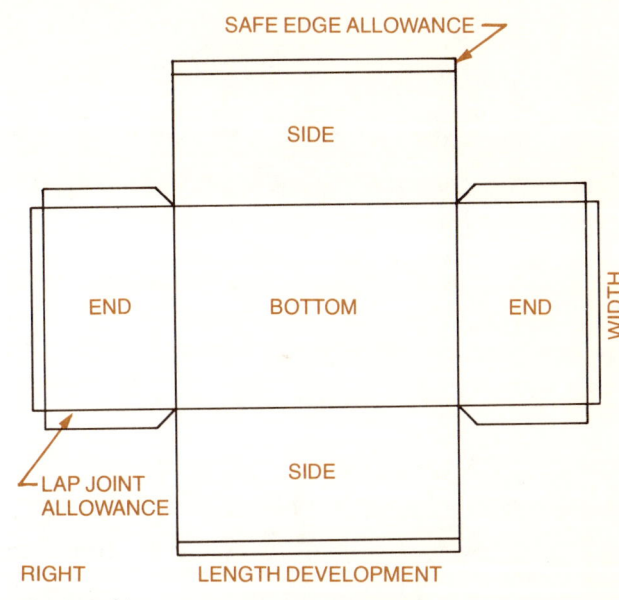

LENGTH DEVELOPMENT

Fig. 16-5(b)

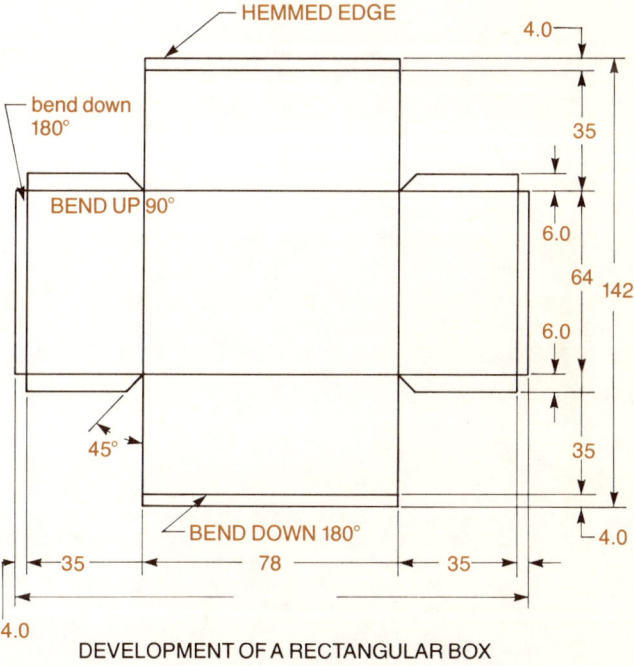

DEVELOPMENT OF A RECTANGULAR BOX

Fig. 16-5(c)

STRAIGHT LINE DEVELOPMENT 221

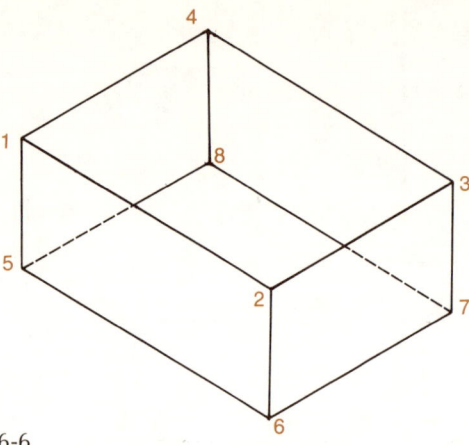

Fig. 16-6

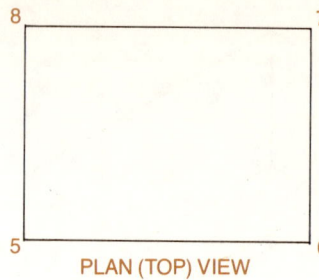

Fig. 16-8

Look at the box again in Fig. 16-6. Numbers have been added to all eight corners of the box to help explain the steps. We can forget about edge seams and joint **allowances** for now.

Steps in Straight Line Development (1)

1. Draw the front and top view as in Fig. 16-7. All measurements are taken from these views.

Fig. 16-7.

allowance—additional space provided for a purpose

There are several ways you could begin. For this, your first development, it would be easier to begin by drawing the top view. Remember you are looking down into the box. This top view is often called the **plan view**.

Note: place this view where space permits.

Fig. 16-9

2. Project lines out from each corner in the plan view.

222 DEVELOPMENT OF OBJECTS

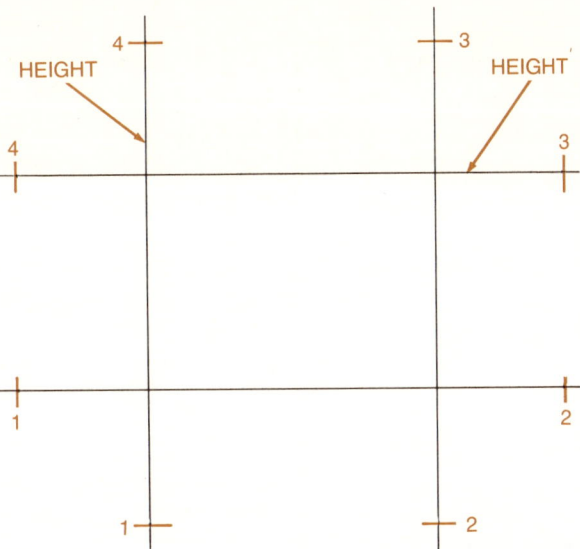

Fig. 16-10

3. Transfer the height to the development by measuring from the corners of the plan view.

view from each of the points you have just drawn.

You now have drawn the basic development except for edge seams and joint allowances. The allowance for edges and joints varies. In this example we will allow 5.0 mm for the edges and joints where required.

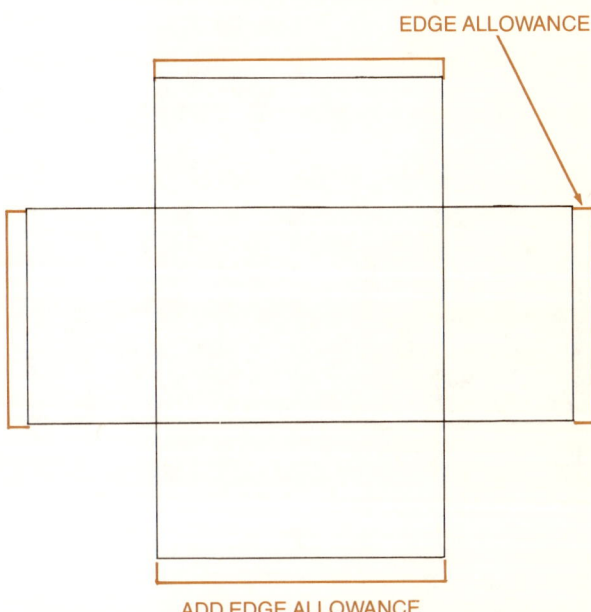

Fig. 16-12

5. Add the 5.0 mm allowance for the edges that will be hemmed later.

Fig. 16-11

4. Draw lines parallel to the edges of the plan

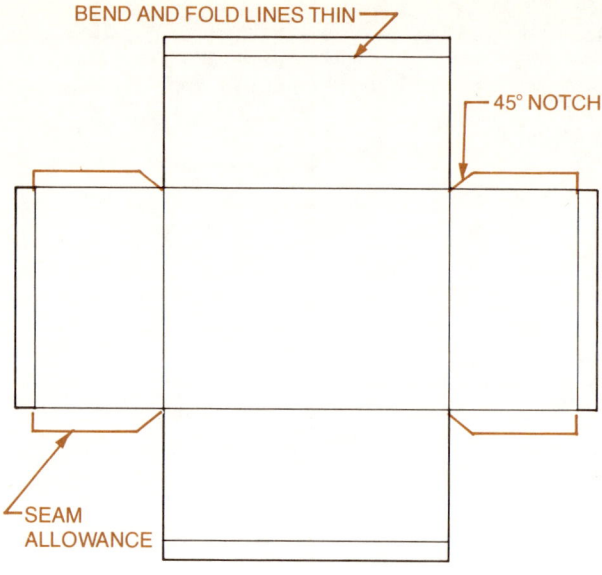

BEND AND FOLD LINES THIN

45° NOTCH

SEAM ALLOWANCE

ADD SEAM ALLOWANCE

Fig. 16-13

Note that the position of each surface as the object is unfolded in Figure 16-15

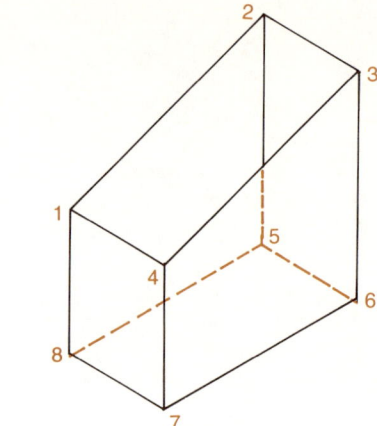

Fig. 16-14

6. Add the 5.0 mm allowance for the lap joints that will seal the box after bending. To prevent overlapping and bulging on seams, a 45° notch is cut away from the corner of the seam allowances.
7. Darken the linework. The outline is the normal object line, thick and black. Lines that indicate where the object is to be bent or folded are drawn thin and black. These lines are called **fold lines**.

For our purposes the development is complete. Dimensions and additional shop instructions may be added later. Now, let's look at another rectangular object and use a slightly different approach to complete the development.

Steps in Straight Line Development (2)

Again, numbers have been added to help explain the development. The object is a piece of rectangular tubing. The top of the tube is cut off at a 45° angle.

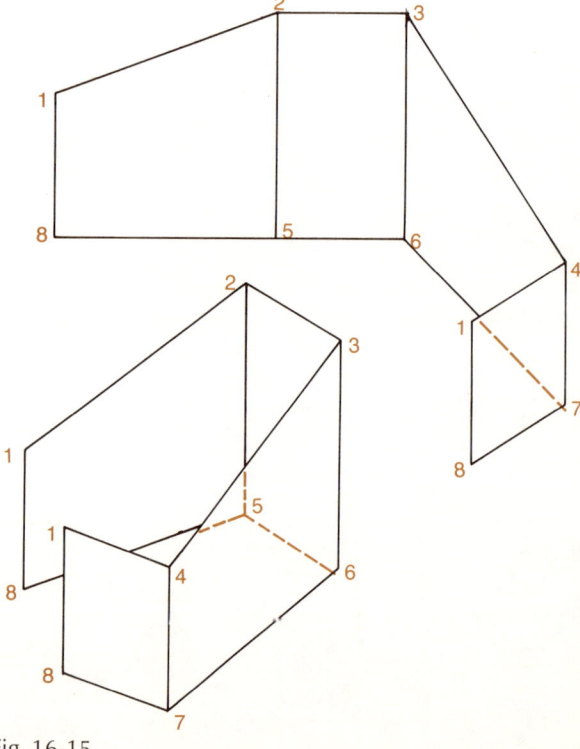

Fig. 16-15

224 DEVELOPMENT OF OBJECTS

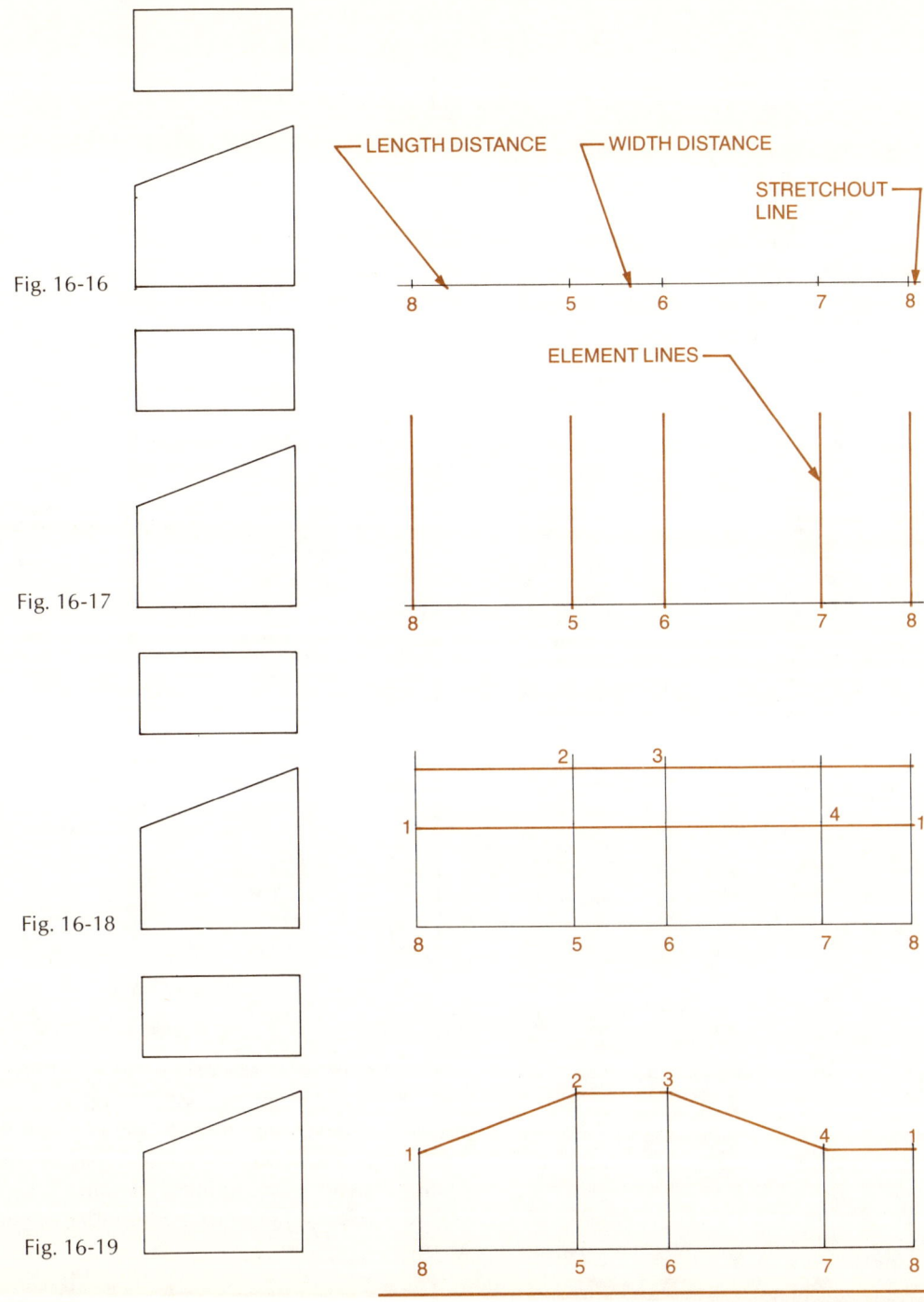

Fig. 16-16
Fig. 16-17
Fig. 16-18
Fig. 16-19

1. Draw the top and front views. Project a horizontal line from the bottom of the front view.
2. Step off the length and width of each side and end, on the line.
3. Draw light vertical lines from each point on the line in Fig. 16-17.
   These vertical lines are called **element lines**.
4. Project light horizontal lines from the corners in the front view across the element lines. Fig. 16-18.
5. Using Figure 16-15 as a guide, pinpoint the corners on each element. Join the corners to complete the development.

PARALLEL LINE DEVELOPMENT

Parallel line developments are used for objects whose basic shape is cylindrical. Following the steps to develop a cylindrical shape would be much easier if we first reviewed some basic facts about circles.

Remember. A circle is a closed curve. The distance around this curve is called the circumference. Each point on the circumference is the same distance from the centre point.

The circle can be divided into a number of equal sectors. If the circle were divided into 12 equal sectors the contained angle of each sector would be 30°. $\frac{360}{12} = 30$

The Greek letter π (Pi) is used as a constant to find the size of the circumference of a circle. The value of $\pi = 3.1416$. The circumference of a circle is found by multiplying $\pi \times$ DIA. (diameter). For example, if the diameter of a circle is 60 mm, the circumference $= \pi \times$ DIA. $= 3.1416 \times 60 = 188.5$ mm.

With the above information fresh in your mind the development of the open ended cylinder in Fig. 16-20 is no problem at all.

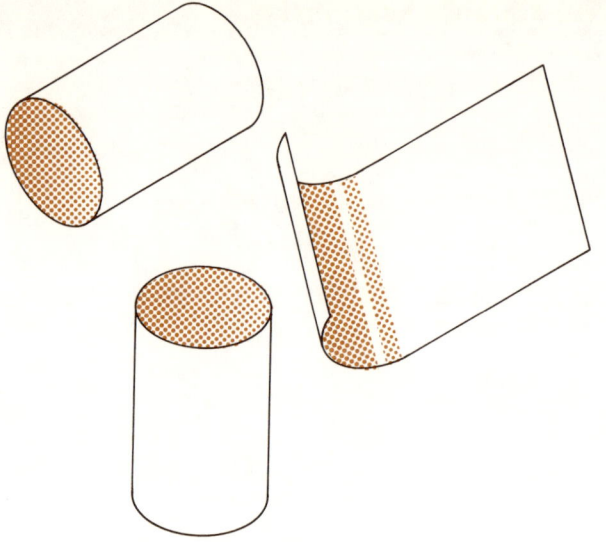

1. VERTICAL POSITION

Fig. 16-20

Steps in Parallel Line Development

1. Draw the top and front views of the cylinder.
   Project the height from the front view to begin the development.

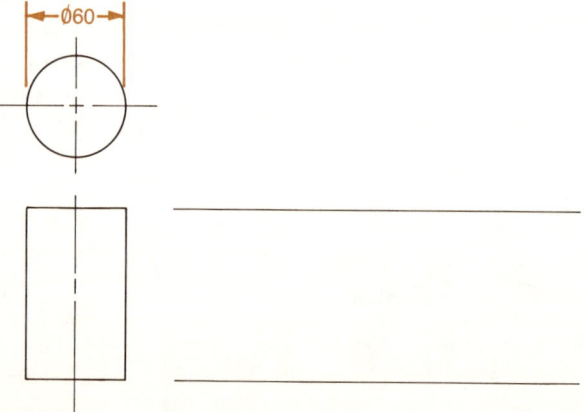

Fig. 16-21

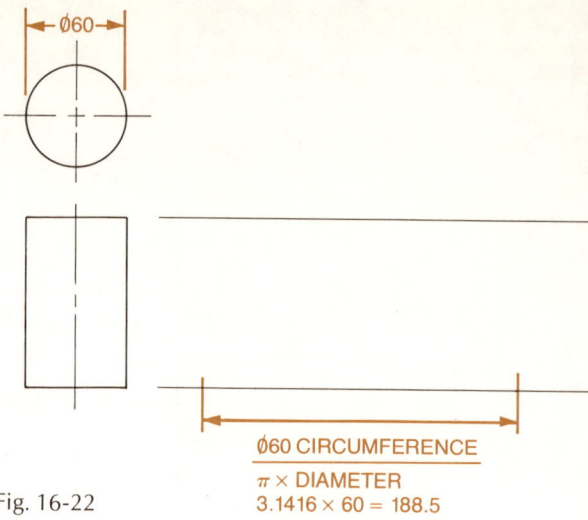

Fig. 16-22

∅60 CIRCUMFERENCE
π × DIAMETER
3.1416 × 60 = 188.5

2. Measure the circumference off on the bottom line.

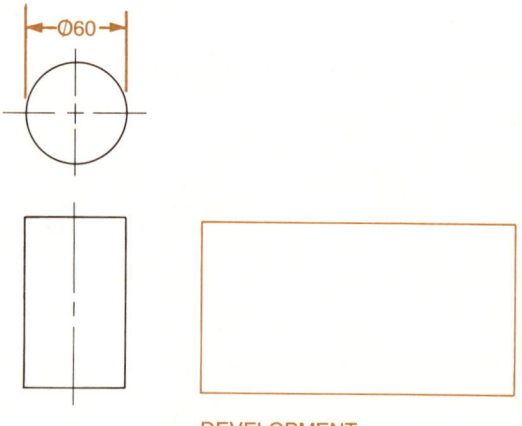

DEVELOPMENT

Fig. 16-23

3. Project vertical lines up from the points just placed on the bottom line to complete the development. Fig. 16-23.

That was easy, you must admit. To show your appreciation, spend a few minutes learning how you can divide a straight line into any number of equal divisions.

226 DEVELOPMENT OF OBJECTS

How to Divide a Straight Line into Equal Divisions

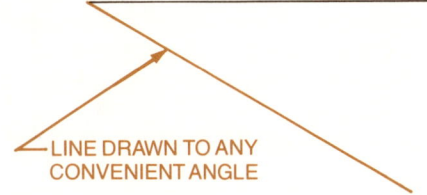
LINE DRAWN TO ANY DESIRED LENGTH

Fig. 16-24

We wish to divide this line into 12 equal divisions.

LINE DRAWN TO ANY CONVENIENT ANGLE

Fig. 16.25

1. Draw another straight line from one end of the line at any angle. Fig. 16-25.

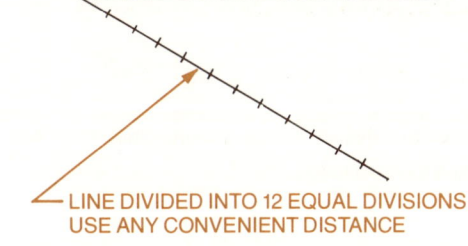
LINE DIVIDED INTO 12 EQUAL DIVISIONS USE ANY CONVENIENT DISTANCE

Fig. 16-26

2. Measure off 12 equal distances on the second line. You may use any convenient distance you wish. Fig. 16-26.

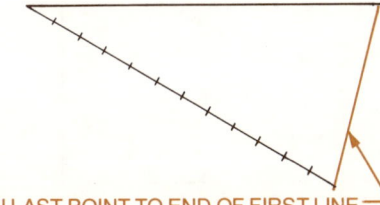
JOIN LAST POINT TO END OF FIRST LINE

Fig. 16-27

3. Draw a straight line joining the last point on the line to the end of the first line. Fig. 16-27.

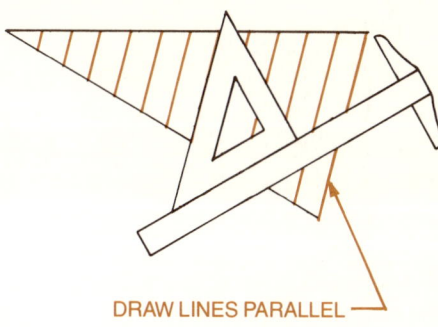
DRAW LINES PARALLEL

Fig. 16-28

4. Draw lines parallel to the line just drawn in step 3, from each point on the line. The original line is now divided into 12 equal divisions.

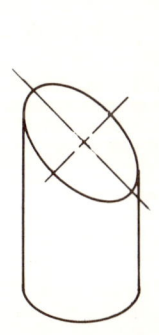 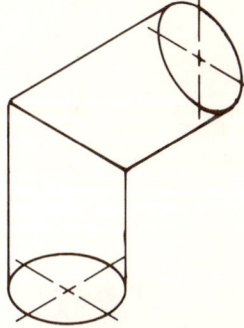

(a) TRUNCATED CYLINDER

(b) TRUNCATED CYLINDERS FORMING A TWO-PIECE ELBOW

Fig. 16-29(a) Fig. 16-29(b)

Now let's apply the above information to help develop the round cylinder shown in Fig. 16-29(a and b). The top part of the cylinder is **truncated** at an angle of 45°. This cylinder can be used as part of a pipe elbow joint to turn a pipe through 90°.
Note: the height of the cylinder changes from each point on the circumference.

truncated —cut off

PARALLEL LINE DEVELOPMENT

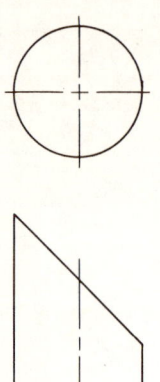

Fig. 16.30

Fig. 16-31

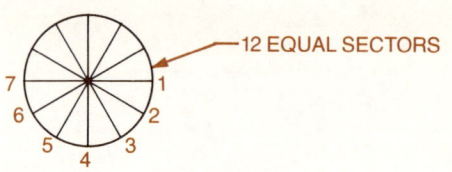

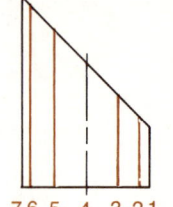

Fig. 16-33

Steps in Developing a Truncated Cylinder

To develop the cylinder follow these steps. Again if we add numbers where necessary the steps are easier to follow.

1. Draw the top and front view of the cylinder.
2. Begin the development by projecting the height from the front view.

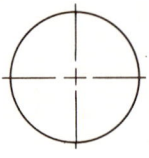
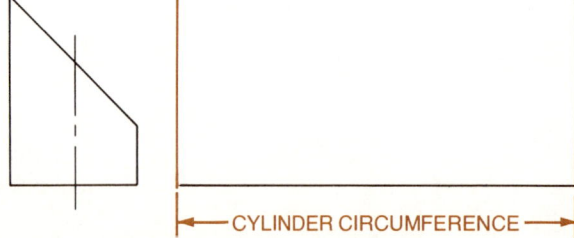

Fig. 16-32

3. Calculate the circumference of the cylinder and draw the ends of the development.

4. Divide the top view into 12 equal sectors. Project light vertical lines to the front view from the top view as shown in Fig. 16-33.

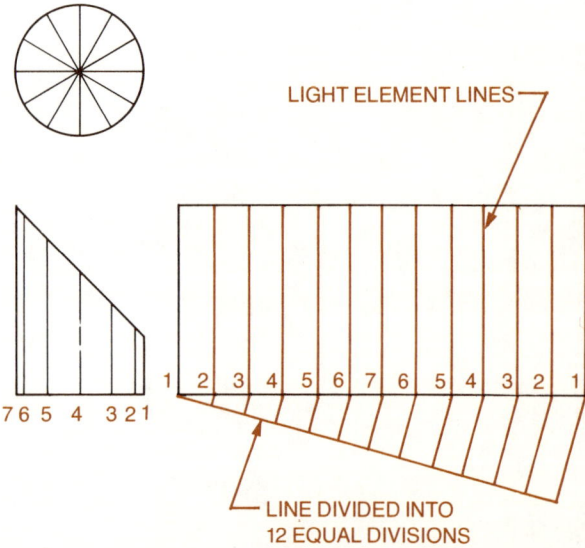

Fig. 16-34

4. Divide the development into 12 equal divisions. First divide the bottom line into 12 equal parts and then draw light vertical element lines as shown in Fig. 16-34.

228 DEVELOPMENT OF OBJECTS

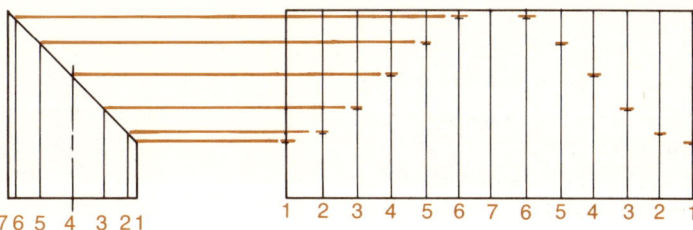

Fig. 16-35

5. Project the height of each element line in the front view to the matching element line in the development.

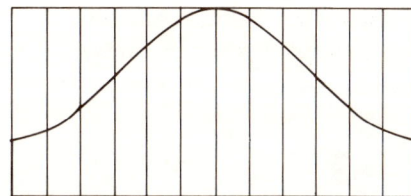

Fig. 16-36

6. Complete the development by joining the plotted points with a smooth continuous curve.

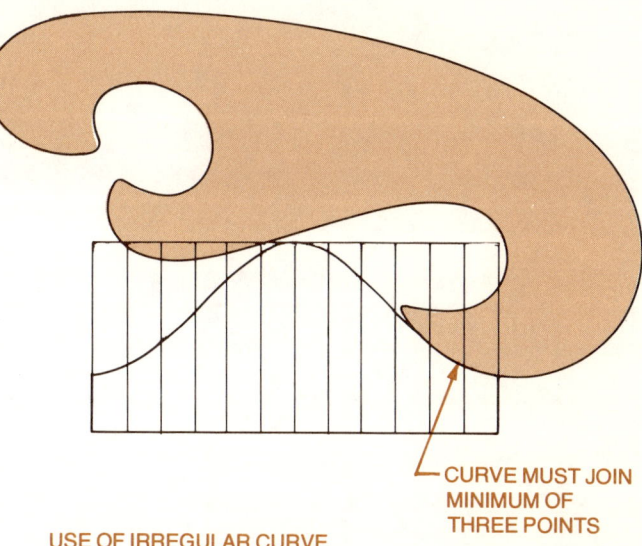

CURVE MUST JOIN MINIMUM OF THREE POINTS

USE OF IRREGULAR CURVE

Fig. 16-37

Irregular or **French Curve**. Drawing curved lines that cannot be drawn with a compass is made easier by using an instrument called an **irregular** or **French curve**. Fig. 16-37. It isn't easy to use. Remember to draw light lines at first. You must join at least three points at one time, never two. When the curve looks reasonably continuous, darken the line.

PARALLEL LINE DEVELOPMENT

POINTS TO REMEMBER

- Many objects are made by bending or rolling thin sheets of metal or other materials.
- A development shows the shape of the surfaces of an object when it is unfolded flat.
- The two most common types of development are straight line and parallel line.
- Straight line development is used to develop objects which have three or more rectangular sides and where the true shape of the surfaces is known.
- Parallel line development is used to develop objects whose basic shape is cylindrical.
- Irregular or French curves are instruments used to draw curves that cannot be drawn with a compass.

QUESTIONS TO ANSWER

1. What does the **development** of an object mean?
2. Name the two most common types of developments.
3. What is each of these developments used for?
4. The Greek letter π has been called a **constant**. (It has only one value.) What is its value? How is it used?
5. Find the circumference of circles whose diameters are:
   (1) 60 mm (2) 45 mm (3) 100 mm (4) 10.5 mm (5) 24 mm (6) 82 mm
6. What is the purpose of an **irregular curve**?
7. How many points must it join each time?

REPLACE THE X's WITH THE CORRECT TERM

1. In the past many cities were XXXXXXXX by strong, high walls.
2. Road XXXXXXXXXX extend beyond the actual pavement and allow for future widening of the road.
3. Heavy windstorms sometimes XXXXXXXX trees by breaking off the upper branches.

PROJECT

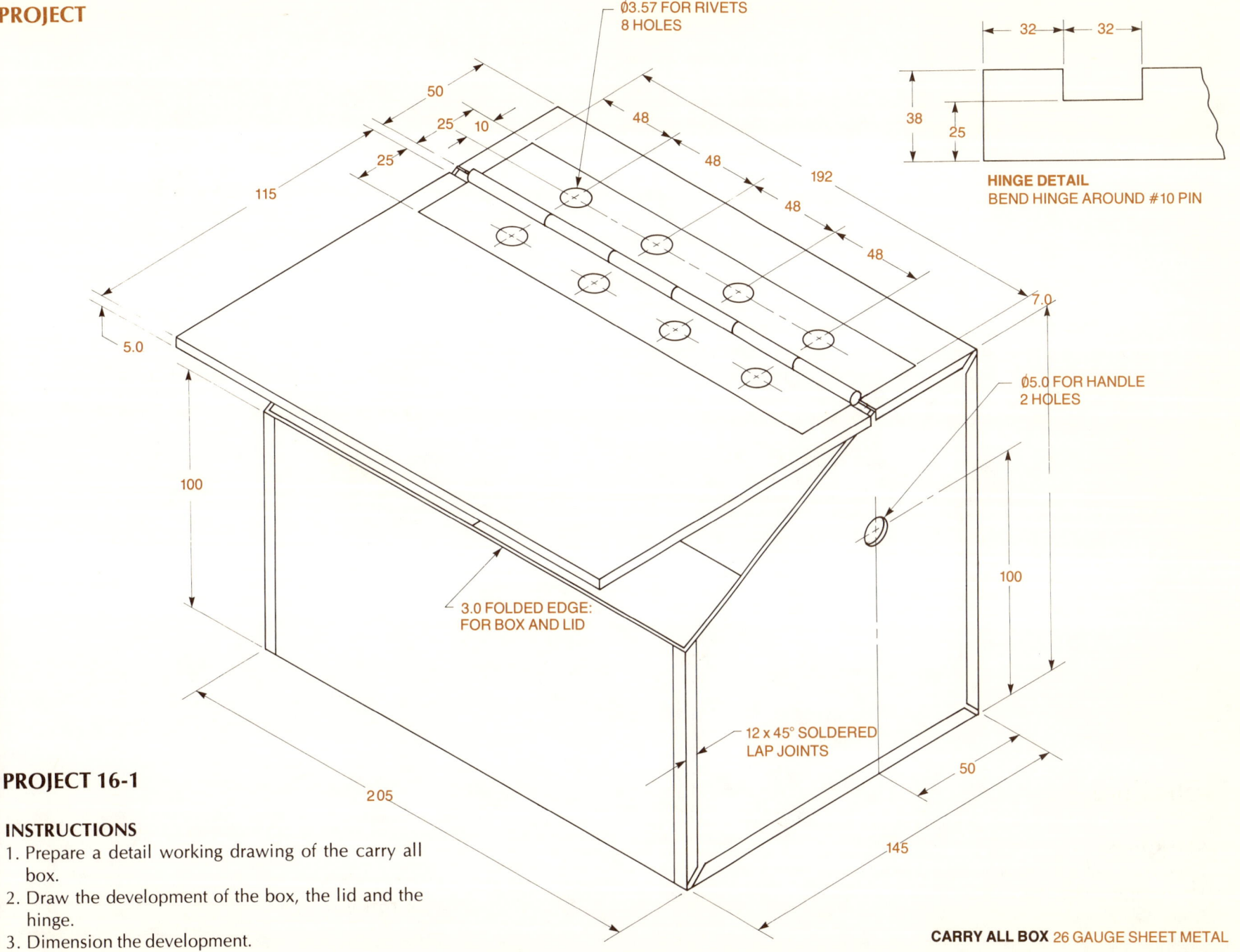

PROJECT 16-1

INSTRUCTIONS
1. Prepare a detail working drawing of the carry all box.
2. Draw the development of the box, the lid and the hinge.
3. Dimension the development.

CARRY ALL BOX 26 GAUGE SHEET METAL

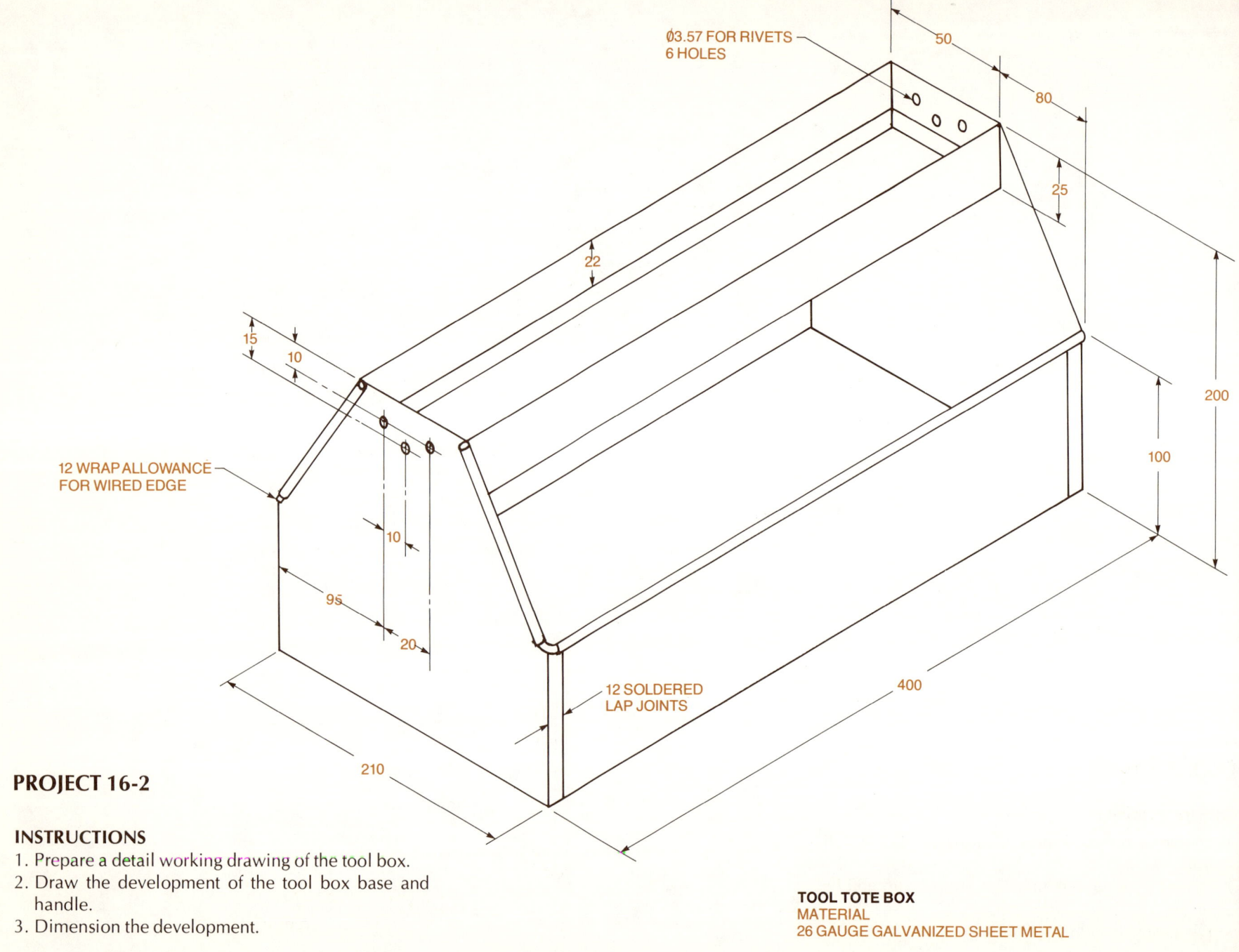

PROJECT 16-2

INSTRUCTIONS
1. Prepare a detail working drawing of the tool box.
2. Draw the development of the tool box base and handle.
3. Dimension the development.

TOOL TOTE BOX
MATERIAL
26 GAUGE GALVANIZED SHEET METAL

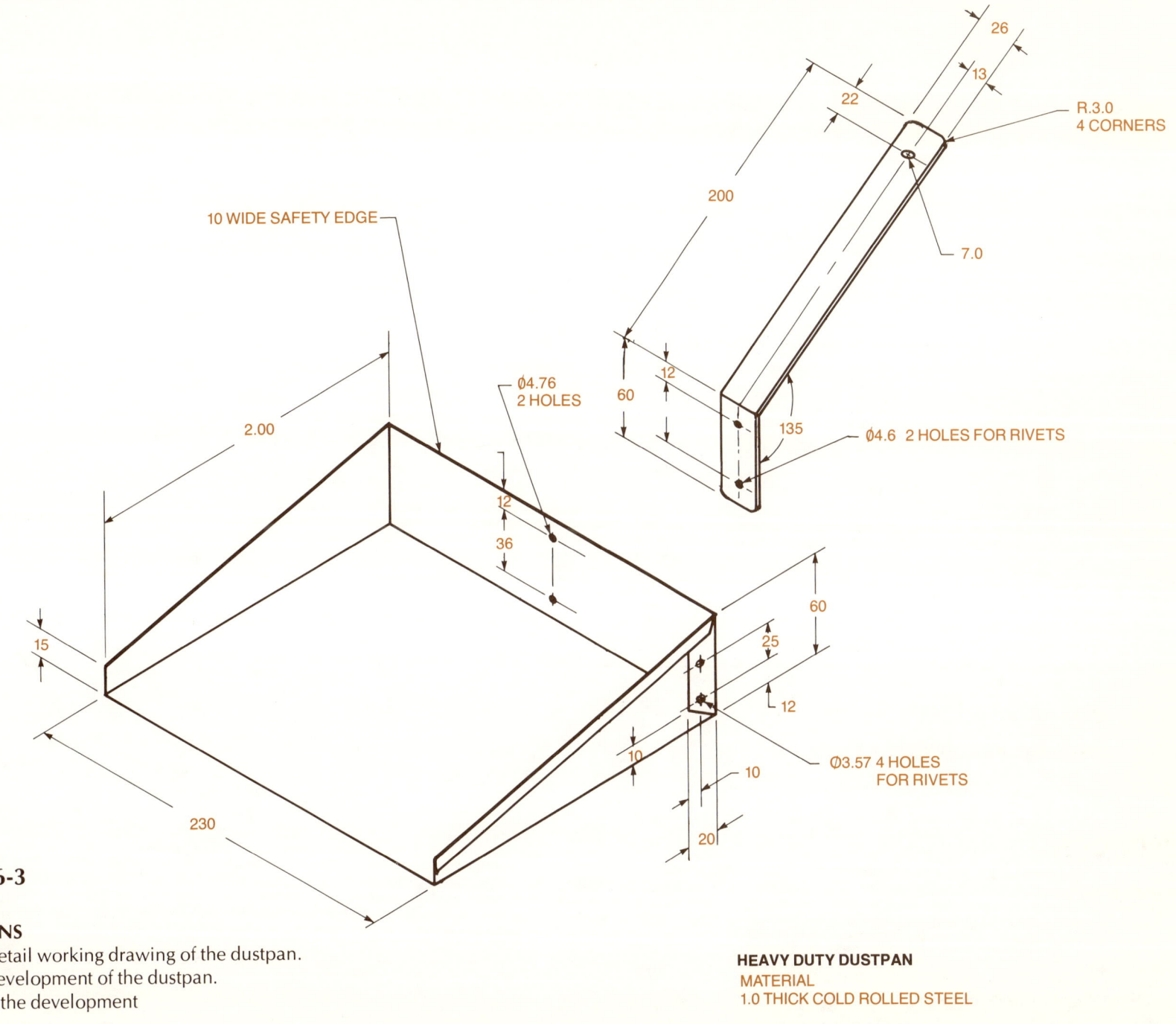

PROJECT 16-3

INSTRUCTIONS
1. Prepare a detail working drawing of the dustpan.
2. Draw the development of the dustpan.
3. Dimension the development

HEAVY DUTY DUSTPAN
MATERIAL
1.0 THICK COLD ROLLED STEEL

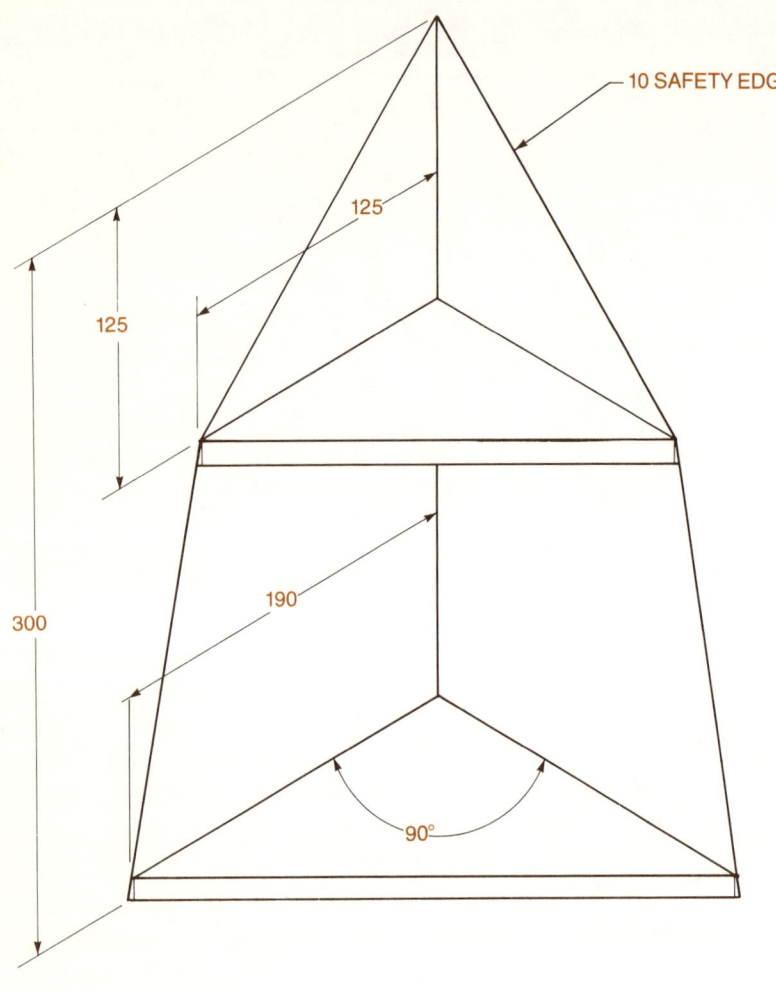

CORNER SHELF MATERIAL TIN PLATE

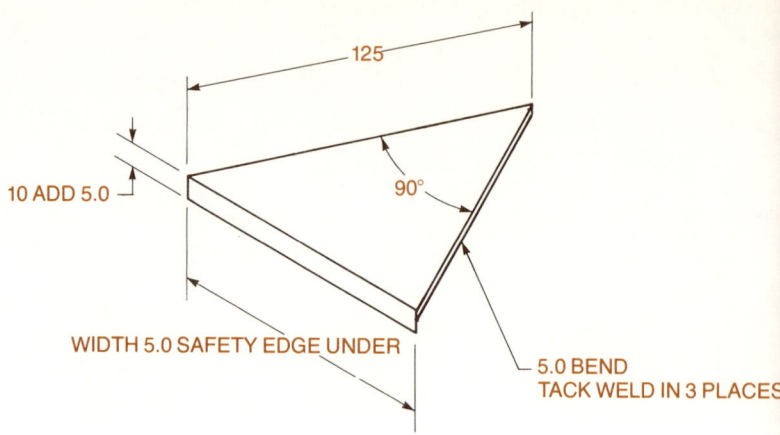

TOP SHELF MATERIAL TIN PLATE

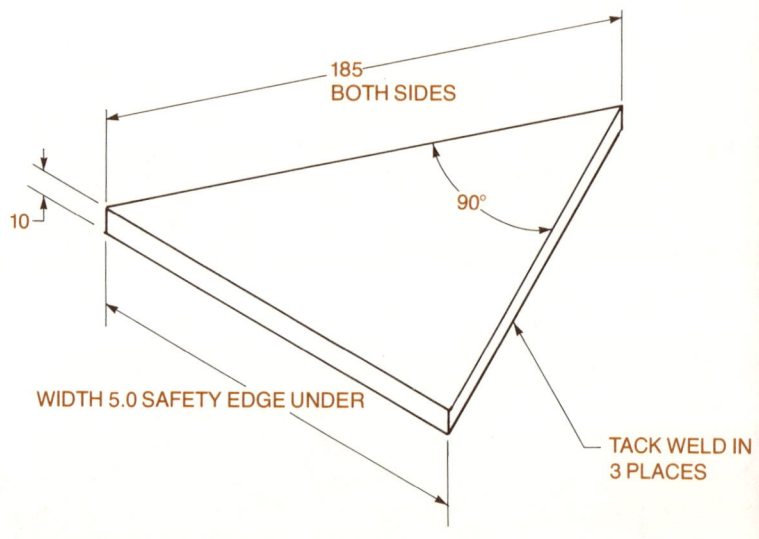

BOTTOM SHELF MATERIAL TIN PLATE

PROJECT 16-4

INSTRUCTIONS
1. Prepare a detail working drawing of the corner shelf.
2. Draw the development of the corner shelf.
3. Dimension the development.

234 DEVELOPMENT OF OBJECTS

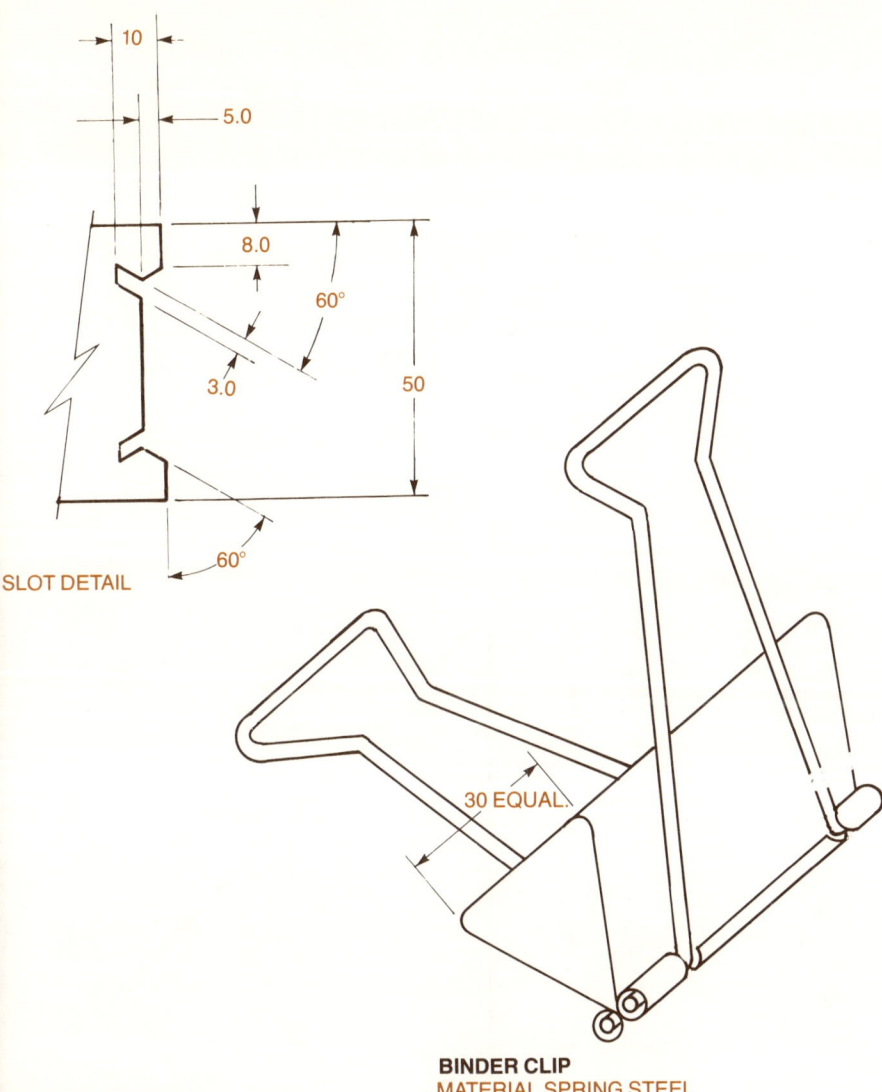

BINDER CLIP
MATERIAL SPRING STEEL

PROJECT 16-5

INSTRUCTIONS
1. Prepare a detail working drawing of the binder clip. Design a suitable wire grip for the binder clip.
2. Draw the development of the binder clip.
3. Dimension the development.

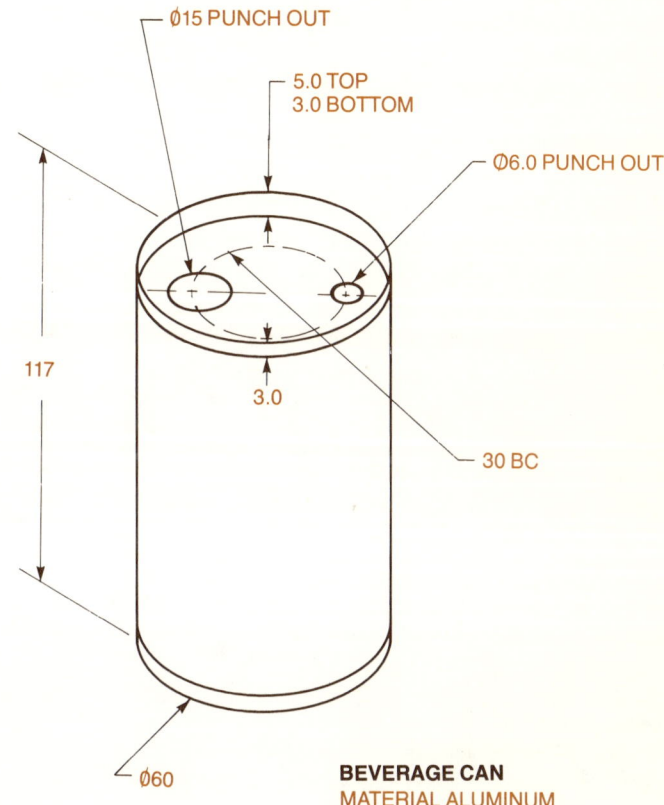

BEVERAGE CAN
MATERIAL ALUMINUM

PROJECT 16-6

1. Prepare a detail working drawing of the beverage can.
2. Draw the development of the beverage can.
3. Dimension the development.

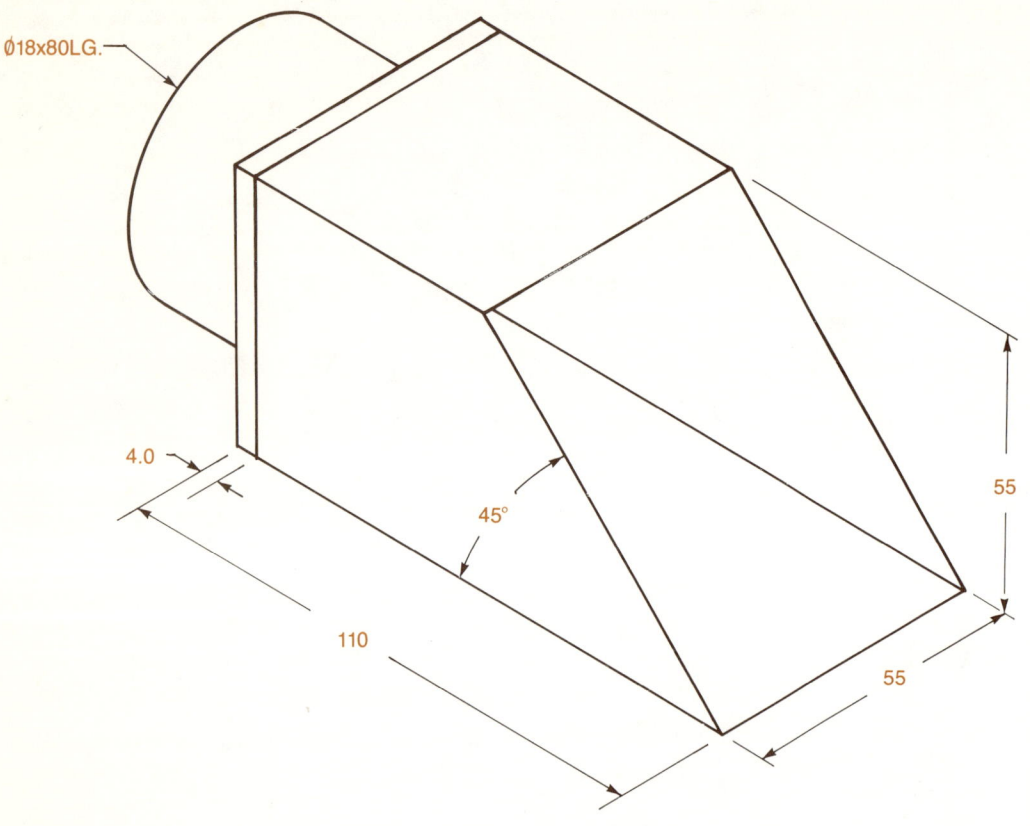

PROJECT 16-7

SCOOP
26 GAUGE SHEET METAL
DRAW A DEVELOPMENT OF THE HANDLE AND SCOOP

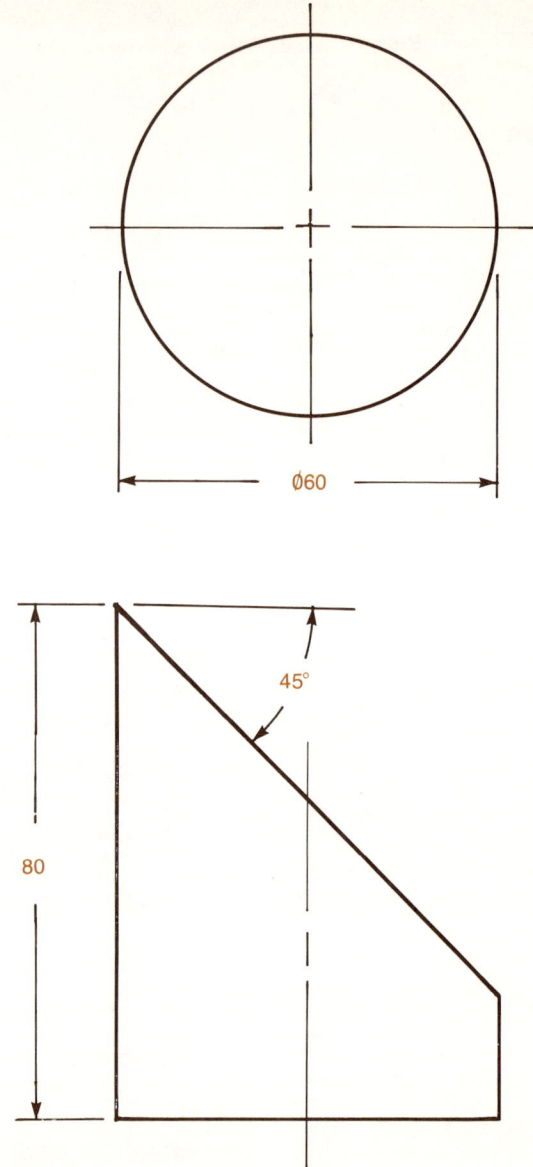

PROJECT 16-8

TRUNCATED CYLINDER
PART OF 90° ELBOW JOINT
DRAW TOP AND FRONT VIEW
PROJECT DEVELOPMENT

PROJECT DEVELOPMENT

DRAW TOP AND FRONT VIEW AND DEVELOPMENT

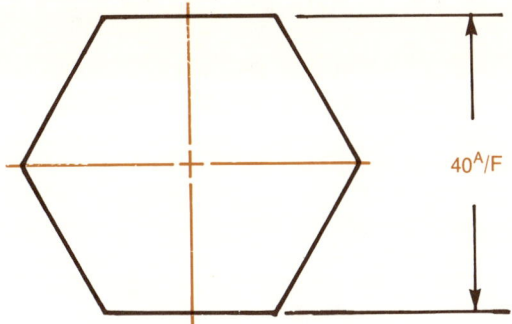

40 A/F

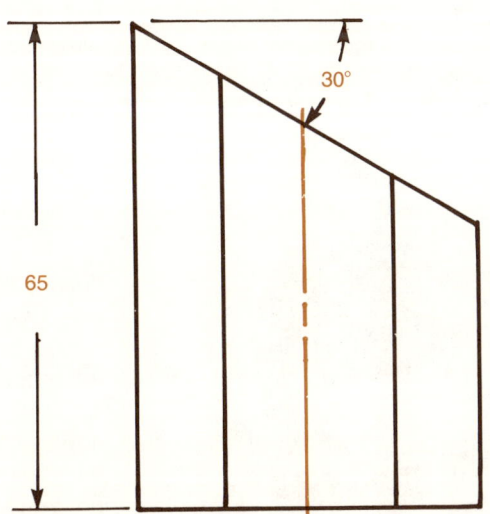

65

30°

PROJECT 16-9
OPEN ENDED HEXAGONAL TUBE   SHEET METAL

Draw top and front-views and development

CHAPTER 17
ARCHITECTURAL DRAWING

WORDS TO LEARN

uncomplicated (un-cóm-pli-cat-ed)

consult (con-súlt)

uncomplicated—easy to understand, simple

Architectural drawing, as you know, deals with all types of buildings: stores, factories, schools, offices, apartments, and houses. Many of us have an image of the ideal home in our mind: the one that we would like to build and live in one day.

Have you ever wondered, how does a house "happen"? Well, you know, like machine parts, houses don't "just happen". We can't go into every detail of house design and construction, but we hope to involve you in some of the basics of planning and building a house. We can begin by putting you in the position of buying the new home that will be built for you.

To simplify matters we will call you the Buyer. The first thing you, the Buyer, will have to think about when purchasing the house is the financing. That is, how much will it cost and how will it be paid for. The amount of money available certainly will affect the style, size and location of the house you choose to buy. Before visiting an architect the Buyer will spend many weekends driving from one housing development to another looking at presentation drawings and model homes.

PRESENTATION DRAWINGS

Presentation drawings of a house are simplified plans that give a general impression of what the finished house will look like. Presentation drawings are **uncomplicated**. Even the untrained reader can see the locations and sizes of the important features of the house. Only the approximate over-all dimensions of the rooms, garages, patios, etc., are noted. These drawings are not used by the tradespeople to build the house. Presentation drawings are usually combined as a set of three drawings. The presentation **floor plan**, as in Fig. 17-2, shows the layout of the house as if you were looking down on the house with the roof removed.

Fig. 17-1.

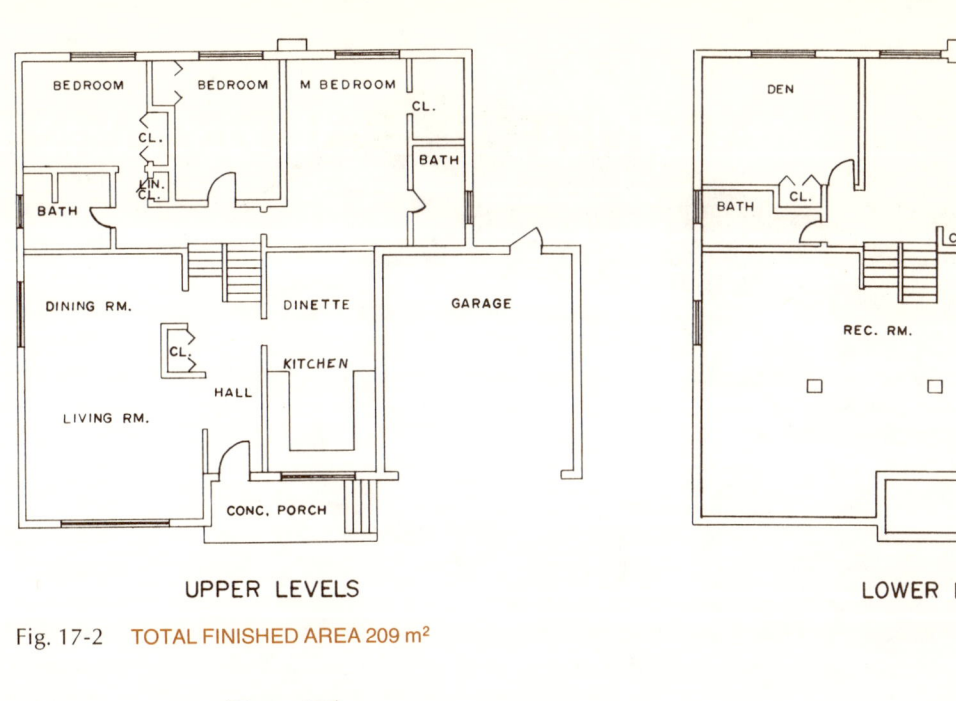

Fig. 17-2 **TOTAL FINISHED AREA 209 m²**

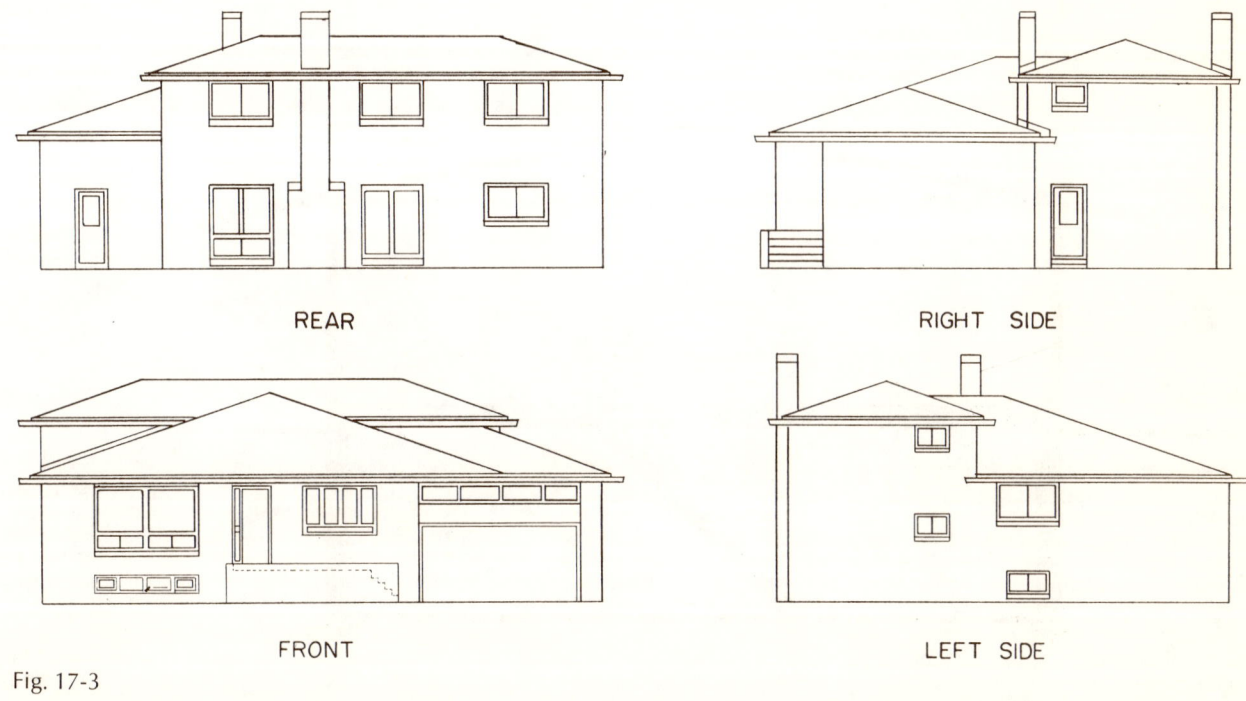

Fig. 17-3

PRESENTATION DRAWINGS

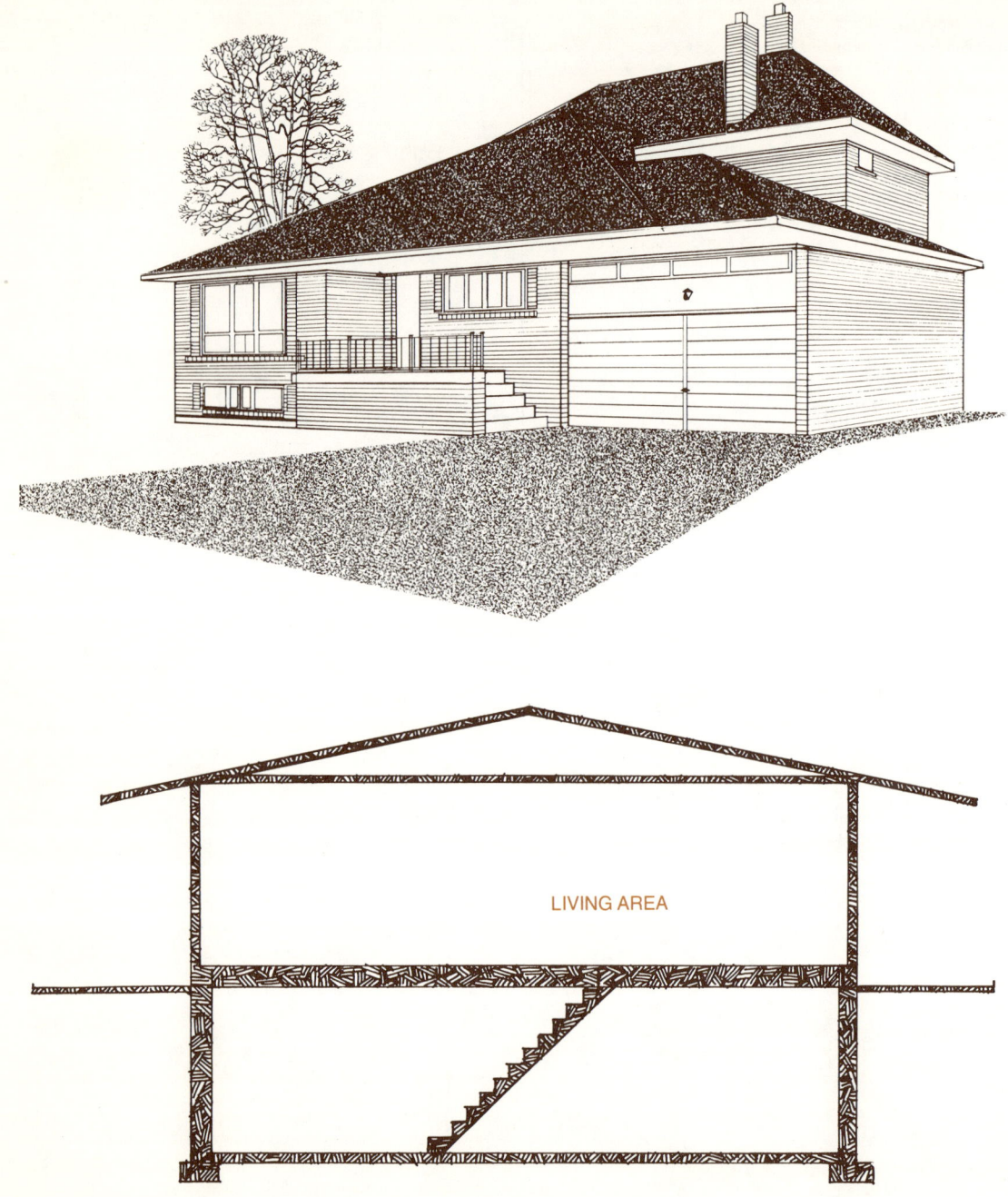

Fig. 17-5

Presentation **elevation drawings** give the reader a picture of what they would see if they were to look at the finished house from four different positions; at the front, the back, the right and at the left sides of the house.

The floor plan and the elevation drawings are used by the drafters to create the **perspective pictorial drawing** of the house in Fig. 17-4. This allows the reader to picture the house as it would look after it was built.

Landscaping, shading, and colour can be added to the pictorial to give a more real effect.

House Types

After a while the buyer will have found that houses are designed in a variety of types. Each house type has its own advantages and disadvantages to consider. We can look at a few of the more popular house types and compare their features.

One-Storey House. A one-storey house, referred to as a **bungalow**, has all the regular living space on one main floor level. There are many advantages. Any room can be reached without going up or down the stairs. It is ideal for indoor-outdoor living. Patios, porches, and major additions can be added more easily and at less cost, than for any of the other house types. One disadvantage is that the bungalow requires a larger lot since it is spread out. The construction and heating costs are also greater, for the same reason.

The Storey-and-a-Half House. The storey-and-a-half house is basically a one-storey house with a steeper roof, making the attic useful as a living area. The storey-and-a-half provides the greatest amount of floor area for the least cost. The house can begin as a two-bedroom, one-bath house, with the upper level left unfinished. When extra living space is needed the attic can be finished to provide extra bedrooms and an additional bathroom. Since a large part of the ceiling is directly under the roof, the attic tends to become very warm in the summer. The sloping ceiling also limits the headroom in the corners of the rooms.

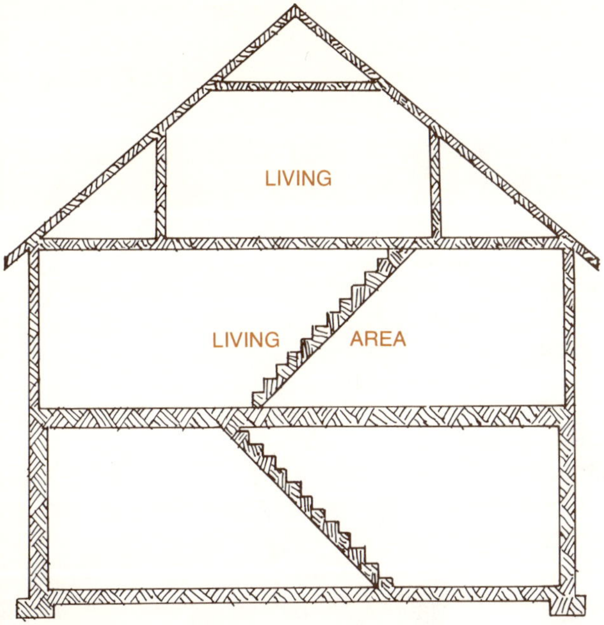

Fig. 17-6

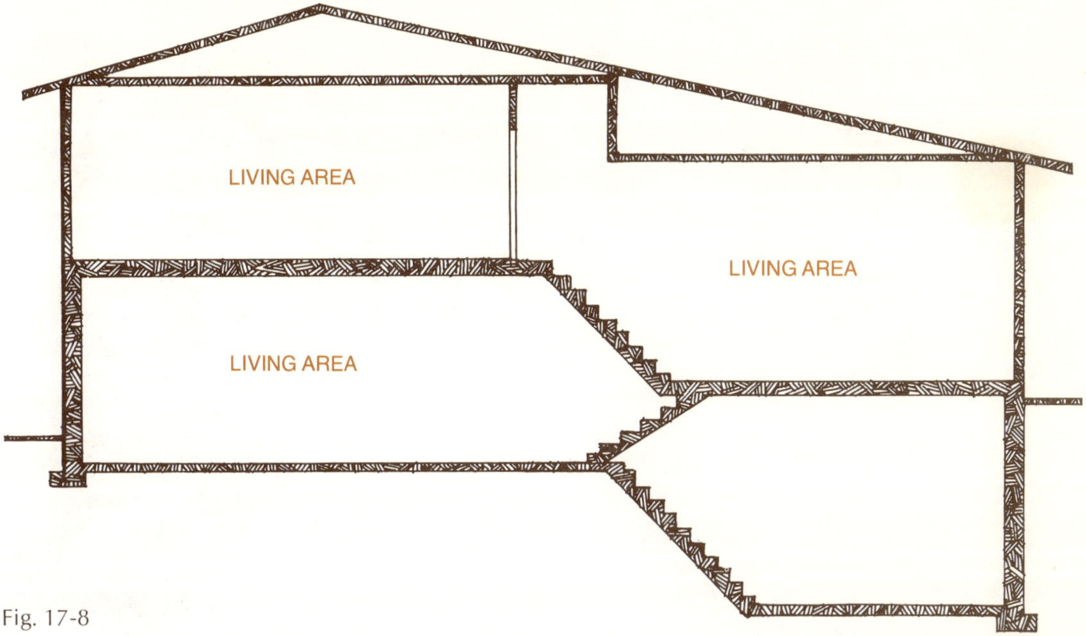

Fig. 17-8

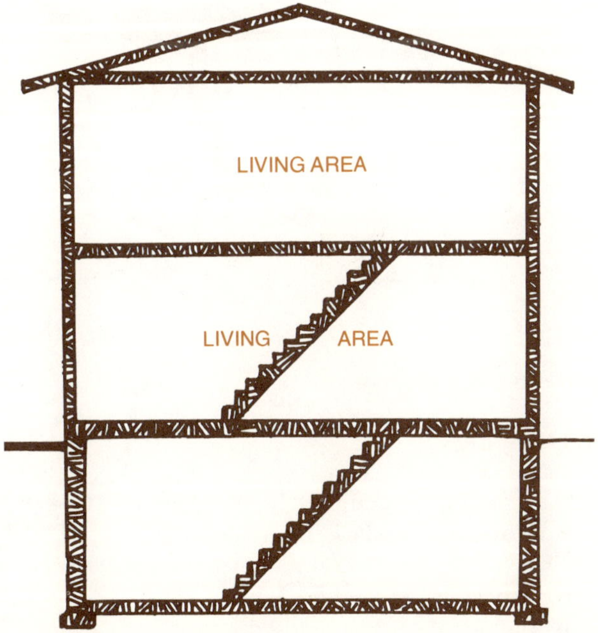

Fig. 17-7

The Two-Storey House. The two-storey is one living area stacked on top of another. It is more economical to build and to heat than a bungalow with the same floor space. This style of house is becoming more popular as land costs rise. The main disadvantage is the problem of climbing stairs from one level to another.

The Split-Level House. The split-level house combines the advantages of the bungalow and the two-storey house types. The split-level separates the sleeping, living and recreational areas on different levels. Fewer stairs are required between each level than in the two-storey house. The split-level house can be placed on a flat lot but is especially suited for the sloping or hilly lot which permits a walkout entrance from the basement to the garden. Split-level houses are usually more expensive to build than the two-storey house. Some areas of the house furthest from the furnace may be harder to heat.

PRESENTATION DRAWINGS 241

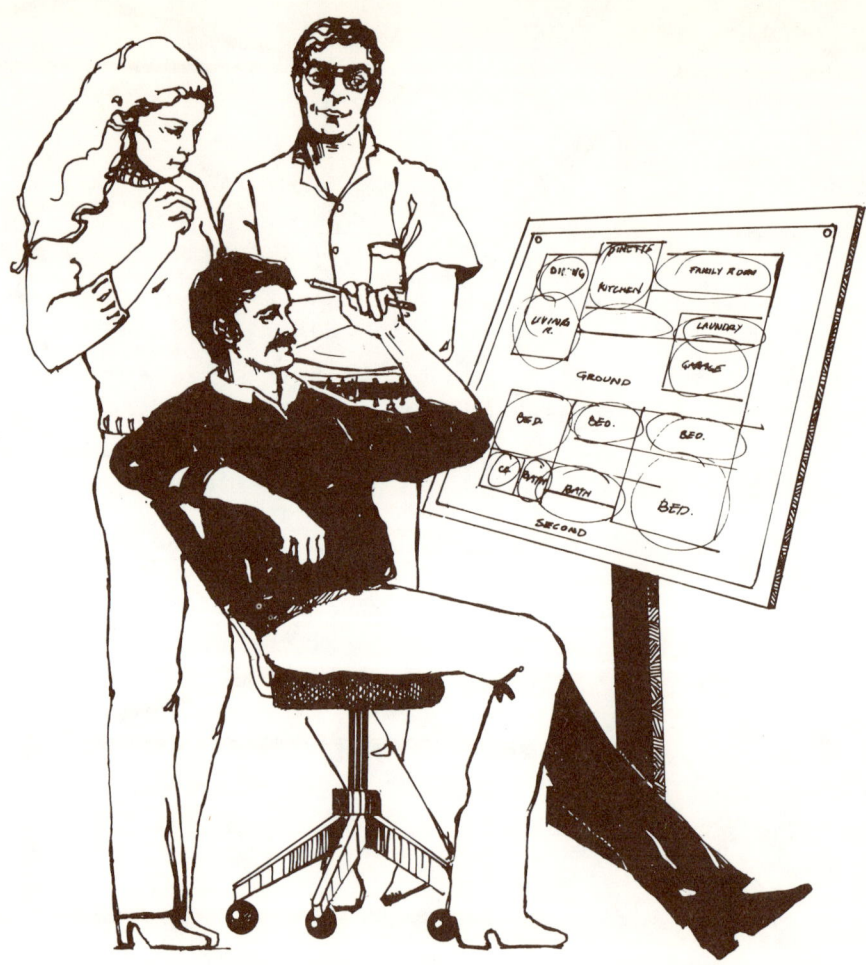

Fig. 17-9

Presentation Drawings

After many weeks of looking and comparing, the buyer finds a site on which to build. The site is also referred to as the **lot**.

The buyer now **consults** an architect who will design the house. The architect asks many questions that reveal the buyer's family size and style of life. The buyer tries to describe the features that would be desirable in the home to help the architect design the type of house to suit the buyer's needs.

Finally let's say that the architect decides that a large two-storey house would take full advantage of the buyer's lot and provide all the features that the buyer wants. The architect shows the buyer the first rough sketches that outline the three main areas of the house.

consult—to ask someone's advice

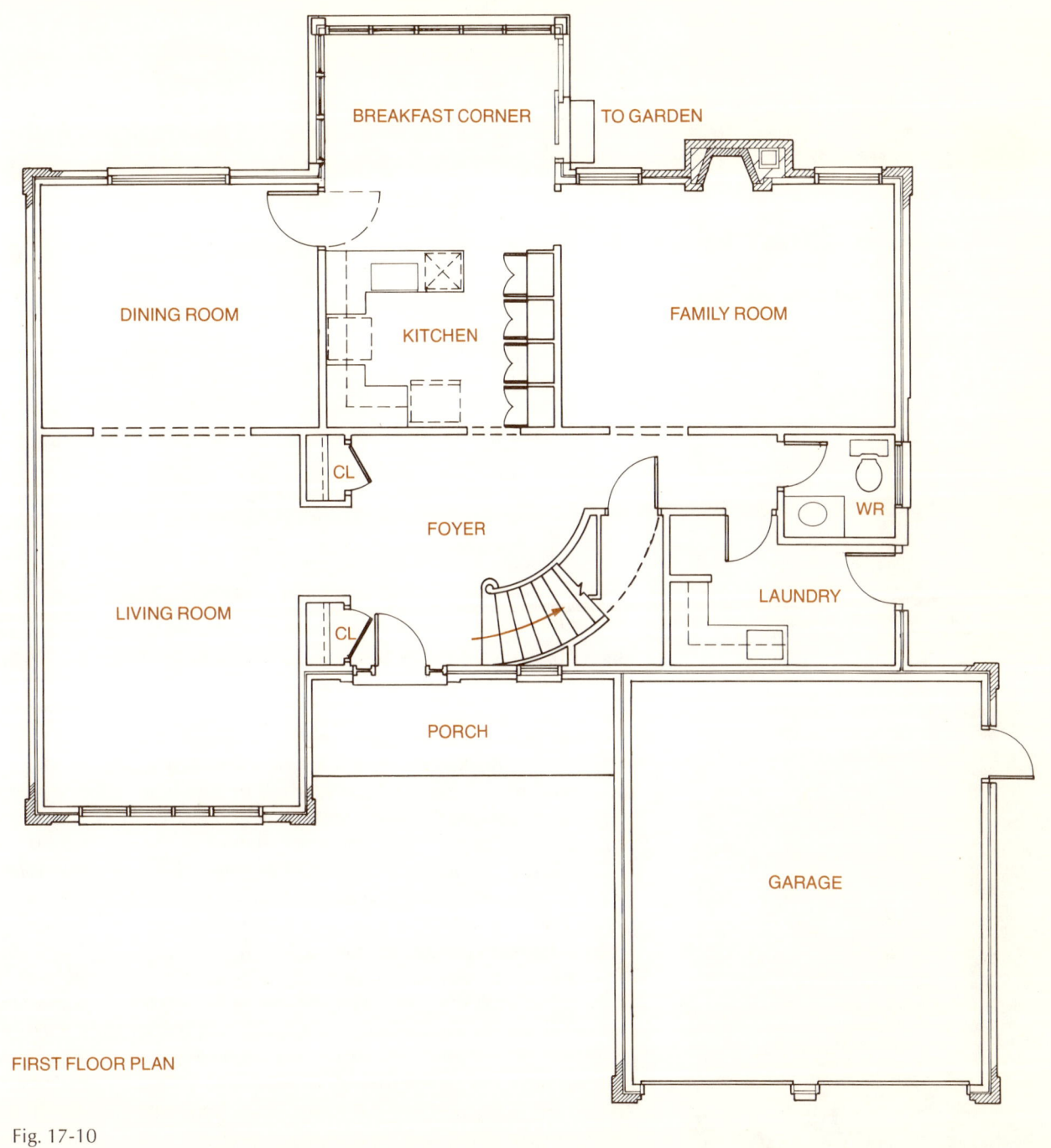

FIRST FLOOR PLAN

Fig. 17-10

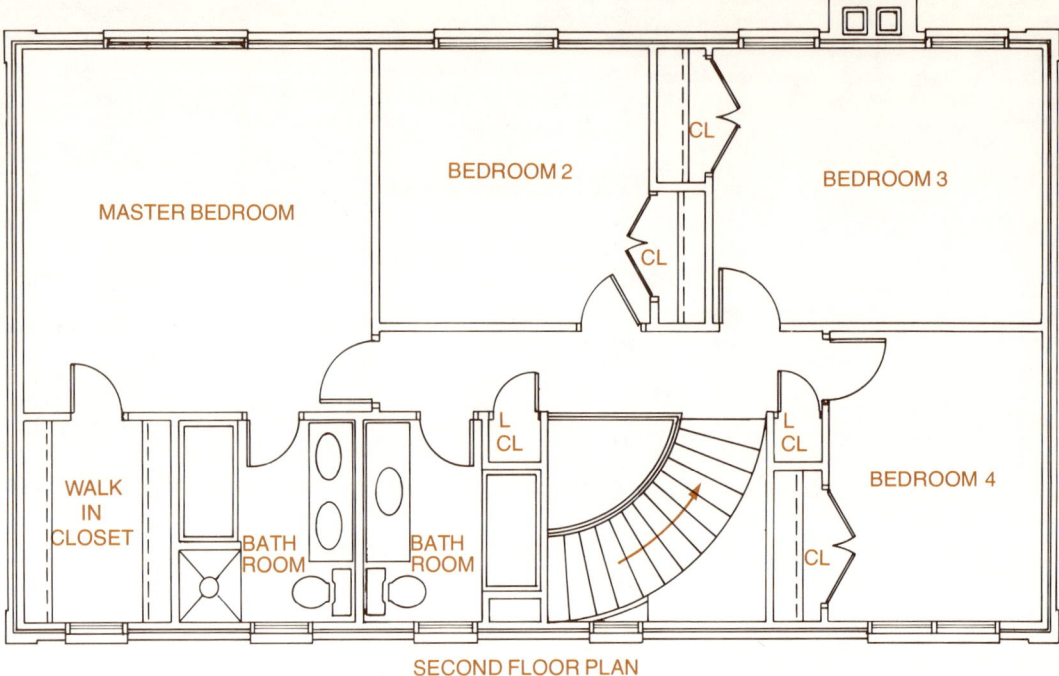

Fig. 17-11

These are living and work areas on the first floor, and the sleeping area which takes up the entire second floor.

Once these plans are approved by the buyer the architect has drafters prepare a set of **presentation drawings** for them and a set of **construction drawings** (also called **working drawings**) for the trades.

To understand the presentation drawings of the buyer's house let us look at the ground floor first. Imagine yourself walking past the two-car garage and onto the front porch. The front door opens to a large rectangular hall called the foyer. The foyer leads directly to every area of the house. We can hang our coats in one of the two closets to the left of the foyer and walk into the living room. The living room leads on to the dining room through a flat archway. By pushing the swinging door we enter the kitchen. The kitchen is divided into two areas. The work area with the stove, refrigerator and sink form a U-shape opposite the pantry. The eating area in the kitchen is sometimes called the breakfast corner. Note that the breakfast room is completely glass-enclosed by windows on two sides and the sliding doors that open to the back garden.

From the breakfast room step into the family room past the fireplace and out into the hall that leads to the washroom next to the laundry. Note that there is an exterior entrance door in the laundry as well. Let's go back to the main hall and up the circular staircase to the upper level.

The large window over the front door adds light and an open feeling to the staircase. The bedrooms and bathrooms have been numbered. Bedrooms 2, 3, and 4 each have their own closets and share the use of a bathroom. The master bedroom is much larger than the other bedrooms, and has a large walk-in closet as well as its own private bathroom. A stall shower is an added feature in this bathroom.

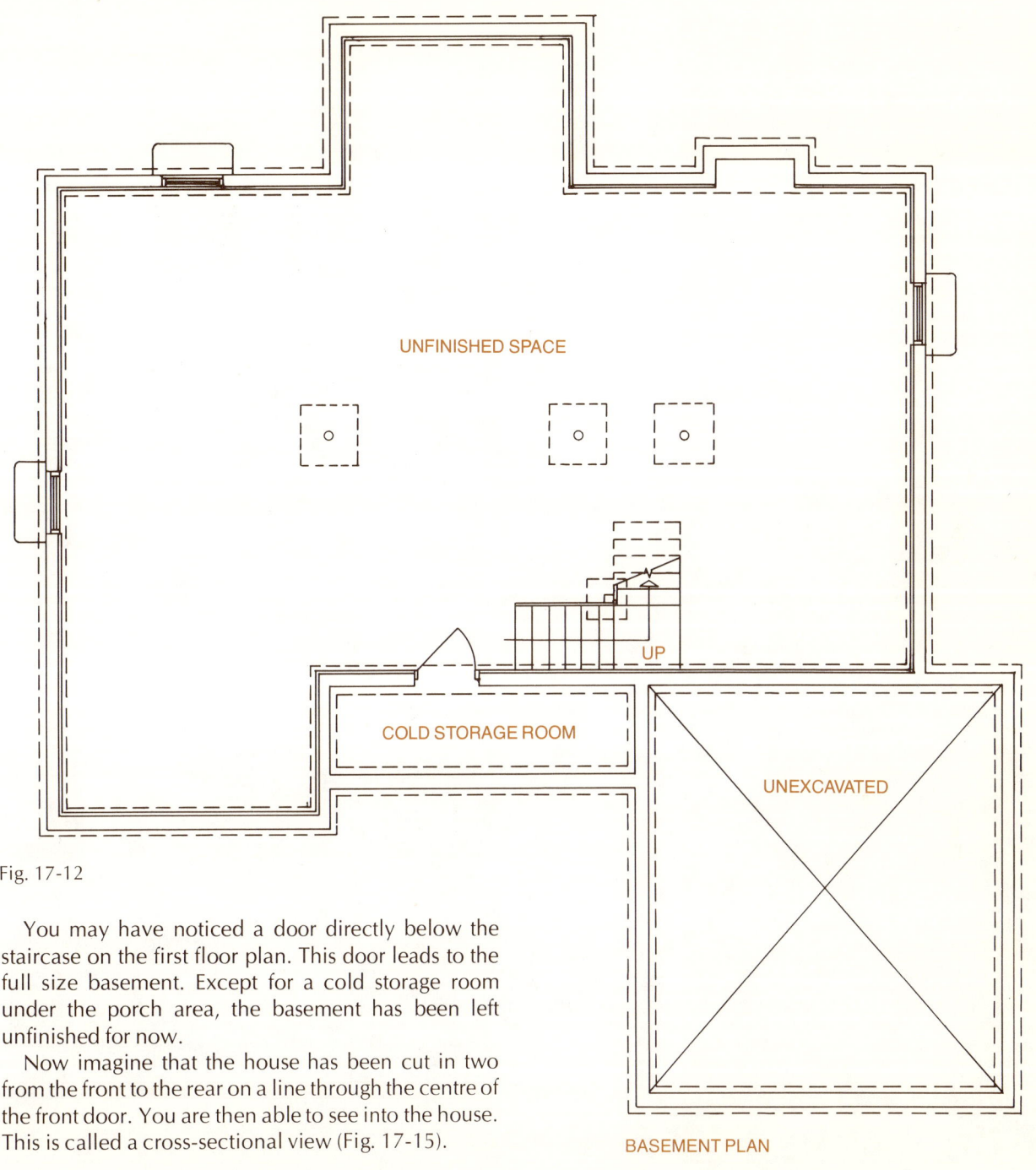

Fig. 17-12

You may have noticed a door directly below the staircase on the first floor plan. This door leads to the full size basement. Except for a cold storage room under the porch area, the basement has been left unfinished for now.

Now imagine that the house has been cut in two from the front to the rear on a line through the centre of the front door. You are then able to see into the house. This is called a cross-sectional view (Fig. 17-15).

PRESENTATION DRAWINGS 245

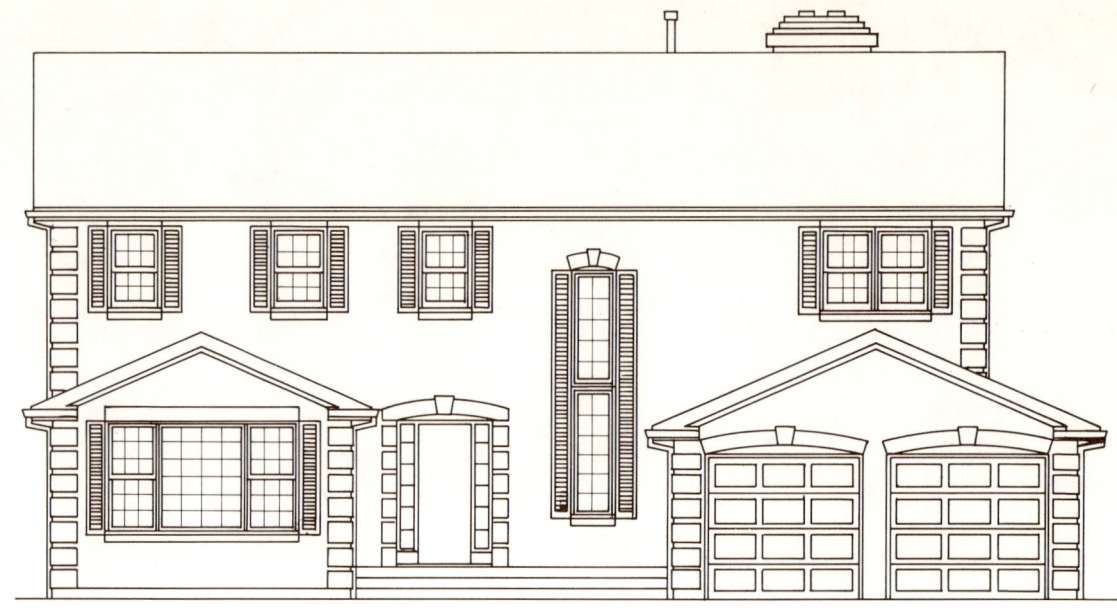

Fig. 17-13(a)

FRONT ELEVATION

Fig. 17-13(b)

REAR ELEVATION

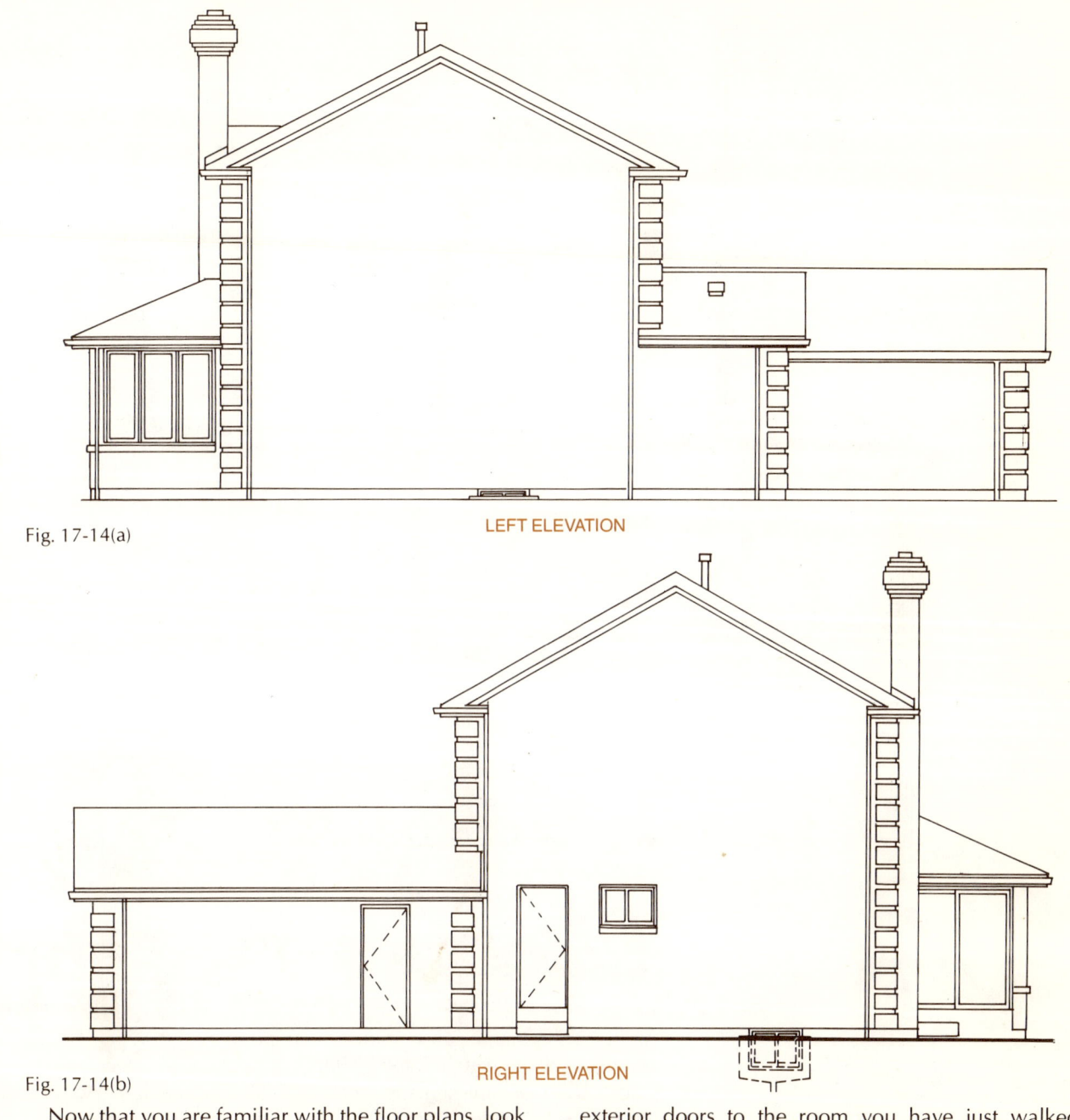

Fig. 17-14(a) LEFT ELEVATION

Fig. 17-14(b) RIGHT ELEVATION

Now that you are familiar with the floor plans, look at the elevation plans and relate the windows and exterior doors to the room you have just walked through.

PRESENTATION DRAWINGS 247

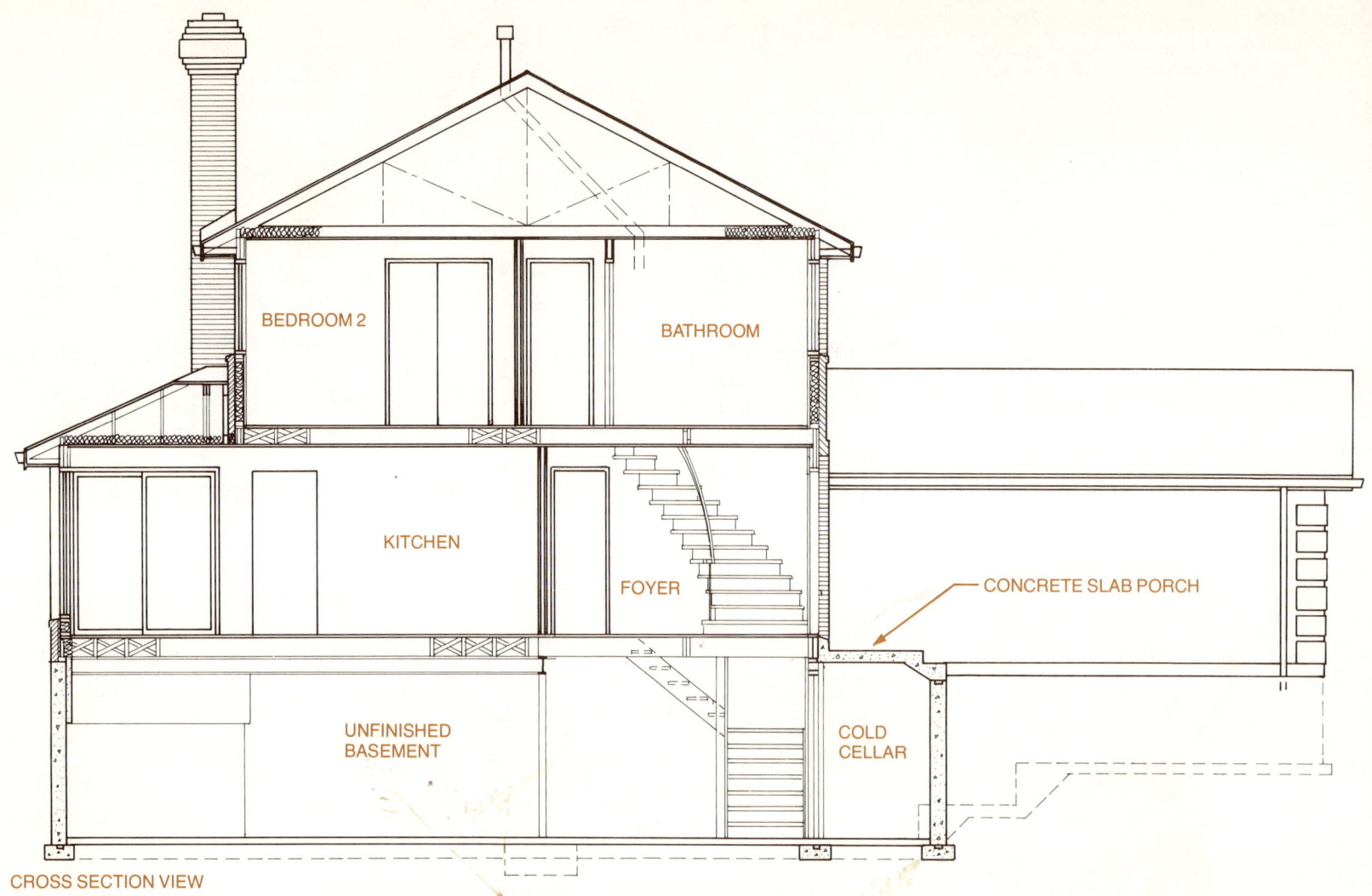

CROSS SECTION VIEW

Fig. 17-15

ARCHITECTURAL CONSTRUCTION DRAWINGS

As you will remember, when the buyer approved the architect's rough sketches, the architect's drafters then made up the set of presentation drawings. At the same time, they also made up a set of construction (working) drawings for the trades.

Architectural construction drawings are used in the actual construction of the house. Every detail and measurement of the house is described by these drawings.

Floor Plans. The floor plan shows the locations of the rooms, closets, windows and stairs as they woud appear from above.

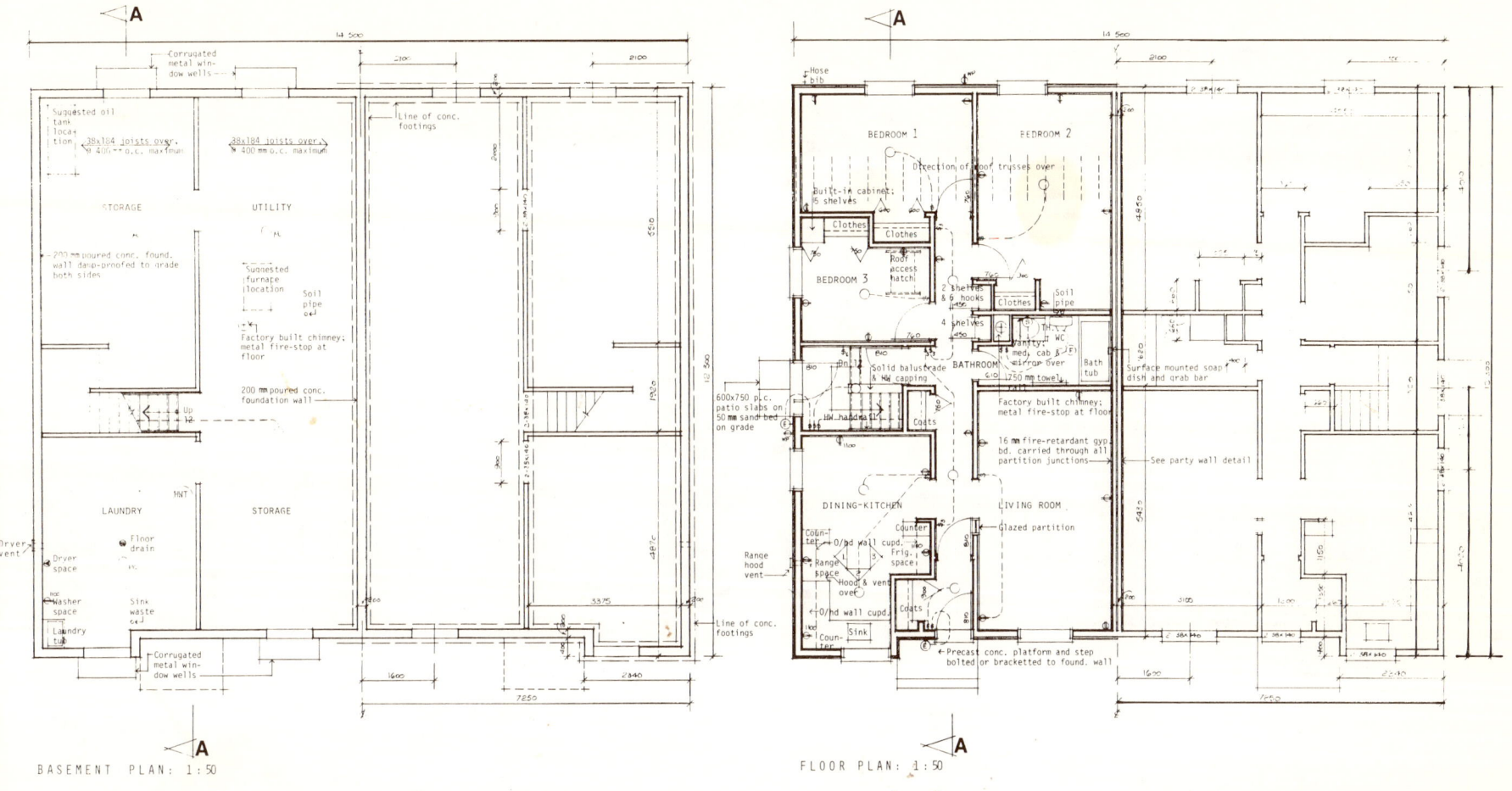

Fig 17-16

Courtesy Canada Mortgage and Housing Corporation

ARCHITECTURAL CONSTRUCTION DRAWINGS

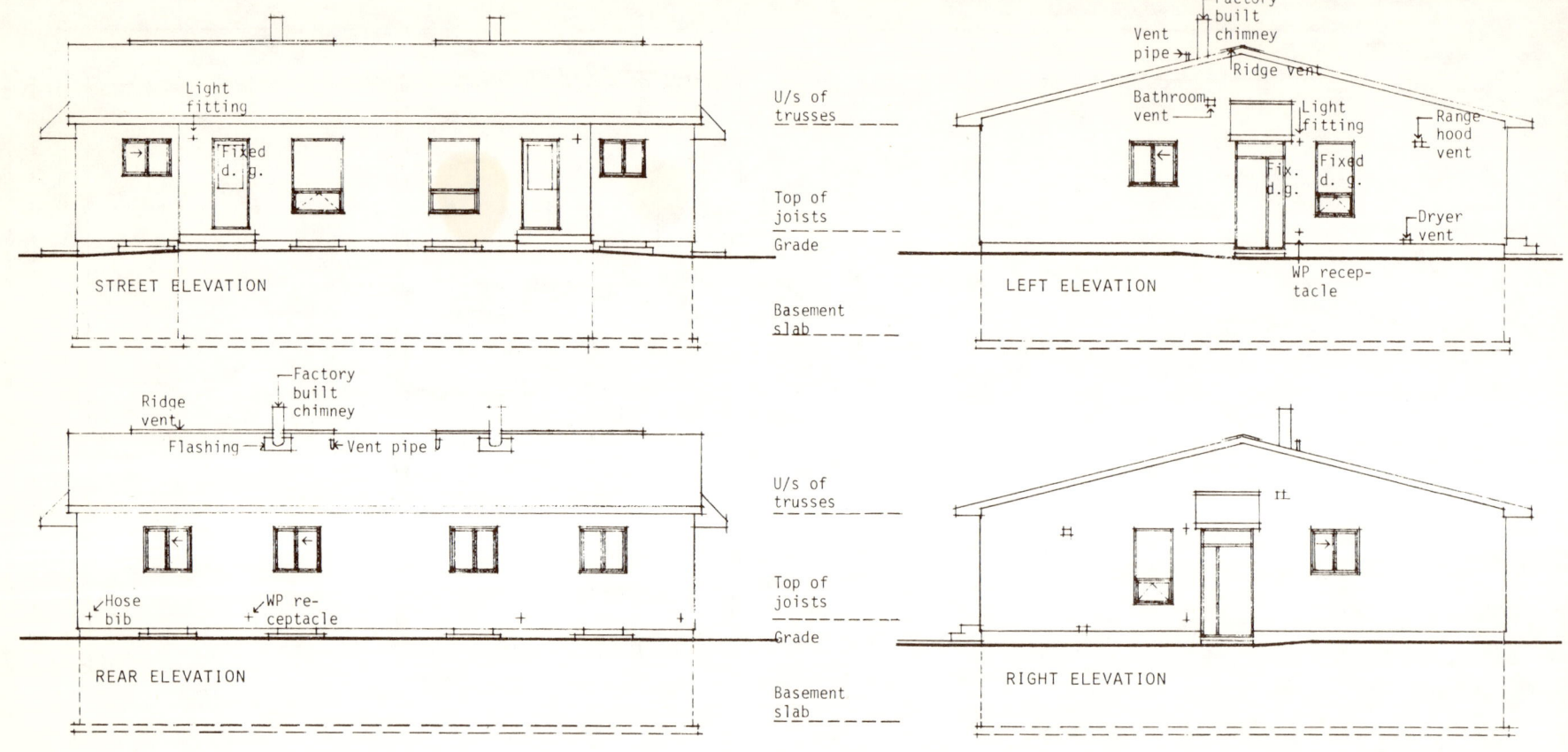

Fig. 17-17

Courtesy Canada Mortgage and Housing Corporation

Elevations. These are views that picture how the house would appear when looking at its sides. There is one elevation for each of the four sides.

Cross-Sectional Elevations. These are the views that show what the inside of the house would look like if you were to imagine the house cut into two parts. This would allow you to look at the interior of the house from the foundation to the roof.

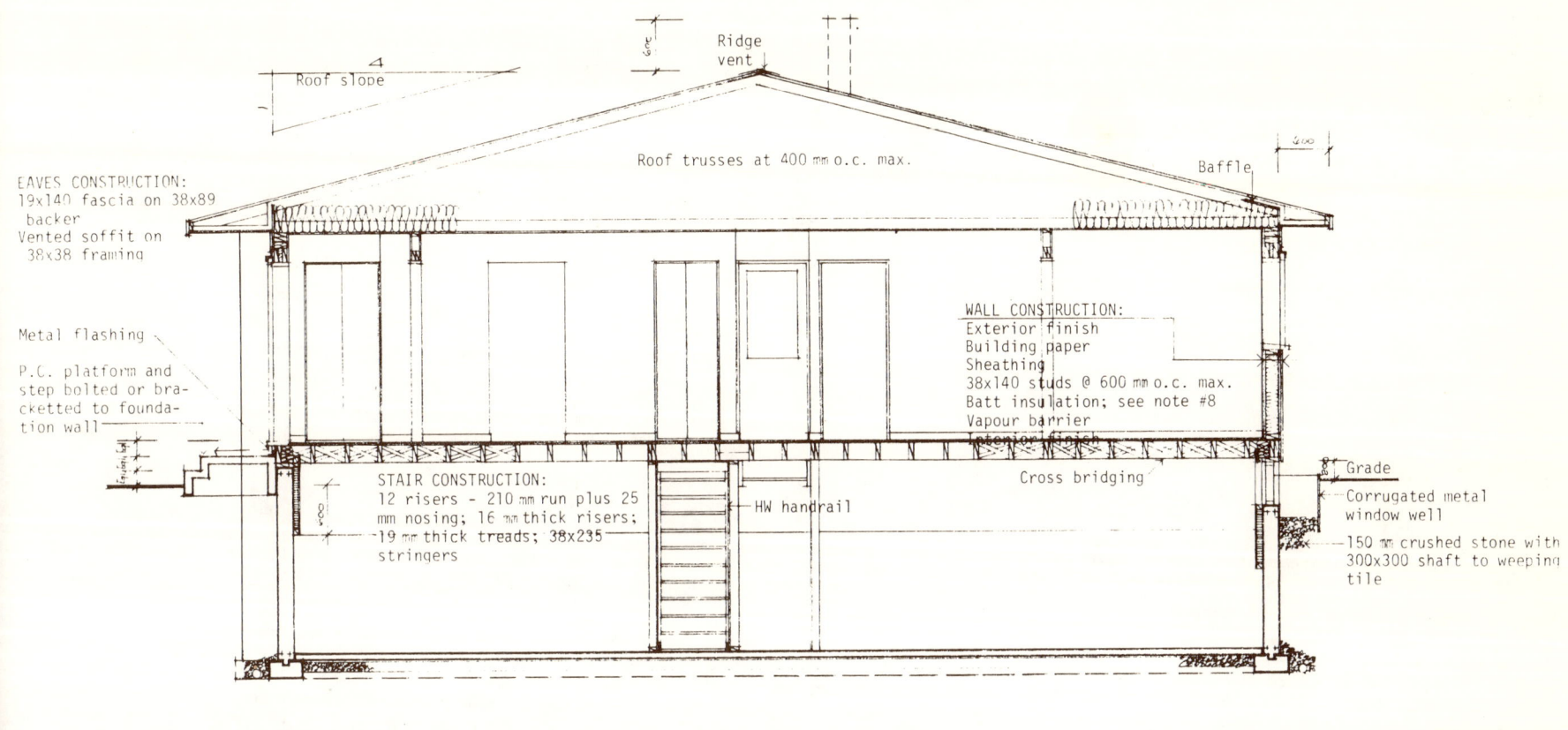

Fig. 17-18

ARCHITECTURAL CONSTRUCTION DRAWINGS 251

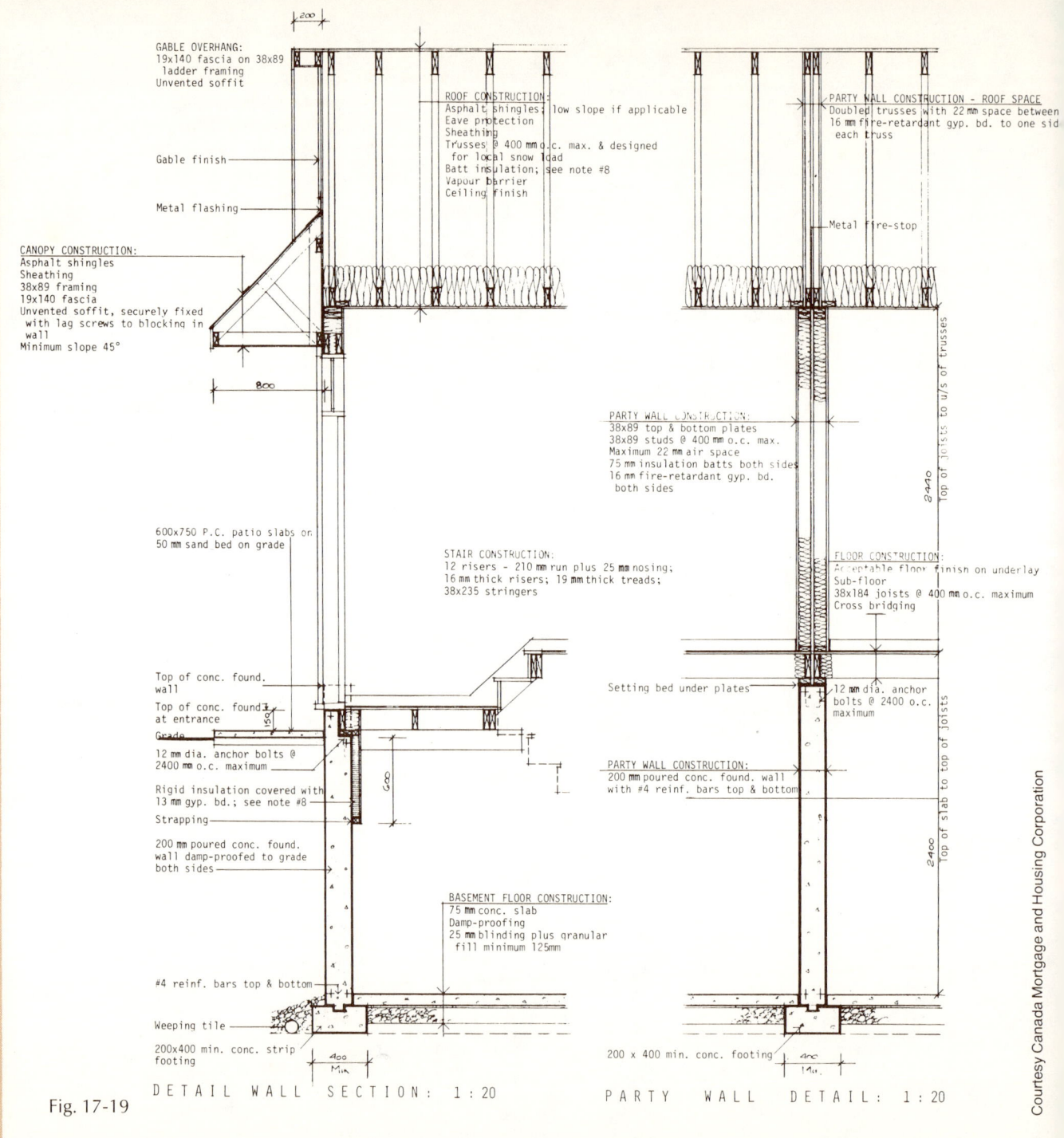

Fig. 17-19   DETAIL WALL SECTION: 1:20   PARTY WALL DETAIL: 1:20

Detail Drawings. These are additional drawings of separate items of a building. They are prepared to help describe the construction of important features such as walls, stairs, fireplaces, eavestroughs, windows, foundations etc.

BUILDING THE HOUSE

Finally the architect and the buyer select contractors who will actually build the house. The contractor then hires the tradespeople, who order the necessary lumber, bricks and other materials, etc., and then the house is begun. Let's watch the house rise as the workers in each trade appear on the site and do their job.

The surveyors stake the position of the house on the lot precisely as planned, using a level and a rod. The excavator removes the earth to the required depth between the stakes.

Houses are heavy and would sink into the earth if not for the **foundation footing**. It's as if you were to walk through deep snow without snowshoes. The broad snowshoes distribute the body mass over a larger area and keep you from sinking into the snow. The concrete footing is poured into forms around the perimeter of the house to distribute the mass of the house over a broader area.

Fig. 17-20

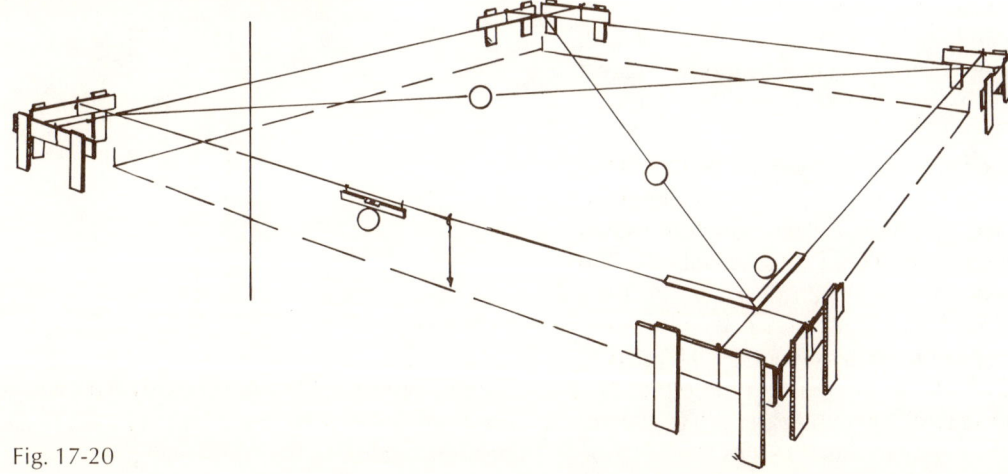

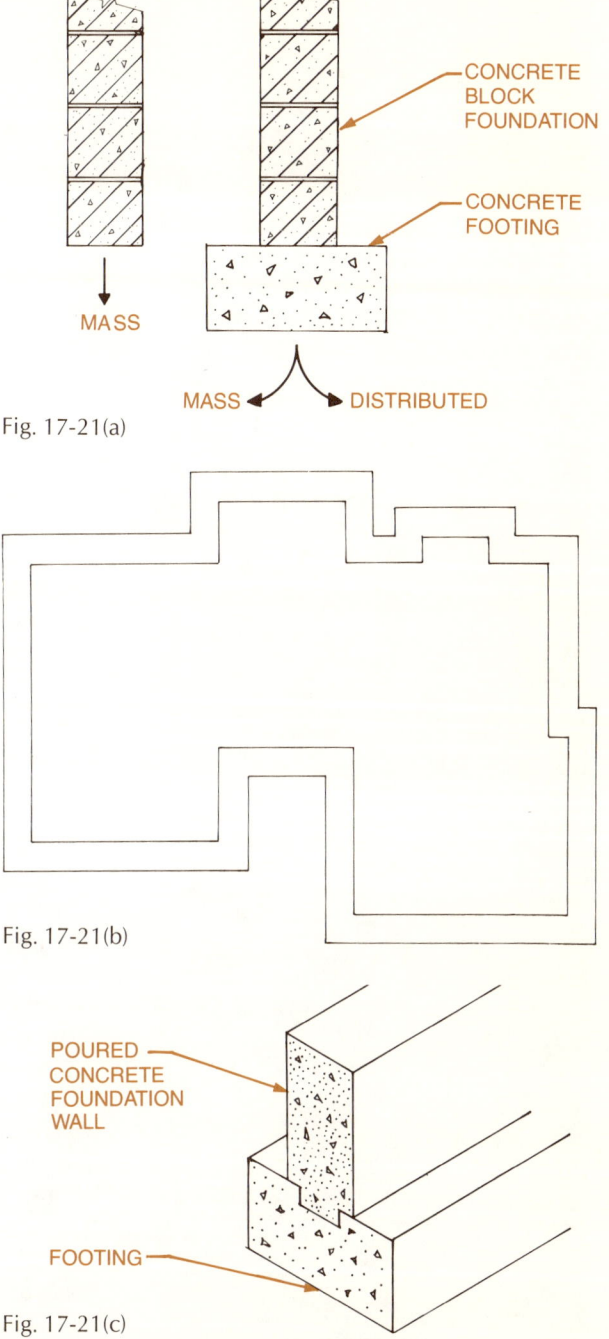

Fig. 17-21(a)

Fig. 17-21(b)

Fig. 17-21(c)

Fig. 17-22

When the concrete hardens after a few days it is ready to support the foundation walls.

The mason carefully builds up the foundation wall using concrete blocks held together by mortar. A level and a string are used for each course to keep the wall straight.

When the foundation wall is the required height the carpenters construct the upper part of the building.

As you can see, a length of wood called the **sill** is fastened to the concrete blocks by anchor bolts. The anchor bolts keep the upper part of the house from shifting off the foundation.

The carpenters nail lengths of wood called **joists** to the sill, from one side of the house to the other. The joists are usually placed 400 mm apart from the centre of one joist to the centre of the next joist. This can be noted as 400 mm O.C. (on centre) on drawings. When the joists are in position, a length of wood called the **header** is nailed to the ends of the joists.

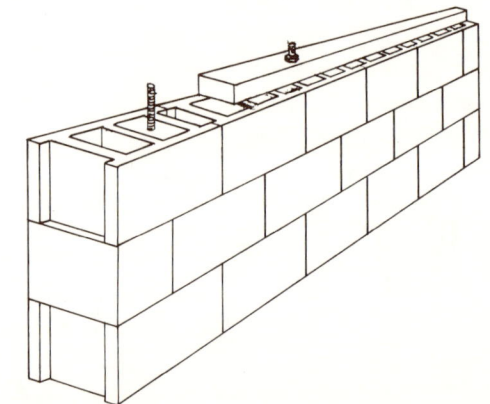

Fig. 17-23

The joists support the **floors** of the house. The sub floor or under floor is nailed over the joists to create a platform for the walls. The finished floor is laid on the sub floor at a later time.

Exterior frame walls and partitions are made up of several members: the **sole plate**, **studs** and the **top plate**. The studs are the vertical supports between the sole plate and the top plate. The carpenters usually construct the walls section horizontally on the sub floor. When each section is complete the sections are raised and nailed into position, as shown in Figure 17-25.

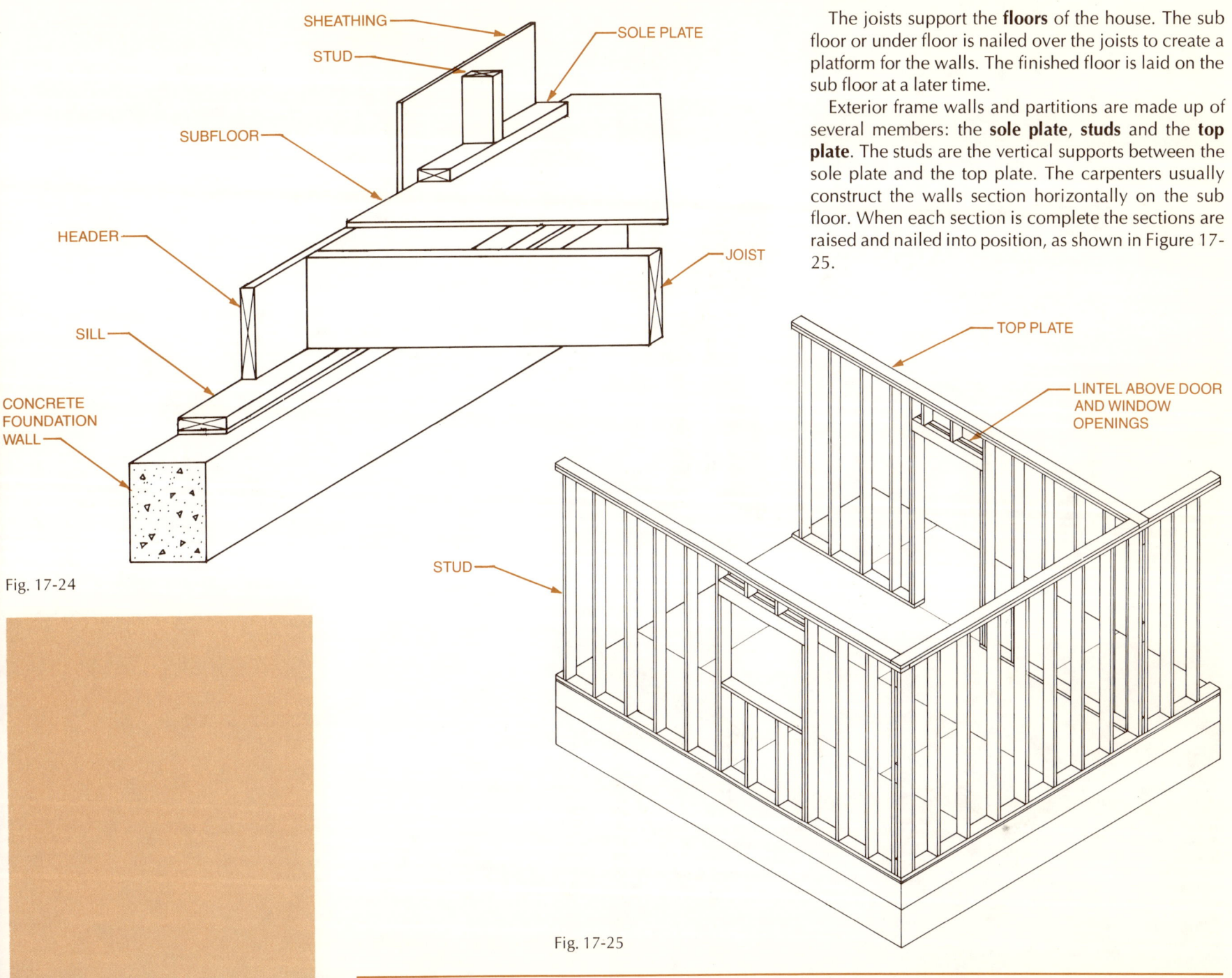

Fig. 17-24

Fig. 17-25

BUILDING THE HOUSE 255

The wall sections are joined by a second top plate to add support for the ceiling joists. The ceiling joists are nailed on end to the top plates usually 400 mm O.C. from each other. They support the finished ceiling and act as ties between each section of the exterior walls. If the house has a second floor they act as floor joists to give support for the floor and roof above.

Once the walls are framed, the outside covering called **sheathing** is nailed to the wall framing members. The sheathing can be any of the following: lumber, plywood, gypsum, fiberboard or particle board.

The carpenters continue their work, constructing the roof. Rafters are usually precut to the proper length and at the desired angle. This angle is referred to as the **pitch**. Pairs of rafters are nailed together to a ridge board to form the top of the roof. The lower end of the rafter is usually notched to fit securely to the top plate

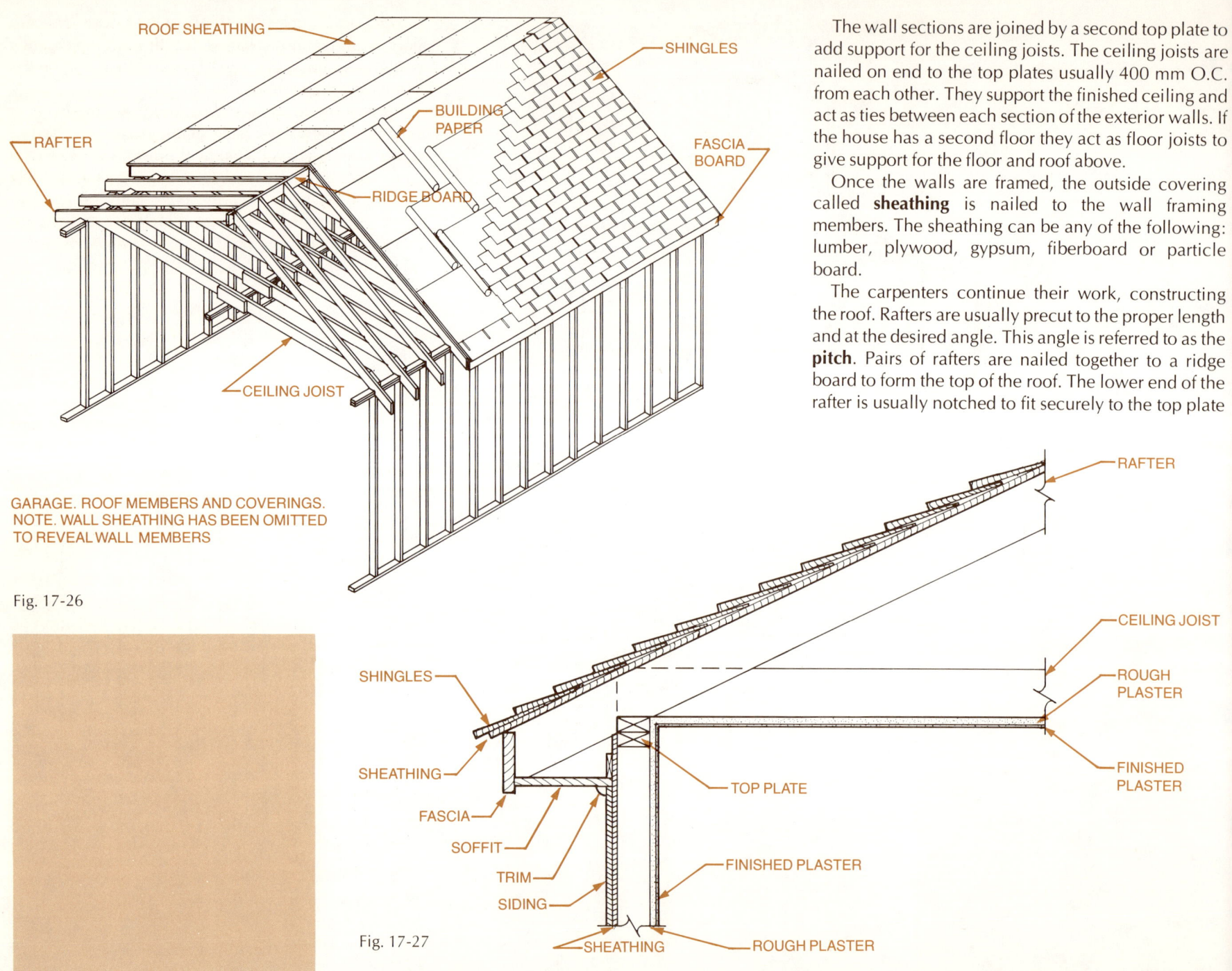

Fig. 17-26 GARAGE. ROOF MEMBERS AND COVERINGS. NOTE. WALL SHEATHING HAS BEEN OMITTED TO REVEAL WALL MEMBERS

Fig. 17-27

256 ARCHITECTURAL DRAWING

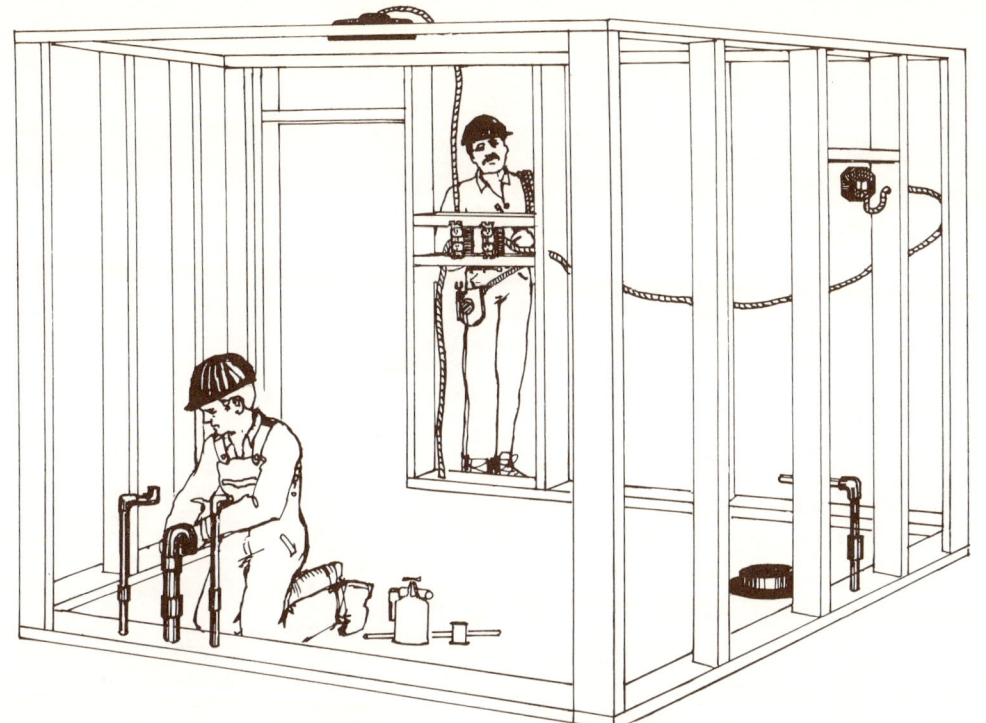

Fig. 17-28

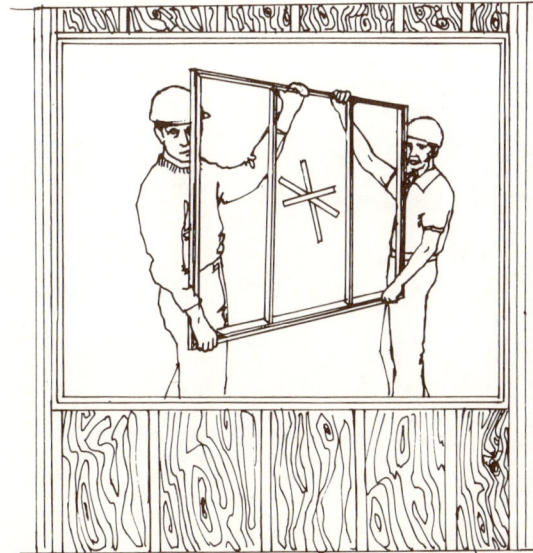

Fig. 17-29

of the exterior walls. The rafters overhang, or extend past the walls of the house. When the rafters are in place, roof **sheathing** is applied to add strength to the roof frame, and provide a surface for the roof covering. As you have seen, the carpenters have been very active, but as the frame of the house begins to take shape the other tradespeople are called upon to help complete the house. The roof must be waterproof. The roofer adds a tarpaper underlay to the roof sheathing, and nails on the shingles. The overhang of the roof is enclosed. For this house, the mason adds the bricks to the outside of the wall sheathing. The plumbers and electricians install all the necessary wiring and pipes. These are almost always placed inside the walls and the floors. Concrete is poured into the basement through a window opening in the wall. The concrete covers the drain pipes that lead to the street and the footings and becomes the basement floor.

From the furnace in the basement, heating experts install all the ducts to each area of the house. When all the pipes, wiring, and ducts are in place, insulation is placed between the studs of all the exterior walls and above the ceiling joists. The glaziers have been active as well, installing all the windows in the window openings in the walls. The interior ceilings, walls and partitions can now be covered with gypsum board by the lath and plaster workers. The cabinetmakers carefully install all the cabinets and counter indicated on the plans. The carpenters hang all the doors and complete the exterior and interior trim as the work progresses.

The tile workers lay tiling in the bathrooms, halls, showers, etc. The plumbers return to install the sinks, faucets, toilets, etc. The painters arrive to decorate the house and the finished floors are laid over the subfloors. The eavestroughs are added to the downspouts and off to the storm sewers. The earth fill has been graded around the house and the sidewalks, porches, patios, driveway and landscaping are completed.

Fig. 17-30

Fig. 17-32

Fig. 17-31

There are a great many steps and items of house construction that we have not mentioned, but which must be added before the house is completed. Perhaps you can think of some that we have not mentioned.

As you have seen, bulding a house is a complicated operation. It requires a construction supervisor who understands every detail of the architect's plans. The supervisor must call in each of the different tradespeople when they are needed at different points of construction. Each worker follows the instructions and information exactly as stated in the plans. The architect has been on the site many times to check with the supervisor and inspect the house at each stage of its construction. We can be sure that you, the buyer, have been by many times as well. Finally the day arrives when all the workers have left. The architect invites the buyer to inspect the completed house. The buyer's dreams, the architect's plans and the skills of all tradespeople have together created a beautiful house: a place to live.

POINTS TO REMEMBER

- Architects produce rough sketches of their house design for approval before making more detailed drawings.
- Presentation drawings give an over-all description of the features of a house.
- There are three types of presentation drawings: floor plans, elevation drawings and perspective pictorial.
- A cross-sectional drawing permits you to "see" into a house as though one wall were removed.
- Architectural construction drawings are detailed and are used in the actual building of the house.
- There are four types of construction drawing: floor plans, elevation drawings, cross-sectional elevations and detail drawings.

QUESTIONS TO ANSWER

1. What type of drawings will an architect first show to a buyer?
2. What are presentation drawings used for?
3. Name the three types of presentation drawings.
4. Describe construction drawings and explain what they are used for.
5. Name the four types of construction drawings.
6. What is another name for construction drawings.
7. Why are house foundations necessary?
8. Name at least six different types of tradespeople who help build a house.

REPLACE THE X's WITH THE CORRECT TERM.

1. The gothic lettering used in drafting has an **XXXXXXXXXXXX** style.
2. When you are sick it is wise to **XXXXXXX** your doctor about your illness.

PROJECTS

PROJECT 17-1

EXTERIOR WALL SECTION
BRICK VENEER
SCALE 1:20

INSTRUCTIONS

1. Prepare a working drawing of the wall section
2. Label each detail that makes up the wall section. Show the dimensions of each detail.
3. The height distance between the finished first floor and the finished ceiling is 2400 mm.
4. All dimensions are in millimetres.

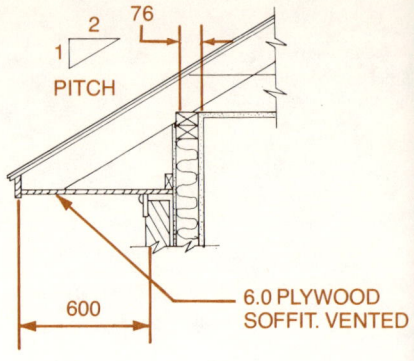

EAVES DETAIL

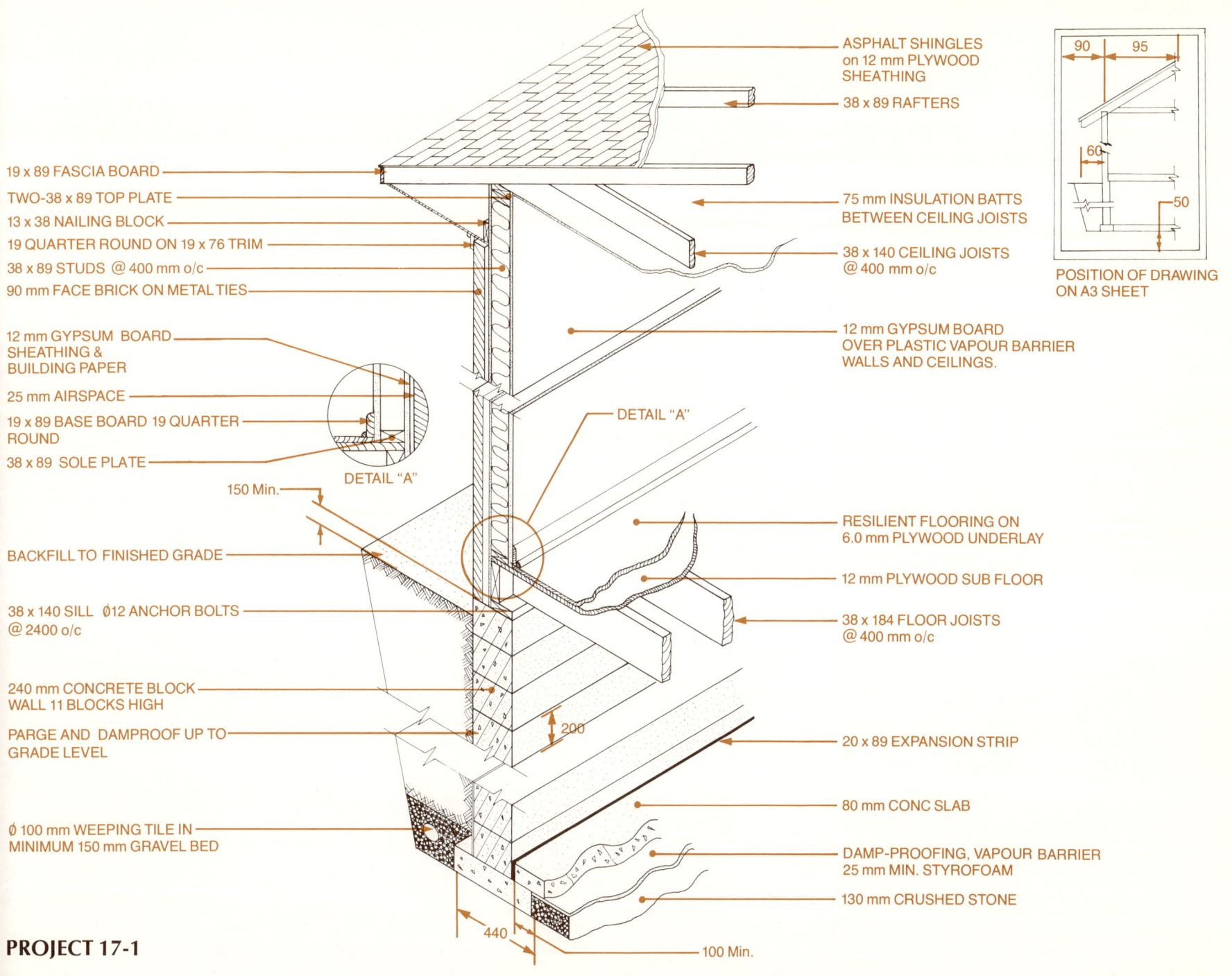

PROJECT 17-1

PROJECT 17-2

**EXTERIOR WALL SECTION FRAME CONSTRUCTION
SCALE 1:20**

INSTRUCTIONS
1. Prepare a working drawing of the wall section on an A-3 sheet. You may follow the suggested layout shown for 17-1.
2. Label each detail that make up the wall section. Show the dimensions of each detail.
3. The height dimension between the finished first floor and the finished ceiling is 2400 mm.
4. The pitch (slope) of the roof is 12 : 5
5. All dimensions are in millimetres.

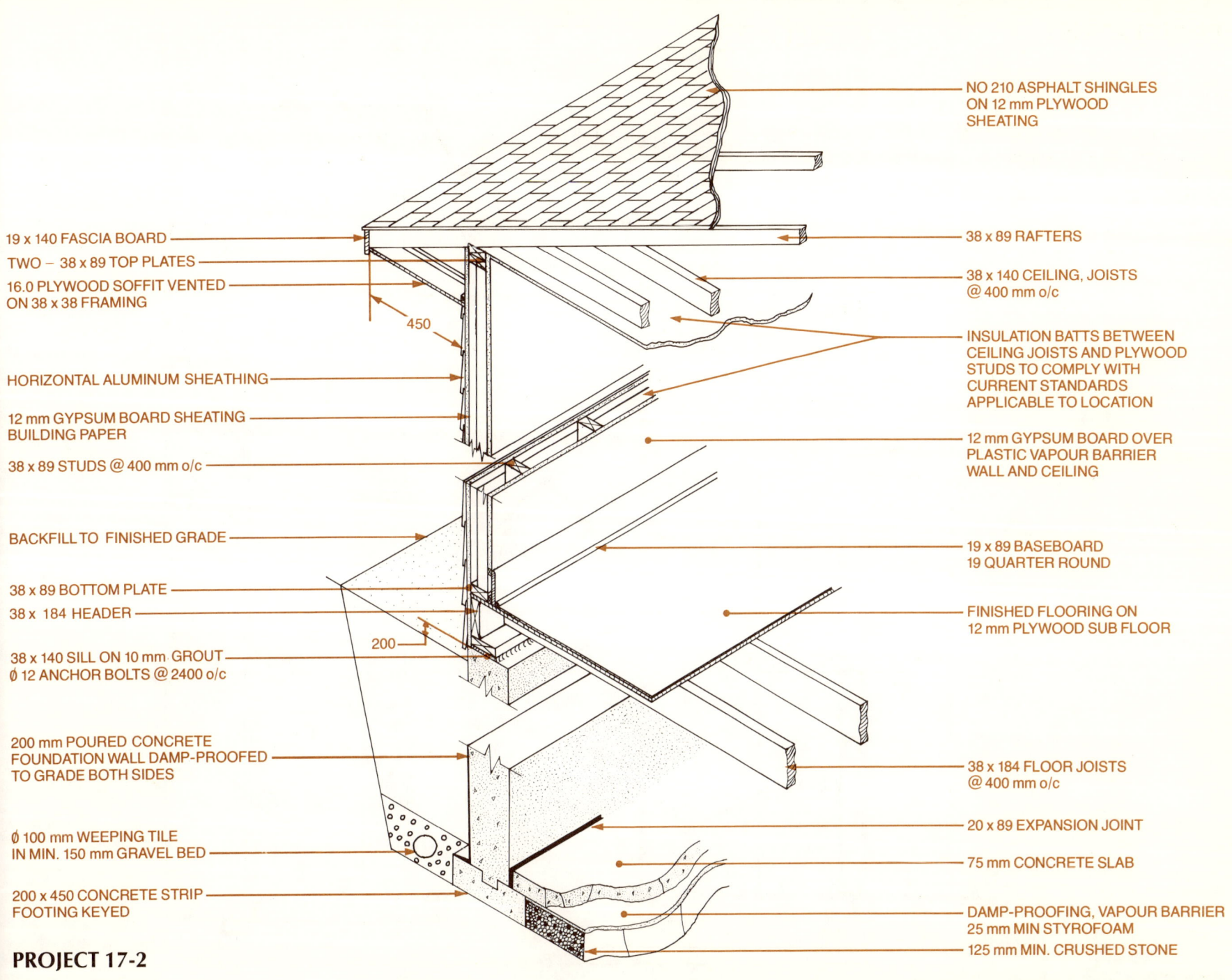

PROJECT 17-2

PROJECT 17-3 (#1)

This project is an industrial style kitchen used in nursing homes recreational buildings etc.
(a) Draw the floor plan of the kitchen
(b) Draw the three elevations of the kitchen.

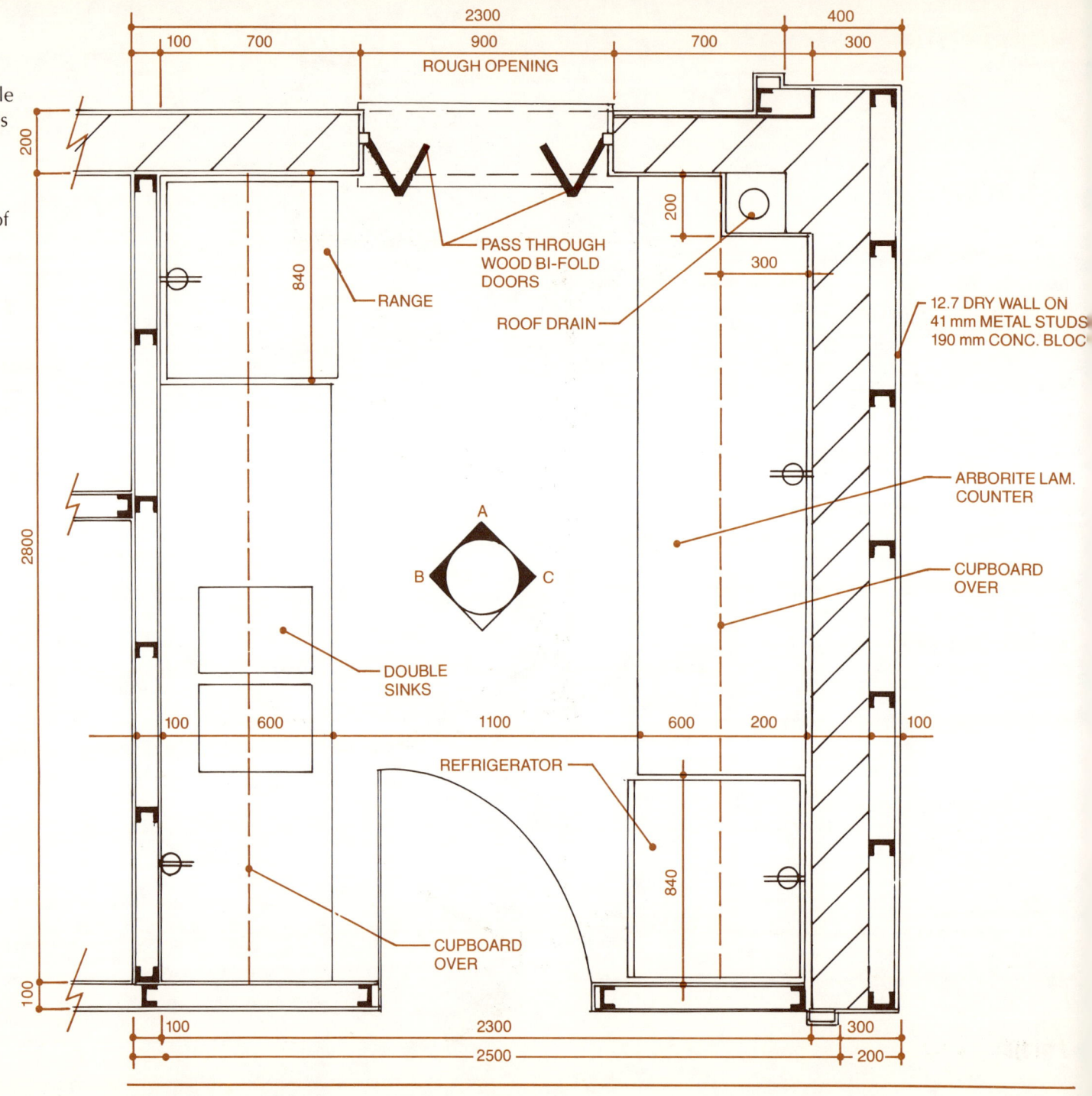

KITCHEN BI-FOLD
FLOOR PLAN
SCALE 1:20

PROJECT 17-3 (#2)

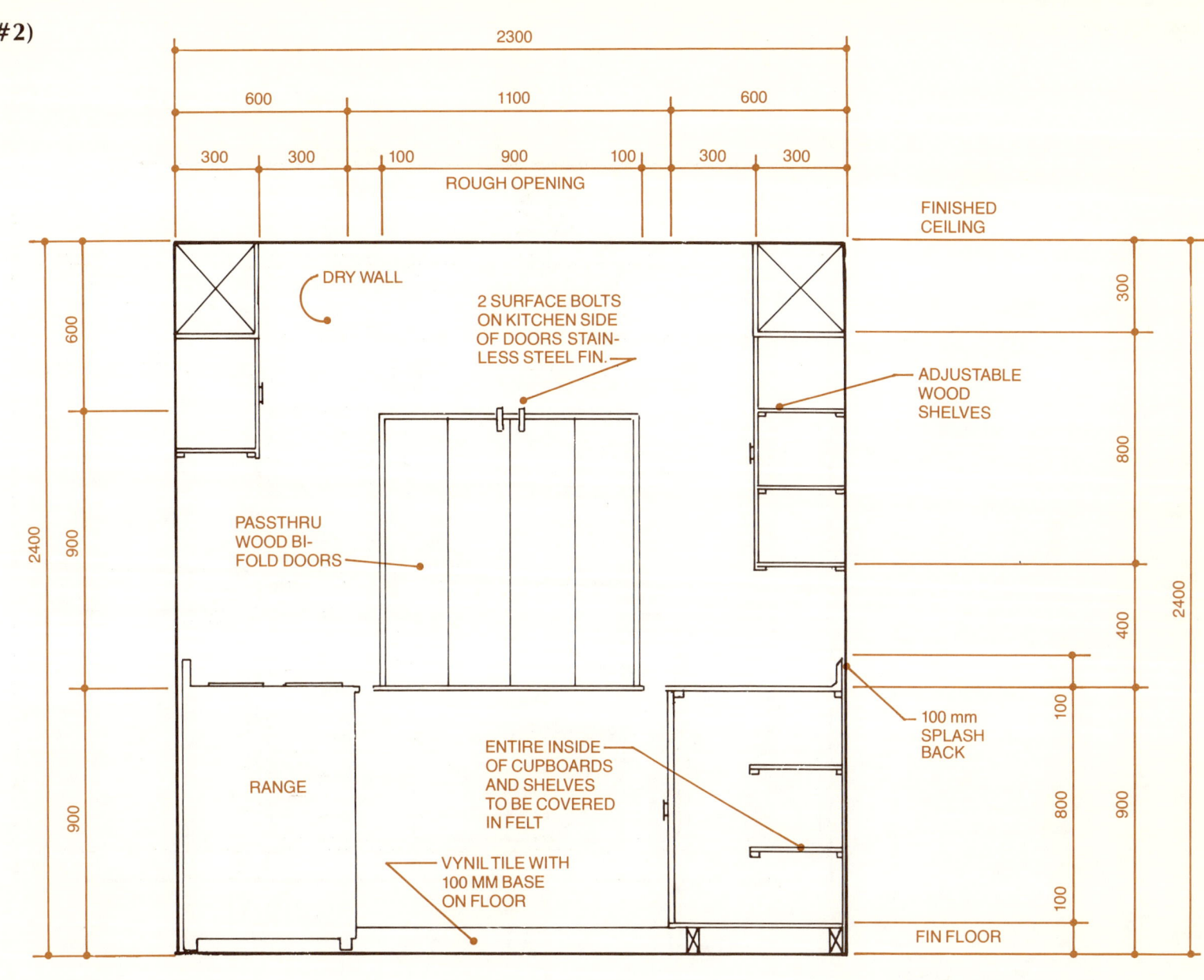

KITCHEN
ELEVATION "A" **SCALE** 1 : 20

PROJECTS 265

PROJECT 17-3 (#3)

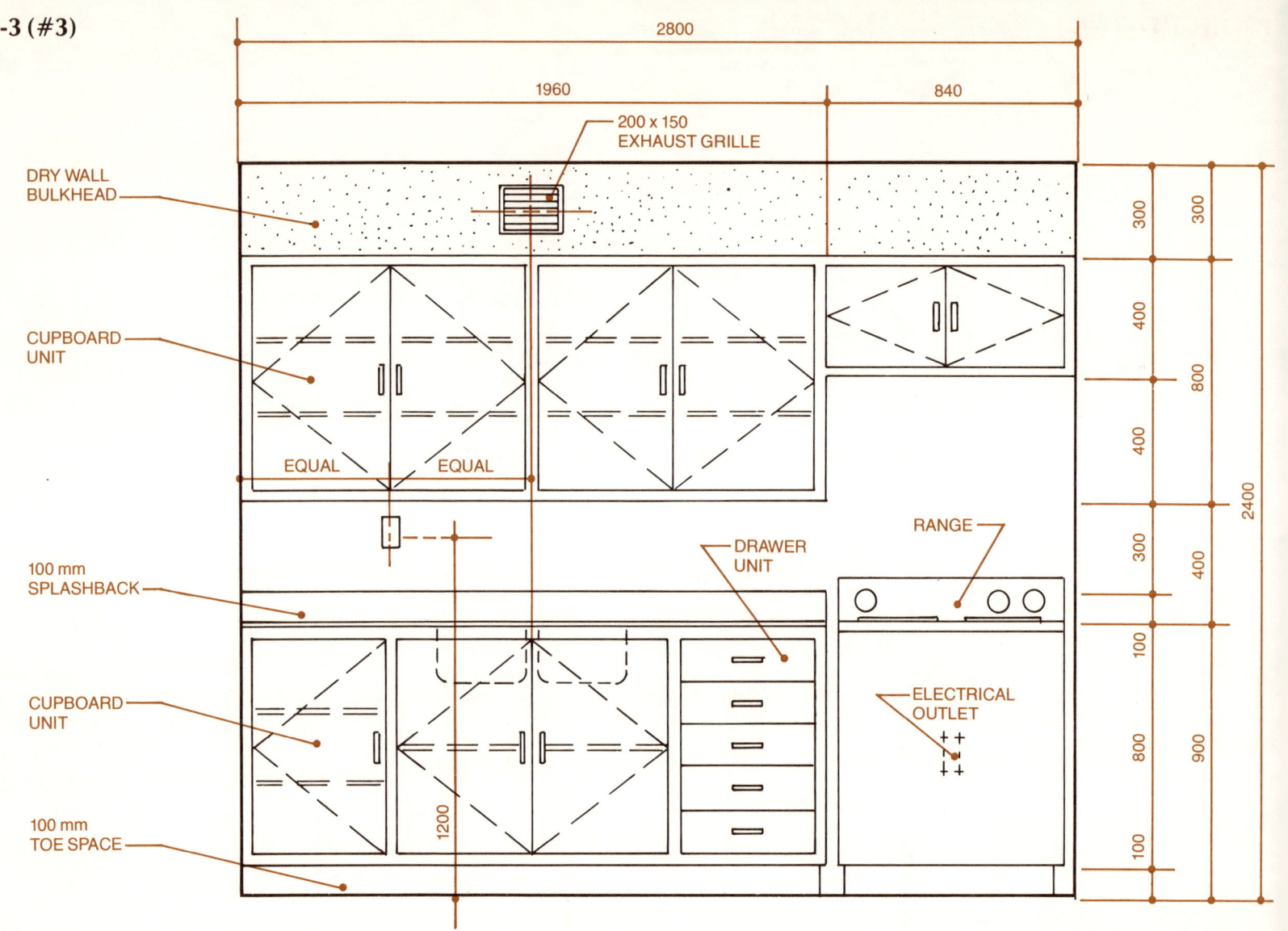

ELEVATION "B" SCALE 1:20

266 ARCHITECTURAL DRAWING

PROJECT 17-3 (#4)

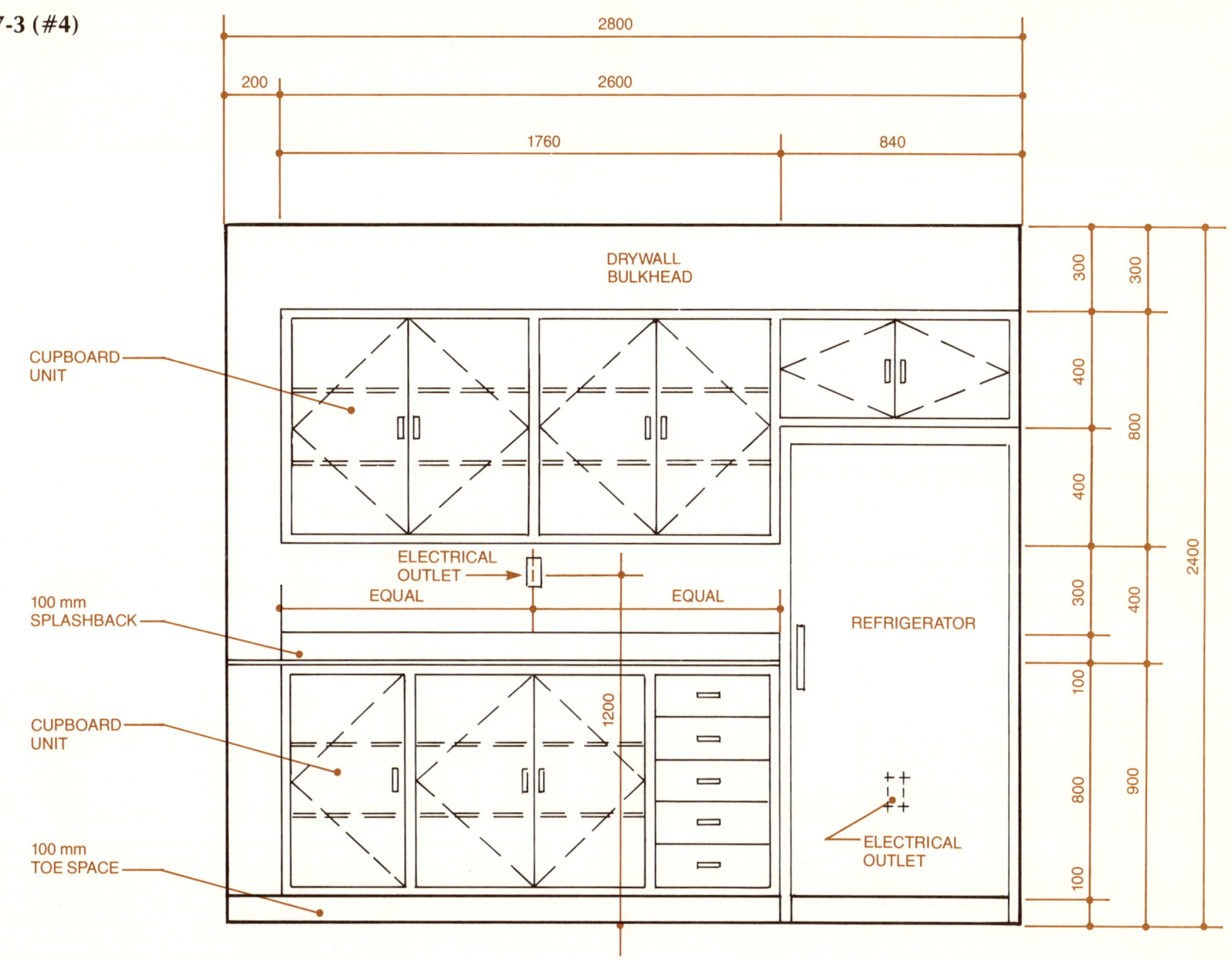

ELEVATION "C"   **SCALE 1 : 20**

PROJECTS 267

PROJECT 17-4

INSTRUCTIONS

1. Using the scale 1:50, prepare a set of presentation drawings of the house the Buyers had built (see Fig. 17-10 to Fig. 17-15.)
2. To determine the necessary dimensions you may measure the drawings (Figs. 17-10 to 17-15) using the scale 1:100.
3. Use your imagination and best judgement for any details and features not supplied.
4. Show only those dimensions required for presentation drawings. Include the approximate floor area for each room.

PROJECT 17-5 (#1)

INSTRUCTIONS

1. Using a scale of 1:50, prepare a set of presentation drawings of the split level house on pages 268 to 272.
2. Use only the dimensions provided. The sizes of features not dimensioned may be determined by measuring the drawings using a scale of 1:100.
3. You may vary the exterior finish and details if you wish, i.e. brick, aluminum siding, vertical or horizontal, etc. Use your imagination and best judgement for any details and features not supplied.
4. Show only those dimensions required for presentation drawings. Include the approximate floor area for each room.

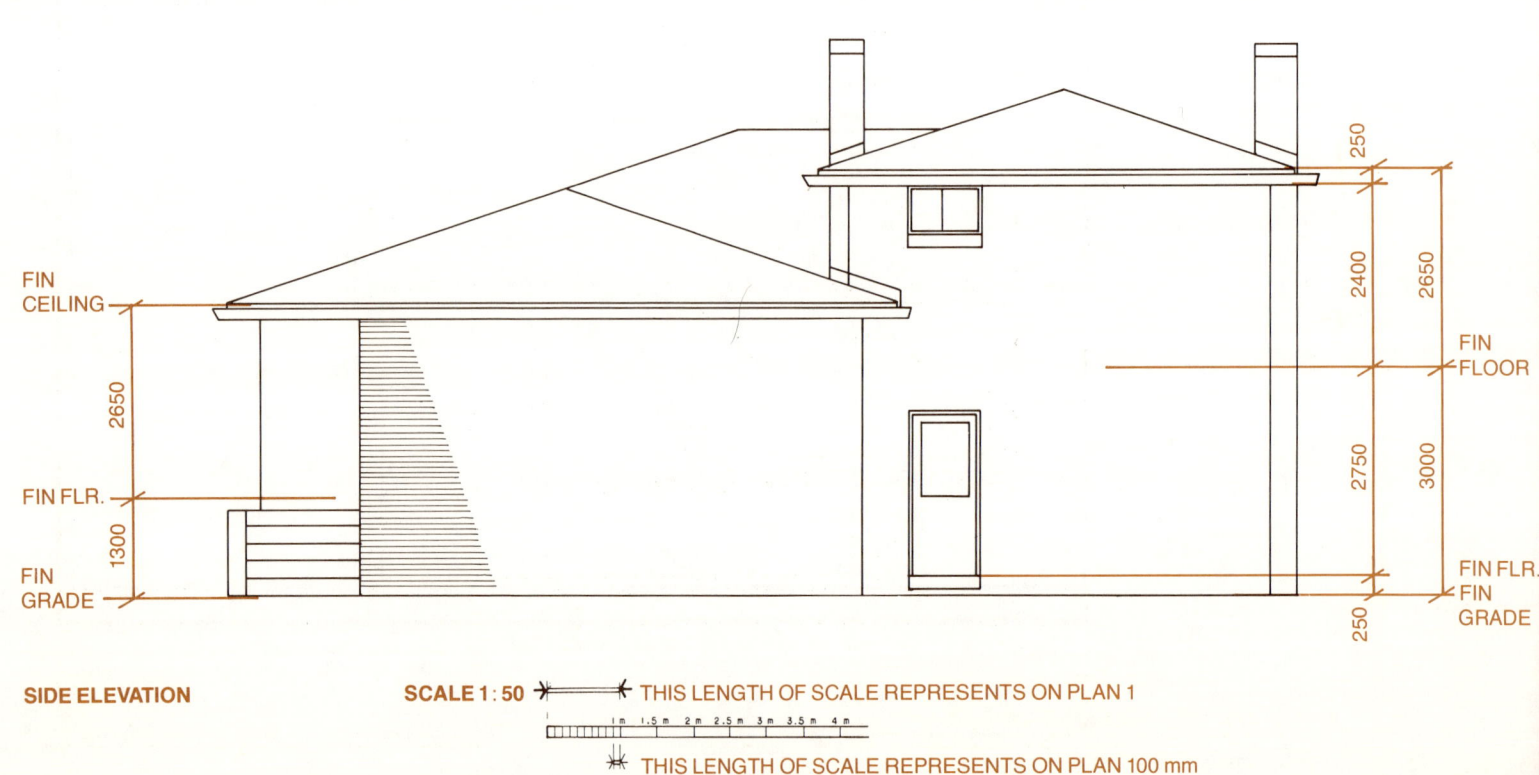

SIDE ELEVATION

SCALE 1:50 — THIS LENGTH OF SCALE REPRESENTS ON PLAN 1

THIS LENGTH OF SCALE REPRESENTS ON PLAN 100 mm

268 ARCHITECTURAL DRAWING

PROJECT 17-5 (#2)

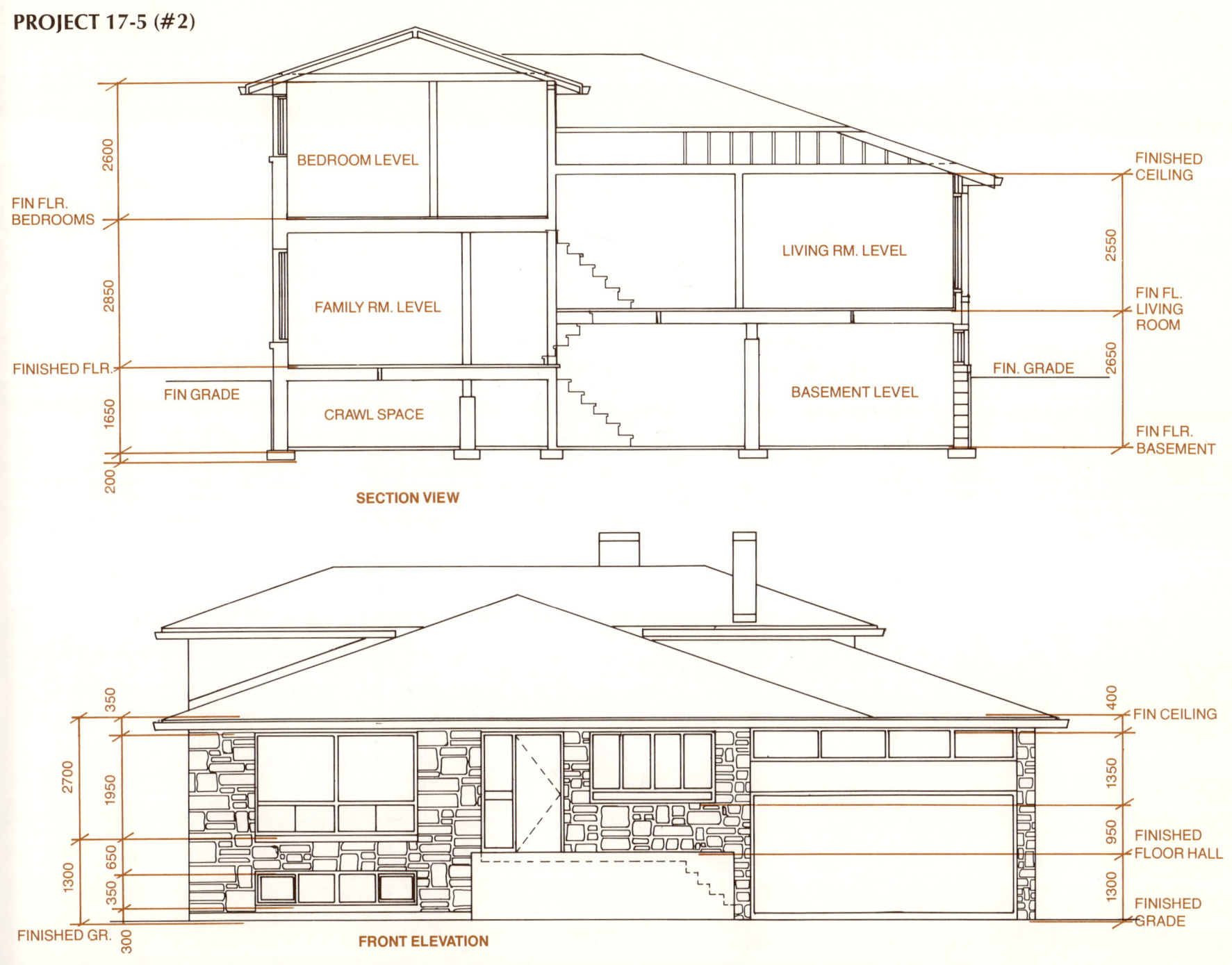

PROJECT 17-5 (#3)

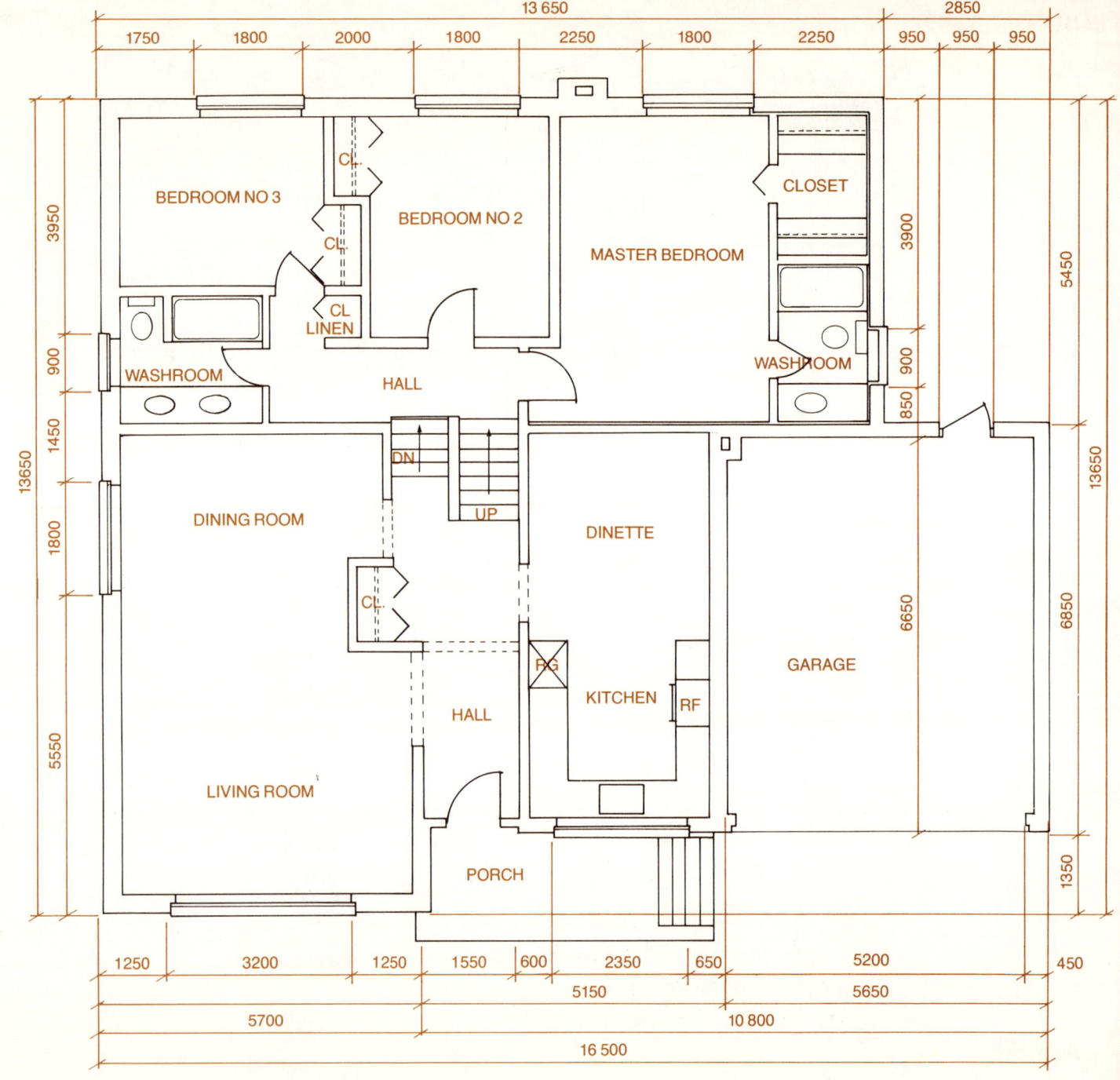

FLOOR PLAN UPPER LEVELS

270 ARCHITECTURAL DRAWING

PROJECT 17-5 (#4)

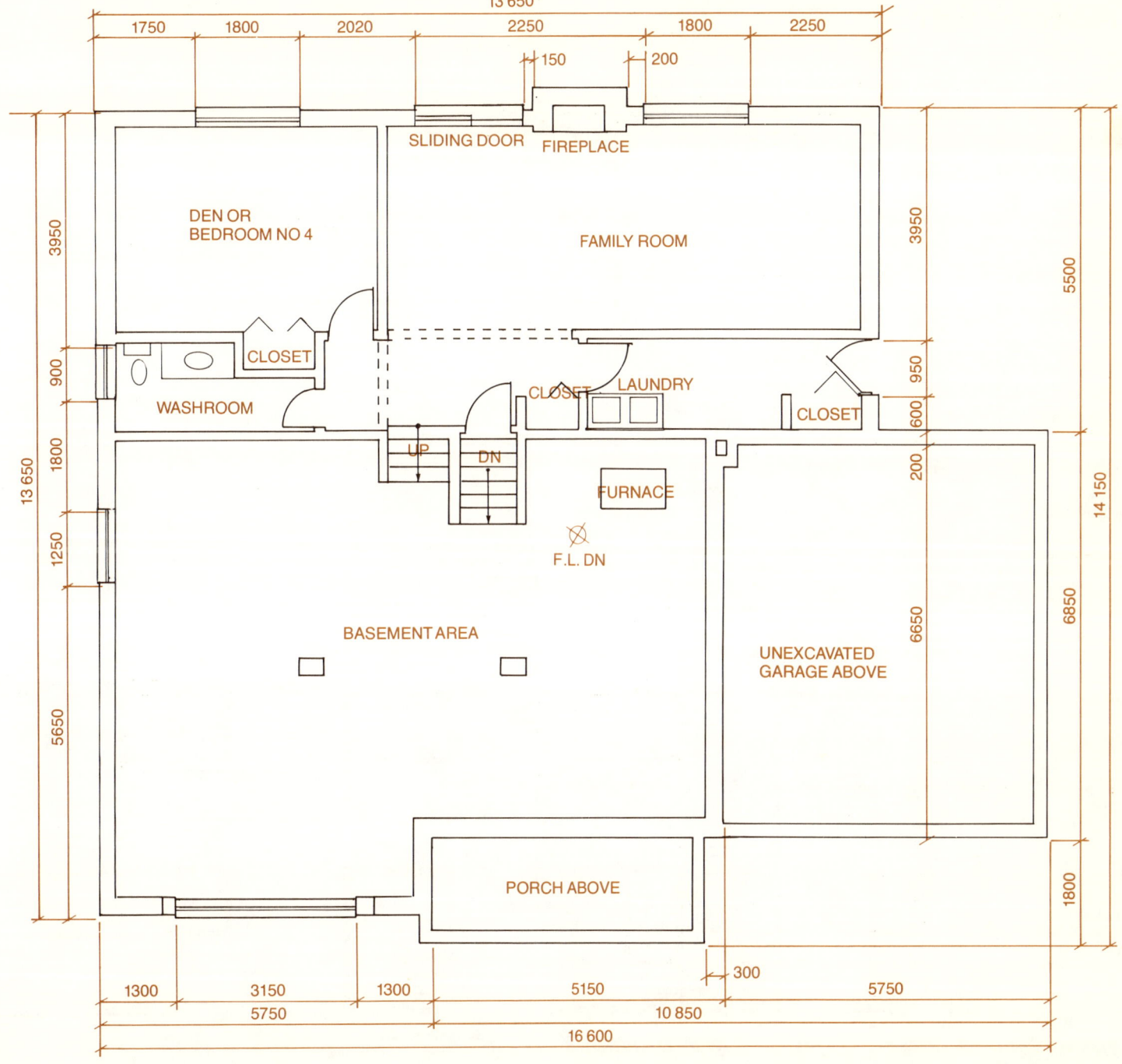

FLOOR PLAN LOWER LEVELS

PROJECT 17-5 (#5)

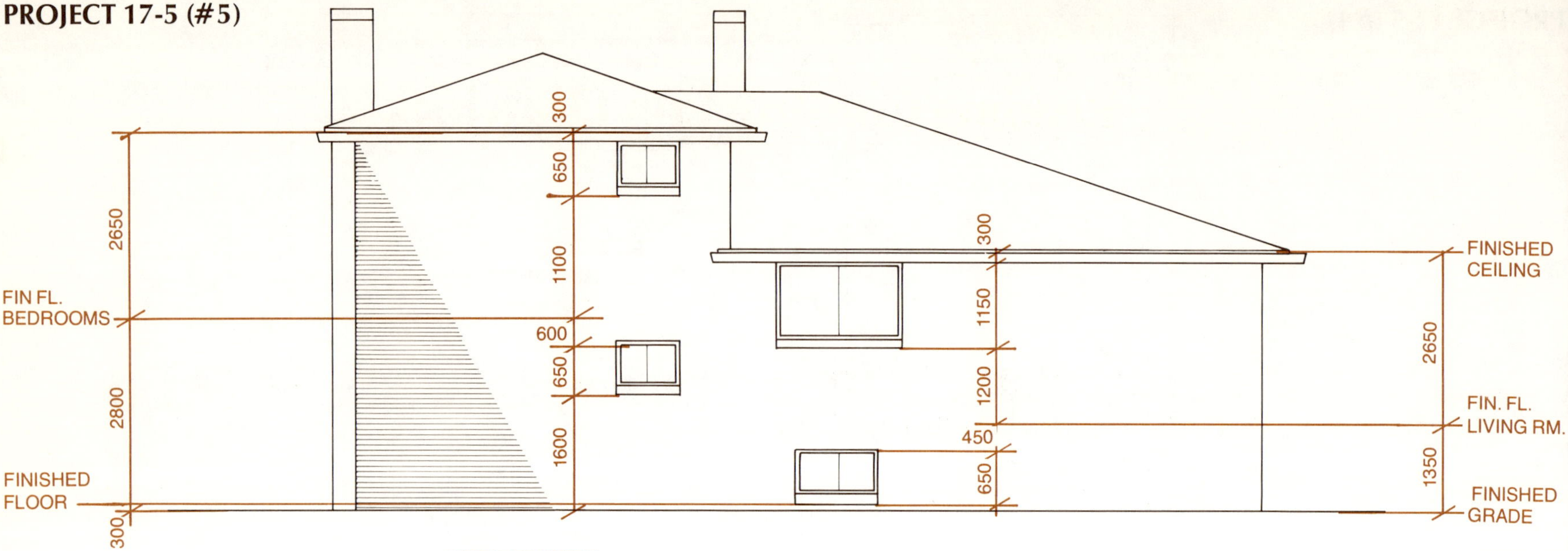

SIDE ELEVATION

REAR ELEVATION

272 ARCHITECTURAL DRAWING

Chapter 18

Reading Construction Drawings

Construction drawings provide all the necessary information so that the builder can erect (put up) the building. A set of construction drawings usually includes
- the plot plan
- the basement or foundation floor plan
- the first floor plan
- the second and third floor plan if necessary
- sectional and detail drawings
- wall, door, window and finish schedules, if the information was not noted on the other drawings.

The Plot Plan The plot plan shows the size and location of the building on the lot.

Basement or Foundation Floor Plans The basement or foundation floor plan includes instructions to construct the house up to the sub-floor of the floor above. It tells us about the footings, wall sizes and other information needed by the masonry and other tradespeople. The plans include the location of doors, windows and partitions as required.

The Floor Plans The first floor plan (and second if required) provides information on how to construct the walls and partitions up to, and including the ceiling joists above.

Sectional and Detail Drawings Sectional drawings of the entire house or certain features clearly describe the internal construction features of the building. Some features such as eaves and footings are often drawn to a larger scale in section views. They inform the builder as to the sizes, materials, finish, trim etc.

Schedules Schedules are charts that note all the information that, for reasons of space, clarity and convenience were not included on the other drawings. These charts may list all the door and window sizes for the building. It is easier to list the floor, wall and ceiling construction details in chart form instead of crowding the other drawings.

A complete set of plans as outlined above is used to construct any building. Of all the plans the floor plans tell us most about the layout of a house as well as provides a great deal of additional information.

Examine the floor plans in this chapter and answer the questions. To help you in these assignments, carefully examine Figures 18-1 and 18-2. Figure 18-1 is a partial view of a floor plan. Note how the windows, doors, and partition walls are dimensioned. The dimensions are taken from the outside of the frame all to the centre of each of the features.

Fig. 18-2 is the same partial view of the floor plan. In this figure the openings in the walls for such features as doors and windows are dimensioned, and are dimensioned to the outside walls.

Both methods of dimensioning are used in construction today, but in time, the use of standardized products will make dimensioning to the centre of features obsolete.

The appendix at the end of this chapter illustrates the symbols commonly used in construction drawings.

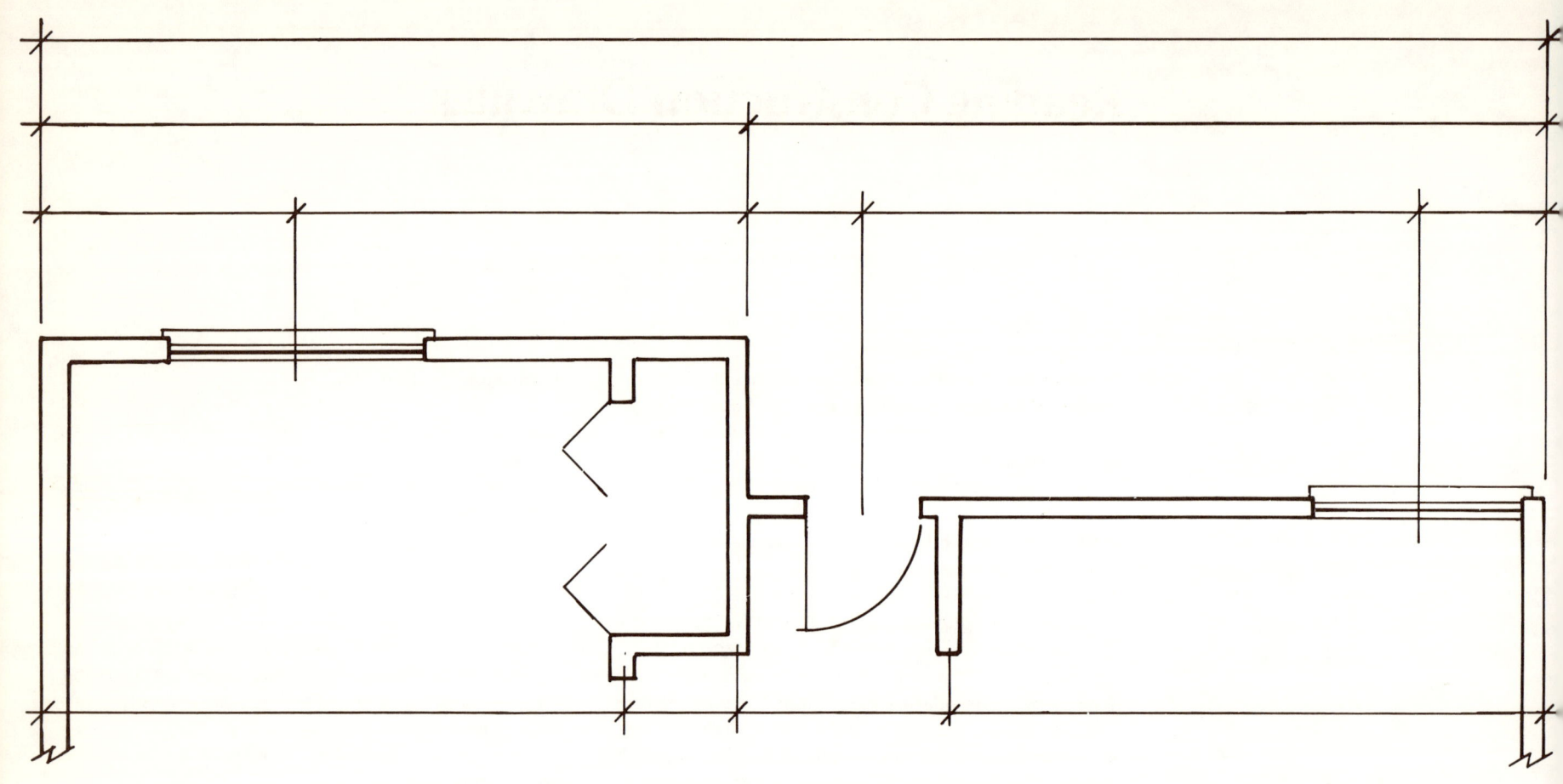

Fig. 18-1 Dimensioning interior partitions and to the centre of doors and windows

274 READING CONSTRUCTION DRAWINGS

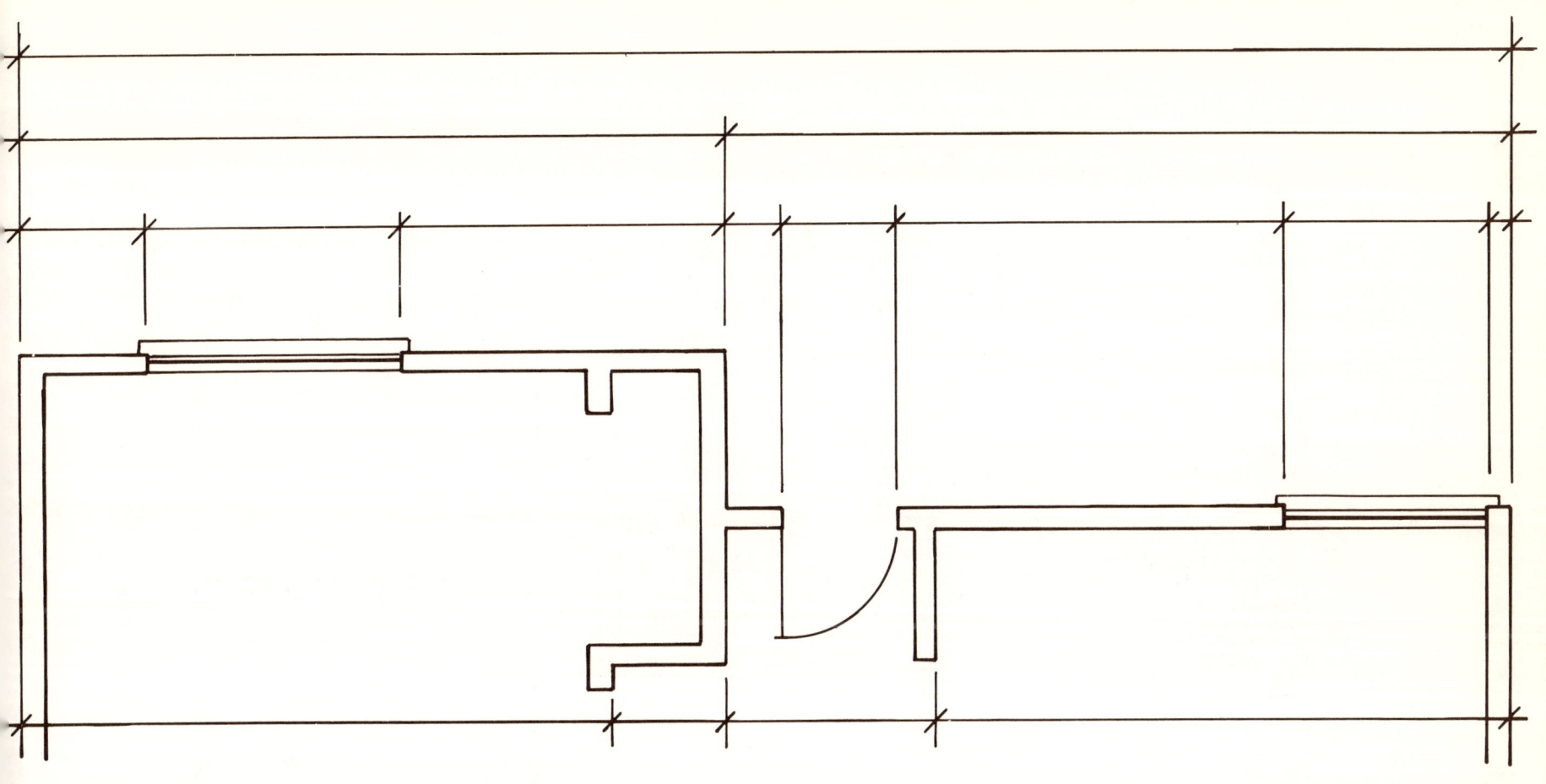

Fig. 18-2 Dimensioning interior partitions and to the openings which doors and windows fit

PROJECT 18-1

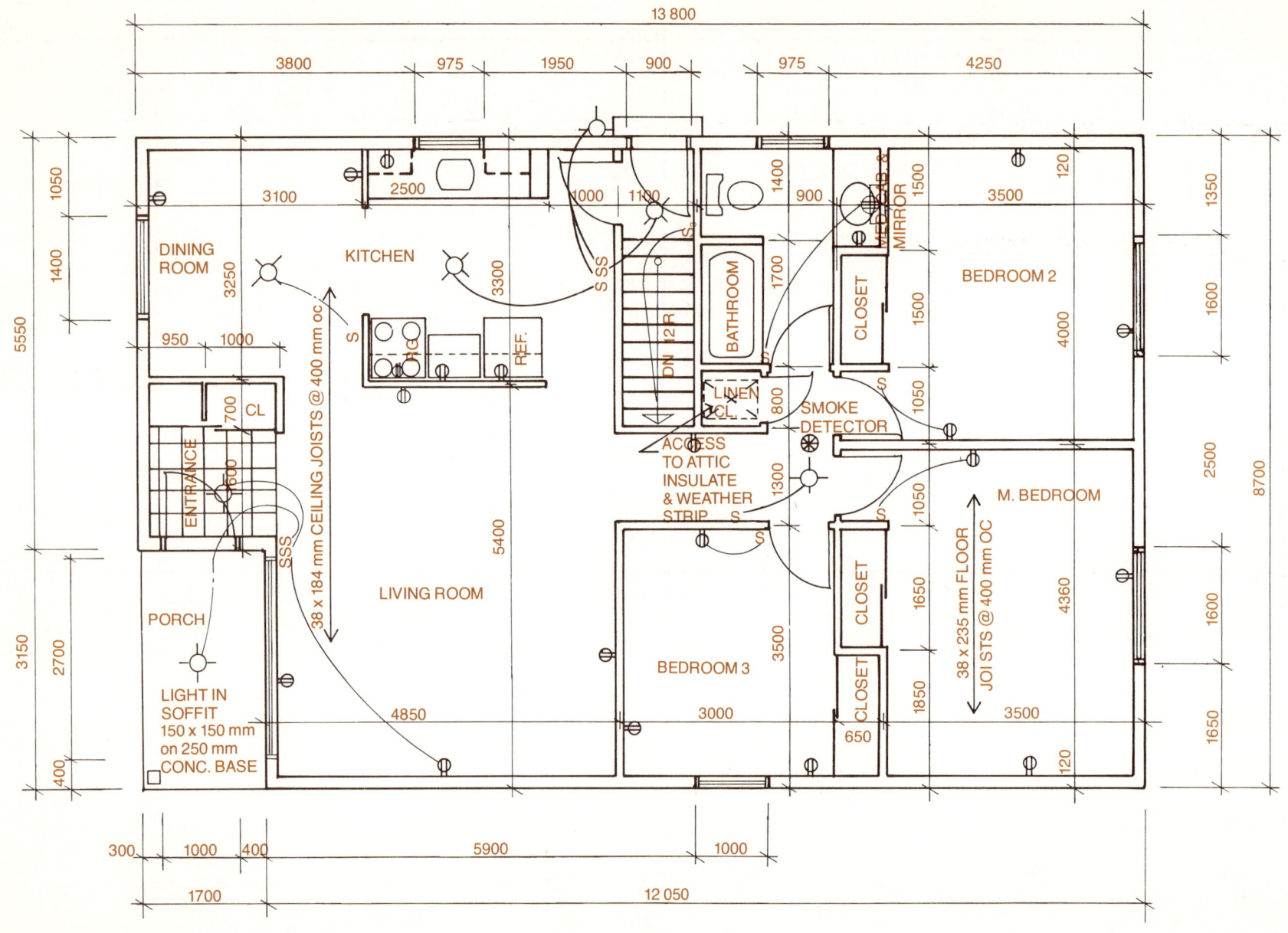

On a separate sheet answer the following questions.
1. What is the style of this house?
2. What type of exterior wall is shown?
3. What are the overall dimensions of the house?
4. Give the directions of the ceiling and floor joists.
5. Give the size and spacing of the ceiling and floor joists.
6. Where are the exterior electric light outlets located?
7. Where is the smoke detector located. Suggest why it is placed in this position.
8. How many risers are there in the stairs to the basement? How many treads would the stairs have?
9. How many closets are shown on this plan? Are all of the closet doors the same type?
10. What is the size of the two exterior door openings?
11. How many window openings are located on this plan? Give the wall opening size for each.
12. What is the total area of the living and dining rooms combined? The inside walls are 110 mm thick.
13. Where is the ceiling opening to the attic located? How did the builder plan to stop heat from escaping into the attic.
14. How many convenience outlets are controlled by a switch?
15. What is the length of the kitchen wall cabinets above the refrigerator and the range?
16. What are the dimensions of the porch?
17. How many square metres of carpeting would be required to cover the three bedroom floors including the closets?
18. Where is the electric light outlet located in the bathroom?
19. Give the total number of convenience outlets.

PROJECT 18-2 (1)

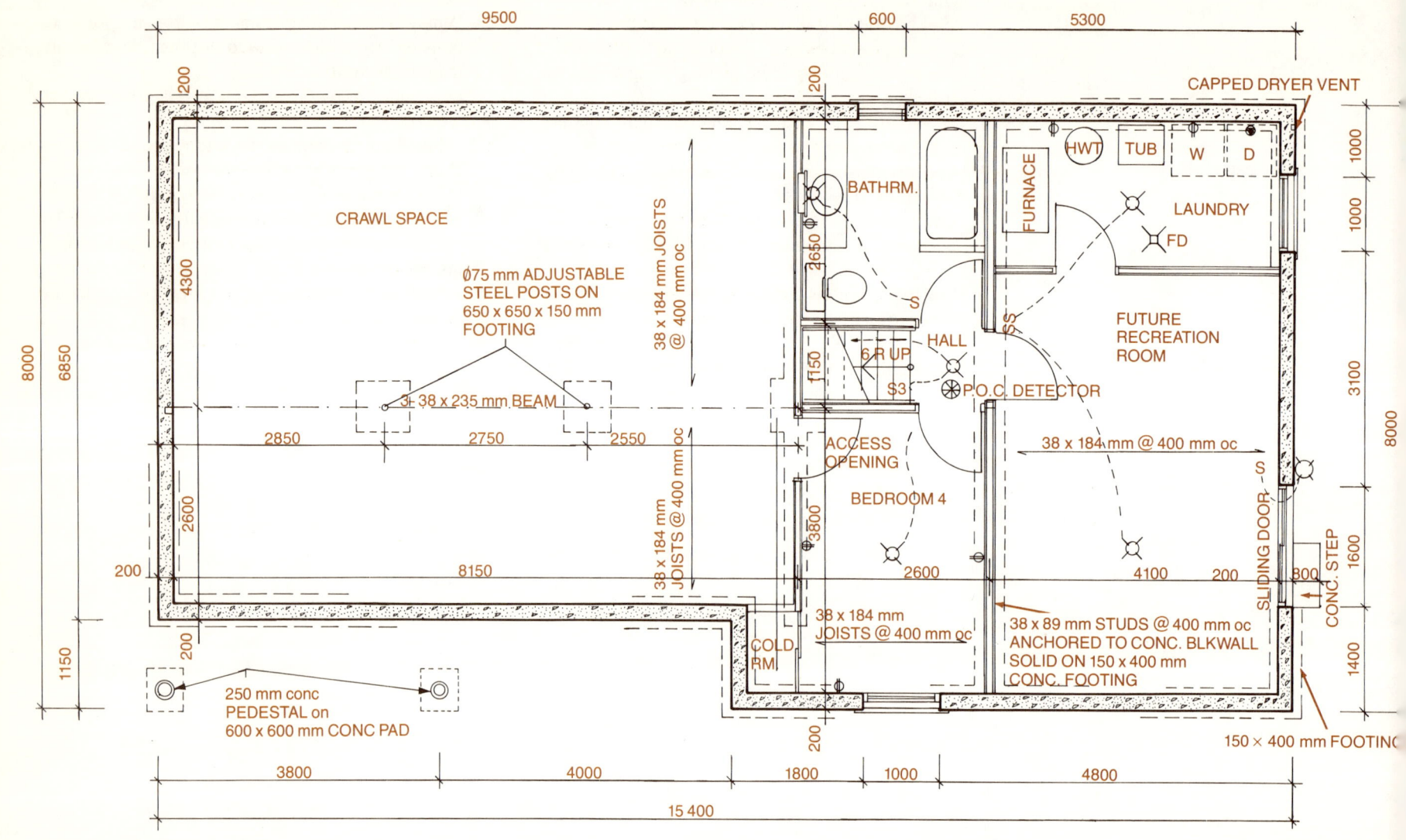

FOUNDATION PLAN LEVEL ONE

SEE PAGE 280 FOR
PLAN OF UPPER LEVELS

On a separate sheet answer the following questions
1. What is the main purpose of the foundation system? (a) the footings (b) the walls.
2. What is the most common foundation material?
3. What other drawing is the foundation plan based on?
4. How are the joists shown on the basement plan supported?
5. What is the size and location of the joists?
6. Describe the construction members of the partition walls.
7. Where is the cold room located?
8. The letters F.D. are noted beside a symbol in the laundry room. What does it tell the reader?
9. Where is the smoke detector located?
10. Where is the entrance into the crawl space located?
11. Suggest why the joists in the crawl space are positioned across the width of the crawl space.
12. What is the functon of the steel posts in the crawl space? How are they supported?
13. Where is the exterior entrance to the basement located? Describe the door.
14. Suggest the purpose for the 250 mm concrete pedestals shown on the plan.
15. How many ceiling outlets are there?
16. How many wall convenience outlets are there?
17. One of the wall outlets in the laundry is different from the others. What does it represent?
18. Where are the switches for the hall light located?
19. What is the area of the living space in the basement?
20. What is the area of the crawl space?

PROJECT 18-2 (2)

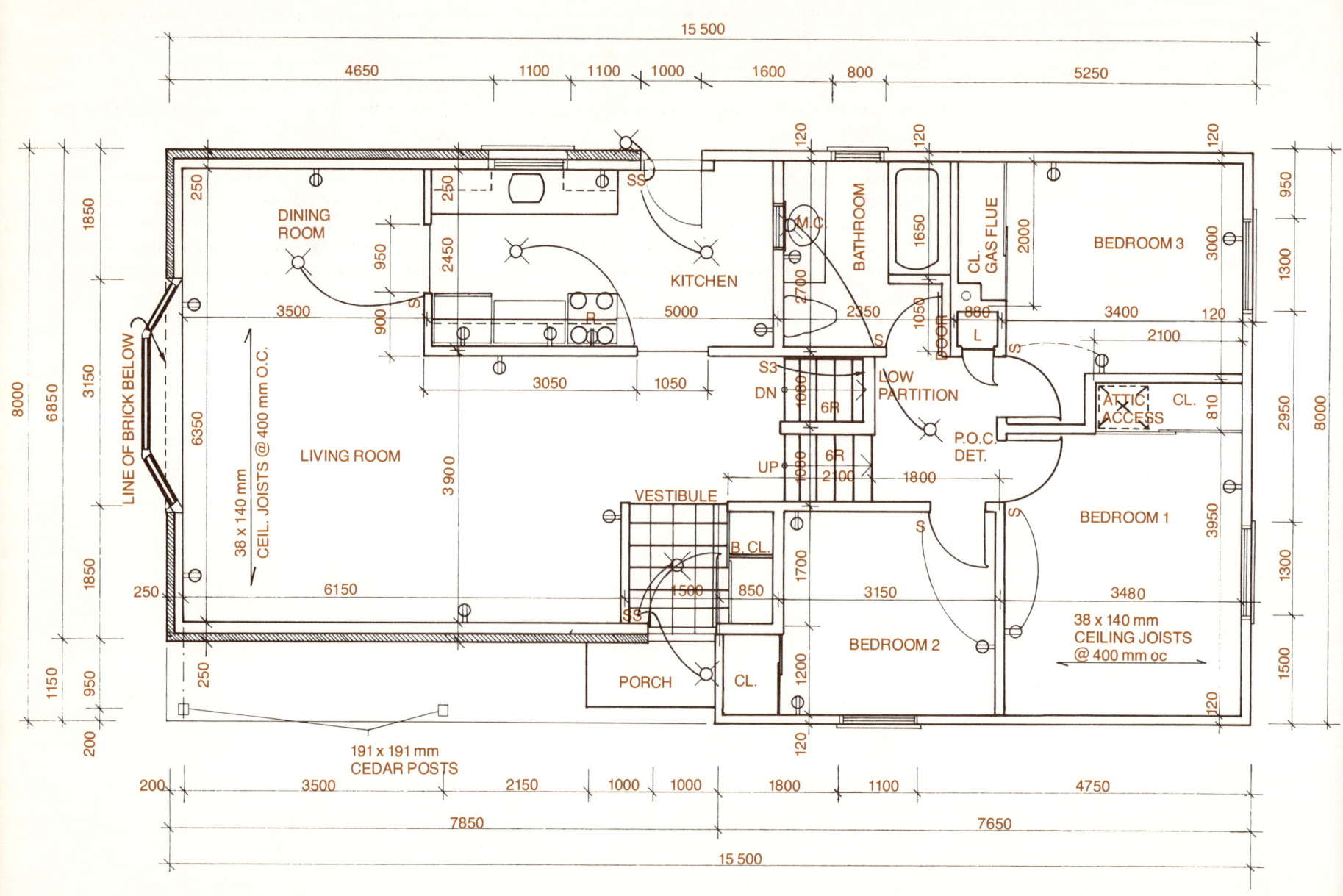

ALL DIMENSIONS IN MILLIMETRES
FLOOR PLAN LEVELS 2 and 3

On a separate sheet answer the following questions.
1. What is the style of this house?
2. What types of exterior walls are shown? Give the thickness of each.
3. What are the overall framing dimensions of the house?
4. Suggest the purpose for the two cedar posts that are in line with the porch?
5. Where is the access to the attic located?
6. Give the direction of the ceiling joists.
7. Give the size and spacing of the ceiling joists.
8. Where are the exterior electric light outlets located?
9. How many closets are shown on this plan? What type of doors are indicated for the closets?
10. How many risers are indicated on the stairs up and down?
11. What is the overall length and width shown on this plan?
12. What is the size of the two exterior door openings?
13. How many window openings are located on this plan? Give the wall opening size for each.
14. The ceiling outlet in the basement hall can be operated by two switches. Where are the switches located.
15. The area just inside the front door is labelled the vestibule. Give two other suitable names for this area.
16. Suggest why there are no ceiling outlets in the bedrooms. What is the purpose for the electric switch in each bedroom?
17. What are the floor areas of each of the 3 bedrooms on this level? The interior walls are 110 mm thick.
18. Where are the cupboards in the kitchen located?
19. What are the dimensions of the porch?
20. Give the sizes of the wall openings into the kitchen.
21. How wide are the stairs?
22. What is the width of the living room?

PROJECT 18-3 #1

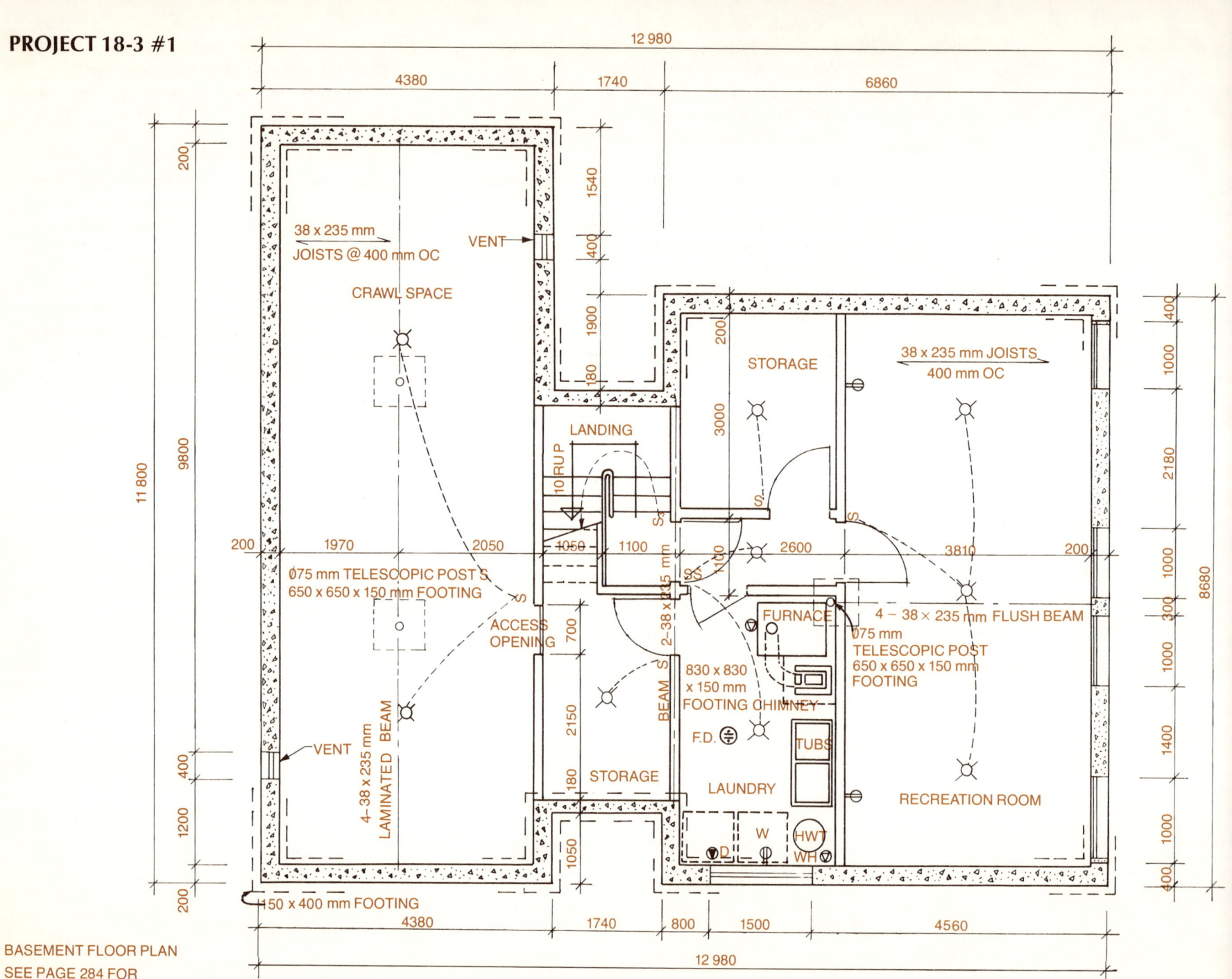

BASEMENT FLOOR PLAN
SEE PAGE 284 FOR
UPPER LEVELS

On a separate sheet answer the following questions
1. Give the overall length and width dimensions of the house.
2. How thick are the concrete walls?
3. What is the main purpose of the foundation system? (a) the footings (b) the walls.
4. What other drawing is the foundation plan based on?
5. What is the size and location of the floor joists?
6. Describe how the main beam shown in the crawl space is supported.
7. Give the size of the beam in the crawl space.
8. Where is the floor drain located?
9. What is the size and location of each of the telescopic posts? How is each supported? What purposes do the posts serve?
10. Where is the entrance to the crawl space located? Give its position to the nearest outside wall.
11. What type of stairs lead up to the first floor? How many risers are there?
12. How many wall convenience outlets are there in the basement?
13. Where are the special purpose outlets located?
14. What is the area of the recreation room?
15. Where are the two vents located? What is the purpose for placing them where they are?
16. Where is the chimney located? How is it supported?
17. How many windows are there in the basement?
18. What is the area of the crawl space? The inside walls are 110 mm thick.

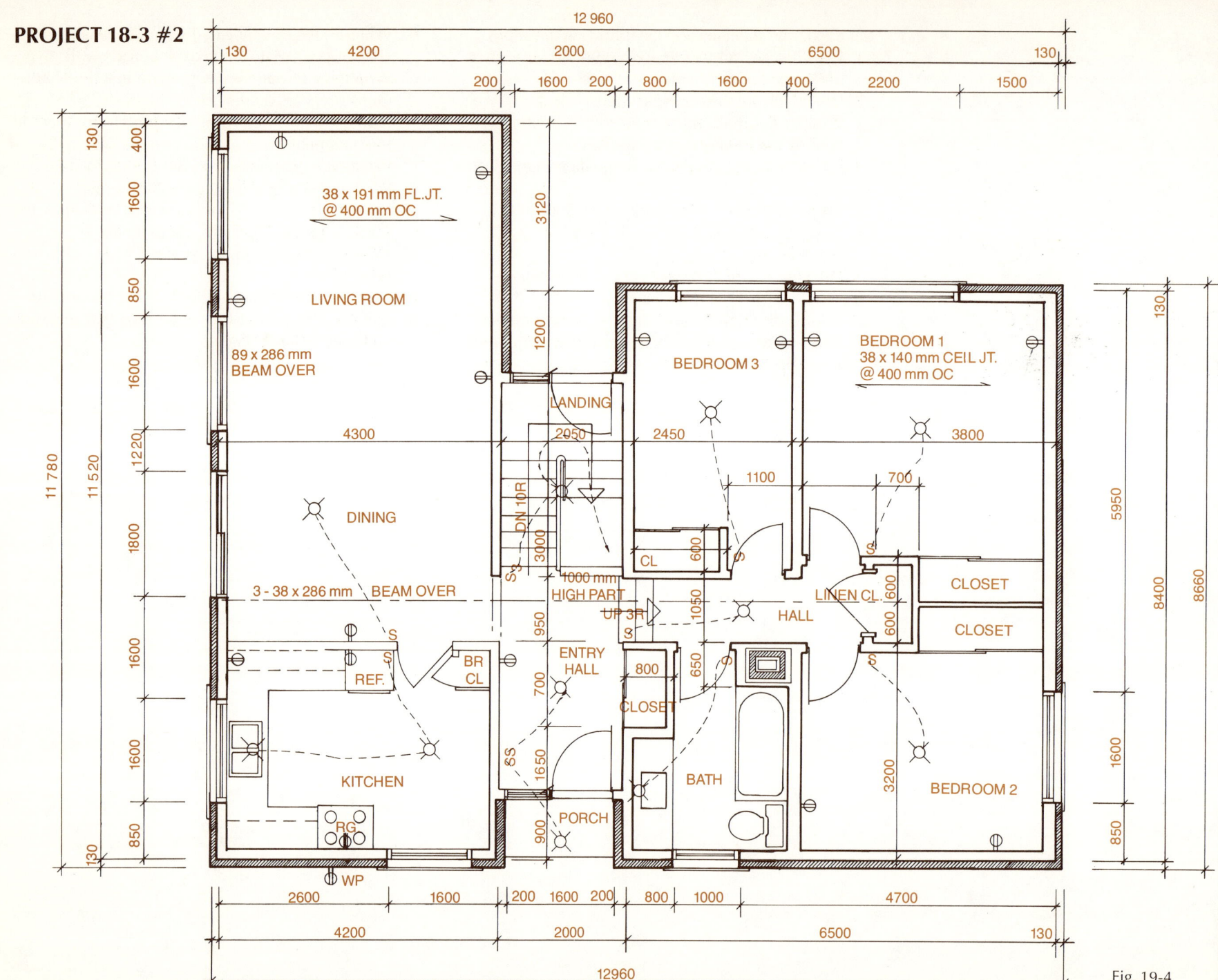

Fig. 19-4

On a separate sheet answer the following questions.
1. What type of exterior wall is shown?
2. What are the overall dimensions of the house?
3. What are the sizes and locations of the beams shown on this plan?
4. What is the style of kitchen in this house?
5. Where are the cabinets located in the kitchen?
6. Give the directions, size and spacing of the ceiling joists.
7. Give the directions, size and spacing of the floor joists.
8. How wide is the entrance hall? The inside walls are 110 mm thick.
9. Approximately how many square metres of carpeting would be required to broadloom the living and dining rooms?
10. Where is the furnace chimney located?
11. What is the style of this house?
12. Suggest why the basement area beneath the living and dining rooms is a crawl space, and not the same height as the rest of the basement.
13. How many risers are there in the stairs to the basement?
14. How many closets are shown on this floor plan? What style of door do the closets have?
15. How many window openings are there in this plan?
16. What is the size of the opening for the front door and side window combined?
17. What is the floor area for each of the three bedrooms?
18. How many convenience outlets are there on this plan? List them for each room.
19. How many ceiling outlets are controlled by a switch?

CHAPTER 18 APPENDIX

BRICK VENEER WALL

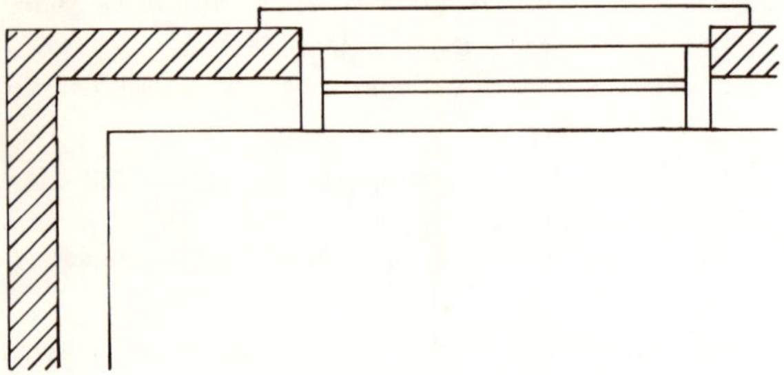

FRAME WALL

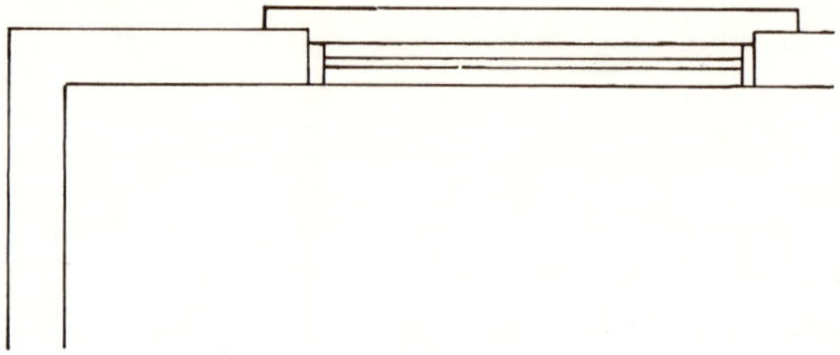

FOUNDATION WALL AND FOOTING

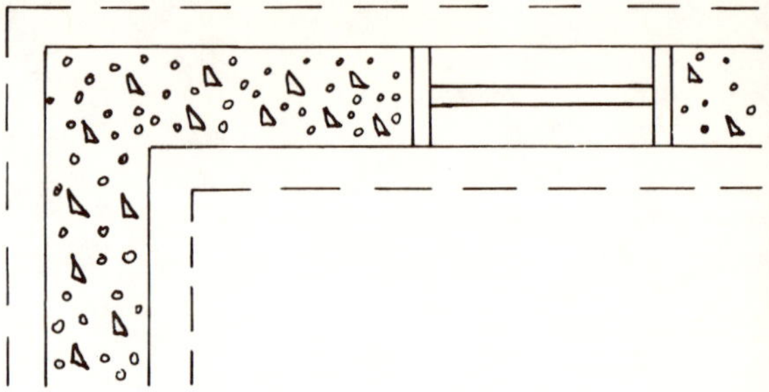

WALL SECTIONS

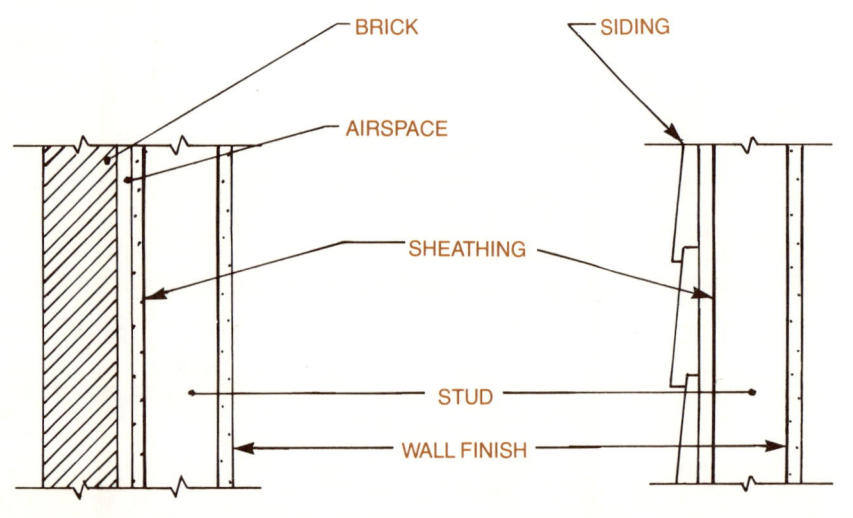

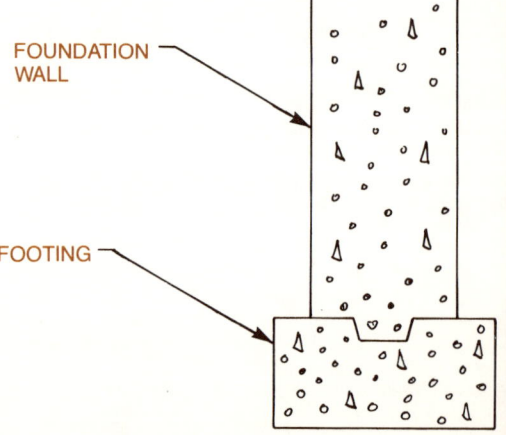

FLOOR PLAN AND WALL SYMBOLS

286 READING CONSTRUCTION DRAWINGS

CHAPTER 18 APPENDIX

ARCHITECTURAL SYMBOLS

MATERIALS

- EARTH
- SAND, FILL PLASTER & GYPSUM BOARD
- BRICK
- CONCRETE
- CINDER BLOCK
- CONCRETE BLOCK
- WOOD FRAMING
- WOOD
- BATT INSULATION
- RIGID INSULATION
- STRUCTURAL STEEL
- GRAVEL

ELECTRICAL

- CEILING INCANDESCENT LIGHT
- WALL INCANDESCENT LIGHT
- FLUORESCENT LIGHT
- S — SINGLE POLE SWITCH
- S_3 — 3-WAY SWITCH
- SWITCH CONTROLLING A CEILING LIGHT
- SWITCH CONTROLLING A CONVENIENCE OUTLET
- TWO 3-WAY SWITCHES CONTROLLING A CEILING LIGHT
- L_{PS} — LIGHT CONTROLLED BY A PULL SWITCH
- SPLIT DUPLEX RECEPTACLE
- WP — OUTDOOR WEATHERPROOF RECEPTACLE
- S — COMBINATION SWITCH AND RECEPTACLE
- DUPLEX RECEPTACLE
- 2W — 2 WIRE SEPARATE CIRCUIT RECEPTACLE
- 3W — 3 WIRE 120/240 V SPLIT RECEPTACLE
- R — RANGE
- D — DRYER
- OR SPECIAL PURPOSE CONNECTION. USE SUBSCRIPT TO INDICATE FUNCTION:
  - DW-DISHWASHER
  - D-DRYER
  - WH-WATER HEATER
- C — CLOCK OUTLET
- F — CEILING FAN
- F — WALL FAN
- DOOR PUSH BUTTON
- CH — CHIME

READING CONSTRUCTION DRAWINGS 287

CHAPTER 18 APPENDIX
DOORS AND WINDOWS

SINGLE SWING DOORS

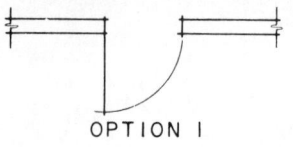
OPTION 1

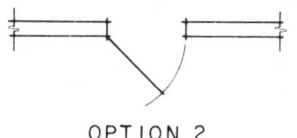
OPTION 2

USE OPTION 1 EXCEPT WHERE SPACE & CLARITY DICTATE THE USE OF OPTION 2

DOUBLE ACTING DOORS

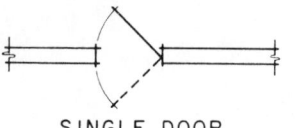
SINGLE DOOR

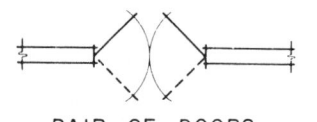
PAIR OF DOORS

IN AND OUT DOORS

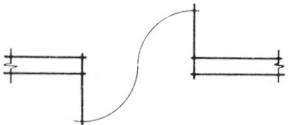
IN & OUT COMBINATION WITHOUT MULLION

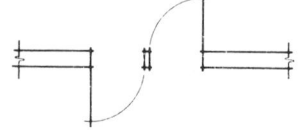
IN & OUT COMBINATION WITH MULLION

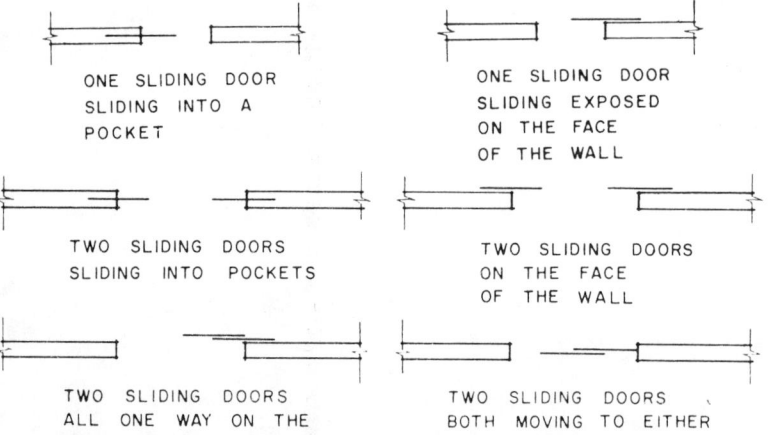

ONE SLIDING DOOR SLIDING INTO A POCKET

ONE SLIDING DOOR SLIDING EXPOSED ON THE FACE OF THE WALL

TWO SLIDING DOORS SLIDING INTO POCKETS

TWO SLIDING DOORS ON THE FACE OF THE WALL

TWO SLIDING DOORS ALL ONE WAY ON THE FACE, LEAVING CLEAR OPENING

TWO SLIDING DOORS BOTH MOVING TO EITHER SIDE BUT NOT LEAVING CLEAR OPENING EG. WARDROBE DOORS

WINDOWS IN PLAN FOR ALL TYPES OF SASH

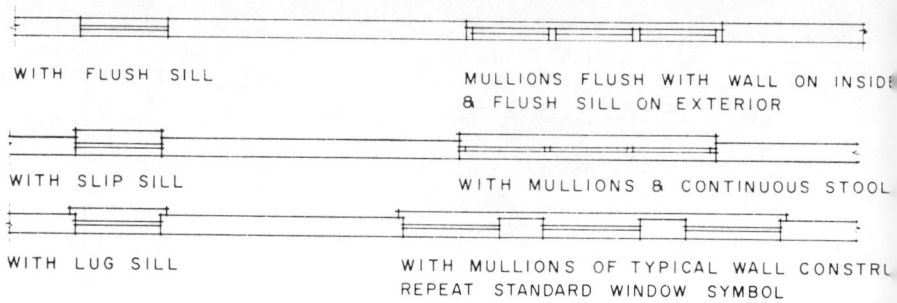

WITH FLUSH SILL — MULLIONS FLUSH WITH WALL ON INSIDE & FLUSH SILL ON EXTERIOR

WITH SLIP SILL — WITH MULLIONS & CONTINUOUS STOOL

WITH LUG SILL — WITH MULLIONS OF TYPICAL WALL CONSTR. REPEAT STANDARD WINDOW SYMBOL

WINDOWS IN ELEVATION

THESE SYMBOLS APPLY REGARDLESS OF THE MATERIAL USED IN THE MANUFACTURE OF THE SASH I.E. WOOD, STEEL, ALUMINUM ETC.

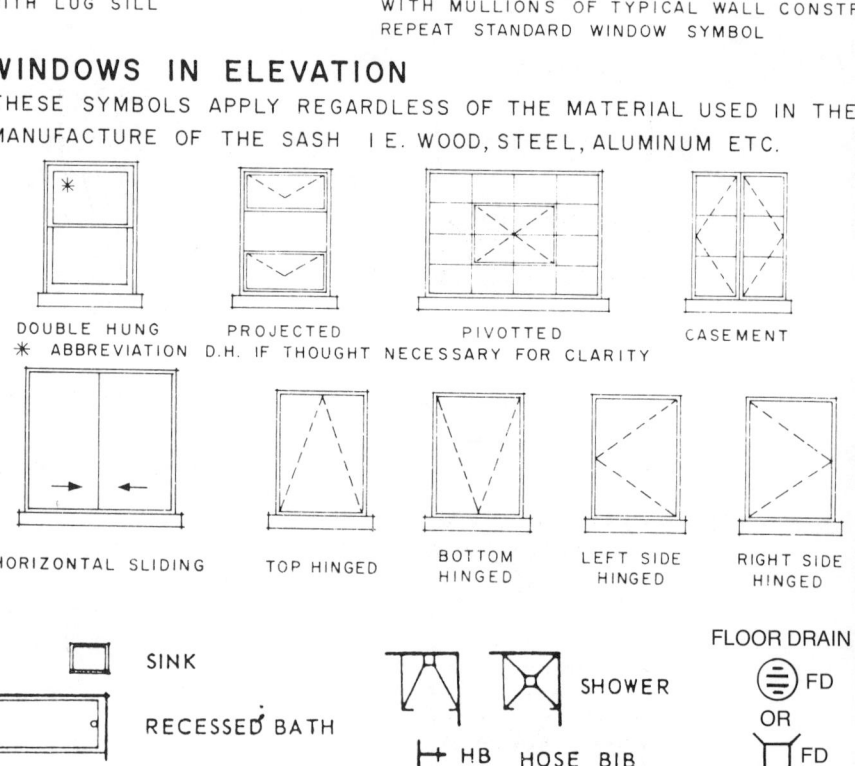

DOUBLE HUNG
✱ ABBREVIATION D.H. IF THOUGHT NECESSARY FOR CLARITY

PROJECTED

PIVOTTED

CASEMENT

HORIZONTAL SLIDING

TOP HINGED

BOTTOM HINGED

LEFT SIDE HINGED

RIGHT SIDE HINGED

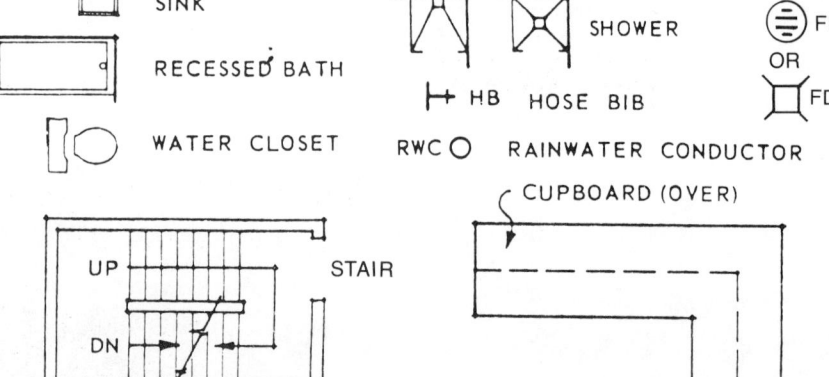

SINK

RECESSED BATH

WATER CLOSET

HB HOSE BIB

SHOWER

RWC○ RAINWATER CONDUCTOR

FLOOR DRAIN ⊜ FD OR ⊠ FD

STAIR UP DN

CUPBOARD (OVER)

288 READING CONSTRUCTION DRAWINGS

CHAPTER 19
READING TECHNICAL DRAWINGS

WORDS TO LEARN

proportion (pro-pór-tion)
recede (re-céde)
project (pro-ject)
contour (cón-tour)

proportion—the relative size of one thing as compared to another

This is an opportunity to demonstrate your knowledge of technical drawings. The projects that have been chosen for this chapter apply the basic principles involved in typical shop drawings. To help interpret each drawing you will first do a freehand sketch of each project on prepared isometric graph paper. All you need is a soft pencil and an eraser. If you feel you need a scale, you may use one. Freehand sketching is not difficult. By following a few basic steps and by having some practice, you will be pleasantly surprised with your results. If you need help, refer back to Chapter 15. One last word: Plan each sketch carefully. Take care to keep the shape of the project in proper **proportion**, whatever the size of your drawing. Always use light construction lines in the planning stage.

Hints in Isometric Freehand Sketching

- Horizontal lines are drawn from left to right, sliding your hand along.   Fig. 19-2
- Vertical lines are drawn from top to bottom using a wrist movement.   Fig. 19-3
- Oblique (sloping) lines are drawn
  (a) from top left to bottom right using a wrist movement.   Fig. 19-4(a)
  (b) from bottom left to top right sliding your hand along.   Fig. 19-4(b)

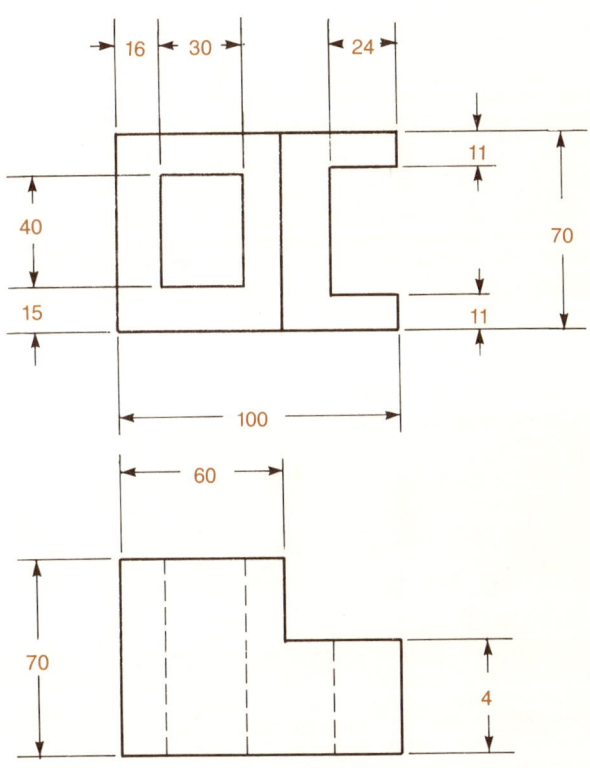

Fig. 19-1(a)

289

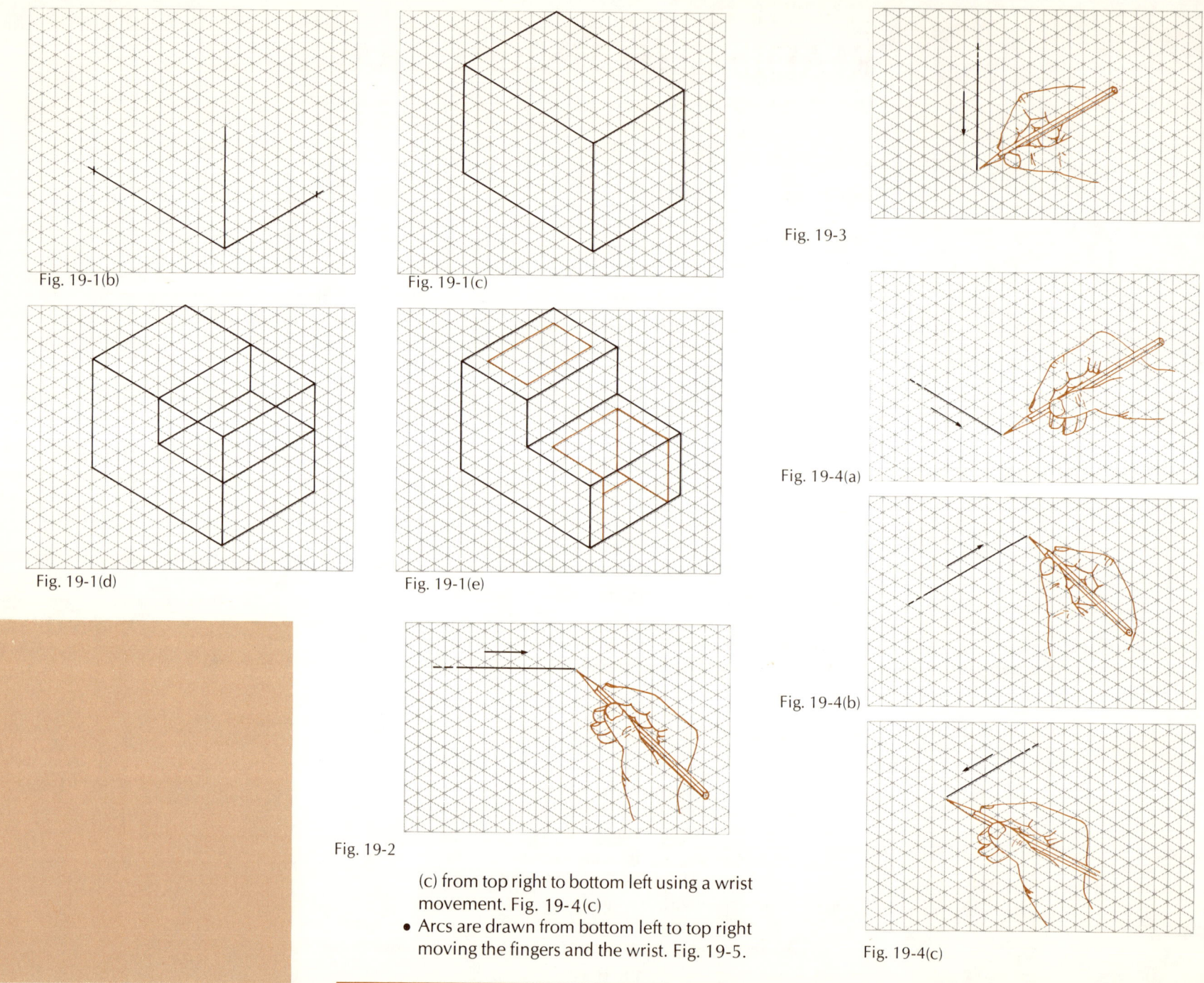

Fig. 19-1(b)

Fig. 19-1(c)

Fig. 19-3

Fig. 19-1(d)

Fig. 19-1(e)

Fig. 19-4(a)

Fig. 19-4(b)

Fig. 19-2

(c) from top right to bottom left using a wrist movement. Fig. 19-4(c)
- Arcs are drawn from bottom left to top right moving the fingers and the wrist. Fig. 19-5.

Fig. 19-4(c)

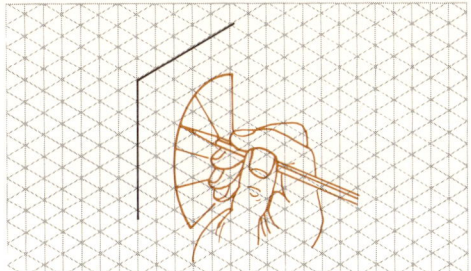

Fig. 19-5

Steps in Sketching a Circle in Isometric

First we will draw the circle in the side position.

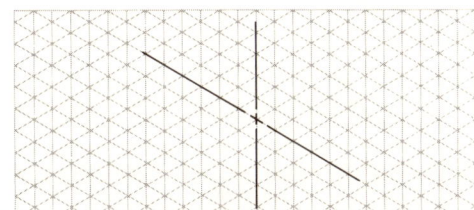

Fig. 19-6

1. Draw the centre lines in the desired position.

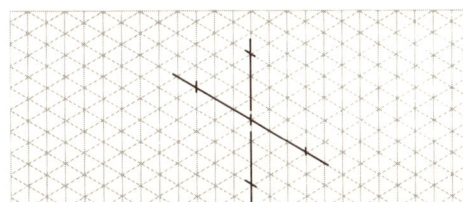

Fig. 19-7

2. Mark off the radius distance on each of the centre lines.

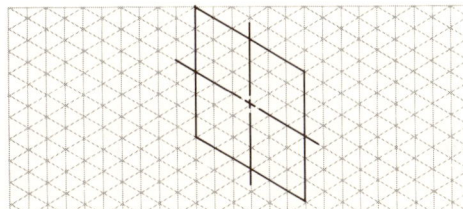

Fig. 19-8

3. Draw the isometric square.

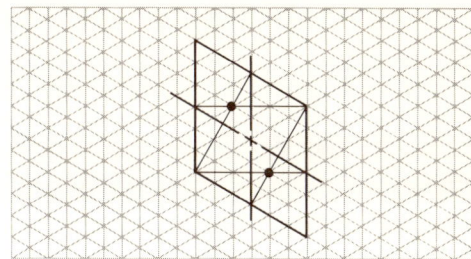

Fig. 19-9

4. From the obtuse angles lightly construct straight lines to the centre of the opposite sides. These lines will intersect at points marked C1 and C2.

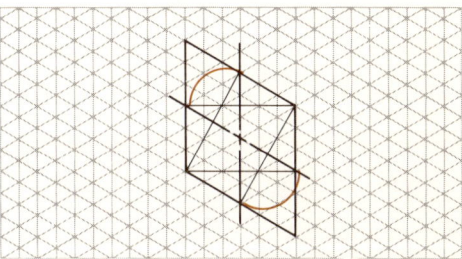

Fig. 19-10

5. Use the intersecting points as centres to guide you. Freehand, lightly draw arcs tangent to the sides of each of the acute angles.

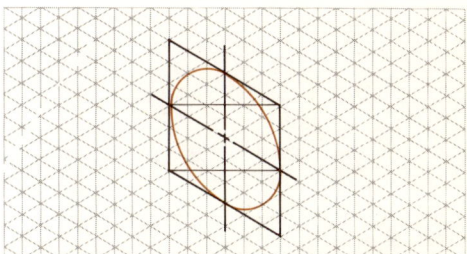

Fig. 19-11

6. Using the construction lines to guide you, lightly draw the other two arcs in the obtuse angles to complete the ellipse.

When drawing the circle in the top position, follow these same steps in the same order.

READING TECHNICAL DRAWINGS 291

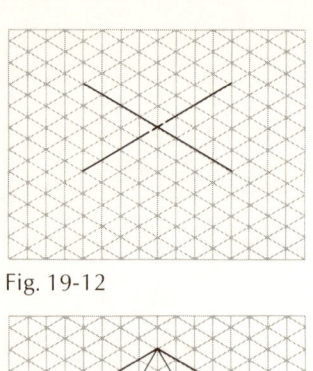
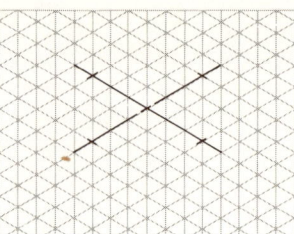
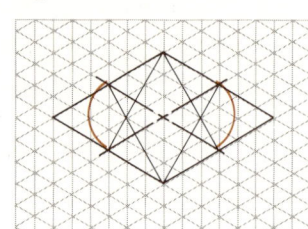
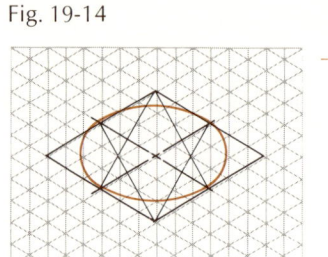
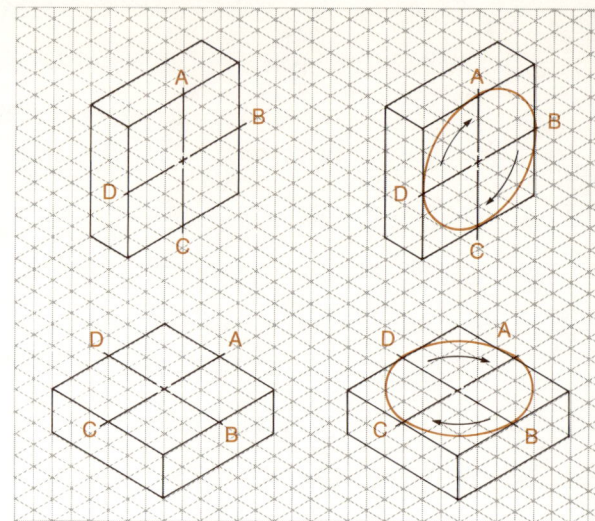

Fig. 19-12
Fig. 19-13
Fig. 19-14 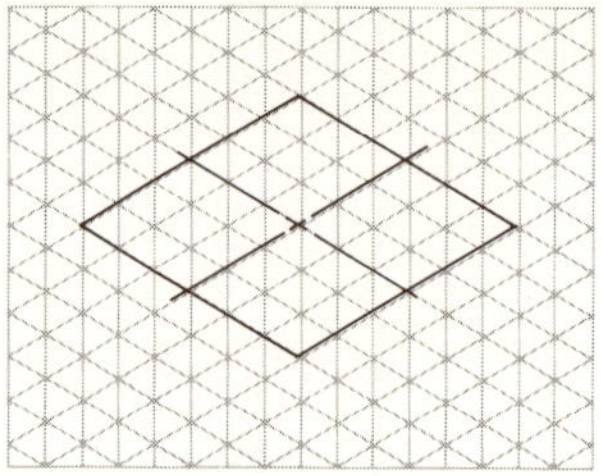
Fig. 19-15
Fig. 19-16
Fig. 19-17
Fig. 19-18

Steps to Show Depth in Circular Contours

1. When drawing each arc that makes up the ellipse use a circular motion lightly back and forth from A to B and from C to D first, then from B to C and from D to A. When you are satisfied with the results darken in the outline.

2. To draw the **receding** arcs and the lower arcs, **project** the centre points to the new positions. Sketch the arcs parallel to the existing arcs drawn before. Draw tangent lines to the arcs where required to complete the **contour**.

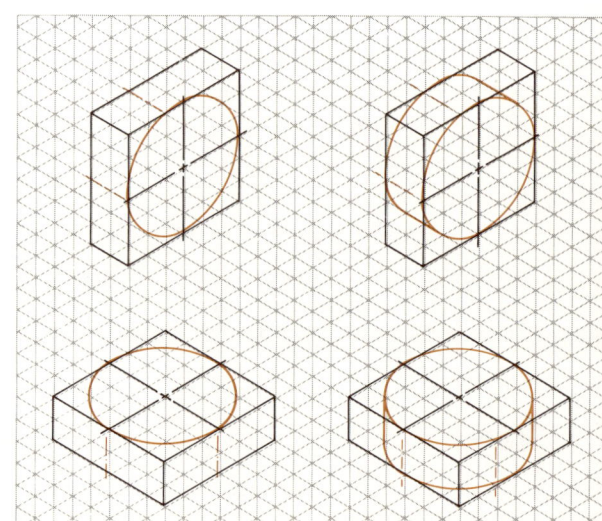

Fig. 19-19

Hints in Sketching Arcs in Isometric

- Mark off the true radius distance for the arc from the corner of the angle.
- Lightly construct lines from these points perpendicular to the sides of the angle.
- Using the position of the centre as a guide, lightly sketch the arc tangent to the sides of the angle.

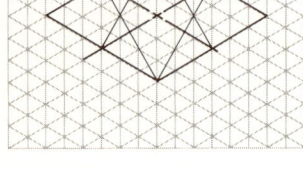

recede—to slope (or move) backward
project—to transfer an image (or voice, object etc) from one position to another
contour—the outline of a body or figure

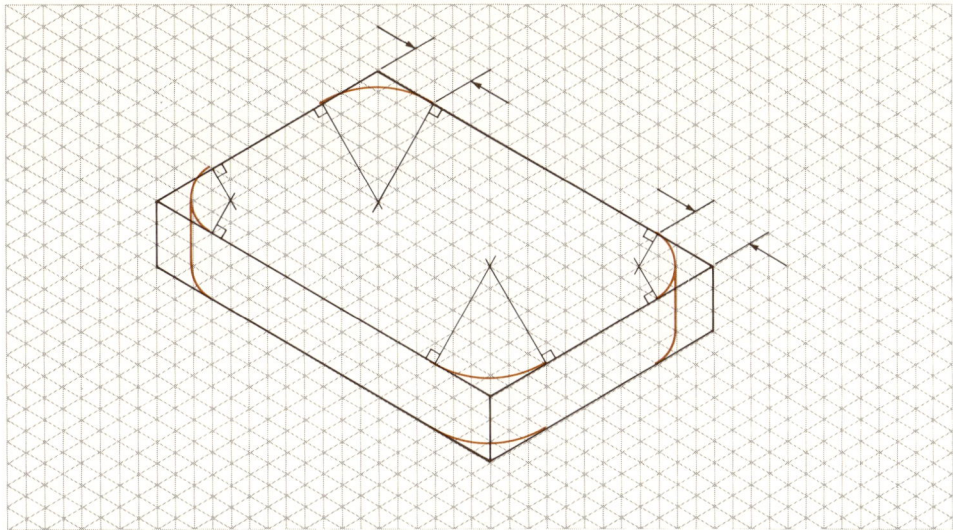

Fig. 19-20

REPLACE THE X'S WITH THE CORRECT WORD

1. If the ingredients in a cake are not measured in the proper **XXXXXXXXXXX** the cake will not turn out the way it should.
2. When the tide goes out water **XXXXXXX** from the ocean beach.
3. A projector **XXXXXXXX** the image of a slide onto the screen for viewing.
4. A **XXXXXXX** map shows varying heights of land.

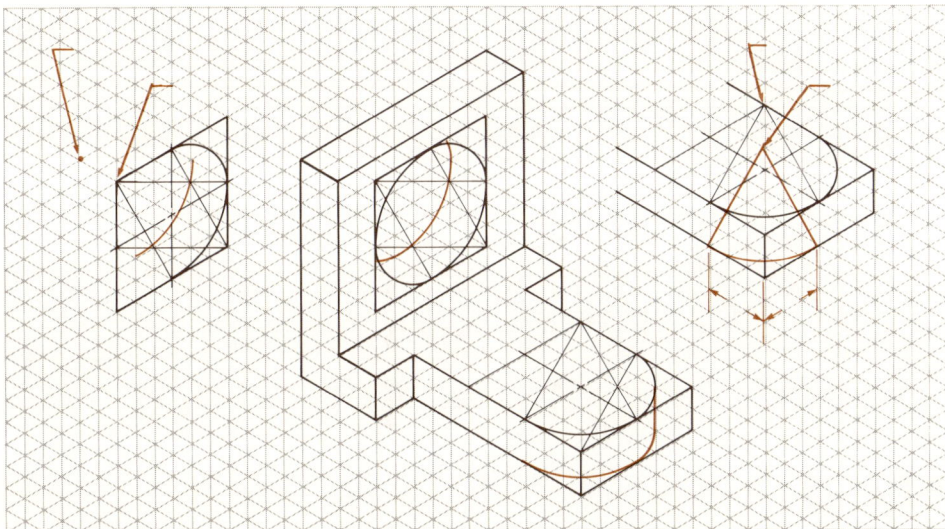

Fig. 19-21

PROJECTS

Projects for Sketching and Reading

1. Prepare a neat sketch of each project on the isometric graph paper. (You may make copies of the graph paper found on the pages inside the covers of this book.)
2. Answer the questions for each project.

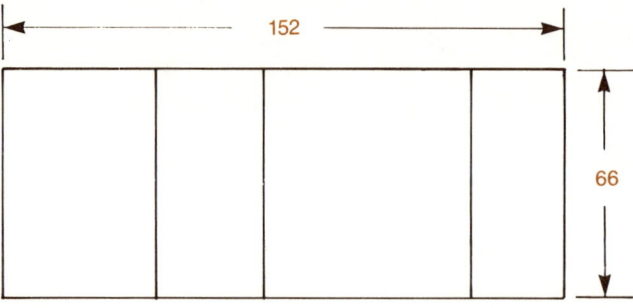

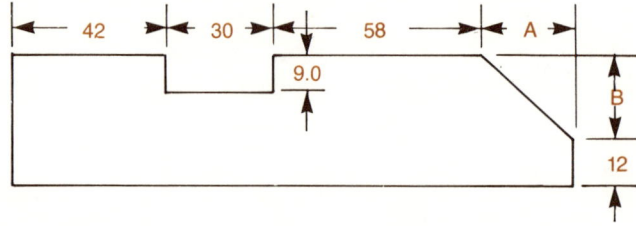 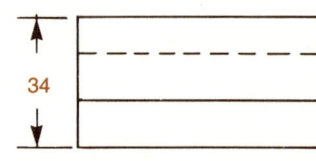

PROJECT 19-1

SLOTTED BLOCK

1. What is the overall length of the slotted block?
2. What is the overall width?
3. What is the overall height?
4. In which view is the slot shown most clearly?
5. How deep is the slot?
6. What line in the side view represents the bottom of the slot?
7. Calculate the dimensions noted as (A) and (B).

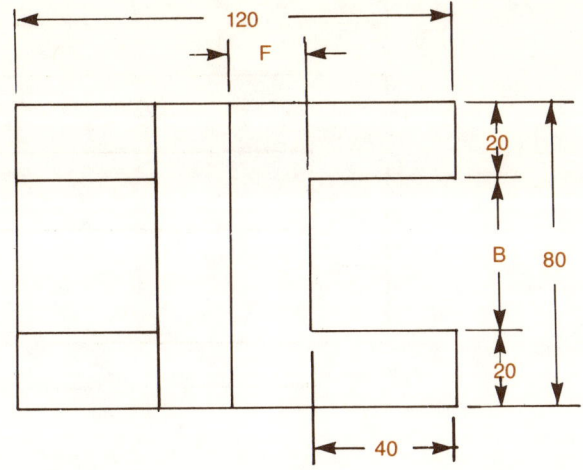
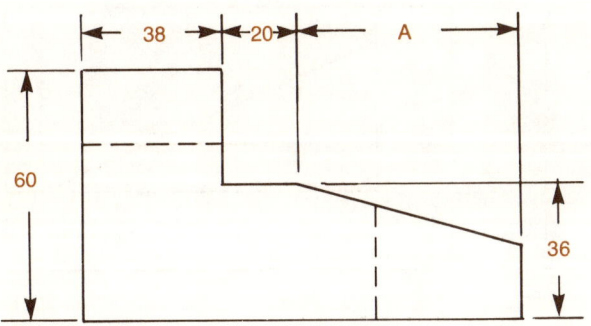
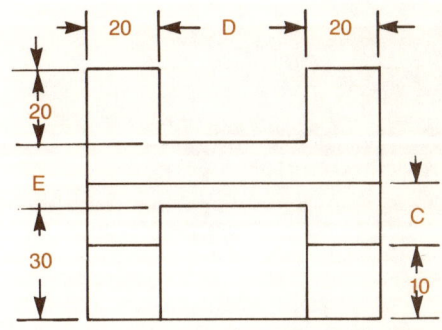

PROJECT 19-2

TOOL BASE

1. Calculate dimensions A to F.
2. What are the overall length, width and height dimensions?
3. What is the length of each of the two slots in the tool base?
4. What is the width of each of the two slots?
5. In which two views is the length seen?
6. In which two views is the width seen?
7. In which two views is the height seen?
8. In which two views is the shape of the slots most clearly shown?
9. Which view most clearly shows the shape of the inclined surface?

PROJECTS 295

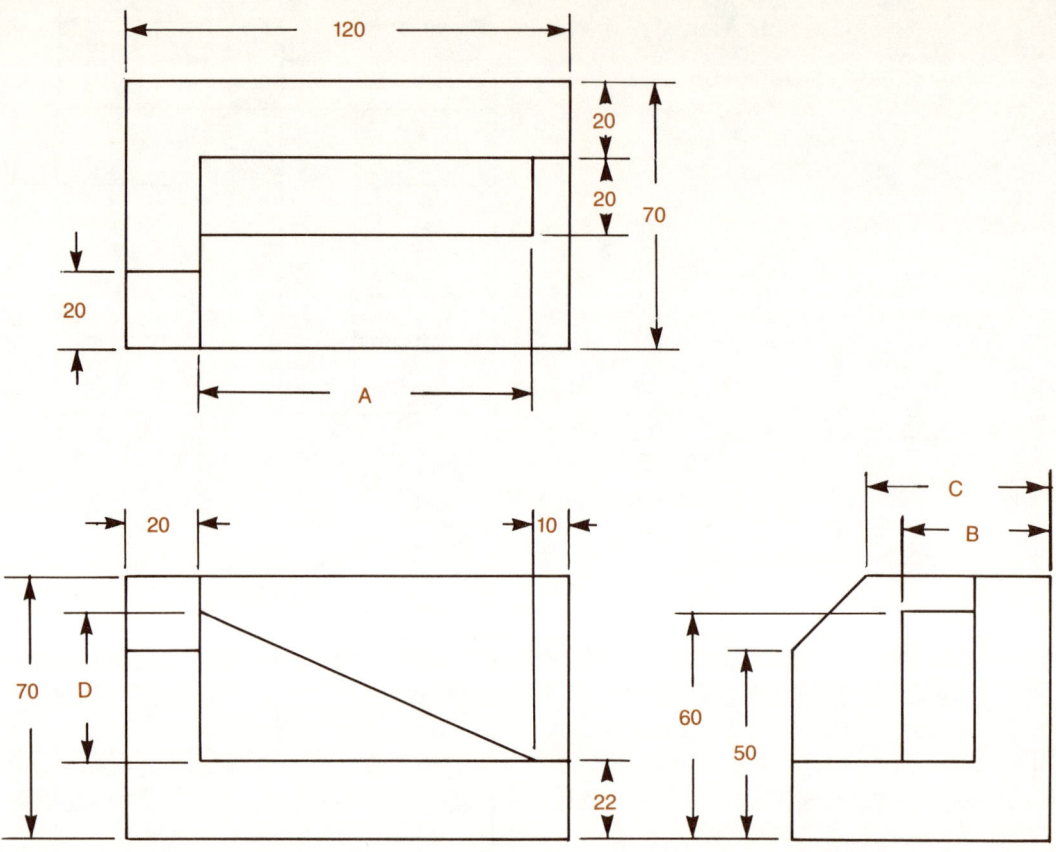

PROJECT 19-3

CONTROL WEDGE

1. What are the length, width and height dimensions?
2. Calculate dimensions A to D.
3. The right side views indicates that the left corner is bevelled. What is the angle of the bevel? Explain how you determined the angle.
4. Would it be possible to describe completely the control wedge with just two views? Explain your answer.
5. In which view is the shape of the inclined surface most clearly shown?

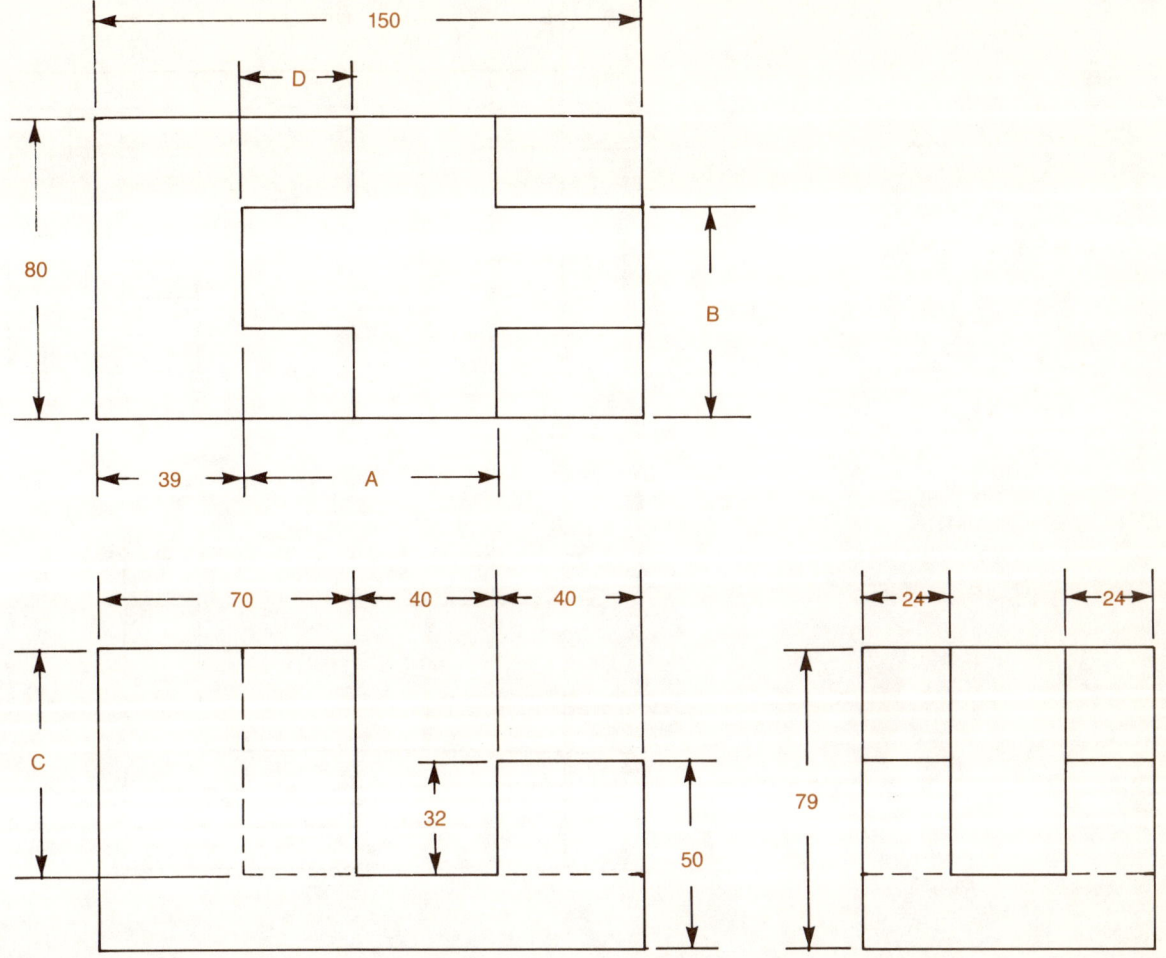

PROJECT 19-4

SLOTTED SUPPORT

1. List the four different types of lines used in the drawing.
2. Give the overall length, width and height of the slotted support.
3. Would it be possible to describe the slotted support with just two views? Explain your answer.
4. Which view gives the most information of the shape of the object?
5. Calculate dimensions A to D.

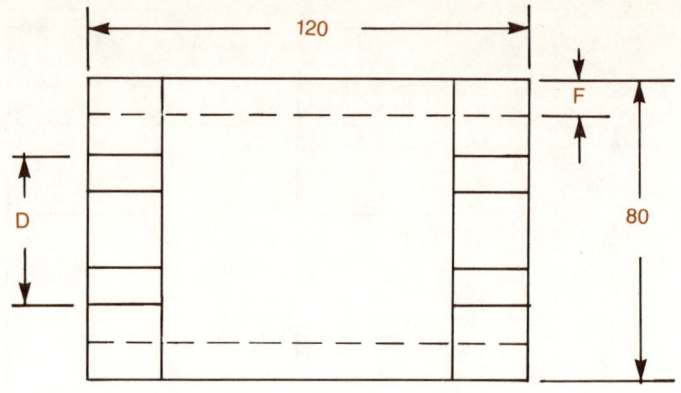
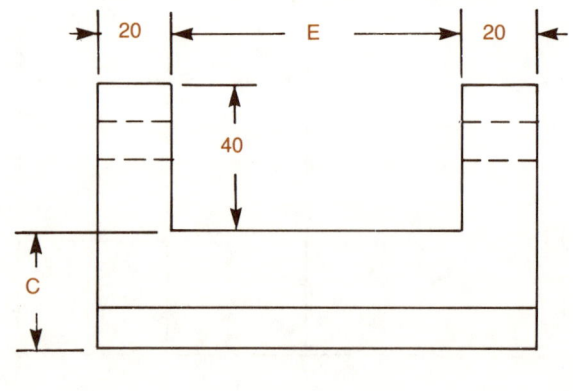
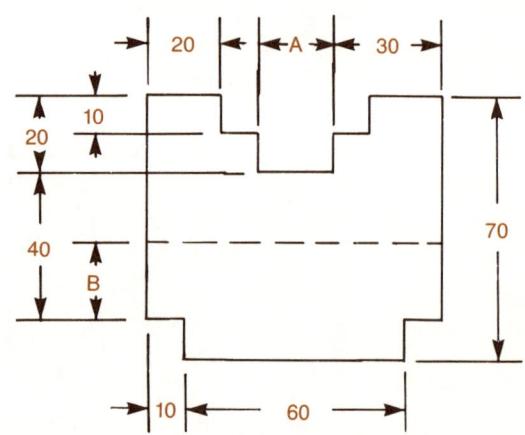

PROJECT 19-5

CARRIER SLIDE

1. What are the overall length, width and height dimensions?
2. What do the hidden lines in the top view indicate?
3. Calculate dimensions A to F.
4. Which two views show the shape of the part most clearly?
5. Could the third view be eliminated? Explain your answer?
6. What do the two hidden lines in the front view tell the reader?

TRACK HANGER

1. What is the size of the square hole in the part?
2. Calculate dimensions A to E.
3. Are all three views necessary to describe the track hanger completely? Explain your answer.
4. Explain why the parallel hidden lines in the top view have a solid line in the centre of them.
5. Why is it necessary to have the hidden lines in the front view end at the object line in each instance?

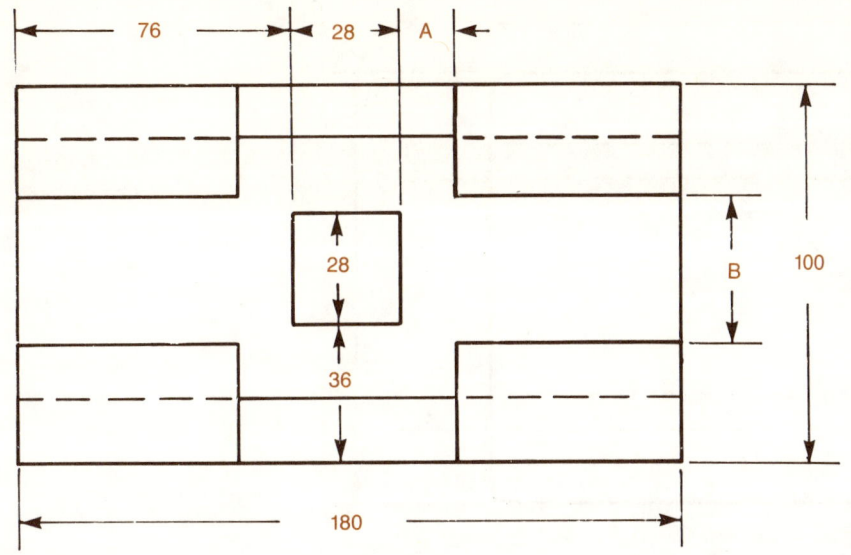
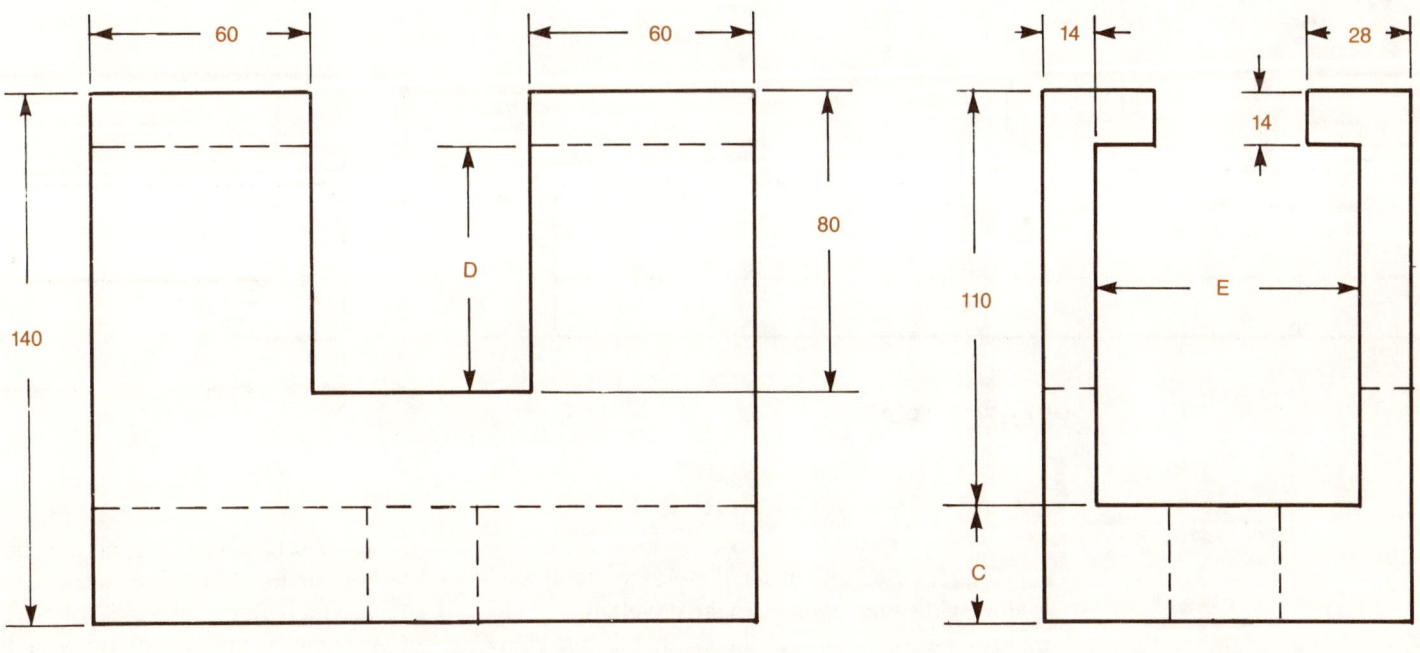

PROJECT 19-6

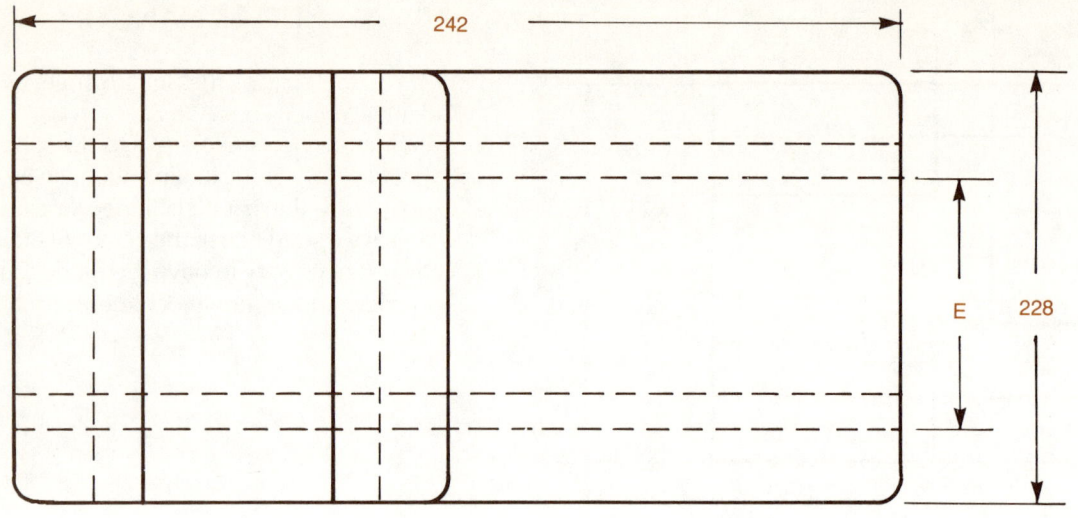
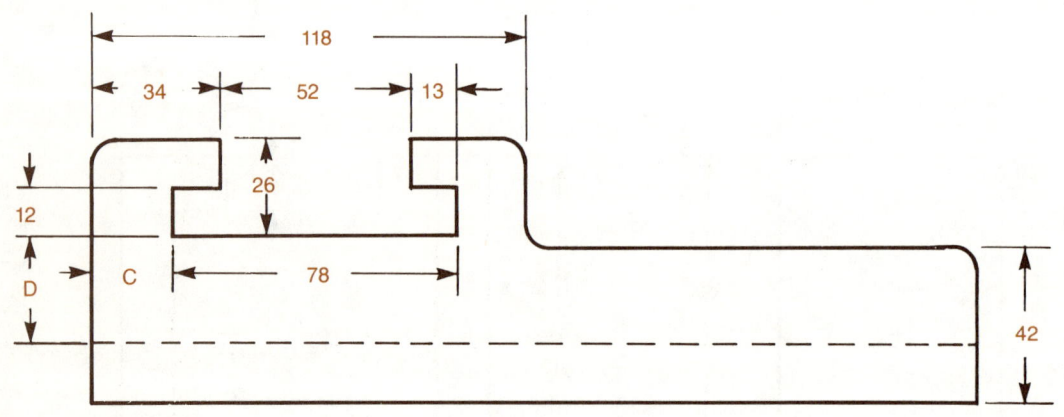
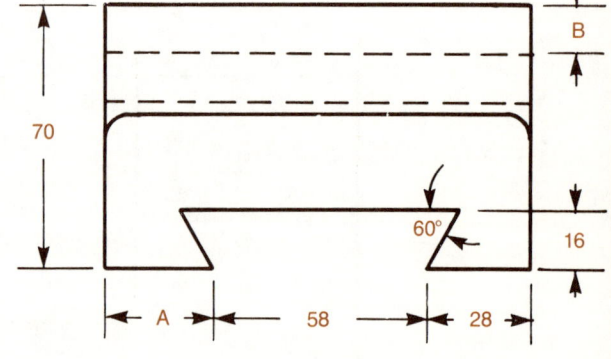

PROJECT 19-7

REST SLIDE

1. In which view is the dovetail most clearly shown?
2. How wide is the opening in the dovetail?
3. How many rounds are shown in the top view?
4. What is the size of the fillet?
5. In which view is the fillet shown?
6. What is the distance separating the parallel hidden lines in the right side view?
7. In which view is the tee slot most clearly shown?
8. What is the unit of measure of angles?
9. What is the angle of the dovetail?
10. Calculate dimensions A to E.

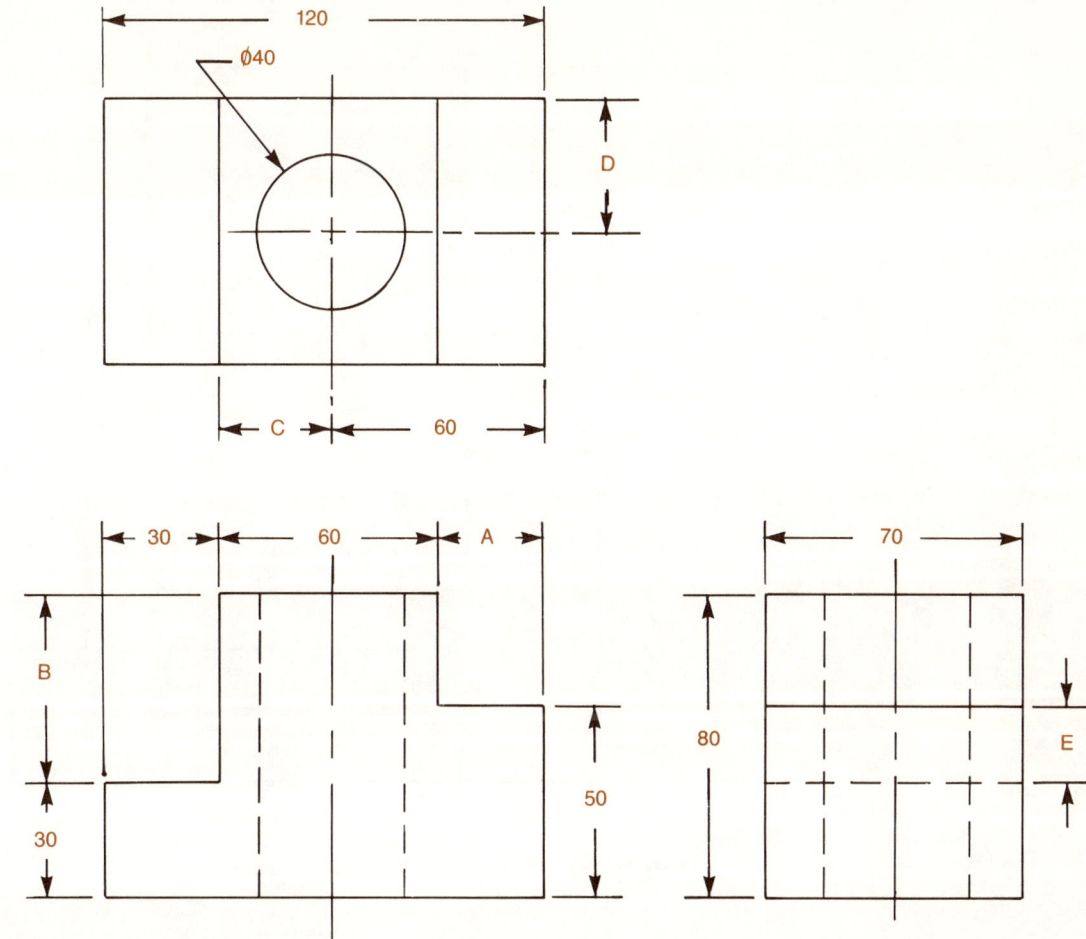

PROJECT 19-8

ADAPTOR

1. What are the overall width, length and height dimensions of the adaptor?
2. Are all three views of the part necessary? Explain your answer.
3. Calculate dimensions A to E.
4. What is the height of the hole in the part?
5. What is the diameter of the hole?
6. What radius would a compass be set at to draw the hole in the part?

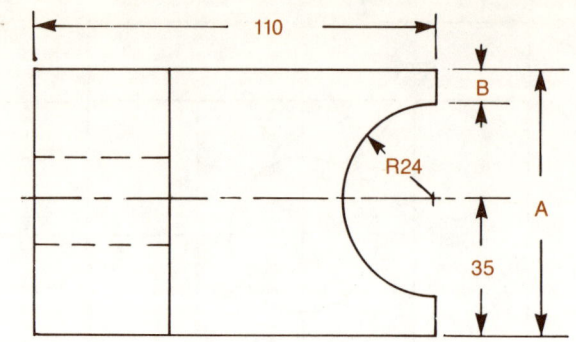

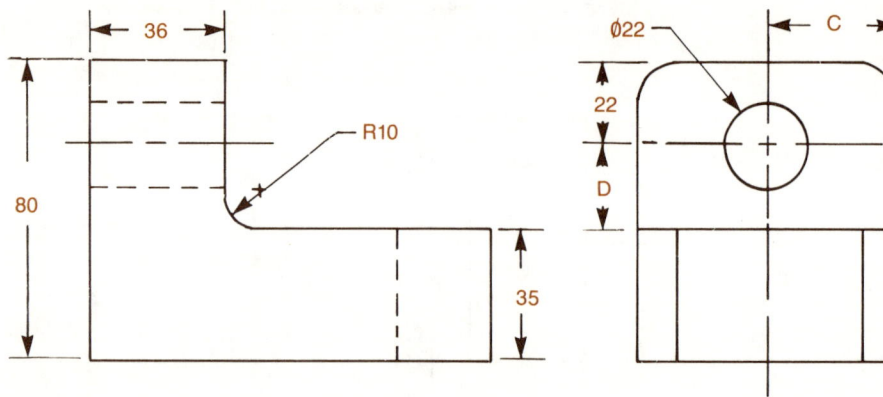

ALL ROUNDS AND FILLETS NOT DIMENSIONED R12

PROJECT 19-9

SUPPORT STOP

1. Give the overall length, width and height dimensions of the part.
2. What is the radius of the largest arc?
3. What is the diameter of the hole?
4. What is the radius of the fillet in the front view?
5. What is the radius of each round in the right side view?
6. What is the distance from the top of the part to the ledge?
7. Calculate dimensions A to D.

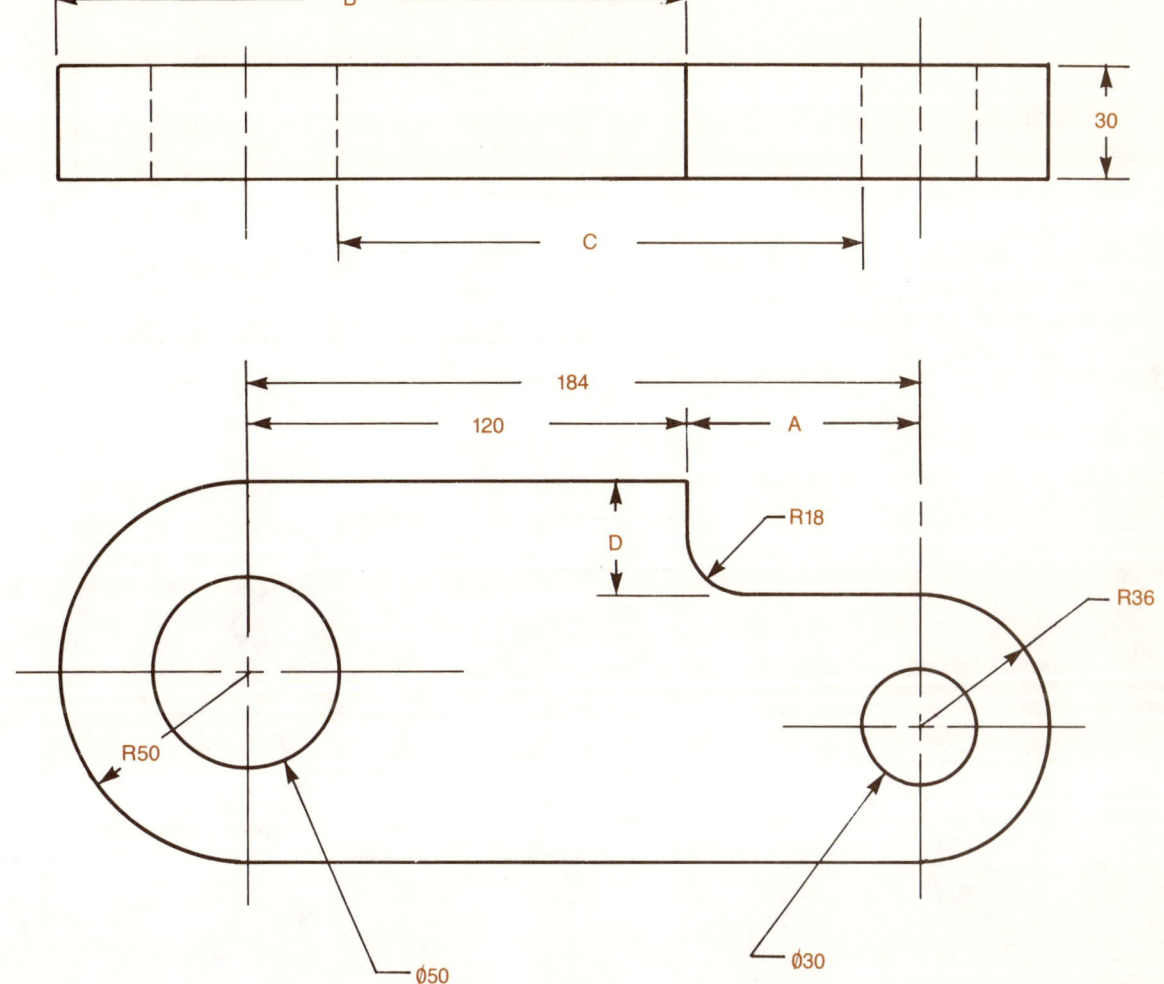

PROJECT 19-10

YOKE PLATE

1. How many holes are in the part?
2. What are the diameters of the holes?
3. What is the distance between the centres of the holes?
4. What is the size of the radius of the fillet?
5. What are the overall length, height and width dimensions?
6. Calculate dimensions A to D.

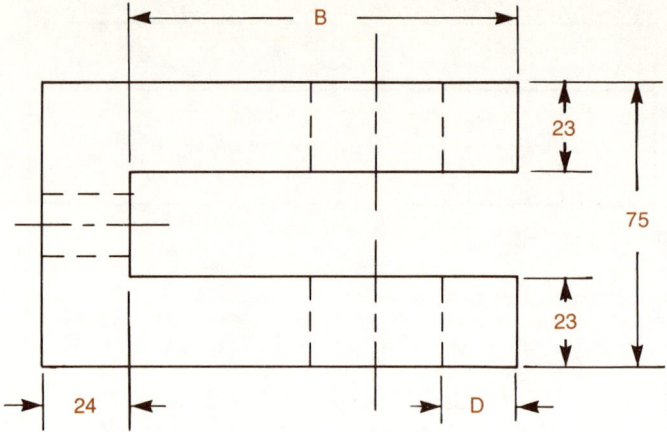
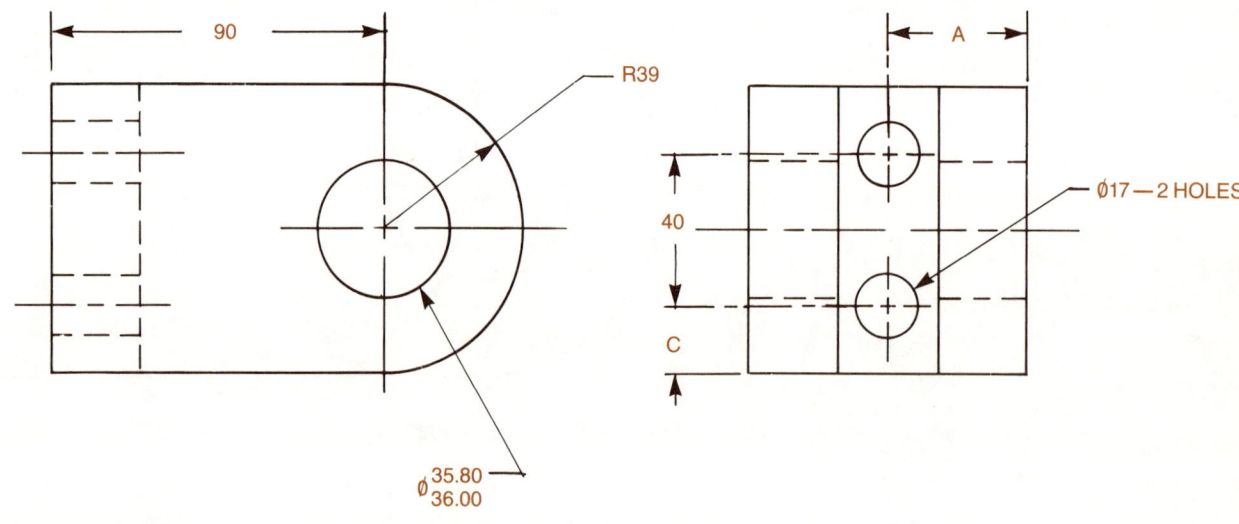

PROJECT 19-11

LOCK FIXTURE

1. How many holes are there in the fixture? State the diameter of each.
2. What kind of line is drawn through the centre of the holes in orthographic views?
3. What is the centre-to-centre distance of the two smaller holes?
4. What is the shop operation used to produce the large hole?
5. What are the length, width and height dimensions?
6. Calculate dimensions A to D.

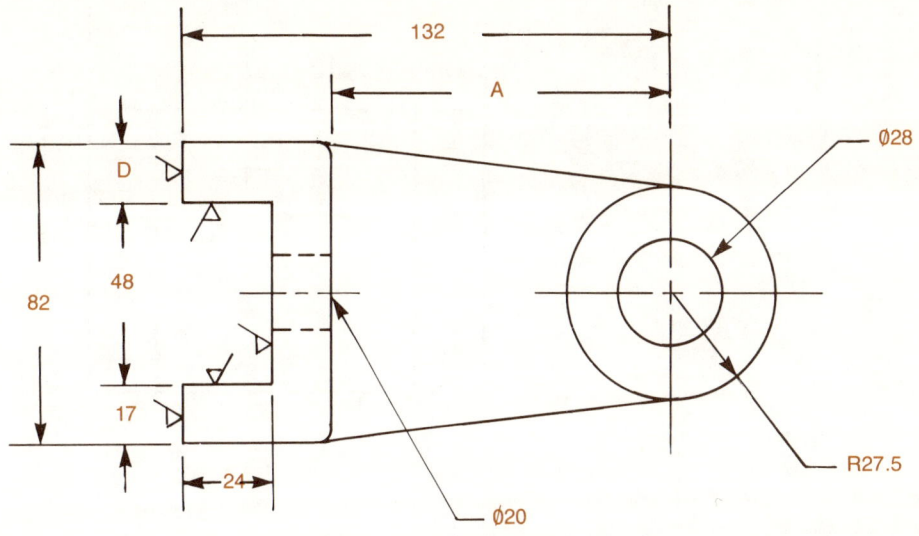
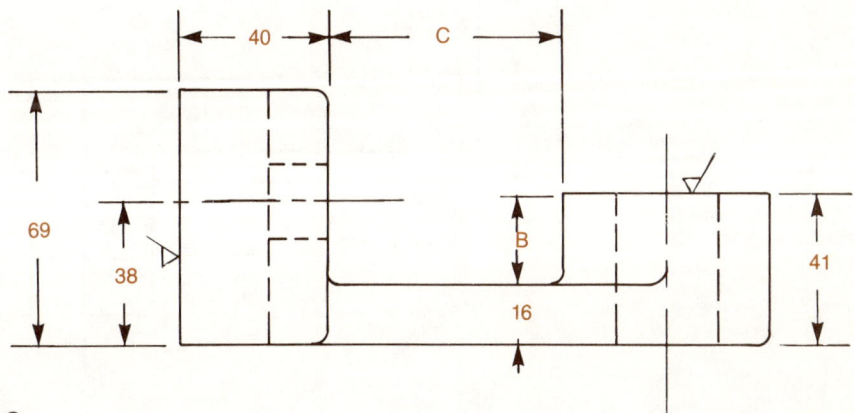

PROJECT 19-12

CONTROL ARM

1. How many surfaces on the control arm are to be machined?
2. Why are four of the corners in the front view not shown as rounds?
3. What are the sizes of the rounds and fillets?
4. What are the overall length, width and height dimensions?
5. Give reasons for drawing a side view.
6. Sketch a side view and neatly position the necessary dimensions.
7. What is the diameter of the boss?
8. Calculate dimensions A to D.

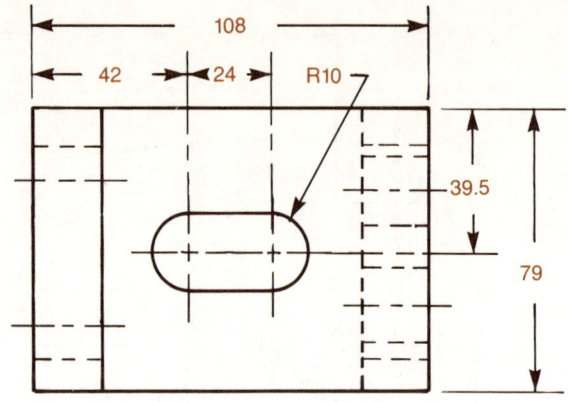
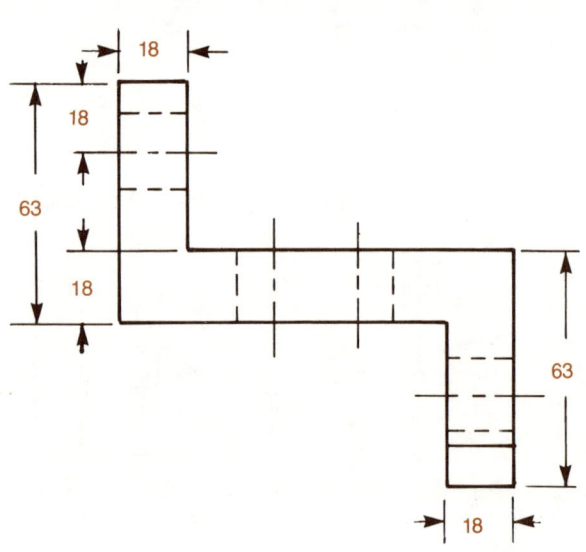
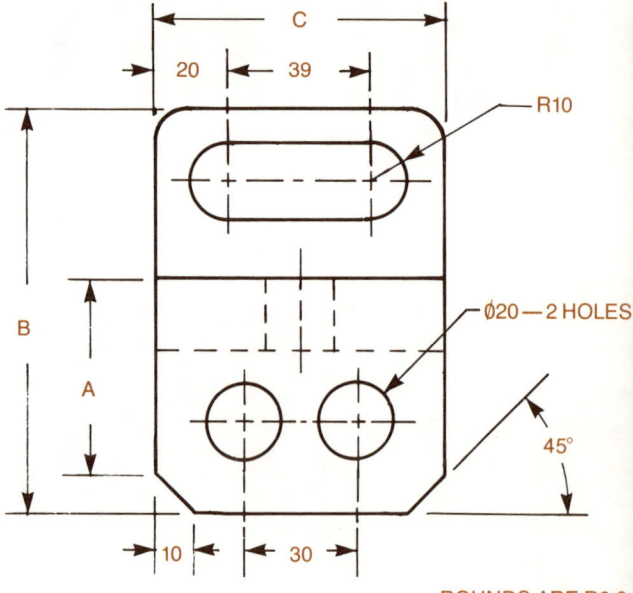

ROUNDS ARE R9.0

PROJECT 19-13

MOTOR MOUNT

1. What is the length of the motor mount?
2. Calculate dimensions A, B and C.
3. What are the dimensions of the slot in the horizontal part of object?
4. What are the dimensions of the slot in the vertical part of the object?
5. What are the diameters of the two holes?
6. What is the angle of the chamfer?
7. What purpose does a slot serve that could not be satisfied by holes?

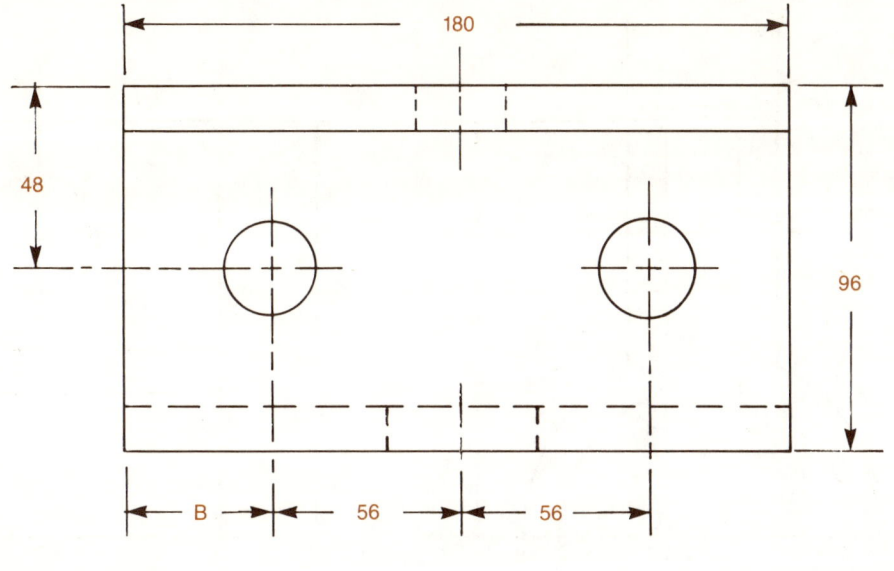
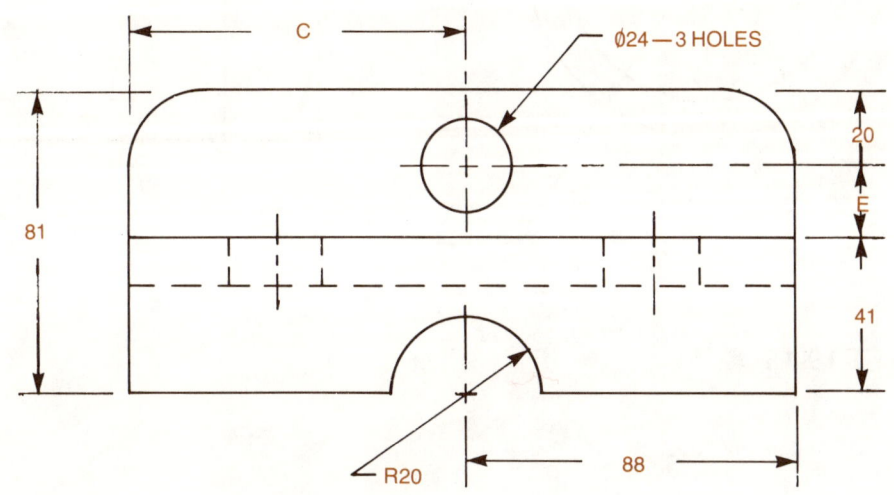
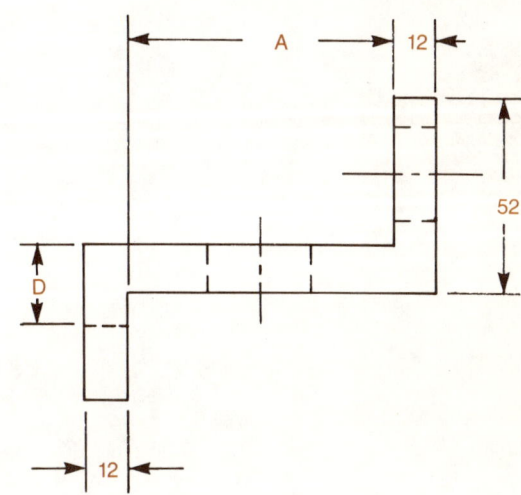

PROJECT 19-14

JACK FASTENER

1. What are the overall length, width and height dimensions?
2. What is the centre-to-centre distance of the two holes in the top view?
3. What are the diameters of the holes?
4. What size are the arcs of the two corners in the front view?
5. Calculate dimensions A to E.
6. What function could the slot serve?

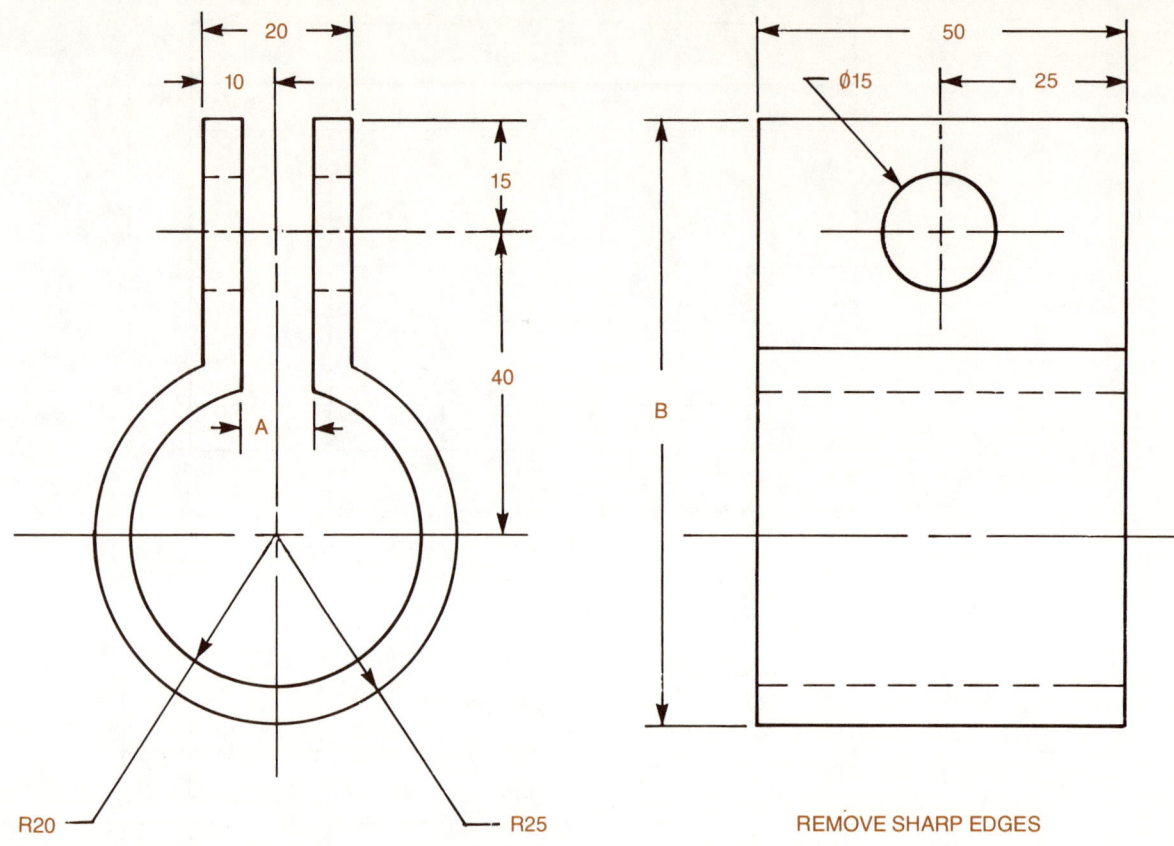

PROJECT 19-15

CLIP

1. Give the length and width dimensions.
2. Calculate dimensions A and B.
3. What is the diameter of the hole in the clip?
4. What surfaces do the hidden lines in the right side view represent?
5. What is the thickness of the material?
6. What is the reason for the note REMOVE SHARP EDGES?

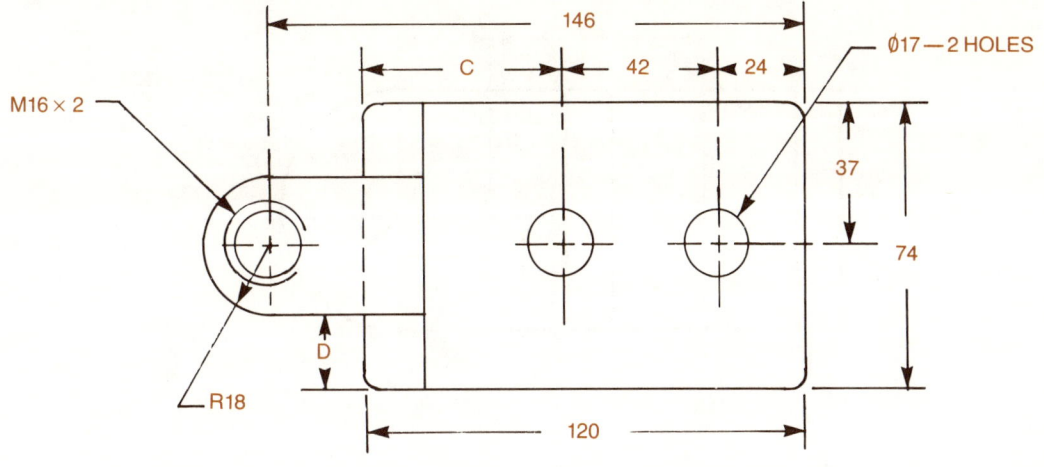
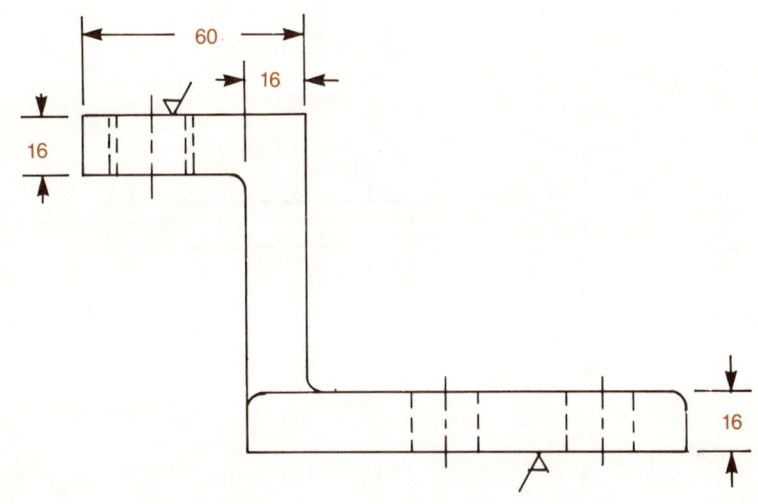
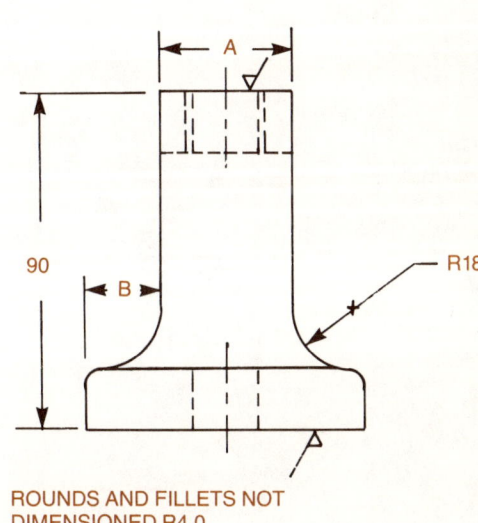

ROUNDS AND FILLETS NOT
DIMENSIONED R4.0

PROJECT 19-16

CLAMP

1. Calculate the dimension A through D.
2. What are the diameters of the three holes?
3. What are the overall length, width and height dimensions?
4. What size are the fillets?
5. What is the maximum height of an objects that will fit under the clamp flange?
6. What is the meaning of the symbol ∀? Why are they shown only in the front and right views of the clamp?
8. What is the size of the tapped hole?

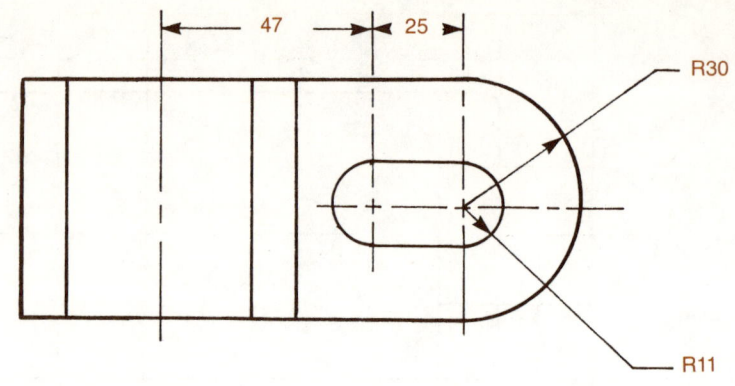

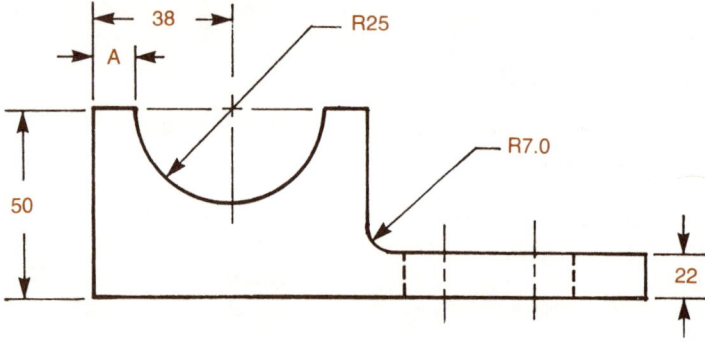

PROJECT 19-17

SADDLE

1. Give the overall length, width and height dimensions of the part.
2. What is the radius of the largest arc?
3. What is the width of the slot?
4. What is the total length of the slot?
5. What is the radius of the fillet?
6. What is the dimension noted as A?

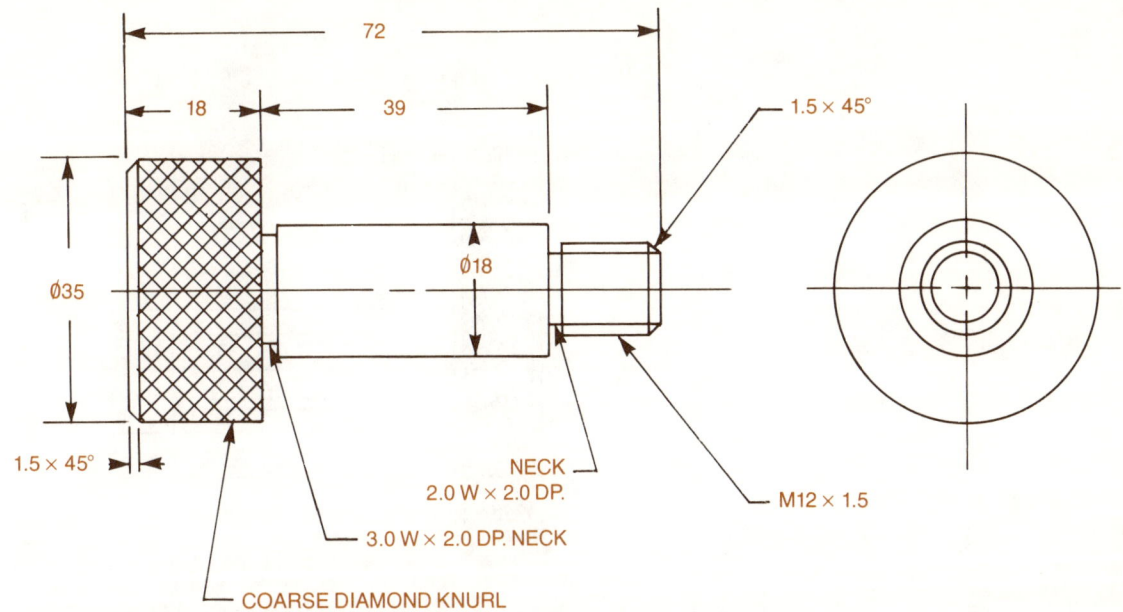

PROJECT 19-18

ADJUSTING SCREW

1. How would you describe the shape of this part?
2. How long is the adjusting screw?
3. What is the overall length of the thread?
4. Explain the note M12 × 1.5.
5. What is the function of the two features indicated as **neck**?
6. Give two reasons for knurling the knob of the part.
7. What type of knurl is indicated?
8. Is the right side view necessary? Explain your answer.
9. The note 1.5 × 45° appears in two positions on the drawing.
   (a) What is the technical name for this feature?
   (b) State the advantages created by each of the two features.
10. What is the largest diameter of the part?
11. What is the smallest diameter of the part?

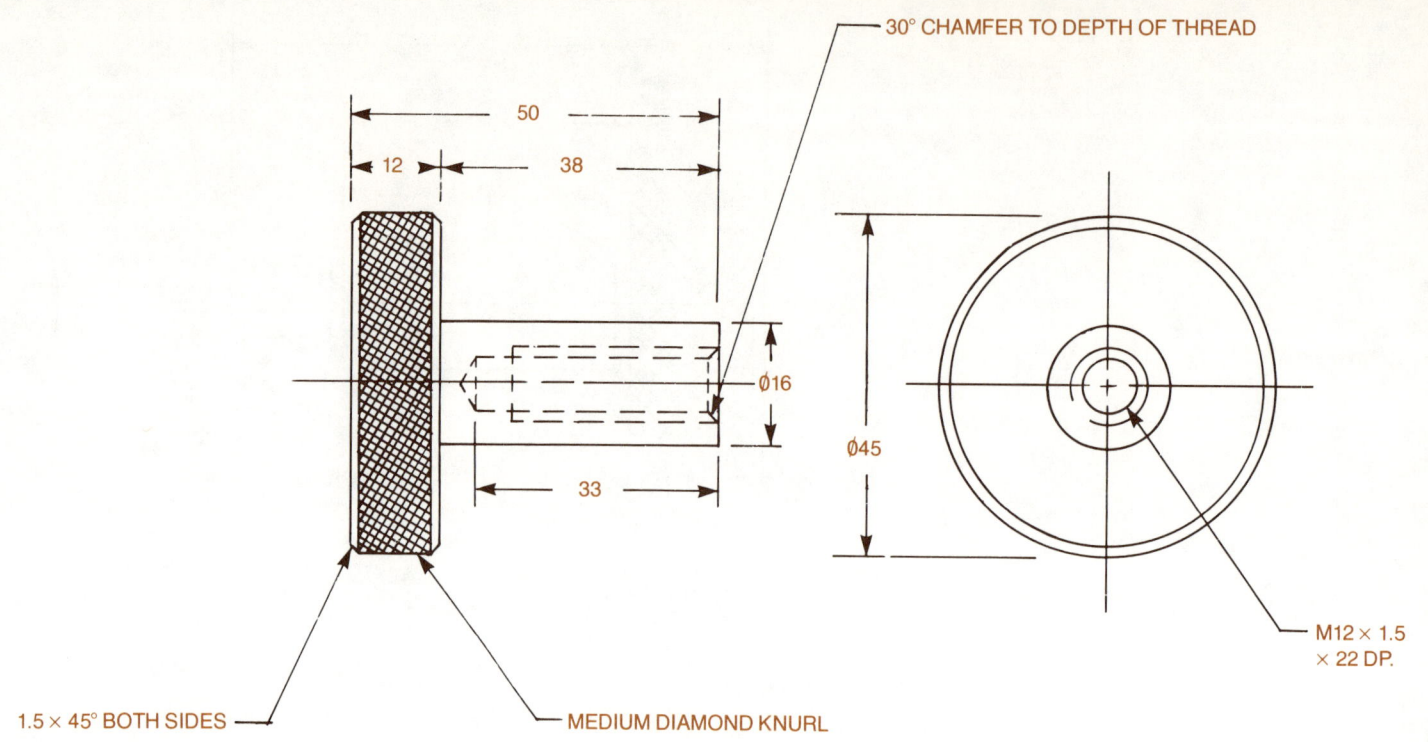

PROJECT 19-19

CLAMP FASTENER

1. Explain the note M12 × 1.5-22DP.
2. What is the purpose of the 30° chamfer?
3. Why is the drilled hole slightly longer than the tapped hole?
4. What is the name given to a hole that does not go completely through a part?
5. Why is the knob of the part chamfered on both sides?
6. Give two reasons for knurling the knob.
7. What is the length of the knob?
8. What is the length of the drilled hole?

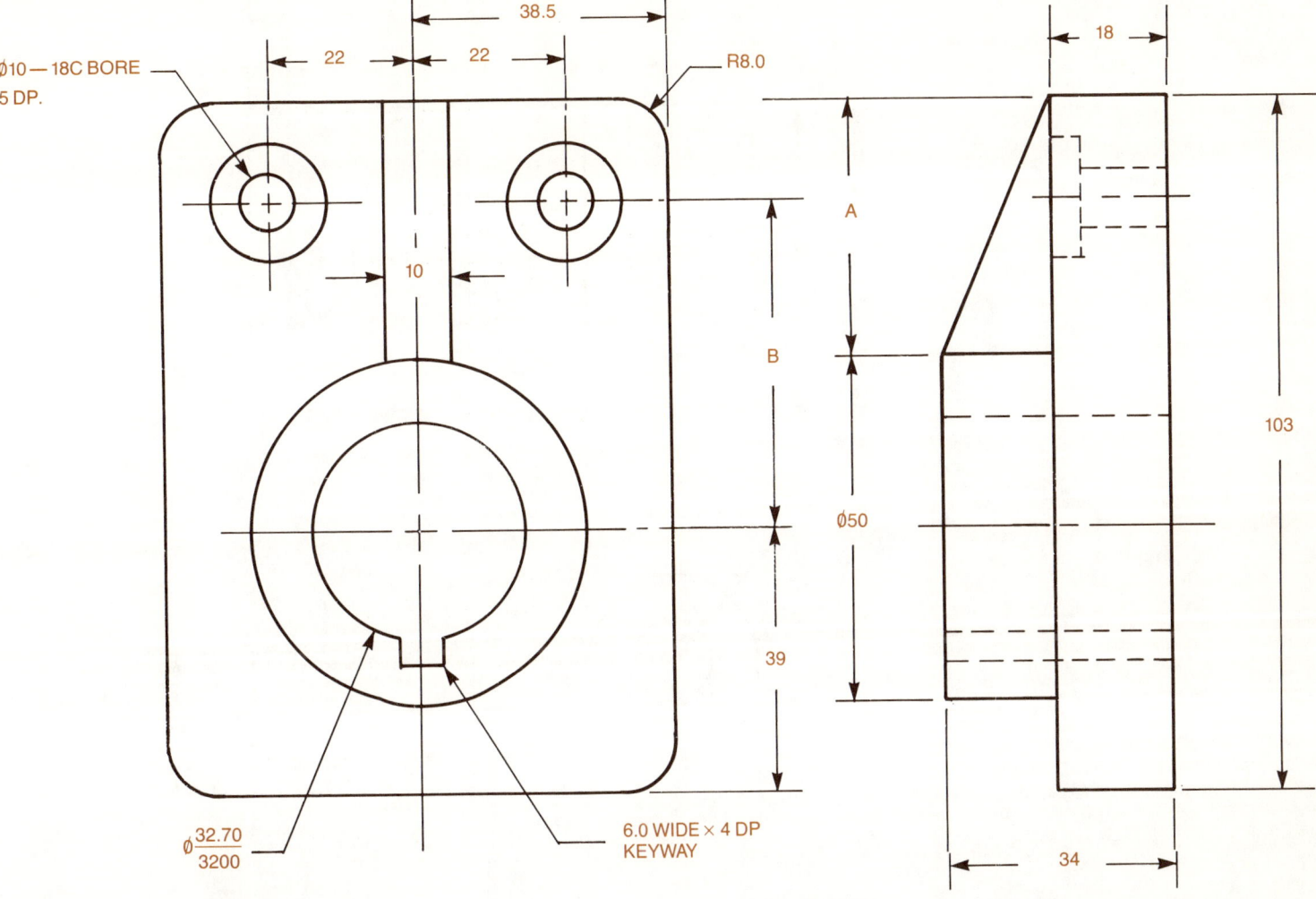

PROJECT 19-20

SHAFT GUIDE

1. What is the diameter of the largest hole in the part?
2. What is the shop operation used to produce the hole?
3. What is the largest and the smallest permitted size of the hole?
4. What is the purpose of the web?
5. What are the overall length, width and height dimensions of the shaft guide?
6. Explain the note ⌀10-18CBORE 5DP.
7. Explain the function of the keyway.
8. Name two types of keys that could be used in the keyway.
9. What is the size of the rounds?
10. What is the thickness of the web?
11. Calculate the dimensions A and B.

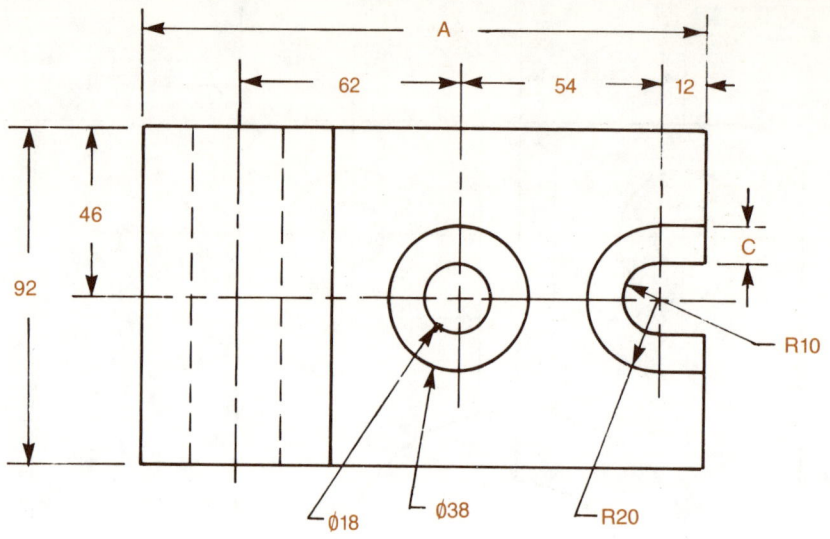

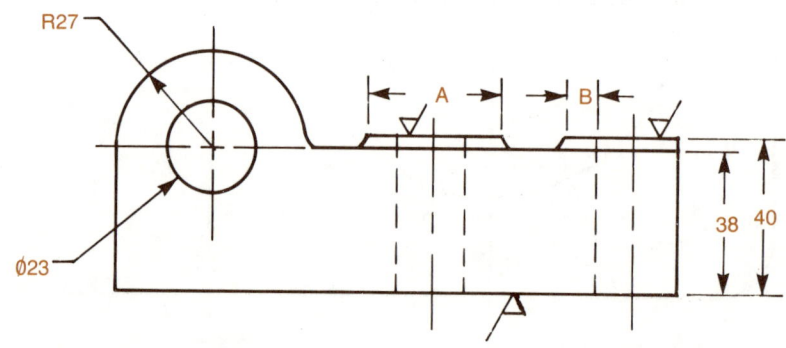

PROJECT 19-21

ANCHOR BASE

1. What is the overall length of the part?
2. What is the height of the boss above the surface of the part?
3. What is the overall height of the part?
4. Calculate the dimensions A, B and C.
5. What are the diameters of the two holes?
6. How long is the slot?
7. How many surfaces are to be machined?
8. What is the overall width of the part?

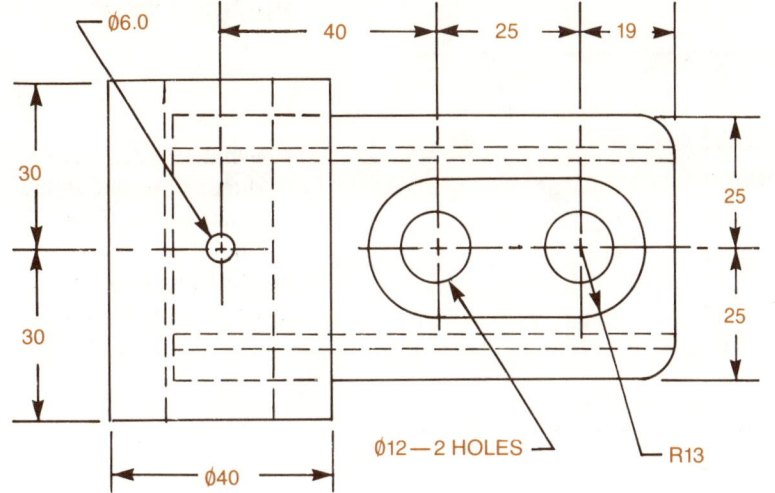

OFFSET SHAFT BASE

1. What is the name given to the raised part of the base with the two Ø12 holes?
2. What is the function of this raised feature?
3. This raised feature has the symbol ∀ on its edge lines. What other features of the part should also have this symbol applied?
4. What is the size of the smallest hole in the part? How long is this hole?
5. What are the overall length, width and height dimensions of the part?
6. Calculate dimensions A to D.
7. What shop operation would produce the largest hole in the part to the dimension indicated?

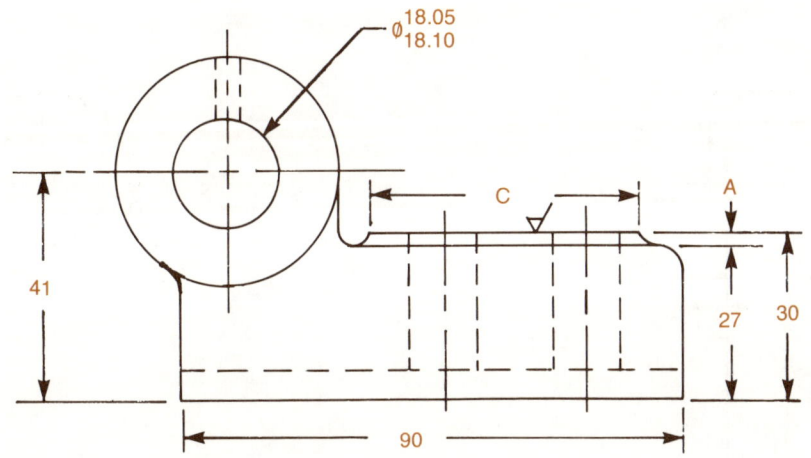
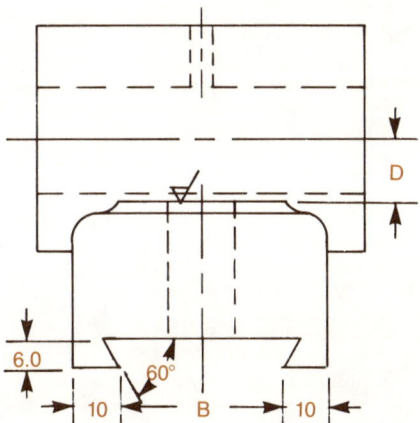

PROJECT 19-22

PROJECT 19-23

CONTROL ARM

1. What are the overall length, width and height dimensions of the part?
2. What are the dimensions of the two holes?
3. Calculate dimensions A to D.
4. Is the part machined all over? Explain your answer.
5. What is the thickness of the web?

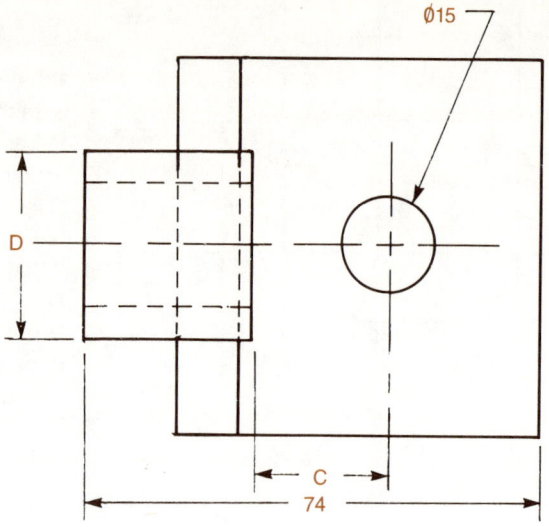

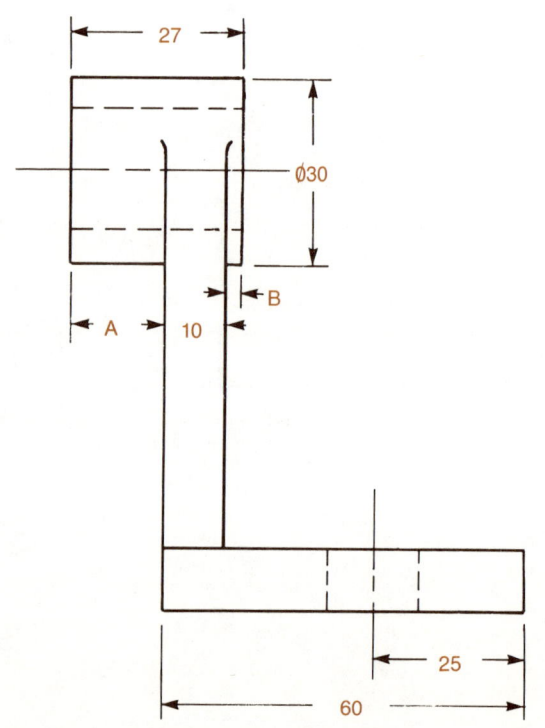

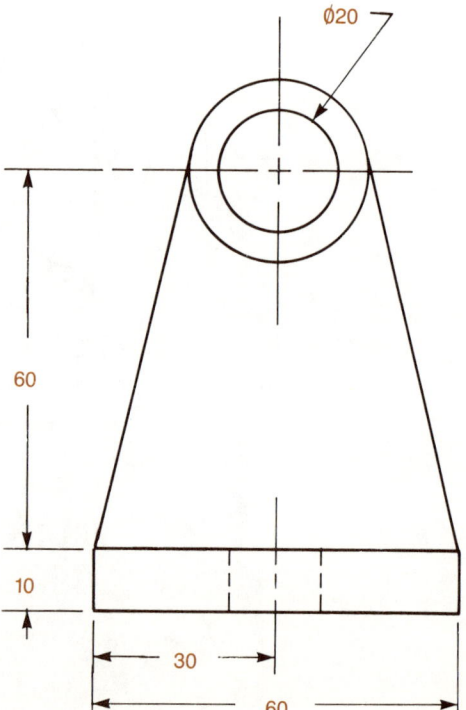

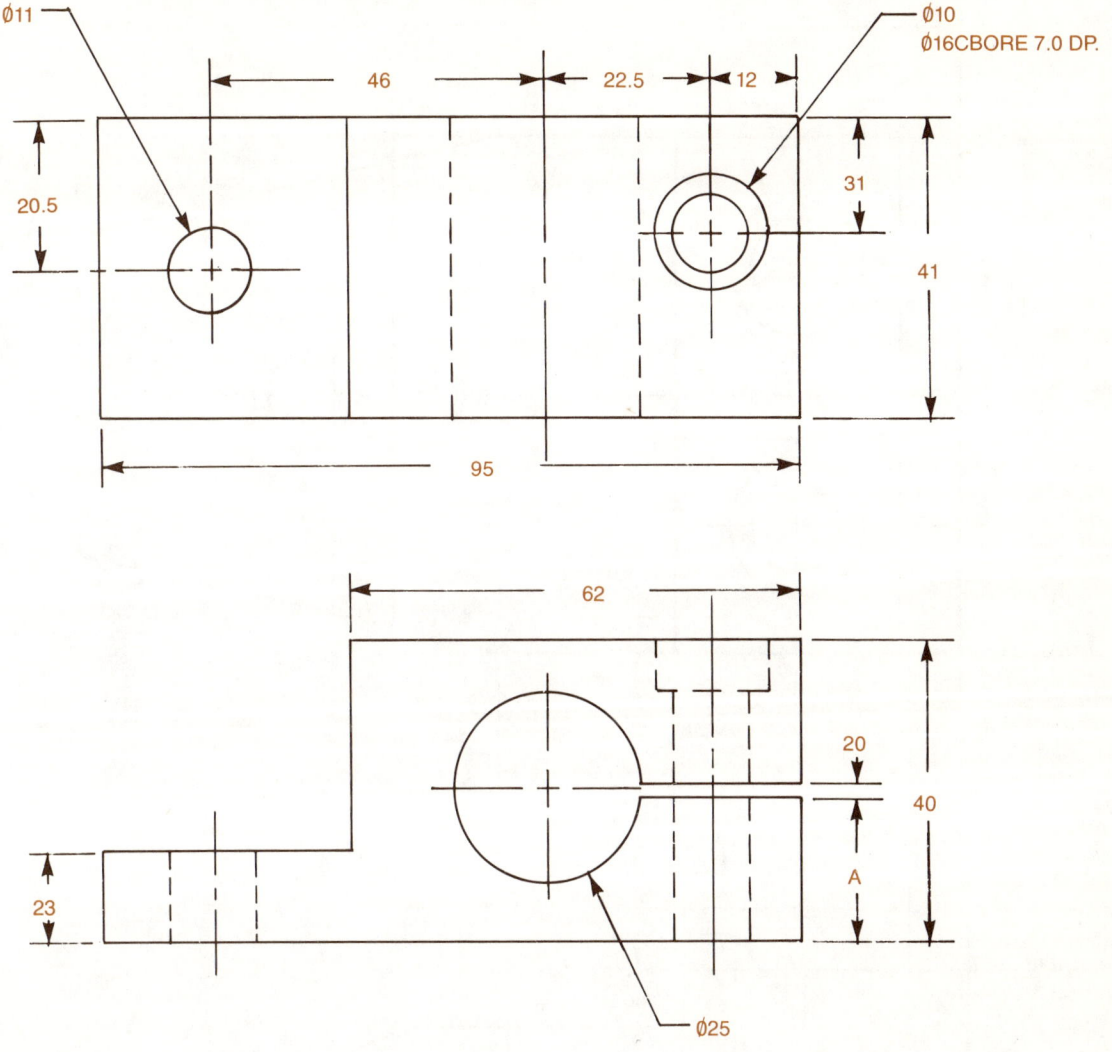

PROJECT 19-24

MOUNTING CLAMP

1. What are the overall length, width and height dimensions?
2. What is the length of the 2.0 slot?
3. What is the purpose of the counterbore?
4. What is the diameter of the largest hole in the part?
5. What is the diameter of the smallest hole in the part?
6. What is the purpose of the slot?

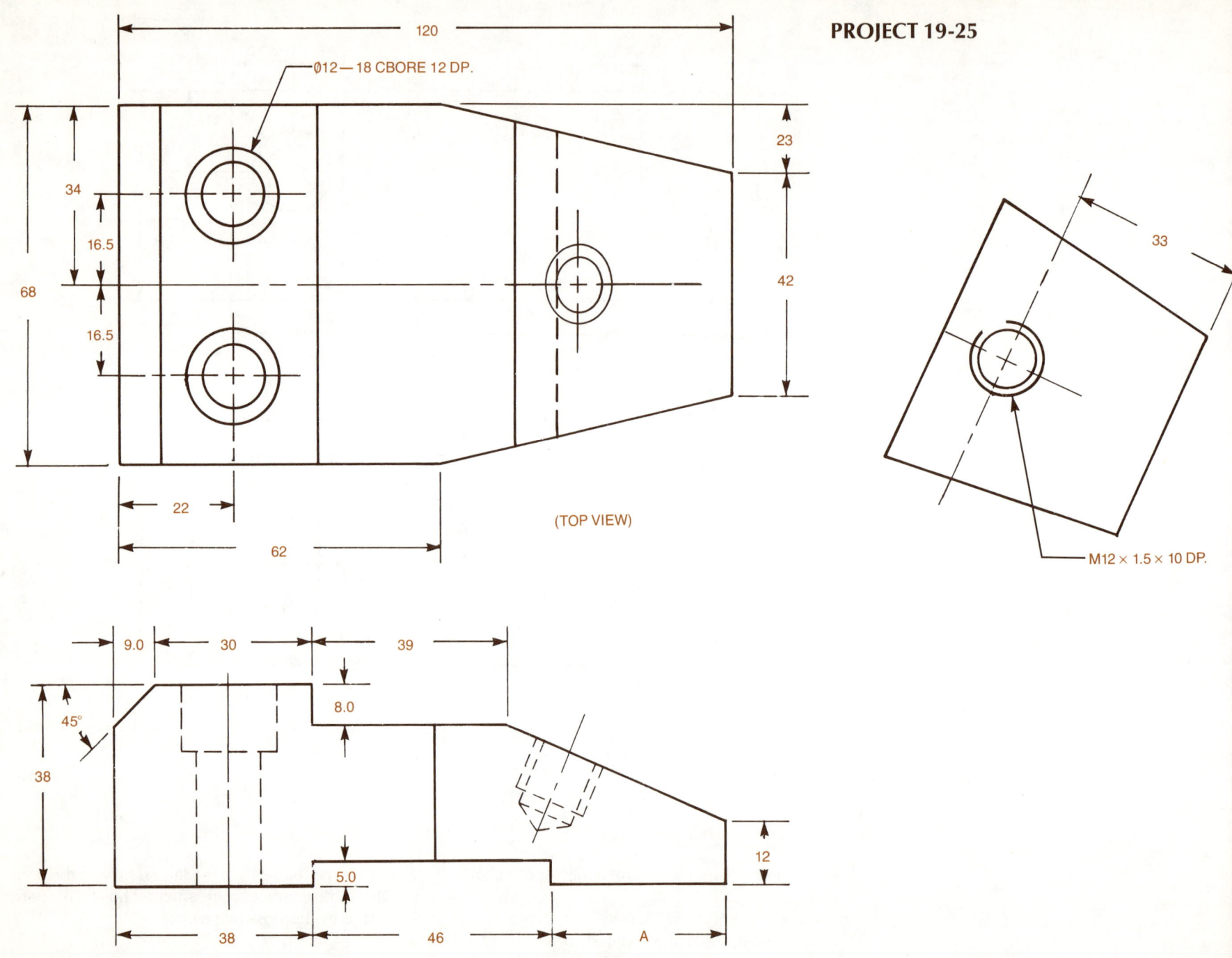

PROJECT 19-25

PROJECT 19-25

1. What are the overall length, width and height dimensions?
2. Give the thread specification for the tapped hole. Explain in your own words each part of the thread specification.
3. What are the dimensions of the other two holes in the part?
4. Give two reasons for drawing the auxiliary view.
5. Why does the tapped hole appear as an ellipse in the top view?
6. Calculate dimension A.

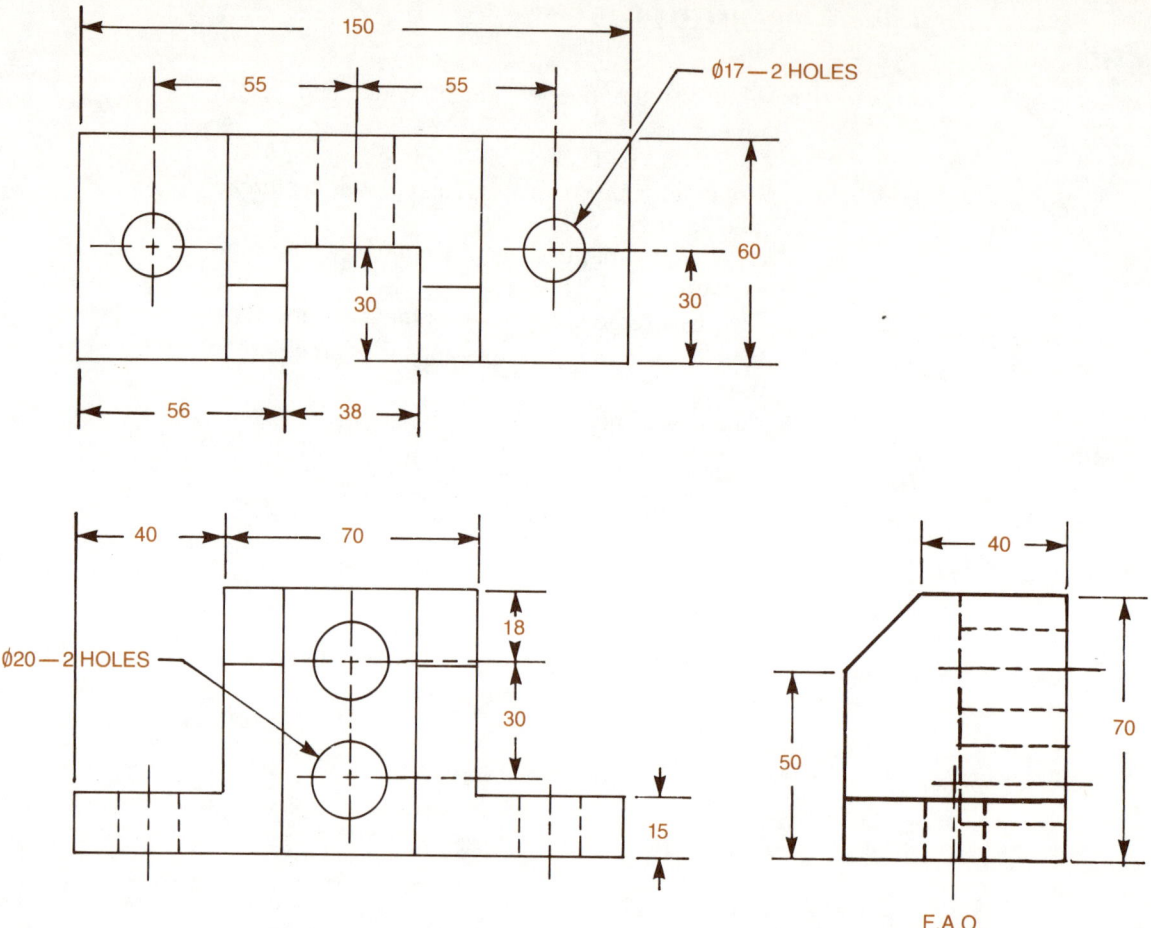

PROJECT 19-26

SUPPORT MEMBER

1. Give the overall length, width and height dimensions.
2. What is the size of the bolting down holes? What is the distance between their centres?
3. What is the size of the holes shown as circles in the front view? What is the distance between their centres?
4. Why are there no fillets or rounds on the part?
5. Explain why the bevelled edge shown in the right side view is drawn at an angle of 45°.

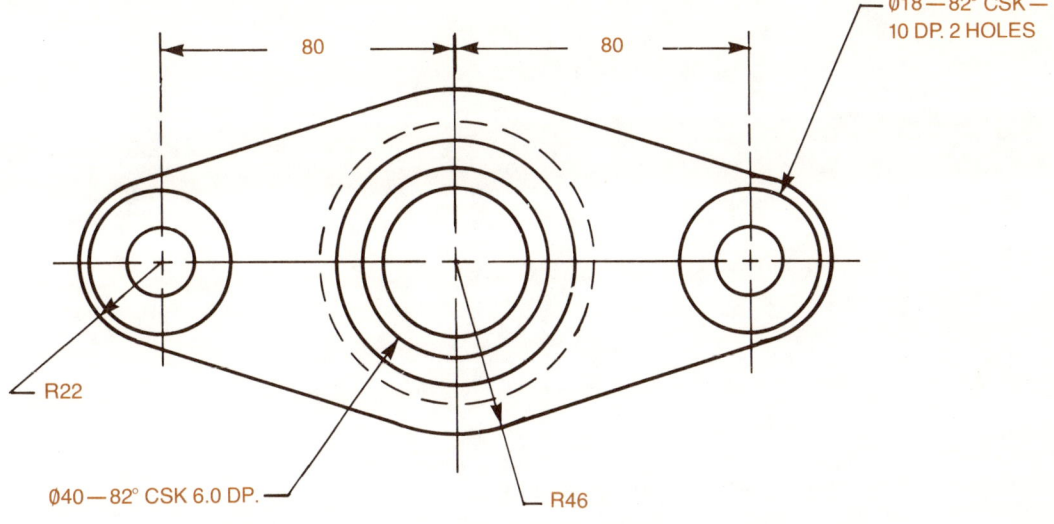

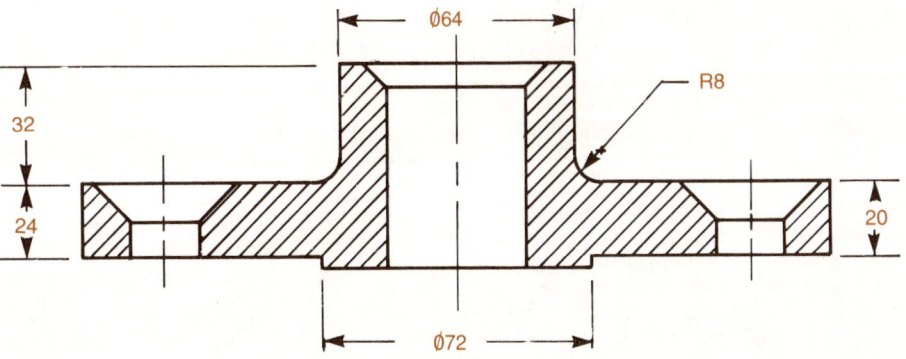

PROJECT 19-27

SHAFT GUIDE

1. What is the overall length of the part?
2. What is the purpose of counter-sinking the holes?
3. What is the overall width of the part?
4. What is the dimension of the fillet?
5. What is the diameter of the largest boss?
6. What is the diameter of the smaller boss?
7. What type of view is the front view?
8. What material is indicated by the section lines?

INDEX

A
Angles, 6,8,70
   arrowheads, 91
   arc, 65, 66, 91
   acute, 199
   dimensioning, 94
   obtuse, 199
   thread, 150
Aluminum, 115
Auxiliary views, 166-171
Assembly working drawings, 177-180
   parts identification, 178-179
   parts in sectional views, 179-180
   steps in drawing assembly working drawings, 181-183
Allowance, 223
Anchor bolt, 254

B
Balloons (parts identification), 179-180
Bauxite, 115
Bends, 224
Blind hole, 116
Bolt circle, 68, 101
Bolts, 154
   drawing bolts, 156
Bore, 118
Boss, 122
Brass, 115
Bronze, 115
Broken out sectional views, 142
Bungalow, 240

C
Cabinet pictorial drawings, 205-207
Cap screw, 155
Casting, 116
Centre lines, 68
Chamfer, 120-121
Circle
   elements of, 65
   template, 69
Circumference, 65
Commercial gothic lettering, 19
Compass, 67
Concentric circles, 66
Construction
   drawings, 244-249
   lines, 10
   symbols, 286-8
Counterbore, 119
Countersink, 120

Cross section, 248
Cylinder (truncated), 227
Cylindrical objects
   dimensioning of, 99

D
Detail
   dimensions, 88
   drawings, 252-3
   working drawings, 113
Diameter, 65
   major, 151
   minor, 151
   root, 151
Dimension figures, 91
Dimension lines, 90, 106
Dimensioning
   angles, 94
   architectural, 274-5
   cylindrical objects and contours, 99
   rectangular objects and contours, 88
   holes, 100
Dimensions overall, 88
   detail, 88
Divide a straight line into equal divisions, 274-5
Drafting machine, 9
Drawing
   presentation, 238
   instruments, 5-9
   steps in spacing single view, 10-11
   steps in drawing single view, 11-12

E
Element lines, 225, 228
Elevations, 239, 246-7, 250-1
Erasers, 6
Erasing shield, 6, 13
Extension line, 90
External thread, 151

F
Fascia, 256
Ferrous metals, 115
Fillets, 69
Finish symbols, 122
Floor plans, 248-9, 255, 273
Foldline, 224
Forging, 115
Freehand sketching, 289-321
French curve, 229
Foundation — footing and walls, 253

G
Gothic lettering, 19
Guide lines, 19, 91, 95
Gib head key, 122

H
Header, 254
House types, 240
Hexagon, 77

I
Internal threads, 120, 151
Iron, 115
Irregular or french curve, 229
Isometric drawing of
   arcs, 204
   axes, 194
   circles, 198-202
   cylinder, 202-4
Isometric sketching, 289-321

J
Joists, 254-5
Joints, seams, 221

K
Knurling, 121
Keys
   keyseat, 122
   keyway, 122
   dimensioning of, 122

L
Leader line, 100, 179-180
Lines
   centre, 68
   construction, 10
   cutting plane, 140
   dimensions, 88
   element, 228
   extension, 88
   fold, 24
   guide, 19
   hidden, 40-41
   object, 10
   projection, 29
   stretchout, 225
Lettering, 19-21
Lintel, 255

M
Machine screw, 155

Machining, 116
Malleable iron, 115
Metals, 115

O
Obtuse angle, 199
Oblique, 192, 289
   steps in drawing oblique pictorials, 205-207
Octagon, 71
Orthographic
   drawing,, 24-30, 78-83
   projection, 27-29
   spacing of views, 41-42
Overall dimensions, 88

P
Pad, 122-123
Parallel line development, 225
Parts identification, 177-179
Pencils
   mechanical, 5
   wooden, 5
   sharpening of, 6
Perspective, 240-242
Pictorial drawings, 192-208
Pictorial thread representation, 152-3
   presentation drawings, 238-244
Pig iron, 115
Pitch
   machine, 151-152
   building, 256
Plan dimensioning, 274-5
Plane figures, 9
Plot plan, 273

R
Radius, 65
Rafter, 256
Reading technical drawings, 289-321
Ream, 117-118
Ridge, 256
Root, 150
Rounds, 65

S
Safe edge, 221
Scale
   full, 8
   reduced, 58-59
   enlarged, 59-60

Schedule, 273
Schematic method of representing screw threads, 152
Screw threads, 120, 150
Seam, 221
Section lines, 137-138
Sectional views, 136, 143
   architectural, 273-248
   broken out, 142
   full, 136
   half, 141
   offset, 139
   removed, 142
   revolved, 142

Set squares, 6
Simplified method of representing screw threads, 154
Sheathing, 255
Shingles, 256
Sill, 254
Site, 242
Split level house, 241
Spokes, 138
Spot facing, 119
Stamping, 116
Standard parts, 117
Steel, 113

Stud machinery, 155
   building, 255

T
Tap, 120
Template, 9
   circle, 69
   ellipse, 205
Thread(s), 150
   angle, 151
   crest, 150
   external, 151
   internal, 151
   pitch, 151
   tables, 152
Top plate, 255
Two-storey house, 241
Truncated cylinder, 227

W
Webs and spokes, 138
Welding, 116

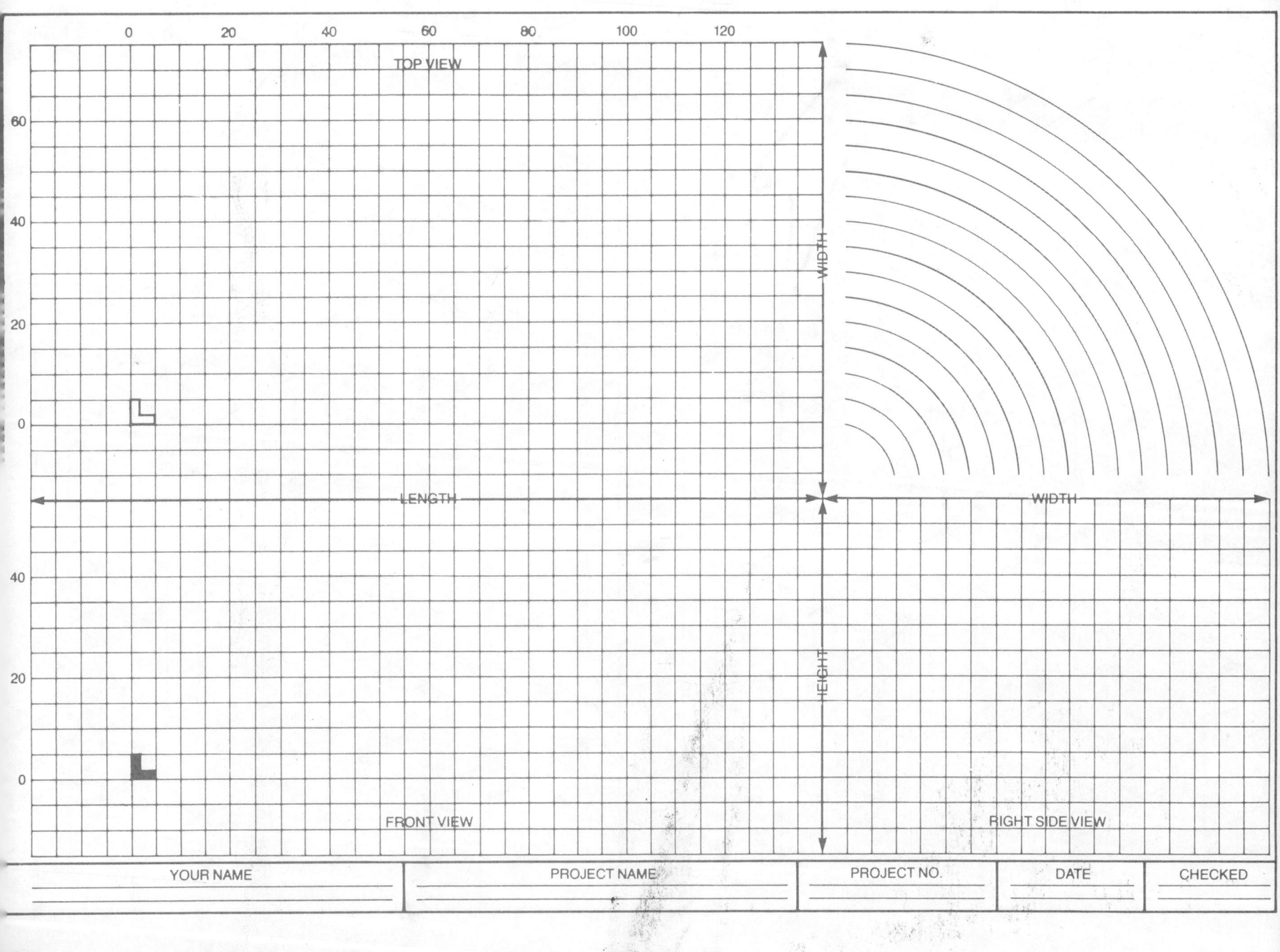

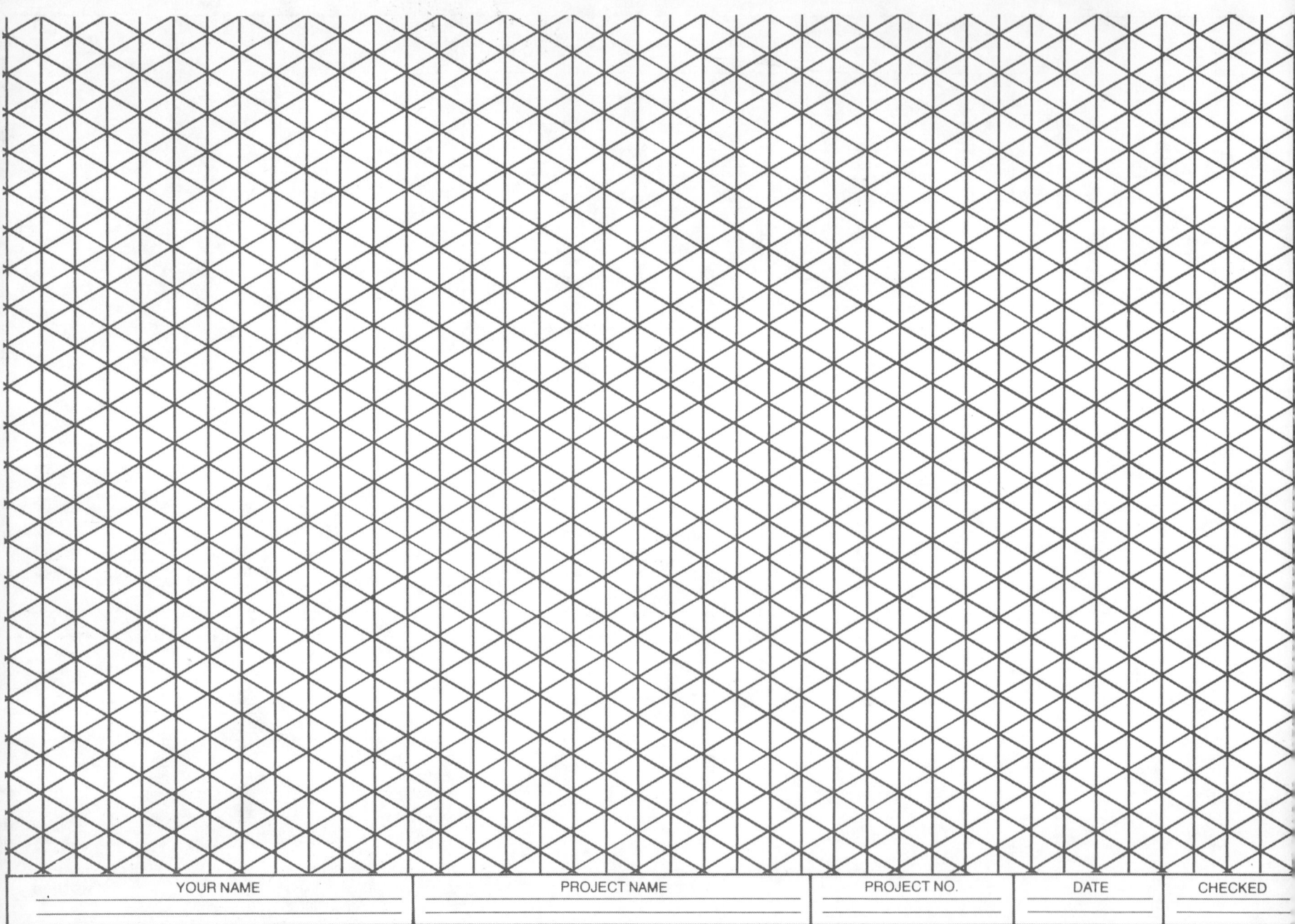